SECOND EDITION

Teaching Reading and Writing in Elementary Classrooms

Rebecca Barr

National-Louis University
Program Officer, The Spencer Foundation

Barbara Johnson

University of Utah

LONGMAN

An imprint of Addison Wesley Longman, Inc.

New York • Reading, Massachusetts • Menlo Park, California • Harlow, England
Don Mills, Ontario • Sydney • Mexico City • Madrid • Amsterdam

---

To our husbands, Bob and Ed, and our children

Teaching Reading and Writing in Elementary Classrooms, Second Edition

Longman, 10 Bank Street, White Plains, N.Y. 10606

Acquisitions editor: Virginia L. Blanford
Associate editor: Arianne J. Weber
Development editor: John Matthews
Editorial assistant: Michael Lee
Production editor: Ann P. Kearns
Senior designer: Betty Sokol
Production supervisor: Edith Pullman
Cover and text design: Joseph DePinho
Photo research: Joseph DePinho
Text photos: Sue Markson
Text art: Fine Line Illustrations, Inc.
Compositor: ComCom

Library of Congress Cataloging-in-Publication Data

Barr, Rebecca.
    Teaching reading and writing in elementary classrooms / Rebecca
Barr, Barbara Johnson.—2nd ed.
        p.   cm.
    Rev. ed. of: Teaching reading in elementary classrooms. c1991.
    Includes bibliographical references and index.
ISBN 0-8013-1677-4

1. Reading (Elementary)   2. English language—Composition and
    exercises—Study and teaching (Elementary)   I. Johnson, Barbara.
Date.   II. Barr, Rebecca.   Teaching reading in elementary
classrooms.   III. Title.
LB1573.B359   1997
372.41—dc20   96-20145
                                                      CIP

Contents

SECTION II   Teaching Strategies: Planning and Implementing Instruction   71

SECTION IV Classroom Perspectives: The Developmental Nature of the Literacy Program 435

Preface

HOW TO READ THIS BOOK

Our goal in writing this book is to help those who are learning to become teachers gain a full understanding of how to teach a balanced reading program in elementary schools. For those who are experienced teachers, the book can be used to encourage further professional development.

Chapter 1 describes in detail our views about the ongoing development of the literacy process, about literacy instruction in the context of classroom realities, and about how teachers develop professionally. We agree with the proponents of whole-language instruction that children learn best how to read and write in environments that integrate reading, writing, listening, and communicating around good literature. We also know that to develop as readers and writers, some children benefit from the special instructional support of a carefully designed program. With this in mind, we present methods of instruction and assessment that are appropriate for *all* children, including children with special needs. Following our philosophical and practical inclinations of inclusion, we discuss the unique problems of special learners as part of instructional planning for all students, within the realities of classroom life. To preview briefly, the book is divided into five sections.

Section I details our ideas on how students develop literacy.

Section II considers teaching strategies and the planning and implementation of instruction. It develops in depth what is known about the components of literacy—knowledge of print, prior knowledge and vocabulary, reading comprehension, and writing—and introduces teaching strategies to foster student learning in these areas.

Section III explores the background knowledge teachers need about children and adolescents' literature and other reading materials, assessment, and organizing students for instruction.

Section IV presents integrated perspectives on classroom instruction, making use of extensive case studies. It examines in considerable detail the structure, characteristics, and activities of effective lessons in order to reinforce and elaborate on concepts described in earlier sections.

Section V examines issues that pertain to the community, the profession of teaching, and ongoing personal growth.

Like learning to read and write, learning to teach is an interactive process. Your prior knowledge, whether gained as a student, as an observer, or as a teacher, is shaped and reorganized to incorporate new understandings. To the extent that you involve yourself while reading the chapters of this book, you will learn the ideas presented. Richly detailed case studies throughout the text expose you to real-life situations teachers face at all levels of literacy instruction. To further promote your interaction with the text, we have included activities that ask you to write your ideas in a journal as you read and think about what you are reading. These journal entries may become the basis for ongoing dialogue between you, other students, and your instructor. The following activities are featured in each chapter.

Tapping Prior Knowledge to Set a Purpose asks you to reflect on the graphic organizer at the beginning of the chapter and to think explicitly about what you want to learn from the information presented.

Pause and Reflect activities encourage new insights by asking you to consider a problem, an activity, or a piece of writing. Writing about it in your journal will help you to objectify your ideas and to identify ideas you wish to learn more about.

Learning from Experience vignettes of classroom lessons, case studies of teacher decision making, and interviews with experienced teachers about their teaching practices provide some of the firmest bases from which you can learn.

Your Turn–Our Turn activities ask you to reflect on various features of the Learning from Experience descriptions (Your Turn). You then have the opportunity to compare your ideas with ours about the same event (Our Turn).

In the Field activities include suggestions for teaching and interview activities that will expand your practical knowledge.

Portfolio Suggestion encourages you to include written activities in your portfolio. It suggests that you select two of your responses to Pause and Reflect activities, and if you completed a field activity, that you include a report about it as well. These samples of your work provide a paper trail showing how your ideas have expanded and become more comprehensive. (Your instructor may want to use these writings from your permanent portfolio as an indicator of class performance. If so, additional guidance for developing and evaluating your portfolio will be provided by your instructor.)

HELP IN WRITING THIS BOOK

In writing this book, we have received the help of many excellent teachers who generously shared their knowledge by talking to us about their teaching, by inviting us to observe and record their instruction, and by letting us write about their classes in the form of case studies. Through the integration of this rich, firsthand material, we have grounded the principles of and approaches to teaching reading and writing that support the development of proficient and enthusiastic readers and writers.

More than anything else we have written, this book is a collaborative enterprise. We are greatly indebted to the teachers who spent hours with us describing their teaching. Although only excerpts from their reflections are included, we learned greatly from them. We thank Mimi Aiston, Terrie Bridgman, Rita Butler, Michael Dunn,

Christina Frank, Ruth Freedman, Carol Ivy, Diane Jenkins, Angelita Johnson, Sue Ann Johnson-Kuby, Claudia Katz, Agnita Keating, Ruth Luke, Peggy Malone, Linda Monahan, Chris Moon, Cindy Morgan Thaler, Sanford Prizant, Beth Rohrer, Barbara Russ, Sue Scott, Kara Shoellhorn, Elly Taheny, Lucia Thoensen, Noreen Winningham, Andi Wisner, and Joanne Zielinsky for their help.

We were enthusiastically invited into classrooms to observe reading and writing lessons. Although transcripts of these lessons fall short of capturing the dynamic interaction we observed, they provide an authentic glimpse of instruction. In some cases, this experience in classrooms enabled us to develop case studies. We are most grateful to Roz Callahan, Ruth Ann Freedman, Sharon Gleason, Agnita Keating, Roberta McCollister, Lucia Thoensen, Pam Pifer, Debbie Radonich, and Sharon Gleason for sharing their teaching with us.

We also want to thank some wonderful professionals who have graciously given time to discuss ideas with us and to review, critique, and recommend changes in the manuscript. Their efforts have made this a better textbook. In particular, we thank Jeanne Chaney, Carol Ivy, Darrell Morris, and Pam Pifer. We also profited from the insightful comments of reviewers.

These reviewers include:

Mariam Jean Dreher, University of Maryland

Lawrence Erickson, Southern Illinois University-Carbondale

Karen Ford, Ball State University

Shirley Long, Eastern Kentucky University

James Mosenthal, University of Vermont

Linda Squier, Ball State University

We are particularly indebted to three outstanding teachers, who contributed chapters to this book. Pam Pifer assumed primary responsibility for writing chapter 12 on early literacy, and Claudia Katz and Sue Ann Johnson Kuby wrote chapter 15 on developing literacy in middle and junior high schools. They shared our frustration during the writing process and our satisfaction in seeing a richly textured book materialize.

This book could not have been written without the insights and knowledge that we have gained from the students we have worked with over the years. They have indeed been our teachers. In particular, we wish to thank the students who provided samples of their reading and writing. Although some must remain anonymous, we have benefited greatly from their work with us. We owe a special debt to our own children, who, through their struggles and pleasures in learning to read and write, have provided an intimate glimpse into the process that could be gotten no other way.

Finally, we acknowledge the support of our colleagues from National-Louis University and the University of Utah, the patient tolerance of our husbands, the artistic photographic work of Sue Markson, and the excellent editorial suggestions of Virginia Blanford, Arianne Weber, John Matthews, and Ann Kearns from Longman.

I..............

How Students Develop Literacy

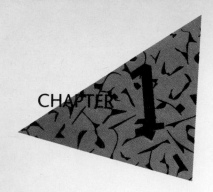

CHAPTER 1

Developing Readers and Writers

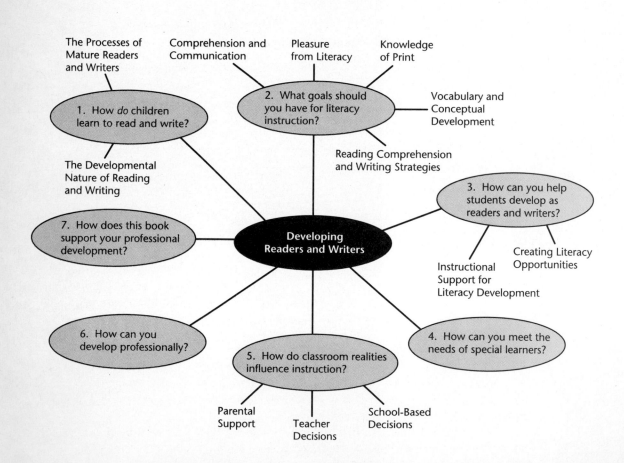

The Processes of Mature Readers and Writers

Comprehension and Communication

Pleasure from Literacy

Knowledge of Print

1. How *do* children learn to read and write?

2. What goals should you have for literacy instruction?

Vocabulary and Conceptual Development

The Developmental Nature of Reading and Writing

Reading Comprehension and Writing Strategies

3. How can you help students develop as readers and writers?

7. How does this book support your professional development?

Developing Readers and Writers

Creating Literacy Opportunities

Instructional Support for Literacy Development

6. How can you develop professionally?

4. How can you meet the needs of special learners?

5. How do classroom realities influence instruction?

Parental Support

Teacher Decisions

School-Based Decisions

▼ CHAPTER GOALS FOR THE READER

To understand mature literacy processes and how they develop

To link these perspectives on literacy to the goals you develop for instruction

To understand the importance of creating a rich literacy environment and supportive instruction

To reflect on how to meet the needs of special learners as part of your instructional program

To understand the realities that shape your classroom literacy program

To reflect on how you can develop professionally

To learn how this book supports your professional development

▼ CHAPTER OVERVIEW

Most of you reading this book either want to be teachers or are teachers already. The book was written with the goal of providing the theoretical and practical knowledge that you need to help your students develop into the best readers and writers they are capable of being. It includes discussions and stories rich in detail, so that you can build understandings about how to be a good teacher of reading and writing. In writing this book, we were influenced primarily by three things: first, our views concerning literacy processes and how they develop over time; second, our beliefs about literacy instruction in the context of classroom realities; and third, our views on how teachers learn, make decisions, and develop professionally.

This chapter first provides an overview of the nature of the reading and writing processes of proficient readers and views on how children acquire this facility. These perspectives form the basis for identifying goals for literacy instruction. Your overall goal will be to support the learning of your students, so they can read and write and love to do so.

The chapter then focuses on how you can develop an engaging instructional program and considers how you may help your students become readers and writers. Creating a rich literacy environment in your classroom and providing instructional support for students who need it are of central importance. Your teaching will be enhanced by the thinking of Vygotsky and the implications that follow for how you plan and teach your students. Because of the importance of supporting the learning of all your students, the needs of special learners such as bilingual children, those who encounter special difficulty with literacy, and particularly talented children are given special consideration. The discussion of instruction is then grounded in a consideration of the realities of classrooms and the challenges they pose for you.

Final sections of the chapter consider your professional development and how this book is organized. The commitment you have made to your professional growth is shown by the fact that you are reading this book. Reflecting on your classroom experiences will be a major contributor to your continued development, as will good relations with the parents of the children you teach, discussions with colleagues, and involvement in professional groups.

 ## TAPPING PRIOR KNOWLEDGE TO SET A PURPOSE

As you read about the perspectives developed in this book, we encourage you to think about your own views. What do mature readers such as you do when you read? What do you do when you write? How do children develop skill in reading and writing? Take a few moments to jot down your thinking about these issues in your journal. Use these ideas, the graphic organizer on the first page of the chapter, and the chapter overview to write questions you want answered about literacy processes and instruction. List these questions in your journal under the heading Chapter 1: Setting a Purpose. Answer these questions when you finish reading the chapter.

HOW *DO* CHILDREN LEARN TO READ AND WRITE?

The road traveled in becoming a reader and writer is lifelong. In the beginning, the journey may be problem free for some children. As they progress, they gain a sense of confidence in their ability to comprehend and express themselves. For others, the road has many curves and obstacles; progress is hard won and children gain a sense of ambivalence about themselves as readers and writers. As a teacher of literacy, you will guide children on this journey; you will accept them with the talents and interests they bring and help them traverse the new literacy terrain.

In order to provide successful guidance, you need to have two things in mind. First, you need to have a conception of mature reading and writing processes—the destination toward which children are headed. Second, you need to understand what it is that children learn as they develop into mature readers and writers. In the remainder of this section, these topics are considered.

The Processes of Mature Readers and Writers

If someone observes that you are literate (because you are reading this page!), what does that person mean? What occurs as your eyes travel across the page? Where does the meaning come from? From the text or from your past experiences? What are some useful ways to think about the processes of reading and writing? In this section, we describe the ways that experts think about literacy processes. We describe the views of Louise Rosenblatt (1978, 1985) in some detail because this is the perspective that has most influenced our own thinking about mature literacy processes.

Controversial Issue

One common way to think about literacy has been to liken the process to that of a computer. Charts showing inputs, processing systems, knowledge systems, and outputs are used to characterize the process of reading. Within these schemes, debates focus on whether the reading process is driven mainly by the text (input) or the knowledge of the reader (knowledge systems). The text-driven system is labeled a "bottom up" system, since it is assumed that readers process print letter by letter in a linear fashion (Gough, 1972). The meaning-based or "top-down" perspective views the reading process as guided by the hypotheses of readers; text is sampled as it is needed to confirm hypotheses (Goodman, 1976). In contrast to these extremes, interactive theories assume that neither text nor meaning dominates the process, but that each informs the other (Rumelhart, 1977).

Yet should we be using a machine metaphor to help us think about literacy processes? Rosenblatt (1985) argues that this way of thinking has as its basis "the mechanistic Newtonian model of research and the behaviorist research model patterned on it" (p. 98). It leads to a tendency to isolate elements, to analyze them separately, and to see them as acting on each other in linear and mechanistic ways. She proposes instead a *transactional theory* in which " 'transaction' designates . . . an ongoing process in which the elements or factors are . . . aspects of a total situation, each conditioned by and conditioning the other" (Rosenblatt, 1978, p. 17).

In this book, we have chosen to organize our thinking about reading processes and their intimate connection with writing using Rosenblatt's transactional theory. Although computer analogs may serve useful theoretical purposes, we believe that the transactional theory, because of its dynamic nature, is a more useful perspective to represent mature reading processes and to inform classroom instruction.

Pause and Reflect

In order to gain an appreciation for how Rosenblatt developed her theory, we ask you to read and reflect on the following lines. Responding to the lines will give you insight into how Rosenblatt's thinking was influenced by studying the processes of mature readers. Rosenblatt's directions are as follows: "Read the following lines. Write down your thoughts as soon as possible after you begin to read. Don't introspect about what you are doing, but simply jot down whatever comes to mind."

> The play seems out for an almost infinite run.
> Don't mind a little thing like the actors fighting.
> The only thing I worry about is the sun.
> We'll be all right if nothing goes wrong with the lighting.*

Before reading further, look over what you have written and jot down any additional thoughts that occur to you. Record your ideas in your journal under the heading Response to the Poem by Frost.

Rosenblatt (1978) had her students read this poem by Robert Frost (1949, p. 555). The reports from some of her students indicated initial confusion—for example: "Upon reading . . . the first time, I couldn't make any sense out of it" (p. 7). Other students did not begin to write until after they had passed this stage. Some notes represented a rudimentary literary response, already at a high level of organization—for example: "Sounds as if it could be a producer of a play giving encouragement to backers" (p. 7). For many readers, the third line created a need for revision: "On second thought, play metaphor—'all the world's a stage'—Life goes on in spite of quarreling, but it won't if the 'lighting' (moral? spiritual?) fails—what does the 'sun' mean? Outside performance? Technical term for stage light? Anyway, war, disagreement, etc., don't matter so much—so long as we still have the 'light' (sun—source of light—nature? God?)" (p. 9).

Based on notes such as these from many students in response to a variety of texts, Rosenblatt developed her "transactional theory." She drew several conclusions from her observations. First, each reader is active, not simply registering a ready-made message. Second, the reader looks beyond the referents to images, feelings, and ideas the words evoke. Rosenblatt (1978) distinguishes between the poem and the text:

> **"Text"** designates a set or series of signs (print) interpretable as linguistic symbols (words). (p. 9)

> **"Poem"** presupposes a reader actively involved with a text and refers to what he makes of his responses to the particular set of verbal symbols. (p. 9)

In doing so, she argues that the poem is not an object or entity, but rather an event in time. She views the act of reading as a dynamic process involving a particular individual, text, time, and set of circumstances. The transaction involves both the present state and interests of readers as well as their past experiences.

This way of thinking about the reading process applies well to the reading of poetry. Does it apply equally well to the reading of a cookbook or newspaper? What is the difference between reading a poem and a newspaper article? What does the reader do when engaged in these different forms of reading? Rosenblatt argues that in both

---

*From "It Bids Pretty Fair," from *The Poetry of Robert Frost* edited by Edward Connery Lathem. Copyright © 1975 by Lesley Frost Ballantine. Copyright 1947 © 1969 by Henry Holt and Co., Inc. Reprinted by permission of Henry Holt and Co., Inc.

forms of reading, the reader responds cognitively and affectively in the transaction with verbal signs. The difference has to do with the reader's selective attention. When reading a newspaper *(efferent reading),* attention is focused on the cognitive aspect, the public meaning, in order to abstract what is to be remembered. When reading a poem or a novel *(aesthetic reading),* attention is focused mainly on what is experienced conceptually and affectively *during* the reading event.

We have spent some time developing Louise Rosenblatt's transactional theory because we draw heavily on it when we think about reading comprehension and reader response to literature. It serves as the basis for our thinking about the integration of reading, writing, and other language arts. Instead of seeing them as separate processes that relate to each other in some linear way, we treat them as part of a unified process that occurs when a reader engages with text.

The theory applies to the mature processes of literacy—to adult readers who have had considerable reading experience. Rosenblatt assumes, for example, that all readers read fluently and are able to translate the series of signs in text to words. Yet as primary grade teachers we know that helping children learn to make this translation is a major goal, particularly in kindergarten through grade three. Some children solve the translation of print to language effortlessly; others need help and guidance and/or direct instruction to acquire the skill and knowledge necessary.

Rosenblatt assumes, as well, that all readers have a reservoir of experiences relating to linguistic symbols. Yet as primary grade teachers we are aware that many children have not yet developed a set of referents corresponding to words they will encounter, let alone a broader array of images, feelings, and related ideas.

Finally, Rosenblatt presumes that readers are able to render cognitively coherent representations, for aesthetic as well as efferent reading. Yet some children need to be taught strategies for comprehension and for sorting out what is sufficiently important that it should be remembered. These strategies call for a special self-awareness by readers of what they are doing. It encourages a more active reading process in which readers have a goal and plan and self-monitor their reading.

In sum, our thinking about reading comprehension, particularly a reader's response to literature, has been informed by Rosenblatt's transactional theory. The theory also provides us with the rationale for the integration of reading, writing, and other language arts. This perspective does not, however, address important developmental issues:

How do children learn about print?

How do they develop vocabulary and related concepts?

How do they develop comprehension and self-monitoring strategies?

In the following section, we consider the nature of literacy development and the theorists who inform our understanding of its development.

The Developmental Nature of Reading and Writing

Most children come to understand why people read and write by participating in acts of reading and writing. They listen to stories read aloud and understand that reading provides entertainment. They help read recipes and understand that reading provides information. They help write lists and understand that reading can aid memory. Active participation in and observation of literacy activities are important, because once children view these activities as pleasurable, useful, and informative, they want to read and write.

As you will learn in the next chapter, we subscribe to many of the tenets of a whole language perspective on literacy activities. That is, we believe that the forms of writing and reading in which we ask children to engage should be similar to those that are valued more generally in our culture: reading stories because they are entertaining, reading an informational passage to gain information, writing to a known audience, and the like. Focus on letters and word parts should occur as part of larger meaningful activities, since items taken out of context tend to be nonsensical.

Although the experience of learning about literacy is a unified one, it is useful for us to consider aspects of the process when we *assess* the development of our students. We distinguish between instruction and assessment. Instruction should involve meaningful tasks. During assessment, in contrast, it may be useful for us to look more analytically. When we study what children are doing when they read and write, we achieve a deeper understanding of their developmental progress and insight into how we can provide effective instructional support. In learning about the development of

In what ways are these children enjoying reading?

children, we recommend that you explore the following three areas: (1) skill with print, (2) prior knowledge and vocabulary, and (3) comprehension strategies.

Skill with Print

We have all listened to a young child "reading" a story. The tone suggests a careful and accurate reading of text, but upon closer examination we may find that the oral rendition bears only an approximate relation to the printed text. Although it is clear that the child has begun to understand some things about reading, the complicated problem of how the signs in text are related to language has not yet been solved. Generally, children at this stage are engaged in exploring text and testing their hypotheses about what it means to read and write. Among other things, they must learn that print is what is read, not pictures. Hiebert (1981), for example, found that many 3-year-olds pointed to pictures when asked what readers should read in books containing both pictures and print. Only gradually do they begin to understand that it is print that people read.

As children make this discovery, they begin to see that spoken words relate to printed ones. Also at this stage, they learn to "read" words in context; that is, they recognize labels and other signs that occur regularly within the same context, like STOP signs or PEPSI in a red, white, and blue swirl. Careful studies show, however, that children do not always recognize the same words out of context, and that when the writing is altered (XEPSI for PEPSI, for instance), they do not detect the change (Masonheimer, Drum, & Ehri, 1984; see also Mason, 1980). Children who identify words this way have not yet reached the stage of word learning when they depend solely on letters to recognize words. They do not yet understand the alphabetic nature of English spelling. This stage is sometimes referred to as *logographic* reading because children identify words holistically in ways not unlike those involved in the recognition of some Chinese characters (Ehri, 1991).

A critical juncture in children's learning occurs when they become aware of the phonemic (sound) composition of spoken words and discover the correspondence between phonemes and printed letters. This stage has been referred to as the *alphabetic* stage (Ehri, 1991) or spelling-sound stage (Juel, 1991). Children at this stage begin to read stories in a word-by-word fashion, searching for matches between spoken words and those in text. They write recognizable words, representing portions of words, usually the initial and sometimes the final consonant, in traditional ways. Over time, through practice and instruction, their representation of words becomes more complete, including the vowels of words and representing them in standard form (Henderson, 1981, 1985/1990).

By reading many easy texts, children enter the stage when their reading and writing processes become automatic and they achieve fluency. Printed words are recognized instantaneously so that attention can be directed to the meaning of text in the way described earlier that is based on Rosenblatt's theoretical work (Stanovich, 1991). Further discussion of how children develop knowledge of print and teaching strategies to support this development are included in chapter 3.

Prior Knowledge and Vocabulary

The knowledge that children acquire through reading and direct experience is incorporated into their developing vocabulary. It is therefore difficult to talk about prior knowledge without considering vocabulary. However, prior knowledge is not limited to vocabulary knowledge. Prior knowledge also includes the personal experiences and the situational context that go beyond vocabulary knowledge. The difference between vocabulary knowledge and more general prior knowledge is somewhat analogous to the difference between a dictionary and an encyclopedia, between a definition and a fully organized body of knowledge. Nevertheless, it is through words that readers gain access to their relevant stores of knowledge—their mental encyclopedias as well as their mental dictionaries.

Prior knowledge and vocabulary, like print skill, underlie the smooth functioning of the comprehension process. The interaction is reciprocal: Prior knowledge enables children to construct the meaning of text, and general comprehension of a text allows them to predict and specify the meaning of unknown vocabulary they encounter.

The words printed on a page are nothing more than graphic forms. It is the knowledge that we bring to reading that gives meaning to text. Consider, for a moment, the comprehension of bilingual students with limited proficiency in reading English text. Many of the words they encounter they are able to pronounce accurately. Yet they are unfamiliar with the meanings of many English words; the printed words fail to trigger meaningful associations that will allow them to reconstruct the meaning of text. Such children often have many relevant experiences and are familiar with terms to describe this knowledge in their first language. Thus, your task as a teacher is to consider how to help them relate their prior experiences and knowledge of their first language to English terms. Accordingly, vocabulary instruction has repeatedly appeared as an important area in second-language learning (Saville-Troike, 1984; Tikunoff, 1988). At the same time, it is important to remember that many bilingual students do not experience such problems since their concepts in English are well developed.

Many English-speaking readers may also have prior experiences and knowledge that relate to text but fail, for whatever reason, to bring this knowledge to bear on the task of reading. They are unable to actively retrieve information relevant to the theme or topic that the author is developing. Such children need instructional support to develop strategies for accessing their prior knowledge.

Pause and Reflect

Think for a moment about how you currently learn vocabulary. Focus on a specific word that you encountered recently that was unfamiliar. What did you do to try to figure out its meaning? Have you encountered the word since the first time you noticed it? Do you feel that you have a good understanding of the word, or are you still trying to specify its meaning and how it can be used? As you reflect on these questions, write your thoughts in your journal under the heading Vocabulary Learning.

To learn vocabulary words, children must engage in an interactive process. On first encountering an unfamiliar word, they must learn as much as they can from the context in which the word occurs. Consider, for example, the following sentence: "At first, the boys were confident, even *cavalier,* pressing close to the edge of the cliff." Students familiar with the word *confident* might be able to form a beginning notion of the word *cavalier;* they might then test this notion through class discussion, reading, or referring to a dictionary; and they might then reconsider their prior experiences to test how the word applies. Other teaching strategies to develop vocabulary are described in detail in chapter 4.

A somewhat different situation exists when children lack the prior experience as well as the words to represent this experience. Limited prior experience will make it difficult for young readers to comprehend text in new topical areas. For these children, your task is to help them build relevant experiences through field trips, film, reading, and class discussion. These and other teaching activities are discussed in chapter 4.

Comprehension Strategies

The prior knowledge of students is intimately connected with their ability to derive meaning from text. It seems evident that understanding a message that is made up of words should require some degree of familiarity with those words. In fact, research indicates that the students with well-developed vocabulary knowledge also tend to be good in reading comprehension and that those with limited knowledge tend to be poorer comprehenders (Davis, 1968; Thorndike, 1973–1974).

And yet, we have not been able to demonstrate a causal relation between vocabulary knowledge and comprehension of texts containing those words. Teaching difficult words to students prior to reading a selection does not necessarily result in comprehension gains (Jenkins, Pany, & Schreck, 1978; Tuinman & Brady, 1974). Results may not be realized because knowing words well enough to accurately select a synonym on a multiple-choice test may not represent sufficient understanding for comprehension of text. Readers must also have a broader understanding of nuances of the word and the situational context in which it occurs. They must know how to activate this prior knowledge while constructing the meaning of text.

Most children become better readers by developing strategies that require their active involvement in reading. These include focusing on a topic or concept and posing some personal questions to guide reading before they read; questioning and rereading to check that comprehension is occurring during reading; and summarizing the main points of the selection and evaluating it after reading. Many good readers develop such reading strategies without instructional support, but many others need specific instruction and guidance.

Similar processes are involved for writing: focusing on a topic or concept or posing some personal questions to initiate the writing process before writing; reflecting and rereading to check that communication is occurring while writing; and rereading, sharing, and editing the text after writing.

Communication and comprehension are transactional processes. Readers and writers must be actively involved in making sense out of print. Active involvement requires them to integrate and organize information across a text and to connect it with what they already know. Good readers can integrate and organize information and have developed reading strategies that enable them to comprehend and learn, while poor comprehenders may be deficient in these areas. Those who cannot integrate and organize information may experience problems with prior knowledge and/or comprehension strategies, while others may lack knowledge of print.

Research also shows that you can help your students to become more aware of comprehension "breakdowns" and how to resolve problems (Garner, Hare, Alexander, Haynes, & Winograd, 1984; Raphael & Pearson, 1982). We describe strategies for helping students develop comprehension strategies in chapters 5 and 6.

WHAT GOALS SHOULD YOU HAVE FOR LITERACY INSTRUCTION?

Your general goals will include developing children's literacy comprehension and communication and enhancing their pleasure from reading and writing. Earlier in this chapter, we discussed perspectives that will help you guide the reading and writing development of your students. We considered the literacy processes of mature readers and writers, as well as the developmental nature of reading and writing as children learn. As children become literate, their knowledge and skill develop interactively in areas pertaining to print, prior knowledge and vocabulary, and comprehension. By delineating these three components, we were not encouraging separate instruction in these areas. We did suggest, however, that these are areas you should consider when you assess and monitor the reading growth of your students (see chapter 10 for further discussion of assessment).

More important for the purpose of this section is that, while your general goals will be to develop children's literacy *comprehension and communication* and *pleasure from reading and writing,* you will have more specific goals that relate to *knowledge of print, vocabulary and conceptual development,* and *reading comprehension and writing strategies.*

Comprehension and Communication

We believe that the main goal of reading is comprehension—understanding the message or meaning of an author. The goal in efferent reading is to carry away a message as accurately as possible. The goal in aesthetic reading is to focus on what is experienced cognitively and affectively *during* the reading event to develop a literary response. By this we mean looking beyond the referents to feelings, images, and ideas the words evoke to form a coherent interpretation. Correspondingly, the main goal of writing is communication—conveying ideas, feelings, and images through carefully selected and ordered words.

Comprehension and communication are dynamic experiences in which readers and writers actively pursue meaning through text. They do so by framing new information in terms of what they already know. For example, in understanding the poem by Robert Frost introduced earlier that Rosenblatt presented to her students, some may have drawn on their experiences attending the theater and others on their memories from being in plays. Similarly, in considering a chemistry experiment, some students may draw on their prior cooking experience; others, on home experiments with soda and vinegar. In efferent reading, this use of prior knowledge will lead to a conceptually coherent understanding; in aesthetic reading, to a personal literary response. Whether readers and writers are young children just beginning to make sense of signs and writing or experienced scholars undertaking a major research project, they draw upon the same processes to construct written messages and understand the writings of others.

Pleasure from Literacy

We emphasize the importance of providing literacy experiences for children through which they will gain pleasure and see reading and writing as personally satisfying activities. From this, they will achieve a sense of the usefulness of literacy and a command over it. It will intrigue their minds by revealing an exciting world beyond the familiar one they know (Olson, 1994). They will be motivated to read and write.

Knowledge of Print

As children develop as readers and writers, they explore and learn about the nature of print. For example, they must learn about how print relates to speech and meaning; they must learn how paragraphs are structured and stories arranged. As their teacher, you need to learn what children already know about print and then develop instruction that allows them to expand that knowledge.

Vocabulary and Conceptual Development

Children must also acquire more general knowledge about people, processes, materials, and events. They organize their prior experiences into categories, and this knowledge helps them make sense of new experiences, including those about which they read and write. As children develop both specific and general knowledge, they become more effective readers and writers. As with the previous goal, you need to learn what children already know and develop instruction that encourages them to expand their vocabulary and conceptual knowledge.

Reading Comprehension and Writing Strategies

Learning to read and write involves developing effective strategies. Observing very young children as they make sense of their experiences shows they are born with the capacity to make sense. Ideally, all children as they become readers and writers should continue to demonstrate this same creative problem solving. All too often, however, they begin to think of reading and writing as routine forms of activity accomplished through rote application of procedures rather than active and speculative use of available cues. One of your goals must therefore be to foster continued application of their "sense-making" capacity as children first encounter stories and as they progress to more complex text. In sum, your overall goal will be to support the learning of your students, so they can read and write and love to do so.

HOW CAN YOU HELP STUDENTS DEVELOP AS READERS AND WRITERS?

In this section, we describe two ways in which you can help your students develop as readers and writers. The first is by creating an environment in which children participate in literacy activities. Children develop their knowledge about print, broaden their background knowledge, and form reading and writing strategies by actually engaging in activities that entail reading and writing. This is the main way in which children become readers and writers. In the first part of this section, we consider how teachers can create literacy opportunities for their students.

Some children, different children at different times, profit from more structured guidance. In order to provide appropriate help, you need to clarify the goals you have for your students, gather information on an ongoing basis in these areas to plan instruction that is responsive to their needs, and provide appropriate support that leads to the gradual development of independence. This set of issues is considered in the second part of this section.

Creating Literacy Opportunities

Children become proficient readers and writers by reading and writing things that are important to them. Any literacy program must include opportunities for students to read and write a variety of texts, discuss the ideas presented, and reflect on the nature of their reading and writing. Students will be motivated to undertake such activities to the degree that they view them as important. We agree with the proponents of "whole language" instruction that children should learn to read and write in environments that encourage communication through the integration of reading, writing, listening, and speaking, and that this integration should be organized around good literature.

The current emphasis on whole language activities is a reaction to reading instruction that fragments the reading process into a variety of skills and teaches each skill separately. In the primary grades, for example, children sometimes are taught letter-sound associations as isolated units or in single words. As a result, young learners fail to develop strategies for word identification that employ cues from context and prior experience as well as letters. Similarly, intermediate-grade students sometimes learn comprehension skills such as identifying main ideas and supporting details and sequencing story events from one or two paragraph selections and consequently fail to focus on the meaning of a text as a whole.

Instead of this fragmented approach, the environment you and your students create should support their engagement in communication and comprehension of ideas with others. Such activities should captivate students in thoughtful ways. Writing is one of the most effective ways in which beginning readers can learn about the relations between letters and sounds (Clarke, 1989). As elaborated in chapters 6 and 7, writing can be encouraged when children have opportunities to share and publish their work. Some writing can be an attempt to capture the ideas of others. Writing summaries, for example, is a natural way to encourage readers to attend to the information contained in text. Students learn from the responses of others; thus, group-based discussion of text is a natural way to encourage new insights. When you encourage your students to read and respond in a constructive, reflective fashion to other students' writing, you are creating a community of readers who share and clarify their comprehension of text (Raphael & McMahon, 1994). We include a more extended discussion of the whole language philosophy in chapter 2 and describe how this philosophical perspective undergirds the creation of a literate environment.

Instructional Support for Literacy Development

Although we agree that reading and writing tasks should be holistic and meaningful, some children are not able to infer all they need to know without special instructional support. Such students profit from carefully designed reading and writing instruction to help them develop as readers and writers.

But what do we mean by instruction? There was a time, not so long ago, when teachers proceeded mainly by following the suggestions in the teacher's manual that accompanied published reading programs. Students were thought of as empty vessels or blank slates to be filled with sight words, phonics skills, and other skills. In other words, a behaviorist philosophy informed instruction.

In contrast to this position is one that views children as already knowing a great deal about literacy, even when they first enter school. They make sense of their new experiences in terms of their previous experiences. This active response to new experiences has been referred to as the construction of events. Children do not passively receive knowledge, as is assumed by a behavioristic perspective, but rather make or construct their unique interpretations of events. This includes events about which they read and write. The instruction of teachers who hold this view of learning is informed by a *constructivist* perspective.

Instructional support is appropriate when it enables students to progress to the next stage of development. Central to instructional planning is the view that instructional support should be geared just beyond what children can accomplish independently in order to help them progress into the next level of proficiency (Rogoff, 1990; Vygotsky, 1978).

We subscribe to the Vygotskian position that learning develops in a social/cultural environment. Children through support and interaction with others forge new ways of thinking and doing. Through talk with others, they monitor their activity. For example, when a child reads with a teacher, the teacher may ask questions pertaining to meaning ("Does that make sense?"). Gradually, with experience, the children may internalize this speech so as to self-monitor their comprehension. Learning in the classroom occurs first interpersonally through social interaction and then, once learned, becomes internalized. We recommend that new concepts and strategies be modeled first by teachers and then reinforced in peer groups. Concepts and strategies developed in this manner will be applied later independently by individuals. Accordingly, the quality of your instructional support depends on goals that are clear, instructional plans based on individual assessment, and teaching support to foster independence.

Pause and Reflect

Reflect on your own style of learning. How have you developed as a reader and writer? Do you learn most from pursuing activities independently? Or do you enjoy the support of a sensitive teacher and/or peers? Write your thoughts in your journal under the heading Style of Learning.

Direction from Instructional Goals.

Goals are a necessary requisite for effective instruction. Goals indicate the specific areas you believe are important for student learning. Like a compass, they provide direction for assessing progress and planning subsequent instruction. Goals provide continuity for instruction from grade to grade. Teachers in some schools develop a common set of goals for literacy instruction, to be translated at each grade level into specific objectives. When the instructional program is designed to realize agreed-upon goals for grades K–8, students receive a consistent message about what is important and what is not. This kind of instructional program provides continuity for learning.

Goals also influence the selection of materials. If one of your goals is aesthetic reading, you will not select text with little or no literary merit. At all grade levels, but particularly in the early grades, you would attempt to find appealing stories written in natural language. Similarly, to develop efferent comprehension, you would select interesting informational text.

Finally, goals influence the instructional methods that you employ. If fluent reading is a goal, for example, you need to encourage your students to read extensively outside the classroom. If you want to expand students' vocabularies, you need to develop prereading instruction that focuses on prior knowledge and vocabulary, and reinforce these areas as students read and respond to text.

Responsive Planning.

Planning responsive instruction depends on detailed knowledge about what students know, what they can do, and what they like. You gain this kind of knowledge by observing students as they read, write, talk, and listen. *Interactive assessment,* then, is observation that occurs during ongoing instruction; it depends on talking with students, considering their reading and writing, providing feedback, and demonstrating instructional strategies.

Supported Independence.

If you expect students to become independent readers and writers, they must be in control of their own reading and writing activities. They must have the opportunity to make choices about what they read and write. Some of these decisions will be made individually during the library time and in the classroom, and also during periods of independent reading. Some decisions will be made by groups of children who want to read books as partners or in small study groups. Similarly, children must have the opportunity to think through what they would like to communicate in writing. These choices help children define and develop their interests.

Independence in reading and writing also results from instructional support that takes children beyond their current level of learning to experience a more complex form of learning. The scaffolding you provide enables them to develop strategies and to internalize and apply what they have learned (Pearson & Gallagher, 1983). The supportive role of teachers changes as students progress through three stages:

1. Teachers model literacy strategies and provide guided instruction to introduce strategies so that students learn how, when, and why they can be used to enhance efferent and aesthetic reading.

2. Students practice strategies with peer support and teacher feedback in order to discuss alternative interpretations and achieve greater independence in using strategies.

3. Students adapt and practice strategies independently according to their individual needs and report on strategy use to the class.

As we introduce instructional strategies in the chapters that follow, we suggest activities that are appropriate for each of these stages.

HOW CAN YOU MEET THE NEEDS OF SPECIAL LEARNERS?

As inclusion of children with special needs into the regular classroom becomes more common, you will be challenged to meet the needs of a diverse group of learners. Many textbooks on teaching elementary school have separate chapters in which the authors discuss the instructional needs of special learners: children whose first language is not English, those with learning disabilities or behavioral problems, those who are developmentally delayed, those who experience difficulty with literacy, and those who are gifted. We believe that children treated in special sections of textbooks have too often been treated separately in the classroom as well. We propose, for both philosophical and practical reasons, to discuss the unique problems of special learners as we discuss instructional planning for all students.

We present methods of instruction and assessment that are appropriate for *all* students. Research, theory, and practice indicate that classroom instructional strategies also work with special learners such as learning-disabled and bilingual students (Anders, Bos, & Filip, 1984; Hollingsworth & Reutzel, 1988; Lyons, 1990). For example, the reading problems of some bilingual students arise from their limited knowledge of English; some of these students also have limited prior knowledge. For those with limited prior knowledge, the teaching support needed is the same as that for learning-disabled children, who, for different reasons, may not have developed appropriate background knowledge. Moreover, the teaching approach is the same for all students asked to understand a new task or assignment for which they lack prior knowledge. In all cases, instruction must be designed to match the developmental level the students have attained. Prereading activities will develop the concepts that enable students to learn from a particular text.

Instruction may be further refined to meet the learning needs of these particular children. For example, students who cannot attend to long and complex text because English is their second language or because of attention deficits may learn the same comprehension strategies as the rest of the class, but may need to have the text broken into two smaller sections to allow for more frequent support and feedback during discussion. The strategy remains the same but is modified to address specific individual needs.

Special learners need to feel respected and valued. When children think that the way they talk or act is misunderstood or not accepted, they are likely to reject instruction (Bowman, 1989). You need to be sensitive to the different ways children from diverse cultures and of diverse abilities learn, think, feel, and express themselves in the classroom. The resulting diversity in interpretation and expression will enhance the learning of all students in your class. Responsive teaching characteristics—sensitivity, a commitment to acute observation, respect for diversity, and a willingness to modify instruction to meet individual needs—are requisites of effective instruction for all students (Ladson-Billings, 1994).

HOW DO CLASSROOM REALITIES INFLUENCE INSTRUCTION?

The teaching approaches we suggest in the following chapters consider the realities of classroom life. Some decisions that influence your work such as those pertaining to curricular materials, time schedules, and classroom composition may be made at the district and school levels. At the same time, within these constraints you have considerable autonomy to form a literacy program that is responsive to the goals you have established. Parents, since they have a stake in the education and welfare of their children, are a potential source of support. In this section, we consider school-based decisions, teacher decisions, and parental support.

School-Based Decisions

Decisions made at a district or school level often determine who and when you teach; they may even specify what reading materials you use. Most teachers work in settings where many decisions have already been made. To this extent, you work within a set of established conditions that you must transform into an effective instructional program (Barr & Dreeben, 1983). The class you are assigned may be easy or difficult to organize, extremely diverse or quite similar in terms of prior knowledge, with many or few special learners. Similarly, materials provided may fit well or not at all with your own instructional goals.

Most schools use literature-based programs, the contemporary version of basal reading series, as the basis for their elementary school literacy programs, although there is an increasing tendency for teachers to develop their own literature programs. Beginning teachers may find that a published program provides a source of support and direction. But as you gain in experience, we urge you to be more discriminating in your use of published programs. You will need to build your class library so that your students can experience a literacy-rich environment. You may develop a program that combines the publisher's graded program with other materials (e.g., children's literature), reorganizes stories into topical units, omits unnecessary skills activities, and develops other instructional strategies. As you gain experience, you can exert considerable influence over the selection of literacy programs and other materials by serving on school or district committees.

The time you have available for instruction influences your effectiveness. The amount of time spent at school each day and year is influenced by state and district policies. School-level decisions typically made by principals with input from teachers determine when students will be out of the classroom for special subjects like library, music, art, and physical education. What remains is your time for instruction. Large blocks of classroom time may permit integration of reading and writing activities; shorter segments may force you to plan more creatively.

Teacher Decisions

Within this set of school-based decisions, you have considerable freedom to organize your literacy program. Indeed, the decisions you make as you organize your literacy program at the beginning of the year are extremely important, because once established, these organizational decisions exert considerable influence on the effectiveness of your reading program. These decisions include:

- the goals you set for your students
- how you assess student progress
- how you group your students for instruction
- how you select and use materials
- how you schedule your classroom time

Perhaps the most important decision you will make pertains to the goals you set for your students. These goals become the "North Star" by which you establish your assessment system and guide your instructional program.

The groups into which students are placed for reading and writing make a difference as to what students learn and how they feel about themselves. The opportunities they have to read directly influence how much they actually read and how much they learn (Allington, 1983b). Too often teachers assume that decisions they make early in the year are carved in stone; in fact, you should evaluate the appropriateness of grouping, scheduling, pacing, and nature of assignments continually as the year progresses.

Parental Support

A final reality of classroom life is that many parents are extremely concerned about how well their children read and write. Parents represent an important source of support and can provide invaluable insights for developing more effective instruction. We recommend that you communicate regularly, try to develop positive relationships, and establish productive partnerships with your students' parents. Suggestions for ways to do this are included in chapter 16.

HOW CAN YOU DEVELOP PROFESSIONALLY?

The fact that you are reading this book means that you are already engaging in professional development. These are exciting and challenging times for teachers: exciting because of increased awareness of the importance of teachers as decision makers in establishing their own literacy programs; challenging because of the responsibility that falls on teachers to be knowledgeable about their own teaching practice.

This task is made easier because many other teachers are currently seeking to learn more about teaching through reading, peer study groups, membership in professional organizations, and inquiry in their own classrooms. Journals currently include many reports by teachers on what they have learned through classroom inquiry. Colleague or study groups provide a hands-on forum to consider alternative ways to support the literacy development of students. Within schools, administrators and other teachers are more aware of the need for mentoring relationships for beginning teachers. Opportunities abound!

We have devoted the final chapter of this book to an extended discussion of how you can continue to learn and extend your knowledge about literacy instruction. The best teachers never allow themselves to be satisfied with solutions that are simply workable; they explore new approaches to assess their strengths and limitations and

How is this teacher furthering her professional development?

to find those that are best for them. They continue to search and learn throughout their careers.

HOW DOES THIS BOOK SUPPORT YOUR PROFESSIONAL DEVELOPMENT?

Our philosophy about literacy development, our views on instruction, and our perspective on professional development guided us as we wrote the chapters that follow. Authors always face many decisions: where to begin, how to divide a complex set of issues into chapters, how to sequence topics. We have organized this body of knowledge in five main sections.

Section I develops our ideas on how students develop literacy. Chapter 1 presents our fundamental beliefs about reading processes and instruction, and chapter 2 describes the history of reading instruction, the philosophy of whole language, and the importance of teacher decision making.

Section II explores teaching strategies and the planning and implementation of instruction. It develops in depth what is known about the components of literacy—knowledge of print, prior knowledge and vocabulary, reading comprehension, and writing—and introduces teaching strategies to foster student learning in these areas. Chapter 3 focuses on how children's knowledge of print develops and how it can be supported by instruction. Chapter 4 considers children's prior knowledge, vocabulary, and purpose setting, and teaching strategies for their development. Chapter 5 focuses on strategic reading and how teachers may guide, facilitate, and empower student comprehension. Chapter 6 considers connections between reading and writing, and how their joint development consolidates and extends students' comprehension and communication. Chapter 7 discusses the research on writing development and considers how you may guide the writing development of your students.

Section III explores the background knowledge needed by teachers about reading materials, assessment, and organizing students for instruction. We discuss the complex decisions faced by teachers in organizing literacy programs at the beginning of the year and consider how they can be modified as the year progresses. Chapter 8 focuses on the importance of knowing and using children's and adolescents' literature in literacy development. Chapter 9 considers published programs for teaching reading and writing. Chapter 10 considers assessment and how it is linked with instruction. Chapter 11 describes a variety of flexible ways in which students can be grouped for instruction and considers how time may be scheduled effectively.

Section IV presents integrated perspectives on classroom instruction. It shows the developmental nature of the literacy program by examining how teachers at different grade levels organize their reading programs. The chapters in this section demonstrate through case studies the interconnections among curricular goals, materials, and teaching strategies. We have included this integrative section because we believe strongly that the truly difficult part of planning and implementing a reading program is to bring all these elements together. Chapter 12 describes classroom programs for preschool and kindergarten emergent readers; chapter 13, for primary-grade children; chapter 14, for intermediate-grade children; and chapter 15, for middle and junior high school students. This section should help you integrate the concepts introduced in Sections I, II, and III into concrete images of how actual classroom programs are formed and change over time.

Finally, in Section V we examine issues that pertain to the community and the profession of teaching. Chapter 16 is devoted to a discussion of professional development. As part of this chapter, we explore ways to establish productive partnerships with parents.

You will no doubt find that much of this text is overlapping and even redundant. Important ideas are developed several times in different contexts and reinforced through repeated and slightly different applications. We hope that by adhering to our own beliefs about effective instruction, we have written a book that allows you to grasp this complex material fully. Rest assured: If an idea seems unclear the first time around, you will have several more opportunities to consider it and to come to an understanding of it.

As we described in the preface, we have planned and included a series of activities that promote thinking and problem solving to facilitate your learning from this text. Just as we believe that learning is an active process for students, we also believe that it should be an active process for teachers.

SUMMARY

In the first part of this chapter, we described the theoretical perspective of Louise Rosenblatt as one that we use to organize our thinking about reading and writing. We considered how literacy develops and discussed three main aspects of literacy development: knowledge of print, prior experience and vocabulary, and comprehension strategies. We used this theoretical discussion to frame what we believe to be important goals for literacy instruction: comprehension and communication, pleasure from literacy, knowledge of print, vocabulary and conceptual development, and strategies for reading comprehension and writing.

We discussed the importance of creating literacy opportunities in the classroom and considered the features of good literacy instruction: clearly specified goals, instructional plans responsive to individual needs, teaching support that develops independence, and the integration of reading, writing, speaking, and listening. We argued that special learners must be considered in ways that encourage their integration into the classroom and their literacy development. Literacy programs are formed through the decision making of teachers working within constraints posed by school-based decisions. Finally, we argue for a career-long view of professional development. We hope that you accept our challenge to reflect as you read this book.

In the Field

1. Interview teachers who are known to be excellent teachers. Ask them about their views on literacy development. What are their goals for literacy instruction? What are their beliefs about instruction and the nature of their classroom environment?

How do they accommodate learners with special needs? What are they currently doing to further their own professional development? Summarize what you learned in a report or in your journal under the heading of Interview of Excellent Teachers.

2. Visit a whole language classroom that includes several children who speak English as a second language. Observe how the bilingual children are encouraged to participate in instruction. Do they seem to be making good progress in reading and writing? Compare what you saw with the descriptions of classroom instruction by Gersten and Jimenez (listed below under For Further Reading). Summarize your classroom observations and your reactions to the Gersten and Jimenez article in a report or in your journal under the heading of Visit to a Whole Language Classroom.

Portfolio Suggestion

Select from your journal two examples of your responses to Pause and Reflect and include these in your portfolio. If you completed an In the Field activity, include your report from it in your portfolio as well. Write a brief evaluation of your work, commenting on what it shows about your learning. (Note: If you are using portfolios for the assessment of course learning, please read the section in the preface on portfolio assessment.)

For Further Reading

Fitzgerald, J. (1993). Literacy and students who are learning English as a second language. *The Reading Teacher, 46,* 638–647.

Gersten, R., & Jimenez, R. T. (1994). A delicate balance: Enhancing literature instruction for students of English as a second language. *The Reading Teacher, 47,* 438–449.

Hoover, N. L. (1985). Teachers' self-reports of critical decisions in teaching reading. *The Reading Teacher, 38,* 440–445.

Kameenui, E. J. (1993). Diverse learners and the tyranny of time: Don't fix blame; fix the leaky roof. *The Reading Teacher, 46,* 376–383.

Pearson, P. D., & Gallagher, M. C. (1983). The instruction of reading comprehension. *Contemporary Educational Psychology, 8,* 317–344.

Rasinski, T. V., & Fredericks, A. D. (1989). Working with parents: What do parents think about reading in the schools? *The Reading Teacher, 43,* 262–263.

Rosenblatt, L. M. (1985). Viewpoints: Transaction versus interaction: A terminological rescue operation. *Research in the Teaching of English, 19,* 96–107.

Ruddell, R. B. (1995). Those influential literacy teachers: Meaning negotiators and motivation builders. *The Reading Teacher, 48,* 454–463.

Strickland, D. S. (1995). Reinventing our literacy programs: Books, basics, balance. *The Reading Teacher, 48,* 294–302.

Teale, W. H. (1982). Toward a theory of how children learn to read and write naturally. *Language Arts, 59,* 555–570.

CHAPTER 2

The Role of Whole Language in a Balanced Reading Program

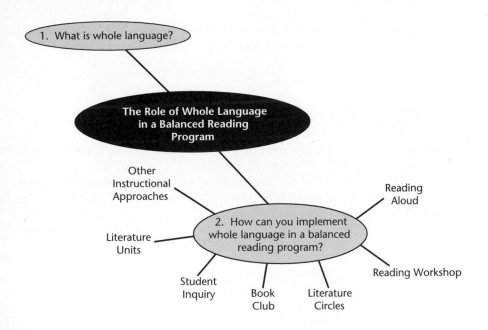

1. What is whole language?

The Role of Whole Language in a Balanced Reading Program

Other Instructional Approaches

Reading Aloud

Literature Units

2. How can you implement whole language in a balanced reading program?

Reading Workshop

Student Inquiry

Book Club

Literature Circles

CHAPTER GOALS FOR THE READER

To understand the philosophical nature of whole language and its basic tenets

To link whole-language philosophy to instructional planning, implementation, and assessment in a balanced reading program

CHAPTER OVERVIEW

The focus of this chapter is whole language, a term we hear in both the public and educational sectors. Whole language conjures up many different feelings and pictures of classroom learning. Many veteran teachers who were very comfortable using the teacher's edition to teach reading and writing became captivated by their students' excitement and investment in reading and writing as they used children's literature and provided students opportunities to select their own book titles and talk about books to their peers. Reading and writing instruction was no more the "teach, drill, test, reteach, and practice" routine they experienced using textbook programs. As a consequence, whole language has created much discussion about how to teach reading and writing in classrooms. In this chapter, you will develop an understanding of whole language and its basic tenets. We then discuss how you can blend whole language into a balanced literacy program.

TAPPING PRIOR KNOWLEDGE TO SET A PURPOSE

Whole language has been discussed in numerous educational journals as well as newspapers and magazines. Have you read about whole language or observed classrooms in which whole language is employed? What did you learn from your reading and observing these classrooms? Write in your journal what you know about whole language. Use these ideas, the graphic organizer, and the chapter overview to write questions you want answered about whole language. List these questions in your journal.

WHAT IS WHOLE LANGUAGE?

Is whole language a technique? Is it a method? Is it a program? No. Whole language is best described as a philosophy—a set of beliefs teachers use to guide literacy instruction. It is not static but evolves as we learn more about language and learning. The term *whole language* provides clues to its meaning. The "whole" refers to the idea that language is considered as a complete unit and not broken into parts. Thus, the four language processes—listening, speaking, reading, and writing—are viewed as a whole in which one process naturally evolves into the other and each process reinforces and develops the other. Hence, whole language embodies the concept of integrating the teaching of reading, writing, speaking, and listening. For instance, children who listen to and tell stories use their knowledge about story structure to read and to write stories. Moreover, reading, writing, speaking, and listening are processes that are used in all content areas and that facilitate the integration of the entire school curriculum.

The "whole" also refers to learning each of the language processes by engaging in listening, speaking, reading, and writing rather than breaking each process into parts from simple to more complex skills. For instance, children learn to write by using scribbles to communicate their first messages. They do not need to know the entire alphabet, the sounds associated with the letters, directionality, letter formation, and so on. They begin to write by writing rather than mastering each sequential step in the writing process; otherwise, learning to write would be daunting. The parts or skills become visible and meaningful to children as they engage in writing for meaning. If they want to show intensity or emotion, they recognize the importance and want to learn how to use exclamation points. End punctuation becomes important and valuable in their writing. The same theory applies to listening, speaking, and reading development. Through engaging in meaningful activities, children learn the many skills inherent in language learning. And as a consequence, it is a never-ending process of becoming more skillful in listening, speaking, reading, and writing. As we use language, we become more adept at communicating our message.

Whole language draws from different disciplines such as cognitive psychology, social-learning theory, psycholinguistics, sociolinguistics, and cultural anthropology. For instance, Frank Smith (1988) and others talk about developing a community of learners in which all children are members of the literacy club. It is from these psycholinguistic and sociolinguistic perspectives that we learn about the power of constructing personal meaning of text. We learn about the effect of personal immersion and involvement in authentic and natural contexts of reading and about discussing children's literature rather than reading rewritten text and answering questions in which only the program or teacher's ideas are given credence. It is from these disciplines that the tenets of whole language are developed. Let's explore some of the major tenets of whole language.

Tenet 1: Reading is a transaction that changes with each subsequent reading. The context, our experiences, the historical, political, and social milieu, and other factors impact the meaning we create. By reading, we create a new text that is different from the author's text. And with each subsequent reading a different text is developed. Louise Rosenblatt (1978) talks about reading as evoking a personal response in which the reader creates a poem. The text serves as a stimulus activating the reader's prior knowledge and experiences; yet the text serves as a blueprint that directs the reader's thinking (Rosenblatt, 1978). Hence no two readings are the same, and no two people will provide the same response. Our experiences and thinking are affected by each reading so that we are not the same people from moment to moment. Moreover, people have their own individual experiences that are unlike the experiences of others, thus affecting what they select as important and what they accept or reject.

Tenet 2: Reading and writing are developed in a similar manner to the ways young children learn to speak. By listening and acting on their environment, children use language to serve a purpose. Oral language learning is not broken down into parts in which children identify and blend the phonemes in each word. Instead children use meaning to construct language. The young child who uses a two-word phrase such as "Mommy sock" uses different intonation patterns to communicate different meanings. Hence this phrase may take on different meanings, such as Mommy, here is a sock; Mommy, I want the sock; and Mommy, is this a sock? From a whole-language perspective, meaning is the base for learning oral language as it is for reading and writing.

Tenet 3: Reading and writing are constructive processes in which readers and writers use their prior knowledge and experiences to create text meaning. The interconnections of these experiences create a scaffold for learning. Students' personal experiences and their reading facilitate students' understanding by creating bridges from the known to the unknown. Hartman and Hartman (1993) talk about book experiences as a part of prior knowledge and encourage students to read across different texts to create a web of understanding that enables the students to understand a story or topic from a number of perspectives. Reading across texts or creating intertextual experiences is an important aspect of developing literacy, as Hartman and Hartman (1993) explain:

> Accompanying this larger vision of reading is an expanded conception of readers. Classrooms become places where students' reading of one text leads to another and another, back and forth across history and across language and cultures; where students are challenged and surprised often by unexpected, serendipitous linking discoveries in their reading; where students continually revise their understandings and responses to previous texts; where students exploit the rich literary and artistic possibilities within, across, and beyond texts; and where students spend their days waist high in works that can be traversed in one direction, and then in another . . . and still another. In the fullest sense, this is what it would mean to become a nation of readers. (p. 210)

Tenet 4: Since language learning is a constructive process and is not learned through rote repetition and memorizing sentence patterns, students must continually take risks to develop literacy. By experimenting and by receiving and using feedback, children become proficient language users. Errors or what psycholinguists call miscues provide a lens for viewing and understanding children's language knowledge. For instance, the child who reads the sentence, "Ron hid the gun in the cellar," with the following miscue demonstrates his use of context to create meaning.

Ron hid the gun in the cellar. (basement)

Another child who reads the same sentence and provides a different miscue shows how phonics plays a role in reading.

Ron hid the gun in the cellar. (cello)

Hence risk taking plays an important role in learning language and is encouraged and rewarded in whole-language classrooms.

Tenet 5: Language learning is a social process. Children learn to talk through social interaction, and in a similar way they learn to read and write. Talk or discussion of text provides another perspective to thinking and understanding of text. It is this social process of conversation that further affects text comprehension and learning. Short and Klassen (1993) point out that as students talk about literature, they are actively examining their understanding and developing a new and deeper understanding about the text. As children discuss an author's work, they learn the different meanings constructed from the same text. Through conferencing, writers learn which parts communicate meaning and which parts are dense. Students learn that reading and writing are transactions that are enhanced and elaborated through the social context of talk. Hence a social-collaborative model of learning is developed in whole-language classrooms.

Tenet 6: In whole-language classrooms, language skills and strategies are developed in the context of authentic, meaningful, and functional activities. In this context, students are reading and talking about books with their peers, writing invitations to their classroom play, discussing and writing rules for their classroom and playground, recording their observations from a science experiment, writing directions to their homes, designing and writing directions to a game, and sharing a book with a younger student. These are the kinds of activities we do daily. The students will not be answering multiple-choice questions after reading, for instance, since it is not an authentic but rather an artificial activity to test story knowledge. When was the last time you and your friend read a book and exchanged questions with multiple-choice responses? Probably never because you were not interested in learning about your friend's story comprehension. Therefore in whole-language classrooms, students are engaged in authentic activities that are meaningful and functional for students.

Tenet 7: Children are curious and become naturally engaged in their own inquiry; hence whole language espouses a child-centered curriculum. Self-selection and choice in literacy activities are derived from this premise about learning. Their role is evident in many whole-language classrooms. In Claudia Katz's eighth grade, children choose their own books to read and discuss in literature circles. They choose their own roles and tasks within literature circles. One person may talk about interesting vocabulary in the chapter, while a second student may discuss the themes the author developed, and a third student may talk about the images formed while reading. In Kara Shoellhorn's first grade, self-selection may entail selecting a buddy to do paired reading. Choice precipitates engagement, increases learning, and encourages children to take responsibility for their learning.

Tenet 8: Observation is pivotal to whole-language classrooms. Yetta Goodman (1978) refers to this process as "kid watching"—identifying the students' strengths and weaknesses so that appropriate instruction can be planned. In whole-language classrooms, it's the child who directs the instructional process rather than a printed curriculum. The curriculum is "negotiated" by observing children's needs and interests. As Weaver (1990) so aptly states, ". . . it evolves as teachers and children together explore topics and themes, generating new interests and goals" (p. 25). For example, if Sarah is using conversation in her writing and doesn't employ quotations, isn't it appropriate to teach her the use of quotations? Kid watching provides valuable information for instructional planning and is the basis for teacher decision making.

Tenet 9: All children are viewed as capable and developing learners and not as immature and disabled. The question in the whole-language classroom is: "What is the child ready to learn next?" Weaver (1990) explains succinctly the importance of viewing children as being capable.

> . . . they (teachers) notice and praise children's strengths and their developing competence as learners and literate individuals. Building upon the children's strengths, whole language teachers create a climate in which children are eager to take risks and grow, rather than afraid to respond for fear of making "errors" and revealing weaknesses that will subject them to remediation. (p. 25)

For the past few months, Edward, a kindergartner in a whole-language classroom, repeats the same two letters in his name as he writes stories. Instead of the teacher labeling his behavior as immature and Edward as possibly being disabled, his teacher helps him during his writing by asking him to identify the corresponding letter to the sound he hears in the word and is attempting to spell. Edward provides five different letters to spell the word *dog.* In this attempt, she notes that Edward doesn't repeat the same two letters and praises him for using several new letters. She follows his first attempt by using Elkonin boxes to indicate the number of sounds in the word *dog* (see Figure 2.1). She tells him there are three sounds in this word and asks him to identify each sound he hears. She carefully enunciates the word, placing stress on each of the three sounds. Edward is able to supply the three letters—d-o-g. Instead of labeling Edward's behavior, this kindergarten teacher tries different approaches to learn about his needs and facilitate his success. Through observation and instruction, she has learned to address his needs.

Tenet 10: Assessment is directly linked to instruction and is often a part of instruction. The purpose of assessment is to gather valuable information for the teaching and learning processes. New goals and appropriate instruction are derived from

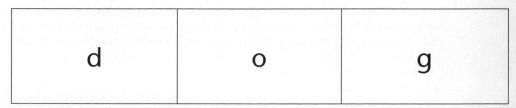

Figure 2.1 Box for Spelling of Dog

assessment. Both instruction and assessment are based on completing authentic-language activities—in other words, tasks that have meaning, purpose, and a function. Whole-language teachers are interested in both students' language processes and the products they create. These teachers are just as concerned about children's understanding and application of instructional strategies for reading and writing as they are concerned about the readers' response or the quality of the written piece. Both process and product are assessed and evaluated by teacher and student to establish new goals and take stock of learning. Self-evaluation is considered an important part of the assessment process so that students become personally involved and take responsibility for their own learning.

Tenet 11: Whole-language teachers' practices may differ from one another since there is no one method that characterizes whole language. Whole language is a philosophy in which teachers hold certain beliefs and are guided by these beliefs to design and implement instruction. It is the teacher and child working together to identify appropriate goals and procedures to help each learner grow and develop. Hence collaborative decision making is an essential part of whole language and makes whole-language classrooms look so different.

Pause and Reflect!

Consider the tenets we just described. What are your reactions to these tenets? Can these tenets be achieved in a classroom? Do these tenets address the diversity of students in today's classrooms? Record your responses in your journal and discuss them with other students in your class.

Controversial Issue

Whole Language

When educators and parents hear the term *whole language,* emotions and strong feelings arise. Camps for and against whole language have been created partly because of educational practices that were supposedly supported or rejected by whole-language philosophy. The hotly contested issue of phonics is a prime example of such a schism forming. Those who believed in phonics maintained that phonics was not being taught in whole-language classrooms. Many whole-language advocates tended to reject the way phonics instruction occurred in commercial programs, since this instruction was separated from the reading of text. In commercial programs, children were learning phonics in isolated skill lessons wherein children did not recognize the relationship of phonics knowledge and reading text, or children focused on sounding out words with little concern for text comprehension. Both views tend to oversimplify the philosophical basis of whole language and to force complex issues into polarities.

Susan Church (1994) points out that whole language is not a set of correct practices or a "right" way of teaching but rather a theory of learning and teaching. During her tenure

How does this type of instruction support the "whole language" theory?

as a classroom teacher, Susan shared her story about whole language and professional development.

> In the early 1980's when I joined a small study group exploring new ideas about literacy learning with Judith Newman, I was confused, challenged, and excited by what I was learning, but I was sure I would someday figure it all out—find a right way to teach. I thought I was exchanging my skills-based practices for meaning-based practices. That was all. I just needed to learn some different things to do in the classroom: Miscue analysis, Big Books, brainstorming, semantic webbing, written conversation, writing conferences, etc.
>
> Although many of those who joined that early study group began with a focus on practice, Judith helped us to see that the really important question is not "What am I doing?" but "Why am I doing this?" She encouraged us to observe our children and learn from them. She continually sent us to the professional literature so that we could ground our practice in a theoretical framework.
>
> This ongoing inquiry into what I believe about learning, teaching, and life has shaped what I do within and outside the classroom. I have shifted my attention from learning how to "do" whole language to learning how to reflect on what I am doing in light of what I understand and believe. I realize that, through this never ending process, my understandings and beliefs will continually evolve.
>
> We need to examine our assumptions continually. We need to consider many different perspectives on important issues—to invite a wide range of viewpoints. Like

Margaret Meek Spencer, we need to ask ourselves, "What if it's otherwise?" Keeping that question at the fore virtually guarantees that there can never be definitive right answers. Instead, there is a constant process of inquiry into both beliefs and practices. (pp. 363–364, 369)*

Susan's story elucidates the heart of whole language and its role in a balanced reading program: By observing children involved in literacy, we become informed about the educational practices in which children will enjoy reading and writing and achieve success. The question is not is this a whole-language activity but rather what am I doing to help children enjoy and learn the reading and writing processes, and why am I doing this? It is from this perspective that teachers are empowered to make decisions about instruction based on their knowledge of literacy and their keen observation of the children they teach. And it is from this perspective that we discuss using a whole-language philosophy to guide literacy instruction and learning.

HOW CAN YOU IMPLEMENT WHOLE LANGUAGE IN A BALANCED READING PROGRAM?

There is no one way to begin applying a whole-language philosophy in your classroom. In this section, we use the ten tenets of whole language to provide different suggestions to help you to begin using whole language within a balanced reading program. As you apply whole language, you will become more adept at planning and organizing instruction. Your thinking and decision making will evolve as you work through questions and problems that surface from daily teaching. You can then seek out other outstanding teachers to discuss educational practices and can also become a member of the International Reading Association (IRA) and National Council of Teachers of English (NCTE).

International Reading Association
800 Barksdale Road
P.O. Box 8139
Newark, DE 19714-8139

National Council of Teachers of English
1111 W. Kenyon Road
Urbana, IL 61801-1096

It is through these organizations that you evolve as a professional by attending local, national, and international meetings, reading their publications, and talking to other professionals about reading and writing instruction. In chapter 16, we discuss professional growth more fully and consider professional development as a lifelong process. We now begin our exploration into helping you initiate whole language within a balanced reading program.

---

*Church, Susan M. (1994, February). Is whole language really warm and fuzzy? *The Reading Teacher*, *47*(5), 362–370. Reprinted with permission of the International Reading Association. All rights reserved.

Reading Aloud

The easiest way for you to begin initiating whole language in your classroom is to read aloud good literature and provide opportunities for personal response. By reading aloud, you involve the entire class in the same activity. Different reading abilities do not become a central issue since you are reading to the students. As a result, students can concentrate on responding to text and constructing its meaning. By encouraging personal response, you can develop an aesthetic reading stance (Rosenblatt, 1989) that nurtures students to become lifelong readers. Personal response can take a number of forms. Journal writing, drama, drawing, and discussions are several ways to develop personal response. Constructing an agreed-upon meaning for text or reading from an efferent stance (Rosenblatt, 1989) can easily be done by incorporating reading strategies. We first consider developing an aesthetic response and suggest you refer to chapter 5 to learn about literacy strategies that can help students to develop efferent responses.

Journal Writing

After each reading, students write and share their personal responses about the reading. Journal writing is to be an expression of their initial thoughts about the text. In Figure 2.2, a third grader's journal response to Robert Kimmel Smith's *Chocolate Fever* appears. This response took only a few minutes to write and demonstrates to children that you value their responses. Moreover, they learn that a wide variety of responses can be made about text, and each has merit and is affected by individual interests, knowledge, and experiences.

A spiral-bound notebook can serve as a journal. Students date each entry and write for five minutes and share their responses with a small group of two to three members. We discuss journaling further in chapter 6.

Drama

Drama is a natural way to respond to literature. Students can interpret the character's thoughts and feelings about events and other characters. Self-expression is manifested through role playing. For example, after having students read Bernard Waber's *Ira Sleeps Over,* place students in small groups and have each group select one of the characters to role play. Students will need time to retell the story as a group and then begin acting out the story. Each group can present their role playing to the entire class, and you can conclude by comparing each person's interpretation of a particular character. The discussion can demonstrate the different responses that can be constructed from text.

Drawing

Students often like to draw while listening to literature. As students listen to text, encourage them to draw their thoughts and feelings about text. Young children may create a picture of how the character felt during the story while older students' drawings may be symbolic and capture the story's theme. Share their pictures by discussing their

Chocolate Fexer

I think Choclate Fever is a good book, because this has a brony named Hennry green. He eats chocolate every day every meal. He has chocolate evry thing. Then one day he gets brown spot, then nerse mesly takes Hemmy to Dr. Fargo's then a bunch of Dorktos are poking Hemmer. I would'int like it if alot of doktor were poking me. I wood run like Henry did.

Figure 2.2 Third Grader's Journal Response

drawings and posting them in the classroom. Students can think of and view the text from a variety of perspectives.

Discussions

Whole- and small-group discussions after reading encourage and develop personal response. Begin with whole-group discussions and gradually move to small groups so that students understand the purpose and content of the discussion. This is the time for students to explain their personal thoughts about text and identify the parts of text that evoked these ideas. These kinds of discussions need to be modeled. Tell your response to text and how these responses were evoked. Encourage students to react to your response by asking questions and comparing their personal reactions.

Reading Workshop

A reading workshop can be easily employed in elementary classrooms. It focuses on students' independent reading and responding to self-selected literature (Atwell, 1987). Reading is the central activity so that students develop "pleasure, fluency, involvement, appreciation, and initiative" (Atwell, 1987, p. 154).

Atwell begins each day with a minilesson in which she talks about a particular author or genre. She and her students read and discuss a piece or part of literature to appreciate text, to analyze meaning, or to understand the author's craft. Both writing and reading processes are considered so as to find out how one can best read and understand text and what the writers' considerations may have been in composing the text. As students ask questions and make comments, you can turn these opportunities into teachable moments. These are the questions that are pertinent to the literature in which the students are engaged. If the questions hold importance to all readers, you can extend instruction and design a subsequent minilesson. It is beneficial to have students contribute texts for reading and sharing during minilessons, to make this session both collaborative and relevant.

Angelita Johnson, for instance, read to her fourth graders Verna Aardema's folktale *Who's in Rabbit's House?* to demonstrate how this author uses onomatopoeia to create interest in the cumulative tale telling of rabbit's problem with an animal taking over his home. They discussed how onomatopoeia created pictures in their minds about what the characters did to resolve the problem. Some students talked about other authors who have used onomatopoeia and shared these books with the class during the next minilesson.

Independent reading follows the minilesson, with the teacher spending a short time walking around checking in with students about their reading needs and progress. The teacher then reads silently, thereby demonstrating the importance of reading for all learners.

Beyond reading literature and engaging in minilessons, students make personal responses to text. Atwell (1987) wanted to recreate a "dining room table" experience that occurred in her own home where readers engaged in conversations about books, authors, and literacy in general. But to have these pleasant conversations with students on a one-to-one basis was difficult because of the number of students and the time constraints of the school day. As a result, oral conversation took the form of written conversations in which Atwell invited students to share their responses about their reading in the form of a dialogue journal.

Dialogue journals take on the form of letter writing, and within this friendly letter form students write their personal responses to their reading and the teacher responds to their journal entries. In the return letter, Atwell points out the importance of expanding students' thinking as readers. The journal is not a regurgitation of the story; it is an opportunity for teacher and reader to communicate about the text.

During the school year, the teacher's responses should accomplish two goals. First, they should help students think about the story as it relates to their knowledge and experiences, including their personal reactions to story elements and confirmation and extension of the students' ideas. Second, they should help students consider the author's and reader's craft in meaning making, such as why the author chose to use flashbacks.

 # Learning from Experience

Helping students make quality responses to books requires modeling, probing, and time. Let's examine a third grader's response to the book *Stone Fox* as well as the teacher's response designed to extend this student's thinking. What did Anna's entry reveal about her reading comprehension? How does Ms. Wong further develop Anna's thinking?

 10/18

Dear Ms. Wong,

I think this story is about Little Willie and Grandpa and doc Smith. I feel bad for Grandpa because he ran out of medicine.

As you can tell he loves cinamen cake. I've never tasted it but cinimen is my middle name. I guess he also likes dogs because he wanted one of stone foxes dog and I'm sorry for Little Willie's eye. Well it was the day of the race. And he was off to the country. I can't believe so many people were there. I can't believe no one wanted Little Willie to win but anyways he was in the race and that's what counts and if I was in the race I would feel good even if no one cheered for me I'd be happy with myself like Little Willie was because he believe he could win and when people say that they do win and whenever I'm frustrated I say I don't need to cry and I won't.

10/20

Dear Anna,

I, too, couldn't believe that the people were not supporting and cheering for Little Willie. If the author chose to have the people cheering for Little Willie, would this change affect your feelings or enjoyment of the story, or would the story plot have to be changed?

Ms. Wong

Your Turn: What did Anna's journal entry reveal about her reading comprehension? How does Ms. Wong further develop Anna's thinking? Write your responses in your journal before comparing it to ours.

Our Turn: Although Anna's journal entry was verging toward summarization, Anna demonstrated her ability to react and connect her experiences and beliefs to the story events in *Stone Fox*. Instead of telling Anna not to summarize, Ms. Wong focuses on Anna's reaction and challenges her to consider the author's thinking as a writer.

Anna's journal entry illustrates another important concept Atwell emphasizes. The journal is not intended to be a final draft, ready for publication. The dialogue journal is to be the reader's initial thinking and reactions to a book. This journal is conceived as a "rough draft," and it isn't intended to go beyond a first-draft stage.

As students demonstrate an understanding of the purpose for dialogue journals, students can respond to each other. Peer communication facilitates learning to write for different audiences. Students' exchanges about literature provide a different perspective on text and further enhance student comprehension.

Atwell discovered that students' responses to each other tended to focus on inquiring whether their peers had similar feelings about the events and characters. The believability and authenticity of a character's feelings, thoughts, and behaviors were explored, and valued when peer responses were added. This exchange added dimension and extended thinking and learning about text.

Atwell has specific procedures for implementing the dialogue journal. She gives each student a letter at the beginning of the year defining the purpose, procedures, and requirements for reading and responding to literature. She recommends that students use a spiral-bound journal to include all correspondence. All correspondence should be dated and returned within 24 hours. Students are to write about their reading at least once a week, and they can do this during or outside of reading workshop. Writing follow-up responses to teacher and peers can also be completed during or outside the class period. Providing specifics about purpose and procedures facilitates implementation; thus students know what is expected of them. Showing examples of different students' responses to literature can also clarify the task. As you show these models, explain how student writers, for example, express their reactions to text and show insights about the author's thinking and choice of words to describe the mood or tone of the story. Analyzing these models provides focus and sharpens students' thinking and writing. As Atwell and others have discovered, writing provides students with opportunities to reflect and rethink their responses to text. Journaling can effectively address the time constraints that individual oral conferences present.

To assess students' reading, there needs to be a match between instruction and assessment. Students should be assessed on the same or similar tasks in which they are engaged during instruction. Atwell uses a point system to designate daily participation in reading workshop, the quality and frequency of entries in the dialogue journal, and the progress students have achieved in the collaboratively developed goals identified by both the teacher and student at the beginning of each quarter. Students take stock of their own growth by reviewing their goals and what they have accomplished during the past quarter and prepare themselves to discuss and show evidence of their growth at the quarterly conference. Assessment is not a special test given one day of the quarter; rather, it focuses on the tasks students do daily.

Reading workshop requires an extensive library to address the different reading abilities and interests of a class. Classroom libraries and school, public, and home libraries can supply students with books. Students should have selected their books before reading workshop begins. Students in grades one and two can select their books at the beginning of reading workshop and need a classroom library filled with short, easy texts to make their selections. These young readers can read up to 10 titles in a 20-minute workshop, so a large quantity of literature is needed.

Adaptations of Atwell's model exist. Some teachers schedule conferences on a frequent basis. Instead of reading during reading workshop, teachers have daily conferences with their students. The conferences may cover a number of different areas, depending on the student's individual needs as well as grade-level goals. During the conference, the teacher notes reading behaviors, so that appropriate instruction can be planned. Some of the instruction can be covered in minilessons or in the next conference.

For beginning readers, conferences tend to focus on reading aloud a scary, funny, interesting, or a favorite part of a story to support word identification and fluency. For the emerging reader, the text difficulty is a major factor. At this stage, students need much practice reading text in which they can easily identify words and develop some fluency. Rereading the same story several times is a common and a recommended practice, and reading workshop provides the time for sustained individual practice.

For students who are beyond the beginning stages of reading, the focus is comprehension. Students, for example, talk about the books they are reading. They may share an interesting, favorite, scary, sad, or humorous part of the story. Or they may talk about the character and share some problems the character resolves. The character's personality, appearance, and actions may be discussed. They may ask questions about confusing parts. The purpose of these conference with developing and mature readers is to share the enjoyment and beauty books can create, develop and extend students' text comprehension, and provide instructional support if needed.

Teachers can typically confer with an individual once every 5 to 10 days, depending on the size of the class and the needs of the students. Many teachers encourage students in grades two and above to keep folders in which they staple a record sheet listing the titles they have read and the date each title was completed. The folder can also contain the student's journal responses, and a list of goals may be stapled to the back of the folder. Some teachers use colored folders to facilitate conference management. A different color is used for each day of the week so teachers can easily identify the students they need to confer with during a particular day. The folders and other management techniques can make reading workshop manageable and also preserve a record of students' reading so students and teachers can review and collaboratively establish goals. Parents also find reviewing the titles their children have read during the past quarter very informative. They learn about their choices and interests in reading.

Some teachers like Nancy Atwell use reading workshop as their entire program. Others use it as one part of a multifaceted program in which reading workshop constitutes a period of 20 to 35 minutes in a 120-minute literacy instructional block.

Literature Circles

Literature circles are small-group discussions about literature. To capture an image of literature circles, visualize students engaged in a conversation about books they are reading. It is an opportunity for students to critically examine literature, to consider the power some books have in transforming ideas, to discuss the magic some books evoke for readers, and to share the laughter and joy a character or a scene can create. It's a time to share the meaning-making process and create extended and new meanings about books. It is a time in which students should be encouraged to take risks while knowing that their ideas are respected.

These conversations don't take place within rows of students; rather they take place in small groups of four to seven students seated in a circle on a carpet, around a table, or in some similar manner that allows students to meet face to face and share their thoughts and feelings about stories, poetry, nonfiction, authors' writing styles, personal experiences related to text, and the like. It is during these "grand conversations" (Peterson & Eeds, 1990) about children's and adolescents' literature that students reflect on and develop new meanings about text. It is through conversation that students learn about what they understand, what they don't understand, and what they need to consider to develop a more complete picture of the meaning of text. Students discover there is more than one interpretation to a given text; many interpretations exist. Moreover, by working together, students "build new ideas that go beyond what could be accomplished individually" (Short & Pierce, 1990, p. 34). They also discover, as Rosenblatt (1987) points out, that each reading is a new event. Discussing text also provides a new interpretation; it, too, is a new event. As Tiballi and Drake (1993) point out, literature circles allow readers "to transcend the text, coming to a deeper understanding of the text by connecting it with personal experiences" (p. 221).

The traditional role of a teacher "firing" questions is not characteristic of literature circles. There is no script of questions at the literal (Who is the main character?), interpretive (How does Joyce feel about the car accident?), and critical thinking (Would you have isolated yourself from your family? Why or why not?) levels. The discussion evolves from the participants' ideas. Students ask their own questions, provide their own reactions, and comment and respond to others' ideas. It is a natural process that mirrors ordinary conversations about books that are likely to occur outside of school. To achieve such a high level of discussion, the students must examine and evaluate discussions by viewing good discussions on videotape and discussing the reasons that a stimulating discussion evolves over an extended period of time.

 # Learning from Experience

Read the transcript of a literature circle discussion from Sharon Gleason's fifth-grade classroom. What do you notice about Sharon's instruction and students' responses to text? Write your responses in your journal.

....

Sharon's fifth graders have just read a Greek myth entitled "Echo and Narcissus" in which Echo, who possesses the gift of storytelling, uses this gift to deceive the Goddess Hera. Echo is punished by Hera and is only able to repeat or echo the words of others. In her grief, Echo meets the handsome youth, Narcissus. He tries to communicate with Echo but only hears his words repeated. Becoming disgruntled and tired of Echo's lack of communication, Narcissus takes rest beside a pond where he spies a beautiful face in the pond. Not realizing this is his own reflection, Narcissus dives into the pool to catch this handsome youth. He drowns seeking and admiring his own beauty while Echo wastes away crying over the loss of her love. To this day, Echo haunts the mountains, caves, and forests with her echo. Let's take a look at a part of their discussion.

Kate: How does Echo compare with Narcissus in the story?

Brian: They don't really compare. They aren't really the same.

Kate: I'm not saying they are the same. What is the same about them? And, what is different about them?

Mercedes: They are completely different.

Kate: That's what I am trying to find out. If Echo really loved Narcissus, they would have to have something in common.

Gena: They were both beautiful.

Caitlin: But the difference in that one is that Narcissus knew but Echo knew it but she really wasn't conscious that she would talk about it. But Narcissus knew it, and he would say it.

Probes

Teacher: Did Narcissus know it the whole time?

Kate: He hadn't seen himself.

Jimmy: He didn't know the reflection was him.

Gena: It said, "But though his face was smooth, and soft as any maiden's, his heart was as hard as steel" (p. 4). I don't think he loved anybody.

Brian: True. The prophecy came true in that story. The prophecy that until he knew himself that as long as he doesn't know himself he would be fine.

Mark: I had some questions on page 3. When Echo was stricken, what solutions would you suggest for her problem, for her plight?

Gena: She could go to Zeus and ask forgiveness.

Mark: She couldn't. Don't you remember she had to repeat?

Cara: She could think. You know Zeus is the God of Gods and he has powers that Hera doesn't. He could probably let her talk to him.

Mark: That was another of my questions. Why couldn't Zeus overrule Hera?

Cindy: He could have overruled Hera.

Mark: But he didn't. Echo kind of worked for him because when he wanted to go find somebody else Echo would go and do it. And then when Hera finally finds out, and does something terrible to Echo, Zeus just sits there and does absolutely nothing.

Ryan: Who said Zeus knew?

Mark: Wouldn't you when one of your nymphs disappeared?

Jimmy: What are nymphs?

Mark: That's what Echo is. Wouldn't you be if it was your favorite nymph?

Caitlin: But it didn't say it was Zeus's favorite nymph; it was Hera's.

Mark: I'm just saying, if Echo is doing something for Zeus, why couldn't Zeus do something for Echo?

Ryan: I think if Zeus knew about it, he'd think she got a punishment for doing something wrong.

Mark: But it was by Zeus's design. Echo was doing that so Zeus could do something wrong.

Heather: It said the nymphs were doing some mischief.

Mark: But look right there. Here. (Mark reads.) "So, when her sisters planned secret fun or mischief, and sometimes even when Zeus sought other company" (p. 3). It wasn't just for the nymphs.

Probes

Teacher: Let's go back and ask, why were myths written? How did myths evolve?

Ryan: To explain something that could not be explained naturally.

Katie: Maybe people thought this is how people lived before them.

Teacher: Tell a little about history?

Heather: They believed there was a Goddess of everything. But nowadays most of us think they are not real.

Probes

Teacher: Can we learn anything from these myths?

Caitlin: Yes.

Guides
Thinking

Teacher: Why do you think Zeus didn't help Echo? Are they possibly trying to teach a lesson?

Mark: But what would be the lesson?

Teacher: What would the lesson be that could possibly be told from this?

Mark: One—don't be so involved in yourself. I don't understand if that was the thing— What did Echo ever do wrong?

Heather: She tricked—helped her sisters go play while she occupied Hera with tales and myths.

Caitlin: She distracted her while they planned to do things.

Heather: She was pretending she was really being nice to her when she was letting her sisters play.

Katie: They were supposed to be under Hera's thumb. Echo pulls her in and she's like hypnotized from these stories.

Mark: She knew what Echo was doing and the nymphs and Zeus. Why did she just punish Echo?

Jimmy: She was pretending she liked her and was helping the nymphs.

The discussion continues.

Your Turn: What did you notice about Sharon's instruction and students' responses to text? Write your responses in your journal before comparing it to ours.

Our Turn: By comparing characters, these fifth graders are able to think at very mature and sophisticated levels of thinking. This discussion continues to be highly advanced and focused. The students easily use text information to support their think-

How are these children increasing their reading ability?

ing. The fifth graders easily demonstrate their ability to manage their own discussions with little teacher intervention. Moreover, Sharon Gleason only probes when students' thinking about text may need to be extended. She does not tell them the answer.

Organization

There are a variety of ways to organize literature circles. Teachers may assign a piece of literature for all to read and respond to. But, typically, teachers provide for student choice, so that ownership, involvement, and motivation are increased. When inviting students' choices, teachers provide book talks about an array of books for students to choose to read. Their selection determines their membership in a literature circle. In other situations, teachers may have identified a theme and selected related books. Students select different books to read and share their thinking about their chosen books with others who have not read them. This type of discussion typically focuses on retelling and comparing the different books read, while in other literature circles students and teachers collaboratively decide on themes and books to read and discuss.

Once the groups are formed, students meet to decide how they will go about reading and sharing their books. Will they read several chapters and meet in literature circles to discuss them? Will they meet at the end of each chapter? This decision can be revised at the end of each circle's discussion. Reading and discussing a few chapters rather than the whole book provide students with opportunities to ask questions, clarify ideas, and consider ideas, issues, and character development from many perspectives. But some literature circles may decide to read the whole book before starting the discussion, in order to develop their own lived-through experience (Short & Klassen, 1993). In this case, short daily meetings may occur to set goals for how much should be read by a particular day and to clarify areas that are not well understood.

It's important for the students to decide and plan for the subsequent literature circle discussion. What do they plan to do before their next meeting? Will they reread sections of the book? Will they read related books? Will they bring in books to share and to compare to the present book under discussion? These and many other questions can be used to establish this "focusing in" and organizing of the next literature circle meeting.

In some literature circles, teachers are participants but do not control the discussion. The teacher is of equal status with the students in terms of what is discussed. All participants have an obligation to respond and share. In other circles, the teacher may serve the role of facilitator to ensure that all participate and all ideas are respected and to encourage reflection and critical thinking. To keep conversations going, the teacher may provide a model of students' personal impressions of the text, so others can respond or share their personal responses. The teacher also needs to observe students' thinking and learning during discussions and provide direction and instruction when needed. Such instruction may occur during the literature circle to facilitate ongoing discussion, but it is more likely to occur after the circle meeting so as to focus attention on constructing meaning.

Implementation

Short and Klassen (1993) suggest beginning literature discussions "with students sharing their impressions of and personal responses to the books. They share favorite parts, retell sections, discuss parts they found confusing, make connections to their own lives or to other literature, and engage in social chatter" (p. 74). Short and Klassen refer to this beginning as "mucking around"—that is, sharing personal responses that support Rosenblatt's point that our first reading evokes personal meaning and later readings move to more efferent responses to literature.

Gradually, students should move toward engaging in critical dialogue about literature. Short and Klassen label this "focusing in," which requires students to listen and to reflect on one another's responses about literature—that is, to make connections with their own thinking of the topic, with other books, as well as with the teacher's and peers' ideas. To facilitate this process, Short and Klassen believe that focus should emanate from the reader's own ideas. Therefore instructional strategies must begin and build upon the reader's ideas.

Webbing can be used to help students focus and home in on a topic, theme, or the like. Students made a web, as illustrated in Figure 2.3, to demonstrate the areas they found interesting and intriguing about their book, *Tuck Everlasting*. From students' comments, discussion can ensue, and later discussions can take place focusing on a particular issue that many students wanted to explore further. In this case, the sixth graders wanted to consider the feelings surrounding mortality and immortality. They wanted to reread sections of the book dealing with living forever and death. A couple of students wanted to share other books they read about death such as Katherine Paterson's *Bridge to Terabithia* and Doris Buchanan Smith's *A Taste of Blackberries*.

Figure 2.3 A Web of Interesting and Intriguing Ideas from *Tuck Everlasting*

Art can be used as a technique for focusing in. Students can, for example, make and discuss the collage representing impressions they developed from reading a particular piece of literature. Other strategies can also be used to help students focus and "dig deeper" into literature.

The class period is not limited to meeting in literature circles; students are given instructional time to read and prepare for literature circles. Some teachers incorporate the use of journals to encourage self-reflection and initiate discussion during literature circle meetings. In this way, students are better prepared because they can read their journal entries prior to discussion. The journal also allows teachers to have knowledge of each student's thinking about literature. The journal serves as a permanent record to help students and teachers to reflect on thinking and learning.

Teachers may have several literature circles meeting simultaneously, with the teacher alternating participation in each of the groups. In other classrooms, teachers meet with each literature circle while other students are reading their literature, writing in their journals, or doing some related literacy project. The more the teacher meets with a literature circle, the more information can be gathered about students' reading needs. Such consistent information gathering can only lead to more effective decision making about instruction.

Assessment

Assessing students' understanding and learning is naturally captured through observation. Listening to students' responses in a literature circle shows, for example, their thinking about character development and demonstrates their use of instructional strategies such as visualization and prediction. If journals are used, reading about students' ideas is another vehicle to assess and evaluate individual thinking. Students should be aware of your criteria for assessment. Providing examples of acceptable and outstanding discussions and journals can help students reach their goals. Showing a videotape of a book discussion and asking students to note how students demonstrated their thinking and learning provides a model for students to achieve. Simulating a small-group discussion, and noting comments that show readers' insights about text as well as strategies for reading and learning, is another vehicle for modeling. Using a grid as illustrated in Figure 2.4 (p. 46) can show how students use personal experiences, other texts, the text under discussion, and other students' ideas to discuss literature. The grid can be used to focus on one student or the entire group.

Pause and Reflect!

Use the discussion grid from Figure 2.4 with the literature circle transcription that discusses the myth of Echo and Narcissus to show how Mark develops meaning about text, and compare it to our completed grid in Figure 2.5 (p. 47).

Using journals and observational tools such as the grid in Figure 2.5 is what Watson (1990) terms learner-referenced evaluation, in which the focus is on the student's individual efforts and achievement. The learner is the focus, not how the learner's performance compares to some particular task such as achieving 80 percent mastery in identifying major ideas and related supporting facts. Nor does our assessment compare learners to other learners, as is done in norm-referenced tests. These latter assessments may be important, but they are not appropriate tools for understanding students' thinking and learning in literature circles. The learner-referenced tools suggested here contextualize assessment so that we can understand the complex interactions occurring during reading and responding to text. We learn about students' meaning-making processes, which can be naturally observed during discussion and to some extent in journaling. This form of assessment extends and provides a more robust picture of our thinking about teaching and learning.

Individual Needs.

Literature circles can address individual needs. If students are second-language learners, teachers can provide books written in their native language about the same topic or title, so that students can read and discuss books that highlight their interests and not be limited by their reading level. Teachers have assisted less skilled readers by providing audiotapes of books in which students can listen and read along. Paired reading of a book is another alternative teachers use to address divergence in reading levels. Choosing a theme or topic allows for an array of books to be selected, so that a text set is formed (Short & Klassen, 1993). In a text set, books can range from easy to more difficult, and students can choose those they can read best, yet share their ideas within a heterogeneous group. These techniques allow students to read and share books together without labeling and grouping students according to ability.

Literature circles expose students to a variety of fiction, nonfiction, and poetry, give opportunities to share different perspectives about text, and provide more instructional time for reading. Practice and exposure will increase proficiency and enjoyment in reading.

Student _____   Date _____   Grade _____

Literature _____

Use of Resources for Meaning Construction	Relationships Focus: Outward	Connections Focus: Inward	Transactions	Discussion
Uses information from something other than book sources	Addresses social issues	Forms new understandings from transaction with text	Recognizes relationships of story and life-themes	Promotes action
Uses reference material	Addresses previous readings by other authors	Moves into the world of the text	Examines story in light of self as audience	Identifies with characters
Frames questions to get information	Addresses previous readings by same author	Shares personal and emotional connections	Sees plot developing	Addresses the reading
Rereads to focus on important details and concepts needed to make sense	Addresses life experiences appropriate to text and readers	Shares a point of view (own, character's, family's, group's, etc.)	Draws from story traits of characters	Retells for own purpose (parts liked, not liked, not understood, to prove something)
Demands meaning by using prior knowledge	Addresses ideas of others	Shares information from text	Discusses setting within context of story (e.g., mood)	Initiates discussion related to text

Figure 2.4 Potential Literature Discussion Responses. *Source.* Reprinted by permission of Dorothy Watson from her article "Show Me: Whole Language Evaluation of Literature Groups" in *Talking about Books: Creating Literate Communities,* edited by Kathy Gnagey Short and Kathryn Mitchell Pierce (Heinemann, a division of Reed Elsevier, Inc., Portsmouth, NH, 1990).

Student _Mark_   Date _10/93_   Grade _5_

Literature _Echo and Narcissus_

Use of Resources for Meaning Construction	Relationships Focus: Outward	Connections Focus: Inward	Transactions	Discussion
Uses information from something other than book sources	Addresses social issues *Zeus does nothing; it was his design when he did something wrong and is protected from Hera. Hera's lack of fairness.*	Forms new understandings from transaction with text *God of Gods Why couldn't Zeus overrule Hera?*	Recognizes relationships of story and life-themes *But what would be the lesson? Don't be so involved in yourself.*	Promotes action *Continues pursuing the idea that Echo was treated unfairly.*
Uses reference material	Addresses previous readings by other authors	Moves into the world of the text	Examines story in light of self as audience	Identifies with characters
Frames questions to get information *When Echo was stricken, what solutions would you suggest for her problem?*	Addresses previous readings by same author	Shares personal and emotional connections	Sees plot developing	Addresses the reading
Rereads to focus on important details and concepts needed to make sense	Addresses life experiences appropriate to text and readers	Shares a point of view (own, character's, family's, group's, etc.)	Draws from story traits of characters	Retells for own purpose (parts liked, not liked, not understood, to prove something) *When sometimes Zeus sought other company.*
Demands meaning by using prior knowledge	Addresses ideas of others *Wouldn't you know if your nymph disappeared? (Zeus is God.)*	Shares information from text *She couldn't. She had to repeat.*	Discusses setting within context of story (e.g., mood)	Initiates discussion related to text

Figure 2.5 Literature Discussion Responses to the Myth of Echo and Narcissus. *Source:* Table outline from *Whole Language Evaluation of Literature Groups* (p. 162) by D. J. Watson, 1990, Portsmouth, NH: Heinemann.

47

Book Club

Consulting the theory and research derived from metacognition and sociolinguistics, Raphael and McMahon (1994) developed the book club. As in literature circles, students in a book club are engaged in journaling and small-group discussions about literature. The difference resides in teacher guidance. In book clubs, teaching and application of reading strategies with literature ensure high-quality discussions and consequently increase reading development. The inclusion of reading logs, McMahon and Raphael (1990) note, further enhances book club discussions. Students consult their reading-log map (see Figure 2.6) to provide them with ideas to initiate writing and discussion. Raphael and her colleagues maintain that many students, especially beginning and less able readers, need strategies or tools for comprehending and learning from text. Through strategy instruction and journaling, students are guided to connect their prior knowledge with the text, to compare books, to understand the author's craft, to understand the thematic and conceptual ideas, and to clarify confusing points. Thus strategy lessons and journals are used to prepare students to engage in high-quality book discussions.

Implementation

We begin book clubs with a whole-group lesson that Raphael labels "community share." During this session, students may discuss different text structures and ways to organize their thinking and learning; be introduced to a particular reading strategy through a direct explanation model (Roehler & Duffy, 1984); or focus on critiquing books. The major goal is to engage students to think critically and analytically about text and to use appropriate reading strategies such as summarizing, predicting, retelling, and visualizing as they read. Through the use of reading strategies, understanding text structure, and critiquing books, higher levels of thinking and learning about text takes place. Students go beyond a general retelling to reflecting, responding, and analyzing literature. Raphael and McMahon (1994) relate that Rachael Silverstone knows the vocabulary in Beverly Cleary's books is challenging for her third graders, so she discusses the important yet complex relationship vocabulary and comprehension share and encourages her students to collect interesting and difficult words from the Beverly Cleary book their small group is reading. In another class, Raphael and McMahon report that Mrs. Pardo's fifth graders are reading several books about World War II and are encouraged to read across texts to develop a broader perspective about a particular topic. To help students synthesize information across texts, she uses a "think sheet" as shown in Figure 2.7. This guide helps readers draw connections among texts and make important intertextual links.

During this same instructional period, students are given time to read and apply the reading strategy and other learnings from the community-share session as well as complete their journal responses. Rachael Silverstone's fourth graders, for example, read a chapter, write a personal response, and collect vocabulary for their reading logs. Some draw pictures to illustrate meaning. Others write synonyms and antonyms, and still others write the page number to remember how the words are used in context. Book clubs then meet and use their logs to discuss the vocabulary as well as discuss their responses to text. Rachael concludes the class with a community-share session to discuss the vocabulary each group found interesting and challenging. As each book

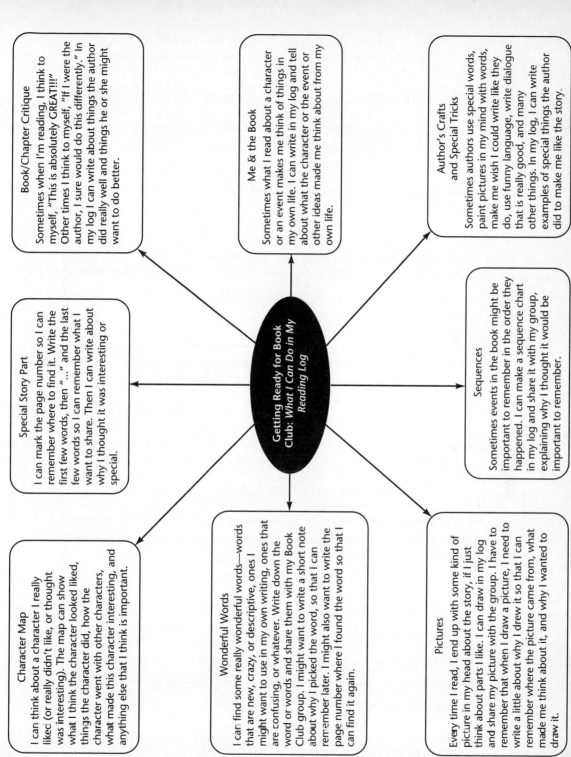

Figure 2.6 Reading Log Map. *Source:* From "Book Club: An Alternative Framework for Reading Instruction," by T. E. Raphael and S. I. McMahon, 1994, *The Reading Teacher, 48,* p. 108. Reprinted by permission.

Book/Chapter Critique

Sometimes when I'm reading, I think to myself, "This is absolutely GREAT!!!" Other times I think to myself, "If I were the author, I sure would do this differently." In my log I can write about things the author did really well and things he or she might want to do better.

Me & the Book

Sometimes what I read about a character or an event makes me think of things in my own life. I can write in my log and tell about what the character or the event or other ideas made me think about from my own life.

Author's Crafts and Special Tricks

Sometimes authors use special words, paint pictures in my mind with words, make me wish I could write like they do, use funny language, write dialogue that is really good, and many other things. In my log, I can write examples of special things the author did to make me like the story.

Special Story Part

I can mark the page number so I can remember where to find it. Write the first few words, then "… " and the last few words so I can remember what I want to share. Then I can write about why I thought it was interesting or special.

Getting Ready for Book Club: *What I Can Do in My Reading Log*

Sequences

Sometimes events in the book might be important to remember in the order they happened. I can make a sequence chart in my log and share it with my group, explaining why I thought it would be important to remember.

Character Map

I can think about a character I really likec (or really didn't like, or thought was interesting). The map can show what I think the character looked liked, things the character did, how the character went with other characters, what made this character interesting, and anything else that I think is important.

Wonderful Words

I can find some really wonderful words—words that are new, crazy, or descriptive, ones I might want to use in my own writing, ones that are confusing, or whatever. Write down the word or words and share them with my Book Club group. I might want to write a short note about why I picked the word, so that I can remember later. I might also want to write the page number where I found the word so that I can find it again.

Pictures

Every time I read, I end up with some kind of picture in my head about the story, if I just think about parts I like. I can draw in my log and share my picture with the group. I have to remember that when I draw a picture, I need to write a little about why I drew it so that I can remember where the picture came from, what made me think about it, and why I wanted to draw it.

49

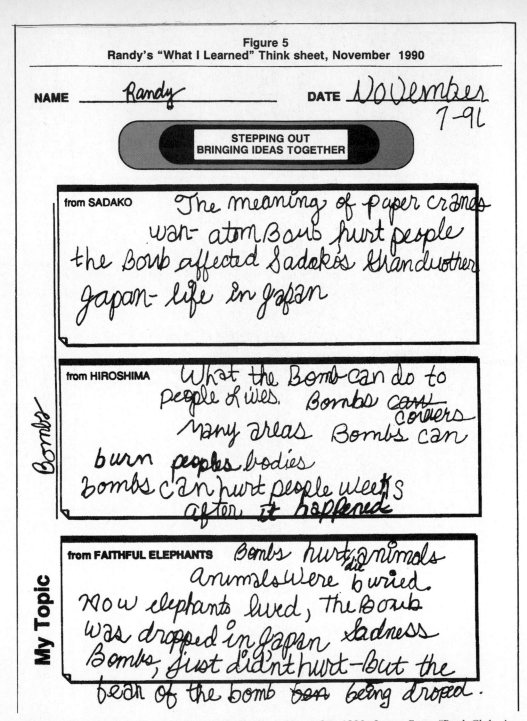

Figure 5
Randy's "What I Learned" Think sheet, November 1990

NAME _Randy_   DATE _November 7-91_

STEPPING OUT
BRINGING IDEAS TOGETHER

from SADAKO
The meaning of paper cranes was- atom Bomb hurt people the Bomb affected Sadako's Grandmother Japan- life in Japan

Bombs

from HIROSHIMA
What the Bomb can do to people & lives. Bombs can covers many areas Bombs can burn peoples bodies Bombs can hurt people weeks after, it happened

My Topic

from FAITHFUL ELEPHANTS
Bombs hurt animals Animals die Were buried Now elephants lived, The Bomb was dropped in Japan sadness Bombs, just didn't hurt-But the fear of the bomb being droped.

Figure 2.7 Randy's "What I Learned" Think Sheet, November 1990. *Source:* From "Book Club: An Alternative Framework for Reading Instruction," by T. E. Raphael and S. I. McMahon, 1994, *The Reading Teacher, 48,* p. 110. Reprinted by permission.

club discusses its vocabulary, Rachael Silverstone writes the words on strips and places them on the bulletin board to review vocabulary.

Raphael and her colleagues also videotape book discussion groups and do simulations. Tapes and simulations of small-group discussions can be beneficial for enabling students to understand and visualize the characteristics of high-quality book discussions. Students can then learn how to share their personal responses beyond the typical comment, "I liked the book." They learn how to elaborate on their feelings by using specific ideas from the book. Through videotapes and simulations, they can learn how to connect their ideas to other students' responses, reflect on other students' ideas, analyze the author's craft, understand the reading and learning process, and ask questions about confusing and vague ideas. The tape and simulation should demonstrate a free-flowing conversation about books that stimulates thinking, curiosity, and enjoyment. Students can then recognize that there are many logical and acceptable interpretations of literature rather than thinking that one correct response exists.

Teachers become participants during student-led discussions; they do not become the focal point, "dispenser of knowledge," and evaluator. Teachers can model responses and questions when necessary so that a natural-flowing conversation can ensue. They also observe students' responses so that they can, in subsequent lessons, provide appropriate instruction.

Assessment

Both teacher and student assessment are used in book club. Teachers can observe book club discussions by making their own evaluation guide based on teacher or student goals and noting whether each student can successfully accomplish the goals. Taping discussion groups can provide further evaluation and direction for instruction. Teachers and students can then review tapes to set specific goals and identify appropriate instruction. Raphael and co-workers (1991) suggest the following teaching idea for small-group evaluation.

> Tape record a book club discussion in which the students are participating. Have them critique their discussion both for what they had done well—such as (a) asking good questions, (b) elaborating on each other's ideas, and (c) taking turns—and for areas to improve—such as (a) off-task behavior, (b) overreliance on written response, and (c) dominant or "bossy" participants. This can be a fun way to address the how to share problems you are having in the classroom discussions. (p. 10).

Reviewing students' log responses can also illustrate individual growth in thinking and responding to literature. The criteria used for discussions can be used with the students' journals. Teacher and students should review journal entries to note growth and development.

By incorporating book club in your classroom, you develop both efferent and aesthetics responses to literature. Collaboration and coconstructing literary ideas among students and teachers can be emphasized through book club discussions and community share. Teaching specific reading strategies can open doors to thinking about text. Reading and applying these strategies to good literature provide a meaningful and functional context for learning. Log writing and discussion provide vehicles for developing literacy; these activities demonstrate the interconnectedness of the language processes.

Student Inquiry

Student inquiry refers to the questions students have and the means and procedures to find out the answers. Student questions organize literacy learning. As students inquire, they become engaged and personally involved in their own literacy learning and moreover develop research skills. They set up the questions, decide the tasks, identify the different sources, and share their learnings. Inquiry is rooted in children's natural curiosity about the world, and this approach can begin around second grade. In an interview with Monson and Monson (1994), Harste explains how teachers can create an environment that engages and supports inquiry. He maintains that teachers need to be aware of the topics and interests their students have and continually rotate these topics under investigation throughout the school year. Teachers need to consider the different disciplines as they view students' questions and develop a broad perspective for their questions. For example, how does a biologist view the nature and use of our water supply? Compare this perspective with manufacturing and industrial needs for water. How does the water supply affect farming and agriculture? How does the water supply affect the canyons and valleys during the springtime? Thus teacher planning is important. You need to be aware of topics that interest your students, note the ways different disciplines address a particular topic, and identify resources to read and study these questions.

During the interview with the Monsons (1994), Harste describes one classroom's use of inquiry. In this classroom, the teacher has organized a Discovery Club in which small groups of students identify a topic for inquiry and the group collaboratively plans and researches the topic. Students begin to read, write, discuss, listen, and engage in further inquiry. In this experience, students see literacy as having a purpose. It has meaning to them and is not something they do to satisfy their teacher or achieve high grades on a test.

We suggest forming small groups with interests in common and asking students to write questions about the topics for which they want to seek answers. Discuss different resources and ways of gathering information. Talk to students about the various perspectives different disciplines may espouse. Discuss these perspectives within the small group and ask the group members to devise ways to share their knowledge with other students.

Student inquiry provides an important dimension to classroom instruction and learning. It demonstrates to students that their ideas and questions have merit and value, shows them how to think about topics and questions from a number of perspectives, and teaches that single, simplistic answers rarely exist. The world is complex, and different perspectives provide different answers. To be knowledgeable, students must consider all these perspectives to solve problems and make wise decisions. In chapter 15, inquiry and research are described in greater depth and an example of inquiry is developed within the context of an eighth-grade classroom.

Literature Units

Literature units can broaden students' horizons and stimulate a keen interest in reading by providing opportunities to explore favorite authors, different genres, universal themes, and personal interests. A literature unit includes a *topic, theme or concept, learning goals, materials* such as literature, videos, computers, and the like, *instructional strategies and activities* to accomplish the targeted goals, and assessment to note students' enjoyment, understanding, and learning and to further facilitate instructional planning. A unit can be a week or more of instruction; many are a month in duration. Flexibility needs to be considered in unit planning and implementation. Observe children's needs and interests and allow them, for example, additional time to investigate further some of their interests or to spend on tasks when they need additional instruction.

Units can be developed in a variety of ways. Some focus on a particular topic or theme that integrates reading, writing, speaking, and listening, and/or that "combines content areas by incorporating concepts, skills, and questions from more than one discipline to examine a central theme, issue, situation, inquiry, or topic" (Smith & Johnson, 1994, p. 200). Other units may focus on an author's works, and still other units may center on a specific type of literature or genre such as fantasy, realistic fiction, or poetry. Units can be developed by publishers, teachers, students, or teachers and students in collaboration. In this chapter, we focus on teacher, student, and teacher-student units. In chapter 9, we discuss literature-based instruction in which publishers organize instruction into units.

To develop a unit, begin by identifying the needs (see chapter 10 for a more detailed discussion) and interests of your students and reviewing the district's curricular goals. Select literature to help students accomplish these goals. Many teachers will ask students to contribute titles or choose from a teacher-developed list. Use the goals to determine appropriate activities and instructional strategies, and create assessment that addresses the unit goals and matches instruction. To develop further understanding of unit planning, we have interviewed an experienced sixth-grade teacher to reveal how she made instructional decisions with respect to identifying topics, goals, corresponding instructional activities and strategies, and assessment procedures.

Learning from Experience

As you read, think about the following question: What does Mrs. Nelson consider as she designs literature units? Write these points in your journal.

Q: Why do you use literature units?

A: I want students to see that reading and writing strategies and skills aren't just used during literacy instruction. They must see the connection between instruction and out-of-school activities and language arts and other content areas, if we expect students to become good readers and writers. It's interesting—when students are involved in a literature unit, they don't think we are having reading and writing instruction. They are involved, for example, with the characters and their lives, or they are focused on teaching others about recycling, for example. It is real and meaningful, not just another story to read and do workbook exercises.

Q: How do you choose topics?

A: I review the sixth-grade curricula primarily in language arts, social studies, science, and math to identify topics that can be easily integrated into a unit. In September, I ask the sixth graders to suggest topics they would like to study. Teaching sixth grade for a number of years, I also know authors, genre, and books students have really enjoyed in the past.

Q: How do you choose your unit goals?

A: I'm using the reading goals our school district decided were important for sixth graders. For this unit, I've chosen several goals. I want students to increase their vocabulary. I also want them to improve their summary writing. Too often when I ask for a summary, they like to tell me everything instead of the important parts of the story. I also want them to become acquainted with science fiction, which my students infrequently read. Themes and concepts are also important for my students to derive from reading text. After identifying a theme or concept, I choose instructional strategies to help students construct the theme or concept. These are the goals for this particular unit. They'll change from unit to unit.

Q: What materials, instructional strategies, and activities will you use to accomplish these goals?

A: For this unit, students will select one of the following titles: *A Wrinkle in Time* by Madeleine L'Engle and *The White Mountains* by John Christopher. Literature circles (book discussions) will be formed based on their selection. To increase vocabulary, I plan to let them identify words that highlight technology, time, and futuristic ideas and place them in a personal dictionary. During literature circles, the students will discuss the vocabulary.

Q: How do you plan to accomplish your second goal, improving summary writing?

A: After each chapter, we'll summarize it. Since my sixth graders like to tell all the details instead of the important events, I plan to explain what a summary is and provide them with two written summaries as models. One summary will include the important points, and the other will include too many details. We'll discuss which is the best summary. Using models for summary writing is only one of several strategies I plan to use.

Q: You mentioned that you wanted your students to become better acquainted with science fiction. Do you have any specific goals?

A: Yes, I hope the sixth graders will choose to read a variety of science fiction books for recreational reading. But I don't think this goal will be accomplished by the end of this unit. I am hoping that the literature circles will cause students to share their books among groups and precipitate more reading. I will also read aloud H. G. Wells's *The Time Machine* and *War of the Worlds*. I plan to encourage students to continue reading and sharing by providing them a bibliography of science fiction that can be found in the school library. I also plan on sending this bibliography to their parents and encourage them to read aloud or encourage their children to read and share science fiction with their family. We will share and evaluate science fiction books they are currently reading to stimulate additional interest and knowledge. As a class, we will also discuss what makes a piece science fiction. All these discussions help them with writing their own science fiction pieces.

Q: How will you assess each goal?

A: Vocabulary will be evaluated by students selecting vocabulary from their personal dictionaries and taping their small-group discussion. For the final evaluation, I want them to write about their favorite story event using 7 to 10 of the words listed in their personal dictionaries. For summary writing, there will be several times students will have to write individual summaries. These summaries will be used to measure growth in summary writing. For readings of other science fiction books, I'll note those who contribute to sharing and those who complete rating cards on science fiction they've read. In USSR (Uninterrupted, Sustained Silent Reading—self-selected reading time), I'll note those who are reading science fiction.

Your Turn: Write your response to the journal question "What does Mrs. Nelson consider as she designs literature units?" before comparing it to ours.

Our Turn: Mrs. Nelson uses the school district's reading goals to help her design appropriate reading goals for each literature unit. She recognizes that reading different genres can facilitate learning and enjoyment. She also uses what she has observed to establish goals for which students need further assistance.

Mrs. Nelson uses instructional time efficiently by selecting topics that combine learning from different content areas. She is also mindful of students' interests and uses them to select topics for literature units.

She uses the goals to help her select instructional strategies and activities that enable students to achieve these goals. She allows students to choose their own vocabulary and books so there is personal investment in learning.

To further promote students' achievement of specific goals, Mrs. Nelson uses sound instructional principles for learning. For example, she uses modeling to enhance students' summary writing. She also involves parents in the curriculum by sending them a bibliography to stimulate recreational reading at home.

Mrs. Nelson has developed a logical plan for evaluating student achievement. Each goal is evaluated and is consistent with the instruction. Assessment complements instruction and can provide a fair evaluation of students' attainment of goals.

There are many ways to organize literature units. Some teachers use what is known as literature webs to provide an overview and organization for thinking about a unit. The web's categories are used to provide the organization. A variety of literature webs do exist and differ according to detail, purpose, and teaching styles.

A web on pioneers was developed by Cindy Morganthaler (see Figure 2.8) that organizes thinking by including the basic rudiments for planning and implementing a literature unit but does not include specifics such as questions and activities for each chapter. The web's foundation is composed of the concept and goals the students are to accomplish. The goals can be developed by teacher, students, or collaboratively. In this example, Cindy selected the concept and goals, since this was her first year teaching fourth graders. The goals focus on content and process. The content, in this instance, is understanding the pioneers' spirit and ability to survive during western expansion of the United States. The process goals include using literacy to appreciate

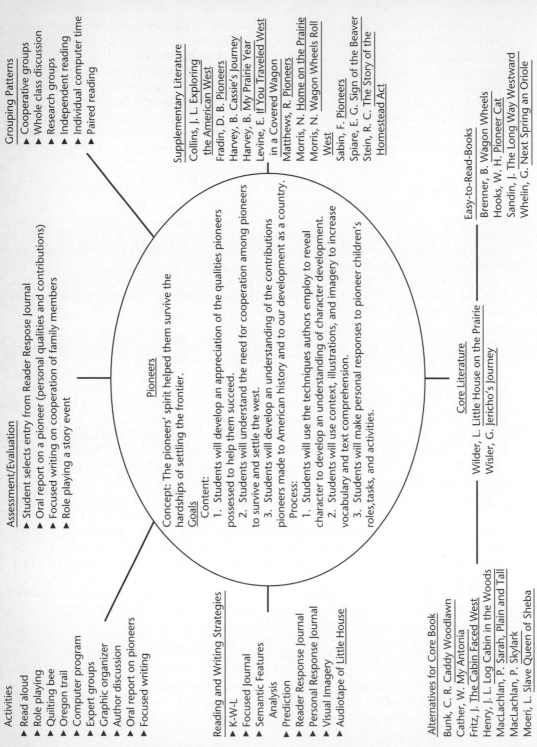

Activities
▲ Read aloud
▲ Role playing
▲ Quilting bee
▲ Oregon trail
▲ Computer program
▲ Expert groups
▲ Graphic organizer
▲ Author discussion
▲ Oral report on pioneers
▲ Focused writing

Assessment/Evaluation
▲ Student selects entry from Reader Respose Journal
▲ Oral report on a pioneer (personal qualities and contributions)
▲ Focused writing on cooperation of family members
▲ Role playing a story event

Grouping Patterns
▲ Cooperative groups
▲ Whole class discussion
▲ Research groups
▲ Independent reading
▲ Individual computer time
▲ Paired reading

Supplementary Literature
Collins, J. L. Exploring the American West
Fradin, D. B. Pioneers
Harvey, B. Cassie's Journey
Harvey, B. My Prairie Year
Levine, E. If You Traveled West in a Covered Wagon
Matthews, R. Pioneers
Morris, N. Home on the Prairie
Morris, N. Wagon Wheels Roll West
Sabin, F. Pioneers
Spiare, E. G. Sign of the Beaver
Stein, R. C. The Story of the Homestead Act

Pioneers

Concept: The pioneers' spirit helped them survive the hardships of settling the frontier.
Goals
    Content:
    1. Students will develop an appreciation of the qualities pioneers possessed to help them succeed.
    2. Students will understand the need for cooperation among pioneers to survive and settle the west.
    3. Students will develop an understanding of the contributions pioneers made to American history and to our development as a country.
    Process:
    1. Students will use the techniques authors employ to reveal character to develop an understanding of character development.
    2. Students will use context, illustrations, and imagery to increase vocabulary and text comprehension.
    3. Students will make personal responses to pioneer children's roles, tasks, and activities.

Core Literature
Wilder, L. Little House on the Prairie
Wisler, G. Jericho's Journey

Easy-to-Read-Books
Brenner, B. Wagon Wheels
Hooks, W. H. Pioneer Cat
Sandin, J. The Long Way Westward
Whelin, G. Next Spring an Oriole

Reading and Writing Strategies
▲ K-W-L
▲ Focused Journal
▲ Semantic Features Analysis
▲ Prediction
▲ Reader Response Journal
▲ Personal Response Journal
▲ Visual Imagery
▲ Audiotape of Little House

Alternatives for Core Book
Bunk, C. R. Caddy Woodlawn
Cather, W. My Antonia
Fritz, J. The Cabin Faced West
Henry, J. L. Log Cabin in the Woods
MacLachlan, P. Sarah, Plain and Tall
MacLachlan, P. Skylark
Moeri, L. Slave Queen of Sheba

Figure 2.8 Literature Web on Pioneers. *Note:* K-W-L denotes Know, Want, Learn.

and understand the content. In this web, there are five basic categories: the selected literature, the reading and writing strategies, instructional activities, grouping patterns, and assessment and evaluation. Cindy has given the students the choice of two core literature books; the students will choose one to read and respond to. Other literature will also be employed for reading aloud, forming research and expert groups, and presenting oral reports. Cindy uses a variety of instructional activities and strategies to accommodate students' diverse interests and learning needs. Many different types of grouping patterns are used to ensure that students are interacting with their classmates while receiving individualized instruction as needed. Assessment is clearly linked to the instructional activities and goals, since daily work is a part of assessment. Moreover, students are actively involved in the assessment process by self-selecting specific items for evaluation.

At a glance, a literature web can help teachers recognize if there is a variety of literature and reading and writing strategies and activities to accommodate the diversity of students' needs. Teachers can check if the goals can be developed from the selected literature, reading and writing strategies, and activities. Lastly, teachers can consider their assessment and evaluation in light of the selected goals, strategies, and activities. Hence this web provides for both organization and examination of the interrelationships among the five basic unit elements.

From this web, a more detailed literature unit can be developed if needed. For the first few units, it is likely that greater detail is needed and will lessen as units become more routine. Since this is one of Cindy's first units, she provides extensive detail, and we use her unit to develop a comprehensive understanding of this unit in terms of goals, literature, instructional strategies and activities, assessment, and grouping. This unit can serve as a model for developing your own units and can be used or modified, as appropriate. This model, however, is not the only way to develop a literature unit. Some teachers prefer using a day-by-day format, and others prefer using a pre-, during-, and postreading format to organize students' thinking about a theme/concept, author, or genre.

As you read the following Learning from Experience, we suggest that you focus on developing a general concept or an overview about unit development. This unit does present reading and writing strategies we discuss in great depth in chapters 4 to 7 and presents ways to group students that we discuss in detail in chapter 11. You should not focus on the implementation of specific teaching strategies and grouping, since this is well developed in the upcoming chapters. After you have read chapters 4 to 7 and chapter 11, we recommend that you reread Cindy's unit so the details about unit planning can be understood better.

Learning from Experience

In this case study, Cindy Morganthaler shows you how to plan and organize a unit. As we examine Cindy's thinking and planning of her pioneer unit, refer to the literature web in Figure 2.8 and note how she plans and organizes the unit on Pioneers and Westward Expansion in the United States. Describe this general process in your journal.

TOPIC SELECTION AND GOALS

Cindy develops the pioneer unit, since the fourth graders cover this topic in the social studies curriculum and there is related literature available for this topic and grade level. As she peruses the social studies curriculum and reads the accompanying textbook, Cindy notes a recurrent message—the pioneers endured many hardships as they traveled westward searching for home, land, and wealth; and their spirit helped them accomplish their goals. She then remembers enjoying Laura Ingalls Wilder books as a child and recalls the hardships the Ingalls family experienced as well as the love and spirit this family exuded. She knows that not all her fourth graders will enjoy reading these books, so she talks to the school librarian about another book that has a male protagonist and highlights the trials and tribulations of a family's experience during westward expansion. The librarian suggests C. Clifton Wisler's *Jericho Journey,* a book that appeared on International Reading Association's Young Adult's Choices for 1995. Cindy reads *Jericho's Journey* and decides this is a good alternative to Laura Ingalls Wilder's *Little House on the Prairie.* She again seeks the school librarian's help to select additional fiction and nonfiction as well as easy and challenging books to address the different interests and abilities of her students. Cindy uses the unit concept and the social studies curriculum to identify content goals: social, cultural, political, and geographical issues of this time period. Cindy then uses the content goals and reviews the two core literature books, *Little House on the Prairie* and *Jericho's Journey,* to identify reading and writing processes that would help the fourth graders achieve the content goals.

DESCRIPTION OF UNIT ACTIVITIES

Cindy then turns her attention to identifying reading and writing strategies and activities to enable students to learn the unit concept and content goals. Cindy thinks about literacy instruction and learning and remembers these theoretical points: (A) Accessing students' prior knowledge helps students make connections between text and their own experiences and thus facilitates learning. (B) Self-selection creates ownership and engagement in learning. (C) Personal response is naturally evoked from good literature and creates interest in reading. (D) Reading strategies help students organize and learn from text. (E) Reading aloud good literature increases students' vocabulary and concept development. (F) Writing enables students to organize, remember, and express their ideas about text. Drawing from these six theoretical points and unit concept and goals, Cindy designs twelve activities and describes her planning and implementation.

    1. Know, Want, and Learn (K-W-L). Cindy decides to begin the unit by employing the reading strategy K-W-L with all her students to access their knowledge of pioneers (see chapters 4 to 6 for a detailed description of K-W-L). On the first day of the unit, Cindy will begin with whole-group instruction by asking her students to tell what they know about pioneers as she writes this information under the "K" or Know section on chart paper posted in the classroom. Cindy plans to help her students group their responses into categories such as shelter, food, transportation, and so on. As a group, they will identify information that may or may not be accurate. For the "W" or want to know portion, Cindy will ask the fourth graders to identify questions they want to find answers to as they read and learn about pioneers. Cindy will record their questions on the "W" section of the butcher paper. Throughout the unit, the fourth graders will independently record answers to their questions, add information they have learned to the "L" or learned column, and correct inaccurate information. When they meet as a large group, Cindy will conduct a debriefing of the K-W-L chart at the end of the unit.

2. Daily Read-Aloud. To develop knowledge about pioneers and westward expansion, Cindy, with the help of the librarian, has selected books related to this unit (see list below). Cindy selects these books since they are too difficult for most fourth graders to read but can be understood and appreciated and can enhance vocabulary development when read aloud and discussed. Cindy plans to do book talks about each one and invite the fourth graders to choose books for her to read aloud. If short picture books are selected, several can be read. She also plans to use the read-aloud book(s) to provide material for teaching the unit minilessons to enhance literacy development

Bial, R. (1993). *Frontier Home.* Boston: Houghton Mifflin.

Harvey, B. (1988). *Cassie's Journey.* New York: Holiday.

Harvey, B. (1986). *My Prairie Year.* New York: Holiday.

Knight, A. S. (1993). *The Way West.* New York: Simon & Shuster.

Lawlor, L. (1989). *Addie's Dakota Winter.* New York: Minstrel.

Speare, E. G. (1983). *The Sign of the Beaver.* New York: Dell Yearling.

3. Cooperative Reading Groups. Cindy knows that students need to work in small groups so they can participate frequently and receive individual feedback. She decides to use cooperative learning groups so students have specific roles to accomplish and can recognize their individual contribution in completing a particular task (see chapter 11 for more information on cooperative grouping). To implement cooperative groups, Cindy will divide the class into groups of three and distribute copies of Ellen Levine's *If You Traveled West in a Covered Wagon.* The students will read the entire book but will be assigned one topic to explore and become experts. Their findings will be shared orally. All members will be expected to contribute to the group discussion and will assume specific roles. The group coordinator will be expected to encourage discussion and participation. The checker will check the book to ensure the group's information is accurate. The recorder will write the information the group members agree is accurate and important. To provide guidance, Cindy will have questions to cover a specific topic but will also encourage students to add questions and ideas of their own (questions appear below). She plans to videotape each oral presentation to help students establish self-selected goals for their end of the unit's oral biographic report on a pioneer. Cindy will discuss different ways to accomplish their goals.

Topics and Guided Questions

1. Wagon Trains
Define. What was the best time to travel? Why was this time so good? What kind of people traveled this way? Describe what it would be like to ride on a wagon train.

2. Covered Wagon

Define. What kinds of things did people pack? Why did they pack these items? How far could pioneers travel in a day? Did they ride all day?

3. Difficulties and Dangers

What dangers did the pioneers experience? List the difficulties the pioneers encountered. What dangers do we experience in our cities and towns? What difficulties do we experience? Compare and contrast the dangers facing pioneers with those we face today.

4. Basic Needs

Where did they sleep? What did they wear? What did they eat? How did they cook and store food? Compare and contrast pioneer children's clothing with your clothes. Compare and contrast how pioneers stored food with how your family stores it.

5. Pioneer Children

Would the pioneer children go to school? Could they read and write? What were their chores? When and how did they play? What chores do you do? Compare and contrast your chores with those of pioneer children.

6. Traveling across Country

What types of animals live on the prairie? How did the travelers receive news? Where did they shop and mail a letter? Compare and contrast the way we communicate with people who live far away with the communication of the pioneers.

7. Finding Their Way

How did they know where to go? What devices do we use to find different locations? Were there roads? Why was the Continental Divide so important? Does the Continental Divide have the same importance today; why or why not?

8. Those Clever Pioneers

What special tricks helped the pioneers? How do we know about them? Can we visit the Oregon Trail today? What would it be like to travel the Oregon Trail as a pioneer?

 4. *Oregon Trail Computer Programs.* Since students typically enjoy computers, Cindy decides to include two computer simulations, Oregon Trail I and II, published by MECC. In these programs, students are challenged to pack up their belongings, buy supplies, and take their family to Oregon in a covered wagon. Students must decide what supplies to take and how much money to bring along. They must make decisions about their route, where to stop, and when to hunt. As students progress through this program, hardships such as drowning, starvation, disease, and death can occur, just like the pioneers faced. Whether students make their goal of reaching Oregon depends on the decisions they make along the trail. Cindy notes that these two simulations engage students in a "lived-through experience" that can help them better understand the pioneers' hardships and spirit as they moved westward. She plans to put students into dyads to play the computer game in 20-minute time segments throughout the unit and when students have free time or finish their activities early.

 5. *Self-Selected Reading and Reader-Response Journals.* Cindy knows the importance of daily independent reading and acknowledges that all students need time to personally select their own books and read at their independent reading or comfort level to enjoy reading, increase comprehension and vocabulary development, and practice fluency. She recognizes that students' interests and abilities vary, so she gathers a wide variety of books covering different genres and levels of reading to provide self-selected reading and to enhance free response in journals. Besides these books, she encourages her fourth graders to choose others about pioneers. Cindy intends to provide 25 minutes for daily reading with 5 minutes for journaling. Her bibliography is included.

Informational Books

Bial, R. (1993). *Frontier Homes.* Boston: Houghton Mifflin.

Collins, J. L. (1989). *Exploring the American West. New York: Watts.*

Fradin, D. B. (1984). *Pioneers. Chicago: Children's Press.*

Freedman, R. (1983). *Children of the Wild West.* New York: Clarion.

Matthews, L. (1989). *Pioneers.* Florida: Rourke.

Morris, N. (1988). *Home on the Prairie.* New York: Derrydale.

Morris, N. (1988). *Wagon Wheels Roll West.* New York: Derrydale.

Sabin, F. (1985). *Pioneers.* New Jersey: Troll.

Stein, R. C. (1987). *The Story of the Homestead Act.* Chicago: Children's Press.

Easy-to-Read Books

Brenner, B. (1987). *Wagon Wheels.* New York: Harper.

Bulla, C. R. (1979). *Daniel's Duck.* New York: Harper.

Hooks, W. H. (1988). *Pioneer Cat.* New York: Random.

Sandin, J. (1989). *The Long Way Westward.* New York: Harper.

Whelin, G. (1987). *Next Spring an Oriole.* New York: Random.

Fiction

Brink, C. R. (1973). *Caddy Woodlawn.* New York: Macmillan.

Cather, W. (1918). *My Antonia.* Boston: Houghton.

Fritz, J. (1958). *The Cabin Faced West.* New York: Coward.

Henry, J. L. (1988). *Log Cabin in the Woods: A True Story about a Pioneer Boy.* New York: Four Winds.

Lawlor, L. (1986). *Addie across the Prairie.* New York: Mistrel.

MacLachlan, P. (1985). *Sarah, Plain and Tall.* New York: Harper.

MacLachlan, P. (1990). *Skylark.* New York: Harper.

MacLachlan, P. (1994). *Baby.* New York: Harper.

Moeri, L. (1981). *Save Queen of Sheba.* New York: Dutton.

Biography

Williams, D. (1993). *Grandma Essie's Covered Wagon.* New York: Alfred A. Knopf. Students can also read any of the "Little House" books.

6. Vocabulary Notebook. To help students better understand the texts written about this historical period as well as increase their vocabulary, Cindy will ask each student to keep a vocabulary notebook. As her fourth graders read, they can choose words that depict transportation, buildings, rooms, objects, or tools pioneers used. They will place the words in their vocabulary notebook, draw and label the item, and write information about how the word, including its use and purpose. Cindy will do a "think-aloud" to demonstrate how she uses context, illustrations, structural analysis, and dictionary to define a word. To assess their word knowledge, students will select several words to share with peers and tape their discussion. Cindy and her students will collaboratively develop criteria to demonstrate word knowledge.

7. Core Literature and Focused Journals. Since choice is such an important aspect of motivation and learning, Cindy allows students to choose one of two books to learn reading and writing strategies and participate in small-group book discussions. She chooses two popular books: *Little House on the Prairie* by Laura Ingalls Wilder and *Jericho's Journey* by G. Clifton Wisler. The first has a female protagonist while the other has a male protagonist that can encourage readers to identify with a main character. To help her fourth graders choose a book, Cindy plans to give book talks for each and display the books for students to peruse. After they make their selections, Cindy will divide the students into groups of four to participate in book discussions. Knowing these two books will be too difficult for some students, Cindy plans to provide audiotapes and do paired reading to support individual needs. To help her students construct and self-monitor comprehension, Cindy designs three minilessons to teach specific reading strategies. She will incorporate a focused journal to check understanding of the particular strategy and help them to better understand text.

To understand text, the reader must be actively engaged in constructing meaning, and Cindy knows that making predictions while reading helps students to become active readers. Thus the first minilesson will be on prediction and reading to confirm, reject, and/or revise the prediction. To initiate prediction making for these two books, Cindy will show a regional map of the Middle West and Wisconsin and Tennessee state maps, and she will read aloud the first chapters of *Little House on the Prairie* and *Jericho's Journey* and share information about the authors. As they read the first third of their books, the students will make predictions, write them in their journal, and record information to support or refute their predictions.

Since vocabulary is very much related to comprehension and is one of the unit goals, Cindy designs a second minilesson focusing on finding words that create visual images of setting, characters, and events. Cindy plans to use the book she is reading aloud to her fourth graders as a model for demonstrating and guiding visual imagery. As her fourth graders read the second third of the book, they will write and discuss the words that created memorable images.

Since students are expected to develop an understanding of the unit concept "The pioneers' spirit helped them survive the hardships of settling the frontier," Cindy believes that teaching students to locate information to support the concept will be helpful. Hence the third minilesson focuses on locating information. Students will be expected to read and find out about the behaviors, chores, and activities of the In-galls children and/or Jericho Wetherby. They will also look for examples of prejudice, since *Little House on the Prairie* may include bias and prejudice toward Native Amer-icans. With the whole group, Cindy will identify and define a concept that illustrates the pioneers' positive and constructive spirit. For example, she may choose the con-cept of cooperation to illustrate this point and think aloud while reading, demon-strating how she identified abstract ideas illustrating cooperation (think-alouds are described in chapter 5). To help the fourth graders remember the concept and ex-amples supporting the concept, she teaches them to use a graphic organizer (see chapter 5). Cindy will begin the graphic organizer by placing the concept of coop-eration in the center of a circle with an example radiating from the map's center. As students read, they are to identify and record their concepts and specific examples demonstrating that idea.

Discussion groups will meet weekly to share their journal responses and other reactions or questions about their reading. The journal entries are to serve as a springboard to discussion but should not be limited by a specific focus and should engage students in discussing interesting and confusing ideas.

8. Focused Writing. Cindy wants students to understand the pioneers' spirit and stamina as they settled the west. She knows that writing can enable students to understand and learn about ideas and concepts. Hence she plans a focused writing activity to encourage her fourth graders to place themselves in the role of the pio-neer children traveling west. By reading *Little House in the Prairie* or *Jericho's Journey* and reading other books, students can develop some ideas about what it was like to be a child during pioneer days. Students will be asked to write three essays describ-ing different experiences they would have if they were living during pioneer times. If students have difficulty identifying different experiences, Cindy will provide sev-eral writing prompts to guide their thinking and writing. (The prompts appear below.) The students will select one of their essays, receive peer response, revise, edit, and share with the class. Some of the prompts apply to *Little House on the Prairie* and/or *Jericho's Journey*. The essay will be evaluated according to the following cri-teria: Is the written presentation organized in a logical manner? Are there enough details presented so the reader can form visual images of the person, place, or event? Has the student edited for end punctuation, complete sentences, capitalization, subject-verb agreement, and the use of quotations?

Prompt One:
Write about your life as a pioneer child leaving home to travel to the prairie. Where did you start? Where are you going? What kinds of things did you pack? Who is com-ing with you? How do you feel about leaving and traveling west?

Prompt Two:
As you travel along, write about what you see, hear, and smell. Describe how you will cross the Mississippi River. Explain an exciting event that happened along the way.

Prompt Three:
Write about camping on the prairie. Where do you stop? What do you cook and eat? How does it feel to travel so far from home? What do you think will happen tonight as you camp?

Prompt Four:
Describe what your day is like as a pioneer child. What are your chores? What do you do for fun? What do you do about school and learning to read and write?

Prompt Five:
Describe building your home. What does it look like? What happens first, second, etc.

Prompt Six:
How is friendship important to you as a pioneer? Write about an event that explains what friendship is about on the prairie.

9. Role Playing. Cindy knows that students learn in different ways. Some learn by writing ideas while others may learn by doing the actual activity to understand and learn the concept or idea. Thus Cindy uses drama to address different learning needs. Cindy will form small groups to pick out a favorite scene in the *Little House on the Prairie* or *Jericho's Journey* and act it out. Students will explain to the class why they picked this scene. By using drama, students can relate to the pioneers' experiences and understand their strong and enduring spirit. The students' performances will be videotaped and evaluated and provide students with a variety of assessment. Students and teacher will develop criteria for evaluating role playing.

10. Biography Reports. Cindy wants to reinforce the qualities that all pioneers needed to settle the frontier. In a whole-class discussion, she will ask students to consider the characteristics and qualities the pioneers needed to possess as they made their way west. As they make suggestions, Cindy will place their ideas on butcher paper posted on a classroom wall.

Cindy will provide a list of pioneers and their biographies (see the list below). The fourth graders will self-select one of the biographies to read and prepare a three-minute oral presentation that includes the following: a short summary of the pioneer's life and a description of the personal qualities and behaviors that helped this person in goal achievement. Cindy will demonstrate the use of the "five w's" (who, what, where, when, why) to help students organize note taking and develop a logical sequence. Cindy and the students will use the criteria developed from the collaborative group presentation to evaluate their biography reports.

Davy Crockett	Johnny Appleseed	Annie Oakley
Esther Morris	Kit Carson	Narcissa Whitman
George Caitlin	Jim Bridger	Abigail Scott Dunway
Dr. B. Owens	Calamity Jane	Wyatt Earp
John Fremont	Lizzie Johnson	John Cotter

11. Semantic Features Analysis. Cindy wants the students to be actively engaged in the oral presentation of the biographies and chooses Semantics Features Analysis strategy to focus students' listening and learning (see chapter 4 for a detailed description). In a whole-class discussion, Cindy will guide her students to identify the different qualities people possess and list these qualities across the top of a Semantic Features Analysis grid. In the vertical column, Cindy will list the pioneers from the oral presentations and students will place a "+" if the pioneer illustrated this quality and a "0" in the square if this quality wasn't evident. At the end of all the presentations, Cindy will review the grid with the class and discuss the qualities that most of the pioneers possessed and those that were uncommon, and they will consider how certain qualities may be helpful while others may hinder the pioneers' progress.

12. Quilting Bee. Since Cindy wants to address different ways to learn, she intends to use quilting, a common activity during this time period, and she reads aloud Ernest's *Sam Johnson and the Blue Ribbon Quilt* prior to designing a class quilt. Students are to design a square apiece for the quilt by incorporating their knowledge of the pioneers and depicting a famous pioneer, an aspect of pioneer life, or a quality they admire in the pioneers.

Materials:

Fabric scraps, scissors, cold glue guns or fabric glue, rulers, fabric pencils, paper (cut into 8″ × 8″ squares), and white fabric squares (cut into 8″ × 8″ squares)

Directions:

1. Discuss what a quilt is and its significance to the pioneers.
2. Have students design their own square on paper.
3. Once the design is discussed with the teacher, students may cut their pieces out on fabric and glue them to an 8″ × 8″ square of white fabric.
4. These squares will be attached to a large piece of fabric that will make up the background of the quilt. Once all squares are attached to the back fabric, turn under the edges and finish seams. If parents are available, three or more of them could volunteer to help finish the quilt. Hang finished quilt in room.

 ## ASSESSMENT AND EVALUATION

Assessment and evaluation are based on the content and process goals and the corresponding unit instruction that Cindy identified for the pioneer unit. Cindy plans to use teacher- and student-selected pieces for assessment and evaluation. A collaborative set of criteria will be developed and used for evaluation and established before students begin the task. The following activities will be evaluated: Vocabulary Notebook, Focused Writing, Focused Journal from Core Literature, Oral Report, and Role Playing. Evaluation procedures were described within the activity description.

 ## ORGANIZATION OF TIME

The unit organization is shown in Figure 2.9 (p. 66). In this figure, Cindy shows how the unit will continue for five weeks and the activities the students will be engaged in daily. Cindy knows that flexibility needs to be considered as she implements the unit. She intends to observe her students' needs and interests and alter the schedule and activities as needed.

 Your Turn: As you examined Cindy's thinking and planning of her pioneer unit, think of what she considered and did to plan the unit. Describe this process in your journal.

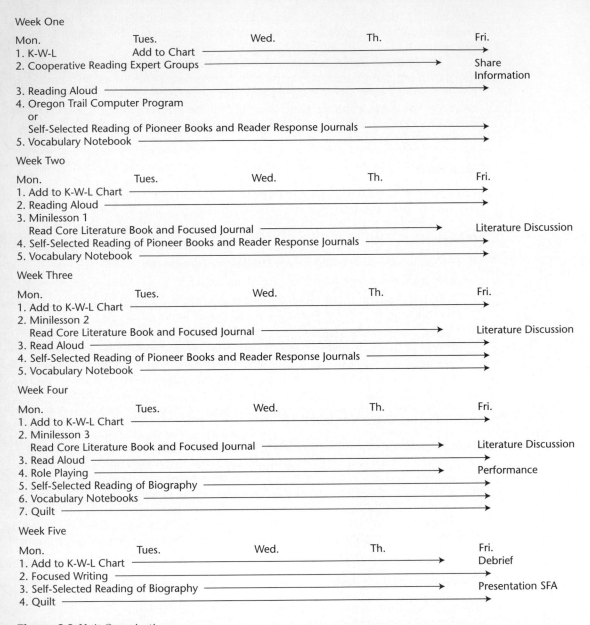

Week One

Mon.	Tues.	Wed.	Th.	Fri.
1. K-W-L	Add to Chart ──────────────────────────────→			
2. Cooperative Reading Expert Groups ──────────────────────────────→				Share Information
3. Reading Aloud ──→				
4. Oregon Trail Computer Program				
or				
Self-Selected Reading of Pioneer Books and Reader Response Journals ──────→				
5. Vocabulary Notebook ───→				

Week Two

Mon.	Tues.	Wed.	Th.	Fri.
1. Add to K-W-L Chart ───→				
2. Reading Aloud ───→				
3. Minilesson 1				
Read Core Literature Book and Focused Journal ───────────────────────→				Literature Discussion
4. Self-Selected Reading of Pioneer Books and Reader Response Journals ──────────→				
5. Vocabulary Notebook ───→				

Week Three

Mon.	Tues.	Wed.	Th.	Fri.
1. Add to K-W-L Chart ───→				
2. Minilesson 2				
Read Core Literature Book and Focused Journal ───────────────────────→				Literature Discussion
3. Read Aloud ──→				
4. Self-Selected Reading of Pioneer Books and Reader Response Journals ──────────→				
5. Vocabulary Notebook ───→				

Week Four

Mon.	Tues.	Wed.	Th.	Fri.
1. Add to K-W-L Chart ───→				
2. Minilesson 3				
Read Core Literature Book and Focused Journal ───────────────────────→				Literature Discussion
3. Read Aloud ──→				
4. Role Playing ──→				Performance
5. Self-Selected Reading of Biography ──→				
6. Vocabulary Notebooks ──→				
7. Quilt ───→				

Week Five

Mon.	Tues.	Wed.	Th.	Fri.
1. Add to K-W-L Chart ──→				Debrief
2. Focused Writing ───→				
3. Self-Selected Reading of Biography ────────────────────────────→				Presentation SFA
4. Quilt ───→				

Figure 2.9 Unit Organization

 Our Turn: Cindy reviewed the fourth-grade curriculum and noted areas she could easily integrate with literacy instruction. She talked to librarians and perused the library to identify literature her fourth graders would enjoy, and she noted that a unit on westward expansion was a good choice. She read the social studies textbook, literature, and curriculum for this topic and developed the unit concept and goals. She used the concept and goals to identify activities and strategies to help her students understand the concept and achieve the goals. Cindy incorporated good literature, self-selection, strategy learning, different types of grouping, and diverse ways to understand and learn the unit concept. Assessment matched the instruction students received and incorporated self-selection and collaborative evaluation. Learning skills and strategies were contextualized and focused on students using their prior knowledge and experiences to construct meaning and actively engaged students and put them in control of their own learning. It's evident that Cindy knew the curriculum and students' abilities and interests, understood literacy development, and was aware of and sought additional resources to identify good literature in order to plan such a comprehensive unit. Good unit planning takes time, knowledge, and good organization.

Other Instructional Practices

Throughout this book, we describe different instructional practices such as writing workshop, language experience, and shared reading approach that emphasize literacy as a constructive process, contextual learning, and the integration of reading, writing, speaking, and listening. Again, whole language is not a program or set of instructional methods; it is a philosophy that teachers use to make pedagogical decisions as they observe children engaged in literacy.

SUMMARY

In this chapter, we defined whole language as a philosophy and not a program or set of strategies. Whole language has evolved from theory and research of many different disciplines such as cognitive psychology, psycholinguistics, sociolinguistics, and cultural anthropology. We presented ten tenets of whole language:

1. Reading is a transaction that changes with each subsequent reading.
2. Reading and writing are developed in a manner similar to the way young children learn to speak.
3. Reading and writing are constructive processes in which readers and writers use their prior knowledge and experiences to create text meaning.
4. Since language learning is a constructive process, students must continually take risks to develop literacy.
5. Language learning is a social process.
6. Language skills and strategies are developed in the context of authentic, meaningful, and functional activities.
7. Children are curious and become naturally engaged in their own inquiry; hence whole language espouses a child-centered curriculum.
8. All children are viewed as capable and developing learners and not as immature and disabled.
9. Observation is pivotal.

10. Assessment is directly linked to instruction and is often a part of instruction.

11. Whole-language teachers' practices may differ since there is no one method that characterizes whole language.

In the last half of the chapter, we suggested ways to implement a whole-language philosophy within a balanced reading program. Reading aloud, reading workshop, literature circles, book clubs, and literature units are a few examples teachers have incorporated in their classrooms. These instructional practices allow teachers to teach language as a whole, to use authentic and meaningful materials that have a purpose, and to encourage self-selection and personal inquiry. The question is not is this a whole language activity but rather what am I doing to help children enjoy and develop the reading and writing processes, and why am I doing this? It is from this perspective that teachers are empowered to make decisions about instruction based on their knowledge of literacy and their keen observation of the children they teach. And it is from this perspective that we discussed using a whole-language philosophy to guide literacy instruction and learning.

In the Field

1. Begin to design a unit for a particular grade level and develop it as you read the rest of this book. Choose a unit organized by topic, genre, or author. Identify the theme or concept and goals. Identify literature. Describe activities and literacy strategies to develop the theme/concept and goals. Suggest appropriate assessment and evaluation.

2. Observe a classroom that incorporates reading workshop. Note the reading and writing behaviors exhibited by the students and teachers. Talk to the students about what they are doing and their feelings toward reading workshop. Discuss with the teacher how the minilessons will be planned, the conferences organized, and the journals implemented.

3. Observe a literature circle or book club discussion. What did you observe? Did all children participate? During the discussion, did students explore and examine characters and theme and motives, and did they go beyond summarizing the plot or topic? If not, how would you help students engage in critical thinking?

Portfolio Suggestion

Select from your journal two examples of your responses to Pause and Reflect, Learning from Experience, or In the Field. Write a brief evaluation of your work. Explain how this chapter affected your thinking about whole language within a balanced reading program.

For Further Reading

Church, S. M. (1994). Is whole language really warm and fuzzy? *The Reading Teacher, 47,* 358–361.

Ernst, G., & Richard, K. J. (1994–1995). Reading and writing pathways to conversation in the ESL classroom. *The Reading Teacher, 48,* 320–326.

Hartman, D. K., & Hartman, J. A. (1993). Reading across texts: Expanding the role of the reader. *The Reading Teacher, 47,* 202–211.

Lapp, D., & Food, J. (1994). Integrating the curriculum: First steps. *The Reading Teacher, 47,* 416–419.

Raphael, T. E., & McMahon, S. I. (1994). Book club: An alternative framework for reading instruction. *The Reading Teacher, 48,* 102–116.

Smith, J. L., & Johnson, H. (1994). Models for implementing literature in content studies. *The Reading Teacher, 48,* 198–209.

II. • • • • • • • • •

Teaching Strategies: Planning and Implementing Instruction

CHAPTER 3

Knowledge of Print: Its Development and Instructional Support

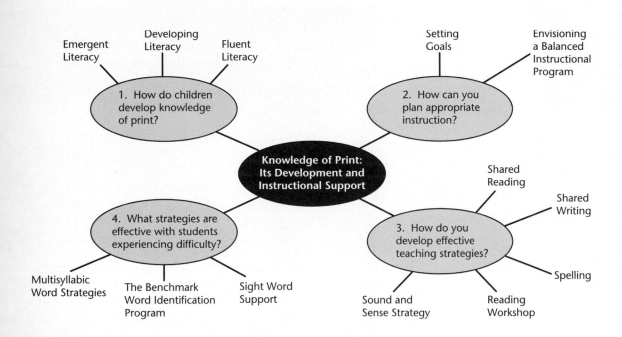

Emergent Literacy

Developing Literacy

Fluent Literacy

1. How do children develop knowledge of print?

Setting Goals

Envisioning a Balanced Instructional Program

2. How can you plan appropriate instruction?

Knowledge of Print: Its Development and Instructional Support

Shared Reading

Shared Writing

3. How do you develop effective teaching strategies?

Spelling

4. What strategies are effective with students experiencing difficulty?

Multisyllabic Word Strategies

The Benchmark Word Identification Program

Sight Word Support

Sound and Sense Strategy

Reading Workshop

▼ CHAPTER GOALS FOR THE READER

To understand how children learn about print

To develop a vision of appropriate instruction

To develop strategies to help your students acquire knowledge about print

To understand alternative teaching strategies for students who experience special difficulty with print

▼ CHAPTER OVERVIEW

What *do* children do when they learn to read? In many respects, it remains a mystery. We do know, however, that they develop skill as they engage in reading and writing activities. Children progress through a series of phases as they gain proficiency in literacy, and these changes can be observed. We also know that many children naturally develop the complex set of skills involved in reading and writing on their own through immersion in print-rich environments. As teachers, then, we are like gardeners trying to encourage healthy growth. If anything, this naturalness of the process makes it all the more remarkable. As gardeners we watch carefully over the growth that is occurring. We quickly see when certain children may profit from greater support through minilessons or more long-term direct instruction. But even when we provide this needed support, we remain respectful of the naturalness of the literacy-learning process.

In this chapter, we consider what it is that children learn about print. The chapter has four main parts. In the first, we describe a useful framework for thinking about how children learn about print through reading and writing activities. In the second part, we focus on planning appropriate instruction: setting goals and envisioning a balanced instructional program. In the third section, we describe instructional strategies for you to support your students as they learn about print.

Instead of "one-size-fits-all" instruction, we recommend that instructional support be responsive to the needs of individual children. We conclude with a description of instructional strategies that will help those children who experience most difficulty in becoming fluent with print.

◆ TAPPING PRIOR KNOWLEDGE TO SET A PURPOSE

Have you recently interacted with preschool children? Did they show any signs of being fascinated with print and writing? Did they try to read the labels on boxes and cans, street signs, and words shown on the television? Have you had any experiences assisting children who are struggling to understand the nature of print? Drawing on the chapter overview and outline and your reflections about your experiences with young children, identify what it is that you most want to learn from reading this chapter. List these in your journal under the heading Chapter 3: Setting a Purpose.

HOW DO CHILDREN DEVELOP KNOWLEDGE OF PRINT?

Learning to read is a complex process in which children solve many problems. One of these is to understand the nature of print and how it works. *Print* can be narrowly conceived of to refer to the process of forming letter sequences or to the letter sequences themselves, or, more generally, to various forms of communication involving printed materials. Children must learn about the alphabetic characters themselves, their symbolic functions in relation to speech and meaning, and their broader communicative functions. The correspondence between speech and writing is complicated, because relationships occur on a number of levels that are by no means always obvious. At the most general level, a written message relates to its spoken counterpart. At a more basic level, a printed sentence corresponds to a spoken sentence, but whereas a capital letter and a period indicate the boundaries of the printed sentence, inflectional characteristics indicate the boundaries of the spoken sentence.

Spoken words also relate to printed words, but whereas printed words are marked by spaces, spoken words are not similarly separated from each other. Indeed, children who are beginning to read often have little awareness of how speech becomes partitioned into word units. As children learn to read and spell, they acquire a visual representational system that allows them to see what they say and hear. Thus word learning as a part of reading instruction involves not only learning about the nature of printed words, but also discovering how language may be segmented into units that correspond to printed words.

Below the level of meaningful words, spoken phonemes (sounds) and syllables correspond to letters or series of letters (graphemes). Establishing the relations between phonemes and letters is complicated for several reasons. First, just as children are not aware of word units in their spoken language, they are also not aware of the phonemes that compose spoken words. In fact, it has been argued that it is experience with let-

Pause a

Think back t
words and h
parent or an
ticularly usef
your journal

Developing Literacy

The discussi
of print and
how stories
meaningful.
ken languag
dence betwe
word is and,
and letters v

Ehri (1
holds word i

Since b
similat
They d
segmer
ory wh

In other wor
form and its
image when
more comple

Develo
ter sounds m
ken with pri
about letter-
times useful
(1) word awa
spell.

Word Awar

An importan
taneously. Tl
With regard
oral language
able to segme

ters that sensitizes children to the phonemes of words (Ehri, 1983, 1991). Second, although there are only 26 letters, some are easily confused because they are mirror images *(b* and *d)* or rotations *(n* and *u)* of each other. Finally, in English it is not always the case that one letter is used to represent one phoneme. For example, the letter pairs *sh, th,* and *ch* each represent a single phoneme. Furthermore, particularly for vowels, the correspondence is more complex. A letter may stand for several different phonemes, and a phoneme may be represented by several different letters and/or combination of letters.

Children grow to understand these complex sets of relationships between print and speech over time. The problems being solved by children first noticing print differ from those of children who have begun to use reading and writing to communicate. Moreover, not all children experience the same problems as they learn to read and write. Given variation in their past experiences, your students will bring different goals and understandings to literacy tasks. It is important for you, as their teacher, to know about the sorts of challenges that children face.

In thinking about the sorts of problems that children solve, we focus first on those that they encounter in the preschool years when they become intrigued by print and the meaning it signals. The literacy that occurs during this period has been called *emergent literacy* (Teale & Sulzby, 1986). Children progress from this exploration to the somewhat more advanced phase that we will refer to as *developing literacy*. During this phase, some students profit from the instructional support and reading encouragement offered by their teachers. Others develop their literacy skill simply through the experience of reading and writing. Finally, students' knowledge about the way print works becomes fairly complete. Through practice they integrate their knowledge to achieve *fluent literacy*. In the remainder of this section, we consider what research reveals about the complexities children encounter during each of these phases and discuss the support that you can provide to help them progress.

Emergent Literacy

During their preschool years, children walking down streets see street signs, advertisements, T-shirt slogans, and printed directions. Inside their home they look at magazines, letters, labels, and trademarks. The parents of many children read stories to them. Almost all children encounter printed words and see people reading and writing. They learn that people make things happen when they are involved in reading and writing: They gain information by reading newspapers, instructions, and mail; they are entertained by magazines, books, and personal letters. Through these experiences, they learn that print has meaning and function. This understanding of the *functions of print* is basic to subsequent literacy learning. In this sense, learning to "read" begins long before children engage in formal reading instruction (Taylor, 1983).

What are the challenges that children meet as they become aware of print? One of the earliest concerns the nature of print. Children must come to realize that print is more than a series of marks (Ferreiro & Teberosky, 1982). Ferreiro (1984), for example, reports that when she asked a 3-year-old (pointing to the text), "What could be read here?" he responded, "Letters." When she asked further, "What does it say in

How is this yo

the letters?'
not discerne
no different
is achieved
that it repre

Childr
quently beli
found that i
they were a
print. Later,
identify nur
ple read and

During
in context.
the same co
within a re
words are ta
when the w
change (Mas
tify words th
ing when th
words. We c

very young children do not know how to segment oral language into parts that relate to printed words (word awareness). They listen to sentences without awareness of the words composing them. This awareness develops gradually over time. Karpova (1955, as described in Slobin, 1966) found that children's word awareness develops in three stages. In the first, at 3 to 4 years of age, children understand sentences as units, without distinguishing individual words. For example, they report that a sentence such as *Dan and Peter went walking* contains two words: "Dan-went-walking" and "Peter-went-walking." During the next stage, children become able to separate sentences into subject and predicate. The sentence *The boys play ball* would be reported as containing two words: "The boys" and "play ball."

A more sophisticated form of word awareness develops as children become emergent readers: They learn to identify the spoken words that relate to printed words. In *learning words,* not only must they learn to discriminate among printed words, but also to forge connections between spoken and printed words. These, however, do not occur as separate processes. For some children, this complex learning seems to be effortless. Others, however, encounter difficulty. Those who fail to develop word awareness (a concept of word) during the initial stages of reading can be identified because their oral reading bears little or no correspondence to the printed words being read. Once children start to develop word awareness, their reading changes. As described by Clay (1967):

> As [the children] developed skill in matching behavior, fingers were used to point to those parts of the text that were supposed to correspond to the vocal responses. Fluency gave way to word by word reading. At this point the child's reading became staccato as he over-emphasized the breaks between words. He could be thought of as "reading the spaces" or "voice pointing" at the words. (p. 16)

Thus when children point to words during the initial stages of reading, this indicates that they are developing awareness of words and an understanding of the correspondence between spoken and written language. Voice pointing and, subsequently, natural phrasing reflect increasing control of print. When children continue to fingerpoint beyond the beginning stages of reading, this may indicate difficulty in visual acuity or coordination.

Most children do not have difficulty becoming aware of words and learning them. Some, however, profit from explicit instruction focusing on printed words and the correspondence between print and language. The instructional methods developed by Morris (1986), described later in this chapter and in chapter 13, show how you can help children to develop a concept of word and the word awareness underlying it.

To learn printed words, children must identify features that distinguish new words from previously learned ones. When children read the book *Brown Bear, Brown Bear,* they may begin to learn the words *brown, red, yellow,* and *green.* Some may rely on picture cues; others may notice that these words begin with different letters and identify the words on the basis of the initial letter. This will work well until the word *blue* is added to the set. The children will then need to consider more than the initial consonant to discriminate correctly, since *brown* and *blue* (as well as *bear*) begin with the same letter.

This discrimination may not be much of a problem in the initial stages of reading when text is highly predictable and picture cues support word identification. But as children progress, they must solve the problem of keeping an expanding set of words straight. Features that are initially useful in discriminating among words are no longer sufficient, and students must attend to other features. In Ehri's terms, the visual images of words being built in children's memories must become more complete (Ehri, 1980). Primary teachers observe this problem in discrimination most often when students encounter words with similar beginning and ending letters but different medial vowels (e.g., *bat, bit,* and *but*). Most children eventually learn to attend to a sufficient number of word features so that words are rarely confused. Writing facilitates this process; as children write, they become conscious of all letters in a word. In addition, contextual information may support word recognition.

Finally, children must develop a system for learning sight words and for relating printed words to their meaning and spoken counterparts. *Sight words* are those words recognized immediately on the basis of sight; they are printed words known by a child. Concrete and meaningful words such as "baby," "ball," and "dinosaur" are easier for children to remember and identify quickly than more abstract words such as "in," "the," and "very." Words that are distinctive in meaning may already be well differentiated in children's memory, whereas the more abstract words may not have been experienced by children as concepts separate from other words.

Within categories of concrete and abstract words, those read frequently are more easily remembered than those rarely encountered. Not so long ago, the stories in published program readers were developed by controlling the repetition of words to help children to remember them through concentrated practice. However, sentences in stories created on this basis such as "Run Spot run. Run. Run." or "Look Sally. Look! Look!" were awkward in structure and did not conform to children's natural language. Consequently, children were deprived of cues from context in the form of predictable language patterns. The same degree of support for children in the initial stages of reading can be achieved by having children read books with limited amounts of print and predictable sentence patterns. Through this rich print and picture environment, children learn and remember words that are read repeatedly. At later stages, children who continue to have difficulty remembering words benefit from reading and rereading stories to provide the experience necessary for sight-word learning.

Practice with isolated words is not the same as practice in context. Through contextual reading, children begin to associate the visual form of a word with its meaning as well as its spoken identity. Drill with isolated words may help children relate the printed words with their spoken form, but without context, they do not have to specify the meaning of words in terms of prior experience and story context. Consequently, the concepts of words in memory are less semantically rich and less easily remembered.

Children also remember more easily words that they have written. As children write words, they focus on each sound component of the word and the letters needed to represent these sounds (phonemes). For example, when Tommy writes the word "ball," he says the word slowly to himself. He emphasizes the initial phoneme, drawing it out "b-b-b," and then determines what letter might best represent it. He then writes the letter "B." This process of continuing through the word in terms of its sounds enables Tommy to become more aware not only of the sound components of the word, but also, through writing, its visual representation. The processes entailed in becoming aware of phonemes and learning letter-sound patterns are discussed next.

Phonemic Awareness and Letter-Sound Patterns

What exactly do we mean by phoneme awareness? When children first learn to speak, they are able to discern differences at the phonemic level in words; they are able to hear the difference between words that differ in only one sound (e.g., *cat* and *hat*) and respond differentially. This is not what we mean by phoneme awareness because these young children have little conscious awareness of phonemes as distinctive units. They are not able to treat phonemes in an objective fashion and to think about them in abstracted form. *Phoneme awareness* is the conscious awareness of sounds within words.

Children become aware of phonemes as separable entities gradually over time. Relatively few children of preschool and kindergarten age are able to segment words into phonemic components; in contrast, many first graders are able to do so (Liberman, Shankweiler, Fischer, & Carter, 1974). It should not, then, come as a surprise that phoneme awareness and reading are very related. It has been shown that reading influences the way children perceive phonemes (Ehri, 1984).

Even more important, it has been demonstrated that instruction to develop phoneme awareness facilitates later reading (Bradley & Bryant, 1983; Lundberg, Frost, & Petersen, 1988). The evidence is fairly conclusive that some children profit from becoming aware of phonemes in words. Just as becoming aware of words in sentences facilitates the learning of sight words, becoming aware of phonemes in words enhances the discovery of relations that hold among letters and phonemes.

While it is possible to develop phoneme awareness prior to reading printed materials, we believe that the teaching that develops phoneme awareness in the context of reading and writing activities is more effective. How do children learn to hear phonemes in words? One natural approach is to encourage children to invent spellings during writing. By saying words in an elongated fashion, children become able to hear the sounds, first, at the beginning and endings of words and then in their middles (Clay, 1979; Elkonin, 1963). The main point here is that hearing sounds within words enables children to relate sounds to letters, which in turn leads to improved word recognition (Ball & Blachman, 1991; Bradley & Bryant, 1983; Clarke, 1989).

Another way is through word families. By hearing and seeing rhyming words, children become aware of how the beginning consonants or consonant blends ("onsets") change while the word endings ("rimes," the part from the vowel onward) stay the same. Treiman (1985) has shown that the linguistic units of onsets and rimes are more easily discerned by children than are individual phonemes. Moreover, rimes relate in a more predictable fashion to phonemes than do the same letters taken individually (Adams, 1990).

Many children learn to read from programs that include instruction in phonics and other word elements. At the same time, an increasing number of children learn *letter-sound patterns* inductively; that is, they discover spelling patterns through writing. This is particularly true for children in whole-language classrooms. There is evidence that those children who learn to read easily also develop knowledge about word elements easily, beyond what has been taught to them through direct instruction. The knowledge of average and less proficient learners, by contrast, tends to reflect the con-

What words or word patterns should these children encounter in their text selection?

cepts that have been taught to them directly through their writing and reading programs (Barr & Dreeben, 1983). If some of your students are not making progress, you may need to provide them with supportive instruction that is similar to what is described later in this chapter, to help them to hear sounds in words and to discover the relations that hold between letters and phonemes (Stahl, 1992).

Pause and Reflect

Think back to your experiences in kindergarten, first grade, and second grade. What do you remember about learning to read? Did you like the stories you read? Were you taught "skills"? Did you do much writing? Did any of your teachers read to you? Were you excited about learning to read and write or was it an unpleasant experience for you? Think about these early experiences. Which do you see as being particularly productive and which a waste of your time? Write your thoughts in your journal under the heading "Literacy Experiences in School."

Fluent Literacy

Our goal as teachers is to help children develop their familiarity with print so that they read without even noticing the print—so that they focus on the meaning of text with little attention and effort diverted toward the recognition of print. By *reading flu-*

ency we mean reading unfamiliar as well as familiar selections with appropriate intonation, phrasing, and rate. It is possible for children to demonstrate fluent reading with familiar stories they have read many times, but unless this same fluency is demonstrated with unfamiliar selections, we cannot conclude that they are fluent readers. The capability to read fluently depends on two conditions:

- instantaneous recognition of an extensive set of printed words
- considerable practice in reading contextual selections

Some skillful young readers achieve fluency in their first year of reading. Many, however, require several years of reading experience before they acquire sufficient word knowledge and contextual practice to read unfamiliar material fluently (see Lipson & Lang, 1991, for a discussion of reading fluency).

Controversial Issue

Reading Fluency

How does reading fluency develop? Some experts in the field of reading believe that fluency comes about through the complex orchestrations of information from a variety of sources (Bussis, Chittenden, Amarel, & Klausner, 1985; Clay, 1979). Goodman (1976), for example, asserts that "skill in reading involves not greater precision, but more accurate first guesses based on better sampling techniques, greater control over language structure, broadened experiences and increased conceptual development" (p. 504). Heavy reliance on print is assumed to cause poor reading. It is believed that fluency will develop as children are encouraged to guess accurately and to rely less on detailed analysis of printed words.

An opposing position has been articulated in recent years: Fluency depends on the efficient and thorough processing of printed words. That is, fluency depends most centrally on mastery of print and its instantaneous processing (Adams, 1990; Samuels, 1979). As Stanovich (1980, 1991) explains, good readers who have developed automaticity in word knowledge encounter few problems with word identification when reading and therefore can direct all their attention toward meaning. They read fluently because the print does not pose problems, and they are therefore able to focus on meaning. In contrast, poor readers who encounter many problems with print are forced to use context to aid word identification, and this diversion of attention from meaning to print results not only in lack of fluency but also in poorer comprehension. Thus, mastery of print enables readers to focus their undivided attention on comprehension.

In this book, we assume that the goal of reading is comprehension, and that adequate comprehension depends on the orchestration of knowledge from different sources, including the reader's background knowledge of a topic, the developing understanding of an author's message, knowledge of language structures, and knowledge of print. At the same time, we believe that fluent processing of print depends on automaticity of word knowledge—the quick recognition of words without effort devoted to analysis.

We recommend that fluency be promoted in two ways. First, children should be given the opportunity through classroom reading and writing experiences to master the relations that hold between the letters and sounds of English. Second, children should reread stories and informational passages that are relatively easy for them so that they experience highly accurate reading. If the text provided poses too many problems, there is no way that a child will come to understand what fluent reading entails.

HOW CAN YOU PLAN APPROPRIATE INSTRUCTION?

Setting Goals

As the prior discussion reveals, children gain knowledge in many different areas as they develop knowledge of print. Instruction should be designed to help children learn about the following aspects of print: (1) functions of print, (2) concept of word (word awareness), (3) phonemic awareness (the ability to hear individual sounds within spoken words), (4) a sight vocabulary, (5) knowledge of the sounds that letters represent (letter-sound patterns), and (6) reading fluency. These goals form a sort of progression. It is important for children to understand the function of print before more formal support is provided for forming the concept of word and phonemic awareness. As they gain experience reading and rereading, children will expand their sight vocabularies, develop their ability to decode, and become fluent readers.

In setting your goals, it is also important to consider the special characteristics of your students. The size of your class and the unique talents and needs of your students will influence the emphasis that you place on different aspects of print. If your students are in the beginning stages of reading, you will emphasize activities that help them to become aware of the functions of print and aware of words and phonemes. If your students have already begun reading, you will want to provide reading and writing experiences in which they expand their sight vocabularies and learn letter-sound patterns. For more advanced readers, you will support their development of fluency. If some of your students are learning-disabled, you will want to think of their special needs in relation to that of the class and consider how you may structure activities to meet their needs. If some of your students speak English as a second language, this will have implications for the literature that you select for your class library, the cultural resources that you have to enrich your class program, and the instructional support you will offer (Crowell, 1991; Hornberger, 1992)

Envisioning a Balanced Instructional Program

We can think about this issue on two levels. At the more general level, what will be the nature of the reading and writing program that you offer to your class? In many districts, school policies in such areas as grouping and material selection shape the form that your reading program will take. If, for example, you teach in a district that encourages teachers to develop their own literature-based reading and writing program, your program will look quite different from the one you offer if you teach in a district that has adopted a published literacy series. Yet no matter what the general form of your literacy program, on a more specific level you have the opportunity to tailor-make the general approach through the incorporation of instructional strategies that are appropriate to the needs of your students. Moreover, as your class changes from year to year, so accordingly will the emphasis of your instructional program.

But is one approach better than others? Should your district select a publisher's program, or should you develop a literature-based program? What are the advantages of creating literature-based programs? Through such programs do children learn to love reading? Do they also develop knowledge of print? Are there some children who need more systematic instruction to develop knowledge of print? Debates about reading approaches have gone on for many years. In the mid-1960s, the controversy focused on whether programs that emphasized meaning were as effective as those focused on phonics in enhancing the reading achievement of students. In her book *Learning to Read: The Great Debate,* Jeanne Chall (1968/1983a) concluded that the majority of studies indicated that children learn best when they experience instruction that focuses systematically on phonics.

The questions are similar today. Do children who read from materials organized according to reading levels with attention to skills learn better than those in whole-language programs in which reading and writing are integrated in response to literature? The results from recent studies tend to show that whole-language programs and more traditional programs involving direct instruction in phonics are equally effective (Stahl & Miller, 1989; Stahl, McKenna, & Pagnucco, 1994). This is most true when they are compared by the use of more formal measures of learning outcomes (e.g., Dahl & Freppon, 1995; Morrow, 1992). On measures of attitude and more informal measures of literacy, whole-language programs tend to show an advantage. Qualitative analyses of classroom activities in elementary school show that the two approaches provide very different learning experiences for children, including greater opportunity for decision making, writing, and application of knowledge about print (e.g., Dahl & Freppon, 1995; Fisher & Hiebert, 1990).

Using results from their meta-analysis of studies of whole-language instruction Stahl, McKenna, and Pagnucco (1994) conclude that eclectic programs, which include open-ended tasks and student-selection of literature but which also stress achievement and include phonics instruction, seem to be effective in improving both achievement and attitude (p. 175). We agree that an either-or choice is simplistic. We recommend that you begin with a conception of a quality literacy program and then from this perspective evaluate the strengths and limitations of the program that has been selected by your district or that you have developed.

In view of the research literature and the practice of outstanding teachers, we recommend that the following components form your literacy program:

- Children's literature read aloud by the teacher
- Children's literature read and reread by children
- Word study, including focus on phonemes and letters
- Teacher-supported writing activities
- Opportunities for children to write

We describe these components here and then develop these ideas more fully in subsequent chapters.

Literature Read by Teachers

Some time each day should be spent reading aloud to students. In kindergarten and the primary grades, you may select books that children will be able to read aloud themselves, and you may wish to reread these books aloud periodically. This experience of hearing books read aloud will encourage and prepare children to read the books on their own. At all grade levels, you may select books based on student interest or relevance to thematic units in such areas as social studies or science. Guidelines for selection of books are described in Chapter 8.

Literature Read by Children

The stories that children read themselves form the core of your reading program. These selections should come from a variety of sources including the classroom library, the school library, and the reading materials selected for students in your school. A published program may be used in your district. If so, you will want to examine the selections included for the range of conceptual and cultural perspectives they represent. To have a balanced literacy program, you will also want your students to read selections from your school or classroom library as well as those from the published program. If some of your students are bilingual, it is particularly important that your libraries include books written in the first languages of your students to enhance the development of biliteracy (Crowell, 1991).

Reading and rereading stories help children to develop their print skill. Through this reading and rereading experience, they form connections between the printed and spoken forms of words and discern how patterns of letters relate to syllables and phonemes. Instructional strategies to support this process are described later in this chapter.

As children enter the phase of developing literacy, it is helpful to identify books that provide contextual support for reading and to encourage children to begin reading them. In helping children to select appropriate books, the concept of *reading level* is important. Children enjoy reading and learning when the match between their skill and the demands of the reading materials is appropriate. If it is too challenging, we refer to this reading as being at *frustration level*. Those books read with the support of a teacher during instruction can be challenging but not frustrating *(instructional level)*. A rule of thumb that some teachers follow is that if children experience difficulty with more than one word in every ten, the material is too difficult. Sometimes children are determined to read books they are interested in that would appear to be too challenging; when they are extremely motivated, their interest and background knowledge may help them overcome the problems they encounter. The books that children select to read on their own should not pose many problems for them; that is, they should encounter relatively few unknown words. We refer to this as a child's *independent reading level*.

It is most difficult to find appropriate books for children who are in the beginning stages of learning to read. A solution followed by some teachers is to read aloud books contained in the class library so that when children read them they are very familiar; they have the memory of the story to support their reading. A similar solution is embodied in the *Shared Book Experience* (Holdaway, 1979), in which a group of children follow along as their teacher reads aloud, pointing to the words read. This works particularly well with Big Books with predictable language and those containing familiar stories. Children enjoy reading along as they learn the story by heart. They are then able to select smaller versions to read on their own or with a friend. The point here is that familiarity with the story provides the support that they need to successfully navigate the print.

What are *predictable pattern books?* These are books such as *The Great Big Enormous Turnip* by Alexei Tolstoy (Scott Foresman, 1971) that build thematic suspense through repetition in sentence frames reflecting the recurring actions of characters. This progression serves to carry the story along. In Tolstoy's story, after the turnip had grown up sweet and strong and enormous, the old man decides to pull it up:

> He pulled—and pulled again. But he could not pull it up.
>
> He called the old woman.
>
> The old woman pulled the old man. The old man pulled the turnip.
>
> And they pulled—and pulled again. But they could not pull it up.
>
> So the old woman called her granddaughter.
>
> The granddaughter pulled the old woman.
>
> The old woman pulled the old man. The old man pulled the turnip.
>
> And they pulled—and pulled again. But they could not pull it up.*

And so the story continues and builds to the climax, which children enjoy greatly. The repetitive language not only builds the suspense of the story, but also provides beginning readers the support they need to deal with the print.

A variety of books with patterned language are included in the description of children's literature for young readers developed by Barbara Peterson and included in the appendix. The list shows how books may be organized according to the level of support provided. The books listed in Levels 1 to 4, for example, are composed of experiences familiar to children, familiar language patterns and vocabulary, and illustrations that correspond closely with the meaning of the story. This degree of support allows children to reconstruct the story and to explore how the story is encoded in print.

Children learn a lot about reading through reading. They learn about how stories and other selections are organized; they gain knowledge about people, events, and places; they experience what Hartman (1992) calls "intertextuality." Making comparisons across texts leads to comparative insight and enjoyment. They also learn about print. As children read, they become able to identify an increasing number of words instantaneously without analysis. As discussed previously, we refer to these words as "sight words." Sight words, words that occur frequently, account for about 70 percent of running text. They usually include some common nouns, verbs, and adjectives; in addition, many words that form the structure of sentences, such as "the," "his," "here," and "but," may be recognized easily on "sight." Most children learn

---

*From "The Great Big Enormous Turnip" by Alexei Tolstoy, 1971, from *Scott Foresman Reading Systems,* pp. 8–16. Reprinted by permission.

these words as sight words because they recur frequently in text. The sight vocabulary that children develop uniquely reflects the stories and other selections they have been reading. Proficient readers develop a large sight vocabulary; the words they see repeatedly become familiar and are recognized on sight.

Some children learning to read have a difficult time learning and remembering sight words. Thus it is useful for you, as their teacher, to note whether they are quickly (without analysis) identifying this set of words. Fluent reading depends on the development of sight words. Thus in considering the oral reading of students, it is important to ask how quickly and accurately they recognize these basic sight words. Furthermore it is instructive to consider how the oral readings of children match with the printed words and sentences.

Word Study, including Focus on Sounds Associated with Letters.

Some children become aware of spelling patterns and their pronunciations without formal instruction. Others profit from some form of support in this area. Still others require instruction that begins early and is direct, intensive, and systematic. The important point is that not all children need and respond to the same form of instruction and the same degree of support.

In order to support the development of children's knowledge of letter-sound associations, it is important to understand the cues that are available to children from alphabet letter names. The best way to understand how children use alphabet letter names in their writing is to think about the cues that letter names provide.

Pause and Reflect

Say the alphabet letter names aloud. As you do so, note which names provide useful cues from spoken sounds to written letters. Which letter names correspond directly with sounds? For which letters are the sounds represented at the beginning of the name? At the end of the name? Which letter names do not relate in any direct fashion? Record your observations in your journal under the heading "Alphabet Letter Names" before reading further.

You may have noted that "A" provides a reliable cue for children writing words containing the long vowel sound such as in "came" and "rain." This is true for the other vowel names as well: E, I, O, and U. Yet the vowel names do not signal to children that a "marker" is also needed to indicate long-vowel pronunciation (e.g., the "e" in "came" and the "i" in "rain"); this needs to be inferred by children from examples or taught more directly.

The letter names of B, D, J, K, P, Q, T, V, and Z include the letter sound at the beginning of the names. The letter names for "C" and "G" also include the sound at the beginning of the name, but they are somewhat more confusing because the letters also represent sounds that are not included in the names, as in "cat" and "get."

In other letter names, the sound is represented at the end, as for the letters F, L, M, N, R, and S. We might anticipate that this cue would be somewhat harder for chil-

What can you learn from this child's developmental spelling test?

dren to hear than those from the beginning, but studies of children's invented writing show that they provide useful cues. Finally, the remaining letter names, H, X, W, and Y, provide less reliable sound cues to letters.

Do children use letter names to represent the short-vowel sounds? Think for a moment about how this might be done. Read (1971) discovered from an analysis of children's writing that they do indeed use letter names, but in a complicated way. What do you think children are writing with the spellings "LAFFT" and "ALRVATA"? The words they have written are "left" and "elevator." If you say "A" slowly, you will notice that the initial sound corresponds to the short "E" sound. Similarly, Read found that they wrote "FES" and "FLEPR" for "fish and "flipper." The letter name for "E" pronounced slowly contains the short "I" sound. This was also found to be true for the letter name for "I," which includes the short "O" sound (children wrote "got" as "GIT" and "clock" as "CLIK)."

In sum, we know that children make use of letter names in their writing and do so in very creative ways. Yet letter names differ in the usefulness of the cues they provide.

Some languages are highly predictable in the relation between letters and sounds. The relation is somewhat more complex for English, but analyses have shown a great deal of predictability. Richek, List, and Lerner (1983) describe the types of letter-sound associations and the evidence of the degree to which these relations are predictable. Most single consonants are consistent in their relations between letter and sound. That is, when children are reading, initial consonants are reliable cues to speech sounds. Similarly, in writing, many consonant sounds are predictably represented by letters. Most first graders master knowledge of consonant letter-sound associations as well as consonant digraphs (sh, ck, ph, and th). Consonant blends, composed of two or three consonants, are also highly reliable and are usually mastered by second grade.

Vowels and vowel combinations are more complicated because of the variety of letter combinations used to represent vowel sounds and the fact that vowel letters represent both long and short forms of pronunciation. Inductive methods of teaching in which children infer relations by seeing a set of word exemplars are particularly useful in helping students to develop their knowledge about vowel-sound associations. You may use a minilesson to list, for example, the following words on the chalkboard and ask children what they notice about the relation between letters and sounds:

can	cane
hat	hate
pan	pane
fat	fate

Through such word study, they will begin to note the letter contexts in which long and short vowel pronunciations appear.

Although many of your students may infer letter-sound relations through their reading and writing experience, there are some who may profit from explicit instruction. Thus it is important for you to understand the nature of English spelling, know which phonic associations are reliable, and think of how to help students develop this understanding.

Teacher-Supported Writing Activities

Through such activities as Language Experience Stories and Supported Writing, you have the opportunity to model the forms of thinking that underlie writing. As children participate in the composing process, they see you represent their words in written form. When Language Experience Stories are read aloud, by pointing to each word being read you help your students to develop an understanding of the match between spoken and written words. Earlier we described this matching behavior, when children develop "concept of word," as critical to the learning of sight words and initial consonants.

Knowledge of print is also developed through shared writing experiences. As part of the composing process, you can model the writing of words by helping students to hear the sounds at the beginning of words you are writing. At a somewhat more advanced level, you may wish to use sound boxes to help children to hear the sounds of words as they write. This instructional approach is described more fully later in this chapter in the section on teaching strategies.

Opportunities for Children to Write

Children, even those in the beginning stage of emergent literacy, should be encouraged to write. Later in this chapter and in chapters 6 and 7, we describe approaches that you may use to encourage children to write. Because children explore the nature of print as they write, writing is one of the best ways for them to develop their knowledge about English spelling.

Pause and Reflect

Janellen Hatch, a first-grade teacher, has just transferred to a new school district that requires its teachers to use a published reading program. Her study of the program indicates that three components seem to be emphasized: the reading of stories, the development of word identification mainly through workbook activities, and enrichment that includes such activities as dramatic reenactments, partner reading, and vocabulary development.

What activities will Janellen need to develop in order to enrich the published reading program? Consider the five components just described (pp. 84–89) in developing your ideas. Record your answer in your journal under the heading "Enhancing a Published Program."

HOW DO YOU DEVELOP EFFECTIVE TEACHING STRATEGIES?

As discussed earlier in this chapter, instruction should be designed to help children learn about the following aspects of print: (1) functions of print, (2) concept of word (word awareness), (3) phonemic awareness (the ability to hear individuals sounds within spoken words), (4) a sight vocabulary, (5) knowledge of the sounds that letters represent (letter-sound patterns), and (6) reading fluency. In this section and the one that follows it, we describe teaching strategies that you can use to help your students develop knowledge of print.

All literacy activities in your classroom should provide experiences through which children come to see the pleasure of reading and writing and understand their functions. Children will engage in listening to stories read aloud and in reading and writing themselves. In addition, classroom activities should include those that are structured to help children focus on and understand the nature of print. A number of teaching sequences have been developed to help children learn about print and we describe some of these in this section. First, we describe a *shared reading* approach that helps children to develop awareness of words and to form a concept of word. Then we describe *shared writing* activities through which children become aware of the sounds composing words (phoneme awareness) and the sounds that letters represent. Another way in which children learn about print is through *spelling*. We discuss a spelling program that features word patterns based on the work of Henderson (1981, 1985/1990). We describe the approach of *reading workshop*, a useful way to have children read intensively and extensively. Through this reading experience, they consolidate their sight vocabulary and become fluent readers. Finally, we demonstrate a *sound-sense strategy* that will help your students to become more independent and fluent readers.

What is the value of choral reading?

Shared Reading

The philosophical and pragmatic bases for Shared Reading come from two related but separate traditions: the *Shared Book Experience* of Holdaway (1979) and the *Language Experience Approach* of Stauffer (1970). Both of these seminal thinkers in the area of early literacy knew the importance of making the strange world of print become familiar to young children. Holdaway did it by bringing children into the process of reading by sharing a focus on print as words were read. Stauffer accomplished a similar goal by having children see their words written as part of language experience stories.

Shared Reading is an effective way to help children develop word awareness and form a concept of word. By pointing to words as you read the words aloud, you model the relation between printed and spoken words (Morris, 1980, 1992). We refer to this as "finger-point reading." This experience is particularly useful for children who are in the beginning stages of print awareness. It also lets more advanced children demonstrate their knowledge of print. Their accuracy in finger-point reading and locating words directly reflects the extent to which they have solved the problem of how printed and spoken words relate to each other, which is to say, the extent to which they have formed a concept of word. The teaching strategy involves the following steps:

1. Select a Big Book or help children to develop a language experience story. (For descriptions of Big Book reading and the Language Experience Approach, see chapter 12.)

2. Read the first line of the story aloud to students, pointing to words as you read. Continue to model the "finger-point reading" procedure as you read the remainder of the selection.

3. Encourage children to join you in choral reading the selection as you read and point to the words read.

4. Mark off the first line and ask if there is someone willing to read it while pointing to the words read. Give other children the opportunity to read the remaining lines in the same way.

5. Ask if any child can point to a word as you name it in the first sentence. Continue by asking other children to locate other words that you name in the remaining sentences.

This set of procedures can be used flexibly. You may begin with the choral reading and repeat this step until the children are familiar with the selection. The final step may be omitted altogether. One interesting observation made by Morris (1980) was the tendency of children to point more than once for words of several syllables. That is, on the second syllable of a longer spoken word they would point to the next printed word on the line. This indicated that they had not yet completely solved the problem of how spoken words relate to print. This instructional strategy is modeled by Marcy Lee with her first graders in chapter 13.

Shared Writing

Shared Writing (Pinnell & McCarrier, 1994) is a variation of the Language Experience Activity in which teachers and children construct a story based on their experiences. Typically with the LEA, the teacher does the writing. In contrast, during Shared Writing, the children as well as the teacher participate in the writing. The purpose of the activity is to make public the process of thinking about words and their sound structure and converting the sounds into written form. Through this joint composing activity, children become aware of the sounds of words (phoneme awareness) and the letters representing the sounds.

The stage can be set for Shared Writing in a variety of ways. Following a nature walk or a visit to a museum or attendance at a play or concert, children can write about the highlights of their adventure. Or if they make or cook something, they can write the steps involved. Alternatively, some teachers designate two children as authors of the day to compose a sentence each about something important that is happening in their lives. Whatever the experience, all children in the group or class will participate in writing the story. The teaching strategies include the following steps:

1. Elicit a sentence from the class or the designated author. Repeat the sentence so that children understand what will be written.

2. Say the first word slowly in elongated fashion and ask, "Do you know the first letter?" Let the child who responds write the letter. You may decide, depending on the length and complexity of the word and the knowledge of the group, to finish writing the word. Alternatively, you may decide to say the word slowly and ask if anyone knows the next letter. On occasion, with a regularly patterned three- or four-letter word, you may wish to draw a sound box (a grid with one

box per sound, e.g., *c a t*) in which you fill in letters as children are able to hear the sounds in the word. (See Clay, 1993b, for a discussion of using a "sound box.")

3. Repeat the sentence again and say the next word in elongated fashion; ask if anyone knows the first letter. (Continue as for step 2.)

4. Have the class read along with you what has been written so far. As you read the words aloud, point to the word being read.

5. Continue the process with the next word until you read the end of the sentence.

Shared Writing is a highly interactive strategy. To be successful, it depends on children being engaged in the writing process. If their interest wanes, you may wish to assume more responsibility for the writing. Read the following Shared Writing dialogue to learn more about how Leslie Shaver engages children in writing.

Learning from Experience

The children in Leslie Shaver's kindergarten class had just finished making popcorn. Leslie pulled out a sheet of newsprint and said, "Let's write what we just did." During the writing process, Leslie uses several different strategies to help her students become aware of the sounds that compose words. As you read the lesson transcript, note the ways in which Leslie supports their developing phoneme awareness. Also consider what her students are learning about print.

Structures
student retelling

Models saying
word slowly to
help children
hear sounds

Mrs. Shaver: Well, what did we do first?

Tommy: First, we put the popcorn in the pot.

Mrs. Shaver: Okay, does everyone agree? *First, we put the popcorn in the pot.* All right, we have to write that down. *First.* Say *first* slowly: *f i r s t.* Hear any sounds in there?

Matt: *fff* F.

Mrs. Shaver: All right, come on up and write that down. [Matt writes *F.*] That's a good-looking F. Does anyone hear any other sounds?

Sarah: First *tt* T.

Reviews sentence

Models saying
word slowly to
help children
hear sounds

Mrs. Shaver: Yes, there's a T, at the end. *f i r s t.* Let me write the letters in between. [Mrs. Shaver writes *irs.*] Okay, Sarah, want to write the *t* at the end of *First*? [Sarah writes *t.*] Great! "First, we put the popcorn in the pot." *First* [points to first] *"we."* Let me say that slowly: *w.e.* Hear the sounds?

Kimba: W.

Mrs. Shaver: Want to write it? [Kimba writes *w.*] A beautiful W. Do you know the next letter?

Reviews sentence

Models saying
words slowly to
hear sounds

Focuses on other
sounds

Kimba: E?

Mrs. Shaver: Write it down. [Kimba writes *e.*] *First, we put the popcorn in the pot. Put.* Hear the sounds? *p u t.*

Maiko: I hear a T [Mrs. Shaver draws a sound box with room for three letters.]

Mrs. Shaver: Now everyone listen carefully. There is a T in *put*. Where does it come? Okay, at the end, so we'll write it here. [Mrs. Shaver writes t in the third square.] What other sounds do you hear: *p u t*?

Peter: A P like at the beginning of Peter.

Reviews writing

Mrs. Shaver: Write that down after *we*. [Peter writes *p*; Mrs. Shaver writes *u*.] Okay, Maiko, want to write the T? [Maiko writes the t.] Now, what have we got? *First, we put* [children read along as Mrs. Shaver points to each word] *the*. Does anyone know how to write *the*? Okay, Matt, give it a try. [Matt writes *the*.] Great. *First, we put the popcorn* . . . Say it slowly so you can hear the sounds: *p o p*. What sound do you hear at the beginning? [Several children say *p.p.p.*] What about at the end? [A chorus saying *p*] Good, *pop*. Watch as I write it. [Mrs. Shaver says the sounds slowly as she writes *p o p*.] Now listen to *corn* as I write it. [Mrs. Shaver says the sounds slowly as she writes *c o r n*.] Now let's read what we've written. [Children read *First, we put the popcorn* as Mrs. Shaver points to the words.] *In the pot*. Let's finish it. *In*—what sounds do you hear in *in*?

Models saying word slowly to hear sound

Models writing word

Models saying word slowly to hear sounds

Rachel: *nnn* N.

Mrs. Shaver: Good, we write *in* I.N. Rachel, want to write it? [Rachel writes *in*]. Oops, not so close, leave a space. Okay, great. *In the.* Who can write *the*? Okay, Sandy. [Sandy writes *the* by copying from the *the* earlier in the sentence.] Did you notice what Sandy did? She knew that we wrote "the" earlier in the sentence, so she looked at it to remind herself how to write it. Great problem solving, Sandy. One word left. *pot*. What sounds do you hear in *pot*?

Requests sounds from children

Paula: It begins with P *pp*, and it ends with T *tt*.

Mrs. Shaver: Want to write the *p* and we'll help you with the middle? [Paula writes *p*.] Who can help Paula with the middle? Okay, Matt, what would you write?

Matt: It would be an O like in *pop*.

Mrs. Shaver: Good problem solving, Matt. Paula, Matt says an O comes next and then T. [Paula writes *o* and *t*.] That was really good writing. Let's read it together: *First, we put the popcorn in the pot.* [Mrs. Shaver points to the words as the children read aloud.]

Reads what is written

 Your Turn: Think about this minilesson. What strategies did Leslie use to help her students develop phoneme awareness? What concepts about print were developed? Write your response in your journal under the heading Shared Writing before reading our response.

 Our Turn: The dialogue shows how the children participated in the writing of the story. Particularly for children for whom writing is still somewhat mysterious, it makes the writing process more transparent. From Leslie's modeling and from her use of the sound box, children begin to see the importance of saying words slowly before writing them in order to hear their sounds better. They develop phoneme awareness or sensitivity to the sound structure of words. Through the shared writing process, children also begin to learn the letters that go with the sounds. Moreover, children can participate in the activity at different levels, depending on what they have already learned about print.

Tim Kindergarten Stage 1	Anne Kindergarten Stage 2	Jonathan First Grade Stage 2	Silvia Second Grade Stage 3	Jane Second Grade Correct
AMINƆ	J	CHIRP	CHIRP	CHIRP
EM3321	SB	SAP	STAMP	STAMP
SEMAꟼS	AT	EDE	EIGHTEEY	EIGHTY
19ИHM	J	GAGIN	DRAGUN	DRAGON
SAMH	P	PRD	PURD	PURRED
MENENA	TP	TIP	TIPE	TYPE
ENIMM	T	CHUBRL	TRUBAL	TROUBLE

Figure 3.1 Spelling strategy classifications for five children. *Source:* From *Teaching Spelling* [Fig. 2.5, p. 50] by Edmund Henderson. Copyright © 1990 by Houghton Mifflin. Used with permission.

Spelling

As children read and write, their knowledge of English spelling (orthography) increases. They gradually develop greater understanding of the elements of words, and they do so in a fairly predictable manner. Longitudinal studies of children show how the early spellings of children change over time. These observed changes have been classified by Henderson according to developmental stages (Henderson, 1985/1990). As shown in Figure 3.1, in the first stage of writing (see Tim), children use letters, numbers, and other marks to represent words; however, the spellings bear no resemblance to correct spellings. Such responses show that children understand that words are composed of a series of letters, but they have not yet solved the problem of the more precise matches that hold between the phonemes and letters of words.

In the second stage, alphabetic writing occurs when children represent some sounds of words in a systematic way, particularly those at the beginnings of words (see Figure 3.2). First, they tend to represent only initial consonants (note Anne's writing); then both initial and final consonants are represented (note Jonathan's writing).

In the third stage, children represent within-word patterns more completely, in particular letters representing vowels and those that mark the pronunciation of vowels (e.g., final-e pattern) are included. Nevertheless, as shown for Silvia in Figure 3.1, spelling still departs in systematic ways from standard spelling for some words. Finally, children learn to spell words in standard form (see Jane's writing). What this development in spelling reflects is growth in the underlying knowledge that children have about words and the letter-sound patterns that compose them.

Learning from Experience

James wrote a story about catching fish. Look carefully at his writing, which is shown in Figure 3.2. Do you know what he has written? In terms of Henderson's developmental spelling stages, where would you classify James? Are there words that come from either a more or less advanced stage?

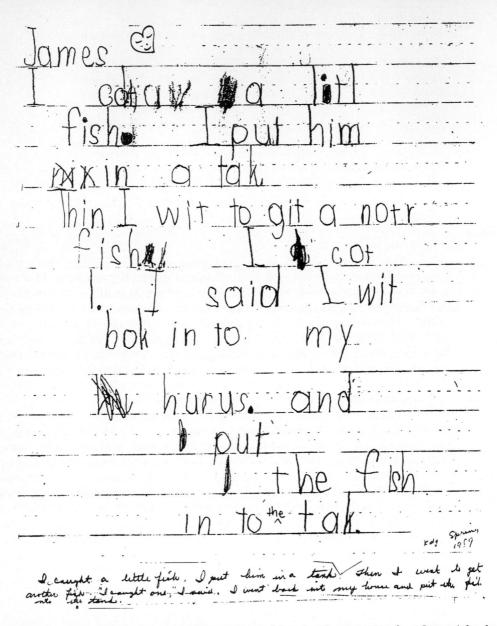

James

I cdaw a litl
fish. I put him
nixin a tak.
thin I wit to git a notr
fishy. I cot
l. I said I wit
bok in to my
hurus. and
put
the fish
in to the tak.

kdg Spring 1959

I caught a little fish. I put him in a tank. Then I went to get another fish. "I caught one," I said. I went back into my house and put the fish into the tank.

Figure 3.2. A Sample of James's Writing. *Source:* Printed with permission from James Ashenhurst. We thank him for this contribution.

Your Turn: Think about what you learned about James's writing. Write your response in your journal under the heading James's Writing and Spelling before reading our response.

Our Turn: Were you able to make out what James wrote? Here is what he wrote: "I caught a little fish. I put him in a tank. Then I went to get another fish. I caught one, I said. I went back to my house and put the fish into the tank."

In terms of spelling stage, James represents some words in standard form (e.g., fish, put, him, said). He may know these words as sight words. Words he hasn't yet learned give insight into his knowledge of spelling. He represents all beginning and final consonants and some medial ones. He is working on vowel sounds: Some are not yet standard (e.g., thin, thin, wit, git, bok). His spelling is similar to that of Jonathan and Silvia in Figure 3.1, somewhere between stages 2 and 3. The analysis suggests that he is ready to focus on how vowels are represented by letters.

Spelling is important in its own right and also because of its close relation to reading development. Research indicates that reading and spelling are reciprocal processes that depend on the same underlying phonological knowledge (Gentry & Gillet, 1993; Morris & Perney, 1984; Ferroli & Shanahan, 1987). Thus spelling activities can be viewed as enhancing reading (Invernizzi, Abouzeid, & Gill, 1994) and should be conceptualized as one aspect of a comprehensive literacy program.

Disagreement exists, however, over how spelling development can best be fostered (Morris, Blanton, Blanton, & Perney, 1995). Traditionalists advocate the use of a textbook, spelling lists, and weekly routines to support spelling (Henderson, 1985/1990; Templeton, 1991). In contrast, reformers call for the use of minilessons to focus on the types of spelling errors that occur in student writing (Wilde, 1990).

We suggest a more eclectic position. The words children study should be appropriate to their developmental level (Morris, Blanton, Blanton, Nowacek, & Perney, 1995); that is, they should reflect the sorts of spelling errors that children typically make in their writing. For example, we believe that the spelling activities for Anne (see Figure 3.1) should be quite different from those for Silvia. Morris, Blanton, Blanton, Nowacek, and Perney (1995) found that low-achieving third graders receiving instruction from a second-grade level spelling book that included spelling patterns more appropriate to their developmental level performed better than comparable children learning from a more challenging and less appropriate third-grade spelling book.

In addition to the appropriateness of the spelling words, we believe that children need more systematic spelling instruction than can be provided through minilessons. Particularly those children who do not easily discern orthographic (spelling) patterns profit from systematic instruction.

Thus we suggest that teachers form groups for word study and spelling based on children's spelling levels. In first and second grade, one group of children might focus on learning consonant sounds, others on simple consonant-vowel-consonant patterns, and still others on more complex patterns. Groups might be formed on the basis of a developmental spelling test such as the one described in chapter 10. In later grades, spelling tests that accompany spelling programs developed around word patterns can be used to determine the grade level at which children perform in spelling.

Weekly spelling activities typically consist of the following schedule. Monday: Introduce spelling words, calling attention to the pattern to be studied. Tuesday, Wednesday, and Thursday: Guide students through recommended spelling activities. Friday: Administer spelling test. Activities can be those recommended in a spelling textbook or you can develop your own activities.

In the final section of this chapter we describe the Benchmark Word Identification Program. Activities that are used to help children learn a set of regularly patterned words can reinforce spelling as well as word identification. Indeed, we encourage the integration of word study and spelling activities—areas that in the past have often been treated as separate subjects.

Reading Workshop

Reading Workshop is a way of organizing students, books, time, and space in a fashion parallel to the widely adopted pattern of writing workshop (Atwell, 1987). You are already familiar with many of the components of reading workshop such as USSR (Uninterrupted, Sustained Silent Reading), literature logs, and book sharing. As with the writing workshop, choice and responsibility are vital ingredients. Children choose the books they read and are responsible for organizing their time for reading and recording their reactions. Through such extensive reading practice, children develop interest in reading, expand their knowledge of word meanings, apply comprehension strategies, develop writing expression, and enhance reading fluency.

The form that Reading Workshop takes will vary from grade to grade and from class to class within grades. Teachers first using the approach may include it once a week; usually children enjoy having it more often. In order to provide an image of Reading Workshop, we provide a sample schedule showing how the time of Reading Workshop might be allocated.

Focus (about 5 minutes): A brief response by class members is called for to the question "What am I reading today?" This creates a public commitment and lets classmates know what others are reading. This activity may be most useful when students are first learning about Reading Workshop.

Minilesson (about 5 minutes): Atwell (1987) recommends starting each session with a brief discussion of a literary topic, such as "What are the key ingredients in a successful mystery?" "What do we mean by 'voice'?" or "What is a first-person narrator?" These discussions may also be rooted in a shared short read-aloud from a passage in a book being read by one of the students.

Reading Time (20 to 40 minutes): Students read books of their choice. As teacher, you can begin the period by moving through the class to give help and answer questions. Then, for the rest of the period, you will read children's literature. This modeling component is crucial to the success of the workshop.

Sharing/Discussion (about 10 minutes): One way to start a discussion is to have students read aloud a short passage that they particularly liked when reading the book, one that might be sufficiently puzzling or controversial to generate discussion. This sharing will also familiarize students with books they may wish to read.

Literature Logs (about 10 minutes): Students will write entries in their logs about the books that they have been reading. As teacher, you may use this time to write in your log or to respond to some of the student journals. Periodically, you will read aloud your journal entry as a way of modeling the kinds of thinking that can occur around books. Literature Logs are written conversations about books that take place mainly between each student and the teacher, although students may also wish to have such exchanges with a student partner—most often on a weekly basis. The logs encourage a discussion around good literature. Student errors are not addressed.

Sometimes it is useful to have the class develop a set of rules for using Reading Workshop time. In classes using Reading Workshop, students' suggestions have included the following: "We cannot do homework"; "we must read a book"; and "we may not talk to or disturb others."

When children are first learning to read and write, Reading Workshop provides the opportunity for them to consolidate their sight vocabularies and to integrate meaning from print and context as they read. You can provide support for young readers in the beginning stages of literacy in a variety of ways. Have your class library well stocked with books that are appropriate for the early stages (highly predictable text due to picture cues and repeated sentence patterns), as well as those for successive stages of reading development. Organize your books in terms of difficulty, in the way that has been done by Reading Recovery professionals (see the appendix). This will make it easier for you to help children find books that will not be overwhelming or too easy.

For students of all ages, Reading Workshop enables children to be in control of their reading and to share their ideas about the books they have selected. It provides the opportunity for students to consolidate their comprehension strategies and develop fluency. More important, it provides the space for students to learn about literature and to learn what they enjoy. The focus is on literature and the responses of students to it.

Sound and Sense Strategy

Readers sometimes have difficulty identifying unknown words. Typically, they come to an unknown word and halt. Some sound out the word, others replace it with a known word, and some just skip over it as if it were not there. The Sound and Sense strategy (Houghton Mifflin, 1981) can be a beginning step to help such readers identify unknown words and self-monitor their reading.

Procedure

The steps children take are these:

1. Skip the unknown words and read to the end of the sentence
2. Return to the unknown word; associate appropriate sounds for initial and final letters of the word

3. Return to the beginning of the sentence and reread, attempting to identify the word

As children apply this strategy, they will use phonics and context to identify the unknown word. They will need to practice the strategy first under your supervision and later independently. The strategy allows them to focus on making sense of print so that reading is meaningful.

As you experiment with each of these teaching strategies, keep in mind that our main goal for our students is to have them read fluently and to develop a love for reading. It is possible for children to read books they have read many times fluently, but when they read an unfamiliar book, their reading is often word by word with inappropriate intonation. You must seek to help children develop the degree of familiarity with print necessary for reading most materials (familiar as well as unfamiliar) fluently. Some young children realize fluent reading early, during their first year of reading; many require several years of reading experience before they achieve fluency in the way we define it here.

Among the ways in which you can help your students develop fluency, two are particularly useful. The first is essential: Have your students read and reread materials that pose few problems for them. The second involves modeling fluent reading so that your students have an idea of how their reading should sound. These approaches are described in detail in chapter 13.

WHAT STRATEGIES ARE EFFECTIVE WITH STUDENTS EXPERIENCING DIFFICULTY?

Although most of these teaching strategies are appropriate for most of your students, in this final section of the chapter we describe more supportive teaching for children who find literacy particularly challenging. We describe *sight word support* to help students develop their knowledge of sight words, *the Benchmark Word Identification Program* to help students with independent word analysis, and *multisyllabic word strategies* to help them deal with long and challenging words.

Sight Word Support

As defined by Harris and Hodges (1981), a sight word is "a word that is immediately recognized as a whole and does not require word analysis for identification" (p. 295). As children engage in reading, words become familiar as units. Most children, through reading and rereading books, build a sight vocabulary; that is, they are able to recognize an increasingly large set of words immediately without analysis. The method is fairly simple. Children expand their knowledge of sight words by reading and rereading stories and other text. For example, after a story has been read by a group or the class with your support, have your students reread the story with a partner. Have them reread it to figure out how they might act out the story. Have them read it aloud to a parent or to a younger child either at school or at home. Rereading familiar text is the most effective way to help children expand the number of words they recognize on sight without analysis.

For those children who do not develop a sight vocabulary readily through repeated reading, what can you do? How can you support the reading of these children? Not every word needs be learned through phonic analysis. Some words, in fact, do not lend themselves to a sounding-out procedure. (Consider these words: *their, the,* and *said.*) Moreover, some children experience difficulties with phonics and can benefit from learning words as sight words. In chapter 12, we describe *word banks* as a method to help children significantly increase their sight vocabularies. Through this approach, each child builds a unique collection of words of importance to that particular child (Ashton-Warner, 1963). These procedures are described in detail in chapter 12, in which a lesson featuring Mary Johnson's kindergarten class illustrates the approach.

The Benchmark Word Identification Program

Word study can occur in a variety of ways. In chapter 12, we describe the word study activity of invented spelling that encourages the development of phoneme awareness. In chapter 13, two word-study activities are described: Making Words (Cunningham & Cunningham, 1992) and word sorts (Temple & Gillet, 1984). In this section, we describe a word study program, the Benchmark Word Identification Program, that was developed for poor readers who failed to profit from one or more traditional decoding programs (Gaskins, Gaskins, & Gaskins, 1991). The Benchmark program is one component of a comprehensive literacy program that revolves around authentic reading and language activities.

The program is built around the idea of analogies (Cunningham, 1979). Students are taught to decode by comparing an unknown word to one they know. These known "key words" represent common spelling patterns (phonograms). One hundred twenty key words are introduced in the Beginning Program, and 94 more in the Intermediate Program. A variety of teacher-directed activities revolve around a set of key words introduced weekly, including language experience stories, phonemic awareness, word sorts, writing, and spelling tasks.

Each daily lesson of the Beginning Program consists of a variety of activities. Monday's activities, for example, include goal setting, teacher modeling of identification strategies, introduction of five key words, writing a language experience story, writing new words while chanting spellings and a review of key words. Activities on Tuesday and Wednesday support and extend Monday's learning. The lessons on Thursday and Friday include many of the same activities introduced earlier in the week. Throughout the week, the teacher encourages application of the compare/contrast strategy in various settings. Students learn *when* and *how* to use the strategy as well as *why*.

The Intermediate Program begins with a review of the 120 key words. The second phase involves a 10-day cycle in which additional key words are introduced, strategies for chunking multisyllabic words are developed, and word meanings are explored. If you are interested in using this approach, you should read the article by Gaskins, Gaskins, and Gaskins (1991), cited at the end of this chapter.

Multisyllabic Word Strategies

Some older students who understand how letters relate to sounds and can apply this knowledge in their identification of one- or two-syllable words become overwhelmed when they encounter multisyllabic words. They need to be taught a system for dividing these words into chunks that they can then identify. For example, a multisyllabic word such as *reinvent* may stump some children until they learn to segment the word *re-in-vent* and then pronounce and blend together the syllables.

These procedures may be introduced as a minilesson or as the need arises when you are working with an individual or a small group of children.

1. Identify the multisyllabic word that may cause difficulty and write it on the chalkboard.
2. Have students look at the word to determine how they might break it into chunks. Have one student draw slashes between syllabic chunks, and ask if other students agree. If not, revise the division until most students agree.
3. Ask students how the first syllable would be pronounced, and then the second, the third, and so on. Then have students blend the syllables together. Analogies from known sight words may aid them in syllable identification.
4. Continue the process for other multisyllabic words as long as the students are interested.

The following small-group discussion led by Mrs. Marshall demonstrates the use of this procedure.

Learning from Experience

Mrs. Marshall's less able fifth-grade students tend to experience difficulties with multisyllabic words that include prefixes, suffixes, and inflectional endings. As you read the transcript, note how Mrs. Marshall helped her students learn to divide multisyllabic words into pronounceable units.

Sets goal

Explains procedure for identifying multisyllabic words

Mrs. Marshall: Before we read the next text selection, let's go over a few words that may challenge you as you read. When you come to words with many syllables that you can't pronounce, try dividing the word into syllables, thinking about how each syllable may be pronounced, and then blending the syllables together. Once you've figured out the pronunciation of the word, does it sound familiar? Also, rereading the sentence in which the word appears can provide a clue to word meaning. Sean, can you pronounce this word? [Mrs. Marshall writes the word lonely on the chalkboard.]

Sean: That's easy! *Lonely.*

Mrs. Marshall: Great. Now break this word into syllables.

Focuses on division of known word into syllables

Wendy: Between the e and the l. [Mrs. Marshall puts a slash between the letters e and l, so it appears as *lone/ly.*]

Demonstrates procedure	**Mrs. Marshall:** So the first syllable would be pronounced as *lone* and the second syllable as *ly*. When we blend these two syllables together, we have the word *lonely*. [Mrs. Marshall demonstrates blending by slowly pronouncing and merging the two syllables together.] Now try this word. [Mrs. Marshall writes *indignantly* on the chalkboard. She gets no response.]
Applies procedure to unknown word	**Mrs. Marshall:** Okay, let's break this word into syllables. Kelly, give it a try. Come to the board and put a slash between each syllable.
	Kelly: [Kelly makes the following divisions: *in/dignant/ly*.]
	Mrs. Marshall: There's one more syllable. Where do you think it may be? It may help you to remember that each syllable has to have a vowel sound associated with it.
	Kelly: [Kelly looks at the word again and places a slash between the letters g and n, so it appears as *in/dig/nant/ly*.]
Guides syllable pronunciation	**Mrs. Marshall:** Right. Now let's try to pronounce each syllable from left to right.
	Fifth graders: [As Mrs. Marshall uncovers each syllable, the students correctly pronounce it.]
Guides syllable blending	**Mrs. Marshall:** Good. Let's blend the syllables together so we can recognize the word. [Mrs. Marshall and the students slowly blend the sounds together.] What is the word?
	John: *Indignantly.*
Focuses on word meaning	**Mrs. Marshall:** Good. What does this word mean?
	Fifth graders: [No response.]
	Mrs. Marshall: What does *indignantly* mean in this sentence? After Charlie hit her, Julie looked *indignantly* at him.
	David: She had a mean and angry look on her face.
	Mrs. Marshall: Good. Try this word. [Mrs. Marshall writes *alarmingly* on the board. There is no response.]
Applies procedure to unknown word for review	**Mrs. Marshall:** If you can't pronounce the word, what should you do first?
	Terry: Break it into syllables.
	Mrs. Marshall: Okay, here's the chalk. Now break the word into syllables. What does each syllable have to include?
	Terry: A vowel sound. [She comes to the chalkboard and puts slashes between the syllables so it appears as the following: *a/larm/ing/ly*.]
	Mrs. Marshall: Good. Now, all of you, try to pronounce each syllable. [The fifth graders individually attempt to pronounce each syllable, aloud but not in unison.] Let's try to blend the syllables together. [Mrs. Marshall leads the students to slowly blend the sounds together.] How do you pronounce this word?
	Courtney: *Alarmingly.*
Focuses on word meaning	**Mrs. Marshall:** What does this word mean?
	Kelly: Upset or scared about something.
Provides practice Reviews procedure	**Mrs. Marshall:** Good. I am giving you a worksheet with four more words on it. Get into pairs and try to identify these words. If you can't pronounce it, what is your first step?
	Kelly: Divide it into syllables.

> *Mrs. Marshall:* What's the next step?
>
> *David:* Say each syllable.
>
> *Mrs. Marshall:* What's the next step?
>
> *Courtney:* Slowly say it together.
>
> *Mrs. Marshall:* Right, slowly blend the syllables together so you can identify the word. All the words on the worksheet are in the story we'll be reading. There are page numbers next to each word indicating where each word appears in the story. Find the sentence where the word appears and define the word. [The fifth graders choose their own partners and begin working while Mrs. Marshall circulates and provides assistance.]

 Your Turn: Think about this lesson. What were the various ways in which Mrs. Marshall helped her students learn to cope with multisyllabic words? Write your response in your journal under the heading Multisyllabic Word Strategies and then read our response.

 Our Turn: Mrs. Marshall began instruction with a known word to instill confidence. Step by step, she explained a procedure for pronouncing unfamiliar multisyllabic words. Initially, she demonstrated the procedure, provided guidance and feedback within the larger group, and followed with semi-independent practice. Following this practice, she had students report on their ability to apply the strategy and whether they understood the meanings of the words. This explicit and structured teaching should minimize the problems these less able readers experience with print and allow them to focus on comprehending the text selection.

SUMMARY

Learning how spoken language is represented in print entails a complex set of learnings. Yet these are understandings that children normally develop through informal experiences with their families and in preschools (emergent literacy), during their first years of school (developing literacy), and later as they use reading and writing for learning and enjoyment (fluent literacy). Many children depend on the instructional guidance of their teachers to acquire this complicated set of learnings. Thus it is important for you, as their teachers, to envision a balanced instructional program based on your goals and an assessment of the knowledge and skill students have developed in the following areas: (1) functions of print, (2) concept of word (word awareness), (3) phonemic awareness (the ability to hear individual sounds within spoken words), (4) a sight vocabulary, (5) knowledge of the sounds that letters represent (letter-sound patterns), and (6) reading fluency.

In the final sections of the chapter, we introduced a number of instructional strategies to encourage students to develop their understanding of print: *shared reading* to help children to become aware of words and to form a concept of word; *shared writing* and *spelling* activities to encourage children to become aware of the sounds in words (phoneme awareness) and the sounds that letters represent; and *reading work-*

shop to help them to consolidate their sight vocabularies and to become fluent readers through extensive reading experience. We also described the *sound-sense strategy* to enable your students to become more independent and fluent readers.

Because some students encounter considerable difficulty learning about print, we also discussed more focused approaches for such children: *sight word support* to help students develop their knowledge of sight words, *the Benchmark Word Identification Program* to help students develop independent word analysis strategies, and *multisyllabic word strategies* to help them deal with long and challenging words.

In the Field

1. Visit a kindergarten class where children are encouraged to write. Get the teacher's permission to engage some children quietly in a discussion of their writing. Ask them to "read" what they have written. On a separate paper, make notes about what the children have read and compare it with what they have written. If their writing includes some letters, to what extent do the letters correspond to the sounds of the words read? In terms of Henderson's model, what underlying knowledge does the child's spelling reflect? Record your responses in a report or in your journal under the heading In the Field: Kindergartner Student Writing.

2. Obtain a Big Book from a school or public library and invite a child of five or six to read with you. As you read, finger-point to the words read in the way described by Morris. Reread the story and invite the child to read with you as you finger-point read the words. Then invite the child to read and point to the words while reading. Is the child willing to engage in this activity? To what extent does the story read match with the printed words? Are the words read also those that were pointed to? Does the child seem to enjoy reading? What do you conclude about the child's concept of word and sight vocabulary? Describe your experience and observations in a report or in your journal under the heading In the Field: Big Book Reading.

Portfolio Suggestion

Select from your journal two examples of your responses to Pause and Reflect or Learning from Experience: Your Turn and include these in your portfolio. If you completed an In the Field activity, include your report of it in your portfolio as well. Write a brief evaluation of your work, commenting on what it shows about your learning.

For Further Reading

Bissex, G. L. (1980). *GNYS at WRK: A child learns to write and read.* Cambridge, MA: Harvard University Press.

Clay, M. M. (1992). Introducing a new storybook to young readers. *The Reading Teacher, 45,* 264–273.

Cunningham, P. M., & Cunningham, J. W. (1992). Making words: Enhancing the invented spelling-decoding connection. *The Reading Teacher, 46, 106–115*.

Gaskins, R. W., Gaskins, J. C., & Gaskins, I. W. (1991). A decoding program for poor readers—and the rest of the class, too! *Language Arts, 68,* 213–225.

Teale, W. H. & Sulzby, E. (Eds.). (1986). *Emergent literacy: Writing and reading.* Norwood, NJ: Ablex.

Yopp, H. K. (1992). Developing phonemic awareness in young children. *The Reading Teacher, 45,* 696–703.

Prior Knowledge, Vocabulary, and Purpose Setting

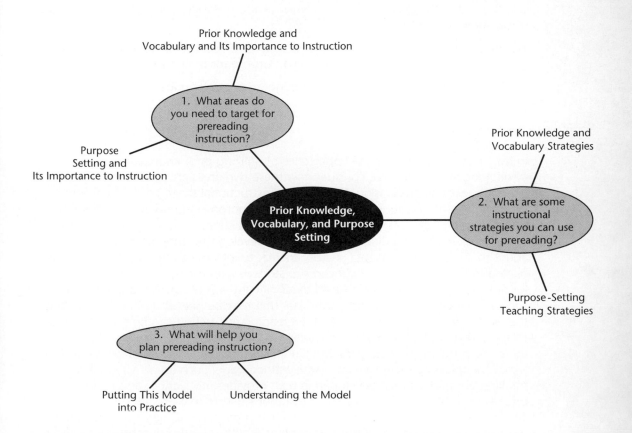

Prior Knowledge and
Vocabulary and Its Importance to Instruction

1. What areas do you need to target for prereading instruction?

Purpose Setting and Its Importance to Instruction

Prior Knowledge, Vocabulary, and Purpose Setting

Prior Knowledge and Vocabulary Strategies

2. What are some instructional strategies you can use for prereading?

Purpose-Setting Teaching Strategies

3. What will help you plan prereading instruction?

Putting This Model into Practice

Understanding the Model

▼ CHAPTER GOALS FOR THE READER

To understand the effects of prior knowledge and vocabulary and setting a purpose to comprehending text

To understand and apply instructional strategies to access and develop prior knowledge, develop vocabulary, and set a purpose for reading

To understand and apply a model for designing prereading instruction

▼ CHAPTER OVERVIEW

In this chapter, we discuss the importance of utilizing prior knowledge and developing vocabulary. We consider how these two areas are related and their effect on text comprehension. We describe instructional strategies highlighting prior knowledge, vocabulary development, and purpose setting and conclude by presenting a model for planning prereading instruction.

The goal of prereading instruction is to develop the students' prior knowledge about the major text concepts or story theme, to introduce important vocabulary related to the important text concepts or story development, and to set a purpose for reading. Students are introduced to specific aspects of the text they will read, such as concepts, themes, and vocabulary that may be new and difficult and affect the overall understanding of the text. Prereading instruction can be thought of as an ice breaker in that it makes the reader feel comfortable and prepared to understand the major ideas presented in text. For instance, students can brainstorm words, people, and ideas they associate with courage. Such an activity activates thinking about a concept developed in text, provides motivation, and builds bridges from the student's mind to the author's text to make reading the text easier. Brainstorming words related to the text topic can naturally guide students to formulate hypotheses about the text content and thus have a purpose for reading—checking their hypotheses as they read. Reading strategies such as brainstorming are described in this chapter to help students connect their knowledge with the author's, to help students focus their thinking to understand text, and to motivate them to read.

TAPPING PRIOR KNOWLEDGE TO SET A PURPOSE

When you were in elementary school, what did your teachers do before you began reading a story or a textbook chapter? Did they ask for your ideas about the text? Were you given a set of words to define and use in sentences? Did your teachers give you a question for setting a purpose for reading? If so, did it help you understand and enjoy text? Have you had more recent classroom experiences that provide different instruction for developing prior knowledge, vocabulary, and purpose setting? Use the chapter overview and your own experiences to identify your purpose for reading this chapter. List those in your journal.

Learning from Experience

Diane Jenkins is an experienced junior high school reading teacher whose class includes children with a wide range of reading ability—learners for whom English is a second language and less able readers as well as above average readers. Elly Taheny teaches first grade. Her students also vary in reading ability; some are nonreaders while others are able to read second-grade materials. We asked them, "Are there specific areas you target for prereading instruction?" As you read, find out what Diane and Elly do to prepare their students to read text.

Diane: I do a lot to activate my junior high students' prior knowledge—I use lots of different strategies to get them to focus in on what they already know and then use that as a springboard to get them interested in the selection. I believe they need to know something about the topic to be motivated to read.

I also want them to make predictions, whether it's an expository or narrative text. I encourage them to use subtitles, titles, pictures, whatever there is in the text to use for previewing, to help them make some predictions. I usually tell them, "Think about what you are going to read before you read it."

Elly: Two years ago I changed my thinking about reading instruction. Before this time, I only expected children to think after they had read. What I'm trying to keep foremost in my mind now is that my first graders need to be thinking before the actual text. For example, if we're using expository text, I'm going to start by finding out what they know about the text topic. If we're going to read about spiders, I might say, "Let's talk about what you know about the way spiders live, what spiders eat, and how spiders look." Another time we had a selection in the reader about days of the week, so I started by reading the Big Book *Monday, Monday I Like Monday* out loud to the class. Then we worked for a couple of days with that—reading it together, writing about our favorite days of the week. Then we were ready to read a second text about days of the week. Knowing something about the topic helped my students comprehend, and it also made word identification easier.

Your Turn: Now that you have read the interview, how do Diane and Elly prepare students to read text? Write your response in your journal before comparing it to ours.

Our Turn: To Diane and Elly, prereading is an important part of reading instruction for both first graders and junior high school students—as well as everyone in between. Both teachers noted different ways to develop prior knowledge. Diane used previewing while Elly used other books to read aloud, discussion, and writing. A variety of activities can be used during prereading instruction to facilitate comprehension.

WHAT AREAS DO YOU NEED TO TARGET FOR PREREADING INSTRUCTION?

Typically, students enjoy and comprehend text more if they receive some preparation that facilitates and motivates their reading. Such preparation should focus primarily on these areas: prior knowledge and vocabulary and purpose setting. Beginning readers, however, typically require print skill instruction, which is developed in the preceding chapter, Knowledge of Print: Its Development and Instructional Support.

Prior Knowledge and Vocabulary and Its Importance to Instruction

We define prior knowledge as an individual's present understanding and organization of a topic, idea, concept, event, object, or person. Vocabulary is the meaning associated with a word. By focusing on prior knowledge and vocabulary in prereading instruction, you inform students that reading is a meaningful act, not limited to decoding words. Consider this idea for a moment. Prior knowledge facilitates text comprehension. How does this work?

Recall the last time you went to a play. Did you know anything about it before you went—whether it was a farce, drama, or mystery? Had you seen a play of this kind previously? Did anyone tell you a little about the play, or did you read the synopsis or order of scenes in the *Playbill*? Did this prior knowledge—assuming you had some—help you comprehend?

As a general rule, linking what you are reading or seeing with what you already know helps you comprehend and learn. Prior knowledge provides a framework for assimilating new information and organizing it into useful categories. Your knowledge about cooking, for example, may include information about tools, recipes, stoves, temperatures, methods, places where food is prepared and served, and so on—all organized in some way and interconnected. Not only do these organized networks of prior knowledge (or *schemata,* as some cognitive psychologists call them) help you make sense of your ongoing experiences, but new information derived from these experiences continually expands our existing prior knowledge.

How will this young boy's investigation of roots affect his reading about plants?

Similarly, reading comprehension is facilitated by the reader's prior knowledge about the topic being read. The more children know about a story before they read it, the more they will understand. Anderson (1984) suggests that prior knowledge enables us not only to comprehend but also to organize new information and remember it more efficiently. Students with prior knowledge are better able to:

- Add information learned from text. These students already have a "location" in which to place new information.
- Generate additional information that goes beyond the author's stated ideas. The ability to make inferences makes the text memorable and complete.
- Search their memories for specific information. The categorical structure of prior knowledge allows naturally for an efficient memory search.
- Focus attention while reading, and therefore they can more easily summarize text. Prior knowledge enables readers to differentiate major and minor points, to select important information, and to use this information to summarize what has been read.

A number of studies (Chiesi, Spilich, & Voss, 1979; Pearson, Hansen, & Gordon, 1979) suggest that readers with substantial prior knowledge comprehend text better and develop more plausible inferences than those without. To facilitate reading comprehension, however, prior knowledge must be accurate; studies indicate that incompatible prior knowledge adversely affects comprehension (Alvermann, Smith, & Readence, 1985; Lipson, 1984), and that children experience difficulties resolving conflicts between prior knowledge and new information (Lipson, 1984). Instructional intervention needs to be considered when prior knowledge is likely to interfere with text information.

Pause and Reflect!

Compare your prior knowledge about reading instruction with that about your favorite hobby. Which of the following two texts would be easier for you: reading a textbook on reading instruction or reading a book about your favorite hobby? Explain your answer in your journal.

Much of our prior knowledge consists of vocabulary and word meanings, but much of it also consists of personal experiences and situational contexts that go well beyond word meaning. The difference between these two components is analogous to that between a dictionary definition and an encyclopedia entry. Readers gain access to their relevant stores of knowledge through both their mental dictionaries and their mental encyclopedias. The dictionary provides the pronunciation and a brief and abstract definition whereas the encyclopedia provides a context that is richer in meaning.

Although prior knowledge and vocabulary have been treated separately in the research literature, these two areas are closely related and can be easily linked during prereading instruction to activate, develop, and reinforce concept development. In this way, prior knowledge is accessed about the concept or theme the students will be reading, and it's likely that vocabulary from the text will be considered and thus easily integrated into the vocabulary lesson.

Vocabulary is closely associated with comprehending text; a reader's vocabulary knowledge is a good predictor of his or her comprehension (Anderson & Freebody, 1981; Chall & Stahl, 1985; Davis, 1968; Thorndike, 1973–1974). Integrating new and known words facilitates learning and develops conceptual knowledge, so that students, including those with learning disabilities (Anders, Bos, & Filip, 1984; Margosein, Pascarella, & Pflaum, 1982; Swaby, 1977) and those learning English as a second language (Gersten & Jimenez, 1994), can better understand text. Readers who know the word *car*, for example, are better able to learn words like *van, limousine,* and *station wagon.* Providing vocabulary instruction by itself, however, does not necessarily increase students' comprehension (Stahl & Fairbanks, 1986). Mezynski (1983) examined eight studies, four of which resulted in comprehension gains because of vocabulary instruction and four of which did not. In the latter four, students were taught simple definitions or synonyms accompanied by illustrative sentences—not unlike the approach used by many teachers. This activity generally neither facilitated comprehension nor motivated students to read.

Pause and Reflect!

Can you remember copying a word list off the board and using your dictionary to find a definition? What were the results of this task? Were you able to use the word comfortably in a variety of situations involving listening, speaking, reading, and writing?

The studies increasing students' vocabulary, on the other hand, employed instruction that went beyond this kind of narrow drill. In one, the additional instruction consisted simply of having students answer two questions about each instructional word. In learning the word *altercation,* for example, students were asked, "Do you have altercations with your teacher?" and "Do you have altercations with a tree?" (Kameenui, Carnine, & Freschi, 1982). Students were given explicit assistance to use context to integrate word meaning and were actively engaged in constructing word knowledge.

With second-language learners, Gersten and Jimenez (1994) noted that effective teachers developed students' vocabulary from the children's literature under study and required students to use this vocabulary as the students discussed and wrote about the story. Within this study, Donna, a third-grade teacher, initiated vocabulary discussion by relating students' personal experiences to learning new vocabulary presented in text. She then highlighted important text vocabulary through demonstrations such as poking a hole in the paper to define the word *pierce,* reviewing the word later in the story discussion, and writing the new words on the chalkboard. Donna provided a scaffold for acquiring vocabulary, combining it with concrete manipulatives, and also employing auditory and visual modalities to support second-language learners' learning styles. Incorporating the use of different learning modalities is essential when students are learning a new language (Gersten & Woodward, 1992).

Active involvement is essential to increasing vocabulary and improving comprehension. It's further supported by Craik and Lockhart's (1972) work on depth of processing in which they maintain that deep processing requires students to actively generate information by relating the "old" to the "new" so learning can occur.

Other vocabulary research indicates the importance of understanding relationships among words, numerous exposures to learn new words, and the speed of accessing word meaning. A study by Beck, Perfetti, and McKeown (1982) considered all three of these variables. Students were provided with target words grouped by category and were engaged in a variety of activities to develop semantic relationships among a given group of words. For instance, students were to identify behaviors or characteristics associated with the target words: accomplice, virtuoso, rival, miser, and so on, and answer questions such as "Could an accomplice be a virtuoso?" Beck and her colleagues found that students increased their understanding of relationships among words as they increased their knowledge of word meanings, and that such learning went beyond memorizing definitions. But they also found that to achieve this level of learning, students needed 10 to 15 exposures to the targeted words and some exercises that focused on speed of accessing word meaning. Moreover, this type of vocabulary instruction produced significant effects on students' general reading comprehension.

We can draw several implications for prereading instruction from this discussion of prior knowledge and vocabulary. First, prereading instruction focusing on prior knowledge must be related to the theme or concept of the selection to be read. Students can make connections between their experiences and the text and thus construct meaning. Second, students must be actively engaged in constructing meaning. If students read from beginning to end of a text with no background knowledge and no predictions to confirm or deny, their reading becomes a passive activity, often laborious and boring. Third, prereading activities that are responsive to prior knowledge can serve an important diagnostic function; unfamiliar ideas can be identified and developed, and misconceptions clarified. Fourth, effective vocabulary instruction will include a variety of strategies and activities that are both meaningful and relevant and focus on words that enhance understanding of thematic or conceptual information in text to make learning easier and more logical. Students do become aware of new words daily through oral and written contexts, but to use these words in comprehending information from a particular text takes a lot of practice over time and justifies the need for vocabulary instruction (Beck & McKeown, 1991). However, vocabulary instruction should not involve simply learning a list of words and their corresponding definitions but rather should engender active involvement. Developing word meaning is complex; it requires seeing relationships, organizing, refining, and elaborating word meaning (Beck & McKeown, 1991). Finally, students must see and discuss the target words many times through repeated study. Students need a variety of opportunities to learn words, beginning in prereading instruction but *continuing during* and *after* their reading of a text selection. Their continued involvement with the same words causes them to reflect on their meaning and use; such instruction provides "depth of processing" (Craik & Lockhart, 1972). Since learning vocabulary requires many exposures to a word, vocabulary instruction is also considered as students read text and also after reading text. Prereading instruction is only the starting place for studying vocabulary.

Purpose Setting and Its Importance to Instruction

Prior knowledge and vocabulary can be related to purpose setting. A purpose provides direction and focus for understanding and thinking about text, and such direction and focus are attained while developing prior knowledge and vocabulary. Students can use this knowledge to set a purpose for reading. In most cases, purpose setting involves a question or pseudoquestion students think about as they read. Such questions are intended to direct thinking, to make reading an active process, to motivate students to read, and to increase comprehension. The most effective purpose-setting questions encourage students to think and reason throughout the text; to answer them, students must integrate prior knowledge with text-based information and/or link together text-based ideas.

Pause and Reflect!

Examine the following purpose-setting questions. Do these questions encourage readers to think and reason?

Compare and contrast Mark and Susan's feelings about their mother's illness.
What are Ira's problems?
How do Jeff's personality and behavior differ from your own?
How are levers different from pulleys? Identify examples of pulleys and levers you use daily.
Discuss the causes of the war between the states. Are these causes similar to those of other wars?

Place your responses in your journal before continuing. Each of these questions and pseudoquestions requires children to synthesize information from the text or from their heads. They are broad enough that students must gradually develop answers while reading the text; they would not be able to find answers in one or two connecting sentences. Some of the questions or pseudoquestions require students to use their prior knowledge while reading to answer the question.

Effective purpose-setting questions focus on important text-based ideas. Your own questions should serve as models for the questions students should develop while they read independently; not all purpose-setting questions should be teacher developed. When students pose their own questions, they have a self-felt purpose for reading, and they are motivated to make responses. Student-generated questions also allow you to assess your students' abilities to formulate questions.

Purpose setting serves as the natural link between prereading and during-reading instruction. The question or pseudoquestion can direct students to establishing a particular goal and using a specific strategy for reading text. This is more fully described in the next chapter, Strategic Reading: Guiding, Facilitating, and Empowering Students' Comprehension.

WHAT ARE SOME INSTRUCTIONAL STRATEGIES YOU CAN USE FOR PREREADING?

In the following section, we present strategies for prereading instruction—prior knowledge and vocabulary and purpose setting. This is not an exhaustive list but should provide a beginning to your thinking about prereading instruction. You need to decide which might be important or useful for understanding a specific text; not all areas need to be developed in prereading for every text. Your decisions should be based on the difficulty of the text and your students' reading abilities, prior knowledge, and motivation. In the final section, we suggest a model for effective prereading instruction and illustrate how you can use this model for instructional planning.

Prior Knowledge and Vocabulary Instructional Strategies

Prereading strategies must do more than simply mention or tell students new concepts. To be effective, instruction must encourage students to think and become actively involved in identifying relations among key concepts. It must help them link their thinking with the author's and cause them to reflect and reconsider their own ideas, concepts, and beliefs. In the next few pages, we discuss several instructional strategies to access and enhance students' prior knowledge and develop students' vocabulary. These instructional strategies do encourage thinking and active involvement and can be used with a variety of age groups.

Knowledge Rating

In the knowledge-rating activity, students learn to self-assess their level of word knowledge so they are better prepared to comprehend text. Knowledge Rating is designed to infuse responsibility and develop word consciousness in students. To initiate this teaching strategy, the teacher selects vocabulary used in text that is important to understanding the major concepts or themes and presents the words to students by pronouncing and writing them on the chalkboard, chart, or overhead projector. Students are then given directions to rate their own level of word knowledge by using the following categories: have no idea; have seen and heard word; can define; can use it in talking and writing. Students can make a grid similar to that illustrated in Figure 4.1 for Amy Tan's *The Moon Lady,* a folk tale from China. To understand these words, students will need to be familiar with the Chinese culture. After students have assessed their knowledge of these seven terms, students and teachers can make decisions about what they will do before reading *The Moon Lady*. If students can define or use the vocabulary in speaking and writing, it's likely they can read the story with ease. For students who have little or no idea what these terms mean, you may want to consider some of the following options before they read. Class discussion can provide ample opportunities for students to ask questions and discuss word meaning before they begin reading. You can form small groups for students to discuss the unfamiliar words with their peers. Students can preview the tale, in small groups, looking for the targeted vocabulary and reading the sentence or paragraph to develop further clues about the word. Or, in small groups, students can use other resources to look up the words, such as a dictionary or encyclopedia, and discuss word meaning.

Context Strategy

Joan Gipe (1980) developed a strategy to help students use context clues efficiently and effectively. Her strategy encourages students to integrate information across sentences and at the same time incorporates the definition of the target word. Students become actively engaged in generating and applying word meaning. Gipe found this strategy to be more effective for third and fifth graders' comprehension of text than more traditional strategies such as using a dictionary, forming associations, and categorizing words. The strategy incorporates active involvement, integration of word

Word	Have No Idea	Have Seen and Heard Word	Can Define	Use it in Talking and Writing
1. Moon Lady				
2. Dragonfly				
3. Moon Festival				
4. Rickshaw				
5. Cleaver				
6. Teahouse boat				
7. Eel				

Figure 4.1 Knowledge Rating for *The Moon Lady*

meaning, and words derived from the text itself, three important aspects for increasing vocabulary. Moreover, other research indicates that skilled readers use context clues more than any other strategy to derive word meaning (Nagy & Anderson, 1984).

To use Gipe's instructional strategy, prepare a four-sentence context employing the target word within each sentence. The first sentence contains a broad but meaningful context to develop understanding, the second sentence provides more detailed information, and the third includes an explicit definition of the target word. In the last sentence, the student is asked to make a response. The multiple exposures to the word can enable the student to develop word meaning. The following example provides a four-sentence context for the word *aeronaut*.

The *aeronaut* was getting the hot-air balloon ready for flying.

The *aeronaut* told her helpers to let go of the ropes so she could fly the hot-air balloon. An *aeronaut* is a person who flies a hot-air balloon.

What do you think the *aeronaut* does while flying in the sky?

The first sentence, read aloud by the teacher or a student, enables students to hear the word *aeronaut* pronounced and to predict that an aeronaut is a person, because of the word's placement in the sentence and the fact that people act on objects. The second sentence confirms that an aeronaut is a person and includes some details about the aeronaut's job, and the third sentence defines the word. The final sentence checks the reader's understanding. To maximize the effectiveness of this instructional strategy, we suggest choosing words that affect thematic or conceptual understanding of the text. Incorporate one or more sentences from the text selection itself and use the selection's content to develop the other three sentences, so that the four-sentence context is very related to the specific text to be read. Sentences taken directly from the text can be used to further link vocabulary learning to text comprehension.

To implement this strategy, we suggest that students read and discuss the four-sentence context. Encourage students to share their responses to the contextual question. Go beyond word meaning and discuss how they derived the meaning by asking them, "What clues helped you figure out the meaning of the target word?"

Related Text Reading

In related text reading, children independently read a text containing important concepts that will be emphasized in a second instructional text selection. Crafton (1983) found that reading a second selection on the same topic has a cumulative effect on students' comprehension. Her study provides support for what we logically would expect—the more we read about a topic, the more we will comprehend from subsequent selections on the same topic.

To put this theory into practice, select a variety of materials: books, magazines, poetry, newspapers that are related to the textbook selection, unit of study, or literature students are expected to read. Students are given time to read and review together any of the related materials before they begin the assigned reading. You may want to encourage students to write ideas they acquired from reading on chart paper, so all have the opportunity to see and think about them. In this format, students are given choices in what they read and who they will share information with.

If you want to provide more structure, choose a short selection from a children's magazine or other source similar in topic to one that will be read for instruction. Ask students to read the first brief selection independently, and provide time for a short discussion. During the discussion, highlight vocabulary and concepts that are important to the subsequent text selection. Write these words and others the students note on the chalkboard or chart paper. This type of activity can be beneficial for beginning readers and less proficient readers such as LD (learning-disabled) students and some second-language learners.

A third alternative is to read aloud a text that has important information related to an upcoming text selection and discuss it. For example, students expected to read a fable may be unfamiliar with the characteristics associated with this genre. Reading a fable aloud and discussing its common characteristics can provide students with a framework for understanding the fable they will be assigned to read. This is very appropriate for beginning readers.

Related Writing

Writing can be an excellent prereading strategy to explore personal ideas, feelings, and knowledge about a topic. It enhances and clarifies thinking about a topic prior to reading. Students can express their own ideas before authors present theirs. For instance, before reading Arthur Dorros's *Rain Forest Secrets,* students can write about what they know about the rain forest and its preservation. Or, before reading Cynthia Voigt's *Dicey's Song,* they can write about issues surrounding the older child who has responsibility for younger siblings. Encourage students to brainstorm before writing so students' "juices" are flowing and they have accessed some ideas. Sharing their writing with others is also a good idea and inviting them to compare their ideas to the author's can do much to enrich thinking and learning.

Semantic Mapping

Semantic mapping is an effective strategy for learning sets of conceptually related words (Heimlich & Pittleman, 1986). Students are given a category and a set of related words to develop a "map" (see Figure 4.2) or network of word relationships (Johnson & Pearson, 1984). As students develop their map, they are actively engaged in constructing meaningful relationships among words (Blachowicz & Johnson, 1994). They can use their map as they read to confirm their thinking about word meaning, to add new words from the text, and to reorganize their map to reflect their present thinking.

There are many effective variations to mapping vocabulary words, but, in all variations, students identify relationships among words and explain how these words are related. If they are encouraged to experiment and develop an understanding of word relationships, each semantic map will be unique, as Figure 4.2 illustrates. In Map A, some students categorized words into subgroups and placed them underneath the major category. In Map B, others employed picture diagrams that included the given set of words.

You can initiate the semantic mapping process by selecting a key or central concept from a topic under study. Select a key concept about which students have some prior knowledge in order to make associations and connections. Place the key term on the chalkboard and ask students to free-associate words related to the key term. Invite students to define and discuss the relationship between the key concept and the associated word to judge its relevancy to the topic under study. You may choose

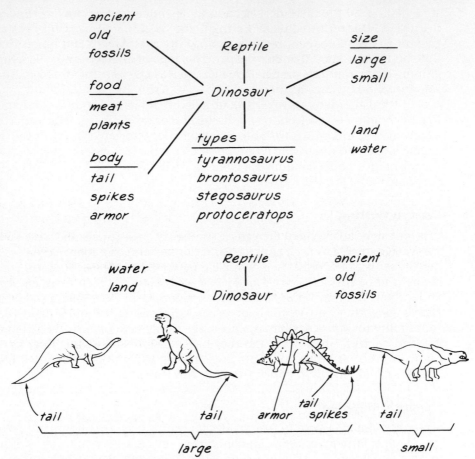

Figure 4.2 Examples of Semantic Maps

to add essential vocabulary associated with the central concept and introduce the words into the discussion. Form small groups so that students can develop a map to indicate their organization of these words. Encourage each small group to add words to help them categorize and organize their thinking. Once the map is complete, the group members are encouraged to explain their reasoning. The verbal presentation reinforces the group's thinking, increases other class members' understanding of conceptual relationships, and provides you with a bird's-eye view of their thought processes.

Semantic maps can also be used with narrative literature, to help students understand genres or themes. For instance, sixth graders may be doing a unit on mysteries. For this unit, you might ask students to identify words associated with mysteries, calling on their prior knowledge. Pose questions to probe their understanding of the particular genre: What kinds of characters do you find in mysteries? Let them write words associated with mysteries and also include vocabulary from the books and short stories they will be reading to develop a greater understanding of mysteries. Words like *gendarme, espionage, secret agent, automatic, passkey,* and *adventure* can further develop students' understanding of mysteries and facilitate text comprehension. After students read different mysteries, encourage them to review their semantic maps to add vocabulary and to rethink their organization of words. Focusing on vocabulary development during the entire unit can increase word knowledge and text comprehension.

Learning from Experience

Mrs. Thoensen's fourth-grade class is going to read a chapter on Alaska in their social studies textbook. Typically, her students experience difficulties with comprehension. Many have little or no prior knowledge about many social studies topics. During class discussion, they exhibit poor understanding of text-based concepts. She has observed that some of her more diligent students attempt to memorize word meanings but do not relate them to familiar words, situations, or ideas. Consequently, after they have finished a chapter, they promptly forget the meanings of these words. A few of her fourth graders also skip over new words and do not develop an adequate understanding of the chapter concepts.

Mrs. Thoensen decides to use Semantic Mapping to help her students identify relationships among words and to get them away from memorizing isolated definitions. As you read this classroom vignette, note how Mrs. Thoensen introduces Semantic Mapping and guides her students' vocabulary development.

Connects prior knowledge to text topic

Mrs. Thoensen: Our next chapter in social studies is about Alaska. What words do you associate with Alaska? [Mrs. Thoensen calls on different students and writes their responses on the board.]

John: Polar bears.

Carlos: Mountains.

Lattice: Long winters.

Miata: Icebergs.

Larry: Kayaks.

Parker: Midnight sun.

Elaboration of vocabulary

Mrs. Thoensen: Tell me about the midnight sun.

Parker: The sun stays out to midnight. I think it's in June and July.

David: Umiak.

Elaboration of vocabulary

Mrs. Thoensen: What is an umiak?

David: It's a bigger boat than a kayak. You can fit more people into it.

Sara: Mount McKinley.

Jeff: Igloo.

Hosea: Oil.

Juan: Cold.

Checks knowledge	*Laurie:* Small houses. *Heather:* Hot. *Mrs. Thoensen:* When does it get hot? *Heather:* In the summer. *Cory:* Dogsled races. *Mrs. Thoensen:* Is there at least one of your words listed on the chalkboard? *Fourth Graders:* Yes.

Laurie: Small houses.

Heather: Hot.

Mrs. Thoensen: When does it get hot?

Heather: In the summer.

Cory: Dogsled races.

Mrs. Thoensen: Is there at least one of your words listed on the chalkboard?

Fourth Graders: Yes.

Connects text to students' prior knowledge

Discusses new vocabulary

Mrs. Thoensen: I'm going to add five words that are related to Alaska. These are probably unfamiliar, but they are important words that we will read and discuss in this unit on Alaska. These words are: *glaciers, volcanoes, peninsula, Aleut,* and *Tlingit.* [Mrs. Thoensen pronounces and writes the words on the chalkboard.] What is a glacier?

Ana: Ice.

Hosea: They covered the earth.

Elaborates

Mrs. Thoensen: That's correct—a glacier is made of ice and snow, and they still cover parts of the earth. Where are glaciers found?

Jeff: In Alaska.

Mrs. Thoensen: What is a volcano?

Laurie: It erupts.

David: And lava comes out.

Elaborates

Uses question to evoke more information

Mrs. Thoensen: Yes, volcanoes can erupt and lava is produced. A volcano is caused when the rock underneath the earth's surface becomes so hot that it melts and pushes through openings in the earth's surface. Where are volcanoes found?

Lattice: Hawaii, and I think there's one in Alaska.

Mrs. Thoensen: How do volcanoes affect people and animals?

David: When volcanoes erupt, you don't want to be near it. The heat and lava can harm people and animals.

Mrs. Thoensen: What is a peninsula?

Jeff: It's like an island.

Provides feedback

Mrs. Thoensen: Well, not exactly; an island is totally surrounded by water. A peninsula has one side connected to land while the other three sides are bordered by water. Let's look at the globe. Hawaii is an island since it's surrounded by water. [Mrs. Thoensen points to Hawaii.] Most of Alaska is a peninsula. [Mrs. Thoensen points to Alaska.] What is an Aleut?

Fourth Graders: [No response.]

Mrs. Thoensen: Aleuts are related to the Eskimo and were the first people to live in Alaska. What are Tlingits?

Fourth Graders: [No response.]

Suggests other sources

Explains procedures and gives example

Mrs. Thoensen: They are a group of Indians who also live in Alaska. You may want to use your textbook chapter and glossary to give you additional information so that you can relate these new words with the more familiar words.

I'm going to divide you into small groups, and your job is to make a diagram or draw a picture to show how different words fit together. It's very likely that your maps will all be different. There is no one way to do a map, but the map must be logical so you can explain how you grouped the words. Can you find two words that relate to each other?

Matthew: Umiak and kayak.

Reasoning

Mrs. Thoensen: What's the relationship between these words?

Matthew: Boats.

Mrs. Thoensen: As a group, you decide how to show this relationship. You must use all the words on the chalkboard, but you can also add words. Are there any questions?

Sara: Do we have to put these words together into sentences?

Mrs. Thoensen: Not into sentences, but show in a picture or a diagram how the words fit together for the topic, Alaska.

Miata: How many words have to be in one group?

Mrs. Thoensen: There is no set number. You have to be able to explain the relationship of the words in each group.

Mrs. Thoensen divides the students into groups of three and four. As children develop their maps, Mrs. Thoensen circulates among the groups to answer questions. She also asks questions to stimulate thinking. When all groups are finished, each group explains its map. Take a look at how one group related the set of words associated with Alaska (see Figure 4.3).

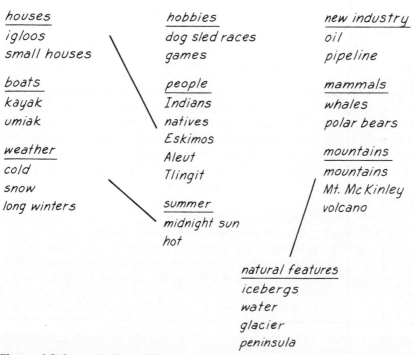

Alaska

houses
igloos
small houses

boats
kayak
umiak

weather
cold
snow
long winters

hobbies
dog sled races
games

people
Indians
natives
Eskimos
Aleut
Tlingit

summer
midnight sun
hot

new industry
oil
pipeline

mammals
whales
polar bears

mountains
mountains
Mt. McKinley
volcano

natural features
icebergs
water
glacier
peninsula

Figure 4.3 Semantic Map of Alaska

> **Mrs. Thoensen:** Juan, will you explain your map?
>
> **Juan:** Polar bears and whales are two of Alaska's mammals.
>
> **Matthew:** Oil is Alaska's new industry. [Matthew points to the group labeled "new industry."] In the last ten years, they've put in a pipeline.
>
> **David:** Cold, snow, and long winters are all part of weather.
>
> **Jeff:** In the summer, there is the midnight sun and it's hot. [Jeff points to the category labeled "summer."]

This group continued to provide logical explanations for each grouping. When they concluded their explanations, Mrs. Thoensen posed some questions to help them see additional relationships. Let's focus on the concluding part of this group's presentation.

Expanding students' connections

> **Mrs. Thoensen:** There are at least two of your groupings that relate to each other. Can you find them?
>
> **Juan:** I have found one. Well, the weather and summer because they both include hot and cold.
>
> **Mrs. Thoensen:** How can you show how these groups are related?
>
> **Juan:** Draw a line to connect them.
>
> **Mrs. Thoensen:** Can you find anything else?
>
> **David:** The mountains, volcanoes, and the icebergs. They are all very big and are natural features. [David draws a line to connect the two groups.]
>
> **Jeff:** The people and houses because the people live in houses. [Jeff draws a line to connect the two groups.]

Your Turn: Now that you have read the Semantic Mapping lesson, how did Mrs. Thoensen introduce and guide her students' thinking about vocabulary? Write your response in your journal before reading our response.

Our Turn: Mrs. Thoensen identified the topic they would be studying in social studies and gave them the opportunity to free-associate words related to Alaska. As students contributed specialized vocabulary, she requested elaboration to increase other students' word knowledge. Mrs. Thoensen added vocabulary from the social studies text to initiate students' thinking and collaboration that can enhance text comprehension.

Once the words related to Alaska were listed, Mrs. Thoensen explained the procedures for mapping but did not show the fourth graders how to design their map. She encouraged each small group to work through this process to demonstrate their conception of the relationships among these words. By developing their own "map," students acquire word knowledge that becomes personally relevant and meaningful. As these fourth graders worked together, they learned that words can be related in numerous ways. There is no one "correct" way to categorize words; many logical ones exist. These fourth graders probably learned that definitions are a small part of understanding words. Knowing how words are related provides a greater depth of conceptual knowledge.

How does forming a Semantic Map help students develop their knowledge?

By having them work in small groups, Mrs. Thoensen shows her students that we also learn from our peers. Learning is a collaborative process. Each student has many, varied experiences that can support and increase other students' learning.

Concept of Definition

In Concept of Definition, students use a framework or word map (see Figure 4.4) to generate word meaning and gain control of vocabulary development (Schwartz & Raphael, 1985). The word map causes students to focus on three important parts of word meaning: (1) the general class to which the target word belongs; (2) the properties or details associated with the target word and those that distinguish it from other words in this category; and (3) examples of the target word. These three areas can be turned into questions to help students effectively use dictionaries and context to decipher word meaning. We will use Figure 4.4 to highlight these three questions. The first question *(What is it?)* refers to the general class in which the target word belongs. In this case: What is tennis? Well, it is a game. The second question *(What is it like?)*

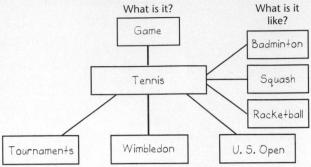

Figure 4.4 Concept of Definition. *Source:* Adapted from "Concept of Definition: A Key to Improving Students' Vocabulary" by R. M. Schwartz and T. E. Raphael, 1985, *The Reading Teacher, 39*, pp. 198–205.

encourages students to provide properties or details that separate tennis from other games. For the target word *tennis,* some games similar to tennis that come to mind include *badminton, squash,* and *racquetball.* The final question *(What are some examples?)* focuses students on specific instances or illustrations. Some specific examples related to the target word *tennis* are *tournaments, Wimbledon,* and the *U.S. Open.*

Concept of Definition is limited to defining nouns and verbs and can be effectively used with students from fourth grade through college (Schwartz & Raphael, 1985; Schwartz & Nicholas, 1982). When you introduce this strategy to the entire class, students need to understand the importance of vocabulary as it relates to text comprehension. Students can then more readily recognize the merit of using this strategy to better understand specialized vocabulary in a unit of study. In class discussion, compare the word *map* to a picture that lends details and clarity to a word's meaning. Provide further direction by asking the three questions and encouraging students to use their prior knowledge and other sources such as glossary, dictionary, encyclopedia, and the text that the students will be reading. Students are likely to provide many appropriate responses to each question that allow for a rich discussion and hence encourage a broader understanding of word meaning. Once students understand the purpose and procedures of this strategy, form small groups to complete word maps on other specialized vocabulary related to the topic under study. As students become familiar with the word map, it becomes a tool or strategy that helps them learn words independently. Students can use the word map both before or after they read text. Using word maps before reading can help focus and facilitate text comprehension. When they use word maps after they read, students can add and revise the maps to confirm and develop greater understanding of text vocabulary.

Semantic Features Analysis

In this instructional strategy, students look for relationships between a noun such as a person or object and a trait or characteristic. Students record the relationship on a grid as shown in Figure 4.5 (Johnson & Pearson, 1984). If the two words, such as *Cinderella* and *good,* share a strong relationship, then the student may use a + to indicate a positive relationship. If the two words, such as *wolf* and *good,* have a negative rela-

Features / Words	Good	Evil												
Cinderella														
Wolf														
Stepsisters														
Little Red														
Goldilocks														
Troll														
3 Billy Goats														

Figure 4.5 An example of a Semantic Features Analysis Grid

tionship, the student can place a – in the intersecting box, as shown in Figure 4.5. Many times a slight relationship does exist between words and can be indicated with a 0. Other symbols or a graduated scale can be employed to indicate varying degrees of relationship as students become familiar with this strategy or have extensive topical knowledge.

To initiate this vocabulary strategy, identify a topic students will be reading. In this example, students may be beginning a folktale unit, and you may want the students to consider familiar folktale characters and their corresponding traits to serve as a precursor to reading more unfamiliar folktales. Ask students to identify familiar folktale characters and list them in the column. Then ask the students to list words describing the characters, such as their actions and appearance, and place these words across the top of the grid. As a large group, students can compare each characteristic to each folktale character to indicate its relationship. Once students understand this comparison task, identify additional familiar characters and traits and then form small groups to discuss these comparisons. As they read more folktales, students can add characters and traits to their grids and continue making these relationships.

By comparing words, Semantic Features Analysis helps students to develop critical thinking, to integrate old and new information, and organize conceptual knowledge. Many students, including those with learning disabilities, benefit from Semantic Features Analysis (Anders et al., 1984; Johnson, Toms-Bronowski, & Pittelman, 1982).

Vocab-O-Gram

In this strategy, students make predictions about how particular words are used to tell a story (Blachowicz, 1986). They are going beyond the definition of the word to consider its application in text and are engaged in much higher level thinking about words and their relationship to text. To develop an understanding of the thinking required in Vocab-O-Gram, we invite you to take part in a simulation of Emily Arnold McCully's picture book *Mirette on the High Wire*.

Pause and Reflect!

In your journal, make a copy of the grid illustrated in Figure 4.6. The five boxed areas represent the elements of a story: setting, characters, problem, actions/events, and resolution. You are to predict how these nine words in the grid will be used to tell the story *Mirette on the High Wire*. Use your knowledge of the words and story structure to predict each word's use in the story. Place each word into a box, indicating if it will be used to describe the setting, character, or something else. The words are: boardinghouse, flailed, hemp, protégée, vagabond, enchanted, commotion, salute, and trance. Make your choices and record them in your journal before reading further.

How did you make your selections? Did you try to define the word? Did you consider whether the word was a noun, verb, or some other part of speech? Did you make associations between what you know about stories and authors' use of words and the target words? Did you want to talk to other people to receive their input? Did you want to consult a dictionary? Did you want to read the story? Were you actively engaged?

You may have provided an affirmative answer to all of these questions, which is what we hope you did. Students engaged in this activity should experience active involvement by making associations, using prior knowledge, conferring with peers, using a dictionary, and being motivated to read.

After students have made their choices, they read the text to confirm and reject their predictions, and this culminates in a discussion about the way the author employed the words to tell the story. There is no one right way to categorize all the words. There will be differences due to the natural variance in readers' interpretations. What is important is that students can provide logic and support for their choices.

Setting	Characters	Problem
Which words tell you about where and when the story took place?	Which words tell about the characters in the story (their feelings, thoughts, appearance)	Which words describe the problem?

Action	Resolution
Which words tell you about the action in this story?	Which words tell about the resolution?

Figure 4.6 Vocab-O-Gram

You may want to read the picture book *Mirette on the High Wire* to learn how the author used these words to tell her story. From our summary, you may get an idea of how she used these words. This story is about a young girl who admired a famous high-wire artist and became his protégée only after she helped him overcome his recent fear of heights.

Teachers have extended this vocabulary strategy by using the target words to predict the story plot, thus establishing a purpose for reading, which is the next area we consider for instruction.

Controversial Issue

When Should You Teach Vocabulary?

Preteaching vocabulary has undergone criticism because research has shown that to learn words well and use them in speaking, reading, and writing requires more than the one exposure that characterizes prereading instruction. Beck and her colleagues (1982) suggest it takes thirteen or more exposures to learn new vocabulary. Thus we suggest that vocabulary instruction not be limited to the prereading phase of reading instruction. A single exposure to a new word won't help students learn. New words should also be discussed and developed during and after the reading of a particular text. In many of the strategies described in this chapter, students can discuss and review word knowledge during and after reading text. For example, in regard to the Semantic Mapping strategy, the fourth graders in Mrs. Thoensen's class reviewed their map from prereading instruction and added or redesigned their maps during postreading instruction.

We suggest you continually develop vocabulary by applying some of the following principles and suggestions.

1. Develop students' interest and curiosity in words. Interest and curiosity can be created by allowing students to choose their own words for personal development. Haggard (1982, 1985) has shown that students' self-selection of words is an important factor in vocabulary development. To stimulate interest in word learning, spend a few minutes each day identifying and talking about new words read or heard during the course of the day. Students can also keep personal dictionaries and add new words they find interesting. On a weekly basis, divide students into small groups to share new words and their meanings. This is a good time to help students develop knowledge about the dictionary. When students design their personal dictionary, meaning and purpose are added to studying dictionary skills such as alphabetization, guide words, special pronunciation, and word meaning.

2. Encourage students to read. The incidental learning of new words from reading should not be discounted. Studies have shown that reading does increase students' vocabulary (Herman, Anderson, Pearson, & Nagy, 1987; Nagy, Herman, & Anderson, 1985). Each day, provide children time for reading their favorite books. Share different genres to expand their interests and to acquaint them with new words associated with a particular genre. Share nonfiction related to topics being studied in social studies and science to reinforce specialized vocabulary learning.

3. Use different learning methods to acquire new vocabulary. Children do learn by hearing and seeing new words in print, but using the other senses can also provide valuable ways to acquire new vocabulary. Drama can enhance word meaning. Give students the opportunity to act out the meaning of new words such as apartheid, anticipation, aroma, grief. Drawing the meaning of new words can also open new doors to learning. We have all heard the old adage "A picture is worth a thousand words." When children have learned to create their own pictures for new words, they have acquired another tool for learning vocabulary. Mnemonic techniques are another helpful aid to learning. Do you use sayings to remember concepts, such as "Every good boy deserves fun" to remember the notes on a musical staff? Such techniques are labeled mnemonic and help us remember. Pressley, Levin, and Delaney (1983), for example, use mnemonics to enable students to learn words through the use of the keyword method. In this method, students create their own mnemonic by connecting a verbal and visual image to remember the meaning of a particular word. For example, to remember the meaning of rainbow, the student may draw the picture of rain coming down on a multicolored hair bow. The strength of the keyword method lies with the children constructing their own verbal and picture associations. Word meaning becomes personal and functional.

4. Provide direct experiences to learn words. Young children learn words best if they can experience the meaning of a word. Reading about different animals isn't the same as seeing and touching the animal under study. Learning about particular kinds of vegetables and fruits is heightened when teachers show them and encourage children to taste them. For example, Ms. Wiese shared Lois Ehlert's *Eating a Rainbow,* an alphabet book of vegetables and fruit, and brought the actual fruits and vegetables for her kindergartners to taste. Employing concrete experiences is time-consuming and can be expensive, but it does much to increase word learning.

5. Use a dictionary in meaningful ways. The dictionary is an important tool for learning words, but it doesn't always appear helpful. For instance, giving students a list of words to look up in a dictionary doesn't do much to increase word meaning. It is a senseless task, since students don't know which meaning to choose and remember. Too often these are activities we remember encountering as elementary school students. As a consequence, the dictionary has received some bad raps. The dictionary needs to be used in a more functional and meaningful way. For example, after reading a story or nonfiction article, students can list words they didn't know and discuss them in small groups or with the entire class. This is the perfect opportunity to integrate the use of dictionary, context, and discussion to develop word knowledge. By incorporating the use of the dictionary with the context of a text and discussion, students can achieve success in locating the appropriate definition and use discussion to develop deeper understanding.

6. Help students to use context clues effectively. Defining a word from context can be tricky. Often, there are not enough clues to help students define the word. Yet at other times the author has clearly used certain types of clues to help students understand a particular word meaning. Take some time to discuss specific types of context clues with students, so they can use them when authors do employ them to make word meaning accessible. There are several types of clues that are most helpful

in deciphering word meaning. In a direct definition clue, the target word is defined in the sentence: A *rodent* is a mammal such as a squirrel, beaver, and mouse. In a figure-of-speech clue, a literary device is used to create meaning: The *volcano* ejected rockets of fire. In comparison and contrast clues, the target word is defined by comparing and contrasting it to something that is familiar: Joanne's humility was in sharp contrast to Luanne's *bravado.* In a synonym or antonym clue, an easier word is used to define the more difficult target word: When Jeremy heard the news, he was *humiliated.* He went home feeling low and degraded. Discuss these clues as students meet new words in the literature they are reading. Encourage students to share how they used the context to develop meaning.

Purpose-Setting Teaching Strategies

Purpose-setting strategies should motivate children to read a particular text and guide students' thinking as they begin to read the text. The strategies we present in this section enhance comprehension and encourage students to want to read. The first strategy is very simple. It uses a single question or pseudoquestion to guide comprehension. The second strategy, Previewing, encourages students to look over the reading to develop some ideas about the text. Story Impressions, the third strategy, is meant to be employed with stories; it develops a purpose for reading and stimulates children's interest in a particular story. The fourth strategy, K-W-L (Know, Want, Learn), is designed to be used with expository text; it, too, develops both purpose setting and interest in reading—in this case, nonfiction. All three strategies can be used with both beginning and advanced readers.

Questioning

A single question or pseudoquestion can motivate and guide students' comprehension of text. The purpose-setting question can be developed by the teacher or generated by the student; both types should be used. The teacher-generated question establishes a model for students to develop their own questions for reading and learning. The student-generated question stimulates motivation, since students develop their own personal questions for reading and learning.

Purpose setting should meet two main criteria: It should address a central idea, and it should encourage children to think. Here are several examples of teacher- and student-generated questions and pseudoquestions:

Teacher-Generated Questions

Compare and contrast Mark's and Sally's attitudes about their friend's death.

What are Cara's problems?

How do dogs differ from wolves?

What are David's feelings about the car accident, and how does he finally learn to deal with these feelings?

Based on the events of the story, what does Linda learn about friendship?

How have U.S. immigration laws and policies changed throughout history?

Teacher Prompts to Create Student-Generated Questions

Given a set of related words, predict the topic of the selection and the major areas to be covered.

Given the time, place, and characters of a story, predict the events of the story.

Read the introduction and predict the content of the selection.

Given an important section of dialogue or section of text, predict the genre, topics covered, or plot.

Considering the title of the story, tell what the story will be about.

To use a teacher-generated question or pseudoquestion for purpose setting, simply ask students to develop an appropriate response to the question. Students should always return to the prereading questions and discuss their findings after they read the selection so purpose setting remains a relevant and meaningful activity.

Previewing

This instructional strategy encourages students to generate their own ideas about the text content. It can be used with both fiction and nonfiction but is most often used with nonfiction. By reviewing the title, headings, illustrations, graphics, and summary, if it is included, readers can anticipate the content and focus their thinking while reading. Previewing can be a motivator because readers have learned something from the activity and have become interested in the topic. It can help them learn, but it can also help them select a good book to read. Who would buy a book before they read the title and the book jacket? This is the essence of previewing, which can be a quick yet effective strategy.

Story Impressions

Story Impressions develop students' understanding of story structure and also establish a purpose for reading text (McGinley & Denner, 1987). This instructional strategy integrates two areas of prereading instruction: prior knowledge and vocabulary with purpose setting. In Story Impressions, important story clues derived from salient points of setting, character, problem, and resolution are selected to guide students' thinking about a particular selection. Referring to these clues, students compose a hypothetical story summary.

A set of story clues for "Down the Hill" by Arnold Lobel is shown in Figure 4.7. In this particular Story Impression, the first two word clues establish the characters and setting, and the later clues identify the sequence of essential story events. Using these story clues in the order they are presented, the students predict the story plot by composing a hypothetical summary. After they complete the summary, they read the text and compare their plot development with the author's.

Learning from Experience

Mrs. Owen's second graders are going to read "Down the Hill." She plans to introduce Story Impressions to help her students use story structure so their comprehension is facilitated and to focus students' thinking as they read text. She has developed a set of story

Down the Hill

Frog and Toad
↓
Winter
↓
Sledding
↓
Scared
↓
Together
↓
Bump
↓
Alone
↓
Tree
↓
Dream

Figure 4.7 Story Impressions: *Down the Hill* by Arnold Lobel

clues to help them compose a hypothetical summary. As you read, think about how Mrs. Owen implements Story Impressions to facilitate students' thinking.

Explains strategy

Mrs. Owen: Before we read "Down the Hill," we're going to guess what happens in the story. The clues that I've written on the chalkboard tell you what the story is going to be about. Let's use these clues to write a summary, or a shorter version of what we think will happen in the story. Let's start! The first clue is *Frog and Toad.* [Mrs. Owen points to the first clue on the chalkboard.] What do you think Frog and Toad are going to be?

Jacek: Two frogs.

Mrs. Owen: Frog and Toad are going to be two frogs?

Jacek: No.

Uses story structure

Mrs. Owen: Right, frogs are different from toads. Who do you think they are in the story?

Michael: Friends.

Elaborates

Mrs. Owen: Okay, they could be friends. They are the characters in our story. [Mrs. Owen points to the second clue, winter, on the chalkboard.]
Winter. What does this story clue tell us about the story?

Sumi: When it happened.

Uses story structure

Mrs. Owen: [Mrs. Owen points to the third clue, *sledding.*] What could this word clue tell us about the story?

Orlando: They could be sledding.

Mrs. Owen: Now think of a story about two friends named Frog and Toad sledding in the winter. Look at the next clue, *scared.* [Mrs. Owen points to the fourth clue.] What would happen in a story where Frog and Toad are sledding? How would this next story clue, *scared,* fit into the story?

Bobby: Maybe they are scared.

Elaborates

Mrs. Owen: So this could be the problem . . . Okay. Look at the next clue, *together.* How does *together* fit into our story?

Michael: Frog and Toad are on the sled together.

Mrs. Owen: The next word clue is *bump.* How does *bump* fit into our story?

Jan: They go over a bump.

Mrs. Owen: What goes over a bump?

Jan: The sled.

Uses story
structure

Mrs. Owen: The next word clue is *alone.* [Mrs. Owen points to this clue on the chalkboard.] Use this clue and predict how the story develops.

Denise: Frog or Toad is going to fall off the sled, and one is left alone on the sled.

Mrs. Owen: *Tree*—how does this word clue fit into our story? [Mrs. Owen points to the word *tree* on the chalkboard.]

Orlando: They hit a tree.

Mrs. Owen: Our last clue, *dream.* [Mrs. Owen points to this clue on the chalkboard.]

Michael: They dreamed it.

Mrs. Owen: You all have ideas about what this story is going to be about. Let's write a group summary of what we think will happen in this story. We have to start at the beginning with Frog and Toad. Give me a sentence to start our summary.

Jennifer: Should I follow what's up there?

Provides feedback

Mrs. Owen: Yes, you have to follow the order of the word clues.

Denise: Frog and Toad are sledding in the winter. [Mrs. Owen writes this sentence on the chalkboard.]

Mrs. Owen: What happens to Frog and Toad?

Jennifer: Toad got scared. [Mrs. Owen writes this sentence on the chalkboard.]

Mrs. Owen: What did he get scared of?

Michael: Toad got scared of sledding. [Mrs. Owen adds this idea to the sentence on the chalkboard.]

Mrs. Owen: How should we include the word *together* in the next part?

Bobby: They got scared together. [Mrs. Owen writes this sentence on the chalkboard.]

Mrs. Owen: Now what happens—*bump?* Give me a sentence that tells us how a bump fits into the story.

Jan: They went over a big bump on the sled. [Mrs. Owen writes this sentence on the chalkboard.]

Mrs. Owen: Now what happens? [Mrs. Owen points to the next word clue, *alone.*]

Michael: On the bump, Frog fell off. [Mrs. Owen writes the sentence on the chalkboard.]

Mrs. Owen: *Tree*—how does this clue fit into our story?

Jennifer: Frog hit a tree. [Mrs. Owen writes the sentence on the chalkboard.]

Mrs. Owen: How does *dream* fit into the end of our story?

Michael: And at the end, it all was a dream. [Mrs. Owen writes this sentence on the chalkboard.]

Sets purpose **Mrs. Owen:** This summary is what we *think* the story will be about, but we may be wrong. Some of our ideas may happen and others may not. I want you to read this story and find out which of our ideas the author included. Which ones did the author not use? Choose a partner and read the story together and discuss your answers to this question.

Your Turn: Explain how Mrs. Owen implemented Story Impressions to facilitate students' thinking as they read. Before reading our response, jot down your ideas in your journal.

Our Turn: When we asked ourselves this same question, we noted that Mrs. Owen provided the second graders an opportunity to brainstorm before composing their group summary so they could experiment and develop an understanding of the writing task. Mrs. Owen used questioning to guide the second graders' thinking about how a story typically develops in a natural and sequential manner, which provided additional support for writing a hypothetical summary. As the second graders became familiar with the activity, Mrs. Owen's questions included less detail so that guidance was gradually lessened. And finally, Mrs. Owen did not try to change the students' ideas. The ideas were logical, so they became part of the group summary. Moreover, all of the second graders' sentences were written verbatim, indicating Mrs. Owen's acceptance of their present language capabilities. We learned that second graders were able to use their knowledge of story structure to dictate a logical summary incorporating all story clues.

K-W-L

K-W-L is an acronym for Know: What do I Know?—Want: What do I Want to Know?—and Learn: What have I Learned? (Ogle, 1986). It emphasizes students' prior knowledge, categorizes their ideas, encourages them to develop questions for reading, directs them to seek answers to their questions, and determines sources to search for answers. This strategy stimulates active reading of expository text and encourages students to put their prior knowledge to work as they read so that comprehension and learning are increased.

To initiate K-W-L with "What do I know?" identify the key concept of the text selection and ask children to tell what they know about this concept. As the children provide important topical information, ask questions so they can link their knowledge to that of the author. For example, if fifth graders will be reading about natural disasters and learning the types, causes, and effects of different disasters, questions should lead students to think about these areas. Your role is to focus and guide students' thinking so they better realize and understand what they presently know. As students identify information about natural disasters, they should write this information on the K-W-L guide under the column labeled "What I know?" (see Figure 4.8).

K	W	L
What I Know	*What I Want to Find Out*	*What I Learn—Still Need to Learn*

Categories of Information We Expect to Use

Figure 4.8 K-W-L Strategy Guide

Before concluding this first step, have the students try to classify the information they already know about disasters so that as they read, their thinking is better organized and they can easily check their knowledge with text information.

In step 2 (What do I want to know?), promote motivation by focusing on what the students want to learn. Encourage students to ask their own questions about the topic under study, and give them time to write their questions on the K-W-L guide under the column labeled "What I want to find out." Not all their questions may be answered, but this can spur them to do additional reading and research. Once students have written their questions, identify which of these questions will likely be answered in the assigned text. Consider other sources to answer the questions that remained unanswered. Ask students to read the text and search for answers and seek additional sources to questions unanswered by this particular text.

The remainder of the strategy (What have I learned?) includes guided reading and postreading instruction, which goes beyond the scope of this chapter. These later steps will be discussed in detail in chapters 5 and 6.

Learning from Experience

As you read about a fifth-grade classroom, note how the teacher guides prereading instruction through the use of the K-W-L reading strategy. Write your responses in your journal.

Mrs. Diener has noted that her fifth graders frequently do not enjoy reading expository text. During recreational reading time, they rarely choose nonfiction other than sport books or magazines such as *Ranger Rick, Geographic World,* and *Cobblestone;* they are not particularly interested in reading the chapters in their social studies and science textbooks and seem to comprehend these chapters less easily than the stories. They usually have difficulties understanding the concepts presented in content-area textbooks.

Mrs. Diener feels that K-W-L might be an appropriate prereading instructional strategy to pique her students' interest in exposition as well as to increase their reading comprehension. To introduce K-W-L to her students, Mrs. Diener selects a short and interesting informational article from *Cobblestone,* a magazine her students have selected in the past.

Identifies strategy and purpose

Mrs. Diener: The selection we'll be reading is about natural disasters. To help you understand and remember what you have read, I am going to teach you how to use K-W-L. Once you have learned it, you should use it when you read informational material. For example, if I assign a social studies chapter, try using K-W-L to help you learn information so that you can participate in class discussion and get better grades on the test. Here's a K-W-L guide. [Mrs. Diener hands each child a copy.] Let's look at the left-hand column, labeled *K* for *know.* Underneath the letter *K,* it says *What I know.* In this column, we write what we know about the topic of our article. Let's start! Can you identify different types of disasters? Write down the types you know. [Mrs. Diener provides some time to think and write.] Jordan, what did you write?

Jordan: Earthquakes. [Mrs. Diener writes *earthquakes* in column *K* on the chalkboard. See Figure 4.9.]

Elicits prior knowledge

Mrs. Diener: What do you know about earthquakes?

Jordan: There have been some in California. [Mrs. Diener writes the word *California* in the *K* column.]

Probes

Mrs. Diener: Do you know why they are found in California?

K	W	L
What I Know	**What I Want to Find Out**	**What I Learn—Still Need to Learn**
1. earthquakes	1. What causes a tornado?	
2. California	2. What does it feel like to be in an earthquake?	
3. faults	3. How long is an earthquake?	
4. floods	4. Why are some mountains volcanic?	
5. people leave homes	5. Which one has killed the most people?	
6. people lose their stuff		
7. tornadoes		
8. homes destroyed		
9. people die		
10. objects are whipped around		
11. wind		
12. Neb.		
13. Ill.		
14. volcanoes		
15. mountains		
16. heat		

Categories of Information We Expect to Use			
1. types	3. effects	5.	7.
2. places	4. causes	6.	8.

Figure 4.9 K-W-L Strategy Guide for Natural Disasters

Jordan: I think it has something to do with faults. [Mrs. Diener writes the word *faults* in the *K* column.]

Probes

Mrs. Diener: What are faults?

Fifth graders: [No response.]

Prediction

Mrs. Diener: Do you think the article will provide information for this question?

Chris: Maybe.

Mrs. Diener: Can you name any other natural disasters?

Elicits prior
knowledge

Kelly: Floods. [Mrs. Diener writes the word *floods* in the K column.]

Probes

Mrs. Diener: What kinds of damage do floods create?

Kelly: Water gets so high that people have to leave their homes. [Mrs. Diener writes the sentence *People leave homes* in the K column.)

Duke: My grandmother lost all her stuff in the basement because the river overflowed from so much rain. [Mrs. Diener writes the sentence *People lose their stuff* in the K column.]

Mrs. Diener: Do you know any other kinds of disasters?

Lauren: Tornadoes. [Mrs. Diener writes the word *tornadoes* in the K column.]

Dakita: Tornadoes rip up homes and kill people. [Mrs. Diener writes two phrases, *homes destroyed* and *people die,* in the K column.]

Salem: Signs and cars are whipped around. [Mrs. Diener writes the sentence *Objects are whipped around* in the K column.]

Mrs. Diener: John, what causes the whipping?

John: The wind. [Mrs. Diener writes the word *wind* in the K column.]

Mrs. Diener: Okay. Do you know where tornadoes occur?

Barry: Nebraska and Illinois. [Mrs. Diener writes the words *Nebraska* and *Illinois* in the K column.]

Mrs. Diener: Any other disasters?

Kelly: Volcanoes. [Mrs. Diener writes the word *volcanoes* in the K column.]

Mrs. Diener: Where are volcanoes?

Duke: Mountains. [Mrs. Diener writes the word *mountains* in the K column.]

Mrs. Diener: Okay. What causes a volcano?

Lauren: It has something to do with heat. [Mrs. Diener writes the word *heat* in the K column.]

Prediction

Mrs. Diener: Do you think this article may tell about what causes a volcano?

Todd: Probably.

Mrs. Diener: Any other disasters?

Fifth graders: [No response.]

Teaches strategy

Mrs. Diener: Let's try to categorize these ideas that appear in the K column. What do you think will be grouped together in an article about natural disasters?

Fifth graders: [No response.]

Provides model

Mrs. Diener: We listed many different disasters. Could one group or category be types of disasters?

Fifth graders: [They nod their heads, indicating yes.]

Mrs. Diener: In the K column underneath the phrase *categories of information we expect to use,* I'll write the word *types.* What are some of the types that you expect we'll learn about?

John: Tornadoes, volcanoes.

Lauren: Floods, earthquakes.

Practice	**Mrs. Diener:** Are there other categories that may be found in the article?
	Mavis: Places.
Provides feedback	**Mrs. Diener:** Yes, they may tell us the locations of specific disasters. [Mrs. Diener writes the word *places* in the *K* column underneath the phrase *categories of information we expect to see.*] Do you see other categories?
	Lorenzo: What happens after disasters?
Provides feedback	**Mrs. Diener:** Good. In other words, what are the effects of natural disasters? [Mrs. Diener writes the word *effects* underneath the phrase *categories of information we expect to see.*] Other categories?
	Duke: What happens before a disaster?
Clarifies	**Mrs. Diener:** You mean causes?
	Duke: Yeah. [Mrs. Diener writes the word *causes* underneath the phrase *categories of information we expect to see.*]
Teaches strategy	**Mrs. Diener:** Let's look at the second column labeled *W* for What do you want to learn? What would you like to learn about natural disasters? Write your questions on the K-W-L guide. [Mrs. Diener provides time for writing their questions.] Latoya, what is your question?
Develops ownership	**Latoya:** What causes a tornado? [Mrs. Diener writes this question in the *W* column.]
	Vanessa: What does it feel like to be in an earthquake? [Mrs. Diener writes this question in the *W* column.]
	Coretta: How long is an earthquake? [Mrs. Diener writes this question in the *W* column.]
	Darnell: Why are some mountains volcanic? [Mrs. Diener writes this question in the *W* column.]
	Jose: Which one has killed the most people? [Mrs. Diener writes this question in the *W* column.]
Clarifies	**Mrs. Diener:** Do you mean which type of disaster killed the most people?
	Lauren: Yeah.
Teaches strategy	**Mrs. Diener:** You've asked some good questions about natural disasters. Tomorrow, we're going to read the article on natural disasters and find out if any of our questions are answered in it. Is it likely that all your questions will be answered in this single article?
	Lorenzo: No.
	Mrs. Diener: Why?
	Lorenzo: No one book can provide all the information about one thing.
Provides feedback	**Mrs. Diener:** That's right! A short article especially has to be focused and limits the number of ideas presented. So if our questions remain unanswered, then what?
	Vanessa: We can ask someone the answer.
Probes	**Mrs. Diener:** Yes, what other sources are available?
	Lauren: The encyclopedia, and it's real fun to use the one on the computer. It shows films and makes sounds.
	Mrs. Diener: Yes, the interactive video does make it interesting. What else?

Jordan: Nonfiction, fiction. Use the card catalog to look up the topic.

Mrs. Diener: You have some good ideas.

Your Turn: How did Mrs. Diener use K-W-L to guide prereading instruction? Write your response in your journal before comparing it to ours.

Our Turn: In this K-W-L lesson, Mrs. Diener was attempting to help her students think about what they already knew and also reflect on areas they understood less well. Mrs. Diener also encouraged her students to classify known information, so that as they read, they would search for new information to put into these categories. Initially, the fifth graders were unsure what Mrs. Diener meant by forming categories. After Mrs. Diener provided a model, her students were able to develop additional categories.

The students easily formed questions about what they wanted to learn from this text selection. Many of their questions were based on the categories developed during class discussion, which may indicate students' interest and involvement during this prereading lesson. Mrs. Diener enabled students to understand that not all their questions would be answered in this short article and helped them identify additional resources to answer their questions.

WHAT WILL HELP YOU PLAN PREREADING INSTRUCTION?

In this chapter we have discussed the theory and research that support prereading instruction and presented some strategies you can use in preparing students to read text. Now we are ready to put this information together and make specific plans for prereading instruction. As we all know, instructional time is always at a premium, and one of our primary tasks is to put it to use in the most efficient ways. As you prepare students to read text, your planning and decision making should focus on three areas: print skill; prior knowledge and vocabulary; and purpose setting. Your plans and decisions must take into account many factors, including your students' interests and abilities. An organized, systematic plan can facilitate wise and logical decision making. Figure 4.10 provides a graphic illustration of the model we suggest. In the next section, we explain how this model works.

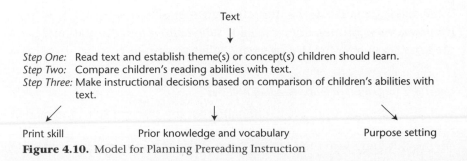

Figure 4.10. Model for Planning Prereading Instruction

Understanding the Model

Step One

Read the text. As you read, identify the theme or important concept that students should develop from their own reading. (A theme is typically associated with narrative fiction and a concept with nonfiction.) We recognize that texts often contain more than one theme or concept; your task is to choose one or two to be learned by all your students. These serve as the framework for designing appropriate activities for the different areas of prereading instruction. This framework provides unity for your instruction; each prereading activity should develop or enhance understanding of the identified theme or concept, so all prereading activities support one another and students are prepared to read and comprehend text as well as develop the concept.

Step Two

Analyze the text students are about to read and compare it to the reading abilities of your students. Focus on the following question: What knowledge do these students need to have in order to learn information from the text? To develop an answer to this question, do three things:

1. Consider text factors such as vocabulary, sentence length, and text structure.
2. Assess your students' reading abilities.
3. Compare the text factors with your students' abilities.

The following questions provide a broad but efficient estimate of text complexity and student ability. Answer both groups of questions and compare your findings; this should help you identify which area(s) you should stress in prereading instruction.

Questions to Estimate Text Difficulty

Does the text include many multisyllabic words?
Are there many long and complex sentences?
Does the text include an extensive specialized vocabulary?
Are numerous concepts or themes presented in the text?
Is the text expository or narrative?
If the text is narrative, is the story structure logical?
If the text is expository, does it include subheadings and illustrations?
Are text ideas presented in a coherent, cohesive manner?

Questions to Assess Students' Reading Abilities

Will the text present print-skill difficulties for my students (e.g., too many new words)?
Do the children relate their knowledge and experience to text?
Will the text-based ideas be familiar to my students?

Will the vocabulary and sentence structure be too difficult?

Will my students be interested in reading this text?

Will my students easily comprehend this selection?

Step Three

Make appropriate plans for prereading instruction. Establish areas where you need to support children's text comprehension as well as develop the preestablished themes or concepts of the selection. And, finally, select those instructional strategies that will maximize comprehension and learning.

Putting This Model into Practice

Let's put this model into practice with a specific text and a group of sixth graders. The sixth graders are going to read *Shiloh* by Phyllis Reynolds Naylor.

Step One

Typically, you would read the book before planning instruction, but since this is an explanation of the instructional model, and it is a long text, we provide a summary. It would be helpful to have a copy of *Shiloh* to review as we discuss this model.

Shiloh is a realistic-fiction novel about an 11-year-old named Marty Preston who lives in the rural hills community of Friendly, West Virginia. Although they experience poverty, the family members are close and include two younger sisters, Marty, and his parents. Marty is kind, respects his parents, and demonstrates an appreciation for living things. On a Sunday-afternoon walk, Marty meets up with a beagle he later names Shiloh. The beagle is initially suspicious of Marty, but eventually Marty is able to coax him to play. The beagle follows him home and won't leave, but Marty's father points out that the dog belongs to someone else and it is likely Judd Travers. Even though Marty tells his father that he suspects Shiloh has been severely mistreated, especially if it is Judd Travers's dog, his father points out that it isn't any of his business, and bad treatment is hard to prove even when it is child abuse. Shiloh does belong to Judd Travers, but Marty decides to hide Shiloh. This begins the struggle between Marty's sense of fairness with respect to animal rights and his honesty and respectfulness toward his parents.

After reading the book, we selected a theme that seems to be repeated over and over in this book. It's the struggle Marty has with his strong beliefs about fairness and truth. He finds himself facing this issue throughout the book because he decides to hide Shiloh after he leaves Judd Travers's home a second time. Although he tries to convince himself that he isn't lying to his father, the underlying truth and deceit continually surface. This recurring struggle led us to select the following theme: Stretching the truth, deceit, and lies can be discomforting when they involve people you love and respect.

Step Two

To complete this step, we analyzed the book in greater detail. We then considered the sixth graders who will read this book.

Reconsider the questions we suggested earlier to estimate text difficulty. If you have a copy of *Shiloh*, review it as we respond to these questions.

Questions to Estimate Text Difficulty

Does the text include many multisyllabic words?

> Difficult multisyllabic words are not included. Inflectional endings such as *-ed, -ing, -ly* make many of the words multisyllabic, and these are typically understood by sixth graders.

Are there many long and complex sentences?

> There are many compound sentences and sentences with subordinate and co-ordinate clauses. Students would need to read text fluently so they can easily construct meaning. An example follows: "Every bit of food saved is money saved that could go to buy Dara Lynn a new pair of sneakers so Ma won't have to cut open the tops of her old ones to give her toes more room." (p. 57)

Does the text include a large amount of specialized vocabulary?

> The vocabulary is not technical or scientific, but the Appalachian dialect is incorporated, which may present some difficulties for comprehension.

Are many concepts or themes presented in text?

> No, the struggle or conflict is often repeated, which makes it accessible.

Is the text expository or narrative?

> *Shiloh* is a narrative.

If the text is narrative, does it follow a logical story structure?

> Yes, there are no flashbacks or other complex imagery.

If the text is expository, does it include subheadings and illustrations?

> That doesn't apply.

Are text ideas presented in a cohesive and coherent manner?

> Yes, references to people, objects, events, and the like are easily understood within and across sentences. The need for a tight, logical text structure of important ideas stated in the top of the paragraph is unnecessary for narrative.

Overall, *Shiloh* is an easily accessible text for sixth graders. It follows story structure, and its theme recurs throughout the book. The vocabulary isn't complex, and the dialect may only provide a slight barrier.

Now consider the sixth graders who will read this book. The sixth-grade class is located in an urban area that is mixed ethnically and economically. Half the class reads fluently with few print-skill problems. The others' print skills are below grade level, but they can read easier materials fluently. There are several who are second-language learners and experience difficulties with vocabulary and prior knowledge. The class selected this book for instruction, and interest plays a large role in their comprehension. If they are interested, they focus, can recall, and can analyze text.

Once we had this information, we responded to the questions we posed earlier.

Questions to Assess Students' Reading Abilities

Will the text present print-skill difficulties to your students (e.g., too many new words)?

> No, *Shiloh* won't be difficult, since the vocabulary is common and not technical. The dialect is likely to present the only difficulty.

Do the students relate their knowledge and experiences to text?

> When the students are interested in the text, they become focused and motivated. Since they selected this book, it's likely they will try to relate to the character, story events, and theme.

Will the text-based ideas be familiar to your students?

> The students will be inexperienced with rural life, hunting, a slower-paced life, and other similar aspects of the story. Some have experienced poverty and cruelty. Many will not understand the idea that food is limited and can't be spared for a dog. Understanding the struggle of truth, deceit, and fairness may be difficult to understand, since they are abstract concepts.

Will the vocabulary and sentence structure be too difficult for your students?

> Since the vocabulary is rather simple, it should not present a problem. The sentence structure, for the most part, should not present a problem. Since the plot is not fast paced and has much repetition, comprehension should not be a problem, even for those not reading grade-level materials.

Will the students be interested in reading the text?

> Yes, since they selected it.

Will the students easily comprehend the book?

> Yes, but some instruction is likely needed about such concepts as fairness and truth.

> These sixth graders are not likely to have difficulties with print skills because of the simplicity of the words. The text structure should be familiar, since it conforms to stories that they frequently read. The students selected this book, so motivation and interest should facilitate text comprehension. The weakest area for these students is knowledge of rural life—for example, its language, culture, and activities.

Step Three

In this step, use the comparative information to plan appropriate prereading instruction for each of the three areas: print skill, prior knowledge and vocabulary, and purpose setting.

> Reflect on the comparative information we developed in step 2 to develop plans for prereading instruction. Although these sixth graders have mixed abilities with respect to print skills, they are reading a fairly simple text, so print-skill instruction is likely to be unnecessary. They will be reminded to use the Sound and Sense strategy as they encounter unknown words. Prior knowledge of rural life and the relationships among truth, honesty, deceit, and respect may be lacking, so these are the areas to focus prereading instruction on.

> As we select instructional strategies for prior knowledge and purpose setting, we need to choose strategies that maximize learning and judiciously use instructional time. Think about the strategies we have learned in this chapter. Reflect on the comparative information we have developed about these sixth graders and the book they are to read. Using both pieces of knowledge, we have chosen three instructional strategies that can facilitate comprehension. Two of these are related text reading and related writing. First, we selected a related text reading to help sixth graders understand the theme: Stretching the truth, deceit, and lies can be discomforting when they

involve people you love and respect. An excerpt from Richard Wright's *Black Boy* entitled "Hunger" helps urban students to relate to honesty, lies, deceit, and respect. Richard Wright descriptively shows how poverty affects urban-area children, and this can later be contrasted with Marty's experiences in a rural area. To understand a broader picture of rural life, reading aloud the book *Where the Red Fern Grows* may help establish universal human relationships and feelings toward living creatures and life itself. Begin reading and discussing this book prior to reading *Shiloh,* and continue reading it daily while students are reading *Shiloh.*

The other prior knowledge strategy is writing. Students will initially share words they associate with three concepts: honesty, deceit, and fairness. The students' ideas will be recorded on the chalkboard, after which they will be asked to explain what one of these three concepts means to them. They may give personal examples or use experiences of others, including those of book characters, to support their ideas. This writing activity provides them with an opportunity to make a personal response, to clarify their ideas, and to begin thinking about the theme they will be experiencing as they read.

This case study is intended to present a model of careful decision making for prereading instruction but should not be considered the *only* correct plan. It is only one of several appropriate plans that should help these sixth graders comprehend this particular text selection. Moreover, there are additional strategies not included in this chapter that can also help these sixth graders comprehend this text.

Planning prereading instruction may appear to be a long and tedious process, but as you become familiar with your students and reading materials, it will go faster and become easier. Eventually, it will develop into a routine activity that is effective and manageable.

SUMMARY

Preparing children to read text is an essential part of reading instruction. This is the step that enables students to comprehend text. It sets the stage for both learning and enjoyment. When you develop students' prior knowledge and vocabulary for the topic of the selection, students are better prepared to comprehend text. Setting a purpose for reading or encouraging students to set their own purpose can both facilitate comprehension and provide motivation. For the very young beginning reader or older students experiencing difficulty with print, teachers also need to develop print skill so that students are better equipped to focus on the meaning of the text.

Planning for prereading instruction involves three steps: reading the text and identifying the theme(s) or concept(s) students should learn from reading; comparing the students' reading abilities to text factors that may hinder their reading; and using that comparative analysis to plan instruction that will appropriately facilitate students' comprehension. Following this three-step model provides a coherent plan for prereading instruction and promotes effective use of instructional time. Students should then be ready to read and enjoy the text selection.

In the Field

1. Choose three words from a text that students may have difficulties comprehending. Write a four-sentence context for each instructional word. With a small group of students, read and discuss the four-sentence contexts. In your journal, write your observations about your teaching experience.

2. Choose a narrative and an expository text selection. Identify the major topic, theme, or genre for each. Develop some questions for each text selection that can help children relate their prior knowledge and vocabulary to the selected topic. Identify specific words in the text that can facilitate comprehension and enhance conceptual learning. In your journal write the topic, theme, or genre, questions, and related vocabulary from the text.

3. Meet with a small group of students and ask them to identify a topic they would like to read about. Choose a text related to their topic. Meet with the group and ask them to identify words related to the topic. Add related words from the text they will be reading. Give them time to design a Semantic Map. Discuss the map before they read text. Read text silently and ask them to reconsider their map and add words or change its organization. In your journal, write your observations about your teaching experience.

4. Choose a short story and identify word clues to establish the sequence of the plot. Choose clues that identify the character, setting, problem, important events, and the resolution. Your selection of word clues should help students construct story meaning, but it should not discourage some diversity in plot development; otherwise, Story Impressions can squelch motivation and the inherent intrigue of prediction. Write your Story Impression in your journal. Try it out with a small group of students. Write your observations of the lesson implementation.

Portfolio Suggestion

Select from your journal two examples of your responses to Pause and Reflect, Learning from Experience, or In the Field. Write a brief evaluation of your work. Explain how this chapter affected your thinking about planning and implementing instruction for accessing prior knowledge, developing vocabulary, and helping students establish a purpose for reading.

For Further Reading

Blachowicz, C. L. Z. (1986). Making connections: Alternatives to the vocabulary notebook. *Journal of Reading, 29,* 643–649.

Dole, J. A., Sloan, C., & Trathen, W. (1995). Teaching vocabulary within the context of literature. *Journal of Reading, 38,* 444–451.

Ogle, D. M. (1986). K-W-L: A teaching model that develops active reading of expository text. *The Reading Teacher, 40,* 564–571.

Strange, M. (1980). Instructional implications of a conceptual theory of reading comprehension. *The Reading Teacher, 33,* 391–397.

White, T. G., Sowell, J., & Yanagihara, A. (1989). Teaching elementary students to use word-part clues. *The Reading Teacher, 42,* 302–308.

CHAPTER 5

Strategic Reading: Guiding, Facilitating, and Empowering Students' Comprehension

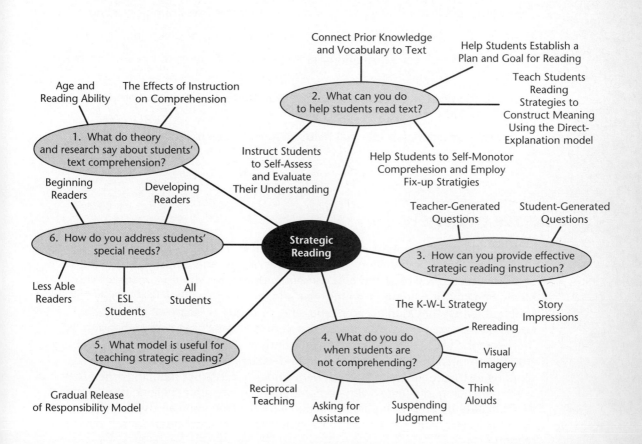

Connect Prior Knowledge
and Vocabulary to Text

Help Students Establish a
Plan and Goal for Reading

The Effects of Instruction
on Comprehension

Age and
Reading Ability

Teach Students
Reading
Strategies to
Construct Meaning
Using the Direct-
Explanation model

2. What can you do
to help students read text?

1. What do theory
and research say about students'
text comprehension?

Instruct Students
to Self-Assess
and Evaluate
Their Understanding

Help Students to Self-Monotor
Comprehesion and Employ
Fix-up Stratigies

Beginning
Readers

Developing
Readers

Teacher-Generated
Questions

Student-Generated
Questions

6. How do you address students'
special needs?

Strategic
Reading

3. How can you provide effective
strategic reading instruction?

Less Able
Readers

ESL
Students

All
Students

The K-W-L Strategy

Story
Impressions

Rereading

5. What model is useful for
teaching strategic reading?

4. What do you do
when students are
not comprehending?

Visual
Imagery

Think
Alouds

Gradual Release
of Responsibility Model

Reciprocal
Teaching

Asking for
Assistance

Suspending
Judgment

CHAPTER GOALS FOR THE READER

To become familiar with the theory and research related to strategic reading

To understand the effects instruction has on students' comprehension

To incorporate a direct explanation model to enable students to become strategic readers

To plan and implement reading strategies that guide, facilitate, and empower students to comprehend text

To use an instructional model that helps all students learn and apply reading strategies as they read text

CHAPTER OVERVIEW

In this chapter, we emphasize an efferent response rather than a personal response to text. We present instruction that guides, facilitates, and empowers students to comprehend as they read and as a consequence creates strategic readers, who identify a plan for reading, monitor their understanding as they read, apply "fix-up" strategies when they don't understand, and conclude by self-evaluating their learning. We begin by considering research on students' text comprehension. We then describe instructional strategies or actions to achieve a goal that can enable students to become active readers who understand and learn from text. We also describe instructional strategies that help students construct meaning when they are experiencing difficulties with comprehension or reading challenging materials. We conclude by presenting an instructional model that you can use to help your students learn reading strategies to become effective independent or self-directed readers.

TAPPING PRIOR KNOWLEDGE TO SET A PURPOSE

Think back to your own schooling experiences. What kind of instruction was provided to help you comprehend and learn from text? Did this instruction help you become actively involved in your learning and help you resolve comprehension difficulties while reading? Why or why not? As a mature reader, what do you do to develop understanding and learning from text? Write your responses in your journal.

Consider the chapter overview and the graphic overview and reflect on your own experiences to help you set a purpose for reading this chapter. Write this purpose in your journal.

WHAT DO THEORY AND RESEARCH SAY ABOUT STUDENTS' TEXT COMPREHENSION?

In this section, we explore the theory and research about how students' reading comprehension is affected by their age and reading ability, and then consider how instruction can successfully affect students' ability to comprehend and learn from text.

Age and Reading Ability

Developmental differences are a factor in the ability of students to monitor their own comprehension of text. To understand younger and older students' abilities to self-monitor comprehension, read the following passage explaining how to play a card game and answer the questions that follow it.

> We each put our cards in a pile. We both turn over the top card in our pile. We look at the cards to see who has the special card. Then we turn over the next card in our pile to see who has the special card this time. In the end the person with the most cards wins the game. (Markman, 1977, p. 988)

Did you comprehend the entire passage? As you read the passage, what happened? Did you stop after completing the sentence about the special card? If so, why did you stop? Or did your eyes revert to the beginning of the passage to see if you had missed information identifying the special card? Or did you continue reading while thinking that the author would eventually tell us more about the special card? If you kept reading, what happened next?

You probably became more confused, since the author never tells us how the special card affects the game and how a player acquires the most cards in order to win. Since you are a good reader, you probably recognized that the passage was ambiguous and poorly written. Do elementary students come to this same conclusion? Do they realize that they do not understand how to play the game?

Markman (1977) read this passage to first and third graders and found that first graders were unaware that they did not comprehend the passage even after being asked questions about the meaning of the passage. It was only when the first graders attempted to play the game that they realized they did not understand. Even third graders did not immediately recognize that information was omitted from the passage. Only after being questioned did the third graders recognize their lack of comprehension. This research demonstrates the importance of playing the game and making the reading experience concrete for younger students. Younger children have a better opportunity to self-monitor comprehension when they are actively involved and are constructing meaning. Although these young students listened to rather than read the passage, research does indicate that listening comprehension surpasses reading comprehension during the primary grades. Thus it is likely that reading this passage may have presented these young children with greater comprehension problems.

When we consider additional research focusing on young students' reading ability, the findings indicate that young children experience difficulty monitoring their own reading (Clay, 1967; Wixson, 1979), and that self-monitoring comprehension develops with age (Forrest & Waller, 1980; Myers & Paris, 1978). Furthermore, poor or less able readers experience greater difficulties with comprehension monitoring than do good or more able readers (Garner & Kraus, 1982; Golinkoff, 1976; Paris & Myers, 1981; Raphael, Myers, Tirre, Fritz, & Freebody, 1981).

In an interesting study, Garner and Taylor (1982) compare younger versus older as well as more able versus less able readers' awareness of meaningful text. Fourth, sixth, and eighth graders read the following passage and were asked if the story was easy to understand or if parts of it needed to be rewritten. If they did not immediately recognize the inconsistency in the passage, the researchers gave the students two additional opportunities to discover the problem.

Read the passage these students read and predict whether there were differences among the grade levels in detecting the inconsistency. If the students were poor at comprehension, would they have greater difficulties than the students who were good at comprehension? Write down your answers after reading the passage.

> The train stopped in Centerville every day at both one o'clock and at five o'clock. Dr. Jones needed to travel from Centerville to Milltown on business. He decided to go by train. He packed his bags. He caught a train at seven o'clock, and was in Milltown in time for his meeting. (Garner & Taylor, 1982, p. 2)

Were there differences among the grade levels in detecting the inconsistency? The results of the study indicate that fourth graders recognize the inconsistency less easily than do sixth graders, and sixth graders less easily than do eighth graders.

Did the less able readers do as well as the more able readers? More able readers are superior at monitoring comprehension. Typically, more able readers and older readers discover the inconsistency when they are asked additional questions and are given another opportunity to reread the passage; this suggests that comprehension monitoring is not a quick, automatic task, even for more able, older readers. Less able readers in grades four, six, and eight never do identify the inconsistency in this paragraph. Less able readers need to be made consciously aware that text must make sense. Hence teacher instruction that includes questioning, discussion, and rereading text should focus students' attention on careful monitoring of their own comprehension.

Paris, Wasik, and Turner (1991) note that both young and less able readers "often focus on decoding single words, fail to adjust their reading for different texts or purposes, and seldom look ahead or back in text to monitor and improve comprehension" (p. 609). These readers need help understanding the goal of reading. They need to focus on self-monitoring comprehension and identifying reading strategies that can "fix-up" comprehension "breakdowns." Paris and his colleagues concur with the research that indicates even 12-year-olds lack well-developed concepts of the reading process and do not possess well-developed knowledge of reading strategies that directly affect comprehension and learning.

The Effects of Instruction on Comprehension

Can we teach students to construct and monitor their understanding of text? A study by Garner et al. (1984) indicates that we can. In this study, less able readers from ages 9 1/2 to 13 were taught a specific strategy for monitoring their comprehension of text that involved *text lookbacks*—skimming text to find answers to questions that cannot be answered from memory. Students were also taught to discriminate between two types of questions: those that can be answered from information found in text and those that are to be answered from their own knowledge.

After three days, the less able readers, who had received instruction, performed better than those without training. The trained less able readers answered more questions correctly based on their use of text lookbacks and used the lookback strategy frequently when they could not answer the questions from memory. This study indicates that comprehension monitoring can be taught. Other studies have also shown that students can use reading strategies to monitor and increase their comprehension (Block, 1993; Gambrell & Bales, 1987; Miller, Giovcalo, & Rentiers, 1987; Palincsar & Brown, 1984; Paris & Myers, 1981). Considering the results of the National Assessment of Educational Progress (NAEP), Applebee, Langer, and Mullis (1988) posit the importance of teaching reading strategies to develop students' interpretive and critical thinking skills.

Text lookbacks constitute only one example of an effective reading strategy. There are numerous others, and we explore many different strategies throughout this book. But let's focus for a moment on the meaning of *strategy*. A strategy is not a skill (Paris et al., 1991). A skill is performed the same way each time. Reading text fluently is a skill. Associating a specific sound with a letter is yet another example of a skill. Reading strategies, on the other hand, are plans or methods to develop understanding and learning from text in which readers consciously employ, adapt, and flexibly use these strategies to fit the task and purpose of reading (Pressley, Johnson, Symons, McGoldrick, & Kurita, 1989). Reading strategies help students construct meaning from text; they facilitate the building of knowledge and are also tools to overcome the incomprehensible parts of text. Strategies help students, for example, to summarize text, select important text information, and ask questions to seek clarification.

Strategies are designed to build independence so students learn to apply the appropriate strategy as needed. Duffy (1993) further points out that skills become automatic. For instance, mature readers don't pay attention to the spelling patterns in words as they read. They instantaneously know the words. But unlike skills, strategies can't be automatized, as Duffy (1993) states, "because the uniqueness of each text requires readers to modify strategies to fit the demands of the text. For instance, how one makes predictions differs from text to text depending on the clues available. . . . Consequently, a good strategy user consciously adapts individual strategies within an overall plan for constructing meaning" (p. 232).

Effective reading strategies typically follow patterns similar to those used in *direct explanation* (Roehler & Duffy, 1984). Direct explanation includes three components: (1) identification, explanation, and modeling of the strategy and its benefits; (2) guided instruction and practice of the strategy; and (3) review and reinforcement. Let's consider these three components in greater detail.

Identification

The teacher identifies the strategy to be learned and its value and describes how students can apply it. To help students apply it, teachers may demonstrate how to do the strategy and explicate their thinking as they read text. Duffy, Roehler, & Herrmann (1988) stress the importance of making thinking and reasoning visible to students by explaining what you do as an expert reader to construct meaning.

Guided Practice

The teacher guides students' understanding of the strategy through a process called responsive elaboration. Duffy et al. (1988) point out that the teacher and student collaborate in order to perfect the use of a particular skill or strategy. The teacher may ask questions to check students' use and understanding of the strategy, may provide additional information about the strategy, or may further extend the students' thinking about the strategy's use and application. In the following example, note how the teacher helps shape the use and application of imagery as Maria reads a portion of Eleanor Coerr's *Mieko and the Fifth Treasure*.

Checks strategy use	**Teacher:** Now I want you to read and draw pictures in your mind about the text. What do you do when you are creating pictures? **Maria:** I tell what it looks like.
Elaborates Checks under-standing	**Teacher:** So you are describing it and providing detail. Maria, tell me about the pictures you create in your mind as you read the next passage. **Maria** [Reads text]: "She would never forget the day when The Thunderbolt—the atom bomb—was dropped on Nagasaki, sending shock waves out to her town. It was like the end of the world. Windows shattered and roof tiles flew through the air. Mieko was knocked to the ground. When she had put up an arm to shield her face, a jagged piece of glass had torn into her hand, ripping a deep gash from her fingers to the wrist." (p. 11)
Probes	**Teacher:** What pictures are created as you read? **Maria:** Windows are broken and the houses are ruined.

Teacher: Yes, what would Mieko's house look like after this thunderbolt hit? Can you use words to describe it?

Maria: Her house wouldn't look the same. It would look rickety and not taken care of.

Elaborates
Provides
support

Teacher: If the house is being destroyed from this thunderbolt and you see a rickety torn house, then how would Mieko look, since she was in her house when the thunderbolt hit? Reread this part and try to describe what Mieko looks like. [Teacher points to the sentence.]

Maria: "Mieko was knocked to the ground." Maybe she has bruises or broken bones. "When she had put up an arm to shield her face, a jagged piece of glass had torn into her hand, ripping a deep gash from her fingers to the wrist." Blood is dripping on the floor and forming a puddle. She is frightened.

Provides
feedback
and
support

Teacher: Good, Maria. If she is frightened, what do you think her face would look like?

Maria: She may be shaking. Her eyes may be large and look scared. Her mouth might be wide open ready to scream.

Reviews
strategy
use

Teacher: Great! You are creating pictures in your mind about what is happening in text. You are creating your own movie of the text which can help you remember and enjoy what you have read.

Review and Reinforcement

The teacher checks students' understanding of the strategy and when it should be employed. Students can discuss how they are using the strategy and if they are combining it with other strategies to increase understanding, enjoyment, or learning. It is during this phase of instruction that you need to encourage students to use it in a flexible manner to accommodate their individual learning.

As Duffy (1993) reports, when reading strategies were taught through a direct-explanation model, the at-risk or less able students revealed a greater understanding of their thinking and learning about a text. Consider the response of one second grader's response when asked in an interview about how he reads:

> Before I read, I think about the story and predict, and if I get stuck, I stop, go back, read it over again, and try to make sense out of it. (pp. 110–111)

ESL and learning-disabled students also benefit from reading strategy instruction that facilitates their text comprehension (Bos & Vaughn, 1991; O'Malley & Chamot, 1987). Moreover, using direct explanation to develop strategy use is also recommended for ESL and learning-disabled students, as it is for grade-level learners. These instructional strategies should be taught with good literature, as is suggested with grade-level students. Activating prior knowledge about the text topic, establishing a plan for reading, self-monitoring comprehension, and self-evaluating learning are important areas to develop with these students.

We know that students can learn instructional strategies to increase comprehension, but do students then apply them as a natural part of learning? Students who recognize the value of reading strategies, and who use them to increase comprehension and learning, are likely to incorporate them when reading (O'Sullivan & Pressley, 1984; Schunk & Rice, 1987). To accomplish this task, you must clearly demonstrate to students when to use a specific strategy and must make sure the strategy has beneficial outcomes. In other words, if students employ a particular strategy as they read and learn from text, then the test or assignment should reflect the type of learning this strategy develops and nurtures. Students can then recognize the value in using the strategy.

Paris, Lipson, and Wixson (1983) point out that students are also likely to apply reading strategies if instruction includes the discussion of declarative, procedural, and conditional knowledge. As the terms are used in this context, *Declarative* knowledge refers to "knowing that." In this context, students "know that" a variety of texts exist. Students "know that" goal setting is essential to learning. Students "know that" different reading abilities and interests exist. They "know that" reading a tennis magazine can be easy, quick, and enjoyable but reading a computer manual to solve a problem can be difficult and uninteresting. Thus students "know that" reading is a process in which they set goals and identify and use appropriate reading strategies.

The *procedural* knowledge, or "knowing how," refers to the students' knowledge of the specific strategy and steps necessary to implement the strategy successfully. For example, do students "know how" to form predictions, "know how" to summarize text, "know how" to ask questions? In this context, students can, for instance, make predictions but also "know how" to use specific procedures such as using prior knowledge, text title, and illustrations to develop their predictions. Thus procedural knowledge includes knowing and applying the strategy successfully.

The *conditional* knowledge, or "knowing when and why," refers to the students' ability to recognize the appropriate time a particular strategy is needed to achieve success in completing the reading task. Students go beyond knowing how to use a particular strategy while reading. For example, before reading a chapter on frogs, students write down their knowledge and experiences with frogs. They consider the text, goal, personal interests, and reading abilities to choose an appropriate strategy for reading. Hence conditional knowledge seeks to answer the question: Under what conditions should I use a particular strategy?

To become expert or strategic readers, students need to consider declarative, procedural, and conditional knowledge as they approach the reading task. Hence strategic reading takes place when readers are aware and in control of their thinking while reading, and take appropriate actions when they don't comprehend text.

Students are also more likely to apply a particular reading strategy if the instructional strategy is taught over a long period of time so that students know the procedures and can use the strategy in a flexible manner to meet their individual needs. They need to become problem solvers by adapting, combining, and developing strategies to meet their own individual needs. At this point of development, strategy use becomes very idiosyncratic. For example, students may have learned to write down and categorize information about a topic prior to reading, but when they read about a familiar topic, students may find reviewing ideas in their minds to be sufficient.

Moving beyond procedural instruction of specific strategies and helping students to use strategies to meet their individual needs constitutes a more advanced and challenging phase of instruction. Pressley, El-Dinary, Brown, Schuder, Pioli, Green, and Gaskins (1994) refer to this level of strategy usage as the transactional nature of strategies instruction in which the focus is not limited to teaching behaviors but "what happens between teachers and students and in the minds of the teachers and students"

(p. 13). Hence, in this phase of instruction, it is important to move beyond the teaching of isolated reading strategies.

You can make strategy use a natural, individual, and routine act if you do the following. Observe students as they read, discuss, and write and provide appropriate feedback and modeling. Continually collaborate with students to construct meaning from text (Pearson & Fielding, 1991). Cue strategy use; that is, discuss different strategies to read and learn from a particular text (Gaskins, Anderson, Pressley, Cunicelli, & Satlow, 1993; Weinstein & Mayer, 1986). Moreover, work with colleagues and administrators by discussing goals and instruction for helping students become more strategic as they construct meaning from text (Gaskins et al., 1993). Observe other teachers during strategy instruction to improve your instruction. Talk to your colleagues about strategies that have made a difference in their students' reading. Discuss strategy use with your students to learn how they use or don't use strategies as they read. From these activities, you can gather valuable information for teaching and learning. Realize that strategy learning is a slow and continuous process in which teachers and students must be engaged throughout students' schooling.

Controversial Issue

Aesthetic or Efferent Reading?

The issue we all struggle with in reading instruction is to achieve balance between efferent and aesthetic reading. Historically, reading instruction has focused on constructing the author's meaning from text with little attention or appreciation about the reader's point of view. The instructional emphasis on achieving the author's meaning can frequently erode the reader's interest and self-felt purpose for reading. As a consequence, reading in school has often become an artificial activity in which students read and complete activities for a grade on a report card rather than a matter of appreciating and enjoying expository and narrative literature. Although, in this chapter, we emphasize instructional strategies for developing an efferent stance of understanding and learning from text, we believe that students must receive a balanced instructional diet. They must be afforded opportunities to read aesthetically if they are to appreciate and enjoy literature. For instance, students need to self-select and develop personal responses to text, as they do in reading workshop. They need to be given activities that encourage personal inquiry rather than be always fulfilling a goal set by the teacher or curriculum guide. As they develop as readers, students need to be encouraged to move back and forth from an aesthetic to an efferent stance as literature presents these opportunities.

WHAT CAN YOU DO TO HELP STUDENTS COMPREHEND TEXT?

Reading is a complex act. To maximize learning, students need to develop strategies for reading text. To develop strategic readers, your instruction needs to include five elements:

1. Guiding students in connecting their knowledge and vocabulary to text concepts and themes and "taking stock" of their topical knowledge.
2. Helping students establish a plan and goal for reading.
3. Teaching students reading strategies to construct meaning using the direct-explanation model.
4. Helping students to self-monitor comprehension and employ fix-up strategies to overcome comprehension difficulties.
5. Instructing students to self-assess and evaluate their understanding of a text as it relates to their goal.

By teaching students to become strategic readers, you make it possible for students to analyze and discuss how they read text. Teachers model and demonstrate effective tools or reading strategies to understand and learn from text. By sharing knowledge, students learn how to use a particular reading strategy and the reasons for employing it, and they learn to use it to meet their individual reading needs. In the remainder of this section, we describe the five aforementioned points more fully.

Connect Prior Knowledge and Vocabulary to Text

Research demonstrates the power in activating and elaborating students' prior knowledge and vocabulary about a topic they will be reading (Pearson et al., 1979). In chapter 4, we described instructional strategies that encouraged students to make connections between their prior knowledge and vocabulary and the text. In helping students to construct and expand these connections, you will accentuate their learning and their ownership of and investment in what they read. Students should be encouraged to continue making these connections while reading.

Help Students Establish a Plan and Goal for Reading

Students need to adjust their reading according to goals and also be conscious of their individual strengths and abilities. Before students jump into reading a particular text, help them develop an appropriate plan for reading. Whole-group discussion and sharing ideas about how you plan and set your goal for reading can be helpful. The plan should take into account not only the purpose you have established during prereading instruction but also include overriding goals or outcomes for a particular text such as enjoyment or information gathering. If they are reading for enjoyment and pleasure, encourage students to skip or read rapidly the uninteresting parts and read, reflect on, and reread the parts that offer pleasure and beauty. If they are reading for information, prompt students to think about the final task—a report, for instance, or maybe a test. Even here the instructional strategies you present will vary according to the type of test. Having to prepare for an essay test, for example, may suggest a different reading plan than preparing for a multiple-choice test. The practice of routinely establishing plans and goals for reading develops over time; thus short and frequent discussions before students read can be beneficial.

Teach Students Reading Strategies to Construct Meaning Using the Direct-Explanation Model

Students can benefit from learning and applying reading strategies that focus on reading comprehension. To learn how to use particular reading strategies, students must identify the strategy and its purpose. You can model how to use the strategy by "thinking aloud" as you apply the strategy to a particular text. You can guide students' practice by providing feedback and elaborating on their use of the strategy. Periodic review and reinforcement of a particular strategy is necessary if students are expected to continue to use it. In this chapter, we demonstrate how teachers use the direct-explanation model as they teach reading strategies.

Help Students to Self-monitor Comprehension and Employ Fix-up Strategies

Instruction should encourage students to self-monitor as they read. Students need to know when they comprehend and when they do not. Lack of comprehension should cause students to employ any number of fix-up strategies to overcome comprehension problems. If they do not understand a sentence in a text, for example, students may read ahead to note if the author provides clarifying information, or they may pose a specific question and reread the difficult paragraph searching for the answer. Only guided instruction can show them how to control and regulate their reading so comprehension does occur. But instruction must encourage students to apply reading strategies in a flexible manner, and to use reading strategies as a way to problem-solve when comprehension difficulties arise (Duffy, 1993). Toward the end of this chapter we describe specific fix-up strategies.

Instruct Students to Self-Assess and Evaluate Their Understanding

Finally, you need to model for students the importance of evaluating whether or not they have accomplished their reading goals. Students should learn that evaluation takes place during and after the reading act. As students read, they need to consider whether they are acquiring the information they need to achieve their goal, and after they have read text, they need to evaluate whether or not they have achieved it. If not, what were the possible reasons? Were their plans inappropriate for the reading goal? Did they rely heavily on the author's ideas, since their prior knowledge was limited? Did they use the most effective fix-up strategies when they encountered difficult parts of text? Without a teacher's instruction, students are not likely to closely evaluate their reading of text. Discuss these questions after using a particular reading strategy or strategies with a text. Frequent discussions can encourage students to practice self-assessment.

These five elements embody the strategic reading process. When students can activate prior knowledge and vocabulary to construct meaning, identify appropriate reading strategies, self-monitor comprehension and employ fix-up strategies when needed, and self-assess their comprehension and learning, they are able to read and learn independently. Strategic reading represents a primary goal that you can help all students to achieve.

Pause and Reflect

Consider your own reading, as you respond to the following questions in your journal. Do you consider what you know before reading about a particular topic? Do you make a plan and establish a goal prior to reading text? Do you use particular reading strategies while reading? If so, which ones? Do you self-monitor reading by using strategies such as asking questions and summarizing? If so, which ones? After reading text, do you check if you have accomplished your initial goal? Why or why not?

HOW CAN YOU PROVIDE EFFECTIVE STRATEGIC READING INSTRUCTION?

In this section, we explain and demonstrate how to provide effective strategic reading instruction so that students focus on constructing meaning and realize this is the main goal of reading. Through descriptions and classroom dialogues of actual lessons, we demonstrate how teachers help students to plan, construct meaning, monitor comprehension, employ fix-up strategies, and evaluate their plans and goals for reading. Each classroom dialogue reflects initial learning of a particular reading strategy. As a result, the teacher provides more direct instruction—teaching students the procedures, value, and conditions in which to use the reading strategy, guiding reading, and providing feedback while the reading strategy is being employed. To enable students to use any of the described strategies independently, you will need to follow the instructional model (Gradual Release of Responsibility Model) suggested in the last section of this chapter. Moreover, we believe that learning a specific strategy is essential but that it is only a beginning in helping students become strategic readers. Students must also learn how to adapt, integrate, and coordinate reading strategies to truly become strategic readers. This second phase of strategy instruction is an important one and cannot be overlooked if we expect students to naturally engage in strategic reading (Duffy, 1993). Once students learn a repertoire of strategies, you need to discuss your own ways of learning from text—making visible your thinking as you read and learn. You also need to engage students in discussing how they can combine and coordinate these strategies to best address their individual learning needs. Students must never lose sight of what strategic reading is all about. Strategic reading is problem solving. It involves flexible ways to help them read and construct meaning. As you read the strategies in the remainder of this chapter, use the procedures as guidelines rather than as rigid procedures. Remember the goal is to comprehend text and not to memorize the strategy.

To teach students to become strategic readers, we connect *prereading* and *during-reading instruction*. At the prereading stage, you and your students employ purpose-setting strategies that can naturally be integrated into this next instructional phase of planning, constructing meaning, self-monitoring, and evaluating their reading.

The first purpose-setting strategy, suggested in chapter 4, employed either a teacher- or student-generated question to focus students' thinking during reading. We consider both types of questions and how you can use them as springboards to provide effective strategic reading instruction while students read.

Teacher-Generated Questions

In chapter 4, we suggested that you generate prereading questions that are broad enough to cause students to think about text-based concepts or themes. Such questions can guide and shape students' planning, understanding, self-monitoring, and evaluating plans and goals. A key to students' understanding of the theme or concept is using *text structure* as they read. Generating pre- and during-reading questions about text structure can help students organize their thinking and understanding so they can easily comprehend text. There are two basic text structures: narration and exposition. *Narration* reads like a story because its structure employs setting, characters, a problem, attempts to solve the problem, and a resolution; *exposition,* often the structure of nonfiction, may employ one or more types of text structure, including comparison/contrast, cause/effect, problem/solution, enumeration, and time order. Let's examine each of these text structures in turn.

Narration

Familiarity with story structure can help students organize their thinking as they read. Since students should expect particular story elements to occur generally in a specific sequence, recognizing aspects of story structure can enable them to distinguish important from trivial information and to self-monitor comprehension. To make students aware of story structure as they read, we suggest using an adaptation of the *Herringbone* strategy (Herber, 1970), the purpose of which is to help students understand and remember the essential components of story structure to compose a summary. A Herringbone diagram looks like a fish skeleton with six bones labeled *who, where, when, what, why,* and *how* (see Figure 5.1, p. 162). Combining the purpose-setting question with Herringbone can help students develop the theme of the story.

 Learning from Experience

Mrs. Santo introduces the Herringbone strategy to help her third graders understand and remember the story plot. As you read this classroom dialogue, notice how Mrs. Santo helps her students become strategic readers and how she guides her students' use of the Herringbone strategy to understand and learn from text.

....

Connects prior knowledge to text

 Mrs. Santo: Yesterday, I read some folktales to you. Remember, you heard "The Gingerbread Boy" and "The Three Little Pigs." We discussed how folktales usually tell a story. Stories have a beginning, middle, and end. They also have characters, a problem, and a solution. We learned that folktales include characters that are good and characters that are evil. We also learned that folktales teach us lessons about what we should or should not do and what happens when we are foolish or disobey rules.

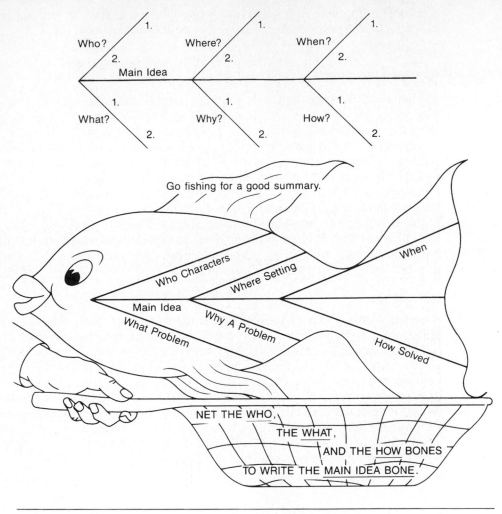

Who + what + how = *main idea*

Cinderella was cruelly treated by her step-mother and step-sisters until she was rescued by the prince.

Who + what + how + when + why + where = *story summary*

Now write the ideas from the bones in sentences and you have a summary of what you have read.

Cinderella lived in a far-off kingdom long ago. Her father died leaving her in the charge of a cruel step-mother with two selfish daughters. All the girls of the kingdom went to the ball in lovely gowns, but Cinderella had none. Her fairy godmother fixed her dress, carriage, and slippers of glass with a flick of her wand. Cinderella joined the party where the prince fell in love with her. She became the princess and forgave everyone.

Dianna Priessman
and Ann Walz

Figure 5.1 Herringbone diagram used to help students identify the essential components of a narrative or story structure. Use a developmentally appropriate illustration.

Identifies plan

⋮

Tells purpose and value

⋮

Explains procedure

⋮

⋮

Guides thinking

⋮

⋮

⋮

Provides feedback
Elaborates

⋮

⋮

⋮

⋮

Today, you are going to read a folktale entitled "Henny Penny." This folktale teaches us a lesson and also includes characters who are good and evil. As we read this story, I want you to think about the question written on the chalkboard, "Who is foolish, Henny Penny or Foxy Loxy?" Henny Penny and Foxy Loxy are two characters in this folktale. To help you answer this question and understand, organize, and remember the important parts of the story, we are going to use the Herringbone strategy. I'm giving each of you a copy of a herringbone. A herringbone is the skeleton or bones of a fish. The questions on the bones will help us organize and remember what happened in the story. By answering these six questions, we can summarize the story. You can use the Herringbone strategy to organize your thinking for a book talk or use it for review before discussing a story. The first bone has the question "Who are the characters?" As we read the beginning of the story, we'll find out who the characters are and write the characters' names on this bone. The next bone has the question "Where does the story take place?" Where in the story are we likely to find this answer?

Jan: In the beginning.

Mrs. Santo: Yes, we usually find the setting in the beginning of the story. The next bone has the question: "When does the story happen?" Where will we find this information?

Jay: The beginning.

Mrs. Santo: You're right. Look at the next bone. This question is "What is the problem?" Where will we find this answer?

Alisha: In the beginning or the middle.

Mrs. Santo: Yes. The next bone has the question "Why did the problem occur?" In this question, you are looking for some reasons or causes for this problem. The last bone has the question: "How is the problem solved?" To answer this question, you find out what the character does during the story to solve the problem. The middle of the story contains story events that tell how the character goes about solving the problem. And at the end of the story, what do we usually find out?

Tyrone: How the problem is solved.

Mrs. Santo: Yes, the resolution to the problem. We're going to complete the herringbone as we read the folktale "Henny Penny," and it should help us remember the important parts of this story. Which questions should we be able to answer first?

Christopher: Who are the characters? Where does the story take place? When does the story happen? And what is the problem?

Mrs. Santo: Good. Go ahead and read the first five pages of the story silently and look for the answers to these questions. You can write the answers to these questions as you're reading to help you remember what you have read. [The third graders read silently and receive individual teacher assistance when requested.]

 Your Turn: Now that you have read the classroom dialogue, reconsider the first two questions: How does Mrs. Santo help her students become strategic readers? How does she guide their use of the Herringbone strategy to understand text? Write your responses in your journal before reading our thoughts.

Our Turn: To connect students' prior knowledge and vocabulary to Galdone's Henny Penny, Mrs. Santo read two folktales to develop some familiarity with story structure and specific literary elements such as good and evil characters and the underpinnings of theme or lesson. By listening to other folktales, students are better prepared to read another folktale and discuss these same literary elements. Mrs. Santo did not choose to develop specific vocabulary, since the folktale was fairly easy to read and she wanted to concentrate on learning the Herringbone strategy. Mrs. Santo made sound decisions by providing related reading to develop or activate the students' knowledge of folktales and story structure. She also read the stories aloud so the children's print skills would not inhibit their comprehension.

To understand the purpose and value of learning the Herringbone strategy, Mrs. Santo explicitly states its purpose—identify important story ideas, organize information, and help students remember the story. She provides examples of when students should use the strategy—to summarize the story for a book talk or to discuss the story after you've read it.

As you read the following section, consider the next question, How does Mrs. Santo guide students to understand and use the Herringbone strategy? Are her students successful at using the strategy?

Mrs. Santo: And what is the answer to the first question, "Who are the characters?"

Kyle: Henny Penny, Cocky Locky, Ducky Lucky, Goosey Loosey, Turkey Lurkey, and Foxy Loxy. [Mrs. Santo writes the characters' names on the chalkboard. See Figure 5.2.]

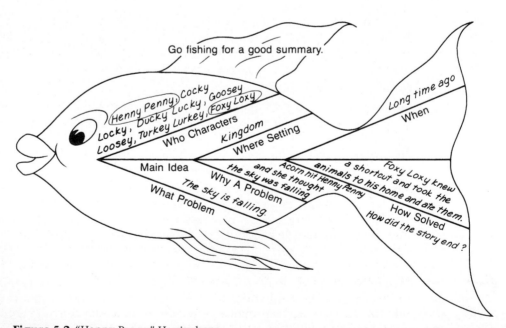

Figure 5.2 "Henny Penny" Herringbone

Mrs. Santo: Which of these animals are the main characters? Which two characters are the most important?

Sarah: Henny Penny and Foxy Loxy.

Reasoning

Mrs. Santo: Why did you choose those two?

Sarah: Because the story's called "Henny Penny." And I think Foxy Loxy is going to hurt all these animals.

Elaborates

Mrs. Santo: Good thinking! Henny Penny is the good character, and Foxy Loxy could be the evil character. Good, you've remembered that folktales include good and evil characters. We aren't sure that Foxy Loxy is evil, but we will find out as we read the story. I'll put circles around the main characters, Henny Penny and Foxy Loxy. We may change Foxy Loxy, if we find out he isn't the other main character.

Mrs. Santo's students answer the other four wh-type questions: where, when, what, and why. We return to the class discussion.

Mrs. Santo: All right, now silently read the last pages and see if you can answer the question "How is the problem solved?" Find out if the prediction about Foxy Loxy is correct. Is Foxy Loxy the evil character? [The third graders read and receive individual teacher assistance when they request it.]

Mrs. Santo: How is the problem solved?

Kyle: It isn't. Henny Penny never gets to tell the King.

Reasoning

Mrs. Santo: Why?

Kyle: Because Henny Penny was silly to listen to the fox and took the shortcut.

Provides clarity

Mrs. Santo: So, maybe we need to change the question from "How is the problem solved?" to "How does the story end?" [Mrs. Santo erases the original question and replaces it with the second question, "How does the story end?"] Okay. Jan, how does the story end?

Jan: Foxy Loxy knew a shortcut and took the animals to his home and ate them. [Mrs. Santo writes this answer on the appropriate bone.]

Mrs. Santo: So, in this story, the problem isn't resolved. Why is that?

Jan: Because Henny Penny was stupid and listened to Foxy Loxy.

Elaborates

Mrs. Santo: Henny Penny is silly and foolish because she doesn't spend time thinking about what she is doing. Let's go back to the question "Who are the characters?" Is Foxy Loxy the evil character?

Josh: Yes. So you can erase the other characters and just leave Henny Penny and Foxy Loxy up on the board.

Reviews goal

Mrs. Santo: Good. Now let's use the herringbone to help us summarize the story. By summarizing, we better remember the story when we want to tell it later. A summary includes the important parts of a story: the setting, characters, problem, and resolution. Which bone will help me begin the summary?

Cara: When does the story happen?

Elaborates and thinks aloud

Mrs. Santo: Good choice. Long ago, Henny Penny felt an acorn drop on her head and thought the sky was falling. While Henny Penny was on her way to tell the King, she told the other animals, including Foxy Loxy. [Mrs. Santo points to the bones as she tells and writes the summary on the chalkboard.] What parts of the story have I used in my summary?

Maria: Setting, characters, and problem.

Mrs. Santo: Good. What questions in the herringbone will help me to tell the things that happened in the story and how the story ended?

Jan: How did the story end?

Thinks aloud

Mrs. Santo: Good. I'll reread what we've included so far. "Long ago, Henny Penny felt an acorn drop on her head and thought the sky was falling. While Henny Penny was on her way to tell the King, she told the other animals, including Foxy Loxy." Now, I'll use the information on the "How" bone to complete my summary. [Mrs. Santo points to the bone labeled "How did the story end?" and writes the next two sentences on the chalkboard.] Foxy Loxy told the animals he knew a shortcut and led the animals to his cave. Foxy Loxy and his family ate the animals for dinner. Does this summary tell the important parts of the story?

John: Yes.

Evaluates

Mrs. Santo: Let's go back and look at our purpose-setting question: Who is foolish, Henny Penny or Foxy Loxy? Look at the summary to help you answer this question.

Cara: Henny Penny.

Mrs. Santo: Why?

Cara: Foxy Loxy tricked Henny Penny.

Mrs. Santo: Good, Foxy Loxy is the evil character, who plays the part of the trickster.

Your Turn: Now that you have read the classroom dialogue, reconsider the two questions: How does Mrs. Santo guide her students' understanding and use of the Herringbone strategy? Are her students successful at using the strategy? Write your responses in your journal before reading our thoughts.

Our Turn: By using the Herringbone strategy, Mrs. Santo effectively linked the purpose-setting question "Who is foolish, Henny Penny or Foxy Loxy?" to helping students construct and self-monitor reading comprehension. In the later part of the lesson, Mrs. Santo extended her explanation about the use and value of the Herringbone strategy by demonstrating how to use the responses on the herringbone diagram to compose a summary. To provide guidance and opportunities for practice and feedback, she taught the Herringbone strategy in a step-by-step fashion by breaking the strategy and the story into small parts. Through discussion, Mrs. Santo demonstrated to her third graders how the herringbone helps them understand the important elements of a story. During this discussion, Mrs. Santo guided their thinking about text through questioning and causing students to reflect further on text, elaborate, and make their ideas explicit. Mrs. Santo was also able to point out that in some stories problems may not be resolved. And, in this particular story, it helped students to develop an initial understanding of the theme of the story. Through questioning, they began to see that foolish characters can lead others to make big mistakes. And thus Mrs. Santo helped her students infer that readers need to question and not just automatically listen, believe, and follow. Once the herringbone was completed, Mrs. Santo used the responses on the herringbone to demonstrate its usefulness in composing summaries. She modeled her thinking by explicitly stating what was going on in her mind while composing a summary of "Henny Penny." Thinking aloud is a powerful instructional strategy we explain in greater detail at the end of this chapter.

The third graders' first attempt with the Herringbone strategy has been successful. The students completed the herringbone diagram correctly. But they will need additional guidance before they can independently compose a summary from a herringbone and can adequately self-evaluate its effectiveness. For an appropriate follow-up activity, Mrs. Santo can divide the third graders into small groups to read another folktale, complete a herringbone diagram, and use it to compose a summary. Small groups can share their summaries and note if the important story elements are included.

Exposition

Authors of expository text frequently use a particular text structure (comparison and contrast, cause and effect, problem and solution, enumeration, time order) to convey an important concept. When students don't know how to use writing patterns to determine important ideas, they have difficulty comprehending and learning from expository text structure (Meyer, Brandt, & Bluth, 1980; Taylor & Samuels, 1983). Using text structure also depends on developmental levels, and differences exist between less and more able readers (Englert & Hiebert, 1984; Meyer et al., 1980). As students get older, their use of text structure improves and more able readers are far more able to use text structure than are their grade-level counterparts who are less able readers (Meyer, 1977). Moreover, more able readers attach more details to important text-based ideas than do less able readers (Meyer, 1977). ESL students also experience difficulty with exposition, partly because of the use of different text structures (Allen, 1994). Hence helping students learn to identify different expository text structures and use them as tools for comprehension is important (Bartlett, 1984; Horowitz, 1985a, 1985b; McGee & Richgels, 1985), especially for less able and ESL students.

To help students use text structure during reading, first explain its purpose; second, help them identify the type of text structure employed; and finally, provide reading strategies such as *graphic organizers* to help students construct meaning, monitor comprehension, and respond to the teachers' purpose-setting question. Identifying the text structure is essential, if students are to use it to organize their learning. These text structures can be identified by looking for specific syntactic and semantic techniques authors employ to signal a particular text structure. Authors often denote text organization in the topic sentence and/or use signal words such as first, second, and third to denote a particular text structure. Piccolo (1987) initially teaches signal words and questions to pinpoint the text structure the author employs. In Figure 5.3, you can examine the different types of text structures, questions to help students identify the text structures, and typical signal words to provide students with assistance in detecting the text structure. Have students read, identify, and discuss the different text structures and the related signal words. Once students understand the different types of text structures, graphic organizers can be introduced as an effective reading strat-

Text Structure	Question	Signal Word
Comparison/ **Contrast**	Is the author showing similarities and differences?	similarly, on the other hand, but, however, while, although, likewise

Paragraph

    Tennis and table tennis share some similarities and differences. Both have a net, but in tennis the net touches the ground while in table tennis it touches the table. In both games, a ball is used. In tennis, a racket with strings is used while in table tennis a paddle is used. Scoring is different in both games. In tennis, scoring is love, 15, 30, 45, and game; however, in table tennis, the score increases by increments of 1 from 0 to 21. Both games require skill and practice and are enjoyed by both young and old. Try both games and note other similarities and differences.

Text Structure	Question	Signal Word
Cause/ **Effect**	Is the author telling why something happened?	if . . . then, because, consequently, thus, therefore as a result

Paragraph

    Ball watching and footwork can have great effects on your tennis game. If tennis players don't have good ball-watching skills, they are likely to lose the game. The racket and body of a tennis player who watches the ball tends to follow through the shot, and a successful shot is the result. Footwork is another important part of tennis. If tennis players use a cross-over step to hit a volley, they can better cover the court and consequently reach more shots. Work on improving these two skills and you'll see your game improve.

Text Structure	Question	Signal Word
Problem/ **Solution**	Is the author identifying a problem and providing some solution?	if . . . then, because, consequently, thus, therefore, as a result

Paragraph

    Good sportsmanship is important in all sports, including tennis. Throwing tennis rackets, screaming at line judges, and yelling at your partner are not examples of good sportsmanship. To overcome these negative behaviors, try some of these positive behaviors. If you miss a shot, instead of throwing your tennis racket in disgust, do a shadow swing of the shot you just missed. The shadow swing reinforces the correct swing and allows you to use energy in a positve manner. If you tend to scream at line judges for their calls, then ask the judge, "Are you sure that ball was out?" This question can cause the judge to better analyze future calls. A partner who is yelled at is likely to feel more nervous; therefore, provide encouragement. A partner you believe in is likely to feel confident and make good shots.

Text Structure	Question	Signal Word
Enumeration/	Is there a topic and a list of details?	first, second, to begin with, next, finally, most important

Paragraph

    In tennis, there are several important shots. The first is a ground stroke in which the ball is hit from baseline to baseline. The second is the volley in which the ball is hit in the air before it bounces. The third is the overhead in which the player hits the shot when it is at its highest peak in the air. And finally, the lob is a shot that is struck with an open-face racket over the opponent's head. These shots take much practice before a player can consistently use them to win.

Text Structure	Question	Signal Word
Time Order/	Is there a list of dates in sequence?	On (date), not long after, before

Paragraph

    The tennis racket has changed over the years. The first rackets which appeared in the 1880s were made of wood and the head was pear shaped. In the 1920s, leather grips were added to wooden rackets. During the 1920s, the first metal racket appeared. In the 1950s, rackets were made with a wood-laminating process to make them stronger. The aluminum racket appeared in the 1970s and made rackets lighter. Graphite and fiberglass are the materials of modern-day rackets. Tennis rackets are likely to change in the future and make tennis more enjoyable and easier to learn.

Figure 5.3 Different Types of Expository Text Structures, Questions, Paragraphs, and Signal Words to Help Identify Text Structures

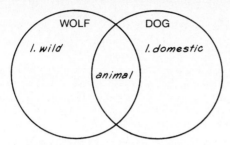

Figure 5.4 Organizing Information from Comparison and Contrast Text Structure: A Venn Diagram

egy to help students understand, organize, and remember information (McGee & Richgels, 1985; Piccolo, 1987).

Students can be taught to use different types of graphic organizers to identify the important information being highlighted within a particular text structure. In the remainder of this section, we describe graphic organizers that capture a particular text structure.

If *comparison and contrast* is the predominant text pattern, constructing a Venn diagram is a useful way to guide and monitor comprehension. Have students draw two intersecting circles and label each circle with one of the ideas or things being compared. As students read, have them write similarities within the overlapping portion of the circle, and differences within the appropriately labeled circle, outside the area common to both circles (see Figure 5.4).

For both *cause and effect* and *problem and solution* texts, students can use columns and arrows to note relationships (see Figure 5.5). Label one column "causes" and the second "effects." As students read, have them note causes and effects, write them under the appropriate column, and draw an arrow between the two to indicate the relationship between these two points. This same strategy can be employed with problem and solution texts.

For *enumeration,* students can make a Semantic Map by placing the topic in the circle's center and drawing lines radiating from the center identifying different points. As they read each subsection, have them look for ideas explaining, describing, or supporting the topic, as illustrated in Figure 5.6.

Teaching students to make a *time line* can be an effective strategy for reading a time-order text structure. The time line allows them to note changes due to time and to detect relationships and discover important text-based ideas. To use any of these expository strategies for organizing and comprehending information, we suggest that you demonstrate the strategy with a short, easy text, since exposition is difficult for many readers. Explaining the purpose of the strategy, the procedures, and the situa-

Figure 5.5 Organizing Information from Cause and Effect or Problem and Solution Text Structures

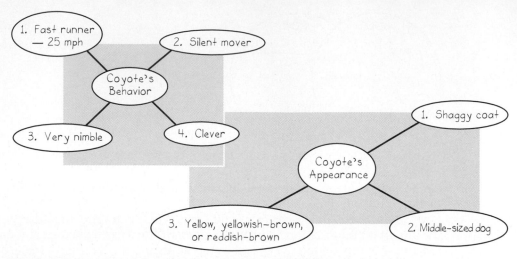

Figure 5.6 Organizing Information from Enumerative Text Structure

tions in which it is useful can be beneficial to comprehending and learning. In the following Learning from Experience, Mrs. Houston introduces her students to a time line to illustrate the important events so that students can develop a generalization from seeing and analyzing the time line.

 ## Learning from Experience

In her sixth-grade classroom, Mrs. Houston teaches her students how to use a graphic organizer as a reading strategy to understand and learn from text. As you read this classroom dialogue, note how Mrs. Houston helps her students become strategic readers by considering the following questions: How does Mrs. Houston connect students' prior knowledge and vocabulary to text? How does Mrs. Houston help her students understand the purpose and value of using a time line to understand, organize, and learn from text? Do her students feel they achieve success by using this strategy to understand and organize important information?

Connects prior knowledge to text

Mrs. Houston: Yesterday we talked about immigration. We discussed familiar words that you related to this topic, and I introduced a few new words. In small groups, you used Semantic Webs to show how these words were related to each other as well as to the topic of immigration. The words I introduced, and some of the words and ideas you discussed, are included in the informational article we're going to read about immigration.

Identifies purpose

As you read, think about this question: How has immigration changed over the years? [She writes this question on the chalkboard.] To help you answer this question, I want you to consider how the author has organized this article. In nonfiction,

Identifies plan

authors organize their ideas by using different types of text structures, including time order. [Mrs. Houston writes the words *time order* on the chalkboard.] In this text structure, authors organize their ideas according to the time they occurred in history. The author chooses this text structure because it seems to best communicate an important concept to the reader. Even though time order helps us organize and focus our thinking, it is sometimes difficult to remember all the different ideas that are presented; so we have trouble developing relationships among the ideas, and the concept we're supposed to learn from text seems vague or hard to understand. One thing that can help you answer the purpose-setting question is to make a time line and record the events and ideas as you find them in the text. [Mrs. Houston points to the question "How has immigration changed over the years?"] After you've finished reading and recording the different points, review the time line, and you ought to develop relationships among text-based ideas and be able to answer the question. Making a time line should increase your comprehension and learning of text. It can also help you review for a test without rereading the entire text. Now silently read the first page of the article, "Deciding Who Shall Come." Find events and ideas showing that immigration has changed.

Mrs. Houston: John, what's the first event and when did it occur?

John: Before we were a country, foreigners were welcome.

Mrs. Houston: About what time period did this occur?

John: I don't know.

Mrs. Houston: Go back to text and reread the last paragraph and see if it provides clues to the time foreigners were welcome. [John silently rereads the paragraph.]

John: Well, it must be before 1800, since foreigners were no longer welcome then.

Miata: It's probably the 1700s, since we weren't a country before that.

Mrs. Houston: Both of your ideas are correct. [Mrs. Houston draws a straight horizontal line across the chalkboard, places a mark at the beginning of it, and writes *1700s* above the mark and *Foreigners were welcome* below the mark. See Figure 5.7.]

Mrs. Houston: Okay. Are there changes in immigration after the 1700s?

Linda: There was xenophobia.

Mrs. Houston: What is xenophobia, and when did it occur?

Mark: Scared of immigrants, and it happened in the 1800s. [Mrs. Houston places another mark on the time line and writes *1800s* above the mark and *Xenophobia* below it.]

Mrs. Houston: Good. Let's read the first column of the next page silently. As you read, find out how immigration changed. [Mrs. Houston waits for them to finish reading.]

Mrs. Houston: Hannah, how did immigration change?

Hannah: The Chinese couldn't come into the country after 1882.

Mrs. Houston: Why weren't the Chinese allowed into the United States?

Tells purpose and value

Guides implementation

Uses text lookbacks

Provides feedback

Checks comprehension

Guides thinking

1700s	1800s	1882	1917	1921
Foreigners were welcome	Xenophobia	Chinese Exclusion Act	Literacy test	Quota system 3 percent of 1910

1924	1943	1960	1965	1978
Quota system 2 percent of 1890	Repeal of Chinese Exclusion Act	Human rights movement	End of individual quotas	Single worldwide quota

Figure 5.7 Time Line for "Deciding Who Shall Come"

Hannah: Because of the Chinese Exclusion Act. [Mrs. Houston makes another mark on the time line and writes *1882* above the mark and *Chinese Exclusion Act* below it.]

Mrs. Houston: Any other changes in immigration?

Jess: Foreigners had to take a literacy test after 1917. [Mrs. Houston makes another mark on the time line and writes *1917* above the line and *Literacy test* below it.)

Mrs. Houston: Were there changes in immigration before 1917?

Veena: I don't think so.

Mrs. Houston: Reread the text and make sure there were no additional changes. [The sixth graders reread text.]

Veena: Well, there was the "new immigration" from 1890 to 1917, and it seemed to cause the literacy test so I don't think it's a change in immigration.

Elaborates

Mrs. Houston: You're right. If you read the first sentence of the last paragraph, the author tells you the literacy test is the result of the "new immigration." Reread this sentence. What words tell us these two ideas are related?

Veena: "To restrict this wave of immigration."

Mrs. Houston: Specifically, the word *this* refers back to the "new immigration" that wasn't accepted by Americans, and consequently a literacy test became a requirement for immigration.

Mrs. Houston used the question "Were there changes in immigration?" to guide students' thinking and reading until they completed the article. To conclude the lesson, she asked the sixth graders to review the time line (see Figure 5.7) and note if it helped them to answer the purpose-setting question "How has immigration changed over the years?" Many were able to answer this question, and in the discussion that followed, many sixth graders said the time line had given them a better understanding of the article. Most felt it improved their comprehension; some noted that it helped them review the article without rereading it and others felt that time lines would be a good tool to use in studying for some tests.

← **Your Turn:** Now that you have read the classroom dialogue, reconsider: How does Mrs. Houston connect students' prior knowledge and vocabulary to text? How does

Mrs. Houston help her students understand the purpose and value of using a time line to understand, organize, and learn from text? How does she guide students to understand and use a time line as a graphic organizer? Do her students feel they achieve success by using this strategy to understand and organize important information? Write your responses in your journal before reading our thoughts.

 Our Turn: Mrs. Houston demonstrated how a purpose-setting question can guide students to select an appropriate reading strategy to accomplish their reading goal. In this case, students were to find out the reasons for changes in immigration laws. Identifying the author's text structure and selecting an appropriate graphic organizer enables students to construct relationships among the historical events and develop a response to the question. In this lesson, Mrs. Houston identified the goal and explained an appropriate plan for accomplishing it. She then provided guided practice so students understood how to use the purpose-setting question in conjunction with the time line. Applying this procedure caused the sixth graders to construct meaning as they read text. Moreover, Mrs. Houston periodically requested that students elaborate on certain ideas or events signifying changes in immigration. When students provided vague responses, she showed them how to use text lookbacks as a strategy to fix up poor comprehension. As she concluded the lesson, the students were asked to evaluate the strategy and consider appropriate situations in which to use it.

Student-Generated Questions

In chapter 4, we suggested that you encourage students to develop their own purpose for reading and thinking because student-generated questions encourage student motivation and commitment. The Directed Reading-Thinking Activity or DR-TA (Stauffer, 1969) encourages active involvement, since students make predictions about text content. Moreover, it supports critical thinking and discussion of the author's development of text and promotes understanding and learning of text. The discussion enables students to construct and self-monitor comprehension as they read either narrative or expository text. As they read additional sections of text, students are able to make more knowledgeable predictions about the text content based on text reading and their knowledge of story structure and/or subject area content. This process—predict and justify, read, and confirm or refute—guides and focuses students' thinking during reading. Encourage students to use the title, subtitles, and illustrations to make predictions about the content and invite them to present their hypotheses. You can break the text into parts so that students can examine their predictions, thus allowing them to revise or change their predictions, if they wish. Encourage them to use the text to support and explain their reasoning.

As you plan a DR-TA, we suggest you begin by selecting a short story with a good story structure that includes characters, a problem, and a resolution. Choose several stopping points so students can make predictions to guide their thinking about how the story develops. A good place to stop reading is where the author sets up alternatives and the reader is unsure what the character will do next or how the story event will develop or conclude.

If you choose an expository selection, use a selection that contains subheadings. The text structure should be logical and easy to follow, with a limited number of fairly explicit—that is, not ambiguous—important ideas. Use a T-Chart (make a large T on ruled paper to divide into halves) to write a prediction for each subheading on the left-hand side of the T-Chart, and write the important information the author included on the right-hand side of the T-Chart. Use the subheadings as starting and stopping points to predict, read, prove, and discuss.

To implement a DR-TA, give the students the title of the story or expository selection and ask them to write or tell what they think the text will be about. You may want to eliminate writing for younger children, since these learners tend to focus on spelling and penmanship and these areas detract from this strategy's main purpose. Give them a few minutes to think. Then have them discuss their predictions as a group. Writing the essence of students' predictions on the chalkboard lets them refer to these during reading and discussion. Then have the students read to find out if their predictions are correct. Tell them to remember the place in the selection that supports or contradicts their predictions.

When everyone finishes reading, have students indicate if their predictions were supported, refuted, or lacked sufficient information by asking questions such as: Did your prediction follow the author's plan? Was your prediction supported? Is there information in the text supporting your prediction? Discuss each student's prediction. At the conclusion of this discussion, ask students to formulate new predictions, and insist that these be logical and supported by text information, prior knowledge and experiences, or a combination of these two. Continue this procedure to the end of the selection, and end with a short discussion of the story's conclusion and theme and the eliciting of personal reactions. If you are reading expository text, conclude by discussing the concepts and their application. In the following Learning from Experience, Mrs. Parker demonstrates how the DR-TA can work in a classroom.

Learning from Experience

Mrs. Parker, a seventh-grade language-arts teacher, is teaching a heterogeneous group of 12 students how to use the DR-TA as they read a story. The text the seventh graders will be reading is "The $43,000 Mistake" by Jean Sharda, a feature story about a former used-car salesman and high-stakes gambler, Old Cotton Thaggard, whose one bank account statement is reported as $43,000 higher than the amount he expected. The dilemma occurs: Should he report it or should he withdraw the money? He checks his account three times to see if the bank realizes it made a mistake. The teller keeps reporting a $43,000 balance so he decides to withdraw it; however, the bank realizes it made an error and demands the money be returned. But Thaggard won't return it, since his bank statement read $43,000. The bankers point out that reasonable people would suspect something was wrong when their bank balance showed such a discrepancy. Thaggard maintains that he believed some of his gambling partners finally paid up their debts so he refuses to return the money.

The bank prosecutes. Thaggard is charged with "false pretenses," and after many court battles, the federal court finally finds Thaggard guilty of bank larceny. Thaggard serves five years in prison, but the bank never receives its money, since Thaggard can't recall where the money went. As you read this dialogue, consider how Mrs. Parker helps her seventh graders understand the purpose and value of the DR-TA and how she helps them predict and use text and prior knowledge to support or reject their predictions.

Tells purpose and value

Mrs. Parker: Today we're going to learn a strategy that you can use as you read stories. The strategy is called the DR-TA, and it can help you understand and remember what happened in a story. The DR-TA is a good strategy to use when you're assigned stories or chapters in a novel and you're expected to know what they're about. It's also a great strategy for leisure reading, since it can increase your enjoyment and understanding of the story.

Explains procedure

Here's how the DR-TA works. Think of yourself as a detective. You are given clues such as a title and maybe a picture to help you predict the story plot. Today you are going to read the story, and the title is "The $43,000 Mistake." Use the title and picture to predict what is likely to happen in this story. Write down your predictions. You don't need full sentences. Phrases are fine. [Mrs. Parker allows a few minutes for students to write, then puts their responses on the board.]

Danny: A mistake that will cost $43,000.

Pat: Someone loses $43,000.

Margo: Someone makes a very expensive mistake, and it's more valuable than money.

Mrs. Parker: What do you mean by "more valuable than money"?

Maurice: Like a friendship.

Olivia: Stock market crash.

Points out goal

Mrs. Parker: Okay. Great start. Let's look at the first part of the story. As you read, think about your prediction. Does your prediction follow the author's plan? Once you finish reading, go back to the text and find the section that proves or disproves your prediction. [Children read silently. When the students finish, Mrs. Parker resumes instruction.]

Mrs. Parker: Okay, let's look at the first prediction. Was the story about a mistake that cost $43,000?

Seventh Graders: Yes.

Asks text support

Mrs. Parker: Where in the text does it indicate that it's a mistake about this amount of money?

Beth: It says, "The Alabama Motor Company showed a balance of $43,498—more than $43,000 over what it should have been!"

Mrs. Parker: Okay, good. Did someone lose money? [Mrs. Parker points to the second prediction.]

Roberto: Well, the bank did.

Asks text support

Mrs. Parker: Why do you say the bank lost the money?

Roberto: Well, there's all this extra money in Thaggard's Alabama Motor Company account. If Thaggard takes this money out, it's the bank that will lose it.

Clarification

Mrs. Parker: But has Thaggard taken the money out of the bank?

Mark: No, not yet, but it looks like he will, since he's been going back and forth checking the account balance.

Mrs. Parker: Did someone make a very expensive mistake that's more valuable than money? [Mrs. Parker points to the third prediction.]

Deepa: No, it's only about money.

Mrs. Parker: Was it about a stock market crash? [Mrs. Parker points to the fourth prediction.]

Callie: No.

Checks ability to self-monitor

Mrs. Parker: When did you find out that it wasn't about a stock market crash?

Callie: In the first paragraph.

Mrs. Parker: Read the specific part that disproves this prediction.

Callie: "This is the story of one such mistake in the big, impersonal world of banking."

Mrs. Parker: Okay, draw a line under your first prediction. Now write on your notebook paper a second prediction. How do you think the story will develop? [Students are given a few minutes to write their predictions.]

Mrs. Parker: What do you predict, Mei?

Mei: I'm not exactly sure what's going to happen.

Uses retelling to develop prediction

Uses text lookbacks, questioning

Mrs. Parker: Try telling what happened in the first part of the story.

Mei: This man went to the bank and found he had a lot of money in his account.

Mrs. Parker: What did he do when he found he had all this money? [When Mei doesn't respond, Mrs. Parker continues.] Reread the last two paragraphs and find out what this man did.

Mei [after silently rereading]: He went and checked it out with the bank.

Mrs. Parker: What did he check out?

Mei: If he had this money.

Mrs. Parker: What did the bank tell him about the money?

Mei: The used-car account was about $43,000.

Mrs. Parker: Did he expect to have this much money in his account?

Danielle: No, his bank account should have been a lot lower.

Mrs. Parker: What do you think Old Cotton Thaggard will do?

Mei: Cash a check for $43,000.

Reasoning

Mrs. Parker: Why?

Mei: The bank said he had that much money in his account.

Mrs. Parker: Logical prediction, Mei. [Mrs. Parker writes the first prediction on the board.] Pat, what do you think will happen?

Pat: He'll take it out and spend it. Then someone will claim it. [Mrs. Parker writes the second prediction on the chalkboard.]

Reasoning

Mrs. Parker: Who is "he"?

Pat: Thaggard.

Mrs. Parker: Why do you think this will happen?

Pat: If you had $43,000, wouldn't you spend some of it?

Mrs. Parker: So this prediction is based on your experiences?

Pat: Yes.

Asks text support

Mrs. Parker: Any other clues from the story that make you think he'll spend it?

Nita: Well, he's in high-stakes gambling.

Jim: The other things he's into don't sound like he knows much about money—jukeboxes and used cars.

Carl: He's going to gamble it and one of two things is going to happen. My first idea is that he'll make a lot of money and he won't know how much money to return to the bank. He knows if he hadn't had the original $43,000 he wouldn't have had the chance to make so much money, so he feels guilty, thinks maybe he should return what he wins, too. My second idea is that he loses it all and is in the hole.

Reasoning

Mrs. Parker: Why is he going to gamble the money? [Mrs. Parker writes the third prediction and its alternatives on the chalkboard.]

Carl: Because it says he's a high-stakes gambler.

Mrs. Parker: What clue led you to think he'll be successful?

Carl: There aren't any clues, but when you gamble, it can go either way.

Mrs. Parker: John, what do you think will happen?

John: I think Thaggard will spend the money on gambling. The bank will find out, and he'll have to give it back. [Mrs. Parker writes the fifth prediction on the chalkboard.]

Asks support

Mrs. Parker: What makes you think he'll have to pay it back?

John: Because the bank will notice that $43,000 is missing. Once they know it's gone, they'll find out who has it and demand it back.

Mrs. Parker: Okay. Read section two and find out if any of these predictions match how the author developed the story. [Students read the second section of the story.]

 Your Turn: Now that you have read the classroom dialogue, reconsider: How did Mrs. Parker help the seventh graders understand the purpose and value of the DR-TA? How did she use the DR-TA to help students develop a plan for reading and guide them to self-monitor their comprehension? Write your responses in your journal before you compare your answer with ours.

 Our Turn: Mrs. Parker explained when and why students would use the DR-TA so that students knew the value and use of this reading strategy. She used the analogy of being a detective to help the seventh graders understand and apply this reading strategy. Mrs. Parker accepted the students' predictions and consistently asked them to support their predictions by using text and/or prior knowledge. She limited her questions to asking for specific support for predictions, requesting clarification of responses, and asking for explanations of their reasoning. Mrs. Parker asked students to read specific parts of the text to demonstrate their understanding and reasoning.

Reading aloud also provided Mrs. Parker an opportunity to observe students' word identification and fluency abilities. She used retelling to monitor and clarify story development.

Story Impressions

During prereading instruction, we suggested that students use story clues to develop a predictive summary about the story they are to read. Developing a hypothetical summary motivates them to think like an author and focuses their thinking while reading. Thus, while reading, their purpose is to compare and contrast their hypothetical summary with the actual story. How can teachers use the hypothetical summary to enable students to construct meaning and monitor comprehension? In the following Learning from Experience section, Mrs. Owen demonstrates how hypothetical summaries can encourage strategic reading and help students self-monitor reading comprehension.

 Learning from Experience

As you read this classroom dialogue, note how Mrs. Owen helps her students become strategic readers. As you read, consider the following questions: How does Mrs. Owen help her students understand the value and use of the Story Impressions strategy? How does she guide students to understand and use Story Impressions?

        During prereading instruction, Mrs. Owen's second graders used story clues to dictate a hypothetical or predictive summary of Arnold Lobel's story "Down the Hill." Since these second graders typically did not pay close attention to comprehension, Mrs. Owen divided a piece of chart paper in half. On the left side, she wrote their predictive summary, with each sentence placed on a separate line so the second graders could easily compare their ideas with the author's plan. She used the predictive summary to identify specific pages where the class should stop reading and compare and contrast their summary with the actual story. On the following morning, Mrs. Owen guided their reading using their predictive summary.

Connects print knowledge to text

Identifies plan

Guides implementation

Mrs. Owen: Yesterday we had some ideas about what would happen in the story "Down the Hill." We used these ideas to write a summary of the story. Remember, a summary tells us the important parts of a story and leaves out the details. I've copied your summary onto this chart so you can easily read and check your ideas. These are your summary sentences, on the left. (See Figure 5.8 for completed chart.) Today we're going to compare our summary with the actual story, so we think about what happens in the story as we read and we can better remember the story. If any of our predictions do not follow the author's story, we'll change our predictions to match. I'll write our changes on the right side of the paper. To make reading easier, we'll read just part of the story at a time and compare it with our predictions. Okay? If there are changes, you'll make them, and I'll write them on the chart. Let's begin by

Predictive Summary	Story Summary
1. Frog and Toad are sledding in the winter.	
2. Toad was scared of sledding.	
3. They got scared together.	3. Frog said, "Sledding would be fun."
4. They went over a big bump on the sled.	
5. On the bump, Frog fell off.	
6. Frog hit a tree.	6. Toad was alone on the sled and he hit a tree and a rock and then fell into the snow.
7. And at the end, it all was a dream.	7. At the end, Toad thought sleeping was better than sledding.

Figure 5.8 "Down the Hill" Diagram for Story Impressions

reading the first part of the story. [The second graders silently read the text.] Chantelle, read the first sentence of our predictive summary.

Chantelle: "Frog and Toad are sledding in the winter."

Checks self-monitoring

Mrs. Owen: Is that what happens in the beginning of the story?

Chantelle: Yes.

Mrs. Owen: Matthew, read the second sentence of our summary.

Matthew: "Toad was scared of sledding."

Mrs. Owen: Did Toad get scared?

Second Graders: Yes.

Mrs. Owen: Vladimir, read the third sentence of our summary.

Vladimir: "They got scared together."

Mrs. Owen: Are both scared?

Vladimir: No.

Mrs. Owen: How should we rewrite this sentence so it tells what happens in the story? Julie, how would you change it?

Julie: Frog said, "It would be fun."

Clarifies

Mrs. Owen: What would be fun?

Julie: Sledding.

Mrs. Owen: Okay. I'll cross out sentence three and write our new sentence on the right side of the chart. [Mrs. Owen writes the following sentence: "Frog said, 'Sledding would be fun.' "] Good. Let's read the next part. [The second graders read silently.]

Mrs. Owen: Deepa, read sentence four of the summary.

Deepa: "They went over a big bump on the sled."

Checks self-monitoring

Mrs. Owen: Did they go over a big bump?

Checks self-
monitoring

Deepa: Yes, but Frog fell off.

Mrs. Owen: So, is sentence five of our summary also correct?

Second Graders: Yes.

Mrs. Owen: What about sentence six, "Frog hit a tree"? Is it correct?

Julie: Yes, Frog hit a tree.

Uses visual
imagery

Mrs. Owen: Everybody reread this section. Try to picture in your mind what's happening to Frog and Toad. [Second graders read silently.] What did you see?

Chantelle: Frog hitting all these things and falling in the snow.

Thinks aloud

Mrs. Owen: Let's reread together and I'll tell you what I see. "Bang! The sled hit a tree." The sled hits the tree, but Toad isn't hurt. "Thud! The sled hit a rock." The sled hits a large rock, but Toad is still OK. "Plop! The sled dived into the snow." The sled is buried in the snow, but I'm not sure where Toad is. "Frog came running down the hill. He pulled Toad out of the snow." Now, I see both the sled and Toad buried in the snow. Let's reread sentence six in our predictive summary.

Second Graders: "Frog hit a tree."

Mrs. Owen: Did Frog hit a tree?

Jason: No, Toad was alone on the sled, and he hit a tree and a rock.

Mrs. Owen: What happened to Toad and the sled?

Scott: They both were covered with snow.

Mrs. Owen: Let's rewrite sentence six to include these two ideas.

Matthew: Toad was alone on the sled and he hit a tree and a rock and fell into the snow. [Mrs. Owen writes Matthew's statement on the right side of the chart.]

Mrs. Owen: Read the last page of the story and compare it with the last sentence in our summary.

Chantelle: It wasn't a dream.

Mrs. Owen: What was it?

Chantelle: Toad thought sleeping was better.

Mrs. Owen: Better than what?

Second Graders: Sledding.

Mrs. Owen: Rewrite the last sentence in our summary so it matches the story.

Jason: At the end, Toad thought sleeping was better than sledding. [Mrs. Owen writes the revised sentence on the right side of the chart.]

Checks self-
monitoring

Mrs. Owen: Let's read our new summary and check if it tells what happens in the story "Down the Hill." [Second graders do choral reading of revised summary.]

Mrs. Owen: Does our revised summary match the story?

Second Graders: Yes.

Demonstrates
strategy's value

Mrs. Owen: Let's try to recall what happened in the story without using our revised summary. [Mrs. Owen covers the chart.] Jason, tell what happened in the beginning of the story. [Students take turns retelling the story.]

Mrs. Owen: You've done an excellent job retelling what happened in the story. Up to now, you haven't been able to do this without going back to the story. Comparing your predictive summary with the actual story helped you remember the story. What do you think?

Chantelle: It's easier to remember.

 Your Turn: Now that you have read the classroom dialogue, reconsider: How does Mrs. Owen help her students understand the value and use of the Story Impressions strategy? How does she guide students to understand and use Story Impressions?

 Our Turn: To improve these second graders' comprehension, Mrs. Owen closely planned and guided students' reading of the story. As she introduced the lesson, she explained how the Story Impressions strategy was an effective plan for improving comprehension and memory of a story. She provided additional guidance by dividing the text into shorter segments so students had less material to comprehend and self-monitor. The discussion and teacher feedback, which occurred after reading each short segment of text, provided further guidance to further facilitate comprehension. Mrs. Owen made the second graders aware of the importance of constructing meaning and self-monitoring comprehension by encouraging them to compare the predictive summary with the actual story and to clarify or correct their responses. Mrs. Owen used fix-up strategies to improve comprehension by including rereading and visual imagery. She asked the second graders to reread the revised summary to help them evaluate their comprehension as well as the effectiveness of the Story Impressions strategy.

The K-W-L Strategy

In chapter 4, we discussed K-W-L (Know, Want, Learn), a purpose-setting strategy used with expository text. During prereading, students listed and categorized information they already knew about a topic. They categorized this information and then identified information they wanted to learn from the text. Students then read the selection silently and used their questions to guide reading and thinking.

You can use K-W-L during reading very much as Mrs. Owen used predictive summaries. Divide the text into sections—usually an easy task with subtitled expository text. Then have students use their W (Want to Learn) questions to guide their reading. As their questions are answered, have students write their responses underneath the question. They use their questions to self-monitor their reading and should be aware that their topical knowledge may not agree with the author's information. It's helpful for students to be conscious of comparing their ideas from the "K" or Know column with the author's ideas. This comparison provides another opportunity for self-monitoring comprehension.

Learning from Experience

During prereading instruction, Mrs. Diener uses the K-W-L strategy to activate and categorize the fifth graders' prior knowledge of natural disasters and to form questions about natural disasters that they are interested in answering. In this lesson, Mrs. Diener demonstrates how she uses her own questions to seek answers as she reads. As you read the class-room dialogue, find out how Mrs. Diener uses the K-W-L strategy to help her students develop strategic reading skills.

Identifies plan

Models

Thinks aloud

Mrs. Diener: Today we're going to use the K-W-L work sheet we began yesterday to help guide our thinking and learning as we read the article "Prepare for Disaster." [Mrs. Diener gives each student a copy of the article.] Yesterday we wrote individual and group questions about natural disasters. Today we'll see if any of our questions are answered by this article. Under the "W" column, I wrote a question about disasters that I'm going to use to guide my reading. My question is "What should you do if an earthquake occurs?" Let me show you how I'd use this question as I read text. From the title, "Prepare for Disaster," it's likely that I'll learn about what to do during a disaster—maybe even an earthquake. [Mrs. Diener reads the introduction aloud.] *"Volcanoes erupt, the earth quakes"*—it's going to be about earthquakes—*"and storms sweep over the land. But much can be done to prevent damage and death during the earth's upheaval."* Preventing damage and death sure sounds like I'll learn about what to do during earthquakes. *"If you heed warnings, remain calm, and are prepared to take the right course of action, you can survive a natural disaster."* The article is going to be about different types of disasters and how to prepare for one so you can survive. The first subtitle is "Earthquakes," so it's likely that my question will be answered in this section. *"California and Alaska are known for their earthquakes"*—I didn't know Alaska had earthquakes—*"but Mexico and New York had quakes in 1985"*—I remember the many deaths in Mexico City's earthquake, but I didn't know about New York—*"and the worst quake in North America in recorded history occurred in the Midwest."* I didn't think the Midwest had earthquakes. Earthquakes seem to occur all over North America. *"It may start with a rumble, like a train passing nearby. Then the ground or floor beneath your feet will begin to shake."* Scary feeling. *"The quake may last less than a minute, but during that time, bridges and buildings may collapse."* How long? I better reread it. *"The quake may last less than a minute."* That's unbelievable that so much damage can be caused in sixty seconds. *"For the next few days, the area may experience aftershocks."* What are aftershocks? Maybe I'll find out in the next paragraph. *"If an earthquake occurs when you are indoors, do not run outside. If you are in a tall building, do not take an elevator because it may get stuck."* Here's my answer. I better read this carefully. *"Flying glass or bricks are dangerous, so stay away from windows, mirrors, and chimneys. And be wary of moving furniture, falling dishes, and light fixtures. Protect yourself by standing in a strong doorway or crawling under a bed, desk, or table."* My question is, What should I do if an earthquake occurs? My answer is, Stay out of elevators, stay away from objects that can move and fly around the room. Get under a heavy piece of furniture. [Mrs. Diener writes her answer under the question.] *"If you are outdoors, stay far from buildings and telephone or electrical power poles that might fall."* Again, objects can fall and kill people. I'll add this information to my answer: *"Stay away from big buildings or other big objects. . . . Do not run, but move quickly toward an open area."* I wonder why you shouldn't run? Maybe it will tell in the next sentence. *"If you are near the ocean, head inland* *or toward higher ground to escape a tsunami"*—what's a tsunami?—*"(great wave)"*—oh, it's a big wave—*"that might sweep high onto the shore."* People should stay away from the ocean so a big wave won't kill them. [Mrs. Diener writes on the K-W-L work sheet this last sentence as a continuation of her answer and puts the article aside for a moment.] I told you what I was thinking while reading and used my question about earthquakes to help guide my thinking. I used the title to make a prediction about the information I would be reading. Prediction helped me focus and think about what I was reading. What other strategies did I use as I read?

Guides implementation

Duke: Asked questions.

Provides feedback

Mrs. Diener: Yes, I asked questions when I didn't understand text. What else did I do as I read this page?

Lauren: You added your own ideas.

Mrs. Diener: Yes, I added some information that I knew about this topic. Combining your ideas with the author's ideas helps you remember what you read. What else did I do as I read this page?

Jose: Once you found the answer, you wrote it down.

Mrs. Diener: Yes, I wrote it under the question on my K-W-L guide. Writing the answer helps me remember it.

 Your Turn: Now that you have read this classroom dialogue, reconsider the initial rephrased question: How does Mrs. Diener use the K-W-L strategy to increase students' strategic reading skills? Write your response in your journal before comparing it to ours.

 Our Turn: Mrs. Diener thinks aloud to demonstrate how to use questioning while reading. The question helps students focus and think while reading; there is direction and guidance. Linking questioning to think-alouds encourages students to elaborate, make connections between reader and text, and construct meaning. Hence students are following a plan while reading, can self-monitor comprehension, and can naturally evaluate their comprehension by developing appropriate responses to their questions.

WHAT DO YOU DO WHEN STUDENTS ARE NOT COMPREHENDING?

Too often students do not know what to do when they do not comprehend text, as illustrated in some of the classroom dialogues you just read. Students lack what we call fix-up strategies. As students were using the reading strategies such as DR-TA and Story Impressions, the teachers naturally included different *fix-up* strategies to further facilitate comprehension. You may remember that Mrs. Owen, for example, used text lookbacks, imagery, and think-alouds to develop understanding when students were confused about the story. These fix-up strategies seemed to put the students' thinking back on track. In this section, we describe several fix-up strategies students can easily use to solve comprehension problems.

Rereading

Many students expect to understand and learn from a single reading. Unfortunately, a single reading is often not enough. Rereading is essential, but subsequent readings should have a definite purpose—for example, to provide a definitive focus and clarity for understanding a new and difficult concept. Rather than rereading the whole text, students reread a particular section to better examine a vague concept or a question they could not answer.

When students cannot answer a particular question, they should think about whether it is a text-based or a reader-based question (Pearson & Johnson, 1978). In other words, can the answer be derived from text, or must readers derive the answer from their own knowledge and experiences? Here are examples:

Text-based question: Does an earthquake last a long time?
Reader-based question: How would you feel if you were caught in an earthquake?

If the question is text based, it is appropriate for the reader to skim the text to find the answer.

Part of using this strategy successfully is to identify important words in the question as clues to locating the section of text most likely to contain the answer. In the following examples, we have italicized important words. Readers can then skim the text to find these words or match them with text subheadings. After discussing a few examples, students can identify key words in questions to help them search the text to find answers. What are the key words in the following two questions?

Does an earthquake last a long time?
How does the water in most lakes differ from water in the ocean?

In the first question, the key words are *earthquake* and *time* because they signify topic and specific detail. In the second question, the key words are *lakes* and *ocean* since they identify the topic, and the other key word is *differ*, which signals the task the reader is to do.

Raphael (1986) has added another dimension to using questions as a strategy for increasing comprehension. In the Question-Answer Relationship or QAR strategy, Raphael uses this same basic question typography to help students seek answers for questions but has extended it further to provide additional guidance. She has also developed a schematic (see Figure 5.9) to guide students' thinking in determining the source of information that is most likely to provide answers to specific questions. Raphael defines four question types (Right There, Think and Search, Author and You, and On My Own) and the likely sources to find answers. Students learn to classify questions by looking for key words within the question and text. In this strategy, students receive visual mnemonics to guide their search for a specific answer.

To teach students how to use QARs, Raphael explains the four types of questions, gives examples of each type of question and explains how the question fits into a particular category. She then asks students to classify specific questions and provide reasons for a particular classification. Students practice by looking for key words, identifying a classification, and providing an appropriate response. QARs have helped elementary students successfully answer questions (Raphael, 1984). It is an especially good tool for students who have difficulty analyzing questions and locating answers.

In the Book QARs	In My Head QARs
Right There This answer **can be easily found** in the book. It is right there on page _____ .	**Author and You** This answer **will not be found in the story.** Readers use information given in the story along with what they already know on their own. *The answer is right here on page 4.* *Well, if that is true, then I think . . .* This is a higher-level question.
Think and Search This answer is in the story, but you need to **put together different story parts** to find it. The words for the question and the words for the answer are found in different parts of the story. *Here is the question on page 12. Let me see, I think I read more about this in Chapter 2.*	**On My Own** This answer will not be in the story. You can even answer the question without reading the story. This **answer comes from your own experiences and background.** *Ah Yes! I remember that once I . . .*

Figure 5.9 Raphael's Question-Answer-Relationship Chart. *Source*: From "Teaching Question Answer Relationships, Revisited," by T. E. Raphael, 1986, *The Reading Teacher, 39,* p. 519. Reprinted by permission of Taffy E. Raphael.

Visual Imagery

Visual imagery can also guide rereading (Gambrell & Bales, 1987). First, identify the part of text students are not comprehending. Before rereading, ask the students to consider what pictures come to mind as they read. They can tell about the pictures or draw them. Younger students may naturally want to draw pictures rather than provide a verbal picture. As students read and make pictures, you should help them to elaborate on particular ideas and provide a model for using visual imagery. Ask students to share their pictures and point out words and phrases in the text that helped them form specific mental images. If the students are unable to identify words and phrases that helped them draw their pictures, ask questions—why did you include trees, flowers, and grass in your picture, for instance. If they excluded important ideas, use your drawings to identify and explain the ideas they have ignored.

For older students, verbally describing the mental images they form as they read text may be preferable to drawing. Ask students to reread the problematic section and form a mental image of what is being presented in text. You will recall that Mrs. Owen asked Chantelle to do this during the reading of Arnold Lobel's story "Down the Hill."

Think-Alouds

Think-alouds are a powerful strategy that we present in a number of different ways throughout this textbook. Teachers often use think-alouds to demonstrate a new instructional strategy. In this case, the teacher models an expert's thinking by employing a particular strategy while reading. Recall that Mrs. Diener employed a think-aloud to demonstrate its use with student-designed questions during the K-W-L reading strategy. Bauman, Seifert-Kessell, and Jones (1993) have empirically demonstrated that think-alouds can also be used as an effective fix-up strategy for self-monitoring comprehension. Within their instructional program, Clark Canine–Super Reporter (CC/SR), students learn to self-monitor comprehension by asking themselves, "Is this making sense?" after reading a portion of text. After asking this question, they are then to think aloud what was going on in their heads while reading. It is the act of verbalizing their ideas aloud that helps students self-check their ability to construct meaning from text. The teacher demonstrates the process by reading a short portion of text and stopping and asking the question, Is this making sense? The teacher then reports aloud what the text meant. If the text didn't make sense, then students could employ a number of strategies such as using a question to guide rereading and employing visual imagery while rereading. In CC/SR, students can use think-alouds while reading to facilitate comprehension. Think-alouds, in this case, allow students to process the text at a deeper level (Craik & Lockhart, 1972), thus increasing comprehension. (For a more detailed account of this program, see Bauman, Seifer-Kessell, & Jones.)

Learning from Experience

Mrs. Rouleau, a fourth-grade teacher, demonstrates the thinking aloud process in the CC/SR program using Katherine Paterson's *The King's Equal* (pp. 5–6). As you read, ask yourself what Mrs. Rouleau does to illuminate her thinking and construction of inferences. Write your ideas in your journal.

 [Teacher reads and thinks aloud.] *"Many years ago in a country far away, an old king"*—does this make sense? Yes, this must be during the times of kings and queens and kingdoms, when King Arthur and Lady Guinevere lived—*"lay dying. Now the king was very wise and very good, and all the people loved him, so they were sad to know that he would soon leave them."* Does this make sense? Yes, I bet the people are worried that the next king may not be so kind and loving and they probably know something about the future king that makes them concerned and sad.

"But what made them even sadder was the knowledge that the king's son, Prince Raphael, would become their next ruler." Ahha! They are worried about the next king. Prince Raphael seems to be unkind—possibly mean. This seems true since the author tells us they were sadder about the king's eventual death because they knew the son's personality and traits. This is typical of fantasy—there are good and evil characters. And the king's son might be evil while the king is good. *"Prince Raphael was as rich and handsome as a prince should be. His father had assembled scholars from all over the world to teach him, so he was highly educated. The people should have been proud to have Raphael as their next king, but instead they were afraid."* Does this make sense? Sure—their fear must stem from his meanness and cruelty because we have learned that he must be wise since he is well educated. The people can't be worried that the prince would be stupid and make foolish decisions as the ruler.

Your Turn: Now that you have read this classroom dialogue, reconsider the question: What does Mrs. Rouleau do to illuminate her thinking and construction of inferences? Write your ideas in your journal.

Our Turn: In this short demonstration of the think-aloud process in CC/SR, Mrs. Rouleau talked about using prior knowledge and text information to make inferences. In the CC/SR model, teachers stop, ask the standard question, and then elaborate on their understanding. The procedure is slightly altered from the way Mrs. Diener demonstrated it in her modeling of the K-W-L, but the essence remains the same. You should adapt think-alouds to accommodate your teaching style and the needs of your students.

For students to learn the power of think-alouds, they will need to experiment with thinking aloud and receiving feedback from you and your peers. Placing students into dyads to take turns thinking aloud is one way to develop proficiency. You can then circulate among the dyads to provide additional feedback. At the end of the lesson, you can ask students their reactions to thinking aloud and if it helped them with the targeted skill.

Suspending Judgment

Another fix-up strategy students need to practice is suspending judgment. Many times, for example, a new term is introduced in text and a clear definition is not developed within the sentence. The reader should continue reading, searching for additional clues to provide clarity to resolve the comprehension problem. Frequently authors present additional information later in the text to clarify the unknown concept.

Encourage students to read ahead when they are unsure about word meaning, a story event, or a newly presented concept. As they read ahead, they should be seeking information to develop clarity. If additional information is not provided or comprehension cannot be constructed, the reader needs to stop and use other tools such as asking a question and rereading, using a dictionary, or asking for assistance.

Asking for Assistance

The most obvious fix-up strategy, asking for assistance, should not be overlooked and can be quite beneficial, unless it is used as a crutch that impedes independence. Students should look to their peers as well as other adults to receive help.

Reciprocal Teaching

Palincsar and Brown (1984) have combined several reading strategies to facilitate the comprehension of learning-disabled students and have labeled the strategy Reciprocal Teaching. The four strategies are predicting, summarizing, asking questions, and suspending judgment. By having learned to predict, summarize, ask questions, and suspend judgment, students have increased their comprehension. Through the use of the direct-explanation model (Duffy & Roehler, 1987) and students taking turns as teachers, students have learned how to effectively use these four learning strategies.

To implement Reciprocal Teaching, students learn each strategy, such as prediction, before they are expected to serve as a teacher and apply all four strategies. To teach each strategy, the teacher follows the steps of the direct-explanation model. Once the students are introduced to the strategies, they take turns as the teacher and demonstrate their ability to make predictions about a particular part of text, ask questions of students in the group formed to discuss this portion of text, summarize the text that has been read, and suspend judgment by pointing out areas that need further clarification. To use this approach, form small groups so students can experience the role of teacher and have active participation within a small group. Have students participate as student teachers in each of the groups so they can receive additional guidance and modeling and thereby increase their strategic reading abilities.

Palincsar (1984) provides an exemplary small-group dialogue of a Reciprocal Teaching lesson. In the first part, the teacher demonstrates the use of the four learning strategies. In the second part, the teacher chooses a student named Jim to be the student teacher. The adult teacher provides guidance, feedback, and elaboration.

> *Teacher:* The title of this story is "Genius with Feathers." Let's have some predictions. I will begin by guessing that this story will be about birds that are very smart. Why do I say that?
>
> *First Student:* Because a genius is someone really smart.
>
> *Teacher:* But why would I say 'birds that are very smart'?
>
> *Second Student:* Because they have feathers.
>
> *Teacher:* That's right. Birds are the only animals that have feathers. Let's predict now the kind of information you might read about very smart birds.
>
> *Third Student:* What kinds of birds?
>
> *Teacher:* Good question. What kinds would you guess are very smart?
>
> *Third Student:* Parrots or blue jays.
>
> *First Student:* A cockatoo like the bird on *Baretta*.
>
> *Teacher:* What other information would you want to know? [No response from students.]
>
> *Teacher:* I would like to know what these birds do that is so smart. Any ideas?

Second Student: Some birds talk.

Fourth Student: They can fly.

Teacher: That's an interesting one. As smart as people are, they can't fly. Well, let's read this first section now and see how many of our predictions were right. I will be the teacher for this section. [All read the section silently.]

Teacher: Who is the genius with feathers?

First Student: Crows.

Teacher: That's right. We were correct in our prediction that this story would be about birds, but we didn't correctly guess which kind of bird, did we? My summary of the first section would be that it describes the clever things that crows do, which make them seem quite intelligent. Is there anything else I should add to my summary?

First Student: How they steal corn?

Teacher: That's a detail that describes one of the ways in which they are clever. For our summary we will not include details. I think I found a word that needs clarification. What does resourceful mean?

All students: [No response.]

Teacher: If I say that you are a resourceful person, I mean that you are able to deal with problems and difficulties easily. Being resourceful is another way in which crows are intelligent. I would like to make a prediction now. The section's last sentence says, "One major reason they have mastered survival against heavy odds is their amazing communication system." How do you think crows communicate with one another?

All students: *Caw-caw.*

First Student: With a special song.

Teacher: Let's read on. Who will be the teacher for this section? [Dialogue follows that shows the student Jim leading the discussion and the teacher providing corrective feedback.]

Jim: How do crows communicate with one another?

Teacher: Good question! You picked right up on our prediction that this is about the way crows communicate. Who do you choose to answer the question?

Jim: Barbara.

Barbara: Crows have built-in radar and a relay system.

Jim: That's a good part of it. The answer I wanted was how they relay the messages from one crow to the other crow.

Teacher: Summarize now.

Jim: This is about how crows have developed a system.

Teacher: Of what? You must include the whole main idea.

Jim: Of communication.

Teacher: That's right. The paragraph goes on to give examples of how they use pitch and changes in interval, but these are supporting details. The main idea is that crows communicate through a relay system. Jim? (pp. 149–151)

The student teacher continues with the remaining learning strategies.

Reciprocal teaching takes a large amount of instructional time, and it is best suited for those who experience difficulties with comprehending text because they don't self-monitor and they lack fix-up strategies.

WHAT MODEL IS USEFUL FOR TEACHING STRATEGIC READING?

Gradual Release of Responsibility Model

The reading strategies we have discussed in the two previous sections teach students to be strategic readers. You guide reading and learning initially and gradually give this responsibility to each individual reader. This means that each strategy should be developed using a variety of different reading selections. Pearson and Gallagher (1983) have called this teaching and learning process "the Gradual Release of Responsibility Model of Instruction" (see Figure 5.10). This model specifies the proportion of responsibility of teachers and students in the learning of particular comprehension strategies.

When introducing a new comprehension strategy, you need to model or demonstrate how readers use the strategy to understand and learn from text. To illustrate how the strategy is to be used, explain what information should be selected and when the particular strategy can be used most effectively. Which goals can best be satisfied by using this strategy? Is the instructional strategy more appropriate for understanding and remembering information for a test, or is it more generally useful to understanding and enjoying text? Give students guided practice, as Mrs. Parker did as she taught the students the DR-TA. Let students practice using the reading strategy and continually provide feedback.

Once students have shown that they need little or no guidance to employ a given

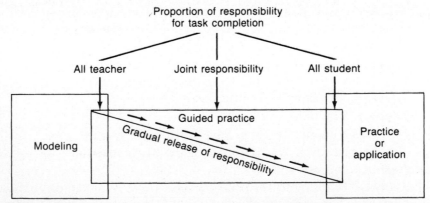

Figure 5.10 The Gradual Release of Responsibility Model of Instruction. *Source:* P.D. Pearson and M.C. Gallagher, 1983, "The Instruction of Reading Comprehension," *Contemporary Educational Psychology, 8,* Orlando, FL: Academic Press, Inc. Reprinted with permission.

strategy, encourage them to use it independently and adapt it to their individual needs. Encourage students to discuss how they have adapted and/or combined strategies to increase their learning. Provide occasional review and prompting when students show they are not understanding text.

The kind of closely guided instruction demonstrated in the classroom dialogues is necessary in the initial phases of learning a new strategy, when students need modeling, guided practice with a variety of appropriate texts, and feedback. As students become proficient with a strategy, however, instructional time can be cut back significantly and students can be encouraged to use their own questions or predictions to guide silent reading of an entire selection. Students need time to experiment with guiding and monitoring their own reading. In the next sections, we suggest how to guide strategy instruction with different types of readers.

HOW DO YOU ADDRESS STUDENTS' SPECIAL NEEDS?

In this section we explore the reading needs of special populations. We address the needs of beginning readers, developing readers, less able readers, and ESL students.

Beginning Readers

Teacher-guided reading instruction is essential for beginning readers, who might otherwise become confused and frustrated with word identification and comprehension. The two areas in which you need to focus to help beginning readers become strategic readers are monitoring of word identification as it affects comprehension and constructing meaning of text. With challenging selections, much of the reading selection needs to be guided with strategies like DR-TA or Herringbone. Students also need numerous opportunities to read and enjoy easy text so they can practice the reading strategies they have learned during instruction.

Developing Readers

Developing readers in grades three through eight require less teacher-guided reading instruction than do beginning readers. In most cases, you should provide guided instruction while students are learning a new strategy and less as your students become familiar with the strategy. You might guide the first portion of a long reading selection, for example, and then assign the remainder to be read independently or in pairs. During subsequent instruction, you may wish to lead a discussion about the selection to provide feedback and to evaluate students' comprehension.

With DR-TA, for example, you would provide the title or first paragraph of a selection to your students to initiate predictions and discussion, then have students read a small portion of text to confirm or refute the predictions, and check students' comprehension in the discussion that follows by having students retell part of the story. Ask students to make another set of predictions, questioning to make sure these are logically based, and then have students revise their predictions as they read the next section of text independently.

With easier text selections, you might help students establish a goal for reading during prereading and then have them self-monitor their reading for the entire selection. Provide feedback through a follow-up discussion.

Less Able Readers

Teacher-guided reading of new text is essential for less able readers, including those with learning disabilities. Typically, these children need your support throughout the text, and selections should be short and varied. Assigning a second, related, but somewhat easier text for independent reading after an instruction-intense guided reading period often helps these readers to develop strategic skills of their own. But these students also need to choose their own selections to read and apply reading strategies. They need to read great amounts of material to increase their reading abilities.

ESL Students

ESL students benefit from reading-strategy instruction that facilitates their text comprehension (Chamot & O'Malley, 1994). Activating prior knowledge and vocabulary about the text topic, establishing a plan for reading, self-monitoring comprehension, and self-evaluating learning are important areas to develop with these students. It is particularly important that you guide ESL students' reading of expository text since they often lack the vocabulary knowledge of content-area disciplines. Teaching these strategies can help to ensure that ESL students have equal access to knowledge by keeping pace with their grade-level peers as they receive instruction in different content areas. We also recommend using literature that is appropriate for the student's age, interest, and cultural background to help ESL students learn how to apply these important instructional strategies as they read independently. Choose literature that uses pictures, graphs, diagrams, and photographs to illustrate and develop important concepts rather than limiting these to printed text alone. Give ESL students opportunities to work in small groups with native-English speakers to apply reading strategies while reading and learning from text. Peer discussion and active involvement help ESL students understand and learn from narrative and expository texts, especially if each student has a specific role in completing the assignment.

All Readers

Teacher-guided instruction is essential for most readers who are encountering difficult materials and new genres, for which they may have inadequate experiences or prior knowledge, or in which a large number of new concepts or vocabulary words may be introduced. Such intensive instruction uses much instructional time, however, so you need to balance difficult materials with easier ones to achieve a balance of instruction and independent reading.

SUMMARY

Research and theory indicate that the process of constructing meaning, self-monitoring, and evaluating comprehension depends on developmental level, and that more able readers are better at this process than are less able readers. But research also indicates that explicit instruction of specific strategies enables students to become strategic readers. However, students need to recognize when to use a specific strategy and how to achieve success when they use it.

In this chapter, we emphasized the importance of teaching students to become strategic readers. Strategic readers make decisions about the purpose or goal for reading a text. As they read, strategic readers construct meaning and integrate prior knowledge and experiences as well as self-monitor comprehension and apply fix-up strategies as needed. And finally, strategic readers assess whether they have accomplished their purpose or goal.

Students benefit from learning a variety of reading strategies to accommodate their different goals and needs. The reading strategies we have suggested do address a variety of reading goals and needs. The strategies are flexible, and most can be used with a variety of ages and materials, including fiction and nonfiction.

Strategic reading is best taught during contextual reading in which students receive teacher-guided instruction. In this context, students can be taught how to plan, construct, and self-monitor comprehension as well as evaluate their plans and outcomes for reading. Daily, guided instruction of contextual reading provides opportunities for you to assess, provide feedback, and adjust instruction. Students need to use a new strategy with many different reading selections. Teacher guidance is gradually phased out so students can strategically plan and learn from text with the ultimate goal of becoming independent readers.

In the Field

1. Choose an expository article and identify the predominant text structure. Select one of the suggested strategies and use it with several students to help them comprehend as they read text. In your journal, describe the lesson and explain how you facilitated and mediated instruction.

2. Plan a DR-TA. Choose a narrative or expository selection and identify specific points at which to stop within the text for discussion. Think about the general questions that promote prediction and reasoning. Implement the DR-TA with a small group of students. In your journal, write a description of the lesson. Reflect on the questions you employed. Did they facilitate students' discussion, thinking, and reasoning? Would you do anything different in designing and implementing the DR-TA? If so, explain.

3. Choose a picture book, a chapter from a trade book such as Beverly Cleary's *Ramona, the Brave,* or a short story and develop a set of story clues for the Story Impressions strategy. With a small group of students, use these clues to help students

write a hypothetical summary. Read the text to compare the summary to the author's story. Discuss the story by comparing and contrasting the summary to the actual story. Critique your lesson by considering the following questions: Did the strategy help students set a purpose and understand the story? Did the students critically evaluate the authors' development of the story? What other behaviors did you observe?

Portfolio Suggestion

Select from your journal two examples of your responses to Pause and Reflect, Learning from Experience, or In the Field. Write a brief evaluation of your work. Explain how this chapter has affected your thinking about planning and implementing strategic reading instruction.

For Further Reading

Bauman, J. F., Jones, L. A., & Seifert-Kessell, N. (1993). Using think alouds to enhance children's comprehension monitoring abilities. *The Reading Teacher, 47,* 184–193.

Davey, B. (1983). Think aloud—Modeling the cognitive processes of reading comprehension. *Journal of Reading, 27,* 44–47.

Duffy, G. G. (1993). Rethinking strategy instruction: Four teachers' development and their low achievers' understandings. *Elementary School Journal, 93,* 231–247.

Herrmann, B. A. (1988). Two approaches for helping poor readers become more strategic. *The Reading Teacher, 42,* 24–28.

Maria, K., & Hathaway, K. (1993). Using think alouds with teachers to develop awareness of reading strategies. *Journal of Reading, 37,* 12–19.

McGee, L., & Richgels, D. J. (1985). Teaching expository text structure to elementary students. *The Reading Teacher, 38,* 739–748.

Palincsar, A. S., & Brown, A. L. (1986). Interactive teaching to promote independent learning from text. *The Reading Teacher, 39,* 771–777.

Pearson, P. D. (1985). Changing the face of reading comprehension. *The Reading Teacher, 38,* 724–738.

Raphael, T. E. (1982). Question-answering strategies for children. *The Reading Teacher, 35,* 186–190.

Schmitt, M. C. (1990). A questionnaire to measure children's awareness of strategic reading processes. *The Reading Teacher, 43,* 454–476.

CHAPTER 6

Making the Reading and Writing Connection: Consolidating and Extending Students' Comprehension

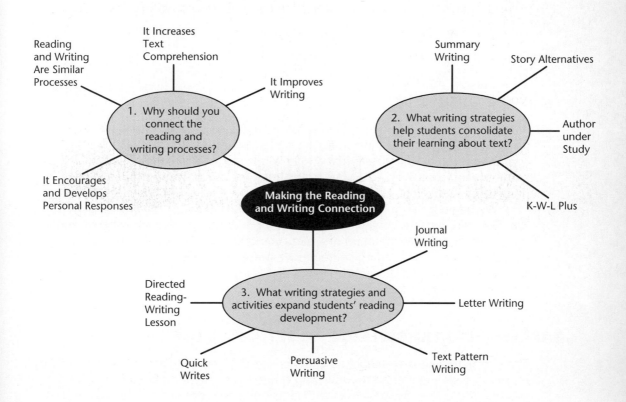

Reading and Writing Are Similar Processes

It Increases Text Comprehension

It Improves Writing

It Encourages and Develops Personal Responses

1. Why should you connect the reading and writing processes?

Summary Writing

Story Alternatives

Author under Study

K-W-L Plus

2. What writing strategies help students consolidate their learning about text?

Making the Reading and Writing Connection

Directed Reading-Writing Lesson

Quick Writes

Persuasive Writing

3. What writing strategies and activities expand students' reading development?

Journal Writing

Letter Writing

Text Pattern Writing

▼ CHAPTER GOALS FOR THE READER

To understand the rationale for connecting the reading and writing processes

To use writing as a way to consolidate students' comprehension of text

To use writing as a way to expand students' meaning of text

▼ CHAPTER OVERVIEW

In this chapter, we provide a rationale for connecting the reading and writing processes and present writing strategies and activities to consolidate students' comprehension of a particular text and enhance students' reading development of narration and exposition. The suggested strategies and activities cover a variety of grade levels and different learners' needs.

We begin by exploring the natural connections between reading and writing. We then demonstrate how you can use writing as a tool to conclude and extend the meaning and interpretation of a particular text. To accomplish this task, we connect the strategic reading strategies we presented in chapter 5 to writing strategies that extend students' thinking and learning of text and discuss additional writing strategies that extend students' thinking and learning of text.

◆ TAPPING PRIOR KNOWLEDGE TO SET A PURPOSE

Think back to your own schooling experiences. Did you write after you read text? If so, was the writing limited to answering questions and writing book reports? Have you had more recent experiences with classrooms that present different writing experiences from those you experienced as a student? Consider the chapter overview and your own schooling experiences to identify your purpose for reading this chapter. List those in your journal.

WHY SHOULD YOU CONNECT
THE READING AND WRITING PROCESSES?

In this section, we explore four reasons for connecting reading and writing instruction. Reading and writing share many similarities and thus provide a natural link for teaching and learning. Writing about what you have read can also increase text comprehension. It can also provide opportunities for personal response and thus create active and interested readers. Moreover, reading and analyzing other authors' works can improve students' writing.

Reading and Writing Are Similar Processes

The cognitive processes underlying reading and writing have many commonalities although some differences do exist. An obvious difference is that the writer is faced with a blank page whereas the reader is faced with a printed page, but the important similarity lies in the fact that both readers and writers are constructing meaning. As Wittrock (1984) points out, readers and writers "create meanings by building relations between the text and what they know, believe, and experience" (p. 77). Likewise, Tierney and Pearson (1983) talk about readers and writers as composers who are both involved in (1) planning that includes setting goals and considering prior knowledge, (2) drafting a text that focuses on constructing meaning, (3) revising that includes refining and self-monitoring meaning, and (4) aligning or accommodating meaning from text with the readers' or writers' conceptual understanding.

From this perspective, meaning is constructed by the reader and the writer. Meaning does not reside in the print; it resides in the mind. For the reader, meaning occurs while reading. The reader's experiences, feelings, and purposes, for example, affect the meaning the reader composes from text. For the writer, meaning also occurs while writing. Similarly, the writer's experiences, feelings, and purposes affect the text the writer composes. Both reader and writer have expectations guiding the composing processes. Once these expectations or hypotheses are not met, the reader or writer revises by rereading or rewriting. As Rosenblatt (1989) points out, "an unexpected juxtaposition of words, the challenge of a new context or an unsettling question may open up new lines of thought or feeling" (p. 165) for both reader and writer. From this perspective, reading and writing are both learning processes. From their own words, writers discover new ideas and thereby learn from their own writing (Emig, 1983), and, similarly, readers learn while reading another author's text.

Although the basic reading and writing processes are similar, the frequency, sequence, and use of particular strategies do vary (Langer, 1986). The focus and perspective of the strategy, such as revising, do differ. Writers, for instance, spend much time engaged in revision to succinctly state and convey a particular perspective and meaning. The amount of time spent in rereading—checking the use of words and structure of sentences—is shorter, and rereading doesn't require the precise and exact wording that is needed for writing.

Reading and writing are related but not reciprocal processes. Because of this relationship, students benefit from instruction that connects reading and writing and

How are reading and writing incorporated in the teaching of science?

examines these differences and similarities, rather than teaching reading and writing as separate and mutually exclusive processes (McGinley & Tierney, 1989). Students can use the similarities in the composing processes of reading and writing to enhance their literacy development.

It Increases Text Comprehension

There are many benefits to linking reading and writing instruction. Writing can improve students' text comprehension and learning. It causes students to generate meaning from text by developing relationships between text ideas and their own topical knowledge (Wittrock, 1984). By writing, students focus, select, and organize important text information and also integrate their own ideas with text.

Summary writing, for example, has been shown to be an effective tool to increase comprehension and learning. Taylor and Berkowitz (1980) found that sixth graders who wrote one-sentence summaries of expository text had better comprehension than those who read and used study guides, read and answered questions, or simply read the text. In another study Doctorow, Wittrock, and Marks (1978) found that sixth graders exhibited the best comprehension if there were text headings and students wrote one-sentence summaries after each paragraph. A review of the reading and writing research also indicates that "almost all studies that used writing activities or exercises specifically to improve reading comprehension or retention of information in instructional material found significant gains" (Stotsky, 1983, p. 636).

As students write, they discover how well they understand text. Writing about a selection causes students to think about a particular topic, pick out relevant text information, integrate prior knowledge, and organize thinking effectively. Students who accomplish this task discover their control over reading and develop a better understanding of text. Such writing can serve as a diagnostic tool as well, since failure to identify the main idea or to provide supporting information can highlight areas in which students need support.

It Encourages and Develops Personal Response

Writing also encourages students to reveal their personal responses to text. Because personal response tends to be open ended, writing frees students to reflect on text and develop more personalized understandings. Students often find characters, for example, with whom they can identify or situations similar to their own. By writing personal responses, readers develop a better understanding of their own thoughts and feelings. Putting thoughts on paper causes students to reflect on and reread text, and the cyclical process of rereading and rewriting can improve both self-expression and comprehension.

It Improves Writing

Reading can improve students' writing. Carson (1990) found that reading rather than grammar instruction and writing exercises improved students' writing. Reading serves as a model for writing; it can be used to prepare students for writing, which is important for all learners but especially for those whose first language is not English (Farnan, Flood, & Lapp, 1994). Moreover, the reading and writing processes are similar in nature for both first- and second-language learners (Grabe, 1991). By integrating these similar processes, all students strengthen both reading and writing development.

WHAT WRITING STRATEGIES HELP STUDENTS CONSOLIDATE THEIR THINKING ABOUT TEXT?

In this section, we connect the reading strategies presented in chapter 5 to writing strategies and activities that help students consolidate text comprehension. The reading strategies from chapter 5 included the Herringbone and graphic organizers focusing on teacher-generated questions, the DR-TA (Directed Reading-Thinking Activity) focusing on student-generated questions, Story Impressions, and K-W-L (Know, Want, Learn). We begin connecting reading and writing by recalling how in chapter 5 the Herringbone strategy was shown to be easily linked to summary writing. We then show how graphic organizers can also be linked to summary writing. The natural integration of reading to writing continues with the linking of the DR-TA to story alternatives, Story Impressions to Author under Study, and K-W-L to K-W-L Plus.

Summary Writing

To guide students' thinking and learning of text, we suggested teaching students to use the Herringbone strategy with narration and graphic organizers with exposition. These two strategies enable students to use text structure to understand and learn important ideas from text.

In chapter 5, Mrs. Santo used the Herringbone strategy to access important information about the story plot. On each bone, students told about a particular story element such as characters, setting, and problem. Mrs. Santo concluded the lesson by using the information on the herringbone to summarize the story. Writing summaries facilitated text comprehension by organizing important information from the story.

Summary writing is also an appropriate and effective tool for understanding and learning exposition. With the use of graphic organizers such as those suggested in chapter 5, students can use text structure to organize and write summaries. These tools make summarizing more concrete; this is especially important for second-language learners, who find the syntactic and semantic features of language to be complex and challenging, as well as for less able readers, who need specific strategies to comprehend text.

Consider the time line Mrs. Houston employed with the article "Deciding Who Shall Come." In a follow-up lesson, Mrs. Houston decided to use the time line to help her students create a summary. She directed her students to review the time line to discover what happened to immigration policies from the 1700s to the late 1900s. In this particular text, the time-order text pattern helps students recognize that immigration policies have changed over the years. The time line highlights change so that Mrs. Houston can ask, "Why were changes occurring?" At this point, Mrs. Houston suggests they use this question while rereading text to explain the reasons for policy changes. The guided rereading allows students to recognize cause and effect as an underlying text pattern within the time-order text structure. As students note the causes and effects for policy changes, Mrs. Houston can write the cause below each time period on the time line. With this added information, Mrs. Houston uses the time line to model her thinking as she composes the topic sentence: "Immigration policies have changed since the birth of our country." She follows this statement by using details from the time line to explain the reasons for policy change. The lesson continues by asking the students to use the outline to provide additional details for the continuation of policy changes. Sentences are then formed to complete the summary.

Mrs. Houston may need to model this lesson a few times with other expository articles and utilizing different text structures, since summary writing is not an easily developed skill. Support can also be provided by having students working with partners to write summaries from graphic organizers. Summary writing takes time to develop, but it has been shown to be an effective learning tool to remember and access important text-based information.

Story Alternatives

To guide students' thinking while reading, we suggested, in chapter 5, using the Directed Reading-Thinking Activity. Using the title and text, students construct meaning by predicting, confirming, reflecting, and revising their hypotheses while reading. In the DR-TA, if students are reading fiction, they are paying particular attention to story development, since they are comparing their predictions to the author's. Frequently, you will hear students say they prefer their ending or story development rather than the author's choices. These comments provide a natural opportunity to rewrite the story. The author's story provides a scaffold for thinking about a particular problem and ways to resolve the problem that are unsatisfactory to the reader. The students have a framework to experiment and think about story development. They are invited to revise and share their thinking with others. Do their ideas work as well as the author's? As they revise, they must consider story elements that affect story development. Characters, setting, and problems affect logical story development as well as reader interest. Therefore, logic and interest are important elements to consider when writing story alternatives.

To engage students in providing story alternatives, discuss the author's use of story elements such as setting, character development, character's actions, and problems within the story as compared to the students' ideas while reading the story. The following questions can stimulate students' thinking prior to writing:

How does this character affect the telling of the story?

If this character's personality, appearance, and actions changed, would the story change? If so, how?

Does the setting affect the story events? If so, how?

How do the story events affect the ending?

If the story events changed, would the conclusion change?

We read stories because they are interesting and stimulating; how would you make this story even more appealing?

Do we know enough about the characters?

Would a twist or change in events make the story more interesting?

This is a sampling of questions that can cause students to respond to text and create ideas for rethinking and revising. These types of questions can stimulate class discussion. The purpose is to analyze story elements such as characters, setting, and problem to help students recognize that stories need to be logical and believable within a particular genre such as fantasy or realistic fiction.

Besides creating a coherent story, stories must arouse readers' interests. As students write a different version of the story, these writers need to consider their audience, and this naturally leads to incorporating sharing and receiving feedback from classmates who read the story. Writing story alternatives naturally causes students to engage in a process-writing approach. Additional revision and sharing seem natural and can be included depending on students' interest, commitment, and increased learning in their particular story alternatives.

You may have used the DR-TA to read a nonfiction text in which students used subheadings to predict the information the author included. In chapter 5, we suggested that students use a T-Chart to write a prediction for each subheading on the left-hand side of the T and write the important information the author included on the right-hand side of the T-Chart. Use the T-Chart to write a one- to two-sentence summary about the important information for each subheading. Guide students by modeling and thinking aloud to demonstrate how you organized and composed the summary.

Author under Study

In chapter 5, Mrs. Owen employed the Story Impressions strategy to guide and monitor her students' comprehension of the story "Down the Hill" by Arnold Lobel. As they concluded the story, the second graders were able to revise their predictive summary to conform to the events that actually took place in the story and were ready to extend their thinking beyond the specific story events. For postreading instruction, Mrs. Owen wanted her students to become familiar with Arthur Lobel's other Frog and Toad books and decided to incorporate the writing activity Author under Study.

Author under Study (Dinan, 1977) involves reading many books by the same author and having students discuss their similarities and differences. During discussion, students analyze the author's writing so that they learn the author's craft. Students then dictate information based on their discussion about the author's style, setting, characters, and plot, and this dictation becomes part of a Big Book about authors. The students conclude this activity by writing their own stories using the author's works as a springboard into their own writing.

Author under Study was used to encourage Mrs. Owen's second graders to develop a greater understanding of character by reading and studying all of Arnold Lobel's books about Frog and Toad. These two characters have defined personalities; their appearances, thoughts, and behaviors are depicted consistently and, consequently, are very predictable. Understanding character development can help Mrs. Owen's second graders comprehend and enjoy these books and extend their thinking by composing their own Frog and Toad adventures.

Mrs. Owen selects several Frog and Toad books by Arnold Lobel, displays them in the classroom, and encourages her students to read them independently or in dyads. As they read, she suggests that they note similarities and differences between Frog and Toad as they participate in adventures.

Mrs. Owen begins Author under Study by reading aloud and discussing the similarities and differences between Frog and Toad. She uses some of the following questions to encourage discussion:

What does Frog look like?

What does Frog like to do?

What kinds of things does Frog say?

What does Toad look like?

What does Toad like to do?

What does Toad dislike?

What kinds of things does Toad say?

Which character would like to try new things? Explain.

How does Frog treat other characters?

How does Toad treat other characters?

What words would you use to describe Frog?

What words would you use to describe Toad?

What makes Frog an interesting character?

What makes Toad an interesting character?

Would you like to be Frog's friend? Why or why not?

Would you like to be Toad's friend? Why or why not?

As the students note similarities and differences during the discussion, Mrs. Owen places their responses in the Frog and Toad Big Book.

Before the students write their own Frog and Toad adventures, they discuss the parts of a story—beginning, middle, and end. To provide support, Mrs. Owen lets students choose a partner to write a new adventure for Frog and Toad. For the next week, the second graders write and share their stories. Mrs. Owen observes that her students reread, change words, and often refer back to the Big Book about Arnold Lobel as well as to the Frog and Toad books as they write. Before publishing their adventures, she asks the second graders to edit, confer, and make book covers. The activity concludes with students reading their books to the kindergarten class and placing them in the school library so others can read these new authors' books.

K-W-L Plus

In chapter 4, we introduced the instructional strategy, K-W-L. Students are given a guide sheet with three columns. The first column is labeled K for what I know about a topic. The second column is labeled W for what I want to learn, and the third is labeled L for what I learned from reading. During prereading, students list and categorize information they already know about a topic they will be reading. They ask questions about information they want to learn from the text in the W column. And, in chapter 5, we described how students should use their questions to guide their reading. In the last phase, students are to write in the L column what they learned from text. Typically, this is a numbered list of items with no organizational structure.

Carr and Ogle (1987) have added a writing component to this strategy, known as the K-W-L Plus. The students organize the learned ideas by using a web, a graphic organizer, to serve as an outline for writing a summary or report. To initiate the Plus portion, direct students to review their list of ideas reported in the L column and to group together common ideas and identify an appropriate label for each grouping. Often the text selection helps students identify appropriate categories; that is, text subheadings become the different categories. Once the categories are derived, ask the students to review the information they knew before they read the text and place it within the appropriate category. Place the title or main topic in the center of the web. Each category is attached to the core, and the supporting information is added to the appropriate subcategory. The web's center becomes the introductory paragraph of the report. Each category and its details become a paragraph in the report. If there are six categories, then there are six supporting paragraphs. To complete the report, the students write a concluding paragraph by pulling together and condensing the essential ideas from all the paragraphs.

The web replaces the traditional outline that a writer uses to organize information in order to write a report. Students can develop a web more easily than a formal outline, and this appears to be because of its simple structure. With outlines, students often bog down in Roman numerals and indentations; it's the form rather than the content that creates confusion. In the subsequent section, we learn how Mrs. Diener helps her fifth graders use a K-W-L Plus as an extension to K-W-L.

Learning from Experience

We divide this Learning from Experience into three parts. First, consider Mrs. Diener's implementation of the L or learned portion of the K-W-L strategy. In this part, Mrs. Diener guides discussion to help students use the text pattern to organize and consolidate their comprehension, thus preparing them to organize this information into a written report. As you read, consider how Mrs. Diener organizes students' thinking and learning about preparing for disasters.

Uses subheading

Mrs. Diener: Okay, we've done the K and the W parts of the K-W-L. Now we have to do the L part—what we have learned from text. To make it a little easier, let's report what we've learned section by section, starting with the first section, earthquakes. Who would like to start? Lauren, what have you learned about earthquakes?

Lauren: You should go under beds, desks, and tables. [Mrs. Diener writes Lauren's response in the L column.]

Reasoning

Mrs. Diener: Why would you do that?

Lauren: For protection.

Mrs. Diener: Jose, what did you learn about earthquakes?

Jose: Stay away from windows, mirrors, chimneys, dishes, and lights. [Mrs. Diener writes Jose's response in the L column.]

Mrs. Diener: Why should you do that?

Jose: Because they may fall and hurt you.

Uses subheading

Mrs. Diener: Let's go on to the next part, about lightning. Vanessa, tell us what you've learned about lightning.

Vanessa: You should stay away from wire fences.

Mrs. Diener: [Mrs. Diener writes Vanessa's response in the L column.] When should you stay away from wire fences?

Vanessa: When it's lightning.

Uses subheading

Mrs. Diener: Let's go on to volcanoes. What did you learn about volcanoes?

Fifth graders: [No response.]

Mrs. Diener: What can you tell me about volcanoes?

Fifth graders: [No response.]

Identifies
inconsistency

Mrs. Diener: This is real difficult because the author has done something real different here. When you read about earthquakes and you read about lightning, you were able to give me information about what?

Lauren: Preparing for a disaster.

Mrs. Diener: Did the author tell you how to prepare for volcanic eruptions?

Fifth graders: [No response.]

Text lookbacks

Mrs. Diener: What does the author say about volcanic eruptions? Reread this section and find out. [The fifth graders silently read this section.]

Duke: It tells about when they happened.

Feedback

Mrs. Diener: Yes, the author doesn't tell us what we should be doing when a disaster occurs. The author doesn't follow the same pattern. Here is the problem and these are the ways to resolve it. Because the author didn't follow this same recurring pattern, it was harder for you to remember information about volcanoes. What should the author have told us in this section? Lorenzo.

Lorenzo: Tell us what we should do when a volcano erupts.

Mrs. Diener: Good, Lorenzo. Let's proceed to the next section, tornadoes. [Mrs. Diener continues instruction until all subsections of the article are completed.]

Your Turn: Now that you've read the classroom dialogue, reconsider: How does Mrs. Diener organize students' thinking and learning about the text "Preparing for Disasters"? In your journal, write your response before comparing it to ours.

Our Turn: Mrs. Diener demonstrated how students can use subheadings to easily and coherently report ideas they have learned from text. When the fifth graders were unable to report learned information about volcanoes, Mrs. Diener asked them to practice strategic reading by using the text lookbacks strategy and reread this section of text to help them recognize "inconsiderate" text—that is, text that does not follow the same predictable pattern, which can interfere with students' comprehension. These fifth graders were unable to respond even though they reread the text, and this gave Mrs. Diener the opportunity to alert students to their dependency on patterns in text and how the organization facilitates their understanding and learning from text.

During instruction, Mrs. Diener frequently asked students to explain why people should do certain things during a disaster to use the text pattern the author employed to highlight important information. The following day, Mrs. Diener introduces the K-W-L Plus. As you read, note how she helps students use K-W-L Plus to organize the information they learned from reading this text.

Explains
procedure
and its
value

Mrs. Diener: On Wednesday, we completed the L portion of the K-W-L. You told me what you learned from reading the article "Prepare for Disaster." What we are going to do today is make a web, like a spider's web, from the information we've learned and use it to help us organize our writing a report about being prepared for different natural disasters. What a spider does is sit in the middle of her web—she's the main focus. She builds strands around her to catch her prey. What we are going to do is take the main topic of this text and put that in the middle of the web and build strands or supports to related subtopics to help us develop an organized report or write a good report. Read the information in the L or learned column. As you read, try to determine the main idea. What is the main focus of this article? That's what we want to put in the middle of our web. [Mrs. Diener draws a circle to represent the middle of the spiderweb.]

Fifth graders: [No response.]

Mrs. Diener: Does the title of the article provide any clues?

Mavis: Safety for disasters.

Feedback   *Mrs. Diener:* You have the right idea. Does the author only present safe places to go during disasters?

Fifth graders: [No response.]

Guides thinking   *Mrs. Diener:* What does it mean to prepare for something?

Duke: To know what to do.

Guides thinking   *Mrs. Diener:* Good. The author doesn't limit herself to telling us about safe places during a disaster, but she also tells us what to do during a disaster so we can be safe. So in the middle of the web I'm going to write the main topic, preparing for disasters. [Mrs. Diener writes the main topic on the chalkboard. See Figure 6.1 for the completed web.] This is the focus of the article—how we can prepare for various disasters. The problem is the disaster, and we can solve this problem by being prepared. Now what we want to do is draw a line from the web's core to show the types of disasters and how we can prepare for them. What is one type of disaster that we learned about? Vanessa.

Vanessa: Earthquakes.

Guides thinking   *Mrs. Diener:* [Mrs. Diener writes *earthquakes* on the chalkboard and connects it to the middle of the web.] Since we have identified one of the subtopics, let's put all the individual pieces of information that we've learned about earthquakes around this subtopic. We need to select specific information about preparing for earthquakes. We have some other information about earthquakes that might not fit under that category. Skim through the L column and see if you can find one idea that tells how we can be prepared for earthquakes.

Jordan: Don't take elevators. [Mrs. Diener writes this information on the chalkboard and attaches it to the subtopic of earthquakes.]

Mrs. Diener: That would be one way to prepare or be safe from a disaster.

Kelly: You can protect yourself by going under beds, desks, and tables. [Mrs. Diener writes this idea on the chalkboard and attaches it to the subtopic of earthquakes.]

Mrs. Diener: That's another strand that relates back to earthquakes. Lauren, do you have an idea?

Lauren: Stay away from windows, mirrors, chimneys, dishes, and lights. [Mrs. Diener writes this idea on the chalkboard and attaches it to the subtopic of earthquakes.]

Mrs. Diener: Anything else that is specific information pertaining to preparing for earthquakes?

Fifth graders: [No response.]

Extends learning   *Mrs. Diener:* Well, we have three pieces of information. As you write a report on preparing for disasters, you may or may not find that this is enough information. We'll have to see when we turn this into a report. What might you do, if that's not enough information? Duke.

Duke: Go to an encyclopedia.

Mrs. Diener: Lorenzo, where else?

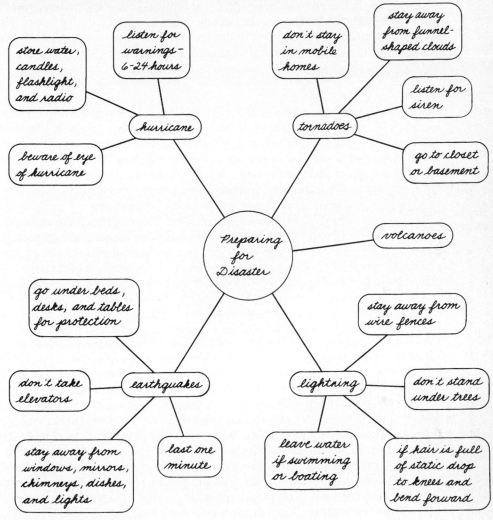

Figure 6.1 K-W-L Plus Web

Lorenzo: Books about earthquakes or about the other disasters we've read about.

Mrs. Diener: Good, Lorenzo. [Mrs. Diener continues to have the fifth graders web the different types of disasters until they identify all the subtopics and their related information.]

Your Turn: In your journal, explain how Mrs. Diener used the K-W-L Plus to help students organize information they learned about disasters.

Our Turn: Mrs. Diener uses the analogy of a spiderweb to promote a simple organization for outlining a report. She uses the title and subheadings to provide additional guidance for the formulation of an outline and demonstrates its formation by writing the students' and her own responses on the chalkboard. Both the verbal and visual presentations help students learn how to outline. She points out that this article may not contain sufficient information about preparing for disasters and helps students to think about other ways to extend their learning.

In the final part of the K-W-L Plus, Mrs. Diener demonstrates how students can write a report from this web. As you read, consider how Mrs. Diener guides report writing.

Explains purpose and procedure

Mrs. Diener: Now, I'm going to show you how to take the spiderweb and turn it into a report so you don't copy information from an encyclopedia or book. We've labeled on our spiderweb different types of disasters. [Mrs. Diener points to each main type on the chalkboard.] The center of my web can act as the introduction to my paper. I would want to mention the topic and then the subtopics. In this introduction, I will include earthquakes,

Uses think-aloud

lightning, volcanoes, tornadoes, and hurricanes as types of disasters for which you can prepare yourself and keep yourself safe. As I write the introduction, I'll explain how I got the information to write it. There are many types. [Mrs. Diener writes these words on the chalkboard and then explains.] See how I got the types? [Mrs. Diener points to each strand coming from the center of the spiderweb. She rereads the beginning of the introduction and continues composing.] There are many types of . . . What kinds of disasters? Natural disasters. [Mrs. Diener writes on the chalkboard the phrase "natural disasters."] Okay, I want to explain to people how they can prepare for them. So I might have to revise this sentence to express that idea. There are many ways people can prepare for natural disasters. [Mrs. Diener erases the original sentence and writes the revised one on the chalkboard.] Do I want to say one type of disaster? No, I want them to know there are what? Different types. So I want to allow my reader to learn about different types. Now, I want them to know the specific types so that when I present this information in the report, readers are prepared and know in their minds that they will learn about these different types. I want them to recognize that's what my report is going to be about. I'll start off with . . . "In this report, you will find information about preparing for . . ." [Mrs. Diener writes this part of the second sentence on the chalkboard.] Hmm, I don't want to say different types of disasters. I want to list the specific kinds. I'm going to say . . . "lightning, earthquakes, volcanoes, and tornadoes." [Mrs. Diener connects this phrase to the end of the second sentence.] Do you see how this paragraph introduces my report? [Mrs. Diener reads the introduction.] There are many ways people can prepare for natural disasters. In this report, you will find information about preparing for lightning, earthquakes, volcanoes, and tornadoes.

Fifth Graders: Yes.

Explains procedure

Mrs. Diener: Now let's consider the body of the report. The subtopics become the body of our report. [Mrs. Diener points to each subtopic on the spiderweb.] Each of these subtopics becomes a different paragraph. Let's take one of these subtopics and as a group compose a paragraph. With which subtopic should we logically start?

Coretta: Lightning.

Mrs. Diener: Why did you choose lightning?

Coretta: Because it's the first one we wrote about in the introduction.

Provides practice

Mrs. Diener: That's a great idea! I then should write these paragraphs in order as they appear in the introduction. Let's try composing a paragraph about lightning. What do you think should be the topic sentence for this paragraph?

Fifth graders: [No response.]

Gives definition

Mrs. Diener: Let me give you an idea. The topic sentence is usually general and includes the main idea of the paragraph.

Fifth graders: [No response.]

Mrs. Diener: Look at the center of the spiderweb. It should provide clues.

Darnell: What to do.

Mrs. Diener: Yes, what to do when there is lightning. Can we incorporate that idea into a topic sentence? Todd.

Todd: "Here is what you do when there is lightning." [Mrs. Diener writes this sentence on the chalkboard.]

Uses questioning to guide thinking

Mrs. Diener: What is it that we should do? This part of the spiderweb should become what? [Mrs. Diener points to the information on the spiderweb surrounding the subtopic labeled lightning.]

Darnell: A part of this paragraph.

Provides feedback

Mrs. Diener: Yes, these are supporting statements or details that tell me what we should do when there is lightning. What is it that we should do? Can you give me one sentence that would include one or more of these ideas? [Mrs. Diener points to the information attached to this subtopic.] John.

John: "If there is lightning out, you are supposed to drop to your knees, bend forward, and put your hands on your knees. Do this if your hair is full of static." [Mrs. Diener writes these two sentences on the chalkboard.]

Provides practice

Mrs. Diener: Barry, how about another sentence?

Barry: "If you're in the water, leave immediately so you don't get struck by lightning." [Mrs. Diener writes this sentence on the chalkboard.]

Mrs. Diener: What about another sentence?

Lauren: "Stay away from wire fences so you don't get electrocuted, and especially stay away from trees." [Mrs. Diener writes on the chalkboard the continuation of this sentence.]

Mrs. Diener: I'd like you to find a partner. Select one type of natural disaster and write a paragraph informing others about preparing for the specific disaster. [Mrs. Diener circulates among the paired students to provide feedback. To conclude the assignment, Mrs. Diener asks the students to share their paragraphs while she and the other students provide feedback. As a group, they compose a conclusion to their report.]

Your Turn: Before reading our response, explain in your journal how Mrs. Diener guides report writing.

Our Turn: As Mrs. Diener introduces report writing, she explains when and how to use webbing. She uses think-alouds and questioning to model the composing process and demonstrate how the web organizes and facilitates writing. She then explains how each strand of the web becomes a separate paragraph and provides guidance as the fifth graders compose a paragraph about lightning. Mrs. Diener gradually releases responsibility by assigning pairs of students to write a single paragraph. They share their paragraphs to receive additional feedback. Since a conclusion to a report differs from the introduction and body, Mrs. Diener reconvenes the class to provide an explanation and model.

What is the teacher demonstrating?

WHAT WRITING STRATEGIES AND ACTIVITIES EXPAND STUDENTS' READING DEVELOPMENT?

In the last section, we showed how writing can be employed during postreading to consolidate students' thinking about text. But this pre-, during-, and postreading instructional plan of one text may not and should not always be employed. Frequently, students are expected to read, respond, and create a new text. Students are thus expected to read independently and use reading as a medium to expand their thinking about text and their knowledge of the world. From this instructional perspective, we consider a variety of instructional strategies and activities that integrate reading and writing and expand students' thinking about text. We include journal writing, informational writing, letter writing, text-pattern writing, quick writes, and the Directed Reading-Writing Lesson.

Journal Writing

Many different types of journals have been employed to encourage students' written responses to text. We present several different types that encourage self-expression, critical thinking, and transactions between author and reader. Journal writing gives students opportunities to reflect on text and enables them to make a cogent presentation of their ideas during class discussions, so that students are better prepared to participate and exchange ideas. As a result, a higher level of discussion can take place. As with any activity, journal writing can be overused. Students do not always want to respond in writing to text. If you use a journal in relation to reading a book, you may ask students to respond to every other chapter, or to write a response to 5 out of 10 chapters of their own choosing. Choice fosters ownership and encourages commitment. We consider three types of journals: reader-response, dialectic, and dialogue journals.

Pause and Reflect

You have been keeping a journal while reading this textbook. How has journal writing affected your understanding and learning of reading and writing theory and pedagogy? Write your ideas in your journal.

Reader-Response Journals

Reader-response journals highlight personal and individual reactions, feelings, and inspirations evoked from text. As readers, we all experience these very personal feelings as we read about settings, characters, and events. At times, we may hear ourselves laugh; we may feel a tear roll down our face; or we may, for example, feel the triumph and excitement of winning the championship. These are a few of the personal responses you try to help students capture in their journals. Giving students the opportunities to express these natural feelings can encourage lifelong reading habits and give students opportunities to recognize that meaning making is very personal. Different meanings are evoked from text. Experiencing these personal responses are the very reasons we all choose to read, and by using reader-response journals you are giving value and credence to these important experiences.

Reader-response journals are appropriate for all ages. Emerging readers may use pictures to express their feelings about text. More mature readers may respond to text by writing a poem or one or more paragraphs. Students' responses develop intensity and depth through learning from teacher and student modeling, sharing and discussing responses, and being given abundant opportunities to read and respond to text. All of these activities provide a scaffold for thinking and learning about text. Real ideas, issues, and problems are considered in a social communicative context of readers and writers.

To initiate reader-response journals, your students need some type of notebook in which to write their entries after reading text. It's a good idea to date the entry and write the chapter, title, or poem evoking the student's response. Choose a story or poem that the students have just read and ask several questions, ranging from the simplest kind (Do you like the story? Why or why not? What is your favorite part? Why? Who is your favorite character? Why?) to the more complex (What pictures does the poem create? As you read, what sounds do you hear? What feelings does it create in you?). Remind them to concentrate on expressing their ideas rather than on sentence structure, mechanics, penmanship, or spelling. You want students to respond freely to the ideas in text. This writing is intended to be extemporaneous in nature and can be likened to stream-of-consciousness writing. It is not meant to be a well-formed essay.

Form small groups and encourage all students to use their journals to discuss their responses to text. They don't have to read their journal entry but can use it to recall their thinking. Conclude the discussion by asking them to write their present thoughts and feelings about the text selection in their journals. Their ideas are likely to have changed as a consequence of the discussion, thus reinforcing the concept that readers do construct their own meanings and that meaning can also be affected by discussion.

Thoughtful and complex journal responses develop over time when teachers model their own personal responses about text and encourage students to share their thoughts with others. Modeling can be accomplished when you read literature aloud and share your thoughts about text and entertain students' reactions. Sharing journal responses in dyads can be another way to demonstrate different personal perspectives about text. Reading students' response journals and writing your responses and questions can guide students to think in more complex ways about character, plot, and theme.

Dialectic Journals

A dialectic journal also promotes personal response. In a dialectic journal, students are focusing more frequently on explicit statements made in text than on general story elements such as character, setting, problem, and resolution. Responding to specific statements provides a different focus on text—a microscopic look, for example, at char-

What can this teacher learn from his students' journal writing?

acters' statements, actions, and thoughts. Similarly, the dialectic journal accomplishes the goals associated with the reader-response journal—that is, personal meaning making, critical thinking, and author-reader transactions.

A notebook is again needed. But in this journal, students make a T-Chart and write the explicit word or statement on the left-hand side of the notebook and their personal response on the right-hand side. To begin, model the process by identifying a word or statement that evokes a personal response. Read a passage aloud. Stop when a word or statement evokes a response. Verbalize the response and write both the author's statement and the response on the chalkboard. Ask students to work with a partner and alternate reading aloud and responding verbally to a particular part of text.

Pause and Reflect

Keep a reader-response journal for the book you are currently reading for pleasure. As you read, write your personal responses down, either in open-ended form or using the dialectic journal format. By writing a journal, what did you experience as a reader? Did you understand or remember the text better than when you just read it and didn't write? Explain. Did you enjoy the book more than when you just read it? Explain.

Dialogue Journals

We discussed the use of dialogue journals in chapter 2. Recall that, in a dialogue journal, the student reads and uses text to carry on a "written" conversation with the teacher or another student. This written conversation focuses on analyzing, making inferences, thinking critically, relating text-based ideas to their own experiences, and asking questions. Students initiate the dialogue with the teacher. The teacher responds to the student writers' ideas and questions and models critical thinking. The dialogue journal provides opportunities to answer individual questions and note personal growth in understanding and relating to text.

Letter Writing

Letter writing gives students experience with a different form of writing that makes them keenly aware of audience, provides them a real sense of the purposefulness of writing and reading, makes writing a natural and authentic experience, and can reveal what students understand and enjoy most about the text. To understand how to implement this strategy, let's look at how sixth graders used letter writing with the novel *A Taste of Blackberries* by Doris Buchanan Smith.

A Taste of Blackberries is narrated by a boy whose best friend dies from an allergic reaction to bee stings. The narrator begins by describing Jamie, their relationship, and the things they enjoyed doing together, despite having very different personalities. On an ordinary summer day, children are removing beetles from an elderly neighbor lady's blackberry vines when Jamie, in a typical overdramatic scene, throws himself to the ground screaming. The narrator returns home, disgusted with Jamie's antics, but soon an ambulance arrives and later that day Jamie dies. The narrator begins the inner struggle to understand how life can go on as usual in the face of death. In the remaining chapters, the boy learns much about life and death through his conversations with the neighbor lady in her beautiful tranquil garden, and at the end, the narrator returns to Jamie's home and continues his friendship with Jamie's family.

We have selected three sections of this book where students can be given opportunities to write letters to friends telling them about the book. After reading chapter 2, the students can write a letter to their friend who loves similar types of stories and would enjoy understanding the main character, Jamie. Before they write, conduct a prewriting discussion using some of the following questions:

1. What does Jamie look like?
2. What does Jamie like to do?
3. As the reader, how do you like Jamie?
4. What do you think of Jamie's actions?
5. What would your friend enjoy learning about Jamie as an enticement to read this book?

After the discussion, students can write an initial draft about Jamie and share it with another classmate to receive feedback and revise it. Have them share this revision with you and then write a final revision to mail to their friends.

After reading chapter 5, students can write a second letter to the same friend telling about Jamie's death. Before the students write their letters, you can use some of the following questions to stimulate discussion:

1. What were the children doing when Jamie got stung by the bees?
2. What did Jamie do when the bees stung him?
3. How did his best friend react to Jamie's screaming?
4. What did Jamie's best friend do after Jamie died?
5. Did Jamie's friend feel guilty?
6. Was Jamie's friend angry at Jamie because he died?
7. How did the elderly neighbor help the boy deal with Jamie's death?

Follow the same process of sharing and revising drafts.

The last letter, written after the students finish reading the book, should include the students' personal responses to the book. The prewriting discussion can focus on some of the following questions:

1. How do you feel about Jamie's death?
2. Do you think death is a natural part of life?
3. How would you feel about visiting Jamie's family after he died?
4. Would you have reacted in the same manner as Jamie's best friend did? Why or why not?

The writing and revising procedures remain the same. This series of letters can help students communicate what they understand and feel about a given piece of literature, and it gives them a chance to share good literature.

Text Pattern Writing

Text pattern writing helps children focus on language patterns and use the rhythm, rhyme, and meaning to build sight vocabulary and develop fluency. As soon as children can read and understand an entire text, they can write a new version and use it as a book for independent reading, or you can use it for classroom instruction. To create their own text, children use the language patterns found in poetry and predictable books to write their own text. Read the first graders' version of the nursery rhyme "Mary's Lamb" and you can see a very simple example of text pattern writing. In this simple rewriting, these young children have changed a few words, but retained the rhythm and repetition of the original. The teacher changed Mary's name to correspond to each child's name, making the nursery rhyme more personal, motivating, and easier for young readers.

Julianne had a little cat,

Its fur was soft as cotton;

And everywhere that Julianne went,

The cat was sure to go.

Nursery rhyme collections from different countries exist and can encourage and facilitate reading for students from diverse backgrounds. The writing in these collections uses rhyming and rhythmic patterns. Using nursery rhymes from other cultures can facilitate acquiring print skills and comprehension as well as respect and understanding of diverse cultures. In Table 6.1 (p. 216), we suggest a few collections and the cultures they represent.

As young children become more familiar with text pattern writing, you can advance to more challenging stories in which repetitive language patterns are still employed but the vocabulary is more difficult and the sentence patterns are longer.

 ## Learning from Experience

As you read about text pattern writing in a first-grade classroom, note how Mr. Carpenter, the classroom teacher, employed this strategy.

 Mr. Carpenter's first-grade classroom included many beginning readers as well as second-language learners. These young readers enjoyed hearing and reading the picture book *Brown Bear, Brown Bear, What Do You See?* by Bill Martin. They liked this book's repetition, rhyme, and rhythm, and Mr. Carpenter felt he could increase their sight word learning by using the kinds of repetitive and rhythmic language patterns used in this book. Mr. Carpenter decided to use group dictation rather than individual writing, since this activity was new and most of his second-language students were developing oral language proficiency. He planned to make the dictation into a Big Book that he could use for group instruction and that several children could read together.

Mr. Carpenter reread *Brown Bear, Brown Bear, What Do You See?* and asked the

Table 6.1 **Nursery Rhymes from Different Cultures**

Author	Title	Culture
Demi	*Dragon Kites and Dragonflies*	Chinese
Wyndham	*Chinese Mother Goose Rhymes*	Chinese
Bodecker	*"It's Raining," Said John Twaining*	Danish
Griego	*Tortillitas Para Mama*	Hispanic

first graders, "Does the author repeat or rhyme words?" They quickly recognized the repetition of phrases and the question, "What do you see?" He then told the children they would write their own version of *Brown Bear, Brown Bear, What Do You See?* by changing the names of the animals but still using the author's repeated phrases and questions. With Mr. Carpenter's guidance, the first graders easily dictated the book during two 20-minute periods. Mr. Carpenter could feel their confidence and ease as they discussed and made decisions about what animals to include and exclude.

After the dictation was completed, the children wanted to illustrate their version, so Mr. Carpenter assigned pairs of children to illustrate each page of text and briefly discussed the notion of illustrations based on text meaning. During the next three days, the children illustrated their pages as part of their seat-work assignments, and then Mr. Carpenter assembled the Big Book and used it for choral reading instruction and independent reading. Mr. Carpenter noted that his students seemed to learn words from the Big Book at a rapid rate and chose to read it more often than Bill Martin's book.

After their experience with *Brown Bear, Brown Bear, What Do You See?* some of the first graders were excited about reading more books with repetitive language patterns, and they used these patterns to create additional Big Books.

Your Turn: How did Mr. Carpenter employ text pattern writing? Respond to this question in your journal and compare it to ours.

Our Turn: Mr. Carpenter chose a book that employed rhythm, rhyme, and repetition to facilitate decoding. He then used this text as a springboard to writing, thereby providing students with a second text that gave them additional decoding practice. By writing their own text, the first graders learned how authors use the rhythm and rhyme of language to create an interesting text. Students then illustrated their text, thus reinforcing text meaning. They practiced reading their text, and since they were the authors, this experience gave them meaningful practice with print skills.

Persuasive Writing

Frequently, students can read and express an opinion about a topic but do not provide supporting evidence. To help students support their opinion, Santa (1993) has developed the opinion-proof reading strategy. Students form a T-Chart and place the word "Opinion" as the heading for the left-hand column. In the right-hand column, the heading is labeled "Proof." As students read, they are likely to form opinions about a character, for example. Students are to ask themselves this question: What words or ideas in the text caused them to develop this opinion? On the T-Chart, students write one or two words that capture their opinion. In the proof column, students write about events, ideas, and other text-based information to demonstrate support for this opinion. Encourage students to reread for the purpose of finding proof for their opinion. Once the T-Chart is completed, the students can verbalize their opinion using supporting evidence. Students are then prepared to write a persuasive piece stating their opinion and using supporting evidence to validate it.

To initially guide students through the process, Santa suggests using a folktale. To connect the opinion-proof reading strategy with persuasive writing, we have chosen the folktale *Red Riding Hood* by James Marshall. After a group of students read this picture book, ask them how they feel about each of the characters. It is easy for students to give their opinions but much more difficult for them to list their reasons. To help them identify evidence for each opinion, reread each page, asking the students to identify information and tell why they feel the wolf was bad and Red Riding Hood was kind and considerate. Rereading page by page and asking questions helped the first graders to provide supporting evidence. As they provide supporting evidence, write their ideas in the proof column, as illustrated in Figure 6.2.

The teacher helps the students use their chart to dictate a paragraph persuading readers to feel the wolf was bad. Before the dictation begins, the students discuss the meaning of the word *persuade,* using synonyms such as *convince* and discussing examples, such as wanting to go to the park and providing reasons for the excursion. To help students dictate a well-developed argument, use questions to guide students' thinking and understanding about connecting opinions to supportive evidence. Some of the questions include these:

How would you begin a persuasive piece?

In this particular folktale, what did the wolf do to make him the evil character?

Opinion	Proof
Wolf is bad.	1. Grandma is sick and he just comes along and eats her.
	2. He eats Red Riding Hood too.
	3. Wolf made her talk because he had such good manners. He was tricking Red Riding Hood.
	4. He tricked Red Riding Hood by telling her to pick flowers for Granny.
	5. He didn't tell the truth to Granny.
	6. He lied to Red Riding Hood.
Red Riding Hood was kind and considerate.	1. She did what her mother said.
	2. She took custard to Granny.
	3. She brings Granny flowers.
	4. She promised that she would never

Figure 6.2 Opinion-Proof Reading Strategy

What are other reasons that made the wolf evil?

How would you end the piece?

A group of first graders wrote the big bad wolf paragraph shown in Figure 6.3. This group paragraph can serve as a model for the first graders to write a subsequent paragraph persuading their readers that Red Riding Hood was kind and considerate. The students can write their paragraph in dyads while you circulate around the room to assist them in writing. Encourage the students to share their persuasive pieces to conclude this writing activity.

Quick Writes

In quick writes, students can write before and/or after they read text. For a short time period before and after reading text, students write about the text topic, thus demonstrating their knowledge and understanding. In a quick write, students write in a stream-of-consciousness form without lifting their pen from the paper. Whatever comes to mind is written down even if it doesn't stick to the topic. The goal is to quickly access ideas and possibly use one of the ideas to develop a more focused piece at another writing session. The students are to focus on their ideas and not on mechanics and spelling. An example of a quick write appears in Figure 6.4. Ed read a New True Book entitled the *Anasazi* and followed his reading by writing for five minutes about whatever came to his mind about the Anasazi Indians.

Using quick writes before students read encourages students to access topical ideas, thus encouraging them to integrate their thinking with the author's. They become aware of what they know and what they don't know and can then formulate questions to use as they read. After reading text, students reconsider their initial writing to elaborate and extend their thinking and to accommodate new ideas through revision. If the teacher only uses quick writes after they read text, students can respond to text by writing down whatever comes to mind for a short time period of three to five minutes and then sharing their ideas with a small group of students. Sharing can be followed by each student selecting one idea and developing it as a short and more focused response to the text.

Second-language learners and learning-disabled students may benefit from discussing their ideas while you write their key points on the chalkboard. Discussion encourages collaboration. For second-language learners and learning-disabled students, peers and teachers extend language learning to facilitate writing and text reading. Writing down their key ideas allows second-language and learning-disabled students to

The wolf is a bad, bad, bad mammal. It's because he just comes along and tricks people. The wolf tricks Red Riding Hood because he wants to eat Little Red Riding Hood. The wolf lies to people. He said to Red Riding Hood that he was Granny. He's bad because he lied to Granny. The wolf said, "I'm Red Riding Hood." If you go near him, he will eat people. He ate Granny for dinner and Red Riding Hood for dessert. He's a bad mammal because he eats, and he tricks and he lies.

Figure 6.3 Persuasive Paragraph

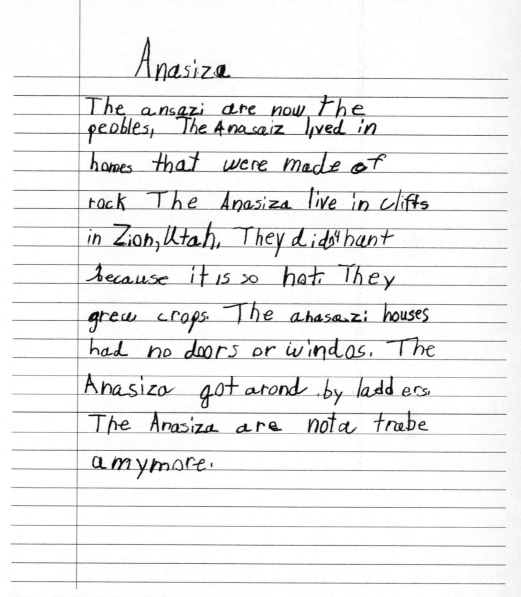

Figure 6.4 Ed's Quick Write about the Anasazi Indians

better express their ideas; they can focus on content rather than spelling. Pairing students to do quick writes can provide guidance and improved writing.

Lapp, Flood, and Farnan (1993) suggest that students do quick writes for both fiction and nonfiction. These help students consider perspectives readers bring to text. Sharing their written pieces provides a forum for learning about different cultural experiences, ideas, beliefs, and values, which in turn broadens students' perspectives about the topic being read. For example, before students read Gary Paulsen's *The Crossing,* ask students to think and write about the feelings and reasons people choose to leave their homeland. You can further facilitate writing by asking questions that tap into their personal experiences and stories. For example, ask: How would you feel about leaving your home? What has caused your family to leave? Students are then being encouraged to connect their experiences with text, and this increases comprehension.

Directed Reading-Writing Lesson

Hillocks (1984) has shown that using written pieces as a model improves students' writing. In the Directed Reading-Writing Lesson (DR-WL), students read and analyze good writers' work, using it as a model to write their own text (Heller, 1995). This reading-writing strategy has seven steps and is likely to require a week of instructional time.

In step 1, the students are involved in activities that focus students on reading and identifying a particular genre, author, topic, or concept so they can use this as a model for their own writing. For example, if the goal is to understand and use the elements of a folktale to write, ask students to share information about folktales. Students are likely to identify specific folktales, identify countries and ethnic groups in which particular folktales originate, and suggest story elements such as characters, problem, and resolution. Some may identify specific folktale elements such as flat characters, enchantment, sleep, *three*'s, and other motifs. You can categorize and list their ideas on a wall chart to help them as they read and write folktales. Encourage students to add ideas to the wall chart throughout the week to further enhance their writing.

In step 2, students are to write a draft, in this case of a folktale. Use a story planning chart, as illustrated in Figure 6.5 to facilitate rehearsal and drafting phrases.

In step 3, small groups of two to four students share their drafts and respond to each others' drafts. Responses should be helpful and focus on meaning, such as

"I can easily understand the story. There is a beginning, middle, and end to your story."

"Is there a problem in your story?"

"What happens, for example, to the evil witch?"

"I am confused about how the problem was solved."

Spend some time modeling helpful responses to writing by using your own writing to elicit comments and questions from the students.

In step 4, students are to become more knowledgeable about their topic. Engage students in lots of reading; independent and paired reading and also reading aloud are good techniques. In this example, ask students to read folktales for the purpose

Name:
Date:
Story Title:

Characters	Setting	Problem	Resolution

Figure 6.5 Story Planning Chart

of understanding how authors develop their craft. Reading, for example, Verna Aardema's African folktale *Who's in Rabbit's House?* can cause students to identify techniques Aardema employs to stimulate interest. Provide time for discussion and analysis. Aardema uses repetition to lend suspense, mystery, and rhythm to the telling of a tale. She also uses onomatopoeia to encourage reader participation by making the sound effects correspond to the word, and hence she encourages appreciation of language and its rhythm.

Step 5 is the time for revision. Students use the information they've learned to improve their written pieces, in the process employing both peer responses and the information they've read. Encourage students to reread books and to talk to peers to further facilitate revision. Respond to students' revisions by focusing on the content rather than on the mechanics. Meet with students individually to discuss their written pieces. Personal and direct communication helps students. They can ask questions immediately, and there is less opportunity for them to be discouraged by many written comments. Conferences can occur as students are revising rather than waiting to confer until the piece is completely revised. To manage conferences, make them short and move to the students' desks so that students aren't waiting and can continue writing. While conferring with an individual, encourage the other class members to revise and receive assistance from peers.

In step 6, students focus on editing for grammar and mechanics. We suggest making a grade-level checklist for grammar and mechanics to guide their editing. (We provide examples of checklists in chapter 7, Guiding the Writing Process.) After students have edited their own pieces, put them in dyads to review editing. Paired editing can provide feedback and additional learning. Review students' writing by looking for improvement in content and strengths and weaknesses in grammar and mechanics. Use this information to plan future instruction.

Sharing is the culminating step. Students celebrate their creations by reading their writing to one or more students and/or making simple books for the classroom library.

SUMMARY

Reading and writing are processes in which readers construct meaning from their knowledge and the text. Writing is also a constructive process in which writers use their knowledge to compose text. Students benefit by connecting reading and writing instruction; their reading comprehension and learning are increased. Writing provides students opportunities to consolidate and summarize text; to organize their thinking and memory of text; to self-assess their ability to comprehend text; and to reflect and expand text meaning. Instruction linking the reading and writing processes can provide students with opportunities to consolidate and summarize text, and it can provide personal responses to text as well as expand students' thinking and writing of a particular text. Reading and writing strategies such as the K-W-L Plus, journaling, letter writing, text pattern writing, and the DR-WL motivate students to compose and generate meaning. These instructional strategies encourage students to focus, select, and organize text information and their own knowledge to create text.

In the Field

1. Meet with one student to select a topic the student would like to investigate. Together select a book and use the K-W-L Plus to identify this student's topical knowledge, questions, and information learned from reading. Organize the information from K-W-L into a web. Use the web to write the report. You will need to plan several sessions to complete this activity. In a short paper, describe what you learned from designing and implementing the K-W-L Plus strategy.

2. Implement a reader-response journal with a small group of students. Select some poems. Meet with these students and ask them to read and respond to one of the poems. Begin by sharing a poem and your personal response to serve as a model. After the students read and write their personal responses, encourage them to share their responses with the other members of the group. Arrange several additional meetings to read and respond to other poems. Note changes in the types of responses students provide, such as providing greater depth and detail in their writing.

3. Visit the children's section of the library. Choose five picture books suitable for text pattern writing. Select books that have a repetitive verse, rhythm, and few words per page. Record the bibliographic information in your journal.

4. Meet with three students and read a poem to them. Follow the reading with a quick write. You and the three students should write for three minutes and write down whatever flows in your minds after hearing the poem. Share and discuss your quick writes. What did you and the students learn from using the quick write strategy?

Portfolio Suggestion

Select from your journal two examples of your responses to Pause and Reflect, Learning from Experience, or In the Field. Write a brief evaluation of your work. Explain how this chapter has affected your thinking about integrating the teaching of reading and writing.

For Further Reading

Beauchat, C. E. (1994). The writer: Another agent in the development of literacy. *The Reading Teacher, 47,* 312–315.

Bernhardt, B. (1994). Reading and writing between the lines: An interactive approach using computers. *Journal of Reading, 37,* 458–463.

Ernst, G., & Richard, K. J. (1994–1995). Reading and writing pathways to conversation in the ESL classroom. *The Reading Teacher, 48,* 320–327.

Sipe, L. R. (1993). Using transformations of traditional stories: Making the reading-writing connection. *The Reading Teacher, 47,* 18–27.

Guiding the Writing Process

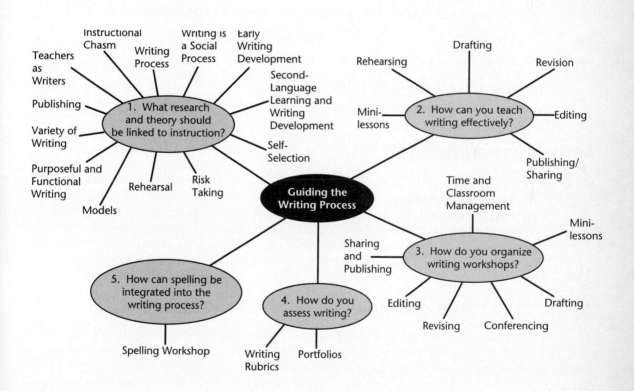

▼ CHAPTER GOALS FOR THE READER

To become familiar with the theoretical and research base of writing

To identify the basic constructs for teaching writing effectively

To organize and implement writing workshop

To help teachers and students assess writing

To integrate spelling with the teaching of writing

▼ CHAPTER OVERVIEW

In this chapter, we explore current theory, research, and practice in the area of writing. We first examine theory and research to help you develop insights about writing instruction. We link theory and research to practice by incorporating these insights into an instructional plan called writing workshop. We then describe how to organize and implement writing workshop and how to assess students' writing, and we conclude with how to integrate spelling instruction in a workshop format.

◆ TAPPING PRIOR KNOWLEDGE TO SET A PURPOSE

Consider your own schooling experiences. How were you taught to write? How often did you write stories, letters, poems? Were you assigned a topic or could you select your own? Were you expected to make an outline, write a rough draft, and finish your writing in a short time period such as 40 minutes? How did your teacher evaluate writing? Were your written ideas important, or were punctuation, spelling, and handwriting more important? Did you enjoy writing? Why or why not? Do you consider yourself a good writer? Why or why not? Consider these questions as you write in your journal about your memories of writing instruction.

Use the chapter overview, the graphic overview questions, and your own schooling experiences to set your purposes for reading this chapter. List these in your journal.

WHAT RESEARCH AND THEORY SHOULD BE LINKED TO INSTRUCTION?

In this section, we review theory and research about writing instruction that will help you make decisions about designing effective instruction for your students. This discussion leads us to an instructional framework that includes best practices for the teaching of writing.

Instructional Chasm

Donald Graves's Ford Foundation study (1976) showed how schools ignored the teaching of writing. Although much time was being devoted to reading instruction, little time was focused on teaching children to compose. How can children learn to write if they are not writing daily? They can't. What Graves made apparent is that the basics—reading and writing—need to be balanced, and his work became the catalyst for an increasing interest in writing research and instruction.

As we visited schools and worked with teachers in the 1980s and 1990s, we observed a major shift in the teaching of writing, when compared to Graves's reports concerning the 1970s. First and foremost, more instructional time was being devoted to writing. Children were composing their own text as early as preschool. All children can and need the opportunity to write: to express themselves, to demonstrate their learning, and to communicate to others. The importance and value of writing have been acknowledged, and writing has achieved an established place in our curriculum. In many of today's schools, students are engaged in expressing their ideas in print. Students, at all grade levels, are self-selecting topics in which they have knowledge and interest, writing a draft, conferring with others to receive feedback, and revising to meet their purposes.

Writing Process

Graves's research extends far beyond simply asserting that schools need to devote more time to writing instruction. His major contributions have concerned the teaching of writing as a process—creating and knowing how to express ideas in print. We learn about the importance of the writing process from the observations of Don Graves (1994) as well as those of Anne Haas Dyson (1989), Janet Emig (1971), and Lucy Calkins (1994), and also from their close examination of elementary and secondary school students during the act of writing. We learn that writing is a very complex process and is idiosyncratic in nature. Each child approaches writing quite differently.

Some may draw before they write while others will sit down and just write. Still others will organize their ideas through diagrams or webs. Puppets and dramatic play may serve as catalysts for some children's writing. Reading may serve as another stepping-stone for composing, in the same way as talking and conducting interviews do.

Not only is writing a complex and idiosyncratic process; it is a process that continues to develop over time. Children's writing develops as children are given opportunities to write frequently about topics they choose. Writing daily for a sustained period of time without interruptions gives children the opportunity to think and try out some of their ideas. Professional writers do not sit down and write a perfectly composed piece. Composing is a slow and thoughtful process that demands time.

Writing Is a Social Process

Writing is a socially developed and acquired skill. On the surface, writing appears to be a solitary and lonely process, since writers are faced with a blank page as they compose. However, this is only part of the writing process. Writing is shaped by our daily encounters with people, books, art, drama, and life itself. To compose, writers spend time observing and talking to others. They share their writing to receive feedback. They read and discuss the ideas that will inform their writing. Hence, writing is not done in a vacuum. It is socially developed through writing conferences, sharing, and publishing.

What are the benefits of collaborative writing?

Early Writing Development

When should writing instruction begin? Researchers demonstrate that writing often precedes and develops alongside learning to read. Sulzby (1985) shows that preschool children initially represent their ideas in print with scribbles and pictures that gradually evolve to letters to signify words and sounds. Young children often come to school knowing the purpose and function of writing. Glenda Bissex's (1980) case study of her son, Paul, from ages 5 to 11 demonstrates how writing is a natural outgrowth of play and other social interactions at home. Paul wrote before he learned to read and created such messages as RUDF (Are you deaf?) and EFUKANOPNKAZIWILGE-VUAKANOPNR (If you can open cans, I will give you a can opener). Paul shows his tacit understanding of letters and sounds; yet he doesn't know how words are segmented—a process he will learn by continued writing and learning to read. The two processes can and do naturally develop together.

We also learn how Paul's growth in writing was either fostered or hindered by the instruction he was receiving in school. When choice and risk taking were not encouraged in the classroom, the frequency, interest, and quality of Paul's writing diminished. The social context of literacy learning does affect development. This child's story causes us to reflect on our own instructional practices. If children choose not to write and limit their writing to what they know is correct, can they become better writers? Probably not. Growth in writing requires risk taking, experimentation, and an environment that supports such exploration (Dyson & Freedman, 1991). We need to carefully consider our role in creating or stifling literacy growth. What do we do in our classrooms to encourage literacy? Do we build from children's demonstrated knowledge by planning instruction that is commensurate with their needs?

Pause and Reflect!

As we learned primarily about Paul's writing at home, we also learned how the home and school fostered or hindered his growth in writing. The purpose of writing is to communicate. It is used to express and share ideas, to acquire things, and to control and stop people and events. Can you remember making or seeing a sign taped to the bedroom door with large printed upper-case letters stating KEEP OUT!? The sign clearly communicated its message. This may have been the only message you could spell correctly, but you knew that words represented meaning. Describe how you used writing as a young child. Were you encouraged to write at home and at school even though you couldn't read or were just learning to read?

Second-Language Learning and Writing Development

Should children write English as they learn to speak it? Hudelson's research with young Latino children suggests that children should explore writing even though they are not fluent speakers of English. Other research indicates that second-language learners use their first language to assist them in writing English (Edelsky, 1982, 1986;

Hudelson, 1984; Zutell & Allen, 1988). Allen (1991) points out that these children need more experiences with print and books to promote writing development. Second-language learners need to be actively constructing, hypothesizing, testing out, and receiving feedback about their writing just as they do in speaking English (Allen, 1991; Dulay & Burt, 1974). As is the case with native speakers, their language reflects their knowledge and use of oral language. Moreover, their informal conversational English is likely to be more fluent and well developed than their knowledge of the more formal language used in school settings for subjects such as science and social studies. Academic vocabulary tends to lag behind informal conversational vocabulary, and this is also reflected in these students' writing. Hence more time is needed for them to develop the formal technical writing students are expected to do in school.

Self-Selection

We also noted that self-selection is essential to enhancing writing development. It's hard, if not impossible, to write about a topic you know little about or in which you have little or no interest. Even if you know something about a particular topic, it still can be difficult to write. Can you remember the perennial theme you wrote about each school year—what you did over summer vacation? You often didn't know where to start. Your mind went blank. Did you do anything over the summer? You couldn't remember anything interesting. You were looking to write about something provocative or some interesting adventure. You probably experienced writer's block. You needed time to brainstorm to identify your own topic—to consider your own experiences and ideas. You needed time to let some of these ideas incubate before immediately writing or you needed to do what some teachers call free writing—that is, "letting the juices flow" and writing whatever comes to mind. Topics and ideas can evolve when you spend a few minutes just engaged in writing what comes to your mind. But it's likely that brainstorming and free writing were not introduced as strategies to select and develop writing topics.

Pause and Reflect

Try out the free-writing strategy. Set a timer for 10 minutes and write or use a computer to compose whatever comes to mind. You can change ideas as you naturally do while thinking. Free writing should be a natural stream of consciousness; it is not focused or precise. What happened as you wrote? Did you uncover a topic? What did you discover about your writing?

To select a topic and write an interesting piece, do the ideas and events have to be provocative? Do you have to create stories, for example, such as Tom Clancy does in his book *Clear and Present Danger?* Although this author's stories are interesting, it is the ordinary daily events we all live through that can be developed into interesting and stimulating pieces. Recall Maurice Sendak's popular picture book *Where the Wild*

Things Are. This story is about a disobedient young boy named Max, who is sent to bed without dinner. He dreams about running away from his mean parents by going on a journey and later returns to the comfort and love of his parents and home. What young children haven't experienced some anger toward their parents, been sent to their room, and dreamed about going on a faraway trip or running away? It is these day-to-day lived experiences that are the beginnings of an interesting piece of writing. It is from our personal experiences that we can create stories that are real and that strike a chord of interest in other readers because they can identify with these experiences.

Risk Taking

Frequent opportunities to write and to select topics do enhance writing development, but so does a classroom atmosphere that encourages risk taking. If you know that each spelling error will be circled, each punctuation mark will be examined, sentences may be labeled "awkward," and word choice may be questioned, you will probably take few risks. Children need opportunities to experiment and take risks while writing. They need time to play with language, practice, and try out some new ideas without the fear of the red pen. Many teachers promote risk taking through journaling. Children are given 10 minutes or more to write anything in their journal without teacher evaluation. This type of journaling develops self-expression and risk taking, since students choose what they write and if they want to share their ideas. The journal becomes a safe place to experiment—for example, with writing more complex sentences or choosing new words to capture the vividness of an event.

Rehearsal

Writers tend to rehearse before they write. They consciously prepare by drawing, daydreaming, reading, making lists, and organizing their ideas. Writers are always observing, and they often take mental or written notes about what they see, feel, hear, taste, and touch. Calkins (1994) talks extensively about the use of notebooks to capture our experiences at the moment they are occurring and then using these notebooks as we write. These written experiences can, for example, open doors to new topics, aid us in reflecting on and rethinking particular topics, and enhance self-expression. Calkins recommends that the notebook become a constant companion both in and out of school. Children write down ideas as they go through the day. If they are on a chairlift in the mountains and see the snowflakes falling on their snowsuits, they can record their observations as to how the snowflakes look, feel, and maybe even taste. It is the immediacy of the experience that allows the writer to capture the precise picture. Curling up with one's new puppy and hearing the soft, low, and contented gurgling and grunting sounds the puppy makes as it fades into sleep is best captured at that moment and not the next day in school. The notebook encourages children to write naturally as the experience occurs rather than during a designated period of the day.

Rehearsal often takes place during the prewriting phase, but it can also occur during the final stages of writing. For example, after composing a story, students may read books to compare how other authors have created interesting and descriptive settings in their stories. Rehearsal, as with other components of the writing process, demonstrates that writing is recursive. Writers go back and forth from one stage to another as they compose.

Pause and Reflect!

Rehearsal comes in different forms and serves an important role in writing even for children who seem to sit down and immediately write. They, too, have been engaged in some sort of rehearsal, such as daydreaming and keeping journals and diaries, that naturally occurs throughout their day.

What do you do before you write? Do you use any of the rehearsal strategies we have mentioned? Do you use one strategy for all types of writing? Or do your strategies change because of the nature of the writing and your knowledge of the topic?

Models

Can models of well-written pieces enhance students' writing development? When you were given a writing assignment, did you ask to see some examples? Did these models provide direction and clarity? Analyzing and studying what good writers do, for example, to create humor and play on language can enhance writing development (Hillocks, 1984). Students should be given permission to imitate patterns they have heard other writers use. Young writers often imitate rhyming patterns that captivated them as they read; and, as a consequence, they used this same pattern in writing their own picture book. For example, after many readings of Audrey and Don Wood's book *Quick as a Cricket*, Julianne, a second grader, sat down one morning to create her own book. Can you tell who influenced her writing? (See Figure 7.1.)

By experimenting with Wood's language patterns, Julianne has developed a sense of using imagery in writing her own books. She will likely develop her own language patterns as she develops other stories.

Purposeful and Functional Writing

Although models can improve writing, students need a self-felt purpose for writing. We write because there is a reason to write, and so do children. If we want to remember what items we need from the grocery store, we make a list. If we want our family to know where we are, we write a note. If a new friend is coming to our house, we draw a map and write directions. Writing serves a purpose. It is real and not artificial.

Contrived assignments to initiate writing do not engage students' motivation and involvement. Students do the assignment for a grade rather than to communicate. Hence writing must be meaningful to students if we want them to be committed to composing their best pieces. Meaningful writing serves a function and is authentic. For instance, writing letters to the school board that list reasons for the purchasing of playground equipment can stimulate students to identify logical reasons,

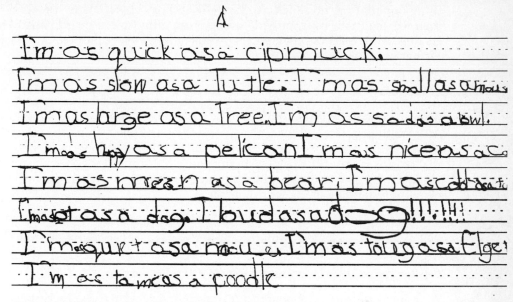

Figure 7.1 Julianne's Partial Version of *Quick as a Cricket*

organize their thinking, and employ correct spelling and punctuation, since there is a real audience who will react to their request. In this case, writing has meaning and is not simply the result of an assignment to learn how to write a persuasive business letter.

Variety of Writing

If we want students to become invested in writing and to develop as writers, we must provide them with opportunities to express their ideas in a variety of different forms of writing. If we introduce students to different genres such as poetry, stories, essays, reports, journals, letters, and memoirs, this experience may strike a chord, or stir interest and thus enhance students' development. Classroom libraries containing different genres on the same topic can cause students to view topics in different forms and choose from these forms for their own writing.

Publishing

Writers need an audience. As Graves (1994), Calkins (1994), and others have shown, writers need to share their work. They need to be published. They need to receive feedback from their teachers, but, most importantly, from their peers. It is through conferencing that authors receive feedback as they compose and revise pieces that are important to them. It is through publishing that authors recognize that they have something important to say. Such rituals as the author's chair, where students read aloud their writing to the class, provide students opportunities to hear firsthand what others think and feel about their writing. Publishing provides purpose and meaning and further validates them as authors.

Teachers as Writers

If we are to teach writing, we need to be writers. Such noteworthy projects as the Bay Area Writing Project and the Chicago Area Writing Project emphasize the importance of teachers as writers. We need to write with children and serve as models to indicate that writing is a continually developing process. Writing alongside our students, sharing and asking for feedback, can help students develop as writers but also further our own understanding of the writing process.

Controversial Issue

Challenges to Theories about Process Writing Instruction

What about the teaching of grammar? Do identifying different parts of speech, diagramming sentences, and punctuating sentences in written exercises help students become better writers? Formal or traditional approaches to writing instruction have emphasized the development of punctuation, grammar, and syntax (Dowst, 1980; Gregg, 1983). Traditional approaches are atomistic in that writing is viewed as a series of skills that once mastered result in the ability to write. Within this model, specific writing-related skills are defined for the student, taught to the student, and practiced by the student. This traditional type of writing instruction functions under the premise that once having learned the appropriate skills involved in the writing process, the student will spontaneously employ these skills in writing.

Research has demonstrated some flaws in this assumption. As early as 1935, the National Council of Teachers of English notes that research clearly indicated that instruction in traditional grammar is ineffective in eradicating errors in written composition. Strom (1960) reviews numerous studies on the relationship of traditional grammar instruction to written composition and concludes that knowledge of grammar does not translate into flawless writing. She further points out that writing activities that develop ideation, sentence structure, usage, and punctuation are superior to drill, diagramming, and memorization of grammatical rules. In their seminal report, Braddock, Lloyd-Jones, and Schoer (1963) conclude that the formal study of grammar does not improve students' writing and that often it replaces necessary instruction in teaching composition. In a meta-analysis, Hillocks (1984) points out that studying grammar (such as identifying parts of speech and diagramming) has no effect on improving students' writing and in some cases has created negative effects. In a more recent study, Calkins (1980) interviewed third graders who were taught by a traditional approach as well as third graders taught by a process-oriented approach. Calkins showed 14 different punctuation marks to each of the third graders and asked the purpose for using them. The third graders receiving traditional instruction were able to explain an average of 3.85 out of 14 punctuation marks while the third graders in the writing-process approach were able to explain an average of 8.66 punctuation marks out of 14. Calkins concludes that this latter group learned effective use of punctuation better through their own writing than did those students doing regular drills and workbook exercises.

It is our contention that, given little time to teach, we need to focus on having students compose and communicate their feelings and thoughts. As they become committed to a piece of writing, they will be interested in using correct punctuation, capitalization, and other parts of grammar. What writers want their pieces of writing published with errors? It is in the context of their own writing that punctuation and grammar become important and meaningful. For example, quotation marks are easily learned when children are writing dialogues in their stories. What better time is there for teaching quotations?

HOW CAN YOU TEACH WRITING EFFECTIVELY?

Theory and research provide us with important insights for instruction. In this section, we link theory and research into practice. According to a social-constructivist viewpoint of learning, students need to write daily and engage in constructing their own meaning. Writing makes us active learners as we create and try out our ideas, point out what we know and don't know, and reflect on and critically respond to ideas. Writing helps us develop meaning. As we write, we ask questions about our own thoughts, and this may cause us to initiate additional thinking, reading, and talking to others. How do we help students discover these concepts? Children need to use the processes authors employ. They need to experience how authors create their books, short stories, poems, and newspaper articles. By understanding and using a process approach to writing, children can and do create interesting and well-developed written pieces. They think of themselves as writers. Learning-disabled students also benefit from a process approach, compared to being taught writing skills in an isolated manner (Englert, 1992). Those who use a process writing approach often refer to it as writing workshop (Calkins, 1994; Daniels & Zemelman, 1985; Graves, 1994).

To teach children a process approach such as writing workshop, we need to examine its components: rehearsing, drafting, conferencing, revising, editing, and publishing. This process is not sequential in nature; rather, it's recursive. Writers may rehearse prior to drafting, and yet may rehearse again before they completely draft their stories. Other writers may discontinue a draft and never publish it. The process is flexible and free-flowing to meet the needs of the writer. Within this process, students develop a variety of writing strategies to gather and organize information, express ideas, and revise. We distinguish one component from another only to facilitate discussion and understanding of the writing process.

Rehearsing

Rehearsing or prewriting is an essential phase of writing. Don Murray (1982) suggests that students spend 70 percent of their time in rehearsal. The writer "tries it out" before committing extensive time and energy to developing a written piece to its completion. During this phase, writers may draw a scene in their stories; they may role-play a particular event; they may brainstorm and write whatever comes to mind; they may interview different people; they may organize a few ideas into a web; or they may engage in other activities that writers refer to as "getting the juices flowing." Tompkins (1994) points out that students are not only selecting a topic but also identifying their purpose and audience, and choosing a specific form of writing that best captures their purpose and audience.

Selecting a Topic

Students need to choose their own topics to develop ownership and commitment to develop as writers. Letting students self-select their topics is not enough. Teachers need to demonstrate in their classroom practices that students possess much knowledge they can use for writing; their knowledge has value and is of interest to others. Publishing students' writing, providing for peer sharing, encouraging students to provide feedback to peer writing are a few examples demonstrating respect for and value of students' knowledge. It is the teacher's responsibility to help students uncover specific topics in which they have sufficient interest and some knowledge to develop in writing.

As discussed in the last section, Calkins (1994) suggests that both teachers and students keep notebooks to record their observations, thinking, and personal responses that occur daily. You can write lists, ideas, ramblings, notes, drafts, poems, or anything at all. It is, as Calkins (1991) states, "a concrete, physical invitation to write without requiring me to view my scrawlings as rough drafts of anything in particular" (p. 38). Calkins maintains (1991) that notebooks "give them the lens to appreciate the richness that is already there in their lives" (p. 35). Notebooks give students the opportunity for free expression and at the same time facilitate their development as skillful writers. They learn how to develop meaning. They discover ideas they never knew existed in their minds. They learn how to use language and include metaphors, similes, and personification evoked from their daily lives. Notebooks demonstrate to students that they can write, and out of their notebooks, ideas emerge, sharing evolves, and writing can begin.

Ed, a third grader, uses a steno pad as a notebook. His initial entries, as shown in Figure 7.2, read more like memorable points during the day. But as we read Ed's journal and talk to Ed about his entries, we can see him playing with imagery. In the first entry, we see the beginnings of personification—"Jeremy was my alarm clock"—and in the second entry we see the boys being described as sleepy heads. Reviewing his other writing, we note this same fascination with creating imagery, and his notebook affords Ed the opportunity to experiment further.

Notebooks help students identify topics and develop their ideas; yet the students are not committed to turning each entry into a formal piece of writing. The notebook encourages free writing that is immediate to the situation the child experiences. Notebooks match the tools professional writers use to record and develop events that are being observed and felt. Students like Ed can also turn to their notebooks as a resource for ideas they can further develop in a written piece.

Earlier in this chapter we mentioned that free writing can help students identify topics. Elbow (1981) suggests a similar strategy called quick writing. In a quick write, students write for an uninterrupted short period of time (5 to 10 minutes) to help them identify and think about a particular topic. During this time, students are not to pause to think or reread their writing. Students are "writing off the top of their heads" about anything that comes to their mind. Using a quick write, students can

3-22-95

When I got to the condo my friends welcomed me. We went to bed because it was so late. We got in at 12:10. I slept with Jermey. Jermey pushime off the bed. Jermey was my alarm clock, because he kicked me. Then I got dressed to go skiing at deer Valley. Eric and Jermey were on level 4. I went skiing with my mom and dad.

3-23-95

Eric slept with me. Eric woke me up by pushing me off the bed. I got dressed and had brakefast. Then the sleepy heads got up. Eric and Jermey are in level 4. I went down ottana bowl.

Figure 7.2 Ed's Notebook

discern if they have sufficient interest in and knowledge about a given topic before they begin drafting. Students can share with peers their writing from a quick write to further assist them in selecting a topic. If students find the short, sustained writing to be frustrating, this may be a clue that another topic should be selected. Quick writes are also good to get the juices flowing. Students can use this writing to help them clarify other important parts of the prewriting process such as purpose, audience, form, and organization.

Students often use drawing as an entrée to writing. They draw and talk about their drawings to select and develop a topic. A first grader drew the diagram or web shown in Figure 7.3 before he selected a topic for a specific story. From the web, he created text and more diagrams to continue story writing.

Purpose and Audience

If students are to grow as writers, they need a self-felt purpose to write as well as a specific audience for whom they are writing. Halliday (1973, 1975) identifies seven different purposes writing serves. These include:

1. Instrumental Language: Language is used to satisfy a need. (Business letter)
2. Regulatory Language: Language is used to control behavior and actions. (School policies)
3. Interactional Language: Language is used to initiate and maintain social relationships. (Invitations)
4. Personal Language: Language is used to express personal responses and opinions. (Diaries)
5. Imaginative Language: Language is used to express creativity. (Poetry)
6. Heuristic Language: Language is used to gather information. (Interviews)
7. Informative Language: Language is used to inform. (Report)

Typical writing assignments, such as writing about summer vacation, lack a genuine purpose, and the audience is usually limited to teachers. Hence students tend to view writing as a contrived process and lacking in authenticity. When classroom activities serve the natural functions of writing, students become engaged in writing. Writing letters to pen pals from another country, providing a friend with written directions to your home, writing questions to ask visiting authors about their books, providing a personal response to books—these are a few examples of the types of writing that

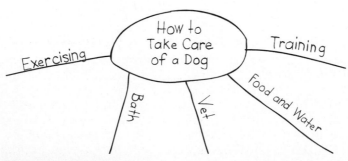

Figure 7.3 Map of Dog Care

are used daily in our own lives. The forms of writing differ as do the audiences. Students can readily recognize the merits in learning to communicate. If clear and correct directions to find a home are not given, friends won't be able to play with them. The end result has meaning.

Forms of Writing

Different forms of writing are needed to address varied writers' purposes as well as meet the needs of particular audiences. Stories and reports are two recognizable forms of writing students learn in school. But do they become familiar with personal forms such as diaries and journals? What about memos, jokes, memoirs, interviews, recipes, and plays? Which of these forms best addresses the writer's purpose? Which addresses the interests and knowledge of the writer's audience? These are judgments writers need to make before they embark on drafting a piece of writing.

Sanford Prizant, a fifth-grade teacher, developed an integrated language arts and social studies unit about the Civil War. He planned to introduce his students to different forms of writing so that they would engage in one of these types as they studied the Civil War. At the outset of the unit, he displayed different genres to illustrate different forms authors employed as they wrote about this time period. During the unit, Sanford gave book talks illustrating how authors used different forms of writing to express their ideas. He read parts of these books and chose to read the Newbery Award winner *Lincoln: A Photobiography* by Russell Freedman to illustrate how an author uses photos to tell about a person's life. The students were also invited to read these books during reading workshop and respond to them in their journal.

Organizing the Written Piece

Students can benefit from developing a general framework for writing their particular piece. From your own schooling, you may remember the infamous outline with main ideas, subpoints, and details, but this is not the organizational framework we are suggesting. Rather, we are recommending the use of mapping strategies and graphic organizers as rudimentary and flexible frameworks to initiate and develop writing. Mapping strategies and graphic organizers are not only beneficial to understanding and remembering information while reading but are also helpful instructional strategies for writing.

If students want to write an informational piece about a particular animal, they may want to think of the categories that are typically included in animal books. Take students to the library and suggest they peruse a number of animal books and note the typical subheadings or chapter titles. They can use this information to form a map to organize their initial draft. For example, Jose, a third grader, is writing a piece about caring for his dog. Before he begins writing, Jose identifies different areas of dog care. He constructs a map as shown in Figure 7.3. The center of his map is the central topic, dog care. The strands emanating from dog care identify different aspects of dog care: grooming, feeding, training, and loving. For each of these parts, Jose provides details. He finds that some areas have fewer details; this causes him to seek additional sources for more information. Jose writes questions to conduct interviews. He uses the electronic card catalog to locate some books on dog care and uses the index in each book to search for specific information on dog care. Jose can easily add the new information to his map and write an organized and more comprehensive piece.

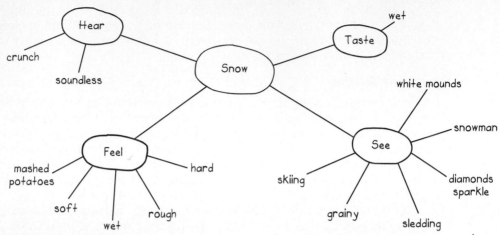

Figure 7.4 Map of Snow

Using a map may also help students write poetry. Tompkins (1994) uses a map highlighting the senses. A fourth grader designed the web shown in Figure 7.4 about snow, which then became the focus of his poem about snow.

For composing stories, you can teach students to use story structure to design a map for writing. Teachers have used simple and complex story structure frameworks to help students think about the different parts of a story. Any framework you employ should highlight the setting, characters, problem, and consequence, since most stories are constructed with these components. Even a simple framework can help students develop the four essential components. This will help them to avoid bringing a story to an abrupt end without developing a solution to the problem. Such frameworks can also guide students' thinking and development of an interesting and compelling story. Two story-structure frameworks are shown in Figure 7.5. The first framework can be employed with younger students while the second one is more applicable to students in grade 5 and above. The latter framework allows for more complex writing and encourages students to think about mood and tone in the setting, several episodes in the plot, development of character, and several problems and conflicts.

To compose analytic pieces involving persuasion, comparison and contrast, cause and effect, or problem and solution, encourage students to use graphic organizers such as Venn diagrams and time lines. You may recall in chapter 5, we suggested that students use these same graphic organizers to organize their thinking while reading text. These organizers can also be employed to help students clarify their thinking as they write text. Peregoy and Boyle (1993) recommend an additional graphic organizer that has achieved success in Leticia Alvarez's classroom, which includes second-language learners. Leticia uses a graphic organizer (see Figure 7.6) to depict the analogy between a train and a coherent piece of writing. The engine provides the power to a train as does the introductory paragraph in an essay. The introduction presents the major points that will be developed in the body of the essay or the cars of a train. The paragraphs are linked together with connecting words or signal words as a train is linked with hitches. Closure occurs with a summary as the caboose func-

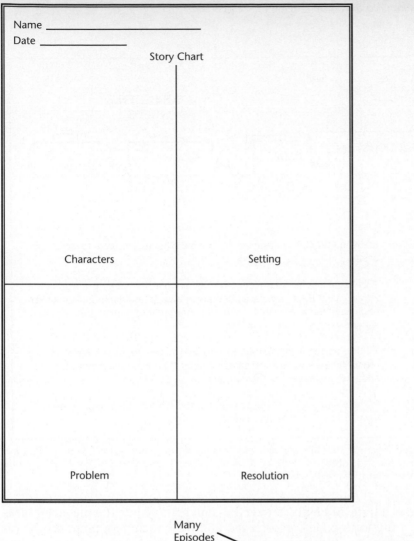

Name _____

Date _____

Story Chart

Characters   Setting

Problem   Resolution

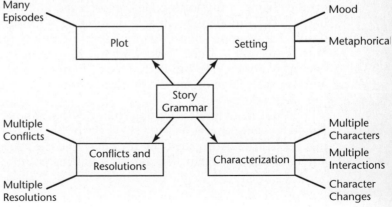

Many Episodes — Plot

Mood — Setting
Metaphorical — Setting

Story Grammar

Multiple Conflicts — Conflicts and Resolutions
Multiple Resolutions — Conflicts and Resolutions

Multiple Characters — Characterization
Multiple Interactions — Characterization
Character Changes — Characterization

Figure 7.5 Story Maps

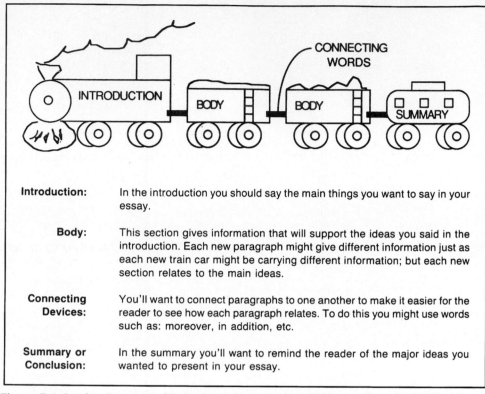

Introduction: In the introduction you should say the main things you want to say in your essay.

Body: This section gives information that will support the ideas you said in the introduction. Each new paragraph might give different information just as each new train car might be carrying different information; but each new section relates to the main ideas.

Connecting Devices: You'll want to connect paragraphs to one another to make it easier for the reader to see how each paragraph relates. To do this you might use words such as: moreover, in addition, etc.

Summary or Conclusion: In the summary you'll want to remind the reader of the major ideas you wanted to present in your essay.

Figure 7.6 Graphic Organizer of Train. *Source:* From *Reading, Writing, and Learning in ESL: A Resource Book for K-8 Teachers,* Second Edition (p. 290), by Suzanne F. Peregoy and Owen F. Boyle, 1997, White Plains, NY: Longman. Reprinted by permission.

tions as the end of a train. Students can use the train graphic to write the major ideas on the engine, a supporting idea on each car, and the concluding point on the caboose. They can identify suitable connecting words for the type of writing they are doing. For example, appropriate connecting words for enumerating ideas include "first," "second," "third," and "finally." In a comparison and contrast piece, connecting words include "similarly," "like," "unlike," and "rather." Displaying the train and its explanation on a bulletin board can serve as a reference for students to organize their writing.

These are only a few writing strategies that can help students organize their initial draft. As students write, they are likely to change the organization by adding, deleting, and consolidating ideas. Or they may find the initial framework was unworkable and have to begin again. This is only a starting point to help students write.

Drafting

During drafting, students are trying out the ideas they have rehearsed. Their focus is on getting their ideas on the page without concerning themselves with punctuation, spelling, and handwriting. Elbow (1981) points out that the student's natural writing voice is hindered when punctuation, spelling, and mechanics are considered during the drafting and early stages of writing. Constructing meaning requires the students' complete attention. Letting the mind consider the spelling of a particular word stops the natural flow of language. The writing that follows may lack cohesiveness, and its coherence is affected by the students' attention to spelling. Once students are pleased with their written ideas, they can then turn their attention to spelling and other mechanical issues.

Drafting takes time and students need more than 40 minutes to write a piece. It often takes many days of 40-minute periods to write a draft. Giving students time to write a draft is essential to increasing writing development. Drafting does not need to be a solitary process. Talk to students as they draft. Ask them questions to facilitate and keep track of their writing. Some of the following questions have created a short two- to three-minute dialogue or conference.

What are you writing?

How is your writing going?

Answers to these questions frequently help students elaborate on their writing and note areas that require more details or need further clarification. The drafting naturally blends into revision and demonstrates that writing is recursive.

To further facilitate students' drafting, suggest that students write on every other line to help them in revising. By writing on every other line, students can easily add words and sentences. They can draw arrows to move sections or do any other type of revision. Many teachers are giving students proofreader's markings so they can write efficiently. First and second graders can learn to use these markings to help writing become fluid.

If computers are available, we suggest that students learn to compose on the computer. Changes are made easily, and students enjoy learning how to use the different computer commands such as Delete, Cut, Paste, and Copy to make writing painless. Unfortunately, we have not seen enough computers in classrooms to make this possible. Junior high and middle schools often have computer labs that have enough computers for a class or sufficient computers for dyads. Take advantage of these resources.

Revision

Drafting and revising are closely linked and do overlap. As students are drafting, they automatically revise. It's hard to compose without changing words, deleting sentences, inverting sentences, and making other alterations. Revision means "seeing again" and is slightly different from drafting. First, when students revise they have committed themselves to sharing or publishing this piece. Additional time is being spent on it, whereas with a rough draft, students can decide to discard it and start another piece. Second, students usually distance themselves from the work before they revise. It may be a day or so before they reread it and make changes. Typically, they share their piece with others and receive feedback before embarking on revision. Many classrooms using a writing process approach establish peer conference groups in which students can read their piece and receive feedback. Students may be a member of a particular group and have a designated day to share their work. Or it may be more informal, and a table in the classroom may be established as a place for conferences. Those who are ready to conference meet at the table. Students then receive feedback from their peers who are also at the revision stage. The membership is flexible, since students may not always be at the same place in their writing. There are advantages to this grouping pattern in that children receive different feedback because of the changing composition of the group. Teachers may also conference with individuals or with small groups and provide another point of view. Authors decide whether to use the conference feedback; they are not obliged to use any of it, even that which comes from the teacher.

Editing

In editing, we focus on mechanics and other written conventions such as spelling, usage, and subject-verb agreement. At this stage, students prepare their writing for publication; standard form and conventions are expected. First, students read and edit their own pieces according to their own capabilities. Teachers often provide checklists, as shown in Figure 7.7, to guide editing. (The checklist in Figure 7.7 is designed for third

---

Name _____   Date _____

_____ I read my draft out loud to make sure it makes sense.

_____ I shared my draft with a friend or a response group.

_____ I improved my writing by _____

_____

(adding information, rearranging ideas, adding descriptive words, rewriting
hard-to-understand passages, etc.)

_____ While editing my spelling, I learned the correct spelling for the
                 following words:
                               _____

                               _____

                               _____

                               _____

                               _____

_____ I checked my writing for: ( ) capital letters
                                         ( ) punctuation (periods, commas, quotation marks)
                                         ( ) paragraphs
                                         ( ) sentence length

_____ I have "paged" my draft to show where each new page will start (if making
                 a picture book).

_____ I gave my draft a title.

Figure 7.7 Editing Checklist

graders.) Some post them on bulletin boards while others staple them to the students' individual writing folders. These checklists make students accountable, but do not impose standards for perfection. Second, teachers or older students also serve as editors to edit for mechanics and other written conventions that are beyond the younger students' grade and ability levels. Ms. Alvarez, a fifth-grade teacher, has her class serve as senior editors for the third graders. In dyads, fifth graders edit the written pieces after the third graders have completed their editing. This provides meaningful practice for the fifth graders and is a service to the third graders and their teacher. Teachers frequently teach students to use the standard system of proofreader's markings. The system is taught and can be posted on a bulletin board to help students produce the final draft. Using this system makes the writing process both functional and authentic.

Publishing/Sharing

Writing needs to be shared. Publishing is one way to share students' work. Publishing can take many forms. Students can make their own bound books (see Figure 7.8 for a simple method to bind books) that can be displayed and checked out of the classroom or school library. The students are published authors just like the authors Jane Yolen and Alan Say. But bound books are not the only types of publications teachers use in their classrooms. Displaying children's writing on the walls in the classroom also reflects the importance and value of students' writing. Students, parents, other teachers, and administrators have opportunities to stop and read individual students' writing. Setting up an author's chair in your classroom does much to promote stu-

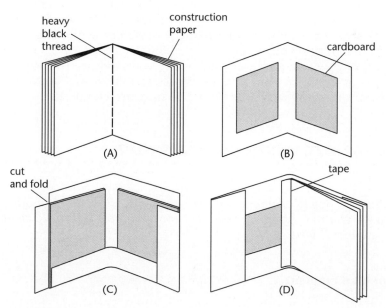

Figure 7.8 How to Make a Book. *Source:* Reprinted by permission of the publisher from Nessel, Denise D., and Jones, Margaret B., *The Language Experience Approach to Reading: A Handbook for Teachers* (New York: Teachers College Press, © 1981 by Teachers College, Columbia University. All rights reserved.), Appendix A: pp. 157–159.

dents as writers. Students look forward to reading their own writing and hearing students' responses in the form of laughter, a smile, a question, or a comment that they too felt the same way. School and classroom newsletters can also serve as another vehicle for sharing students' work. Some students may also want to share their writing in national magazines such as *Stone Soup, Scope,* and others. The submission guidelines are listed in these publications.

Minilessons

To help children improve their writing, incorporate minilessons as a routine part of writing workshop. These lessons are short in duration and focus on students' writing needs. For example, if students are writing dialogues in their stories, then it may be appropriate to teach the use of quotations and speaker tags. Learning this skill in this way is meaningful, and students can put it into practice as they continue their writing of stories. Using your own writing as a model, teach students how you use quotations and include different words in speaker tags. Use books to show how other authors use conversation. As students read books, ask them to note different verbs to tell who and how the speaker said the sentence. Students can choose interesting book conversations to share in the next minilesson or copy them to share on a bulletin board about quotations.

Choose minilesson topics that emanate from students' writing. Get students actively involved in the minilesson so they are constructing their own understanding of the task they are to learn. Use models for learning the task such as showing how outstanding authors use a skill, style, or genre, for instance, to stimulate interest and provide clarity. Provide students with opportunities to review the lesson by displaying authors' work that demonstrates a particular task in the minilesson and by having students design a bulletin board display to illustrate the task. Such opportunities provide meaningful reinforcement and different ways to learn through visual, auditory, kinesthetic, and tactile means. Keep the lessons short—no longer than 15 minutes. The heart of writing workshop should be students' composing.

HOW DO YOU ORGANIZE WRITING WORKSHOP?

In this section, we describe one way to organize writing workshop, but others do exist. We encourage you to experiment with this configuration and make changes to address your students' needs.

Time and Classroom Management

To begin, establish a daily time for writing workshop. For young children, 15 to 20 minutes may be sufficient and can be lengthened as they become more engaged in writing. Older students can start with 25 and gradually work up to 40 minutes. Begin by making your students aware of the daily schedule so they can promptly begin writing workshop by getting their writing folders from file boxes located in the designated writing area. Using two file boxes to store writing folders maximizes efficiency so students aren't standing in line. In these folders, students keep their daily writing. On one side of the folder, students staple a sheet of paper to record writing topics and their progress On the other side of the folder, students staple a checklist to help them edit. Some students also staple a third sheet to their folders indicating their goals for improving writing. On one side of the folder, Miata notes the topics she has completed and the piece that she is presently writing. On the other side, she has a list of editing guidelines and her list of writing goals. To make it easy for students to locate their folder, teachers can use five different-colored folders and alphabetize the folders by the students' surnames.

Within the writing area, place writing tools such as dictionaries, thesaurus, spelling dictionaries, Franklin speller (electronic spell check), and computers. Students whose writing fluency is affected by spelling difficulties can be helped through the use of the Franklin speller as they edit their writing. Spell checks on computers are also helpful for these students. Word Walls (Cunningham & Allington, 1994) can help students who have difficulties with invented spelling. Primary-grade teachers alphabetically display high-frequency words and content words from thematic units in large print on a classroom wall to help students write. Many of these high-frequency words can't be sounded out and have to be memorized; therefore, the Word Wall can help those who have difficulties with spelling. Students who have difficulties with handwriting because of poor small motor-skills can benefit by using the computer for composing. For younger students, different types of paper should be made available such as unlined paper, primary paper, primary paper with a space for a picture. Provide pencils, markers, crayons, and the like, so young students can draw and write text.

In Figure 7.9, we show how one teacher organized her classroom for writing workshop. There is a writing area with files and tools for writing. Along one wall are several computers for students to compose and produce final drafts. Other classroom areas are also designated. One area is used for teacher-student conferencing. Another is used for conferring with peers. A third area is considered the quiet area so that students can read and write without interruption. Carrels are also located in this area for students who are easily distracted.

Minilessons

Writing workshop begins with students getting their folders, going to a particular writing area, and being prepared to participate in a minilesson. The minilesson is short—about 10 minutes in duration. It is intended to address students' writing needs and thereby improve their writing. At the beginning of the year, minilessons focus on the organizational procedures of writing workshop. Students learn the purpose of writing workshop and its routines. For example, in one minilesson you can explain the daily routine: students get folders from the classroom file box, return to their desks for minilesson, write for 10 minutes, begin teacher and peer conferences while writing continues, share writing, and return that writing folder to the classroom file.

As students demonstrate their understanding of classroom routines for writing workshop, minilessons shift in focus to the writer's craft, such as the purposes writing serves in students' lives, different strategies to select writing topics, the tools

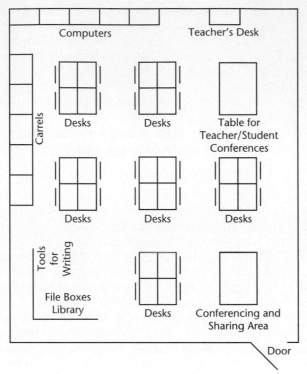

Figure 7.9 Classroom Layout

they use for writing, methods for gathering ideas, and strategies for revision and editing. A typical minilesson for students who are novices to writing workshop would
focus on enabling students to self-select writing topics. Self-selection can present
some discomfort, since students are used to teachers assigning the topic. Telling them
to choose a topic and begin writing for 10 minutes can be very intimidating for students. Many students feel they have nothing to say. Typical retorts include: "Nothing exciting happens to me. I lead a boring life. Who would want to read about my
experiences in a new school?" As a consequence, students sit for 10 minutes staring
at the blank page. They need to learn that their lives are full of rich experiences and
that many other students are interested in their feelings, ideas, and knowledge about
different topics. In the following Learning from Experiences, Ms. Ramirez, a fourth-
grade teacher, provides a minilesson to help students select topics and begin writing.

Learning from Experience

Ms. Ramirez demonstrates in this minilesson how to select topics and use the writing strategy Reading the World (Graves, 1994) to discover a variety of meaningful writing topics.
Before proceeding, try to anticipate the sources she will emphasize for topic selection. Write
your ideas in your journal before reading the dialogue.

Taps prior knowledge	**Ms. Ramirez:** Where do you think authors get their ideas to write books?
	Fourth graders: [No response.]
Focuses information	**Ms. Ramirez:** Where do you think authors such as Beverly Cleary and Judy Blume get their ideas to write books?
	Julianne: From her childhood. She might have had sisters that drove her nuts. She might of had a little sister, like little Ramona.
	Ms. Ramirez: Why would authors use their personal experiences to write books?
	Jeremy: Because they know their experiences well more than someone else's.
	Eric: They can use their own experiences and make it more exciting by exaggerating.
Gets students to think as writer	**Ms. Ramirez:** Do you use your own experiences to write?
	Ed: Yes, I use my experiences.
	Ms. Ramirez: Why do you use your own experiences?
	Ed: Because they are exciting.
Tries to extend thinking	**Ms. Ramirez:** Why else?
	Ed: Because I do a lot of stuff that is exciting.
Tries to extend thinking	**Ms. Ramirez:** Is it easier to write when you use your own experiences?
	Ed: Yes, because I know what happens, and I don't have to think as much about what I should do next.
	Jeremy: I don't use my own experiences.
	Ms. Ramirez: Jeremy what do you use?
Discovers ideas through writing	**Jeremy:** I use other experiences such as aliens—things that don't happen. I am the kind of writer that I just start writing. I get my ideas from thin air.
	Ms. Ramirez: Where do you get that idea?
	Jeremy: I think of a character or a book and use that to do something else.
Tries to extend thinking	**Ms. Ramirez:** So are you using experiences from reading books to write?
	Jeremy: From reading books, watching TV, and movies. We had to write about Milo meeting a new character after reading *The Phantom Tollbooth*. I used the genie from Aladdin to be my character.
Identifies strategy	**Ms. Ramirez:** I use books to help me write too but I also tend to use my daily experiences. I use a strategy, Reading the World, to help me discover what I know and what I want to focus in my writing. Let me show you how I can read the world.
Demonstrates strategy	Yesterday I was driving from my home in Lake Forest to Springfield. I was traveling on the expressway through urban areas in lots of traffic. There were lots of buildings—a span of industrial buildings, large areas of apartment buildings, high-rises,
Initiates participation	office buildings, railroad yards. As I traveled further, the landscape changed to large expanses of land—flat fields with black soil. I could see for miles. There was nothing obstructing my view. As I think about these experiences, I can then write about them. What did I seem to mention the most?
	Mia: How the scenery changed.
Thinks aloud to identify topic	**Ms. Ramirez:** Why did I talk about this? Because I observed such dramatic changes within a short time as I traveled from the northern to the central part of Illinois. Do

Selects form or genre

I want to use this as a topic to write more about? As I wrote about my travels, I discovered the things that I observed that were most memorable. I developed an interest in pursuing this topic. I discovered that the vast contrasts in Illinois were appealing. How could I best express these contrasts? Should I write a poem, a comparison and contrast piece, or what? I think a poem may best point out the dramatic changes because of its brevity.

Your Turn: Now that you have read this minilesson, reconsider the question: What sources did Ms. Ramirez emphasize for identifying writing topics? What did you learn about topic selection?

Our Turn: Ms. Ramirez encouraged students to share the sources they used to identify writing topics and was able to assess their thinking and adjust her instruction accordingly. She discovered that some fourth graders used their own experiences but may feel these experiences had to be exciting if they were to write about them. Other students seemed to limit their ideas to those authors used in their books or to TV programs and movies. Some comments indicate that students felt quite comfortable relying on the teacher generating the writing topic through the use of prompts. Daily experiences did not appear to be an automatic source for all of these students' writing. Thus Ms. Ramirez's minilesson addressed the needs of her students. It provided them with a strategy to identify writing topics. Using her own ordinary experiences, she used a think-aloud to show students how they can use their daily experiences to discover writing topics.

As Ms. Ramirez demonstrated in the preceding minilesson, many teachers use their own writing to develop learning. Some read books, show videos, or filmstrips about authors to illuminate the writer's craft. Other teachers invite authors into their classroom or school to talk about their writing, while other teachers have older students discuss their writing with beginning writers. Mrs. Seger, a third-grade teacher, for example, invited former third-grade students to share their publications with her present students. These students read their books and talked about how they created them during writing workshop. From these discussions students can develop an understanding of and appreciation for writing and learn how the process of writing evolves in a natural and authentic manner employed by professional, mature, and novice writers alike.

Drafting

The minilesson is followed by students quickly reporting what they will be doing during the day's writing workshop. This short report has become known as "status of the class." It encourages students to set goals and have a plan for the day's workshop, and it also allows teachers to keep track of students' progress. To make this report, students use their writing folder to keep track of their progress. They use the recording sheet in the front of their folder to know which topic they are engaged in writing. This same recording sheet also indicates other topics they want to write about in the future, what they are doing with a particular piece, and which ones they have finished. Using this recording device, students can sustain their daily writing. They develop a routine to move from topic to topic. They do not look to the teacher to furnish the next topic when they have completed a piece.

Sustained writing then commences in which the teacher and students are all writing. By writing, the teacher shows the importance writing has for all individuals. During this time, students are at different stages in the writing process. Some may be beginning a new piece while others may be revising. The goal is to write without interruptions and to get the "ball rolling" so that students are focusing and using this time in a proficient and productive manner. They should be using the writing strategies that help them draft and organize their writing, such as writers' notebooks, mapping, and story structure. Each of these writing strategies can be developed in minilessons throughout the year. Students' writing benefits from learning and using these strategies. Their writing addresses a purpose or goal, is organized, and is more completely developed over time. Moreover, students feel they have direction and know how to approach writing.

Conferencing

After 10 minutes have elapsed, the teacher and students begin conferencing. Students may conference with each other to seek feedback about their writing. Conferences may be very informal and occur in dyads in which, for example, one student wants quick clarification on words used to describe a fight breaking out during the hockey game. Other peer conferences may be more formal; in these, several students may sit together to get feedback on a piece they are intending to publish. This is a longer and more involved conference in which several students are commenting on the entire piece. This type of conference requires training. Students need to provide constructive feedback without telling writers what they need to change in their piece. In a peer conference, the writer should begin by summarizing in one or two sentences the contents of the piece and identify the purpose for writing this piece. This summary can help students respond more effectively during a peer conference. As a consequence, the students are ready to listen; they have a purpose; they can better focus their attention, and they can give meaningful feedback. Peers can also be encouraged to identify memorable parts of the piece, confusing parts, vague areas that need additional development. These types of comments can also provide guidance for revision.

While writing and peer conferences are taking place, the teacher begins short two- to three-minute conferences with students. The teacher moves to students to inquire about their writing. Typical questions include:

1. What are you writing about?
2. How is your writing going?
3. Will you read the part you are working on now?
4. Will you read the part of your writing that you are pleased with?
5. Will you read the part of your writing that you have been struggling with?

As you are moving from student to student, it is helpful to carry a clipboard to note the date you met with the student and comments about the student's writing. A sam-

Date	Student's Name	Comments
3/25	Ricardo	Short, choppy sentences
3/25	Sarah	Story doesn't have a problem. Good beginning
3/25	Ramell	No description
3/25	Chanda	Has good beginning, middle, and end

Figure 7.10 Writing Conference Sheet

ple conference sheet is pictured in Figure 7.10. Keep comments to a minimum so you can confer with many students.

You may recall that we suggested using five different-colored folders to organize writing workshop. Colored folders help students quickly locate their folder, but it also helps you schedule weekly conferences. For example, you may confer with those students who have green folders on Monday, those students with red folders on Tuesday, and so forth. This system helps students know when they can meet with you. They have one day they can discuss their writing on an individual basis. Although you meet with individual students on a weekly basis, some students need further assistance. By conducting short two- to three-minute conferences, you should have time to meet with those two or three students who may need extra assistance. It may be helpful to confer with these students first so they can focus on writing and experience less frustration.

To facilitate conferencing you may ask students to supply the following information the day before their scheduled conference. Graves (1994) suggests that students include the following information:

This is what my piece is about: _____.

This is what I set out to do: _____.

This is where I am in the piece
and I am still working on my goal:_____.

This is what I want to work on next: _____.

As a consequence of having this information, when you meet with the student, you can ask better questions about his or her writing.

Revising

When we think about conferencing, we tend to think about revising; otherwise, why would we seek feedback during conferences? It is likely that students will revise after the conference; however, revising isn't that straightforward and sequential in nature. Students naturally revise as they compose, thereby demonstrating the fact that writing is recursive. Moreover, many writers note that writing is revision.

We focus on revision at this point because the interactions that occur during conference allow authors to receive feedback about their work. Although authors are in charge of their work, conferencing can provide some important feedback for creating a better piece. It is this feedback we want authors to hear so they improve their written piece and grow as writers. We now focus on ways to help students revise; these include the use of conferences but also go beyond conferencing.

As students engage in peer conferences, ask them to ask themselves several questions:

1. Based on this conference, what am I going to do to revise this written piece?
2. What are the things that I heard that I need to think about before I revise?
3. What are the things that I heard that I don't think will improve this written piece?

By responding to these questions, students listen carefully to their peers' responses and make the effort to revise their writing. Ask students to attach their responses to their original draft and the revision. In this way, you can see how students are increasing their abilities to revise. Your weekly conference can focus on their thinking and implementation of this revision. Or you can review their work outside of class and provide them with a written response.

A second technique to increase students' abilities to revise is to periodically review their writing folders and provide written feedback. By looking at the students' recording sheets on the inside of their folders, you can note the order in which different pieces were written. You can further learn which pieces were revised. Read only those pieces that were revised. Read the drafts and their revisions to note the types of changes students are making. Are they superficial changes such as adding or deleting words? Are the changes substantial such as reorganizing a piece and adding lots of detail or additional information to provide clarity or stimulate interest? Record your observations so that you can talk about your comments at the subsequent conference. Noting these observations for all students can help you to identify a pattern many students are exhibiting in revision. Use this information to design instruction for future minilessons.

A third technique focuses on students reviewing their own writing folders and reflecting on their growth in revision. Ask students to reread the pieces they have revised from the beginning of the year to the present. Ask them to consider these questions as they review these pieces:

1. What kinds of revisions do you make?
2. Which of these revisions improved your writing the most? Explain.
3. What helps you to revise?
4. What have you learned about revision?
5. Identify a piece that you felt was your best revision. Explain.
6. Identify a piece that you felt helped you learn the most about revision. Explain.

Use two or three of the above questions to help students in their review and ask them to provide written responses or to discuss their answers individually; however, the typical two- to three-minute conferences won't be sufficient and you'll need to alter the conference length. Another alternative is to ask students to share their learning with another peer. In this way, students can learn from each other about how others revise to improve their writing.

The last technique involves reading good authors' works to examine how professional writers stimulate interest, create clarity, and organize their work. You may remember in chapter 6 that we discussed the instructional strategy Directed Reading-Writing Activity (Heller, 1995). This strategy incorporates students' reading and analyzing of professional writers' works to enhance their own writing of a particular genre. This part of the DR-WL can be applied to revision in writing workshop. If students are writing fantasy, for example, encourage them to read authors who write fantasy, such as C. S. Lewis, Mary Norton, and Lloyd Alexander. As they read, they can note how these authors use elements of fantasy to create different worlds, enchantment, and magic. As you become familiar with the genre students like to write, acquire the literature they are choosing to write. Display these books, give book talks, and use them for minilessons to share how good authors write a particular genre.

Editing

Students need to edit their work if they are planning to publish it. This is the time when students need to be conscious, for example, of punctuation, usage, and spelling, since the piece will be made public. Because it's public, students are likely to want their work to look the best it can. This is especially true of students in grades K–5. Adolescents may not always demonstrate an appreciation of this value unless they enjoy writing and it satisfies their need to communicate. Since writing workshop emphasizes self-selection and encourages ownership, adolescents become involved in writing.

To help students edit, we suggest that you examine your curriculum, identifying the punctuation, usage, and grammar students are to learn at your particular grade level. Use this as a guide to make an editing checklist for their writing folders that students can apply while editing. Use this same checklist to plan minilessons so that students can easily apply it to their writing.

Sharing and Publishing

Writing is a form of communication; thus sharing and publishing are natural outcomes of writing. Sharing and publishing can be either informal or formal. Both are appropriate forms that should be incorporated into writing workshop. Sharing may be as simple as students reading their stories to a good friend or as elaborate as publishing a story in a hardbound text that will become part of the school library. In any case, students need to write for a real audience. Their work needs to be shared beyond what is shared with the teacher. Students need to know they are authors who are valued for what they have to say. They have valuable information and interesting ideas that others enjoy reading. What seventh grader who creates a picture book to share with a kindergarten class doesn't experience the enjoyment writing can bring when there is a real audience! And what parents don't giggle when they receive the letter (shown in Figure 7.11) from their son persuading them to purchase a pair of skis? The classrooms that stand out above all others are the ones that display their students' work. And what is better reading than reading second graders' riddles displayed in the classroom, or the poster displays about their favorite animals and the information they gathered? These are all different forms of sharing and publishing for real purposes and for different audiences.

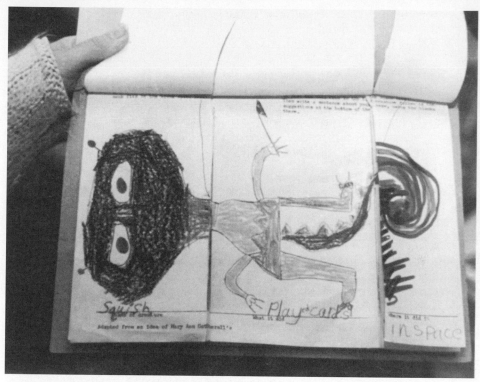

Why do children enjoy reading child-created materials?

Sharing and publishing can be easily incorporated in writing workshop. First of all, not all the writing students do is shared or published. After writing a single draft, a student may abandon the piece and decide to write on another topic. Also some writing is so private that the student does not care to share it.

Sharing can be the easiest and most simple way for student authors to be heard. At the conclusion of writing workshop, Graves (1990) had an author's chair for students to sit in and share their writing with peers. The author's chair provided students with an audience and an opportunity to get additional feedback.

When publishing becomes more formal, such as seventh graders producing picture books for younger students, revising, conferencing, and editing become more intentional. In this particular case, the seventh graders need to carefully develop and reflect on their writing. Many revisions and conferences may occur to develop the setting, characters, problems, actions to solve the problem, and resolution. Getting feedback in peer and teacher conferences may occur many times before students consider editing. Editing becomes important, when this is a formal publication that is to be shared with other classrooms. This more formal type of publishing, which takes considerable time and effort, should be experienced by all students. This type of publication is labor-intensive and should occur less frequently during the school year. Yet students do need to see their writing published if we want students to value and improve their writing.

SCHOOL
DISTRICT

LAKE FOREST
*A COMMUNITY
OF LEARNERS*

Dr. Lynn McCarthy
Principal

March 16, 1995

Dear Mom and Dad,

These are the reasons I need the new Volcal P-10 skis. Please read this carefully and you will see why it is important that I get them very soon.

First, my skis are too small. If I get the bigger skis, I will go faster and I will be a better skier.

Next, I have had my skis a long time. I am sick of them because they slow me down. They also have a lot of scratches on them.

Last, I need new skis to grow into as I get bigger. If I get new skis they will last a long, long, long time. You will save money because you will not have to buy me new skis for a long time.

I hope you understand why I need new Volcal P-10 skis. I also hope you consider buying them for me because you know I how much I love skiing! Besides, if I get new skis I will be the best I can be!

Your son,

Edward Johnson

Edward Johnson

Ed

475 E. Cherokee Road • Lake Forest, IL 60045 • 708-234-3805 • Fax 708-615-4467

Figure 7.11 Persuasive Letter

HOW DO YOU ASSESS WRITING?

Writing should be assessed by you and your students. Your opinion and your students' own opinions about their writing are important to increasing their writing ability. Students need guidance in learning how to assess their own writing. They need to identify elements of good writing. Minilessons during writing workshop can develop this aspect by exploring professional writers' pieces and noting elements of good writing such as imagery, character development, word selection, and the like. Create a bulletin board identifying aspects of good writing. Encourage students to add elements of good writing as they discover them. In the next two sections, we explore two ways to assess writing. The first entails student-developed portfolios and the second, establishing writing rubrics.

Portfolios

You and your students can create portfolios to show different aspects of writing you have learned. Your portfolio can serve as a model; it illustrates that adults do write and are always seeking to become better writers. Graves (1994) points out that portfolios allow students to identify goals for becoming better writers and can establish appropriate plans to accomplish this goal.

To help students develop a portfolio, Graves suggests (1994) that students choose and examine six to seven pieces in which they have different feelings about each piece. They can use the following criteria to make their selections:

1. Choose a piece that you like.
2. Choose a piece that was hard to write.
3. Choose a piece that shows you understood a particular writing element (e.g., sequencing ideas logically).
4. Choose a piece that illustrates your understanding of imagery.
5. Choose a piece that you wish you hadn't written.
6. Choose a piece that illustrates a variety of sentence structures.
7. Choose a piece that shows your ability to develop your own voice in writing.

As they choose pieces, students need to briefly explain the reasons for their selection. Students can use Post-its® or attach index cards to write their explanations. They can place their selections and reasons for choosing these pieces in their portfolios for you to review. Students can also share their portfolios with another peer, and you may want them for parent-teacher conferences because they show students' personal assessment of their own writing.

Change the criteria to help students think in different ways about their writing so they continuously set new goals and develop plans for becoming better writers. Encourage students to develop their own criteria for portfolio selection.

After they have made their portfolio selections, ask students to establish new writing goals and ways they intend to accomplish these goals. They can attach these goals and plans to their writing folder so they can review them. These goals and plans can be easily reviewed and discussed during writing conferences.

Writing Rubrics

Students' writing development and progress can be assessed through the use of writing rubrics, and many school districts and state assessments use this system to note such progress. Teachers tend to use this assessment at major points during the school year. For instance, some teachers will use this system at the beginning of the year to gather baseline data on their students' strengths and weaknesses in writing and then again at the conclusion of the school year to measure growth.

What are writing rubrics? A rubric is a criterion that guides the teacher and student to assess and evaluate a written piece. An example of a set of writing rubrics from Deerfield, Illinois, District 109 appears in Figure 7.12. The grade 5 teachers developed these rubrics to assess, evaluate, and guide instruction. To develop these rubrics, all the fifth-grade Deerfield teachers identified specific points that described exemplary, acceptable, and developing written pieces for fifth graders. They then classified the specific criteria into three general rubrics: (1) style, (2) organization, and (3) mechanics. To ensure that the fifth-grade teachers' expectations were reliable, they asked their fifth graders to write about a particular topic within a 40-minute period at school, after which they read the papers and sorted them into these three levels: (1) exemplary, (2) acceptable, and (3) developing. This task concluded with teachers using the sorted papers to describe each general rubric more fully. The fifth-grade teachers then compared their initial writing expectations to the actual written pieces and identified the specific criteria for the three general rubrics that are included in Figure 7.12.

At the beginning of the year, Deerfield teachers provide a topic and score it according to these rubrics. They share their assessment and evaluation with each student, identifying areas of strength and weakness. Goals are then established for each student. Again, at the conclusion of the year, a second topic is given, and students are assessed and evaluated with these same rubrics. Student and teacher meet to discuss this writing and compare it to their initial written piece. Most of these teachers use these same rubrics throughout the year to help students continually self-evaluate their writing.

To sort papers into the three levels of exemplary, acceptable, and developing, Farr and Tone (1994) suggest that teachers ask themselves the following three questions as they sort their students' writing:

1. What are the characteristics of this written piece that make it strong (exemplary)? Do the written pieces in this category share common characteristics?

2. What are the characteristics of this written piece that make it weak (developing)? Do the written pieces in this category share common characteristics?

3. What attributes do the in-between (acceptable) pieces have?

By reading students' writing, you can best identify criteria for your particular grade level and specifically for your particular class. You can also show students examples of acceptable and exemplary writing to further guide instruction.

Name: _____ Date: _____ Exemplary _____ Acceptable _____ Developing _____

	Exemplary (3)	Acceptable (2)	Developing (1)
Style	Well-developed purpose (clear and evident) Rich and vivid language containing depth of feeling and insight Wealth of ideas Shows originality/creativity to a great extent Uses sentence variety appropriately	Purpose is stated. Appropriate vocabulary for grade level Attempt at developing ideas Some variety in sentence use	No purpose is evident. Uses simple vocabulary Underdeveloped ideas No creativity or originality evident Uses simple sentences
Organization	Has easily recognized beginning, middle, end Paper is clearly focused on topic. Appropriate use of paragraphs Paragraphs have a topic sentence and supporting details.	Has a beginning, middle, end Attempts to focus on topic Demonstrates use of paragraphs some use of topic sentences and supporting details	No discernible beginning, middle, end Lacks focus Minimum use of paragraphing Ideas disjointed
Mechanics		Few mechanical errors interrupt the flow of ideas.	Mechanical errors impair meaning (grammar, spelling, capitalization, and punctuation).

Figure 7.12 Deerfield School District #109 Writing Rubrics for Grade 5

HOW CAN SPELLING BE INTEGRATED INTO THE WRITING PROCESS?

The effect spelling has on writing changes as students progress from emergent to more mature writers and readers as a result of their changing knowledge of English orthography. As emergent writers and readers, students spend a great deal of time focusing on sounding out words to put them into print. Their ideas are often compromised because of their emphasis on words. As students progress through the grades, they become familiar with English orthography because of their experiences in reading text, exploring writing using invented spelling, and participating in word activities such as word sort (Morris, 1988) and making words (Cunningham & Allington, 1994). As a consequence, they are able to focus on constructing meaning.

In the early stages of literacy, students should be encouraged to "work through" the spelling of words, since this makes them conscious of our system of English orthography. Foorman et al. (1991) found that first graders made progress in reading and spelling when they received letter-sound instruction during spelling and received meaning emphasis and explicit phonics instruction during reading. Students are actively engaged in making sense of spelling patterns and phonics instruction encourages them to look for these patterns as they read. Other word activities such as shared writing, word sort, and making words (as described in chapter 3) can further develop correct spelling. As students enter the transitional stages of spelling (Gentry, 1981) in which they demonstrate knowledge of some vowel spelling patterns, they are ready to begin a more formal spelling program. Gentry and Gillet (1995) talk about this stage as moving from spelling by ear to spelling by eye. In other words, students are now sorting out the patterns they construct in writing to those patterns they read in text. This transition typically occurs around second grade, when orthographic consistency develops. A formal spelling program needs to be directly linked to writing; otherwise students do not see the relationship. Unfortunately, too many formal spelling programs are viewed as a separate subject, since the spelling words have no relationship to the writing. In this section, we show how spelling can be an integral part of students' writing.

Spelling Workshop

Gentry and Gillet (1995) have developed a program called spelling workshop that is based on the following principles:

1. Students are actively involved in constructing part of their own learning.
2. Students are developing spelling consciousness by self-monitoring their spelling.
3. Students are learning high-utility words used in writing.
4. Students are learning spelling patterns that appear regularly in English.

To implement this program will require an additional 15 minutes devoted to spelling instruction each day for a 5-day cycle. Each week, students are given a set of words that conform to a particular spelling pattern. On Monday, they are given a pretest on these words, a minilesson to discuss this pattern, and strategies for learning to spell words. On Tuesday, students form dyads and become "word hunters" by constructing their own spelling list of 10 words. Some words conform to the spelling pattern while others are based on the students' interest. There are many sources they can use to construct their list:

1. Words from their pretest
2. Words from their writing
3. Words from their reading

On Wednesday and Thursday, the students, in dyads, use different strategies to practice their word lists, such as employing a flip chart as illustrated in Figure 7.13 using different learning modalities: visual, auditory, kinesthetic, and tactile. Use a file folder to make the flip chart. Divide the top of the folder into three parts and label each third with one of the following phrases: "Look and Say," "Cover and Visualize," and "Write

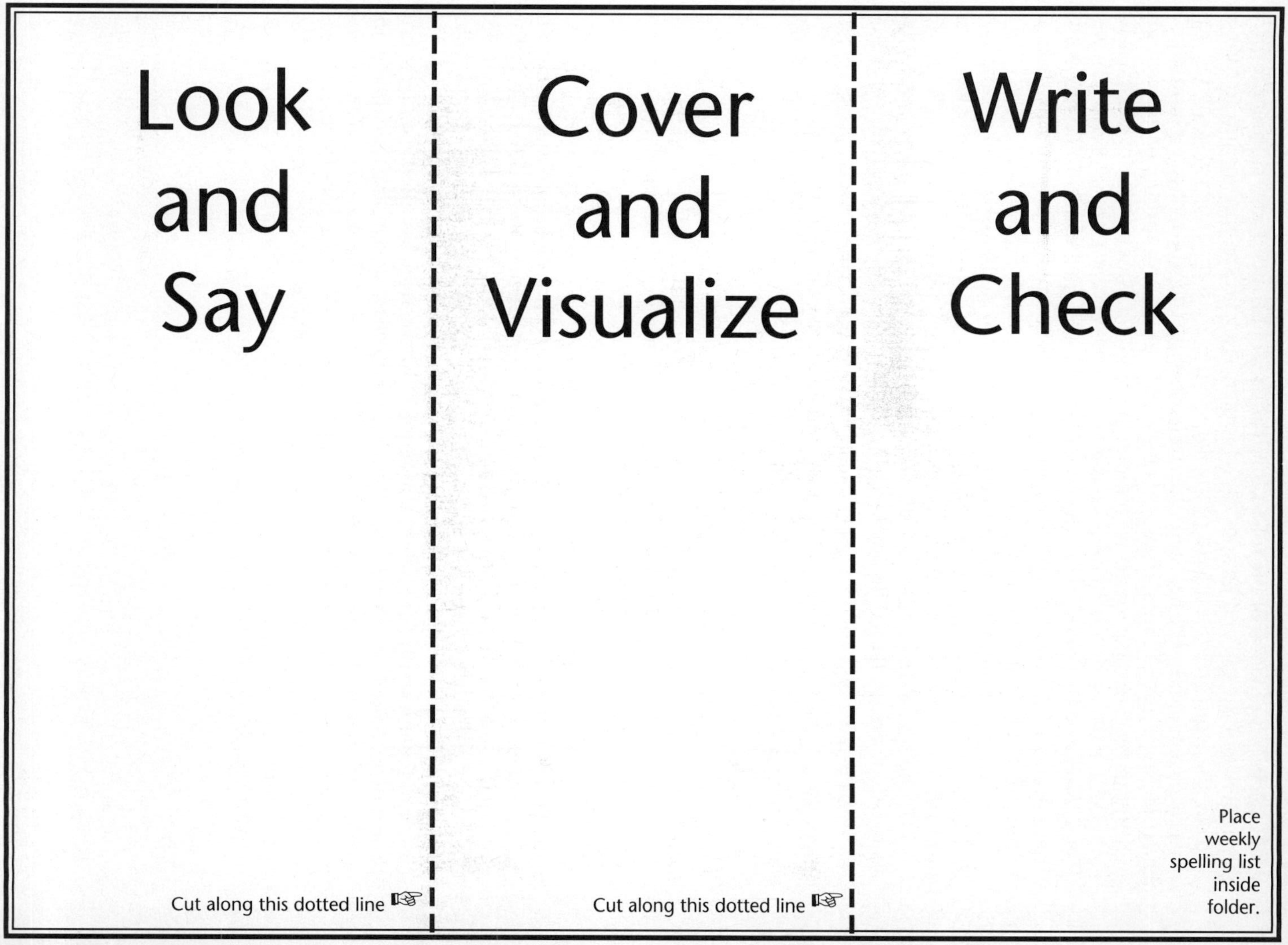

Look
and
Say

Cover
and
Visualize

Write
and
Check

Cut along this dotted line ☞

Cut along this dotted line ☞

Place weekly spelling list inside folder.

Figure 7.13 Spelling Flip Chart

259

and Check." Cut the top of the folder into thirds. To use this strategy, students place paper between the top and bottom of the folder. They lift the top portion to look at and say the word and to notice a particular spelling pattern. They close the tab and visualize the word. In the last step, the students write the word, check it, and repeat the three steps several times. If students have difficulties with specific patterns, highlighting those spelling patterns with a marker can help. Mnemonic devices can also be helpful, such as the traditional saying "i before e except after c." Keith Topping (1995) provides a list of strategies that can help students spell words (see Figure 7.14). These strategies can be discussed with your students and posted in your classroom to remind students to use them.

On Friday, group two dyads together so they can exchange word lists and give each other the posttest. After each posttest, students self-correct their words. One partner spells each word to the other partner.

To help you develop word lists, we suggest you use high frequency word lists such as Fitzgerald's Basic Life Spelling Vocabulary. You can group these words into spelling patterns such as:

anybody   anyhow   anyone   anything   anyway   anywhere

You can give students contrasting patterns such as

mat   mate;   rat   rate;   hat   hate

Students need to add spelling words that may not follow a particular orthographic pattern, such as: their, were, thought, because. These words are frequently used in writing and can be troublesome to some students. Students can also be encouraged to add a few words from thematic units from science, social studies, and other subjects. As dyads form their word lists, encourage them to, first, include the pattern; second, choose words that are chronically misspelled in their writing; and, third, choose words they want to learn to spell. By formulating their own word lists, students become motivated to become better spellers, and they see the relationship between spelling and writing. To further develop the spelling and writing relationship, we suggest that students review their writing weekly and circle misspelled words. As they do this activity, they develop spelling consciousness and recognize words they need to add to their weekly spelling list.

Implementing spelling workshop requires instruction. You need to know how to teach procedures for pretesting, building word lists, developing and practicing spelling strategies, and posttesting, as well as oversee such managerial matters as working together in dyads. To facilitate management, use a spelling folder to collect dated spelling lists, pretests, and posttests. After a month, remove contents. Students can record their spelling pretests, posttests, and the patterns they covered on a recording sheet stapled to their folders, as pictured in Figure 7.15.

Name:

Date	Pretest	Posttest	Spelling Pattern

Figure 7.15 Spelling Recording Sheet

Figure 3
Cued spelling: Mnemonic strategies

Rules	Some spellings do follow logical rules (like "i before e, except after c," which most people remember). The learner may be helped by rules like this, but (a) make sure you've got them right, and (b) keep them simple and few in number.
Words in words	Just breaking words into bits like syllables helps us to remember them, but if you can break them into smaller words that mean something, it's even easier to remember them. Words like shep/herd, care/taker and water/fall are examples.
Fronts and backs	Many words have the same sort of start or finish. Starts and finishes can be looked at closely in a set of words that start or finish the same. Starts (e.g., *sta-*, *pre-*, *un-*) are often not as hard as finishes (e.g., *-tion*, *-ate*, *-ous*, *-ght*).
Families	Words that have the same start and finish can be put in groups or families. Sorting words into families can be a game. This can be done with words that have the same middles or other families or categories.
Make a picture	Making a picture in your mind about the word will help you remember it (like thinking up a picture of two people getting married [wed] on a Wednesday to remind you how to spell the name of that day). Some mind pictures or visual images will seem really silly, but this is good, because if they are funny you will remember them better.
Shrink and grow	You can remember a short hard bit of a word or just some initials for each part (e.g., *par* in separate). Often it helps to grow the initials into new words, to give you a saying or rhyme to remember. Like: - b / e / a / u / tiful big elephants aren't ugly n e c e s s ary one *collar* and two *socks*
Fix and stretch meaning	It helps if you really understand what those hard words mean. You might choose them because they seem interesting. Talking about meaning and use will make the word even more interesting and help fix it in your mind.
Funnies	Work jokes and other silly and comic things into what you do with cued spelling. Funny things are much more likely to be remembered.
Rhyme and rhythm	Rhyme is very good for helping you remember, like in "i before e, except after c." If finding a rhyme is too hard, try to get some rhythm into the mnemonic so it is easier to say. You could even try singing some of the words!
Highlight	We usually get only one bit of a hard word wrong. Try highlighting the hard bits with colours (green for easy bits, red for hard bits). Or like this: station*E*ry

Your must try these out to see what will work best for you. Different learners find different ways more helpful.

Cued spelling will not do much good if you don't get lots of practice with writing as well. To become a better speller, you need to practise writing, wherever you are.

This list may give you some ideas, but it's better if you think of your own ideas. You will have to remember your strategies quickly and easily when writing, so the ideas must be short and sweet. Remember—1. Keep it simple. 2. Do what's easy for you. 3. Find reasons to write.

Figure 7.14 Keith Topping's Cued Spelling Strategies. *Source:* From Topping, Keith. (February 1955). Cued spelling: A powerful technique for parent and peer tutoring. *The Reading Teacher, 48* (5), 374–383. Reprinted with permission of Keith Topping and the International Reading Association. All rights reserved.

Learning from Experience

Mrs. Evans has planned a spelling minilesson for her fourth graders. The spelling list highlighted three important concepts: (1) changing the "y" to an "i" as in "baby" to "babies," (2) knowing the meaning of different inflectional endings, and (3) learning the spelling of inflectional endings. As you read about this spelling lesson, note how Mrs. Evans helps the students understand the meaning and spelling of a particular spelling pattern.

Reviews strategy's purpose

Mrs. Evans: You have just finished taking the spelling pretest. Instead of memorizing the spelling of those words you spelled wrong, I want to make it easier for you. Look for spelling patterns and use these patterns to help you learn the words you misspelled and to spell other words that have this same pattern but are not on your word list. Let's begin by looking for similarities in the words on your spelling list. What do these words have in common?

Skyler: Some of the words end in "ed."

Mercedes: Some end in "ies."

Leticia: Some end in "iest."

Carmen: Other words end in "ier."

Active engagement in learning

Mrs. Evans: Take out your file cards. On each card, write one spelling word. [Mrs. Evans pays particular attention to several of her learning-disabled students who have difficulties copying words and those who have difficulties with spelling. Assistance is provided when needed.]

Mrs. Evans: Sort your word cards into categories. [Students sort their word cards into groups while Mrs. Evans walks around the room providing help as needed.]

Mrs. Evans: What groups did you form? As you tell me the words, I will list them on the board. Check your own groupings to see if you agree with the list on the blackboard. Derek, tell me the words in one of your groups.

Derek: prettier, earlier, heavier.

Mrs. Evans: Do you all agree with this list?

Fourth graders: Yes.

Mrs. Evans: I do too. What is the ending?

Dylan: "ier."

Examines pattern

Mrs. Evans: What are the root words, and how do you spell each of the root words?

Diego: pretty, heavy, early.

Mrs. Evans: What did you have to change in the root word to add the ending?

Paige: Change the "y" to an "i" and then add the "er" ending.

Mrs. Evans: Good. How does the ending affect the word meaning?

Dana: It means that someone is prettier than someone else.

Uses meaning to reinforce spelling pattern

Mrs. Evans: You have the idea. The "er" ending means more. So heavier means more heavy or, in other words, one box of chocolate weighs more than another. I want the heavier one because I love chocolate.

Mrs. Evans continues this minilesson by asking her students to identify the other categories describing the spelling words. They then examine the spelling pattern of changing the "y" to an "i" and discuss the meaning of each inflectional ending.

Your Turn: How does Mrs. Evans help her students understand the meaning and spelling of a particular spelling pattern? Write your ideas in your journal.

Our Turn: Mrs. Evans gets the students actively involved in learning by writing each word on a file card and categorizing the word cards into groups. Using concrete manipulatives can facilitate learning as students write each word, examine spelling patterns, and move word cards around to form groups. Mrs. Evans also uses questioning to help her students discover spelling patterns and their related meanings. Note that Mrs. Evans does not assume that her students can naturally identify the spelling patterns in the weekly word list. Moreover, she points out the importance of looking for spelling patterns to help them learn how to spell words correctly. Examining and applying a spelling strategy ensures that the fourth graders aren't likely to memorize the words for the test and promptly forget them. Strategy teaching gives them a tool to spell and, with this particular pattern, to learn the meaning of inflectional endings.

SUMMARY

In this chapter, we examined the research and theory of writing development. In the first section, we considered how teaching the writing process can improve students' writing; how writing is developed in a social context; when children should begin writing; why, with second-language learners, writing should be developed simultaneously with speaking and reading; why self-selection is so important to writing; why students need to take risks to improve their writing; why rehearsal is crucial to good writing; why examining good writers' work enhances students' writing; why writing should be purposeful and meaningful if we expect students to increase their writing ability; why students need to be exposed to and given the opportunity to write different genres; how teaching grammar in the context of students' writing can improve students' understanding and application; why publishing and celebrating children's writing constitute important parts of writing; and how sharing our work as writers with students improves our knowledge of teaching and learning.

In the second section, we examined the elements of the writing process: rehearsing, selecting, and organizing a topic; identifying a purpose and audience; identifying an appropriate writing form or genre; and organizing the piece. We focused on the process of drafting and revision and learned that writing is recursive. We then considered editing and sharing and publishing.

In the third section, we considered how teachers and students can assess students' writing. We suggested the use of portfolios and ways to select items for portfolio assessment.

In the fourth section, we suggested that the writing process can be best developed through writing workshop. We discussed its components and implementation.

In the final section, we considered the role of spelling in writing. We suggested using spelling workshop as a way to connect the teaching of spelling with writing.

In the Field

1. You and a child keep a writer's notebook for two weeks. Both of you should carry your notebooks everywhere and write down observations, feelings, and ideas. Share your entries with each other and identify topics you want to pursue in writing workshop.

2. Graves uses the writing strategy Reading the World to facilitate topic selection. Take a piece of paper and write for several minutes about yesterday's experiences and activities. You are listening and observing your life to note what might be there to write about. As you write, ask yourself questions and include the answers in your writing. After you have completed your writing, read it, and note if a topic seems to be developing. Try this strategy with a child. Model it and help the child to use this strategy.

3. Develop a minilesson to help students revise a piece of writing.

Portfolio Suggestion

Select from your journal two examples of your responses to Pause and Reflect, Learning from Experience, or In the Field. Write a brief evaluation of your work. Explain how this chapter has affected your thinking about planning writing instruction and assessment.

For Further Reading

Calkins, L. M. (1994). *The art of teaching writing*. Portsmouth, NH: Heinemann.

Gentry, J. R. (1987). *Spel . . . is a four-letter word*. Portsmouth, NH: Heinemann.

Jackson, N. R., & Pillow, P. L. (1992). *The reading-writing workshop: Getting started*. New York: Scholastic.

Lobach, M. R. (1995). Kids explore heritage through writers' workshop and professional publication. *The Reading Teacher, 48,* pp. 522–525.

Wray, D. (1994). Text and authorship. *The Reading Teacher, 48,* pp. 52–59.

III.

Background Knowledge: Organizing for Literacy Instruction

CHAPTER 8

Knowing and Using Children's and Adolescents' Literature

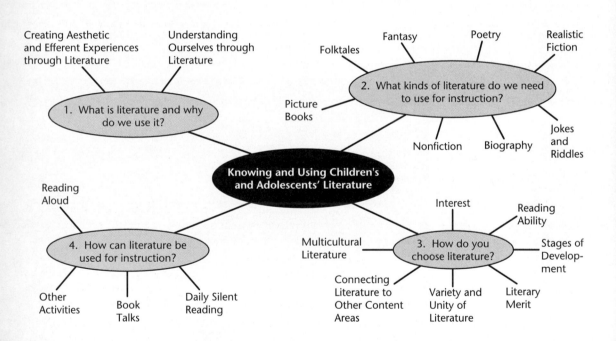

Creating Aesthetic and Efferent Experiences through Literature

Understanding Ourselves through Literature

1. What is literature and why do we use it?

Folktales

Fantasy

Poetry

Realistic Fiction

Picture Books

2. What kinds of literature do we need to use for instruction?

Nonfiction

Biography

Jokes and Riddles

Knowing and Using Children's and Adolescents' Literature

Reading Aloud

4. How can literature be used for instruction?

Other Activities

Book Talks

Daily Silent Reading

Multicultural Literature

Connecting Literature to Other Content Areas

3. How do you choose literature?

Interest

Reading Ability

Stages of Development

Variety and Unity of Literature

Literary Merit

CHAPTER GOALS FOR THE READER

To define literature and understand the importance of using literature to develop literacy

To identify different genres as well as multicultural literature

To be able to select good literature

To learn how to use literature for instruction

CHAPTER OVERVIEW

"I became convinced that the literacy achievement of African-American children would improve if they could see themselves and their experiences, history, and culture reflected in the books they read" (Harris, 1992, p. xvi). Harris's ideas can be easily expanded to all cultures. Children and adolescents who read about themselves in natural and authentic settings, and about events capturing the thoughts and emotions people experience, are likely to become readers and choose reading as an enjoyable, relaxing, and stimulating experience. But it's quality literature children and adolescents need to be experiencing. How can you then invite children and adolescents to experience reading, and how can you help them to become immersed in quality literature?

In this chapter, we provide a definition of literature and reasons for using it in the classroom. We identify different genres, or types of literature, their characteristics, and some titles students may enjoy reading. We present guidelines for evaluating literature and resources for selecting quality literature. We discuss multicultural literature and its impact on students' lives. We explore the different responses students can make to literature and the importance of developing students as critics of literature. Lastly, we discuss how teachers can infuse literature

267

in their classrooms through the use of teacher read-alouds, daily silent reading, and book talks to create lifelong readers.

TAPPING PRIOR KNOWLEDGE TO SET A PURPOSE

Consider your childhood experiences with literature. What were your instructional experiences with literature when you were a child? What enticed you to read? Was it an author? Was it the suspense or adventure of a fast-moving plot? Was it your insatiable curiosity and quest for knowledge? Or was it the experiences and feelings surrounding the reading event? Consider one first grader's response to why she enjoys reading: "I like reading because I can read with my Mommy."

After reviewing the graphic overview, reading the introduction, and reflecting about your experiences with literature, what are your purposes for reading this chapter? List these in your journal.

WHAT IS LITERATURE AND WHY DO WE USE IT?

Literature can be broadly defined as "any kind of printed material" (*Random House Unabridged Dictionary,* 1993, p. 1122). But in this chapter, we limit our discussion to fiction, nonfiction, and poetry. Literature provides both the "heart" and the "backbone" for enabling students to become good readers and writers.

Authentic literature or, in common parlance, the author's original work uses the natural rhythm and cadence of language, provides imagery, develops story plot or concepts, and includes voice with little or no concern for difficulty in vocabulary, sentence structure, and length. The text is natural rather than contrived—that is, no sentences are shortened presumably to make them easier and no vocabulary is replaced with high-frequency, simpler words.

Using authentic literature accomplishes a variety of tasks. Authentic literature stimulates and clarifies thinking. It encourages students to explore, to imagine, to laugh, and to cry. It opens up windows of new opportunities for students to experience historical events and to understand the values, beliefs, and customs of different cultures. Literature develops insights into human development, including behaviors, feelings, and emotions. It provides opportunities for enjoyment and escape from boredom and problems by creating a new world filled with action, intrigue, surprises, laughter, levity, and/or knowledge. By reading literature, students can develop an appreciation of our language. Both visual and auditory images are developed and enhanced. Students expand their knowledge of language patterns and increase vocabulary development. As a consequence, teachers report that students' cognitive, social, and emotional development is enriched by using literature for instruction. But, most importantly, students enjoy good literature and are motivated to read and learn.

Teachers who adhere to a whole-language philosophy or literature-based instruction maintain that their reading program is different from the traditional programs from years past. Students are no longer bored by adapted basal stories or short excerpts and are interested and excited about reading and sharing good literature. Teachers who believe in whole-language or literature-based instruction realize the importance of knowing literature, facilitating students' self-selection, and expanding students' enjoyment to a wide variety of literature.

Pause and Reflect!

Think about children's and adolescents' literature you have read. Which stories made you laugh? Which ones expanded your thinking? Which ones allowed you to escape after a bad day at school or work? Which ones helped you appreciate the struggles of African-Americans or other ethnic groups? Write your selections in your journal. Share your titles with another student colleague.

Creating Aesthetic and Efferent Experiences through Literature

We read literature because it evokes a personal response. Developing and nurturing readers' personal responses to print is an important part of becoming a proficient, mature, and lifelong reader. The initial reading often evokes an aesthetic response in which readers naturally express their feelings and ideas about the text (Rosenblatt, 1978). It's a personal response that draws sustenance from the reader's prior knowledge and experiences and thus is meaningful and motivating for the reader. It's personal meaning making that entices and commits students to read. For example, children who have read Roald Dahl's *BFG* enjoy and respond to the language play and images Dahl creates when the Bloodbottler giant is searching for Sophie while the Big Friendly Giant—BFG, for short—distracts Bloodbottler by suggesting he try eating his favorite food, the snozzcumber. In the following excerpt, we can appreciate Dahl's use of language, the images it creates, and the responses it can elicit from children.

> The Bloodbottler stares suspiciously with small piggy eyes at the snozzcumber.
> Sophie, crouching inside the chewed-off end, began to tremble all over.
> "You is not swizzfiggling me, is you?" said the Bloodbottler.
> "Never!" cried the BFG passionately. "Take a bite and I am positive you will be shouting out oh how scrumdiddlyumptious this wonderveg is!"
> The BFG could see the greedy Bloodbottler's mouth beginning to water more than ever at the prospect of extra food. "Vegitibbles is very good for you," he went on. "It is not healthsome always to be eating meaty things."
> "Just this once," the Bloodbottler said, "I is going to taste these rotsome eats of yours. But I is warning you that if it is filthsome, I is smashing it over your sludgy little head!"
> He picked up the snozzcumber.
> He began raising it on its long journey to his mouth, some fifty feet up in the air.

Sophie wanted to scream *Don't!* But that would have been an even more certain death. Crouching among the slimy seeds, she felt herself being lifted up and up and up.

Suddenly, there was a *crunch* as the Bloodbottler bit a huge hunk off the end. Sophie saw his yellow teeth clamping together a few inches from her head. Then there was utter darkness. She was in his mouth. She caught a whiff of his evil-smelling breath. It stank of bad meat. Then there was utter darkness. She waited for the teeth to go *crunch* once more. She prayed that she would be killed quickly.

"Eeeeeowtch!" roared the Bloodbottler. "Ughbwelch! Ieeeech!" And then he spat. (pp. 55–57)*

But reading is not limited to an aesthetic response and is also efferent in nature, in which case the reader constructs a new text incorporating the author's ideas. The reader is "carrying away" or learning information from text; this is the typical activity engaged in schools. Literature enables students to identify the author's message and gather new information about a topic.

Good literature incorporates both the aesthetic and efferent responses in that mature readers fluctuate from an aesthetic to an efferent response. Ruth Heller's *The Reason for a Flower* naturally evokes both an aesthetic and efferent response:

Seeds travel far and wide. Some even like to hitch a ride upon a bike or on a shoe. Squirrels hide them and forget they do. Some have burrs that stick to furs and travel at a gallop. Seeds can settle anywhere they find water, sun and air and then grow roots and stems and leaves. (unnumbered)†

Ruth Heller's book is only one example of many that encourages both aesthetic and efferent responses. Using this type of literature for instruction can facilitate learning and serve as a catalyst for creating lifelong readers.

Understanding Ourselves through Literature

We read literature because it provides opportunities to understand our own journey through life, and it allows students to imagine who they are and who they can be. As students experience many different types of literature—romance, tragedy, satire and irony, and comedy—they begin to recognize that their own lives mirror many of these same aspects captured in literature. Literature provides insights for our own journey in life and allows us to recognize the universality of human experiences and development. We begin to shed our narrow and stereotypical views about different people and their cultures and begin to recognize the common bonds we do share

---

*Excerpts from *THE BFG* by Roald Dahl. Copyright © 1982 by Roald Dahl. Reprinted by permission of Farrar, Straus & Giroux, Inc.

†Excerpt from The Reason for a Flower, copyright © 1983 by Ruth Heller. Reprinted by permission of Grosset & Dunlap.

as human beings, and we respect the differences that allow us to imagine a better world. To help develop these insights about humanity, students need to read, discuss, and write about a wide variety of literature. Sloan (1991) suggests that elementary school students should be exposed to the "circle of stories" (see Figure 8.1), which provide a broad spectrum of literature within a coherent and unified framework. The circle of stories can be best described as a movie of life. There are no boundaries; one story runs into another so that we recognize how life is a continuous and unified whole. Through story, we realize our dreams as well as experience our worse fears. But hope for a better world is not lost as we recognize the irony and comedy that exist within our lives. Sloan recognizes the unity of literature; stories are interrelated and reflect human imagination and symbolize different aspects of our lives. They capture our quest for identity. Stories mirror our "quests" in life and educate our imagination about achieving the ideal while at the same time always being made aware of reality. Literature reflects the constant conflict between innocence and experience as we search for human identity.

Life begins with a focus on youth, strength, ideals, and innocence, and so does the circle of stories begin with romance. We see young strong, beautiful, handsome heroes and heroines who are in search of the ideal. The romantic story is captured, for example, in the King Arthur tales. In Selina Hastings' retelling of *Sir Gawain and the Loathly Lady,* the young, innocent Sir Gawain is challenged and must find the solution to a riddle. He solves the riddle, and his bride is transformed into a beautiful lady. This is a typical romance in which the protagonist is young, powerful, good, and innocent, faces and overcomes the challenge, and lives happily ever after.

▶ Positive/upbeat
▶ Likable, ordinary character
▶ Rebirth/renewal
▶ Love/hope
▶ Magical/surprising transformation

▶ Hero/heroine
▶ Good vs. evil
▶ Victory and happiness
▶ Quest/adventure

▶ Hope for future
▶ Humor/exaggeration
▶ Characters are victims/weak
▶ Unfulfilled quest

▶ Human limitations
▶ Death/destruction
▶ Character retains dignity/honor
▶ Character has flaws/faults

Figure 8.1 The Circle of Stories. *Source:* Reprinted by permission of the publisher from Glenna Davis Sloan, *The Child as Critic: Teaching Literature in Elementary and Middle Schools, Third Edition* (New York: Teacher College Press, © 1991 by Teachers College, Columbia University. All rights reserved.), Figure 5.1 on p. 59.

Tragedy portrays the limitations all humans possess and shows the darker side of life. We are sometimes victims and are not always in control of our own lives. Much literature exists in this category such as Doris Buchanan Smith's *A Taste of Blackberries* in which Jamie, a young energetic boy who loves to play jokes and be adventuresome, gets stung by a bee, has an allergic reaction, and dies. The tragic loss is felt by his best friend, who has to learn to deal with human limitations.

Irony and satire present the world of experience in which life is hard and cruel. We can see irony and satire in such books as Gary Paulsen's *Nightjohn,* in which Nightjohn, once a freeman, returns to slavery to accomplish his mission of developing literacy among the slaves and experiences extreme cruelty to accomplish his dream.

Comedy presents the hopeful and lighter side to our lives. People's spirits are renewed and opportunities for growth are realized. In Jerry Spinelli's book *Maniac Magee,* the reader experiences Maniac's homelessness and his attempts at eliminating racism and bigotry between Caucasians and African-Americans through a series of humorous and bittersweet adventures. Although segregation still exists, hope for understanding and tolerance prevails.

None of these stories are discrete and embody the characteristics of a single story type: romance, tragedy, irony-satire, and comedy. There is overlap among story types, which is what we experience in our own lives. For example, romance and comedy are captured in John Steptoe's *Mufaro's Beautiful Daughters* in which the beautiful yet kind daughter, rather than the evil and mischievous sister, marries the prince. Good triumphs over evil and living happily ever after characterizes the romance, while comedy is portrayed in the belief that love and hope transcend life's darker side.

Since literature chronicles our lives and provides us with an educated imagination, students are naturally drawn to reading and to responding to good literature. As teachers, we need to build from this natural desire of seeing ourselves through text, seeking self-understanding, and developing an educated imagination by using a wide variety of literature that captures this insatiable desire. By reading and comparing books within this framework, students recognize the underlying principles of literature and view literature as a whole rather than as a set of unrelated titles.

Pause and Reflect!

Identify and briefly describe children's and adolescents' literature that fits the different categories of romance, tragedy, satire-irony, and comedy. Write your responses in your journal. Share your titles with other students in your class.

WHAT KINDS OF LITERATURE DO WE NEED TO USE FOR INSTRUCTION?

Students need to read a wide variety of literature that should help them understand their search for identity (personal quests). But along with the circle of stories conceptual framework, students need to understand different genres or categories of

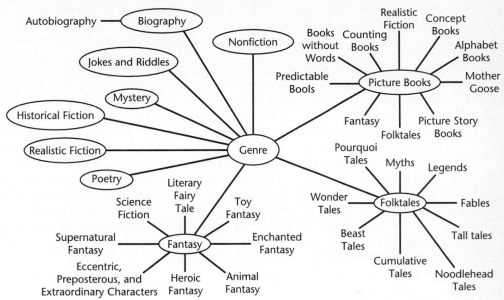

Figure 8.2 Types of Genre

books. These categories should include picture books, folktales, fantasy, science fiction, realistic fiction, mysteries, poetry, biography, historical fiction, and informational books (see Figure 8.2). The categories are not discrete and do overlap. Understanding the characteristics of each genre can help students enjoy and comprehend the authors' ideas and write their own stories, poetry, and informational texts.

In the following sections, we define each genre, providing basic characteristics and a sampling of titles and authors representing a particular genre. Come join us on our adventure of exploring books. We provide a sampling of good books, but we encourage you to go beyond our suggestions by reading additional authors' works. Reading children's and adolescents' books is an important and necessary part of professional development and commitment to providing current and improved instruction.

Picture Books

Picture books can cover a variety of genres such as Mother Goose, alphabet, counting, and concept books, as well as realistic fiction, folktales, and fantasy. What sets off a picture book is its illustrations; yet both illustrations and text are of equal importance in telling the story. The text and illustrations should be complementary; a similar message should be conveyed and the mood and tone developed in text and picture should be in harmony. In the picture book *Zomo the Rabbit,* both text and illustration create a similar feeling and mood of African folklore. The simple flat figures and the bright, primary colors contrasted with the black figure of Zomo, the rabbit, characterize the simple yet clever tricks so common to African trickster tales.

Picture books usually are children's first experiences with books and provide a connection between oral and written language. After hearing the text of many picture books and savoring the illustrations, most children automatically use the pictures to tell the story. Children who have these literacy experiences typically seek out books, sit down, and "read" the pictures, thus demonstrating their emergence as readers. The use of picture books in early childhood and primary classrooms is intended to increase vocabulary, develop the rhyme and rhythm of language, enhance story development, and develop concepts. Of prime importance is that picture books are intended to stimulate enjoyment and a love of literature.

It is a fallacy to think that picture storybooks are only for young children. Many address more mature readers' needs. Such titles as Selina Hasting's *Sir Gawain and the Green Knight*, Chris Van Allsburg's *The Stranger and the Wretched Stone*, Diane Stanley and Peter Vennema's *Shaka King of the Zulus*, and Eve Bunting's *The Wall* explore complex topics and present sophisticated themes. Even with these more sophisticated topics, illustrations are still very important to the telling and meaning of the story and cause it to become a picture book.

In this section, we limit our discussion to Mother Goose, alphabet, and counting books as well as picture storybooks, concept books, and books without words. We begin our book adventure with Mother Goose.

Mother Goose

Mother Goose books help young readers use rhythm, rhyme, and repetition to develop print skills as well as to develop a sense of story. Children often enjoy the humor and exaggeration of these rhymes. Many fine collections exist, such as Greenaway's *Mother Goose*, Tomie dePaola's *Mother Goose*, and *The Tall Book of Mother Goose*.

Alphabet Books

Alphabet books help young readers learn letters and sounds and to increase vocabulary. A wide variety of alphabet books exist. They range from simple ones such as Dr. Seuss's *ABC's* to others that demonstrate the sound and rhythm of language, as developed in Bill Martin's and John Archambault's *Chicka, Chicka, Boom Boom*, to the more complex ones that focus on a particular topic and enhance vocabulary development, which can easily be used with older readers. For example, *Under the Sea from A to Z* is based on the theme of fish and crustaceans while *Jambo Means Hello* engages students in understanding Swahili. John Hunt's alphabet book, *Illuminations*, does much to increase conceptual understanding of people, events, and objects during the middle ages by its use of such words as alchemist, portcullis, and unicorn.

Many alphabet books can be used to facilitate young children's growth in literacy if they include upper- and lowercase type or letters, use common scripts, and illustrate the different sounds associated with the same letter, such as "g" with both hard and soft sounds. With alphabet books such as Graeme Base's *Animalia*, the kindergartners in Mrs. Russ's and Mrs. Moon's class developed literacy skills by using invented spelling to identify the numerous pictured objects on each alphabet page. These young children enjoyed the challenge of exploring the intricate illustrations to search for the many objects, animals, and people beginning with a particular alphabet letter and writing their word lists in their logs.

Counting Books

Counting books develop identification of numerals, number words, and one-to-one correspondence. Many also use rhythm and rhyme to enhance print skills and its appeal to young readers. Such counting books as *Ten Bears All Alone* and *One Wooly Wombat* use rhyme and rhythm to develop print skills as well as number relationships. These books are easily linked to the mathematics curriculum so young children can, for example, learn to count, associate numerals with number words, and do simple addition and subtraction.

Picture Storybooks

Picture storybooks are the most typical types of picture books. Stories follow the elements of story structure: they have setting, characters, a problem, attempts at solution, and resolution. These picture storybooks include simple, realistic, fanciful, and complex stories. Emerging readers benefit from using very simple stories with few words per page that exhibit rhythm and cadence; these have been labeled predictable books because of these characteristics. Predictable picture books such as Ruth Kraus's *The Carrot Seed* and Margaret Wise Brown's *Goodnight Moon* help young readers blossom and feel great accomplishment because they can complete an entire book. Predictable books are often the mainstay of kindergarten and first-grade reading programs. Programs such as Reading Recovery have carefully sequenced picture books from simple to complex (see the Appendix). Although young readers use pictures to help them decode, mature readers benefit from reading and analyzing the illustrations to develop insights about the story and its theme. Review the illustrations in Shel Silverstein's *The Giving Tree* and note how they suggest the secrets of life itself. Although the text is simply written, it has a mature theme that is better understood by older readers.

Concept Books

Concept books are informational in nature and are intended to provide enjoyment, yet at the same time teach concepts such as developing the senses, time, objects, and animals. The content is presented in a simple and logical manner. Some examples are Byron Barton's *Dinosaurs, Dinosaurs,* Tana Hoban's *Circles, Triangles, and Squares,* Donald Crews's *Freight Train,* Gail Gibbon's *Fire! Fire!* Anne Rockwell's *Trucks, and* Lois Ehlert's *Color Zoo.* These and other authors have created many books young children enjoy reading several times. Both boys and girls enjoy learning about animals and discovering how things work; such books can be as popular and appealing as picture storybooks. Too often we may have missed cultivating some young students' love of reading because we limited our focus to reading stories rather than including informational books. Even young readers need a balanced diet of exploring a variety of genres.

Concept books should not be limited to young readers, since many do address mature and complex topics. For example, the Eyewitness Books published by Alfred A. Knopf are developed around illustrations that explain intricate parts and functions of animals and objects that would be interesting and challenging for older and mature readers. Concept books have a broad appeal and can be incorporated at a variety of grade levels.

Books without Words

Books without words are a favorite of students because they can use their imaginations to create stories to accompany the illustrations. Teachers have used these books to develop oral and written language. Students can preview the entire book before they begin telling or writing a story. Many titles are available, and they range from easy to complex, such as Mercer Mayer's *Frog Goes to Dinner* and John Goodall's *The Story of an English Village*. We suggest a few of our favorites:

Titles of Books without Words

Anno	*Anno's Journey*
Alexander, M.	*Bobo's Dream*
Briggs, R.	*The Snowman*
Collington, P.	*The Angel and the Soldier*
Day, A.	*Good Dog, Carl*
Hutchins, P.	*Changes, Changes*
Krahn, F.	*A Flying Saucer Full of Spaghetti*
Mayer, M.	*The Great Cat Chase*
McCully, E.	*Picnic*
Mordillo, G.	*The Damp and Daffy Doings of a Daring Pirate Ship*
Spier, P.	*Rain*
Tafuri, N.	*Jungle Walk*
Turkle, B.	*Deep in the Forest*
Ward, L.	*The Silver Pony*
Winter, P.	*The Bear and the Fly*

Predictable Books

Predictable books are easily read literature for emergent and beginning readers. These books contain three salient elements: (1) simplistic story form, (2) one or two sentences per page, and (3) a predictable language pattern that may be repeated throughout the book and/or words that can be deciphered from the illustrations. These books help young children achieve success and feel a sense of accomplishment. Many of these books exist. Some of the more popular ones include Bill Martin's *Brown Bear, Brown Bear, What Do You See?* Anne Mclean's *The Bus Ride,* Audrey and Don Wood's *Piggies,* Janet and Allan Ahlberg's *Each Peach Pear Plum,* Mirra Ginsburg's *The Chick and the Duckling,* Charles G. Shaw's *It Looked Like Spilled Milk,* and Brian Wildsmith's *The Lion and the Rat.* In chapter 3, we discussed how to use predictable books for beginning reading instruction.

There are many wonderful picture books that students need to hear and read. We provide a sampling of authors and encourage you to extend this list. The authors suggested are well known for their works. Many are longtime favorites of children and have received distinguished book awards. The alphabetical list of authors is given, with only a single representative title. For example, many of Robert McCloskey's other books also provide realistic and enjoyable stories for children. His large and simple illustrations in *Make Way for Ducklings* allow a large group of children to see and enjoy the story during story time. With such favorites as *Blueberries for Sal* and *One Day in Maine,* children take delight in the charcoal or watercolor drawings and the simple but realistic stories.

A Suggested List of Picture Books

Aardema, V. (1976). *Who's in Rabbit's House?* New York: Dial Books for Young Readers.

Ahlberg, J., & Ahlberg, A. (1986). *The Jolly Postman.* New York: Little, Brown & Co.

Aylesworth, J. (1992). *Old Black Fly.* New York: Henry Holt & Company.

Barton, B. (1991). *Dinosaurs, Dinosaurs.* New York: HarperCollins Children's Books.

Bunting, E. (1989). *The Wednesday Surprise.* New York: Ticknor & Fields.

Carle, E. (1986). *The Grouchy Ladybug.* New York: HarperCollins Children's Books.

dePaola, T. (1980). *Knight and the Dragon.* New York: Putnam Books.

Ehlert, L. (1991). *Red Leaf, Yellow Leaf.* New York: Harcourt Brace Jovanovich, Inc.

Fox, M. (1988). *Hattie and the Fox.* Macmillan Children's Book Group.

Gibbons, G. (1986). *Fill It Up!* New York: HarperCollins Children's Books.

Mother Goose (1973). Illustrated by Kate Greenaway. New York: Evergreen Press, Inc.

Henkes, K. (1991). *Chrysanthemum.* New York: Greenwillow Books.

Hoban, R. (1965). *Bread and Jam for Frances.* New York: HarperCollins Children's Books.

Hutchins, P. (1965). *The Doorbell Rang.* New York: Greenwillow Books.

Keats, E. J. (1976). *Snowy Day.* New York: Puffin Books

Kellogg, S. (1985). *Tallyho Pinkerton.* New York: Dial Books for Young Readers.

Lionni, L. (1974). *Alexander and the Wind-up Mouse.* New York: Pantheon Books.

Lobel, A. (1972). *Frog and Toad Together.* New York: HarperCollins Children's Books.

Marshall, J. (1982). *George and Martha One Fine Day.* Boston: Houghton Mifflin Co.

Mayer, M. (1990). *There's a Nightmare in My Closet.* New York: Dial Books for Young Readers.

McCloskey, R. (1976). *Make Way for Ducklings.* New York: Puffin Books.

McCully, E. A. (1992) *Mirette on the High Wire.* New York: Putnam Books.

McKissack, P. (1986). *Flossie and the Fox.* New York: Dial Books for Young Readers.

Minarik, E. H. (1960). *Little Bear's Friend.* New York: HarperCollins Children's Books.

Rey, H. A. (1973). *Curious George.* Boston: Houghton Mifflin Co.

Ringgold, F. (1991). *Tar Beach.* New York: Crown Publisher, Inc.

Rockwell, A. (1985). *Boats.* New York: Dutton Children's Books.

Sendak, M. (1963). *Where the Wild Things Are.* New York: HarperCollins Publishers.

Steig, W. (1969) *Sylvester and the Magic Pebble*. New York: Simon & Schuster.

Steptoe, J. (1984). *The Story of Jumping Mouse*. New York: Lothrop, Lee & Shephard Books.

Van Allsburg, C. (1987). *The Z was Zapped: A Play in Twenty-six Acts*. Boston: Houghton Mifflin Co.

Vincent, G. (1982). *Ernest and Celestine's Picnic*. New York: Greenwillow Books.

Waber, B. (1973). *Ira Sleeps Over*. Boston: Houghton Mifflin Co.

Wahl, J. (1987). *Humphrey's Bear*. New York: Henry Holt & Company.

Wells, R. (1985). *Max's Birthday*. New York: Dial Books for Young Readers.

Yashima, M., & Yahima, T. (1977). *Momo's Kitten*. New York: Puffin Books.

Yolen, J. (1991). *The Greyling*. New York: Putnam Books.

Zolotow, C. (1972). *William's Doll*. New York: HarperCollins Children's Books.

Folktales

Folktales have their roots in oral tradition before the printing press existed. Stories were passed from generation to generation by families to maintain their cultural heritage, morals, virtues, and religious beliefs, as well as to explain natural phenomena. These stories have wide appeal and are enjoyed by young readers through adulthood. The same stories can be seen in many different ethnic and cultural groups and are known as variants. We see the same good and evil characters, transformations, virtues, and similar plot structures. For example, there are many Cinderella variants that young children may enjoy comparing and contrasting. Examples include such titles as the *Egyptian Cinderella, Korean Cinderella, Moss Gown, Tattercoats,* and *Mufaro's Beautiful Daughters*. Young children will especially laugh at William Wegman's *Cinderella,* a spoof that uses dogs as the characters in this tale. Other variants of favorite folktales are interesting for students to explore and analyze, and we list some here.

A Sampling of Folktale Variants

Cinderella

Ai-Ling-Louis. (1982). *Yeh-Shen*. New York: Philomel.

Bushnaq, I. (1986). The little red fish and the clog of gold. In *Arab folktales*. New York: Pantheon.

Climo, S. (1989). *The Egyptian Cinderella*. New York: Harper-Trophy.

Crump, F. (1990). *Cinderella*. Nashville, TN: Winston-Derek.

Jackson, E. (1994). *Cinder Edna*. New York: Lothrop, Lee, & Shepard.

Jacobs, J. (1989). *Tattercoats*. New York: Putnam.

Obyefulu, O., & Safarewicz, E. (1994). *Chinye: A West African folk tale*. New York: Viking.

Perlman, J. (1992). *Cinderella penguin*. New York: Viking.

Phumla M'bane. (1972). *Naomi and the magic fish: A story from Africa*. New York: Doubleday.

Sierra, J. (1992). *Cinderella*. Phoenix, AZ: Oryx Press.

Steptoe, J. (1987). *Mufaro's beautiful daughters*. New York: Lothrop, Lee, & Shepard.

Wegman, W. (1993). *Cinderella*. New York: Hyperion.

The Three Little Pigs

Bishop, G. (1989). *The three little pigs*. New York: Scholastic.

Galdone, P. (1970). *The three little pigs*. New York: Clarion.

Marshall, J. (1989). *The three little pigs*. New York: Dial.

Pene du Bois, W. (1971). *The three little pigs*. New York: Viking.

Scieszka, J. (1989). *The true story of the three little pigs*. New York: Viking.

Trevizas, E. (1993). *The three little wolves and the big bad pig*. New York: McElderry.

The Three Billy Goats Gruff

Arnold, T. (1993). *The three billy goats gruff*. New York: McElderry.

Galdone, P. (1973). *The three billy goats gruff*. New York: Clarion.

Rounds, G. (1993). *The three billy goats gruff*. New York: Holiday House.

The Three Bears

Brett, J. (1987). *Goldilocks and the three bears*. New York: Dodd, Mead.

Marshall, J. (1988). *Goldilocks and the three bears*. New York: Dial.

Little Red Riding Hood

Galdone, P. (1976). *Little red riding hood*. New York: McGraw-Hill.

Goodall, J. S. (1988). *Little red riding hood*. New York. McElderry.

Perrault, C. (1972). *The little red riding hood*. New York: Henry Z. Walck.

Stone Soup

Brown, M. (1947). *Stone soup*. New York: Charles Scribner.

Haviland, V. (1985). The old woman and the tramp. In *Favorite fairy tales* (pp. 299–306). Boston: Little, Brown.

Sapienza, M. (1986). *Stone soup*. Middletown, CT: Weekly Reader.

Stewig, J. W. (1991). *Stone soup*. New York: Holiday House.

Many teachers use Venn diagrams to show similarities and differences as is illustrated in Figure 8.3, which compares Young's Chinese version of Little Red Riding Hood, *Lon PoPo,* with Perrault's *The Little Red Riding Hood* and James Marshall's more humorous version, entitled *Red Riding Hood.*

Besides their variants, folktales also are known for their motifs or recurring patterns that are shared universally or associated with a particular culture or ethnic group. Long sleep, magical powers, transformations, and wishes are some of the common motifs, and some stereotyped characters include the Russian witch, Baba Yaga, the Norwegian trolls, and the African spider, Anasi. Reading and discussing several folktales gives students an opportunity to identify specific motifs and to use these to write their own.

There are specific types of folktales: noodlehead tales, cumulative tales, wonder tales, pourquoi tales, myths, legends, and tall tales. A folktale can appear in more than

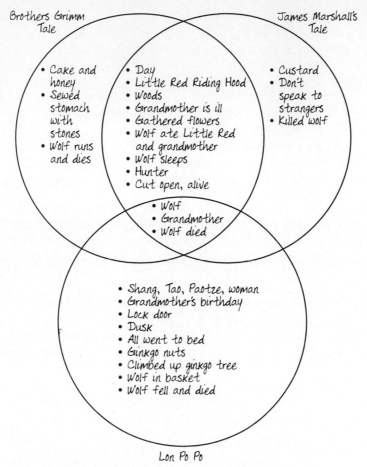

Figure 8.3 Venn Diagram of *Little Red Riding Hood* Stories

one category. For example, Beauty and the Beast is both a beast and a wonder tale. Next, we explore these subcategories of folktales and list a few examples.

Noddlehead Tales

Some folktales are humorous in nature and are called noodlehead tales. In these tales, the protagonist outwits the other characters and exposes them as simple, greedy, and snobbish. Paul Goble writes about a Native American trickster called Iktomi who attempts to cleverly outwit nature, but in the end the fool turns out to be Iktomi. In *Iktomi and the Boulder*, Iktomi boasts about his great looks and gives a boulder his blanket because of the discomfort caused him by the blazing hot sun. He later takes the gift away because the rain will ruin his beautiful appearance. But the boulder gets revenge by chasing him and eventually running over his legs. The boulder continues to outwit Iktomi. This is a great tale that illustrates Native American teachings about respecting nature.

Cumulative Tales

In cumulative tales, the story isn't important; rather, it's the repetition of details building up to the climax. Verna Aardema uses repetition to create action and suspense that lead to the solution of the problem in her retelling of the African folktale *Who's in Rabbit's House?* In this tale, animal after animal tries to help rabbit remove the creature inhabiting rabbit's house. Repetition provides clues to identifying the animal living in rabbit's house. Young readers can easily learn to read the repetitive verse as it is read aloud, and this helps to develop their print skills.

Pause and Reflect!

The Great Enormous Turnip is an example of a cumulative tale. Can you remember others from your childhood? Write your titles in your journal.

Beast Tales

In beast tales, animals are personified and symbolize human beings. These anthropomorphic tales include such the favorites about Chicken Licken, the Three Billy Goats Gruff, and the Three Little Pigs. *The Tall Book of Nursery Tales* published by Harper and Row contains numerous beast tales that young children delight in hearing over and over. More contemporary ones include *The Wolf's Chicken Stew, Awful Aardvark,* and *The Three Javelinas.*

Wonder Tales

Another type of folktale is the wonder tale, which focuses on magic, transformations, royalty, and the virtues of kindness, loyalty, and humility. *Sleeping Beauty, Rapunzel,* and *Beauty and the Beast* are typical examples. In Mordecai Gerstein's *The Seal Mother,* a selkie seal, upon leaving the sea, is wondrously transformed to a beautiful human being.

Older students, especially, enjoy reading satires of wonder tales, such as Jon Scieszka's *The Frog Prince Continued* and *The Stinky Cheese Man and Other Fairly Stupid Tales* by Jon Scieszka and Lane Smith. These two books provide a good opportunity for students to investigate and understand how satire works by comparing it to the familiar tale being satirized. Another favorite is *The Jolly Postman* by Janet and Alan Ahlberg, which provides a unique format of humorous letters and postcards about favorite folktale characters. Students can use this format to write their own letters about other folktales and to also learn another form of writing—that is, letters.

Porquoi Tales

Pourquoi tales explain natural phenomena such as the reasons animals behave in specific ways or look the way they do. Mollel and Morin's *The Orphan Boy* explains how the planet Venus helps the Masai of Kenya and Tanzania. In Martin's *Honey Hunters,* a tale originating from the Ngoni people of Africa, the concept of quarreling is shown to have supposedly begun when animal and beast no longer could share. Kobeh's

Tigers and Opposums focuses on tales from Mexico that provide explanations for the appearance of particular animals.

Myths

Myths focus on the origins of the world and on gods and goddesses; within these tales, science, religious beliefs, and mores are combined. The most well known are the Greek, Roman, and Norse myths, but authors such as Virginia Hamilton, in her book *In the Beginning,* are making us aware of other ethnic myths coming from such places as Africa, Greenland, China, Guatemala, and Australia. Similarly, Barry Lopez's *Crow and Weasel* focuses on Native Americans' spiritual relationships with nature and their obligations to one another.

The older reader tends to understand and enjoy the complex, heroic, and mystical stories such as "The Pea-Pod Man" and "An Endless Sea of Mud." Some easier myths exist for the primary and intermediate readers; they are found in picture books such as Gerald McDermott's *Daughter of Earth and Sun Flight* and Edna Barth's *Cupid and Psyche.*

Legends

Legends are tales about people and events that occurred a long time ago and were passed down over the centuries. Some parts may be true while other parts are exaggerated or, more than likely, did not occur. The "Sword in the Stone" from Robin Lister's *The Legend of King Arthur* is one story whose complete accuracy has been questioned. The power and magic surrounding King Arthur and his sword Excalibur are most likely exaggerated, but they enhance the human imagination. San Souci's *Young Guinevere,* a beautifully illustrated legend of Guinevere, incorporates both history and the legend of the Round Table in telling how Guinevere met Arthur. Jamichael Henterly's illustrations in the *Young Guinevere* are based on the famous *Book of Kells* and employ the gilded illuminated border the monks used during this century. Young Guinevere's embroidery is also captured and reflects the famous Bayeux tapestry of the eleventh century. Students may enjoy such legends from Central and South America as *The Hummingbird King, A Guatemalan Legend,* and *The Sea Serpent's Daughter,* a legend from Brazil.

Fables

Fables tend to be didactic. Their purpose, while still providing enjoyment, is to communicate a moral or ideal human beings should aspire to achieve. Animals are the chief characters in fables, and they personify feelings, values, and behaviors of human beings. Fables tend to be short and are best understood and enjoyed during the intermediate and upper grades. The most well recognized are Aesop's fables, but fables from other cultures exist. John Bierhorst's *Doctor Coyote: A Native American Aesop's Fables* has its roots in the Aztec culture and other Latin cultures. More contemporary Aesop fables include Arnold Lobel's picture-book collection *Fables* and Michael Hague's *Aesop's Fables.* Fables by LaFontaine such as *The Lion and the Rat* have been popularized by the contemporary author Brian Wildsmith.

Tall Tales

Tall tales are rooted in American history. These "larger than life" characters represent the development of the United States—the tales are exaggerations of the might and brute force it took in the making of our nation. The most famous tall tale characters include Paul Bunyan and Babe, his blue ox, Pecos Bill, Johnny Appleseed, Davey Crocket, and Calamity Jane. But there are others who are well depicted in Robert San Souci's *Larger than Life,* such as Strap Buckner, Old Stormalong, and John Henry. Steven Kellogg has written several enjoyable tall tales, such as *Pecos Bill, Paul Bunyan,* and *Johnny Appleseed.* The illustrations in these picture books add much to the telling of these humorous exaggerations. Reading tall tales presents a great opportunity to look at similes and metaphors and their use in creating exaggeration and humor.

Fantasy

Fantasy is related to folktales, since magic, wonder, and transformations are also often employed in this genre. In fantasy, the characters and story plot are original; they are not based on people who once lived or stories once told and passed down from generation to generation. Authors create imagined worlds, characters with supernatural powers, and animals who talk. As is characteristic of folktales, themes having to do with virtues and ideals and with conflicts of good versus evil are also found in fantasy. Adventure and enchantment are pivotal to fantasy. Books such as *Alice's Adventures in Wonderland* and *The Wizard of Oz* immediately come to mind, for in these tales the reader travels from one adventure to another, meeting new exciting characters on their journeys.

Fantasy allows students to escape, dream, and create a better and more ideal world. Authors such as Roald Dahl allow readers to enter into exciting and fanciful worlds. Dahl's *The BFG* is an intriguing story about the Big Friendly Giant, who comes to children's bedrooms to blow in their ears beautiful dreams, while all the other big giants want to be mean and hurt children. In this fanciful adventure, the BFG goes to Sophie's bedroom to blow into her ear a sweet, beautiful dream, but Sophie discovers him and so begins their adventure to save all the children from the mean giants. Dahl's language develops the imaginative world of the giants, and the author also creates new words to describe the giants and their actions. Through Dahl's creative ability to use language, he provides a fascinating and imaginative piece of literature. *The BFG* is only one of the many works of his artistry. If students enjoy this book, they can be directed to his other books, such as *Charlie and the Chocolate Factory, Charlie and the Glass Elevator,* and *Fantastic Mr. Fox.*

Fantasy includes a number of classifications: literary fairy tale; animal fantasy; toy fantasy; enchanted journey; heroic fantasy; tale with eccentric, preposterous, and extraordinary characters; supernatural fantasy, and science fiction.

Literary Fairy Tale

In the literary fairy tale, the author creates an original tale of heroism and royalty, and it is not based on a tale from the oral tradition. In Jane Yolen's *Dove Isabeau,* children can readily recognize the stock characters from folktales: the beautiful, fair, young maiden, and the stepmother who is a witch. The conflict of good versus evil, the spell, and the transformation of Dove Isabeau into the fiery dragon enable students to use their knowledge of folktales to facilitate comprehension and enjoyment of literary fairy tales. Students who are familiar with folktales delight in predicting the different events in the story and discussing which folktales are similar to Dove Isabeau.

Animal Fantasy

The animal fantasy is a favorite among students. In these tales, animals are not only personified but are well-developed characters, so readers can develop insights into their personality, actions, and feelings. Favorite fantasies include E. B. White's *Trumpet of the Swan,* in which a young boy befriends Louis, a swan, who is born without a voice. The main focus is on the swan's family as they work together to get Louis a "trumpet" so he can be like other swans and lead a normal life. In this story, students get to know and understand each of the characters, and they recognize the father swan's unswerving devotion to his son and his determination to find and keep his son's "trumpet" even at a time when the father himself is facing a life-threatening situation.

E. B. White's other classic is *Charlotte's Web,* the beloved tale of Wilbur, the runt pig, and Charlotte, the spider, who sacrificed her life to save Wilbur from being slaughtered. Other famous and enjoyable animal fantasies include Beatrix Potter's *Tales of Peter Rabbit,* George Selden's *Cricket in Times Square,* Beverly Cleary's *The Mouse and the Motorcycle,* and Robert O'Brien's *Mrs. Frisby and the Rats of NIMH.* In all these fantasies, readers become absorbed in the adventure representing high quality literature that precipitates lifelong reading habits.

Toy Fantasy

In toy fantasies, toys are enchanted and personified, but unlike animals in animal fantasies, toys are not considered to be mortal human beings. Jane Hissey's delightful adventure about several stuffed animals—Little Bear, Old Bear, Rabbit, Bramwell Brown, Duck and others—can evoke a warm emotional response from young children. In Anthony Browne's *Gorilla,* Hannah's father is very busy and has been unable to take her to the zoo. Hannah receives a toy gorilla from her father as a substitute for the real gorilla Hannah wanted to see in the zoo. As Hannah sleeps with her new stuffed toy, her toy gorilla magically comes alive, dresses in her father's clothes, and takes Hannah to the zoo. She wakes up the next morning and discovers that her father will take her to the zoo for her birthday. Other favorite tales about toys include Don Freeman's *Corduroy,* A. A. Milne's *Winnie the Pooh,* Margery Nicholson's *The Velveteen Rabbit,* and Edward Ormondroyd's *Theodore* and the sequel, *Theodore's Rival.*

Enchanted Journey

The enchanted journey is an all-time favorite. In this type of fantasy, the characters travel to a magical land of make-believe in which wonder and amazement are commonplace to those who live there but extraordinary to those who visit. Favorite classics fit into this category, such as *Peter Pan, Adventures of Alice in Wonderland, The Wizard of Oz,* and *Charlie and the Chocolate Factory.*

A more contemporary enchanted journey is depicted in Elizabeth Winthrop's *The Castle in the Attic.* In this fantasy, a young boy named William goes on a journey into a magical kingdom to find the other half of the magic token that will free him and his governess to return to their home. Finding the token is only part of their quest. William and Sir Simon also need to win back Sir Simon's kingdom from the wicked Alastor. Castles, knights, and chivalry await William and the reader as they embark on their journey in *The Castle in the Attic.* If students enjoy reading about knights and kings, they would also probably like reading Jon Scieszka's *Knights of the Kitchen Table.*

Heroic Fantasy

Related to the enchanted journey, the heroic fantasy has a hero and/or heroine who saves humankind from a disaster or villain. Unlike the usually ordinary characters in the enchanted journey, the characters in the heroic fantasy have supernatural powers. A popular heroic fantasy for intermediate-grade students is C. S. Lewis's Chronicles of Narnia; *The Lion, the Witch, and the Wardrobe* and *Prince Caspian* are two of the titles in this series. Older Readers have enjoyed Tolkein's Lord of the Rings, Susan Cooper's *The Grey King,* and Lloyd Alexander's *The High King.*

Fantasies with Eccentric, Preposterous, and Extraordinary Characters

This type of fantasy focuses on the wildly exaggerated peculiarities of the protagonist who infuses the fantasy with humor. Who can forget Amelia Bedelia and her ability to see and interpret everything literally? After Mrs. Rogers tells her, "Draw the drapes when the sun comes in" (p. 25), Amelia Bedelia draws a picture of the drapes as the sun shines through the window. In addition to *Amelia Bedelia,* beginning readers will enjoy William Joyce's *George Shrinks,* about a young boy who dreams of being very small and uses toys and other objects to creatively complete the tasks his parents give him.

Favorites for students of early intermediate grades include Astrid Lindgren's unique character, Pippi Longstocking, a Swedish waif who lives with a horse and a monkey and has many outlandish adventures with Tommy and Annika. Mary Norton writes about the fascinating little people in *The Borrowers* and *The Borrowers Afloat.* Another favorite is Richard and Florence Atwater's *Mr. Popper's Penguins,* in which Mr. Popper decides to raise penguins in his own home and then tours the country with his performing penguins. Can you imagine seeing a group of penguins walk out of a New York City taxi? The older reader will be drawn to Carl Sandburg's *Rootabagga Stories,* which use rhythm and poetic devices to create humorous but exaggerated characters such as Ax Me No Questions.

The second-grade teachers in Deerfield School District use cooperative grouping to explore humor in literature. They divide their classes into groups of three and four. Each student selects and prepares a humorous book from which to read parts aloud and to share with the others in the group. The reader then facilitates discussion focusing on the humorous portions of text and the ways authors create humor. Students gain much from this experience, such as understanding humorous and funny characters, conversations, and events. By sharing their reading, these second graders discover new books to read and develop a greater interest in this particular genre while developing reading fluency.

Supernatural Fantasy

In supernatural fantasy, time, events, and people are invested with special or divine abilities that do not exist in the real world. When you think about the supernatural, ghosts immediately come to mind. Generations of readers have been delightfully frightened by *The Legend of Sleepy Hollow.* Often, the reluctant reader can be enticed by a good spooky story. Some surefire winners for those who experience difficulties with print skills are Alvin Schwartz's *In a Dark, Dark Room,* Eve Bunting's *Scary, Scary Halloween,* and Deborah Hautzig's *Little Witch's Big Night.* The older reader will enjoy Alvin Schwartz's *Scary Stories* and *More Scary Stories* as well as Margaret Mahy's *The Haunting* and Sheila Anne Barry's *World's Most Spine-Tingling "True" Ghost Stories.*

Science Fiction

Science fiction is a form of fantasy in which technology often plays a part in the adventures. Some of these uses of technology in the adventures have a scientific basis, if only loosely conceived, while others do not. Time warps, space travel, and the future of the universe are frequent topics. For the younger reader, science fiction typically means stories about space travel—for example, Marzolla's *Jed and the Space Bandits* and *Jed's Junior Space Patrol* and Slobodkin's *The Spaceship under the Apple Tree.*

For older readers, Madeline L'Engle has written intriguing science fiction, such as *A Wrinkle in Time.* Other notable authors include Isaac Asimov, Ray Bradbury, and John Christopher. These writers provide interesting and intriguing plots that deal with highly technical futuristic ideas and objects.

Poetry

Poetry can be a wonderful experience of rhythm, rhyme, and song that provides many beautiful sensory images of our world, encompassing such large subjects as nature, animals, and people and their feelings. Poetry provides opportunities for self-expression and truly evokes an aesthetic response from readers. There are a variety of forms of poetry. One is the narrative, in which a story is told; for example, *Thirteen Moons on Turtle's Back* contains 13 narrative poems from different Native American cultures about the moon and its relationship to the turtle. Diane Siebert's *The Truck Song, Mohave,* and *Heartland* are contemporary examples of narrative poetry that tells stories of our country.

In lyric poetry, poets present their feelings, thoughts, and ideas about nature, people, ideas, and events. The haiku, the cinquain, the limerick, concrete poetry, and free verse are different forms of lyric poetry. The key to poetry is the imagery and imagination employed, and the feelings poets evoke from their readers. Some poets use end rhyme while others use alliteration or assonance to capture the rhythm of language. Adjectives and adverbs help to develop imagery so the reader can feel, taste, smell, see, and hear the image being created. Figurative language such as similes and metaphors also help to create imagery.

Poetry is often neglected for many reasons. Too often, students have learned the technical aspects of poetry and have spent little time focusing on the response poetry evokes. Others have experienced writing poetry to conform to a particular style and form, thus making poetry more formula driven than a matter of capturing an image, feeling, and thought. We suggest that poetry be read aloud to capture the sensory images the poet attempts to create. Response can be in the form of movement, drawing, music, and writing. Shel Silverstein's humorous works *Where the Sidewalk Ends* and *Falling Up* have caused both teachers and students to enjoy, discover, or rediscover poetry. Jack Prelutsky and Jeff Moss are poets who exhibit a similar style and who humorously portray ordinary things such as human relationships, food, holidays, and animals—topics that appeal to children. Shel Silverstein's "Sarah Cynthia Sylvia Stout" provides a good example of the merriment, humor, and playfulness that the poet brings to his poetry.

Reading aloud favorite collections can be a wonderful way to introduce students to many different poets such as Eve Meriam, John Ciardi, Arnold Adoff, David Mc-Cord, Robert Louis Stevenson, William Blake, Dorothy Aldis, Myra Cohn Livingston, and others. Some of the better poetry collections for primary- and intermediate-grade students are *The Random House Book of Poetry for Children* and *Sing a Song of Popcorn*, both of which include a diversity of topics and poets. Teachers may follow the reading of this broad collection of poems with the reading of specific poets and/or topics. Students can participate in poetry readings and share their favorite poems with others and thus create enthusiasm for poetry. Teachers can use a particular poem to introduce a unit in science or social studies. For example, when the class is studying the Revolutionary War, they can read Eve Meriam's poem "George Washington," or if the students are studying whales, they can read poems from *If You Ever Meet a Whale*, a collection of selected poems by Myra Cohn Livingston.

Adolescents who are hesitant about poetry enjoy the humor and free spirit exemplified by Paul Fleischman's *A Joyful Noise: Poems for Two Voices* and *I Am Phoenix*. These two poetry collections allow two readers to participate in reading a poem together. At times, they read a line chorally, and, at other points, they alternate voices. Partner reading can be an easy way to entice adolescents to read poetry out loud. Introduce them to poets from these collections such as Langston Hughes, Roberto Felix Salazar, Nikki Giovanni, Edna St. Vincent Millay, and Robert Frost.

 ## Pause and Reflect!

Choose some poets and read some of their poems. As you read the poems, consider what responses are evoked. Write your responses in your journal and share the poems and responses with another student in your class.

Realistic Fiction

Realistic fiction is a popular genre that is frequently read by students of all ages. In realistic fiction, readers are provided with a mirror of their life. Characters face real problems; they experience joy, sorrow, challenges, laughter, and surprises, as we do in our own lives. Realistic fiction illustrates characters' growth and development, thereby enabling readers to reflect and learn about events and situations they might face in their own lives. By reading realistic fiction, readers can develop insights about life. These insights growing out of a story's theme increase a reader's self-understanding, enjoyment, and learning. What makes realistic fiction powerful is a fast-paced plot and/or well-developed characters. In Bauer's *On My Honor,* Joel deceives his father and goes with his boisterous, show-off friend, Tony, to the Rock River to swim, even though Joel knows the river is polluted and dangerous. The action sequence depicting the swimming, Tony's eventual drowning, and Joel's guilt and cover-up keeps the reader glued to the page. The quick-moving events as well as the author's ability to convey an in-depth understanding of Joel's thoughts about the drowning increase a reader's interest in this story.

Students can benefit from discussions that enhance understanding of plot and character development. For example, during discussion, ask students to consider the techniques authors employ to reveal character. Use these techniques to organize a character map to heighten understanding, learning, and enjoyment of story. In Figure 8.4, Andi Wisner provides a character map and summary for her sixth graders to demonstrate character development. Using Spinelli's *Maniac Magee,* she provides text-based information about Grayson's appearance, actions, and thoughts as well as other characters' thoughts and statements about Grayson. From this map, Mrs. Wisner writes the story told from Grayson's viewpoint. Mrs. Wisner then asks her sixth graders to write a description about a particular character based on their character maps.

Primary-grade children enjoy reading Cynthia Rylant's *Henry and Mudge,* which captures the daily activities of a boy and his dog. Ludwig Bemelman's books about Madeline, a young orphaned Parisian schoolgirl, continue to charm young readers. Dick Gackenbach's *Harry and the Terrible Whatzit* depicts the fears young readers experience when Mom goes to another part of the house, especially when she descends

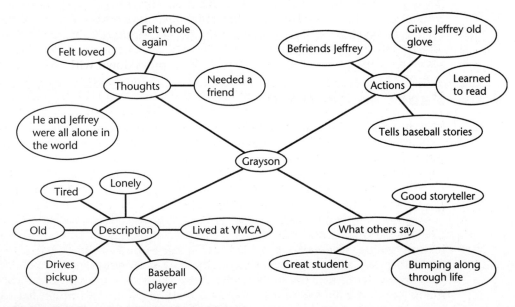

Figure 8.4 Character Map for *Maniac Magee*

to the cellar. Also appealing are Crockett Johnson's memorable books about Harold, who fantasizes by taking a purple crayon and drawing some made-up adventures on the walls. Young readers also respond to sad events, such as Judith Viorst's *The Tenth Good Thing about Barney,* in which a little boy learns to cope with the loss of his dog. Vera Williams also presents a more serious but real-life situation young students might experience. In her book *A Chair for My Mother,* Rosa, her mother, and her grandmother lose their possessions in a fire. Family members begin saving for another comfortable chair for Mother that can replace the one destroyed by fire. Through pain and persistence, Rosa's family remain positive and happy. They show their pride and satisfaction in achieving their goal. Eve Bunting also focuses on serious real-life situations in picture books; for example, her book *The Empty Window* deals with death.

During the intermediate grades, students' realistic fiction interests do not change greatly; they are fascinated by the world of work as they learn to do things their parents do and experience playful, humorous, real-life situations. For the intermediate-grade student, the story needs to include characters of the same age group and a longer, more complex and challenging plot. Typical favorites include such authors as Beverly Cleary and her well-known characters Ramona, Beezus, Henry, and his beloved dog Ribsy. Cleary provides a sense of humor, playfulness, and adventure within real-life situations. Other authors who also write about real-life situations that captivate the reader at this age include Thomas Rockwell, who wrote the humorous book *How to Eat Fried Worms,* in which Billy, challenged by a bet from his peers, goes through a worm-eating ordeal. Judy Blume is an all-time favorite because her characters experience the same feelings and live through the same events many children have experienced. Who can forget Fudge's antics in such books as *SuperFudge, Fudgeamania,* and *The Tales of the Fourth Grade Nothing;* Sheila Tubman from *Otherwise Known as Sheila the Great;* or Margaret and her experiences in arriving at the stage of puberty in *Are You There God? It's Me Margaret?* Jamie Gilson's realistic novel *Do Bananas Chew Gum?* presents the daily experiences involved in being learning-disabled. Lois Lowry writes about a self-assured and articulate girl named Anastasia Krupnik who lives in a Boston suburb. Robert Kimmel Smith writes a hilarious tale entitled *Chocolate Fever,* which is about Henry Green, who loves chocolate and comes down with (what else?) Chocolate Fever. Louis Sachar has three humorous tales, *Wayside School Is Falling Down, Sideways Stories from Wayside School,* and *Wayside School Gets a Little Stranger,* that contain hilarious stories about teachers and students at Wayside School. These tales make children laugh and chuckle and motivate reluctant readers to read.

Stories about real-life experiences with animals also captivate intermediate-grade students and stimulate them to read. Included in this genre are enduring titles such as *King of the Wind, Little Rascal, Big Red, The Black Stallion, Where the Red Fern Grows,* and *Julie of the Wolves.* In Phyllis Reynolds Naylor's book, *Shiloh,* Marty deceives his parents and the dog's owner by befriending a dog who is cruelly treated by his owner. This is a sensitive story that demonstrates love, truth, loyalty, and fairness, as well as how a boy faces the consequences of his actions.

Adolescents frequently look for realistic fiction that helps them develop a sense of adventure, challenge, and identity. These books help adolescents with their questions: Who am I? What will I become? Why do adults and society break or manipulate rules? Why can't I make my own decisions? Favorite authors who address these topics and issues include Gary Paulsen, Paul Zindel, Robert Cormier, Betsy Byars,

M. E. Kerr, Cynthia Voigt, Judy Blume, and Katherine Paterson. At this developmental stage, adolescents are more influenced than before by their peers. These and other authors write about peer pressure and its positive and negative effects on adolescents.

There are two distinct categories of realistic fiction: historical fiction and mysteries.

Historical Fiction

Historical fiction is a distinct type of realistic fiction that is popular with elementary-age students. Historical fiction heightens students' interest in historical events and people and their cultures. Through dramatic story, students can vicariously visit different periods of time and develop insights that nonfiction writing rarely provides. They can learn about the people, values, beliefs, hardships, traditions, and a particular period in history. This genre also helps students consider the present and project what the future ought to be (Blos, 1993).

Reading, for example, Scott O'Dell's *Sing Down the Moon* can help students understand the feelings that adolescent Native American men and women may have experienced as they were driven from their homeland to a reservation, as well as examine the social and political issues of this time period. History textbooks tend to lack a human perspective and do not include the feelings and emotions stories tend to provide.

Although the characters of these works are fictitious, the historical events, setting, experiences, conflicts, and resolutions should be authentic and accurate. In Gary Paulsen's well-researched *Nightjohn,* readers learn the interconnectedness between literacy and freedom—something that a statement such as "Slaves were punished for learning to read and write" cannot express. The human suffering, tenacity, and passion entailed in becoming literate isn't felt and internalized in informational books the way it is when portrayed in *Nightjohn.*

Historical fiction for the younger reader includes Alice Dalgliesh's *The Courage of Sarah Noble.* Dalgliesh's work provides a more peaceful and harmonious perspective on Native Americans and the Europeans who settled in North America. For intermediate-grade students, Elizabeth George Speare's *Sign of the Beaver* captures a sensitive relationship between a Native American and an Anglo-American during the 1700s. Her other book, *The Witch of Blackbird Pond,* provides insights into the 1600s witch trials that occurred in New England. Of course, Laura Ingalls Wilder's many books about the Ingalls family has brought readers hours of pleasurable reading about pioneer life during the settling of the Midwest in the 1800s. Likewise, Patricia MacLachlan's more recent pioneer books, *Sarah Plain and Tall, Skylark,* and *Baby,* and Laurie Lawlor's *Addie across the Prairie* provide rich accounts of pioneer life. Louise Rankin's *Daughter of the Mountains,* set in India, depicts the experiences of a Chinese girl, Momo, under British rule.

Historical fiction portrays societal attitudes prevalent at the time it was written and may portray attitudes and language offensive and not acceptable to people living in today's world. Consider, for instance, Wilder's portrayal of Native Americans in some of her books. The question becomes whether students should read such literature. One way to address differing attitudes is to read and compare literature expressing different perspectives. In this way, students develop an understanding that historical ideas, beliefs, and mores evolve, thus making the events portrayed a "living" history.

Historical fiction can be integrated with content-area textbooks such as social studies and science. For example, students can develop insights about major historical events such as World War II and the Holocaust by reading such books as *Daniel's Story, Journey to Topaz, Number the Stars, The Upstairs Room, The Day Hitler Stole Pink Rabbit,* and *The Hiding Place.* Libraries Unlimited publishes a reference book, *American History for Children and Young Adults,* that relates historical topics and events to historical fiction titles. The book is divided chronologically and by subject and includes an annotated bibliography.

Mystery

Mysteries focus on a puzzle, riddle, and/or the concept of "Who done it?" Intrigue and surprise create the interest in a mystery since readers search for clues to solve it. Characters are often mysterious and secretive and thus contribute to the suspense. Frequently, the setting provides a spooky and erie mood that makes for a good backdrop for the suspense and intrigue. Students see these books as a fun and gamelike experience. Young readers enjoy reading Marjorie Sharmat's *Nate the Great,* in which the author reviews the clues after the mystery is solved. Ken Platt's *Big Max* series infuses some fantasy as Big Max travels by flying umbrella to solve his cases. *Encyclopedia Brown,* another favorite, provides explicit clues so young readers feel successful at solving the mystery.

For the intermediate-grade student, Louise Fitzhugh's *Harriet the Spy* and *The Long Secret* focus on a female protagonist as detective. Ellen Raskin's books, which also provide suspense and surprise, include such titles as *The Westing Game, The Mysterious Disappearance of Leon (I Mean Noel),* and *The Egypt Game.* Deborah and James Howe's *Bunnicula: A Rabbit Tale Mystery* is a wonderful combination of animal fantasy and mystery and is a children's favorite.

Series books such as those about the Boxcar children and Cam Jansen are fast-paced and good books for recreational and independent reading; with these, third- and fourth-grade students can apply reading strategies while enjoying a quick and relaxing book.

Adolescents will enjoy E. L. Konighsburg's *From the Mixed-up Files of Mrs. Basil E. Frankweiler,* Arthur Conan Doyle's classics about Sherlock Holmes, Agatha Christie's mysteries of Detective Hercule Poirot. Edgar Allan Poe and O. Henry wrote fast-paced, suspenseful, and mysterious short stories that adolescents enjoy.

Jokes and Riddles

Humor is an important part of life. It provides release, enjoyment, and relaxation. Jokes and riddles use humor, exaggeration, and word play to create laughter and entertainment. Higher-level thinking and reasoning are easily tapped with these books, since word play is an essential element of riddles. These are also the books that reluctant readers are apt to pick up and read because they are short and usually provoke a chuckle. Readers enjoy memorizing jokes or riddles and telling them to friends. Some surefire winners include Joseph Rosenbloom's *Biggest Riddle Book in the World, School's*

Out Great Vacation Riddles and Jokes, and *The Gigantic Joke Book.* For beginning readers, try *Spacey Riddles and Snakey Riddles,* which is part of a great series of riddle books.

Biography

Biography chronicles a person's life. Authors of biographies are obliged to carefully research the person's life. The author should not idealize the person but rather retain the human flaws and faults all people exhibit. People's lives or parts of their lives should be told more as a story than as a set of facts and concepts. Themes are included to provide a cohesive work that enables the reader to recognize life's challenges. As with historical fiction, biographies are often told from the social, political, and economic perspective of a particular era. Elizabeth Yates's *Amos Fortune, Free Man,* published in the early 1950s, presents a different perspective on African-Americans than does Hamilton's *Anthony Burns: The Defeat and Triumph of an Escaped Slave,* published in the late 1980s. Perspective and bias form a part of biography, but we recommend that students read several books about a person to compare and contrast perspectives and detect if a particular bias exists. Biographies placed in a functional and meaningful context provide an opportunity for critical reading.

There are two forms of biographies, the authentic form and the fictionalized form. They are quite similar because both must be factual in their telling. The main difference lies in the use of dialogue in the fictionalized form. For example, in Jean Fritz's fictionalized biography *George Washington's Mother,* George is depicted having a conversation with his mother. Fritz designed a believable conversation between mother and son, but she had to devise the conversation. A beautiful picture book about Beethoven entitled *Beethoven Lives Upstairs* is written by Barbara Nichol and illustrated by Scott Cameron. This wonderful book is accompanied by an audiotape/CD of Beethoven's beautiful music and also a videotape of Nichol's story about letters written by a boy name Christoph to his uncle Ludwig Beethoven. This is a wonderful fictionalized story that creates interest both in reading and in classical music.

Biographies are written by authors who are not the subject of the book, whereas an autobiography is written by the person whom the story is about. Roald Dahl's book, *Boy,* is autobiographical, and students who enjoy his imaginative books are likely to be interested in reading about his childhood. After reading many of Bill Peet's fascinating books, such as *Pamela Camel,* students enjoy reading Bill Peet's autobiography, which explores his childhood and his inspirations for writing his books.

Around grades 2 or 3, students begin to develop an insatiable appetite for reading biographies. They enjoy reading about athletes, authors, entertainers, and famous people in history. Sports Illustrated for Kids publishes biographies of athletes such as *Shaquille O'Neal.* Millbrook Sports World also publishes a series about famous athletes, such as *Michael Jordan, Basketball Champ,* and *Jennifer Capriati, Teenage Tennis Star.* Learner Publications publishes such sports stories as *Hakeem Olajuwon.* These are great books to motivate students to read, to help student athletes to connect prior knowledge to text-based information, to make inferences, and to read critically.

Biographies present a wonderful opportunity to read, share, and celebrate diversity. They provide role models for different ethnic groups whom students can identify with and whom they can aspire to emulate. John Gillies's *Denor Alcalde: A*

Biography of Henry Cisneros captures the personality of the dynamic Mexican-American mayor of San Antonio. Hawxhurst's biography *Antonia Novello,* about the U.S. surgeon general in Bush's administration, tells the accomplishments of this Puerto Rican-American woman. *Diego* is a wonderful pictorial biography about a famous Mexican artist; also admirable are Eloise Greenfield's *Rosa Parks,* a picture book about an African-American who did much for the civil rights movement, and Davis's *Black Heroes of the American Revolution,* which focuses on African-Americans' roles during the war for independence. Raintree/Steck-Vaughn publishes a number of easy-to-read biographies, such as Nicholas Mohr's *All for the Better: A Story of El Barrio,* which is about a Puerto Rican Bronx lawyer and activist, Evalina Lopez, and Dean Walter Myers' *A Place Called Heartbreak: A Story of Vietnam,* which tells the story of an African-American pilot in the Vietnam war.

Adolescents may enjoy reading Klein's *Edgar Allan Poe: A Mystery* and Coretta Scott King's *My Life with Martin Luther King Jr.* in which the author relates her memories of her husband during the civil rights movement. *Lincoln: A Photobiography* is a Newbery Award–winning biography by Russell Freedman told through photos and text. In *Anthony Burns: The Defeat and Triumph of a Fugitive Slave,* the author, Virginia Hamilton, adds interest to the fictionalized biography by alternating factual chapters about Burns with hypotheses about Burns's thoughts. Joan Kane Nichols's *A Matter of Conscience: The Trial of Anne Hutchinson* recounts Hutchinson's life during the Salem witch trials. Two other well-written books include short biographical selections about women: Polly Schoyer Brooks's *Dreams into Deeds: Nine Women Who Dared* and Susan Beth Pfeffer's *Women Who Changed Things.*

Nonfiction

Nonfiction or informational books present facts and concepts about topics, ideas, events, and people. These books need to be accurate, yet interesting and inviting. The ideas need to be presented in a clear, organized, and coherent manner so they are easily understood by students. National Assessment of Educational Progress (NAEP) data indicates that those who read nonfiction score higher than those who do not report reading nonfiction. Our experiences show that young children of ages three and four show an interest in nonfiction. Ruth Luke and Mimi Aiston designed their junior kindergarten curriculum around the study of animals. They read much nonfiction from books and magazines. These young students showed continued interest in learning about animals by reviewing books and magazines that they heard read in their classroom. These young children also enjoyed rereading and hearing their class dictations about animals. Hence notification seems to be an important area of reading in which to develop student interest.

More recently, we have seen many good informational books published for students in grades ranging from kindergarten through eighth grade. Many informational books appear in a series covering many different topics. Scholastic, for example, has published a number of informational books in their series, A First Discovery Book, which is geared toward young scientists. In this series, there are such titles as *The Egg, the Earth and Sky, The Ladybug,* and *Bears.* Colored photographs are used to illustrate how, for example, the egg appears both inside and outside of the shell. Eyewitness and Eyewitness Junior Books, published by Alfred Knopf in the United States and by Dorling Kindersley in Great Britain, provide incredible illustrations of different parts of objects, animals, and insects. The venerable and ever popular New True Books, published by Children's Press, have enabled primary- and intermediate-grade students to access information about a variety of topics in science and social studies. The type size is large for primary readers, and the books include many photographs depicting the information presented in text. Intermediate-grade students can easily apply reading strategies to access information, and the photographs remain appealing. The Fascinating World of a series published by Barron, presents large illustrations to show such phenomena as the chambers in an anthill and the actual sizes of different species of ants. Aliki has written about many different topics in the series Let's Read-and-Find-Out Book, published by Harper Trophy. In *Digging Up Dinosaurs,* Aliki combines a comic strip format with traditional running text to present information about different species of dinosaurs. The following is a more complete listing of these and other series that may increase students' knowledge as well as their enjoyment.

A Sampling of Nonfiction Series

A First Discovery Book. New York: Scholastic.

A Let's-Read and Find Out Book. New York: Harper Trophy.

Amazing Animal Facts. Chicago: Children's Press.

An Animal Information Book. Los Angeles: Price Stern Sloan.

A New True Book. Chicago: Children's Press.

Eyewitness Books. New York: Alfred Knopf.

Eyewitness Juniors. New York: Alfred Knopf

Friends in Danger. Hillsdale, NJ: Enslow.

Keeping Minibeasts. New York: Franklin Watts.

Picture Library. New York: Franklin Watts.

Rookie Reader—About Science. Chicago: Children's Press.

Your Body. New York: Franklin Watts.

In this section, we reviewed many types and subtypes of children's and adolescents' literature. It is evident there is a variety of genres students can explore and find fascinating and enjoyable. You need to open the doors of literature to your students by selecting the best of literature, providing opportunities for student choice, and giving students numerous opportunities to hear, read, and share literature; you are then likely to develop lifelong readers who want and choose to read.

HOW DO YOU CHOOSE LITERATURE?

Your choice of children's and adolescents' literature for instruction directly affects students' involvement and engagement, and hence their learning. When choosing literature, a number of important factors need to be considered. These factors include students' interests, abilities, and stages of development, and the works' literary merit. The variety of books selected should help students to recognize the unity of literature, should develop literary connections with other curricular areas, and should permit students to experience a diverse and global society. In this section, we consider students' interest, reading ability, and stages of development, works' literary merit, variety and unity of literature, connecting literature to other content areas, and multiculturalism in selecting literature for instruction.

Interest

Student interest should have high priority when selecting literature for instruction. Literature that is interesting to students promotes active involvement, engagement, and commitment to learning. Gathering information about students' interests and using it to select literature is a positive step toward learning. Interest inventories, interviews, and informal discussions can provide information about students' interests. The interest inventory that follows is one information-gathering example and taps students' reading habits, favorite books, authors, and outside interests. Using this inventory in a classroom, teachers can (1) identify groups of children who have similar interests; (2) provide appropriate books and identify authors and genres that may need further investigations; and (3) identify students who have not found reading to be a stimulating activity.

Reading Interest Inventory

Directions: Respond to the following questions.

1. What are some things you like about reading?
2. What are some things you don't like about reading?
3. Are you a good reader? Why or why not?
4. Provide a definition of reading.
5. Why do people read?
6. What things does a person have to learn how to do in order to be a good reader?
7. Name some of your favorite books and authors.
8. Do you prefer fiction or nonfiction?
9. What are some of your interests and hobbies?
10. Do you read for enjoyment? Why? If so, how often and for how long?

Teachers can accommodate students' interests by reading aloud a favorite author or reading aloud about a favorite topic, allowing students to self-select a book or topic for reading instruction, developing units based on students' interests, and bringing books representing students' interests into the classroom.

Reading Ability

The student's ability to read a specific text is an important area to consider when selecting literature. Students benefit from reading literature that presents a challenge but does not frustrate or overwhelm them. Students should be able to read about 95 percent of the words and construct meaning. Reading an easier book can be enjoyable but easy reading as a steady diet does not create a challenge or will most likely not increase students' reading ability. Reading literature that is always frustrating and needs to be continually supported by taped or buddy reading does not provide students an opportunity to apply strategies.

Since reading is a social process, students need to interact with each other. Such interaction may be difficult when a variety of reading levels are found in a typical classroom. To accommodate both interest and reading levels, Ruth Freedman asked her third graders to identify a topic for study and checked out of the school library books on this topic representing the wide variety of reading levels in her classroom. Her third graders did not read the same titles but were able to come together to share what they learned on the topic. Sharing information was the focus for instruction and caused students to read additional books on the topic.

Reading some literature beyond or below a student's instructional range can be appropriate, as, for example, when teaching a particular skill or strategy the entire class needs to develop. Since all Joanne Zielinsky's third graders needed to learn how to use prediction while reading, she chose a text that was at an instructional reading level for most of her students; however, for some it was easy or too challenging. Within 30 minutes, Joanne was able to teach the entire class the meaning of prediction, the steps involved in using prediction as a reading strategy, and its importance to comprehension. Through demonstration and guided practice, the third graders learned how to use this strategy. Choral and buddy reading were used to help all students read and apply the strategy. After the third graders learned the strategy, Joanne had the students apply it with materials at their respective instructional levels.

Students who are reading below grade level often lack vocabulary and language development to read content-area textbooks. As a consequence, these students fall further behind their grade-level peers. These students need to hear and read more complex language patterns and advanced vocabulary. Thus their spending some time listening and reading along with a tape can be beneficial to them in increasing their conceptual knowledge and reading ability.

Stages of Development

Child development researchers have identified several stages of language development (Brown, 1973), personality (Erikson, 1983), and moral development (Kohlberg, 1981), as well as how gender issues affect moral development (Gilligan, 1982). The characteristics of these different stages can guide you in selecting appropriate books for reading instruction. For example, using Erikson's stages of personality development, you can select books that emphasize students' learning the tasks they will need to use during adulthood. Erikson describes the stage from the ages of 6 to 11 as the "Sense of Industry." In this stage, children rely on adults to learn how to take care of themselves and to teach them particular tasks such as reading, gardening, designing buildings, babysitting, and so on. Many books for this age group describe these developmental needs, such as Wilder's *Little House in the Big Woods,* Cooney's *Hattie and the Wild Waves,* Estes's *Rufus M.,* Naylor's *Shiloh,* Arnold's *Mirette on the High Wire,* and Cleary's *Muggie Maggie* and *Henry and the Clubhouse* This happens to be the literature that is most popular with elementary school students.

During adolescence, Erikson says, teenagers seek to find their identity. They question previously established values, learned tasks, and authority figures such as parents and teachers. Much literature exists to enable adolescent exploration, such as Avi's *Nothing but the Truth,* Gary Paulsen's *Hatchet,* Jamaica Kincaid's *Annie John,* Katherine Paterson's *Jacob, Have I Loved,* S. E. Hinton's *The Outsiders,* and Paul Zindel's *A Begonia for Miss Applebaum.* This is the literature this age group seeks to read; too often, teachers don't provide enough time to accommodate their interests, and this often affects their engagement and commitment to literacy.

Most children's and adolescents' literature textbooks provide specific information about the characteristics of each stage of development, its educational implications, and specific books that address the stages. (See Donna Norton's *Through the Eyes of a Child* for a list of titles that meet the needs of particular developmental stages.)

Literary Merit

What makes a book "good"? In this section, we discuss the elements of fiction and nonfiction that lead us to conclude that a book has merit.

Fiction

Choosing good fiction for children may seem like an awesome task. How do you evaluate fiction? In fact, there are six areas that you can use to evaluate literary merit in fiction: setting, character, plot, theme, style, and point of view. One or more of these areas can make a book or story memorable and worthy of children's reading.

The *setting* should be clear, believable, authentic, vivid, and naturally embedded in the telling of the story. Look at the following excerpt from Elizabeth Winthrop's *The Castle in the Attic.* What makes this a good setting?

> William arrived in the vicinity of the castle just as the sun was setting. Even before he reached the castle itself, he knew he was getting close because the land was becoming more and more parched. The houses looked abandoned, and the last people he passed were driving their small herds of scrawny goats and pigs along ahead of them. William could practically count the animals' ribs. "You don't want to go that way," an old woman called out to him. "You'd do best to turn around and come with us. We're all leaving."
>
> William begged for a little water and continued on his way despite their urgings. In the distance, the sky was a dull gray color, and large pieces of ash floated past him on the hot rise. He could see the soldiers patrolling the upper battlements, so he ducked behind a tree. The site had been well chosen, a rocky hill with a path that curled back and forth until it reached the top. A tower stood at each corner, and arrow windows dotted the exterior walls in a random pattern. A single black pennant flew from the corner of one tower. William pulled out his binoculars and focused in on the main gate.
>
> The dragon, a brownish-green, scaly creature, prowled in front of the double wooden doors, endlessly turning on himself so that the occasional bursts of flame from his mouth barely missed his tail. As William watched, the dragon

spied a bird that had flown too close, and he shot his tongue of flame high into the sky. The bird dropped like a stone. (pp. 132–133)*

Winthrop paints this ominous scene of danger and death as a warning of the adventures young William will experience. The author uses setting to highlight William's quest; such a vividly descriptive setting makes the story's events memorable and enhances the quality of this book.

Characters must be believable, authentic, and consistent. Any growth or change that they undergo during the story must seem real, and their behaviors and thoughts throughout must be true to the person that the author has created. Except in folktales and fables, characters should be fully developed, so readers can get inside their heads and become fully involved in their stories. Read the following excerpt from Wilson Rawls's *Where the Red Fern Grows*. What makes this character interesting?

> It's not easy for a young boy to want a dog and not be able to have one. It starts gnawing on his heart, and gets all mixed up in his dreams. It gets worse and worse, until finally it becomes almost unbearable.
>
> If my dog-wanting had been that of an ordinary boy, I'm sure my mother and father would have gotten me a puppy, but my wants were different. I didn't want just one dog. I wanted two, and not just any kind of dog. They had to be a special kind and a special breed.
>
> I had to have some dogs. I went to my father and had a talk with him. He scratched his head and thought it over.
>
> "Well, Billy," he said, "I heard that Old Man Hatfield's collie is going to have pups. I'm sure I can get one of them for you."
>
> He may as well have poured cold water on me. "Papa," I said, "I don't want an old collie dog. I want hounds—coon hounds—and I want two of them." (pp. 7–8)†

We learn about Billy in this excerpt by learning about his thoughts and feelings. The manner in which he describes his yearning for coon dogs is realistic and believable, especially since he lives in the Ozarks, and it is this believable portrayal of character that makes *Where the Red Fern Grows* such a marvelous book.

Children's stories usually have *plot* structures that make them stimulating and compelling. The characters have problems to solve or goals to accomplish. Typically the problem is introduced in the beginning of the story, worked through during the middle, and resolved at the end; the conflict develops logically and sequentially.

Barbara Douglass's *Good as New* is a picture book with a well-developed plot. In this book, K.C., a very young child, is allowed to play with Grady's teddy bear, even though Grady objects. K.C. gets the bear so sticky and muddy that the bear is not al-

---

*Copyright © 1985 by Elizabeth Winthrop. Reprinted from *The Castle on the Attic* by permission of Holiday House.

†From Where the Red Fern Grows (pp. 7–8), by Wilson Rawls, 1961, New York: Doubleday. Reprinted by permission of Books for Young Readers, a Division of Bantam, Doubleday, Dell Publishing Group, Inc.

lowed back into the house. Grady's parents offer to buy him a new bear, but Grady wants his old bear fixed. His parents shake their heads, but Grady's grandfather says, "I can fix that bear." Grandpa disassembles the bear so completely that Grady looks on in despair. But Grandpa keeps working until the bear is, as promised, good as new. As Grady looks at the bear, he says to Grandpa, "I thought you could fix anything. But this bear isn't good as new. It's better than new!" Now when K.C. comes over to visit, Grandpa, Grady, and the bear all go out for a walk.

This picture book has a beginning, middle, and end. Readers are introduced to the characters and the problem; they learn how Grandpa goes about saving the bear (as well as Grady's reactions to each step); they learn how the problem is resolved, and finally they understand and see Grady and Grandpa's reactions to the resolution and discover how the characters will prevent the problem from recurring.

Good as New allows young children to become involved in the story. Children can empathize with Grady, whose parents insist that he share his favorite toy with a preschooler; moreover, children can easily identify with Grady's feelings for his grandfather. Largely because of the elements of its plot, this book provides a memorable and enjoyable reading experience for young children.

The *theme* is the author's central message; it reflects values or developmental learning about life itself. The theme, as Lukens (1976, p. 87) suggests, "does not teach; it helps us understand."* Of course, not all fiction has an identifiable theme; folktales and realistic fiction typically do, while mysteries and science fiction often do not. Stories should not, of course, "preach" to children but should allow them to understand the implications of specific behaviors.

Buchanan Smith's *A Taste of Blackberries* has two well-developed themes for adolescents: the main character begins to develop an understanding of life and death; moreover, he learns to appreciate and value friendship. Both themes develop naturally, through the synergistic effects of plot, characterization, and setting.

Pause and Reflect!

Identify at least three books that have memorable themes. Explain why these themes are so memorable. Share these titles with another student in your class.

An author's individual *style* is the element that allows a particular work to come alive, that provides the alluring enchantment that sets exceptional fiction apart from the norm. The author's choice of words, the rhythm of the sentence patterns, and the use of imagery all work together to create an enjoyable text. Why learn to read if the language all sounds the same? Even young readers can appreciate different styles. What young reader doesn't enjoy the rhythm and word choices in Eric Carle's books, such as *The Very Busy Spider*? How does Carle use language to stimulate interest? Here is one example.

---

*From *A Critical Handbook of Children's Literature* (p. 87), by Rebecca Lukens, 1976, Glenview, IL: Scott, Foresman. Copyright © 1976 by HarperCollins College Publishers. Reprinted by permission of Harper-Collins College Publishers.

> Early one morning the wind blew a spider across the field. A thin, silky thread trailed from her body. The spider landed on a fence post near a farm yard and began to spin a web with her silky thread.
>
> "Neigh! Neigh!" said the horse. "Want to go for a ride?" The spider didn't answer. She was very busy spinning her web. "Moo! Moo!" said the cow. "Want to eat some grass?" The spider didn't answer. She was very busy spinning her web.
>
> "Baa! Baa!" bleated the sheep. "Want to run in the meadow?" The spider didn't answer. She was very busy spinning her web. (pp. 1–8)*

You can almost hear the young reader chanting this text and sensing the rhythm the author creates through repetition of sentence patterns. Carle uses these techniques to create style and to tempt children to read this book repeatedly.

Point of view is, quite simply, the viewpoint from which the story is told or narrated. If the story is told in the first person, we learn about the characters and events through the eyes of the person telling the story. Third-person narration is of two types: omniscient and limited omniscient. In the former, we are shown the thoughts and ideas of every character; in the latter, we are shown the thoughts and ideas of one character and have limited knowledge of the others. An objective point of view provides readers with knowledge of events but not of the inner thoughts of the characters; readers must interpret these for themselves.

Point of view can best be evaluated by reading a selection and noting whether or not you become involved in the story. Can the story be understood and appreciated by the age group for which it is intended? First-person narration, for example, may prove difficult for 6-year-olds, whose developmental stage suggests that they believe everyone thinks as they do. First-person narration in a story that includes events and thoughts universal to children of that age, however, may be very engaging and more comprehensible to very young readers. The picture book *Ira Sleeps Over* by Bernard Waber is told from the first-person point of view, but young children can easily identify with Ira's hesitations about sleeping overnight at a friend's house for the first time and taking along his bear, Foo-foo. Ira's fears—will his friend laugh at his bear's silly name? will he be able to sleep without the bear?—are best conveyed through first-person narration. Readers easily become involved in the story; Ira becomes more real; and the story is more convincing and believable.

We have presented story structure in the order characteristic of the Western tradition: setting, characters, problem, attempts at solution of the problem, resolution. In contrast, in Eastern cultures a plot containing a beginning, middle, and end is likely to be nonexistent. Goal-oriented stories do not reflect, for example, the traditions of Buddhism (Aoki, 1992). Hence the use of story structure or grammars (Stein & Glenn, 1980) to evaluate some Eastern literature is inappropriate. Both types of literature should be read and discussed so all children's knowledge of story is honored and appreciated for its beauty and thinking.

---

*From *The Very Busy Spider* (pp. 1–8), by Eric Carle, 1984, Northampton, MA: Eric Carle Corp. Copyright © 1984 Eric Carle Corp. All rights reserved. Reprinted by permission.

Awards

Consider award-winning books when making literature selections. The Caldecott and Newbery Medals are the two most widely known awards. These two awards are given annually by the American Library Association. The Newbery Medal is given to the most distinguished book written in a given year, while the Caldecott Medal is given to the book with the most distinguished illustrations in a given year. All runner-up books are labeled as Honor Books and are also worthy of consideration. As noted earlier, these books may not always represent people of color in positive and realistic ways, often because of the era in which they were written. Other awards of distinction include the Coretta Scott King Award, the Hans Christian Andersen Award, the Carnegie Medal, Rebecca Caudill Young Readers' Book Award, and the Kate Greenaway Medal.

Nonfiction

Choosing good nonfiction is equally important for reading instruction. In nonfiction, you should be particularly concerned with these questions: Is the text coherent? Are the central ideas readily identifiable and located at the beginnings of paragraphs? Does supportive information follow the central idea?

Nonfiction or expository text should provide a unified set of ideas that are coherently stated. The text structure (cause and effect, problem and solution, comparison and contrast, time order, and enumeration) should highlight the important ideas and concepts. Shorter sentences are not always better; they may be ambiguous and force the reader to make questionable interpretations. If cause-and-effect relationships are important concerns, for example, then the relationships are better stated explicitly in one long sentence than in two short ones (Pearson, 1976). Which of these examples is more easily understood?

"Before the whale dives, it takes in fresh air." (*Running Free,* p. 76)
The whale dives. It takes in fresh air.

The longer, complex sentence provides a framework for time order, which we lose by breaking the sentence into two parts.

Expository text should place central ideas at the beginnings of paragraphs, and supporting details should follow. Important ideas should be stated explicitly. As you read the following excerpt from Herbert Zim's *Dinosaurs,* check for coherence, placement and explicitness of central ideas, and inclusion of essential details.

> Fossils of dinosaurs are hard to find. Land animals do not get buried under preserving layers of sand and mud as often as shellfish and other water animals do. Besides, rocks which are old enough to contain fossils of dinosaurs may be buried deep under layers of newer rocks. Where these rocks do come to the surface, there is only a small chance that fossils will be exposed in them.
>
> It takes patience, skill, and luck to find dinosaur bones. When such bones are found, they are carefully uncovered by experts who know how fragile fossil bones can be. Then the bones and the rock close to them are covered with plaster and burlap for protection. They are carefully removed, packed, and shipped to one of the great museums or universities. Here the bones are cleaned, studied and mounted. The experts compare them with other fossil

bones and with the bones of living animals. Each detail is important. A lump on a bone may show where muscles were attached. The form of teeth tells whether the dinosaur was a plant eater or flesh eater.

The expert must start with a thorough knowledge of living animals. Using this knowledge as a guide, he may build from the bones he has found a complete skeleton of the dinosaur, or even a model as it may have looked when it was alive. (pp. 9–11)

In each paragraph, the important idea is stated in the first sentence, so students can organize their thinking and can easily predict what information they will learn in the rest of the paragraph. The author provides additional help by explaining the process of dealing with fossils sequentially, and this makes the text coherent and easier to comprehend.

Variety and Unity of Literature

From kindergarten through Grade 8, students should experience the different genres and recognize the characteristics associated with each. Students need to compare and contrast books to educate their imagination and enable them to achieve their ideals (Sloan, 1991). To accomplish these tasks, teachers need to consciously plan so that students read broadly both in and out of school. As you devise curriculum, you need to develop a plan to enable your students to study different genres in depth so that they can make informed decisions about daily life situations.

Many teachers address this issue through literature logs, in which students record the books they read for instruction and recreation as well as respond to these books through writing about their literary elements. Teacher and students review their logs to note if different genres and authors are read. They discuss the types read or not read to understand and broaden interests. School districts are also making curricular efforts to highlight particular genres each year so all students will have had intense study of all genres by the end of grade 8.

Connecting Literature to Other Content Areas

When selecting literature, consider the topics being studied in mathematics, social studies, science, and the fine arts. Reading connected to such content areas can expand prior knowledge and vocabulary and thus enhance comprehension. By reading related literature, students develop greater depth and understanding of historical time periods and concepts presented in science and social studies, for example. Students also begin to recognize that learning in each content area is not meant to be isolated and separated but rather connected and reinforced.

Many teachers go beyond selecting a single title to connect a topic in one subject such as science to creating interdisciplinary units that integrate the language arts across the curriculum. This can be done successfully with careful planning, coordination, and/or collaboration. (Such curricular development is described in chapter 2.)

Multicultural Literature

Multicultural literature usually refers to literature focusing on people of color. In the past, this literature was often neglected and ignored. Multicultural literature only accounts for 1 to 2 percent of all children's literature (Bishop, 1992). All students need to read about their own cultural heritage and people. They need to have role models that reflect the values, beliefs, and customs of their culture. Moreover, all students can benefit from reading about different ethnic and cultural groups to better understand humanity, to respect as well as appreciate both similarities and differences, and thus to develop a world vision of society. Multicultural literature can help make society more equitable; it can alter the way we see the world (Bishop, 1992). Moreover, multicultural literature provides an understanding of history, geography, and social studies from a different perspective than that of a textbook. Bieger (1995–1996) points out the importance of multicultural literature by stating, "Through reading, we briefly share in the lives and feelings of the characters rather than dealing only with facts. Literature provides food for both the head and the heart" (p. 309).

Although more multicultural literature is being published, there is not an even distribution among ethnic and cultural groups. For example, there is more African-American literature than there is Latino. Furthermore, Asian literature, for example, represents many different ethnic groups such as Vietnamese, Chinese, Japanese, and Korean, whose traditions and beliefs can vary greatly and thus will be presented differently in literature.

The limited number of multicultural books becomes a more complex issue when we further consider the quality and authenticity of the literature. For example, stereotyping does exist even in award-winning books. Thus multicultural literature must be considered in light of authorship, stereotypes, and authentic and appropriate illustrations.

Controversial Issue

Authorship

The issue of who can write about a particular people and culture has been scrutinized and debated. Can an outsider really know and write about a different people and culture? Or are insiders, who are members of the ethnic and cultural group and familiar with and know its beliefs, values, and traditions, better able to write about their culture? The heatedness of this topic is best illustrated in Seto's (1995) statement:

> I feel very strongly that it is morally wrong for Euro-American writers to "steal" from other cultures in order to jump on the multicultural bandwagon, unless they have direct, personal experience in the country where that culture originates—more than simply being a tourist or doing research in the library.

> In such writing there is a noticeable lack of integrity—something is missing at its core. Writing is above all else a moral issue. If a writer is not honest at the deepest level,

her work will be hollow, no matter how well she knows her craft or how well-developed and interesting her characters and plot may be. (p. 169)

But there are children's authors who do not hold this view. Jane Yolen (1994) points out that if we limited storytelling to only those belonging to the specific ethnic and cultural groups, there might be no literature appearing on the bookshelves about extinct cultures and groups such as the Gypsies and the Amazonian forest people, who tend not to write books. In her interview with Claudia Katz (1995) Suzanne Fisher Staples discusses the qualifications of an author that should be considered rather than the author's ethnicity and culture. She states, "Authors who write literature about other cultures should be informed, analytical, nonjudgmental, and passionate about cultural details and issues" (p. 51).

Although outsiders more than likely have completed research so as to be able to write accurate and authentic books, often, they are at a disadvantage because they are not members of the targeted group and lack the lifelong experiences that undergird cultural authenticity. Although they may be at a disadvantage, does this mean they can't be sensitive to and learn about other cultures and provide another perspective? We believe that students need to read books by insiders so that cultural authenticity is maintained. But we also believe that students should read good literature by outsiders who have spent the time to know ethnic and cultural groups other than their own. Students can benefit by comparing and contrasting perspectives, understanding biases if they exist, and examining the historical era in which the work was created. Such analyses offer students meaningful opportunities to be involved in critical thinking.

Aside from the issue of whether they are insiders or outsiders, authors present particular perspectives that are affected by societal beliefs and local, national, and world events. For example, children's literature on Christopher Columbus frequently presents a narrow and single perspective about Columbus, depicting him as a hero who was strong and insightful but without considering the perspective of the natives who were overridden, transformed, and conquered. Consequently, readers do not develop the perspective of the natives, such as the perspective of the Tainos, from whom Columbus took land and whom he enslaved. By reading and discussing Jane Yolen's *Encounter,* students can develop another perspective of Columbus's explorations, since in this picture book she presents the Tainos's point of view about Columbus's explorations.

By reading and finding out something about the author and noting the book's copyright, students can learn about and also discuss both the perspectives being presented and those not represented. In this activity, research and critical thinking skills are being employed and provide an authentic setting for learning. For instance, students can compare Peter Sis's *Follow the Dream: The Story of Christopher Columbus* to Milton Meltzer's *Columbus and the World around Him* and Adler's *Christopher Columbus, Great Explorer.* As they read each book, ask students to note words that describe Columbus and those used to describe Native Americans. This is a great opportunity to compare and contrast people from different authors' perspectives. Students can then consider implications about reading a single title and one author's viewpoint. Readers may obtain clues about the social, political, and economic thinking of a particular period through careful analysis of multicultural literature. For example, discussing the historical time period when a book was written and how societal views have changed can provide insights about progressive and regressive changes in society.

Stereotypes

Have you read books in which Native Americans have been portrayed as savages, Mexican-Americans as happy-go-lucky, poverty-stricken, members of gangs, and as people who take siestas and procrastinate until "mañana"? Such stereotypical literature does nothing to promote human and cultural understanding, and it tends to perpetuate racism. The language employed to tell the story should be authentic and should characterize the time, place, and people, but it ought not to stereotype the ethnic or cultural group. Moreover, the language should not be denigrating and offensive. Sims (1982) recommends that such words as "savage," "primitive," and "backward" should be avoided when writing about people of color.

If children read books containing stereotypes, they then need to read others that highlight a broader and better understanding of a particular ethnic and cultural group. For example, by reading Virginia Hamilton's *Zeely*, students develop positive images of African-Americans and experience a nurturing, loving environment provided by the parents and extended family members that the author describes.

Pause and Reflect!

Have you read books that have stereotyped different ethnic and cultural groups? Can you identify some of these titles and your responses to these books?

Illustrations

Illustrations need to be considered as being representative of the ethnic group. For example, faces of Asian people should be individual and not identical. The skin color should accurately represent that of members of the ethnic group. For example, yellow doesn't capture the skin color of Japanese people. Moreover, a variety of physical features should be shown, so stereotyping does not occur. The dramatic slanted eyes used in some book illustrations are not characteristic of people of Asian cultures. Cultural clothing and traditions also need to be accurate. These are important points to consider as you evaluate multicultural literature.

Students can benefit from reading culturally specific books that illustrate the cultural heritage or daily experiences of the particular ethnic group. We have selected multicultural books that are considered culturally authentic and that have been recommended by the authors in *Teaching Multicultural Literature in Grades K–8*, edited by Violet Harris. Within this book, Bishop (1992) makes a good case for providing a variety of multicultural books that represent diversity within the world. The following list reflects that kind of diversity.

A Sampling of Multicultural Books

African-American
Bryan, A. (1986). *Lion and the ostrich chicks and other African folktales.* New York: Atheneum.

Dorros, A. (1991). *Abuela*. New York: E. P. Dutton.

Flourney, V. (1985). *The patchwork quilt*. New York: Dial.

Greenfield, E. (1988). *Grandpa's face*. New York: Philomel.

Hamilton, V. (1967). *Zeely*. New York: Macmillan.

Howard, E. F. (1991). *Aunt Flossie's hats (and crab cakes later)*. New York: Clarion.

Johnson, A. (1989). *Tell me a story mama*. New York: Orchard Books.

McKissack, P. (1988). *Mirandy and brother wind*. New York: Knopf.

Myers, W. D. (1990). *The mouse rap*. New York: Harper & Row.

Myers, W. D. (1988). *Scorpions*. New York: Harper & Row.

Price, L. (1990). *Aida*. New York: Harcourt Brace Jovanovich.

Ringgold, F. (1991). *Tar beach*. New York: Crown.

Steptoe, J. (1980). *Daddy is a monster . . . sometimes*.

Taylor, M. (1981). *Let the circle be unbroken*. New York: Dial.

Taylor, M. (1976). *Roll of thunder, hear my cry*. New York: Dial.

Taylor, M. (1990). *The road to Memphis*. New York: Dial.

Asian

Anno, M. (1983). *Anno's USA*. New York: Philomel.

Bang, M. (1985). *The paper crane*. New York: Greenwillow.

Lord, B. B. (1984). *In the year of the boar and Jackie Robinson*. New York: Harper & Row.

Say, A. (1994). *Grandfather's journey*. Boston: Houghton Mifflin.

Say, A. (1989). *The lost lake*. Boston: Houghton Mifflin.

Uchida, Y. (1981). *A jar of dreams*. New York: Atheneum.

Uchida, Y. (1971). *Journey to Topaz*. New York: Scribner.

Uchida, Y. (1983). *The best bad thing*. New York: Atheneum.

Yashima, T., & Yashima, M. (1977). *Momo's kitten*. New York: Viking.

Yep, L. (1977). *Child of the owl*. New York: Harper & Row.

Yep, L. (1975). *Dragonwings*. New York: Harper & Row.

Yep, L. *The star fisher*. (1991). New York: Harper & Row.

Native American

Cannon, A. E. (1990). *The shadow brothers*. New York: Delacorte.

Girions, B. (1990). *Indian Summer*. New York: Scholastic.

Strete, C. K. (1977). *The bleeding man and other science fiction stories*. New York: Green Willow.

Strete, C. K. (1979). *When grandfather journeys into winter*. New York: Green Willow.

Yellow Robe, R. (1979). *Tonweya and the eagles and other Lakota Indian tales*. New York: Dial.

As previously discussed, multicultural literature needs to appear in all curricula so that students can better understand themselves and humanity, and develop an understanding and respect for all cultures. The literature must be authentic, should not patronize or disparage people of color, and should exclude stereotyping. All students need to read about their cultural groups, seek models, gain insights, and develop pride in their heritage. Bieger (1995–1996) recommends using folktales to promote multicultural understanding, because, as she states, "[multicultural books] give insight into the dreams, customs, and philosophy of life of a group" (p. 309). We believe that folktales are a good beginning and also encourage you to move beyond folktales to using realistic fiction and nonfiction to further develop multiculralism. The above-mentioned recommended list of books provide a beginning, but these suggestions should not limit your selections. American Library Association also publishes a reference book for selecting books by African-American authors. You can also update these lists by referring to monthly and/or quarterly publications such as *Book Links,* published by Edpress, and *The Bulletin,* published by the University of Illinois Press.

Many generic and specific resources are available to help you select good literature for children. Each year the International Reading Association and the Children's Book Council survey 10,000 children across the United States and publish an annotated list of their favorite books in "Children's Choices," which appears annually in the October issues of *The Reading Teacher* and the *Journal of Adolescent and Adult Literacy,* both of which are journals of the International Reading Association.

In addition, book-selection aids can be found in any public library. Reference books published by the American Library Association, Libraries Unlimited, National Council of Teachers of English, and the International Reading Association are invaluable for identifying new authors and a wide variety of titles. We have identified a few of these resources.

Resources for Book Selection

Books

Arbuthnot, M. H. (1980). *Children' books too good to miss* (7th ed.). New York: University Press Books.

Barstow, B., & Reggle, J. (1989). *Beyond picture books: A guide to first readers.* New York: R. R. Bowker.

Carlsen, G. R. (1967). *Books and the teenage reader.* New York: Harper & Row.

Elleman, E. (Ed.). (1985). *Children's books of international interest* (3rd ed.). Chicago: American Library Association.

Lima, C. W. (1985). *A to zoo: Subject access to children's picture books* (2nd ed.). Ann Arbor, MI: R. R. Bowker.

Lipson, E. R. (1991). *The New York Times parents' guide to the best books for children.* New York: Random House.

Monson, D. (Ed.). (1985). *Adventuring with books: A booklist for pre K–grade 6.* Urbana, IL: National Council of Teachers of English.

Rollock, B. (1984). *The black experience in children's books.* New York: New York Public Library.

Ryder, R. J., Graves, B., & Graves, M. F. (1989). *Easy reading: Book series and periodicals for less able readers* (2nd ed.). Newark, DE: International Reading Association.

Sutherland, Z. (1980). *The best of children's books: The University of Chicago guide to children's literature. 1973–1978.* Chicago: University of Chicago Press.

Trelease, J. (1989). *The new read-aloud handbook.* New York: Penguin Books.

Periodical Resources
The Bulletin. University of Illinois Press.

Integrating Multicultural Literature.

Banks (1989) has an instructional model for integrating multicultural literature into the curriculum. We describe the four levels of this hierarchical model. The first level is a contributions approach. At this initial level, students listen, read, and discuss books about cultural holidays, heroes, and customs. The next level is entitled "ethnic additive approach." Cultural content, concepts, and themes are discussed and developed within the existing school curriculum. The third level is called the transformation approach. At this level, teachers and students read and discuss literature about societal problems, themes, concerns, and concepts from different cultural and ethnic perspectives. Reading literature by different cultural and ethnic authors or that reflects the insider's point of view constitutes the focus of this level. The fourth and final level Banks calls the social action approach. At this level, students choose social issues to read about. They discuss, write, and make decisions about social, cultural, and ethnic problems. At this level, they try to make a difference in society by carrying out some of their own plans. The Banks model is one way for you to begin integrating multicultural literature into your classroom.

HOW CAN LITERATURE BE USED FOR INSTRUCTION?

There are many ways to organize and use literature in the classroom. We explore a few ways to initiate the use of literature. Using literature in the classroom should be a main, integral part of instruction, and it is highlighted throughout this book.

Reading Aloud

The easiest way to begin is to select literature to read aloud to students. No matter what their age, students benefit from listening to their teachers read: Young students learn more about language and develop an appreciation for reading, and older students learn to enjoy new genres and authors they have never encountered. Best of all, reading aloud encourages lifelong reading—a goal we should have for all our students.

How do you select a book for reading aloud? First, choose a book that you enjoy. Students will sense your pleasure. Choose books that highlight students' interests. Choose books that illustrate the beauty and rhythm of language, so students can see the images or hear the sounds that authors create with words. Choose books that stimulate students to read a new genre or author. Read about different cultural groups to develop insights about humanity. Try to choose literature that students have not already read, and finally, choose books that are too difficult for independent reading, so that students' vocabularies and knowledge of language can expand. Jim Trelease's *The New Read-Aloud Handbook* is one of the best resource books for identifying books for reading aloud.

You also need to consider how to make reading aloud an interesting, captivating experience for your students. Before reading, review the book yourself, so you are prepared to make a good presentation. When you begin, provide some background information to increase students' interest and understanding. You may also want to share information about the author (available, for example, from the resource book *Something about the Author*). Set a purpose for reading, so students become active listeners, or encourage students to make predictions and to listen for information to support or reject their predictions. (See pp. 131–132 in chapter 4 for examples of purpose-setting questions.)

While reading, be expressive. Change the tone of your voice as the characters change their moods or feelings. Read at a comfortable pace, and alter your pace according to the story line. Consider the mood, tone, and rhythm being suggested by the language the author uses.

If you are reading a long book, try to complete an entire chapter at one sitting. If this isn't possible, stop reading at a suspenseful point in the story so that students will look forward to the next installment. Help them make predictions about what will happen next, and before continuing, ask the students to review what has already happened.

After reading aloud, ask students to respond to literature. There are many ways to elicit personal responses from students. Discussion is likely to be an automatic personal response to literature. Large- and small-group discussions can accomplish different purposes. Large groups allow a few people to participate but you, as the teacher, can hear, respond, and evaluate students' understanding. With small groups more students can participate, but you are unable to listen to all conversations. Journaling can give all students opportunities to respond and to receive your feedback. Give students five or so minutes to respond and an additional five minutes to discuss their personal responses in small groups while you mingle among the groups. Students should be encouraged to use their written responses as a springboard for discussion rather than reading their responses verbatim. Drawing pictures is often a natural response to literature and can be accompanied by students sharing their pictures with their peers. Drama is another way to respond to read-alouds. Students can choose a character and do role playing.

Daily Silent Reading

Daily silent reading is another easy way to encourage the exploration of literature. Both teachers and students have an opportunity with this activity to visit new people, lands, ideas, and events. It allows for what Sloan (1991) calls an educated imagination so students can develop a better understanding of their own world. Daily silent reading is an essential activity to motivate and encourage lifelong reading habits. You can call this period anything you like: USSR (Uninterrupted Sustained Silent Reading), SSR

(Silent Sustained Reading), and DEAR (Drop Everything and Read) are some of the familiar acronyms. During this time, students should read materials of their own choice without interruptions.

To establish a daily silent reading time, identify a time period during which students can read without being disturbed—perhaps just before or just after lunch. Designate an appropriate length of time. For young students, 10 minutes may be enough, but 20 or 30 minutes may be better for older students. During this time everyone reads, including the teacher. No other activity can take place—no sharing of the text with a friend, no filling out grade books. Hence students need to select their materials before the period begins.

Explain the rules carefully. We suggest that you begin with a short time period, regardless of the grade level you are teaching. Students need some time to get accustomed to reading as a daily activity. Enforce the rules by discontinuing the activity when a student does not comply. Peer pressure will quickly cause students to follow the rules so that all can get on with enjoying their reading. After two weeks, increase the time, and after a month, provide the full 10, 20, or 30 minutes. Once silent reading is an established activity, students will have their books out to begin without teacher reminders. In fact, students often become disgruntled when recreational reading time is shortened or eliminated for special events. When your students ask for recreational reading time, your goals have been accomplished.

Book Talks

Book talks are short, persuasive accounts to stimulate reading of a particular author, poet, or book. Both teachers and students should give book talks to instill the love of reading, and to develop speaking and listening communication skills. You should model a book talk so that students have a concept of the task. Mrs. Johnson provides an example of a book talk on Virginia Hamilton's *House of Dies Drear*.

> What would it be like to live in a house that was used as part of the underground railroad? Thomas Small, an African-American, and his family move to Ohio and rent Dies Drear's house, which was a place used to hide and transport slaves from bondage to freedom. Thomas and his family share unique and frightening experiences in their new home. They make new discoveries about people and historical as well as current events. Upon arriving at their new home, Thomas looks around for traces of the underground railroad and suddenly finds himself falling into an underground stairwell that leads to tunnels back into their house. The mystery begins with Thomas's fall and his insatiable desire to learn about Dies Drear's house, the murder of two slaves and the white antebellum leader, Dies Drear, and his relationship to Mr. Pluto, the neighbor and house caretaker.

Providing a model and thinking aloud while doing a second book talk can help students plan their own talk. While thinking aloud, talk about providing a backdrop for the story (telling about characters and setting), sharing one event, or highlighting the problem to stimulate reading. Encourage your students to share why they did or did not enjoy a particular book.

What are some ways to learn about children's and adolescents' books?

Other Activities

Shared reading (Holdaway, 1979), Book Club (Raphael & McMahon, 1994), literature circles, and Reading Workshop are exciting and engaging activities that highlight literature. Using literature units is another way to stimulate students' interest in literature. We have explained these activities in chapter 2, and many have been further explored in other chapters. We encourage you to review these activities.

SUMMARY
• •

Literature refers to all printed material, but we have limited our discussion to trade books that include fiction, nonfiction, and poetry. It is the reading of good literature that causes students to like reading and to want to learn how to read. It is the beauty of language, the laughter and tears, the opportunity to escape, the ability to travel in time to experience our ancestors' heritage and learn about other people's history and culture, the chance to better understand ourselves, and the power to find answers to our questions that makes literature both exciting and motivating. These are the natural and most captivating materials we should be using for literacy instruction. Teachers who subscribe to the whole-language philosophy or literature-based instruction have experienced the positive and genuine feelings good literature provides students and the learning that is its outcome. To achieve both enjoyment and learning, teachers have to know a variety of literature to make appropriate selections for instruction and to provide opportunities for different responses to literature.

To enjoy, appreciate, and learn about literature, engage students in meaningful, functional, and purposeful responses. Both aesthetic and efferent responses need to be a routine part of instruction. Students' personal responses encourage interest, desire, and imagination and form the springboard for developing efferent responses concerning the authors' purposes and the ideas and themes suggested in text.

Responses are rooted in the types of selections we choose as teachers. Rich responses can be developed from a wide variety of quality literature. To develop students' responses, interest, and wide reading, become familiar with books. Being aware that picture books are not limited to the young child, teachers can use these books with older students to extend their thinking. Knowing different genres and their related characteristics helps us expand students' horizons for learning and enjoyment. Being able to use, share, and recommend a few good authors within a particular genre can increase the likelihood students' will read, explore, and compare and contrast. Students need to hear, for example, specific folktales and learn that different cultures have similar tales about such attributes as kindness, goodness, cruelty, beauty, and foolishness. By reading fantasy, students experience the author's and their own imagination as they read about castles, new worlds and countries, and extraordinary characters. Each genre has its own characteristics to be experienced and enjoyed, and it's our familiarity, as teachers, with this literature that can do much to stimulate students' selections, understanding, and attitudes.

Developing a keen interest in reading is paramount, and for this reason we can readily see that all children need to see themselves reflected in literature. Unfortunately, there is limited literature representing people of color such as Latino and Asian peoples. And even smaller numbers of books are written about specific Latino groups such as Cubans and Puerto Ricans. There are even fewer publications that can be considered authentic literature reflecting diverse peoples' accurate beliefs, traditions, and language patterns without stereotypes in text and illustrations.

Literature can be integrated into instruction in a number of ways. First and foremost, students need to hear good literature; thus, reading aloud is an important activity for all age levels. Students need designated time to read their own selections, so independent reading time such as Silent Sustained Reading needs to be part of the school day. Book talks, literature circles, Reading Workshop, and literature units also promote the use of literature for literacy instruction.

Students ought not be limited to the textbook to learn in today's schools. There is a wide variety of quality literature that is accessible to kindergartners and older students. Open this treasure chest for students to see and you can create some avid explorers of the world's finest treasures—books.

In the Field

1. Visit the children's section of the library and look at the books suggested in this section. Note these authors' abilities to communicate information in an easy and enjoyable fashion and how authors encourage both aesthetic and efferent responses. Consider, for instance, Ruth Heller's *How to Hide a Butterfly*. The illustrations and poetic verse help the young reader understand the concept of pollination and other important concepts about flowers. Joanna Cole's The Magic School Bus series of books present conceptual information utilizing story and a comic strip format to convey scientific ideas. What second or third grader wouldn't enjoy *The Magic School Bus inside the Human Body*? Lois Ehlert also brings science to the very young child from preschool through kindergarten. Look especially at two of her books: *Growing Vegetables, Red Leaf, Yellow Leaf* and *Planting a Rainbow*. The Journey through History book series presents historical time periods such as the Middle Ages and the Renaissance in a story format that includes the essential vocabulary, lifestyle, and events of this time period. One of the following books in this series will help you recognize how easily students can learn as well as enjoy learning about history: *Prehistory to Egypt, The Greek and Roman Eras, The Middle Ages, The Renaissance, Modern Times,* or *The Contemporary Age,* or choose one of the aforementioned titles to review a particular author's works. List your responses to these books in your journal.

2. Administer the interest inventory to a child or adolescent. Now that you have this information, what literature and topics would you include for instruction and recreation? In what specific ways would these books be used?

3. Choose a children's book and evaluate it by employing the techniques suggested for each area of literary merit: setting, character, plot, theme, style, and point of view. Would your evaluation lead you to recommend this book to students? Respond to this question in your journal.

4. Visit the children's library and critically review the illustrations in multicultural books. Begin your review with the following books: *The Seven Chinese Brothers, Mirandy and Brother Wind, Diego, Pocahontas, The Patchwork Quilt,* and *The Fortune Tellers;* identify others as to their authenticity and appropriateness. Take a moment to respond in your journal about the illustrators in these multicultural books.

5. Choose a children's or adolescents' book for which you will have students create a design and tape a book talk.

Portfolio Suggestion

Select from your journal two examples of your responses from Pause and Reflect or In the Field activities. Write a brief evaluation of your work. Explain what you learned and how it will affect your use of literature in the classroom.

For Further Reading

Alvermann, D. E. (1995). Peer-led discussions: Whose interests are served? *Journal of Adolescent and Adult Literacy, 39*, 282–289.

Banks, J. A. (1989). Integrating the curriculum with ethnic content: Approaches and guidelines. In J. A. Banks & C. A. McGee Banks (Eds.), *Multicultural education: Issues and perspectives* (pp. 189–207). Boston: Allyn & Bacon.

Bieger, E. F. (1995–1996). Promoting multicultural education through a literature-based approach. *The Reading Teacher, 49*, 308–311.

Chaney, J. H. (1993). Alphabet books: Resources for learning. *The Reading Teacher, 47*, 96–105.

Kutiper, K., & Wilson, P. (1993). Updating poetry preferences: A look at the poetry children really like. *The Reading Teacher, 47*, 28–35.

Moss, J. (1982). Reading and discussing fairy tales—old and new. *The Reading Teacher, 35*, 656–659.

Wiseman, C. (1992). African tales on stage. *Book Links, 1*, 24–26.

CHAPTER 9

Published Programs for Teaching Reading and Writing

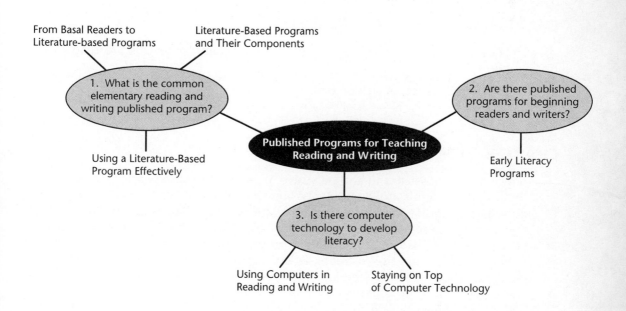

From Basal Readers to
Literature-based Programs

Literature-Based Programs
and Their Components

1. What is the common elementary reading and writing published program?

2. Are there published programs for beginning readers and writers?

Published Programs for Teaching Reading and Writing

Using a Literature-Based
Program Effectively

Early Literacy
Programs

3. Is there computer technology to develop literacy?

Using Computers in
Reading and Writing

Staying on Top
of Computer Technology

CHAPTER GOALS FOR THE READER

To become familiar with a variety of published programs for teaching reading and writing

To encourage reflective decision making in the use of published programs

CHAPTER OVERVIEW

Although there is a strong and pervasive movement toward whole language and the use of children's and adolescents' literature, many teachers incorporate published programs for teaching reading and writing. Elementary school teachers use these programs for a number of reasons. Classroom teachers have little planning time to design an entire program to teach reading and writing. Others lack the expertise to create an entire program; still other teachers recognize that programs used judiciously can enhance students' learning and enjoyment. A program needs to be critically reviewed as to philosophy and instructional practices before employing it with children. And no published program is a panacea; students will need other methods, literature, and programs to become effective readers and writers. You need to consider your students' needs, goals, and desires along with the school's and your own instructional goals as you make instructional decisions about what and how much to use in published programs.

In this chapter, we explore different types of published programs in reading and writing. We consider how these programs can be effectively used to develop literacy, and identify specific points to help you critique and selectively employ publishers' programs to teach reading and writing.

TAPPING PRIOR KNOWLEDGE TO SET A PURPOSE

Think back to your own schooling experience. What books did you use for learning to read and write? Did you have a grade-level reader and workbook—what is called a basal reader? Can you remember what the stories were like? Were the sentences short and choppy? Did you do workbook pages in which you filled in the blanks and circled a response in a multiple-choice format? What were your feelings about these textbooks? Did they engage you in thinking and learning? Did these textbooks help you to become a proficient reader and writer? Why or why not? Did these textbooks help you enjoy reading and writing? Why or why not? Talk to a family member or another student in your class to help you recall your schooling experiences. After you have read the chapter overview and reflected on your own experiences, identify what it is that you most want to learn from reading this chapter. List these in your journal.

WHAT IS THE COMMON ELEMENTARY
READING AND WRITING PUBLISHED PROGRAM?

The most common type of published program is a literature-based program. In this section, we describe how the literature-based program evolved from the basal reading program. We then describe the components of this program and provide some suggestions to enable you to make effective decisions if you decide to use this published program.

From Basal Readers to Literature-Based Programs

Literature-based programs have replaced what was known as the basal reader. Do you remember reading controlled text such as the following?

A Game for Kim*

Kim is not happy.

Kim wants to play.

She wants to have fun.

Kim looks at Dave.

She wants him to play.

Source: From "A Game for Kim" (pp. 6–9), *Outside My Window.* An American Traditional Basal Series, 1987, Glenview, IL: Scott, Foresman. Copyright © 1987 by Scott Foresman. Reprinted with permission.

Dave says, "I can't play.

I am painting."

Painting looks like fun.

Kim says, "I can help."

The ball falls into the paint.

The ball is green.

Dave says, "What a mess!

I do not want your help.

Take your ball and go."

Kim says, "This is not fun."

If so, you may have learned to read from a basal reader. It is likely that you learned from a basal reader, since basals have been used since the 1800s (Anderson, Hiebert, Scott, and Wilkinson, 1985; Durkin, 1978–1979; Vacca, Vacca, & Gove, 1995). Since basal reading programs were the mainstay of instruction and have evolved into a literature-based program, it's important that you become familiar with and knowledgeable about these programs so that you can provide the best literacy instruction for your students.

Basal means base or foundation, and this program served as the core for reading instruction from kindergarten through the sixth or eighth grade. Typically, basal reader programs were developed by scholars through educational publishers, and they included graded reading materials, teacher's editions, and other ancillary materials. Each program was self-contained; that is, teachers had all the materials necessary for implementing the reading program. This last sentence provides the primary clue to the popularity of basal programs in our schools. Basal programs were complete. Teachers did not have to look for materials or develop their own instructional plans. As we all know, none of us have unlimited amounts of planning time. Prepared materials and instructional plans made the basal reading programs very appealing, especially when there was so much to do and so little time to plan.

Recently, publishers have replaced the basal reading program with a literature-based program that serves a similar function. It is the base or foundation of literacy instruction. The change from a basal to a literature-based program has come about because of contemporary theory and research about reading and writing instruction. Several bodies of theory and research precipitated a need for change in the traditional basal reading program. One of the most notable needs for change was the actual material children were using for reading instruction. Researchers also showed a burgeoning need for the teaching of comprehension that wasn't adequately covered in the basal program. A large body of theory and research indicated that writing and reading were related processes and were mutually supportive; yet writing was a neglected area of the curriculum. Research on beginning reading and writing demanded sweeping changes in the way we deliver instruction. The continued instructional effort to help students transfer reading skills to literature was also not being achieved through the use of basal reading programs. Let's further explore each of these changes and the metamorphosis of the basal to a literature-based program.

What do you suppose this child is learning about the reading process?

The Call for Authentic Literature

The materials teachers use for reading instruction have an enormous effect on children's attitudes about and interests in reading. If the materials are engaging, intriguing, or delightful, children will want to read. If the materials are dull and monotonous, children will not choose to read. The indelible effects of poor instructional materials are best illustrated by the following story of a young child's experience with reading, adapted from *The Ordeal of Lady Godiva* by Gwen Wallace.

Learning from Experience

Penny Galsworthy lay awake thinking about her new discovery—the name she had found that would provide her, at long last, with membership in the magical family reading hour over which her father presided each evening. She would be Lady Godiva—surely a worthy name. Penny's home was built around books. Her father, an English professor, made books come alive, and Penny had looked forward as long as she could remember to joining her brothers and sisters who met every evening and became known as the Group.

But when Penny introduced her chosen name that evening, the Group still refused to admit her. She was too little, too young—and she couldn't read. Reading, Penny suddenly understood, was the key to everything.

When Penny started school the following year, she could hardly wait to receive her first book for reading instruction. What would she learn? What fascinating characters would emerge from her reading? She opened the book her teacher gave her—but the phrases that met her eyes were only those that her older brother had teased her with when she went off to school the first day: "See Mary. See Fred. Oh, oh, oh." Was this reading? Where was the magic, the excitement? Penny's eager anticipation faded.

All the children read aloud in dull, singsong tones. When it was Penny's turn, she decided to put her own excitement into the process. She stood and read in dramatic tones—"See Mary! See Fred! Oh, oh, ohhh!"—Penny had caused quite a stir. Her teacher even called to talk to her parents that evening. Sure she had disgraced her family as well as herself, Penny went directly to her room after dinner.

But late that evening, Penny's sister, Betsy, came to get her. The Group demanded her presence. Penny was reluctant, but finally she went downstairs with Betsy.

Betsy knocked on the door. "Who goes there?" a voice asked.

"The Lady Genevieve," Betsy answered, "and the Lady Godiva." The Group had accepted Penny as a member. Her brothers and sisters, she suddenly realized, had endured the same boring materials that she was facing at school—and they had survived, eventually to find their ways to books that provided wonder and magic. (This story was adapted from Gwen Wallace's [1958] "Ordeal of Lady Godiva," published in the *Ladies' Home Journal*.)

Penny's story suggests some of the effects that basal readers can have on children's attitudes and interests. Penny's overwhelming desire to read was almost squelched by the lackluster materials presented to her at school. Penny agreed to endure the ordeal at school, however, because she knew from her experiences at home that it would eventually lead to better things. Can this same insight into the excitement of reading be developed in children who have little or no experience with good literature? Probably not. Dull, monotonous, unengaging instructional reading materials may have devastating and lasting effects on children's attitudes and abilities.

Materials are the heart of any reading program; they affect children's attitudes toward reading, as well as what children learn. Penny Galsworthy was almost turned off to reading by the above lackluster materials. In her mind, reading opened doors to new horizons, but the materials used for reading instruction in her school did not do this. Luckily, Penny's father read to his children, and their home environment was built on real, authentic literature, so Penny knew that reading was more than the stilted sentences she found in her basal reader. But what happens to children who lack these reading experiences outside school? How can they find out that reading is stimulating and inspiring if they are exposed to the kind of materials that Penny was provided? A steady diet of monotonous reading materials can suppress children's interest in reading. There is nothing magical and exciting about reading, "See Mary. See Fred. Oh, oh, oh."

Typically, basal readers did not excite children about reading. For young readers, reading wasn't meaningful. Children were reading high-frequency words in short sentences in an an attempt to help novices "break the code"—that is, decipher the black squiggle marks on the page. How can beginning readers become motivated and invested in learning to read the following text, which is representative of the controlled vocabulary and contrived text of basal readers?

Get up, Get up.

This is a big day.

A big day for us.

Here.

Help me with this.

Make it go up.

Up, up, up.

And now come here.

Here is one for you.

(Margaret Hillert, *Let's Go Dear Dragon*, 1981, pp. 5–7)

We've learned several things about reading. First, children use knowledge about oral language patterns and meaning to break the code, and neither of these possibilities can be pursued in the above text. What child talks in this manner? Do we naturally say, "Up, up, up"? Meaning is also difficult to construct, since there are too many pronouns without referents. Meaning begins to develop only when illustrations are added. What does this say to beginning readers? That print is meaningless. That illustrations are meaningful and important. Is this the concept that you want young readers to develop? No. You want children to read materials that are meaningful and that are designed to communicate an appropriate message about the significance of the activity of reading. Only then will children develop appropriate attitudes toward and understandings of reading.

Second, we know that children's interest plays a large part in learning. Reading good literature that is authentic and not rewritten engages children and stimulates the desire to read. As Penny showed in the story, reading good literature can create enchantment, be an escape from the everyday world, provide an opportunity to dream, and be an adventure to the past or future. Such experiences lead children to read outside of school, which is as important as the instruction they receive in school.

And, finally, reading about white, middle-class, intact families, who typify the characters of the stories in many basal readers, does not represent the diversity of our classrooms. Children need to read about people in their own culture and see themselves in literature (Harris, 1992). Their hopes, their dreams, and their values must be portrayed by people from their own culture if children are to feel they have a place in school and society in general.

The issue of incorporating authentic literature has had an impact on publishers. Creating contrived texts and rewriting text to help children decode are a part of the past that has given way to literature-based programs.

The Need for Comprehension Instruction

Durkin's research in the latter part of the 1970s and early 1980s initiated interest in classroom research having to do with reading instruction. Durkin (1978–1979) showed that little comprehension instruction was occurring during reading instruction, and her follow-up study (1981) showed that the instruction suggested by basal reading programs did little to develop students' comprehension. Comprehension instruction was not developed in depth and tended to be mentioned in isolated skill lessons that were developed with single paragraphs written to teach the skill. When children tried to apply the skills to children's literature, they experienced difficulty. This research promoted changes in publishers' programs. With the development of literature-based programs, we see a greater emphasis on teaching comprehension. Specific strategy instruction is employed by modeling and demonstrating strategies as students are reading literature. By learning instructional strategies while reading, students are becoming strategic readers—that is, they learn the skills that characterize mature and able readers (Paris, Lipson, & Wixson, 1984).

Discovering the Natural Connections between Reading and Writing

During the same time, Stotsky (1983), Tierney, Leys, and Rogers (1986), and others were looking at the similarities between the reading and writing processes. Reading and writing share some important elements that contribute to their mutual development. Both require active involvement in which readers and writers draw upon their prior knowledge of language and daily experiences to construct meaningful text. As when they are writing, readers create a new text as they read (Rosenblatt, 1989). Reading good literature provides models for writing text. Readers have the opportunity to analyze the writer's craft by discussing, for example, how writers create suspense, excitement, and sadness.

During this same time period, Donald Graves (1976) studied writing instruction and discovered that writing was a neglected area of instruction. Students were not writing for functional and meaningful purposes. Although professional authors used a process approach to writing, this approach was not used in classrooms. Moreover, students wrote for a limited audience, which in most cases was the teacher. Seeing the natural connections between reading and writing along with the acquired knowledge of teaching writing as a process promoted changes that are reflected in current literature-based programs. The name itself suggests that reading is not the sole focus of instruction.

The Need to Transfer Reading Skills

At about the same time period, classroom teachers observed that children could not transfer the skills they learned in the basal reading program to children's literature and other materials. Teachers noted that reading skills instruction in the basal program was broken down from complex to simple tasks and taught in isolation rather than in the context of reading a complete text. Reading was taught in bits and pieces and not as a whole, the way we learned oral language. The work of Goodman (1976) and Smith (1988) and other psycholinguists maintained that language is learned as a unified process in context and not developed in parts from simple to complex. For example, if students tried to apply an infinitesimal number of skills during the act of reading, they would develop tunnel vision and would be unable to comprehend. Goodman showed how students who come to an unknown word and use phonics to sound out the word have to reread the sentence to reconstruct meaning, and this illustrates the effects of tunnel vision. From Goodman's theory and research as well as that of other psycholinguists, we see the roots of whole language that led to changes from basal reading programs to literature-based programs.

Developments in Beginning Reading

During the 1970s and 1980s, the issue of assessing children's readiness to begin reading instruction and teaching visual, auditory, and visual-motor skills as prerequisites to reading was being examined. Research indicated that teaching children to do such perceptual tasks as discriminating differences in pictures and letters and drawing lines from left to right did little to increase their reading achievement (Wiederholt & Hamill, 1971). Skill development needed to be directly related to reading.

During this same time, Marie Clay (1979) achieved much success with teaching young readers in New Zealand by having them read and write simple text. Skills were taught in the context of reading and writing meaningful text. Beginning readers, or what became known as emerging readers, used their fingers as they read to develop left-to-right directionality, concept of word, and visual acoustic matching of the printed word. These young children wrote by using their tacit knowledge of sound and letter relationships to spell. Clay's work showed how emerging readers can be directly engaged in the real tasks of reading and writing and thus bypass isolated instruction on auditory, visual, and visual-motor instruction. These emerging readers were reading simple and predictable books that employed natural oral-language patterns that included rhythm, rhyme, and meaningful repetition.

Work by another New Zealander, Don Holdaway (1979), demonstrated how children's natural development of oral language could be translated into the teaching of reading. Through repeated storybook reading of enlarged versions of children's literature or Big Books, children learned to read naturally as they learned to speak. By rereading predictable literature, emerging readers engaged in reading along with the teacher and learned the act of reading.

Other researchers in the United States were also looking at beginning-reading development. Adams (1990) concluded that letter and phoneme knowledge along with reading meaningful text facilitates young children's reading development. Ehri and Robbins' (1992) work also demonstrated the importance of phoneme segmentation and sound blending to develop reading proficiency, although Stanovich (1980) showed that beginning readers use context as they learn but use sound and letter knowledge as they develop reading proficiency. It is the less-skilled reader who compensates by relying only on context.

This body of research on beginning reading has influenced the instruction and materials of publisher's programs. Literature-based programs no longer talk about reading readiness. Children learn how to read and write by reading and writing. Children are listening and reading along as teachers read Big Books, with subsequent reading of the accompanying little books. Children are writing as they learn to read by using their tacit understanding of letter-sound knowledge. Moreover, skill in letter-sound relationships is being developed as children read literature.

Literature-Based Programs and Their Components

Unlike the basal reading program that focused solely on the teaching of reading, literature-based programs are more extensive and address the teaching of reading and writing and include grammar, mechanics, and spelling. Like the basal reading program, the literature-based program is *comprehensive*. By comprehensive, we mean that it helps children learn how to become effective readers and writers, helps children use reading and writing as learning tools, and encourages children to develop positive attitudes toward literacy so they enjoy reading and writing.

The literature-based program also provides *systematic* instruction and continuity across grade levels. Reading and writing instruction is developed in a continuous manner across grade levels to maximize and reinforce learning. Literature-based programs provide continuity by employing a common instructional format and using engaging materials at all grade levels.

Systematic instruction is also achieved through recurring activities. Some programs provide systematic instruction by using three components: Reading Workshop, Writing Workshop, and a literature unit. Other literature-based programs provide systematic instruction by focusing instruction on a particular text and dividing instruction into three phases: pre-, during-, and postreading. Both formats have been described in previous chapters. A consistent instructional process is employed that typically includes modeling and demonstration, guided practice and feedback, application, assessment, and review of reading and writing strategies and skills.

Like the basal programs, literature-based programs provide developmentally appropriate instruction. By developmentally appropriate instruction, we mean that text, activities, and skills are loosely organized according to difficulty, from simple to more difficult. Text changes according to reader development. Beginning readers read short picture books with repetitive and predictable text such as Bill Martin's *Brown Bear, Brown Bear, What Do You See?* while mature readers read complex plot structure such as Jerry Spinelli's *Maniac Magee*.

Activities and instructional approaches are also based on developmental appropriateness. For example, dictation or language experience approach may be used in kindergarten and first grade and no longer used as students become mature readers and writers. Finger-point reading would be suggested for emerging readers, to reinforce concept of word and visual and vocal word matching, but it would not be used with more developed readers.

Skills are also loosely sequenced into a vertical arrangement to ensure continuity and reinforcement. In other words, students are taught to read from left to right before they are asked to concentrate on developing fluency. Belief in the hierarchical nature of literacy development has dissipated since we know that reading and writing require novices to employ the skills experts do (Smith, 1988). Research further indicates that skills overlap and work together to facilitate literacy development (Davis, 1968). Hence a discrete set of sequential skills cannot be clearly discerned. For example, students can read a story and may be able to do higher level thinking such as evaluating a character's decision but may not be able to sequence story events requiring literal recall. As compared to the basal reading program, literature-based reading programs introduce skills based on children's stages of literacy development within the context of reading and writing text rather than teaching skills separately and hoping students will automatically be able to apply the skill as they read independently. Emergent writers create meaning using invented spelling just as mature writers create meaning by easily applying spelling conventions. Both are engaged in communication; yet the level of skill differs.

Literature-based programs provide a plan for *classroom management.* Numerous suggestions are provided to help teachers organize instruction. For example, suggestions for whole-group, small-group, and individualized instruction are often provided. Guidelines for pacing instruction are also given. Addressing the needs of divergent learners is considered such as altering and modifying instruction for gifted students, second-language learners, and learning-disabled students. These suggestions can be helpful but must be critically reviewed to make effective decisions.

Literature-based programs include many components to help you plan for instruction and to address different students' needs. Common components include (1) children's literature and/or anthologies containing authentic children's literature, (2) the teacher's edition that provides suggestions for planning literacy instruction, (3) a consumable student practice book that encourages students to provide written responses to fiction or nonfiction, and (4) assessment tools that may include portfolios. Many programs include other supplementary materials such as Big Books, computer software programs, and audiotapes.

In the following subsections, we limit our discussion to the major components of literature-based programs: children's literature and/or the anthology students read, the teachers' edition, student practice materials, and assessment. We suggest that you have a recent edition of a literature-based program at hand to review while reading the following subsections.

Children's Literature and/or Anthologies

Literature-based programs have students read authors' original works. The literature is not rewritten to include simpler vocabulary, high-frequency words, and shorter sentences, as was characteristic of the basal readers. When the author's original work is used, the vocabulary and natural flow of language are retained, and this allows students to be challenged by the complexities of natural text (with teacher and peer support) and thus facilitates students' independent reading of children's literature. Since children's literature is the prime reading material, knowing authors and understanding the author's craft have become integral parts of these programs. Students learn something about the authors' lives, how they became interested in writing, and from where their ideas were derived. Often photographs of the author are included to personalize the program and highlight the variety of people who find writing to be professionally rewarding. Students learn that authors come from diverse backgrounds and ethnic groups and are ordinary people who have feelings and experiences that are similar to their own.

Each program packages literature differently. In some literature-based programs, students are reading the actual trade book that appears in libraries and bookstores, while in others the literature is combined into grade-level books or anthologies. Although programs may be packaged differently, a variety of literature is included. Fiction, nonfiction, poetry, and multicultural literature are provided at each grade level and address students' abilities and social and emotional needs. The literature selections often are clustered by themes, topics, genres, or authors. Clustering allows teachers and students to make intertextual connections and to integrate literature with other content areas and, thereby, create greater depth in thinking and learning.

Pause and Reflect!

Choose a literature-based program and look at the literature the students are expected to read. What kinds of literature are included? How is the literature organized? Is it organized, for instance, by theme, topic, and/or author? Is there sufficient variety to broaden students' interests and increase their understanding of the world and its pluralism? Why or why not? Are the authors well known? Place your responses in your journal and discuss these with other student colleagues.

Publishers provide the literature you need to implement their program, and this facilitates management and organization. However, your students may be quite different from the publisher's profile of students in a typical grade-level classroom. Thus you need to compare your students' abilities (see chapter 10) and their emotional and social needs to the literature in the program (see chapter 8) and make appropriate decisions. Teacher decision making is a critical part of using publishers' programs. Few teachers use all the literature suggested by the publisher. Teachers make modifications and adjustments by eliminating particular pieces of literature, replacing them with something more appropriate, or providing additional instructional support.

Even though you may not use all the literature in the program, students are still limited to the publisher's selections. As a consequence, students' motivation and interest may be lessened. Student inquiry is limited by the program's literature and thus open-ended inquiry may be compromised. Again, teacher decision making becomes an important factor. Students need instructional time to choose their own literature, to formulate their own questions, and to develop their own projects. If you use a literature-based program, you can still provide students with free choices in a number of ways. For instance, include Reading Workshop as a daily activity in which students freely choose their own books. Or give students opportunities to conduct student inquiry: Let them identify a topic and questions, choose resources to address their personal questions, and design a project to report their findings. Finding instructional time can be accomplished in a number of ways. Some teachers devote one day per week to student inquiry while other teachers focus one or more weeks on this endeavor.

Teacher's Edition

The teacher's edition provides an overview of the entire program, since it explains the philosophy, theory, and goals for learning to read. Its purpose is to guide teachers' planning and the implementation of instruction. The bulk of the teacher's edition is made up of organizational plans for guiding daily instruction, and these include teaching strategies and activities.

At the beginning of the teacher's edition, the publisher presents the program philosophy—beliefs about the reading and writing processes and how students develop literacy. These beliefs are translated into programmatic goals, pedagogy, and assessment. As you read the program's philosophy, you'll want to compare it to your belief system and what you've learned from this textbook. If your beliefs do not match the program's, you're likely to experience difficulty in its implementation, since the foundation of instruction is its philosophy. The daily instructional plans should reflect the program's philosophy, develop the goals, and put into practice the theory described. However, the literature-based program's philosophy, theory, and goals do not always match suggested instructional practices. The program may espouse the idea that students' experiences are an integral part of comprehending a reading selection, but the reading and writing activities might not delve into students' previous experiences or knowledge about the topic presented in the literature.

The program goals also appear in the teacher's edition and are embodied in its listing of reading and writing skills and strategies. This listing of goals is better known as the program's scope and sequence. "Scope" refers to all skills and strategies developed in the literature-based program from grades Kindergarten through 6 or 8. The "sequence" refers to the order in which skills and strategies are introduced, developed, and reviewed. It's highly detailed, can be overwhelming, and can easily lead to teaching skills in isolation. Most programs recognize that reading and writing skills and strategies are loosely ordered and an empirical sequence does not exist, since literacy is an interactive process requiring students to use all skills and strategies simultaneously. A scope and sequence chart from Scott, Foresman's Celebrate Reading! program is shown in Figure 9.1. It illustrates a broad, comprehensive scope for reading, listening, speaking, writing, and genre study. Skills such as classifying, generalizing, and summarizing, as well as strategies such as "Use Prior Knowledge," "Track and Synthesize Information," and "Generate Questions" are represented. In addition, it shows where these skills and strategies are developed in Scott, Foresman's organizational plan: before reading, during reading, and after reading.

The greater part of the teacher's edition focuses on daily guided instruction. Typically, instruction is based on a particular piece of literature. Specific goals or objectives are identified to provide direction and accountability. Instruction may be broadly organized into pre-, during-, and postreading activities. Many teacher's editions provide a lesson planning guide, to help teachers organize instruction. In most lesson planning guides, they provide an overview of the lesson and list the materials, teaching strategies, skills, and instructional pacing to facilitate planning.

Prereading instruction. Most teacher's editions focus on particular areas of prereading instruction—presenting vocabulary that will appear in the text; activating and/or developing background concepts and experiences necessary for comprehending the text; and establishing purposes for reading. Some teacher's editions also teach one or two specific reading and writing strategies or skills and encourage students to apply these as they read. Different instructional activities are suggested to meet the needs of a diverse population.

We include an example of prereading instruction from Houghton Mifflin's Invitations to Literacy program (see Figure 9.2, p. 330). The fourth graders will read A Sierra Club Book entitled *The Great Yellowstone Fire*. To prepare for their reading, students discuss their knowledge about forest fires by employing a K-W-L (Ogle, 1986),

Comprehension Strategies and Skills	Grade(s)	Before Reading	During Reading						After Reading
		Preview, Question, and Predict	Connect Ideas	Judge Ideas	Become Personally Involved	Use Cueing Systems and Cross Check	Fix Up Trouble Spots	Keep Tabs and Organize	Respond and Reflect
Adjust Method and Rate: reread, read on, change pace	1-8						▒		
Author's Purpose	3-8	■				▒		▒	
Author's Viewpoint/Bias	3-8		▒	▒	▒			▒	
Cause and Effect	K-8		▒					▒	■
Classify	K-8							▒	■
Compare and Contrast	K-8		▒					▒	■
Details and Facts	K-8	■	▒					▒	
Draw Conclusions	K-8		▒	▒				▒	
Fact and Opinion	3-8			▒				▒	■
Generalize	K-8		▒					▒	
Generate Questions	K-8	■						▒	■
Main Idea	K-8		▒					▒	
Make Connections: to personal life; across texts	K-8		▒		▒			▒	■
Paraphrase	K-8							▒	
Predict	K-8	■	▒					▒	■
Purpose for Reading: consider and set, check	K-8		▒					▒	■
Realism and Fantasy	K-5							▒	
Sequence	K-8		▒					▒	■
Skim and Scan	K-8							▒	■
Summarize	K-8		▒					▒	■
Track and Synthesize Information: highlight, take notes, outline	1-8							▒	
Use Illustrations	K-8	■						▒	

Strategy	Grades
Use Language Clues to Gain Meaning	K-8
Use Prior Knowledge	K-8
Use Text Features	K-8
Use Text Structure/Genre	2-8
Visualize	K-8
Word Referents	1-5

Author's Craft

Element	Grades
Alliteration, Onomatopoeia	4-8
Characterization	K-8
Dialogue	2-8
Figurative Language: idiom, metaphor, simile	1-8
Flashback	5-8
Foreshadowing	5-8
Imagery	4-8
Irony	6-8
Mood	3-8
Personification	4-8
Plot	K-8
Point of View	4-8
Repetition, Rhyme, Rhythm	K-8
Setting	K-8
Symbolism	6-8
Theme	K-8
Tone	5-8

Figure 9.1 Scott, Foresman Scope and Sequence Chart. *Source:* From *"Celebrate Reading!" Overview of Reading Strategies* (p. 13), 1993, Glenview, IL: Scott, Foresman. Copyright © 1993 by Scott, Foresman. Reprinted with permission.

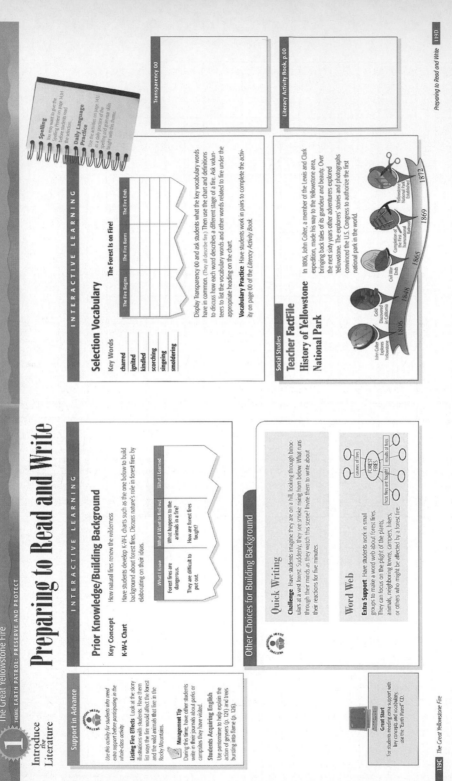

Figure 9.2 Houghton Mifflin's Invitations to Literacy Prereading Strategies and Activities. *Source:* From *Invitations to Literacy*, Teacher's Edition (pp. 119C–119D), 1996, Boston: Houghton Mifflin. Copyright © 1996 by Houghton Mifflin. Reprinted with permission.

write their thoughts and feelings as they imagine seeing a forest fire, develop concepts about the selection's vocabulary by classifying words, and learn about the establishment of national parks. Other features are also included, such as computer technology to develop students' conceptual knowledge about the environment and teaching strategies and activities to address the needs of diverse learners.

Would you use these instructional suggestions? To answer this question, you need to consider your students' needs and identify the teaching strategies and activities that will increase their learning and enjoyment. At the same time, you need to consider if these teaching strategies and activities are supported by theory and research, and your own beliefs about theory and practice. Use these three guidelines to assist you in decision making. However, it is likely that you will not use all the suggestions as they are presented, since literature-based programs provide more activities than you will have time for and need to use. Most teachers eliminate, modify, and develop their own activities according to students' needs, their instructional beliefs, theory and research, and time for instruction.

Pause and Reflect!

Look at the teacher's edition of a literature-based program. Choose one literature selection and review the activities the students are to do before they read the selection. What instructional areas do they include? Are the suggested activities supported by research and theory? Are there activities to meet the needs of diverse learners? Write your response in your journal and compare your response with that of another student colleague.

During reading instruction.   Teacher's editions also provide suggestions for guiding students through the reading itself, often by dividing the text into shorter segments and guiding students to employ a specific reading strategy to monitor comprehension and learning. Specific reading strategies such as previewing and predicting, visualizing, summarizing, and categorizing are identified. The teacher is directed to explain the procedures of the specific strategy along with its purpose and value for understanding and learning while reading a particular text. Often, the teacher is supposed to demonstrate the strategy by modeling, thinking aloud, guiding practice, and providing feedback. Teaching students to use instructional strategies to guide reading is based on theory and research in metacognition that have shown that good readers establish goals and plans for reading text, actively construct meaning, and use fix-up strategies when needed. Such best practices have frequently become a part of literature-based programs.

We include a section of the suggested activities for during-reading instruction from Scott, Foresman's Celebrate Reading! program (see Figure 9.3). First graders read *The Great, Big, Enormous Turnip,* and it is suggested that teachers model previewing and predicting strategies to guide student thinking and learning from text. Further guidance is suggested in the form of supported reading to identify the story problem by using clue words such as "first," "second," and so on. Teachers are encouraged to include their own teaching ideas to foster teacher decision making. Again, you need to consider students' needs, your instructional beliefs, and instructional research and theory as you guide students' reading. Eliminating, modifying, and de-

332

Read

Generate Purposes

Have children plan their reading by previewing and raising questions. Think aloud as necessary to help.

1. Preview and Predict
   - Based on the title, can children predict how large a great, big, enormous turnip might be?
   - Can children use the illustrations to guess what sort of trouble such a large turnip might cause?

2. Set a Purpose
   Consider modeling your own purposes—for example: *I want to find out how the turnip grew so large and what the people in the story will do with the enormous turnip.*

   Invite children to share their purposes for reading the selection.

Idea Exchange

Awards

Helen Oxenbury has won these awards:
- ALA Notable Book
- Kate Greenaway Medal
- Parents' Choice
- Smarties Prize for Children's Books

AWARD

About the Author

Helen Oxenbury was involved in theater, film, and television before turning to illustrating children's books. She is married to John Burningham, an author and illustrator of children's books.

THE GREAT, BIG,

ENORMOUS

TURNIP

Retold by

ALEXEI TOLSTOY

Illustrations by

HELEN OXENBURY

Once upon a time, an old man planted a little turnip and said,

"Grow, grow, little turnip, grow sweet. Grow, grow, little turnip, grow strong."

48

49

FYI—Turnips
- The turnip is a vegetable whose leaves and fleshy roots are edible.
- Turnips were probably first grown in Asia and Europe. Today they are grown in Europe,

Canada, and the United States.
- Turnips thrive in cool weather.
- Although 90% water, the roots and leaves of the turnips are good sources of vitamins A and C.

Your Ideas

Supported Reading

Read pages 48–55 with children to introduce the problem caused by the turnip and the story's predictable pattern.

Remind children that they can use the following strategies as they read:
- To keep track of the order in which things happen in the story, ask yourself what happens first, what happens next, and what happens last. **(ask questions; sequence)**
- Think about why each event happens in the story. Why can't the old man pull up the turnip? Why does he call to the old woman? **(cause/effect)**

D-48

D-49

Figure 9.3 Scott, Foresman's During-Reading Strategies and Activities. *Source: From Teacher's Guide to "Celebrate Reading!"* (pp. D48–D49), 1993, Glenview, IL: Scott, Foresman. Copyright © 1993 by Scott, Foresman. Reprinted with permission.

signing your own instructional strategies to guide reading constitute the capstone of good teaching.

Guided reading has its benefits. By reading and discussing shorter segments, teachers can provide support before frustration begins. When a small part of the text has been read, you can more easily detect possible causes for poor comprehension. For example, you can have the student read aloud the part of text that appears to present difficulty and check if decoding is a problem. You can also ask questions about the concept being developed and note if the student lacks background concepts necessary to understanding text. Check if technical vocabulary prevents comprehension. Ask if reading strategies are being used to develop understanding and learning.

On the other hand, guided reading can deter the enjoyment of reading. Breaking every text into short segments can make reading tedious. Be judicious about guided reading. For instance, teach students to use a strategy through guided reading, but also allow them to use the strategy as they independently read another selection. Follow this reading by discussing the selection content and their interest in the text as well as their use of a particular reading strategy. Another option is to use literature circles, in which students read the selection and divide themselves into groups to discuss the selection and talk about the strategies they employed to construct meaning.

Pause and Reflect!

Look at the teacher's edition. Refer to the text selection you used for prereading instruction. What suggestions does the publisher provide to guide students' reading of text? Will the publisher's method help students comprehend the text selection? Why or why not? Can students use the method for independent reading? Explain. Use your journal to record your responses. Discuss your responses with a student colleague.

Postreading instruction. Teacher's editions also provide strategies for postreading instruction that tend to be extensive and typically include responding to the literature selection, developing reading skills with this selection, connecting text ideas to other language arts and content areas, and reading related literature independently.

Literature-based programs include more opportunities for personal response. Children are using journals to respond to literature. Literature circles are suggested to encourage free response about characters, plot, setting, theme, and other ideas presented in text. For example, Harcourt Brace's Treasury of Literature program uses literature circles and text sets to encourage reader response (see Figure 9.4).

Literature-based programs include much skill development. The skills are derived from the program's scope and sequence chart and systematically appear throughout the grade levels. Typically, literature-based programs integrate skill development with the literature selection. Hence, students are more likely to recognize the connection between learning skills and becoming a proficient reader. However, not all skills are taught with the literature selection. Some activities are taught in isolation with different materials and short paragraphs that present new and unrelated information. Reading a sentence or short paragraph—often written on the chalkboard by the

RESPONSE CARD 12

Text Sets

What are text sets?

Text sets are things that

- have the same topic,
- have the same theme,
- have the same genre (nonfiction, fiction, poetry, biography),
- are written by the same author, or
- are illustrated by the same illustrator.

Text sets include selections in your reading anthology; articles found in magazines, newspapers, encyclopedias, or other reference sources; and books.

Comparing Text Sets

1. Have everyone in your group read *all* of the selections. After everyone has read the selections, use some of these questions for discussion:

To compare texts, use *one* of these ideas.

- What are the similarities in the way these stories were written?
- What information did you find presented in more than one of the texts?
- What other selections have you read that are related to these similarities or differences?

2. Have each group member read one of the selections that have the same theme, are by the same author, or are the same genre.

- Each group member should share what he or she has read.
- Everyone should discuss the similarities and differences in the selections.
- At the end of the discussion, the group may want to brainstorm how to present the comparisons.

Show Your Group's Comparisons

* Create a comparison chart to display your findings.
* Write a drama or a Readers Theatre that fits the text set.
* Make a game showing the comparisons.
* Create a mural and display it in your classroom.

Harcourt Brace School Publishers

RESPONSE CARDS

Figure 9.4 *Treasury of Literature* Reader-Response Activities. *Source:* Excerpt from *Treasury of Literature,* Teacher's Edition, 4-1, copyright © 1995 by Harcourt Brace & Company, reprinted by permission of the publisher.

teacher—does not fit a student's concept of book or magazine reading and thus may not enhance student understanding of the relationship between skills and reading.

Literature-based programs also extend learning and enjoyment of the literature selection with writing, speaking, listening, art, music, computers, and drama activities. These extension activities encourage students' desire to read and develop their competency. These activities address different individual interests and learning needs, thereby encouraging student self-selection.

Many literature-based programs suggest related literature. Some include bibliographies, and some suggest different levels of related literature with such labels as "easy," "average," and "challenging." Some publishers suggest specific titles and accompanying activities, and list books for teacher read-alouds.

There are numerous postreading suggestions, so you need to decide which activities are appropriate and beneficial. Some activities may be more appropriate for some students than others; hence matching activities to a child's need is an effective way to use the suggested activities in the teacher's edition. If many of the activities are appropriate, why not let students choose their own activity? When selecting postreading activities, use the following questions to help you make decisions.

1. Which activities motivate students to read?
2. Which activities encourage personal responses to text?
3. Which activities further develop essential goals for increasing literacy development?
4. Which activities integrate this text with other content-area topics your students are presently learning?

Pause and Reflect!

Look at the teacher's edition. Refer to the text selection you used for prereading and during-reading instruction. What kinds of postreading activities does the teacher's edition suggest? What specific reading and writing skills are suggested for postreading instruction? Does the teacher's edition provide separate and isolated skill activities, or does it provide suggestions for teaching reading skills with the text selection? What kinds of activities are recommended for extending students' learning and enjoyment of literature? Which activities would you consider using? Write your responses in your journal. Share these responses with a student colleague.

Workbooks/Practice Books

Historically, workbooks covered the reading skills listed in the scope and sequence chart of the basal reading program. These skills were typically grouped into major areas, such as decoding (which includes phonics), comprehension (which includes getting the facts and main idea), study skills (which includes using an encyclopedia), and literature (which includes identifying differences between fiction and nonfiction).

Basal workbooks served many purposes, including that of providing students practice with specific reading skills, independent work, and individualized instruction, and providing teachers assessment information about their students' learning.

Much criticism has surrounded the development and use of workbooks (Osborn, 1984). Reading skills in workbook exercises were isolated in that they did not relate to the text selection. Moreover, the workbook exercises appeared in artificially written text composed of contrived sentences and short paragraphs rather than using naturally written text to demonstrate a skill. Students learning skills in this way experienced difficulties applying their learning when reading literature. The exercises often were lackluster; they emphasized low levels of learning such as memorization and identification rather than critical thinking. Frequently, students filled in the blanks or selected multiple-choice answers. Very little critical, creative, and connected writing was required. Because of these criticisms, workbooks were either changed or eliminated. For example, Pegasus, Kendall-Hunt's literature-based program, does not include workbooks and uses some black-line masters or worksheets occasionally to teach and reinforce skill learning and strategy development. In Silver Burdett Ginn's literature-based program, New Dimensions in the World of Reading, workbooks have been replaced with what is called the *Reader's/Writer's Notebook*. This notebook looks very different from the traditional workbook. One example shown in Figure 9.5 demonstrates an open-ended format that invites higher level thinking. The notebook examples are directly related to the literature reading. In the "Packing Up" example, students receive direct instruction about making inferences and are asked to apply this learning as a response to the literature selection, "The Circuit."

Like the basal workbooks, the practice books also provide for independent practice and reinforcement but in a more meaningful and functional manner. The contemporary practice books allow teachers to learn more about their students, since students are writing connected ideas and engaging in higher level thinking activities. As a consequence, teachers and students can make more informed evaluations, and teachers can plan more effectively for instruction.

Pick and choose practice-book pages. Not all practice-book exercises are beneficial, and not every exercise is needed by every student. Choose practice exercises that provide students with skill reinforcement they really need to increase literacy. Choose pages that require higher levels of thinking, and limit those that require mere recognition, like underlining or circling multiple-choice answers. Use practice-book exercises to help you assess a student's literacy proficiency. Avoid assigning practice exercises to keep students busy so independent or small-group instruction can proceed uninterrupted; instead, let students read books, magazines, or newspapers. As the Commission on Reading (Anderson et al., 1985, p. 75) so aptly stated, "Many workbook exercises drill students on skills that have little value in learning to read."

Assessment

With the development of literature-based programs, assessment has changed from testing isolated reading skills in a multiple-choice format to performance-based assessment in which children are reading and writing to demonstrate their knowledge and learning—for example, by reading a story and writing a response to illustrate their critical thinking skills. Literature-based programs have incorporated the use of rubrics or standards to assist teachers and students in evaluating performance. Performance-based assessment serves to link instruction to assessment and makes assessment more meaningful. Portfolios are incorporated in which students for instance may self-select specific written pieces or projects and explain their literacy development.

Packing Up

In "The Circuit," the author doesn't really tell you how Panchito feels about moving at the end of the story. But by thinking about story clues and using your own experience, you can make an inference about those feelings.

If you think you know how Panchito felt, write your inference in the inference box. Then write the story clues and the experience clues that support your inference.

INFERENCE
Panchito was very sad about moving.

(If you're not sure how Panchito felt, go back to the story and look for clues. Write your clues.)

(Think about what the story clues tell you and write down your thoughts.)

STORY CLUES
Responses will vary but should include references to how sad Panchito was over his previous move and how joyful he felt in anticipation of trumpet lessons with Mr. Lema.

EXPERIENCE CLUES
Responses will vary.

Writing Every Day On a separate sheet of paper, describe how you might feel if you found out that you had to leave your best friend and move with your family to another part of the country.

Figure 9.5 Silver-Burdett-Ginn Workbook Example. *Source:* From Reader's/Writer's Notebook for *Wind by the Sea* of the *New Dimensions in the World of Reading* program, © 1993 Silver Burdett Ginn Inc. Used with permission.

Pause and Reflect!

Choose a literature-based program and examine the forms of assessment they include. What types of assessment are employed? Are they meaningful and do they help teachers plan appropriate instruction? Why or why not? Are standards or rubrics suggested for evaluating performance-based assessment? How do students evaluate their own learning? Write your responses in your journal. Share your responses with another student colleague.

Using a Literature-Based Program Effectively

Limiting literacy instruction to a literature-based program does not provide students with a complete and balanced program to increase their literacy development and enjoyment of reading and writing. Literature-based programs are to be used in a flexible fashion in which you pick and choose according to your students' needs and interests. Since each program is different, you need to review and evaluate the specific program and identify areas that are not developed (Dole & Osborn, 1989). For example, some literature-based programs develop the writing process by using Writing Workshop. But in other programs, the writing process is limited in scope and depth because students only write in response to literature. To help you review and evaluate a literature-based program, consider the following points so you can supplement the program and thus provide a more complete and balanced program for your students.

1. According to the philosophy, are reading and writing viewed as constructive processes that can best be developed in meaningful and functional activities? Students become engaged in activities that hold personal meaning, have a definite purpose, and permit self-selection.

2. Do the goals sufficiently cover reading and writing development and address the needs of your students? The goals should focus on helping students understand reading and writing as processes used to communicate, to learn, to enjoy, and to increase understanding of self and others as part of a global society. And, within this context, the goals need to match the needs of your students.

3. Does the program provide literature that all students can read? To increase their reading, students need guided instruction with literature that challenges but does not frustrate them. In other words, students need to have opportunities to read at their instructional level. But this should not be interpreted as a need to form static ability groups. Students also need to read and discuss literature with students of varied abilities. Time for students to practice reading literature at their independent level is also needed. Reading literature with fluency and meaning can enhance enjoyment and increase development.

4. Does the program encourage self-selection of goals, literature, and activities? Students become engaged and committed to learning if there is choice. Letting students choose their own questions to find answers and select their own literature, for instance, encourages natural and authentic forms of learning in which they satisfy their own curiosities and, at the same time, develop strategies for how to think and problem-solve as they read and write.

5. Does the program develop both efferent and aesthetic responses to literature? Most programs do a good job developing the efferent or purposeful side of reading

and writing. For instance, students learn how to summarize and make inferences from text, but are the aesthetic and personal responses to text valued and developed? In your review, consider the quality and quantity of activities that develop personal response to literature.

6. Does the program emphasize performance-based assessment by using meaningful and functional activities that mirror natural and authentic literacy tasks? Assessments should encourage teachers and students to use criteria or rubrics to analyze strengths and weaknesses in reading and writing. Teacher evaluation and self-reflection by students are important tools for increasing learning and developing independent learners. Through self-reflection, students can set their own goals, track their own progress, and develop self-efficacy.

7. Does the program meet the needs of diverse learners within your classroom? Does the pedagogy address and honor the learning styles of students from different

How might independent reading of these books build upon a published program's unit on astronomy?

cultures? For example, are students expected to always read and write independently? Or are reading and writing developed as social processes in which students work cooperatively together to answer questions, complete projects, and discuss literature?

8. Does the program minimize isolated skills instruction? Although most literature-based programs tend to use the literature to teach skills, the skill may still be unnecessary and may not enhance reading development. If skills are presented in isolation, it is likely students will not see the relationship of skills to reading books, magazines, and stories. Eliminate skills instruction (such as identifying nouns and verbs) that does not help students become proficient, independent, interested readers.

9. Does the program suggest meaningful instructional strategies and activities? Not all the instructional strategies and activities that literature-based programs recommend actually help students read the literature selection or become better readers. Choose those activities that are beneficial and eliminate or revise those that are not. Prereading activities suggested in the teacher's edition should help students read and understand the text. During-reading activities should guide students' understanding and self-monitoring of the literature. Postreading activities should help students develop a deeper and broader understanding of the text itself and literature in general.

It is unlikely that any literature-based program can satisfactorily answer all nine of these questions. If you use a literature-based program, you will need to supplement it by addressing its weaknesses. Observe your students and take into account their needs, interests, and abilities in order to make appropriate instructional decisions about the amount of time students should spend with a literature-based program.

 ## Learning from Experience

We talked to Christina Frank, an experienced first-grade teacher who has just completed her master's in reading, to learn how she uses a literature-based program in her classroom. As you read, note how she uses the program.

This September will begin Christina's third year using Kendall-Hunt's Pegasus literature-based program in her first grade class. She uses the program's instructional framework by incorporating the core literature trade books, Writing Workshop, and Reading Workshop. She relies mainly on the philosophy of Calkins (1986) and Graves (1983) to develop and organize her Writing Workshop, rather than focusing on or adhering to the workshop format suggested in Pegasus. She uses Reading Workshop daily, as suggested by the program, but has altered the program according to her students' needs. At the beginning of the school year, Christina asks for parent and grandparent volunteers to support literacy activities. She provides several 30-minute workshops after school to train her volunteers in choral reading, echo reading, and other supported reading approaches. She teaches the volunteers how to note students' strengths and weaknesses by showing models of record keeping from the previous year. Two to three parents come into her classroom daily to assist with Reading Workshop and read with and listen to individual students. Christina points out that Reading Workshop is an important part of the program because it addresses individual needs. Children read according to their capabilities. Those who are at the very beginning stages may listen to the volunteer read while others who are reading independently share their responses to books.

Overall, Christina likes Pegasus because it's comprehensive. It provides instructional plans and direction so teachers can cover the full spectrum of the reading and writing processes. But she notes that no program addresses all students' needs and modifies the program accordingly. She adds phonics instruction, since it isn't adequately covered in the program, and includes additional reading and writing strategies to help students become better readers and writers.

Your Turn: How did Christina use a literature-based program? Write your response in your journal.

Our Turn: Christina had developed her own philosophy about learning to read and write and used it to guide her decision making about literacy instruction. She critically evaluated the program and noted the program's merits and limitations as she adjusted instruction to meet the needs of all her students. She invited volunteers to support Reading Workshop and used Writing Workshop, but she relied more on the specific teachings of Calkins (1986) and Graves (1983), furthermore, she used the core books but also added her own teaching strategies. As with all good teachers, her decision making played an important role in her use of a literature-based program.

Controversial Issue

Published Programs

There is much discussion about the use of published programs. Should teachers be using "canned" programs that may not address their students' needs? Do these programs encourage teachers to be professionals and develop their own programs and make their own decisions? Do teachers become "puppets" and "slaves" to the teacher's edition? Do these programs emphasize authentic and natural literacy development? Are the activities and materials contrived, lacking purpose and not engaging students in personal inquiry? These questions and others have been posed to teachers, and they have caused many teachers to question using published programs and have caused others to develop their own literacy programs that are more sensitive to the needs of their students.

The movement toward teacher decision making and the collaborative designing by teachers and students of their own literacy programs has encouraged professionalism and a greater understanding of literacy instruction and development. Yet, at the same time, it has presented some new challenges. If teachers develop their own literacy programs, is there continuity and consistency of instruction for students? Can all teachers develop effective literacy programs, and are good literacy programs developed immediately and easily? Do teachers have the time to create their own programs? These questions and others are the ones being debated today. There are no simple answers to these questions. We do know that teacher decision making is the essential component in effective instruction. We believe that teacher decision making needs to be a part of all literacy programs, regardless of whether the program is developed by teachers or whether it is a published program. Teachers learn and know their students through careful observation and thereby they adjust the program to meet their students' needs. It is the teacher who is the driving force in guiding literacy development, with all other factors being secondary.

ARE THERE PUBLISHED PROGRAMS FOR BEGINNING READERS AND WRITERS?

Early Literacy Programs

Published programs for beginning readers and writers are becoming more popular because of current theory and research about literacy development. Most of these programs, such as the Wright Group's The Story Box program, emphasize a whole-language philosophy. Children are engaged in meaningful and functional reading and writing activities. A shared reading approach is employed that encourages teachers to read Big Books aloud, with repeated choral readings, to provide young readers the support they need to become proficient readers. Other materials and teaching strategies are provided that develop reading and writing from a holistic framework as children develop proficiency in oral language. The publishers of such programs use theory and research to address the needs of emerging readers by providing materials with the following characteristics:

1. *Short Books.* By reading short books, beginning readers develop book-handling skills such as identifying title, author, illustrator, front, and back. Moreover, they achieve a sense of accomplishment because they read many books.

2. *Predictable Text.* The text contains natural oral language patterns with rhythm and rhyme, has few words or sentences per page, is meaningful, and is interesting to young children.

3. *Big Books and Little Books.* Teachers use big books to model the reading process and to provide the natural support students need in the initial stages of reading development. The little books allow for teacher-assisted instruction and partner reading and encourage independent reading of the same text. The natural repetition and support entailed in rereading big and little books promote reading development. As a consequence, young readers develop fluency and vocabulary.

4. *Graduated Levels of Difficulty.* The big books and little books gradually increase in difficulty so that students can read at their instructional level and experience increasing competency in learning to read. At each level, there are many titles to pick and choose for reading. Teachers and students can select the titles they want to read, and they have opportunities to read additional titles at the same level. The multiple titles at each level give young readers time to develop and practice without having a sense of being "pushed" to the next level.

5. *Language Centers.* Centers are created to provide individual practice on a variety of language skills. Examples include a Big Book center where students create their own versions of Big Books, an independent reading center where students are read-

ing the program's little books, a pocket chart center where students may be engaged in recreating the sequence of the story by placing sentence strips into pocket charts, a skills center where children may be engaged in manipulating cut-up letters to form words they are reading during Big-Book instruction, and a listening center where students can listen to audiotapes of Big Books.

6. *Teacher's Edition.* A guide accompanies the program to provide instructional suggestions for literacy development.

IS THERE COMPUTER TECHNOLOGY TO DEVELOP LITERACY?

Computer technology is an important learning tool and has incredible capabilities to access information from worldwide networks. It can increase students' literacy development as well as stimulate curiosity and enjoyment of learning. Young and older students, including students with learning disabilities and other special needs, benefit from using computers for literacy development. Computers can be used in a variety of ways to increase literacy development.

Unfortunately, too many teachers still look askance at computers in education. Some see computers as a gimmick and a passing phase. Others remember the computer software from earlier days, which tended to be electronic work sheets in which students engaged in skill and drill in isolation. These programs are still being published, but computerized learning has become more sophisticated and can increase students' critical thinking and problem-solving skills. The number of skeptics is dwindling with the spread of knowledge about the latest computer capabilities that are now available.

Other educators note that computer technology is expensive, and there are not enough computers for the large numbers of students in their classrooms. In many cases, this is a problem. There are limited resources, especially in large urban districts. With one computer in a classroom, teachers find it difficult to make effective use of it. To overcome this problem, some schools have placed all their computers in one location, so that there is a computer for every two students in a classroom. Teachers schedule a specific time for using the computer facilities. Moving computers out of the classroom makes implementation less convenient, and spontaneous use can't be accomplished. Sometimes the computer becomes part of the writing and publishing center.

Using Computers in Reading and Writing

Students can use different software programs for word processing, developing the reading process, and reinforcing reading and writing skills, as well as use information access systems such as the Internet to communicate and receive information. We begin by exploring word processing programs.

Word Processing

The most frequently used software programs are word processing programs. Many different companies have published computer-friendly word processing programs for elementary-aged students, such as Scholastic's Bank Street Writer. These programs have directions and symbols on the screen to assist students in revision. With a simple command, young students can compose, change, and move text without the cross-outs, erasures, and generally messy text that occurs with the use of pencil and paper. Students can easily read their writing, thereby making composing and revision an easier task. Many word processing programs provide additional aids such as spell and grammar checks as well as a thesaurus. These are important tools for all writers but especially for those learning-disabled students who experience difficulties with spelling. Children who have problems with small-motor skills often find writing to be a challenging task because of the need for letter formation, but with the use of the computer, these same children begin to enjoy the writing task. They can freely compose and are not concerned with penmanship.

There are software programs that go beyond being tools for making typing or mechanics easy. These programs help children with the writing process. Meec's Storybook Weaver, for instance, includes graphics so students can use it for brainstorming. A variety of settings and characters can be used for the illustrations. Students can choose a split screen for text and illustrations or just choose text. The program also spells words and thus helps young students focus on composing rather than spelling. When the student clicks on the program's graphics, the correct spelling of the word appears. To produce a book is easy, since the graphics and text are included in one program. This program and others like it have their limitations. The student is limited to the program's graphics, which do not allow students to use self-selection to its fullest. For students who experience difficulties getting started writing, the graphics provide a support and engage reluctant writers to compose. Students who have spelling difficulties can more freely compose and experience less frustration because of the associated pairings of the graphic and the spelled word. Students who can write but cannot illustrate well enjoy the graphic capabilities so their books can have a more professional look.

Davidson and Associates publishes Kid Works, a program that is similar to Storybook Weaver and that allows students to create their own text and have it read back to them. This program combines a word processor, a paint (graphics) program, and speech capabilities to convert text into illustrations and illustrations into text with the added dimension of sound. Besides sound, this program has an icon maker that allows students to create their own custom illustrations. Hence students do not have to limit their writing to the program's illustrations as they do with Storybook Weaver. This program is easy to use for students from Kindergarten to grade Four.

Hyperstudio is a far more sophisticated authoring program that allows students to include photographs in a report or story by scanning the photo to be included. Laser disc footage can also be integrated in this program, thereby making it a multimedia text.

These are only three of many software programs that encourage children to become writers. Different word processing programs come out regularly, as well as updated versions, so more sophisticated versions will become readily available.

CD-ROMs

Some of the most interesting and exciting programs available use CD-ROMs (compact disc read-only memory), compact discs that hold video clips, music, and text. Many of these programs develop the reading process in a holistic and contextualized manner. For instance, entire books can be held on one disc, from picture books to a 20-volume encyclopedia. Such technology has changed the way we think about books, through its hypermedia capabilities. Students not only read text but can interact with it. For example, some CD-ROMs read the book to students, allow students to click on text to have it reread, or click on text or an illustration to learn additional information or achieve animation.

Some of the most popular programs are Broderbund's Just Grandma and Me by Mercer Mayer and Arthur's Teacher Trouble by Marc Brown. These two programs, as well as other "talking book" programs, help students become fluent readers. Students click on the read-only section, and the book is read aloud; words are highlighted as they are being read, and thus links between the auditory part of the word and the visual image of the word are created. With this technology, beginning or struggling readers can read along with text and receive the additional auditory support. Students can also read the text alone and receive help with words by clicking the mouse on the unknown word. Additional interactive capabilities are available by clicking the mouse onto different parts of the illustrations. Click the mouse, for instance, on the character Arthur and he talks; this tends to stimulate interest and provides an incentive to reluctant readers. On these same CD-ROMs, the books can be read in Spanish and Japanese. Limited English Proficient students can listen and read the book in their native language and then read it in English. By previewing the book in their native language, LEP students can more easily read it in English. English-speaking students can learn how to read the book in a different language, and this helps them learn a second language and communicate with Spanish- and Japanese-speaking peers.

There are CD-ROMs for mature readers that access text and allow students to select their own path as they read. For example, students may be reading about hot-air balloons and use the mouse to click on a symbol to watch a movie on hot-air balloons. The added dimension of sound and movement makes conceptual learning more concrete and goes beyond the ordinary capabilities of a book. There are many paths to select, and therefore students repeatedly use the same CD-ROMs. Choosing different paths makes the text different for each reader. Whereas some students after reading about volcanoes may choose to read about Hawaii, others may choose to read about Mount Saint Helens. This makes reading a different and individual experience and allows for self-selection and ownership. Rosinsky (1994) points out that students are never finished reading cyberbooks, the term for interactive books on CD-ROMs. There is no beginning, middle, or end—just different paths to continually choose to continue the adventure of reading.

Other CD-ROMs are designed to promote critical thinking and problem-solving skills. Programs such as Book Lures' Who Stole Cinderella's Slipper? and Oregon Trail and ICOM Simulations' Sherlock Holmes place students in simulated experiences that require reading and problem solving. For instance, in Sherlock Holmes, students need to consider the facts and use logic to solve the mystery. In the Oregon Trail, students choose different roles to "play out" the adventure. Students choose such roles as blacksmith and carpenter as they travel from state to state while encountering different problems to solve. With this program, students also read across the curriculum by engaging in social studies and mathematics exercises. These adventure games create enjoyment as well as enhance thinking and learning.

Pause and Reflect!

Choose a CD-ROM program such as The New Grolier Multimedia Encyclopedia or Maxis's SimFarm or SimCity and explore the world of hypermedia. Record your reactions to these programs in your journal. Discuss your experiences with other student colleagues.

Learning from Experience

As you read about this case study, note the benefits of using computers with ESL students. Write your response in your journal.

Marcy Lesser is a reading specialist who provides reading services to ESL students at Heinking School in Glenview, Illinois. She points out that ESL educators such as Krashen emphasize that children who are learning a second language need pictures, actions, and objects to supplement the reading of text (Lesser & Blachowicz, 1995). She has found that computer technology helps teachers use these cues to address ESL students' reading needs. To help her first, second, and third graders with reading, she used the CD-ROM storybook Who Wants Arthur? and a Kid Works 2, a writing/painting/speech program. Kid Works 2 is a dictation program in which teachers or students can write stories that can be read aloud via computer technology. The program has such features as designing your own rebus pictures to substitute for words in text, drawing illustrations, and using primary lined paper.

Marcy began by having a small group of students listen to the story, view the illustrations without seeing the print, and make predictions. The students listened to the story several additional times. During these repetitions, the students viewed the text along with the illustrations. Marcy encouraged her ESL students to use the cursor to point to different parts of the illustrations to stimulate discussion. After listening to the story several times, the ESL students used Kid Works 2 to retell the story Who Wants Arthur? Some students did individual or group dictations. When the groups were made up of more than two students, Marcy used an LCD (liquid crystal display) projection panel so her students could dictate and view the story on a TV monitor. Marcy noted that the ESL students could easily edit their work because of computer technology. It was also easy for them to produce multiple copies of their dictations and make their own books by using the paint portion of the program. Her students could substitute a rebus picture for difficult vocabulary and thus facilitate comprehension. She found her students were motivated to reread the story and were able to match print and sound because of the way the computer highlighted words as the story was read aloud. She noted that her students were also motivated to retell the story, since they could use the computer for dictation.

Your Turn: What are the benefits of using computers with ESL students? Write your response in your journal before reading ours.

Our Turn: We believe that motivation is a big factor in using computers. Furthermore, ESL students are correctly matching the print and its sound because of the highlighting capabilities. Hence students are receiving appropriate instruction and reinforcement. By connecting writing or dictation to reading, ESL students can use writing to increase their abilities to read. The speech capability of the computer provides another support for learning to read.

Software That Reinforces Skill Development

Historically, computers have been used to reinforce skill development. It is this function that has made educators skeptical of their importance and value to learning. At the onset of computer usage, software programs were primarily electronic work sheets through which students would develop skills in isolation. These programs employed a behavioral model in which students received positive reinforcement with a correct response and no reinforcement with an incorrect response. Although many of these programs are questionable, there is some value to drill and practice software programs. Unlike most paper and pencil exercises, drill and practice programs provide immediate feedback. Students know immediately if their responses are correct or incorrect. Students do not keep making the same mistake, thereby reinforcing incorrect learning. As compared to their attitude to workbooks, students are enthusiastic about drill and practice on the computer. Most students enjoy it and are motivated by it. Children even choose to do these software programs at home. The machine and the game-like format intrigue students. Usually there are graphics and sound associated with each program, thus making it even more inviting. Correct responses are rewarded to make students feel good about themselves. Incorrect responses usually receive encouragement rather than criticism. Some drill and practice can be beneficial, so why not use a tool like the computer to make learning more interesting? But practice should be limited, since it isolates the skill from reading and composing natural text.

One drill and practice software program that can be beneficial is Mario Teaches Typing. It uses a game format to help students learn keyboarding, an important skill for using a word processing program. Because it's a game and uses the popular character Mario, children learn hand position and how to make appropriate keystrokes. The program provides practice but can't be a substitute for using keyboarding skills while using a word processing program. A short 10-minute segment is long enough to practice, with additional time devoted to using word processing to compose text.

Other popular programs for reading and writing include work on phonics, spelling, and grammar. Each program is different and may have merits for specific students who need additional individual practice to learn a concept, but students also need opportunities to use the skill in context. Using phonic programs such as Reader Rabbit may reinforce phonics generalization, but the same students who use them need more time spent on reading text to learn to apply the rule. As a general rule, we suggest limiting these programs to a short 10-minute time period.

Internet

The internet is a worldwide system of voluntarily interconnected computer networks containing millions of documents, resources, and databases. There are over 25,000 networks connecting over 30,000,000 people worldwide. Students can access this information by using a modem and communications software or computer account assists such as CompuServe, Delphi, and America Online. Internet is the wave of the future in education and has been compared to the greatest invention since the printing press. It provides current information about almost any topic. For example, students can access library card catalogs, discussion groups, and information resources such as ERIC (Educational Resources Information Center) and have their own electronic mail address to send and receive messages anywhere in the world.

For teaching reading and writing, the Internet allows students to engage in authentic reading and writing tasks. By using electronic mail, students can write, send, and receive messages to one or more people—that is, they can electronically send the same message to one or more E-mail addresses. Students can form discussion groups about their hobbies and interests and "talk" to students in the same state, across the United States, or even in another country. Reading and writing in this venue is meaningful and serves a personal purpose. It's likely that students won't even think about becoming better readers and writers by using E-mail; they just naturally will.

E-mail facilitates communication but so do the other Internet services. When students are interested in reading and learning about a very specific topic, often the school library has little or no information on this topic. With the use of the Internet, students are no longer limited to the school library; they can peruse libraries across the country to find information about their topic. They can also access other information from other sources such as ERIC and obtain the most current information.

Within the Internet system, there exists a fascinating writing and reading experience called TinyMUDs. Children are involved in creating worlds through writing. Via computer, students read and participate with others in these creative writing adventures. When you participate in a TinyMUD, it's as if you are a character in a novel. An example of a TinyMUD appears in Figure 9.6. In this example, one player has created the Old Browning Kitchen, and the other player responds to the command symbol > by writing a response.

Scholastic's Literacy Place literature-based program has already tapped into the Internet and has made electronic information access a part of its program. In Scholastic Network, students are encouraged to research topics related to the unit of study by using their electronic Network Message Board to contact other students in the system to discuss the unit topic. Or students may want to use the on-line database to do further research on the unit topic.

Staying on Top of Computer Technology

Since the software industry is developing new programs daily, its difficult to keep up with all the available programs for reading and writing. To keep current, we suggest several resources. First, become a member of a computer educators' group such as Illinois Computing Educators. This organization provides newsletters, courses, and workshops on new technology, and it provides free services to educators. Second, become

The Old Browning House

RIGHT: The author's photograph appears in the picture frame.

In this front room of the huge old house, a lazy array of windows brings in warm sunlight, some of them open, some of them half covered by lacey old curtains. Little tables with glass tops, some with marble tops, sit beside pieces of old leather-clad furniture and rest their clawed feet in dark red Persian rugs with tassels. The ceiling is high, and fans turn with no commitment. The doors are huge and propped open with old gray vases with messes of dried flowers in great clumps, dropping petals onto the ground. There is a kitchen through a large door to the west, a sitting room to the north, and a magnificent wooden staircase with a thick banister leading up carpeted stairs. The house is in pleasant disarray, porcelain knick-knacks and beautiful nothings in glass cases, too many umbrellas in the brass container by the front door and the rest.

> west

You walk beneath the high wooden arch of the door and into the kitchen. . . .

The Old Browning House [Kitchen]

A huge old kitchen with white and light blue tiles on the floor, giant sunny windows over the big sink, and a light wood island in the middle — a modern feature — with a grill and a polished cutting board on which a display of knives sits. The sink is deep and double, a shining metal with rusty faucets that are tarnished with use. The counters are long and white and mostly clean, toppling over with bags of marshmallows and jars of preserves and tall glass containers of pasta green and red and spirals. A closet at one end is a deep pantry, and there's a large groaning refrigerator by the back door — which is ajar and leads to the back yard. A kitchen table sits at one corner surrounded by a bay window and tangles of English ivy. A cluster of bowls on the floor indicate cats — lots of cats. Glasses and plates sit around in general disarray.

> open cupboard

You open up one of the wooden cupboards, the hinge creaking.

> look inside cupboard

Inside the cupboard are iced tea glasses, and some old china plates.

> take glass

You take a glass down from the cupboard. It's chipped.

Keir walks in from the back yard, the screen door banging shut behind her.

Keir has arrived.

Keir says, "Hello Claire! Helping yourself?"

> say Yes, thanks. . . . Hope you don't mind.

You say, "Yes, thanks. . . . Hope you don't mind."

Keir says, "Not at all!"

"Keir" is the name of a persona, or character. The person actually typing what Keir was saying to me (Keir's player) could be anyone, anywhere in the nation. In real life, Keir's player is an English major at a university and writes for magazines, but on a TinyMUD she can be a virtual persona, who roleplays Keir (that is, pretends to be Keir) to explore creatively the aspects of being, in this case, a wealthy young woman with a large house. In this way, the participants in a TinyMUD create places (like the Old Browning House), landscapes (if I left the Browning House I would be on Keir's estate, with lots of hill country), interactions between people and objects (such as when I was trying to get a glass of water), and interactions between people and people (like the conversation we had), and create a real-feeling virtual reality. On a TinyMUD, you can learn something about living, literally, through the art of writing.

collage by Elizabeth Brown

Figure 9.6 TinyMUD Simulation. *Source:* From *ODYSSEY's* November 1994 issue: *Cyberspace,* © 1994, Cobblestone Publishing, Inc., 7 School St., Peterborough, NH 03458. Reprinted by permission of the publisher.

349

a subscriber to one of the many magazines such as *Macworld*. These magazines review software and the latest in computer hardware. Third, talk to the media expert in your school and/or your community library; they are a wealth of information. They know which programs work and which ones are the favorites of students. They know the ones that are computer friendly and those that increase learning. And, finally, take a computer course at your local university or library.

To help you become a critical consumer of software, we suggest you try out the program yourself and use these guidelines to help you select software for your classroom.

Guidelines for Selecting Software

1. Does the computer software provide meaningful instruction in reading and writing?
2. Are the directions easy to read and implement?
3. Is the content functional and does it provide for interpretive and critical thinking?
4. Does the software challenge students but without discouraging them?
5. Does the software program require active student involvement?
6. Does the software program provide meaningful feedback?
7. Are there different levels of difficulty so the program continually increases students' learning?
8. Does the student demonstrate interest in the software program?
9. Are colorful graphics, animation, and sound effects used to keep students' attention without detracting from learning?

If a positive response can be given to the majority of the questions, the software program's quality is above average. But in the final analysis, you must be the decision maker.

SUMMARY

Materials are an important part of the reading and writing program. They affect students' motivation and interest in literacy. They affect what students learn and influence the type of instruction teachers provide.

Literature-based programs are used in a majority of elementary classrooms to teach reading and writing. Significant changes have been made in these programs because of recent theory and research in reading and writing. Literature-based programs are comprehensive in nature, provide systematic instruction, and facilitate classroom management. These graded programs present a total package of materials and include children's literature and/or anthologies, teacher's editions, practice books, and assessments.

With these programs, children are reading good literature that does not contain rewritten text that controls the length of the reading selection, the difficulty of the vocabulary, and the number of new words for that grade level. A variety of literature is included—fiction, nonfiction, and poetry—that addresses the needs of a diverse student population.

The teacher's edition is the source of instruction information. When you use a literature-based program, identify goals your students need to develop and select complementary instructional strategies and activities to achieve these goals. Be careful not to use all the materials or ideas the program suggests; otherwise, there will be no time for such supplementary materials as a variety of books, magazines, and literature units. The key is to be selective. Not all the literature selections need to be read. Consider your students' needs and interests as you choose literature. Invite your students to help you make choices. Pick and choose from the recommended teaching suggestions for pre-, during-, and postreading instruction. Some suggestions help students to read and enjoy the literature selection and become better readers while others do not.

Early literacy programs have developed popularity because of their holistic philosophy and the great number of big and small books that provide for meaningful reading and redundancy and sufficient practice to develop fluent readers. These programs address the K–2 child's developmental needs by using centers and incorporating a hands-on approach for developing literacy.

Computer technology is an important tool for reading and writing development. With the use of software programs for word processing, developing the reading process, and reinforcing reading and writing skills, computers are becoming an important part of literacy instruction. With the present and future usage of the Internet through a modern and communications software, children are able to easily and quickly communicate and access information.

But with all these published programs, teachers are the key to making decisions about what is beneficial for their students. It is the teacher who can best teach and not a program.

In the Field

1. Interview classroom teachers about their usage of literature-based programs. Here are some suggested questions: How do you use a literature-based program? What components do you frequently use? Does the program meet the needs of all students, such as LD, LEP, and gifted students? If not, what do you do? What is particularly helpful about the literature-based program? Which parts are the least beneficial for students?

2. From a literature-based program, choose a children's literature title and the accompanying lesson plan to review. Identify the reading and writing goals you want students to achieve from reading this text. Use the teacher's edition to help you plan instruction. Make decisions by eliminating, modifying, and developing your own activities to accomplish the selected goals.

3. Interview a few students about their thoughts and ideas about computerized instruction. How do they use computers for reading and writing in their classroom? What are their favorite reading and writing software programs? Why do they like these programs? Do they use the Internet in their classroom? If so, how?

Portfolio Suggestion

Select from your journal two examples of your responses from Pause and Reflect or In the Field activities. Write a brief evaluation of your work. Explain what you learned and how it will affect your planning and your implementing of instruction.

For Further Reading

Dillner, M. (1994). Using hypermedia to enhance content area instruction. *Journal of Reading, 37,* 260–271.

Guthrie, L. F., & Richardson, S. (1995). Turned on to language arts: Computer literacy in the primary grades. *Educational Leadership, 53,* 14–17.

Lungren, L. (1995). Strategies for gaining access to the information superhighway: Off the side street and on to the main road. *The Reading Teacher, 48,* 432–436.

McCarthy, S. J., & Hoffman, J. V. (1995). The new basals: How are they different? *The Reading Teacher, 49,* 72–75.

Wepner, S. B. (1991). Technology-based literature plans for elementary students. *The Reading Teacher, 45,* 236–238.

Linking Instruction
with Assessment

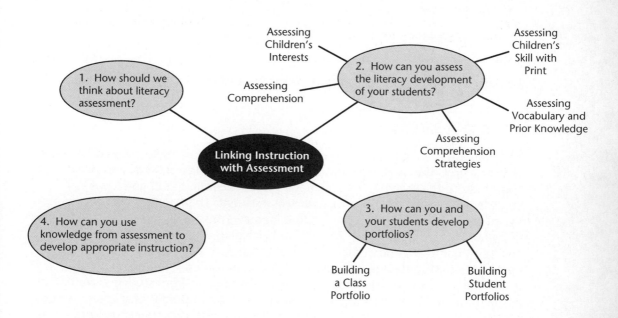

Assessing
Children's
Interests

Assessing
Children's
Skill with
Print

1. How should we
think about literacy
assessment?

2. How can you assess
the literacy development
of your students?

Assessing
Comprehension

Assessing
Vocabulary and
Prior Knowledge

Linking Instruction
with Assessment

Assessing
Comprehension
Strategies

4. How can you use
knowledge from assessment to
develop appropriate instruction?

3. How can you and
your students develop
portfolios?

Building
a Class
Portfolio

Building
Student
Portfolios

▼ CHAPTER GOALS FOR THE READER

To understand different perspectives on literacy assessment

To develop strategies for assessing literacy development

To learn to create student and class portfolios

To learn how to use knowledge from assessment to develop good instruction

▼ CHAPTER OVERVIEW

The title of this chapter reveals our bias: Assessment, to be useful, should be linked to instruction. That is, assessment of children's knowledge of literacy should contribute to the shaping of instructional experiences. In this chapter, we first consider various perspectives on literacy assessment. Then, in the second section, we introduce a model for thinking about literacy assessment and show how aspects of literacy can be assessed by teachers. In particular, we will focus on assessing children's comprehension, skill with print, vocabulary and prior knowledge, comprehension strategies, and interests. This information is more useful in instructional planning when it is combined with samples from students' work. Thus, in the third section of the chapter, we discuss the development of student and class portfolios. In the final section, we consider how we can use knowledge from assessment to develop good instruction.

◆ TAPPING PRIOR KNOWLEDGE TO SET A PURPOSE

Think back over your experiences in schools. What comes to mind when you think of assessment? What are your experiences with assessment? As a teacher, how do you believe that you will use assessment in the classroom? After you have read the chapter overview and reflected on your experiences, identify what it is that you most want to learn from reading this chapter. List these in your journal under the heading Chapter 10: Setting a Purpose.

HOW SHOULD WE THINK ABOUT LITERACY ASSESSMENT?

Many different terms are often used interchangeably—assessment, evaluation, testing, measurement. How are they different? Usually *testing* and *measurement* refer to the act of gaining evidence; they assume a metric or a norm group against which the person or thing being tested or measured is compared. Our use of the term *assessment* goes beyond the process of gathering data to include a better understanding of some area. It also goes beyond placing a value on a performance, as is usually the case in *evaluation,* although evaluation may be part of the assessment process. An important part of assessment includes making judgments about areas of strength and weakness. It is a comprehensive judgment related to comparing measured performance in a number of different areas. The purpose of assessment is to understand the nature of students' literacy development and their relative strengths and weaknesses, and, on this basis, to establish a plan for instructional support.

During the past decade, teachers and educational researchers have been rethinking assessment. This reassessment has been motivated by concerns over accountability. More states have developed their own state assessment systems, and a national assessment is being planned (here "assessment" is used in the sense of evaluation). At the same time, teachers have found that more general measures of learning unrelated to their curricula are of limited value in instructional planning. Considerable progress has been made in the development of alternative assessment procedures, including the use of portfolios. In this book we focus on assessment by teachers because of our belief that you need to know how well your students are learning in order to plan and modify your instructional program.

Controversial Issue

There is little disagreement among educators that some form of assessment is a necessary component of educational planning. If you do not know how well your students are doing, so the argument goes, how can you make plans for the next steps? In the field of literacy, as our views of the process of reading and writing changed from that of a collection of specific skills to that of a unified process, the need for new assessment procedures became obvious. Measures were needed that would capture the reading process rather than parts of it (Calfee & Heibert, 1991; Valencia & Pearson, 1986). This search for process measures led to the development of a variety of alternative assessment procedures, such as portfolio assessment, interviews, think-aloud procedures, and teacher observation (Linn, Baker, & Dunbar, 1991; Valencia, 1990).

Concurrently, forces for educational accountability gained momentum. District administrators as well as educational policy makers and legislators were particularly interested in having evidence to document how well students were learning in different content areas (Paris et al., 1992; Kist, 1991). Standardized tests have long been used for this purpose. They involve short passages and tasks that measure the development of skills, but they may not truly reflect the reading and writing children can do under more natural circumstances. Because of these concerns about the validity of these measures, considerable attention has been directed toward the development of alternative assessment systems (Linn et al., 1991). In the states of Illinois and Michigan, for example, assessment procedures involve longer reading selections that are similar to what children read in their classes (Wixson, Peters, Weber, & Roeber, 1987). In states such as Kentucky, Maryland, and Vermont, explorations are under way to determine whether portfolio assessment can serve both the needs of teachers and the state needs for accountability.

As the amount of testing in schools increases, teachers are becoming more concerned about the amount of time devoted to testing (Smith, 1991). Many find that in addition to formal tests to meet the accountability needs of districts and states, they also need to develop their own assessment systems to determine how well their students are progressing. In most states, the standardized tests of districts and states do not provide the detailed profiles of student learning that are needed for instructional planning. Most professionals agree that some form of assessment is needed by teachers for instructional planning and by administrators for accountability. The debate, still ongoing, concerns the form of the measures, the time they take, usefulness of the information provided, and whether a single assessment procedure can serve purposes of accountability as well as instructional planning.

In the first chapter, we considered the goals you may have for reading instruction and how these will influence your planning. In chapters 8 and 9, we examined published programs, literature, and other materials that you typically use in developing programs to achieve your goals. And yet, although the materials you select may be appropriate to your goals, they may be inappropriate for the students you are teaching. For some students the selections may be so difficult that they lead to frustration and little learning; for others, the materials may be so easy that they are not challenging and students learn little from them. The purpose of this chapter is to introduce you to methods for assessing student learning so that you will be able to make good decisions about materials and about instruction. Because the topic of writing assessment was addressed in chapter 7, the emphasis of this chapter will tend to be on reading assessment. Nevertheless, because of the intimate connection between reading and writing, both will be discussed in this chapter, particularly in the section on portfolios.

How can you judge whether the materials students read are appropriate in difficulty for them? In order to make decisions about the appropriateness of reading selections, you need to become an astute observer of how well your students respond to your questions, how well they read aloud, and how well they do in their written work. You need a map in your mind to know what to look for, and when problems are encountered, what further questions to ask.

The approach we recommend is one in which reading comprehension or the ability to construct meaning from printed text is viewed as the central and most important goal (Barr, Blachowicz, & Sadow, 1995). If, however, a student experiences difficulty comprehending the reading selections that are normally assigned to students in a class, it is important to examine not only the nature of this student's strategies but also the underlying processes that contribute to reading, such as skill with print and vocabulary knowledge. This way of thinking about reading is represented in Figure 10.1.

"Normal reading task demands" constitutes the framework within which to assess reading proficiency. These demands refer to the basal selections, literature, or other materials that are typically assigned by teachers at particular grade levels. The double arrows in the model between "Normal reading task demands" and "Reading comprehension" refer to the match between the difficulty of the materials and the proficiency of students. Students may have difficulty reading a selection for several reasons: They may not be interested in the content, they may lack the ability to decode the print, they may lack prior knowledge needed for comprehension of the selection, or they may not have learned appropriate comprehension strategies.

Teachers typically ask students questions about a selection to judge their reading comprehension. Think for a moment about the questions that you ask students during instruction (or that you have been asked by your teachers) and how this lets you judge whether or not a student comprehends a passage. You may also sometimes ask students to retell a story or the main points from an article. From the responses of students, you soon learn which students have comprehended a selection and which ones have encountered difficulty. If you are teaching older students, you may also ask them to respond in writing to questions based on a selection or to summarize the main points.

When students fail to understand a selection, you need to determine the reasons for this. One area to keep in mind is motivation. If students are not interested in a topic, if they are not motivated to report what they understand, their performance may suggest problems when none exist. One condition for valid assessment is the active involvement of students. Thus you need to be able to detect lack of motivation on the part of students in order to know if your assessment of reading is valid. The

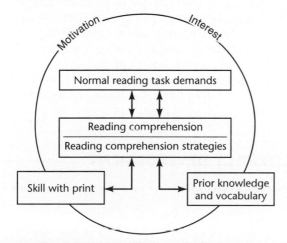

Figure 10.1 Basic Model of the Reading Process

most direct way to assess interest and motivation is to observe students and ask them if they are interested in reading a selection on a particular topic. The important point here is that if students are experiencing literacy problems because they lack motivation, you need to concentrate on capturing their interest instead of developing strategies for reading development.

For most students, however, difficulty with reading comprehension reflects inadequate development in one or several areas related to reading. One such area may be skill with print—the ability of the reader to translate printed symbols efficiently into spoken language or meaning. This includes the ability not only to identify previously unknown words but also to recognize a set of printed words instantaneously and to use information from context to facilitate efficient and fluent reading. For example, some students may not comprehend a selection because they were able to read only a portion of it during the time allotted; their slow reading rate has limited their comprehension. In this case, they probably focus on word identification to the neglect of constructing meaning.

Another possible reason for comprehension difficulty is lack of prior knowledge and vocabulary—the ability to understand key words contained in particular reading selections and the encompassing concepts that are being conveyed, as well as the ways in which word meaning is revealed by context. For example, to understand a passage about the discoveries of Copernicus and Galileo, students must be familiar not only with the meanings of such words as "planet" and "telescope," but also with the concept of "movement." Students differ in the extent to which they can comprehend a passage, and their comprehension often reflects their prior knowledge of a topic.

Finally, students may have difficulty comprehending a selection because they have not yet developed effective strategies for focusing their attention while they read in order to construct meaning. Some students need help in organizing themselves to integrate information across sentences and paragraphs; others need to learn to monitor their own comprehension process more effectively.

In sum, the model in Figure 10.1 identifies aspects of reading that can be observed by teachers: general comprehension, interests, print skill, prior knowledge and vocabulary, and comprehension strategies. The main purpose of this chapter is to show you how you can gather information about each. We believe that you need to learn how to assess children's retellings, how to ask appropriate questions to evaluate the comprehension and motivation of students, how to listen to children read passages and words to judge the development of their skill with print, how to identify central concepts and vocabulary in reading selections and judge student knowledge of these concepts, and how to assess whether children have developed and apply strategies for monitoring their comprehension.

HOW CAN YOU ASSESS THE LITERACY DEVELOPMENT OF YOUR STUDENTS?

There are specific procedures that you can use to become more aware of your students' comprehension, interests, print skill, prior knowledge and vocabulary, and comprehension strategies. While reading about these methods, remember that you gain skill in observation only by doing it. As a beginning, treat the Pause and Reflect activities seriously. They will let you identify questions that you have about the procedures. Even more important, the In the Field activities at the end of the chapter will lay the foundation for good classroom observational skill. If you wish to become proficient making records of a child's oral reading, you must practice listening to a child read aloud and making a record. If you wish to become good at asking questions, you must learn how to study the selections children are reading in order to devise appropriate and penetrating questions. We can't emphasize enough that you will learn about assessment only through actually doing it.

You will learn about the literacy development of students by working with them individually during conferences, by studying samples of their writing, and by observing them during class interaction. When working with students, you will become aware of how much you can learn simply by talking with students. It is important to find time to have brief conversations with your students. When they understand that you are interested in their reactions to instruction and how it might be made better for them, they become eager informants. Ask the questions, "What did you learn from that activity [story, task]?" and "How did you feel about it?" The comments of students provide insight into their thinking about the tasks on which they are working and about their learning. Sometimes what you hope is learned is not what in fact is being learned.

Assessing Comprehension

The selections that children read are many and varied. A major distinction can be made between those that are narrative in style and tell a story and those that are expository in style and convey information. The methods for assessing comprehension differ somewhat for these two major types of text. Thus we first consider ways in which you can assess narrative comprehension and then ways to assess the comprehension of informational text.

Story Comprehension

After students have read a selection, their discussion reveals how well they understood it. Frequently, the discussion begins with children "retelling" what they believe to be important events or points in a selection. Sometimes students will disagree with each other. But usually there comes a time during the discussion when you intervene with questions. For example, when your students' understanding is vague or inaccurate, your questions can direct them to consider more specific information. Other times, particularly when students seem to understand the gist of a selection, your questions may direct them toward greater elaboration and higher-level interpretation, critical evaluation, and personal reflection.

Your ability to assess the comments of students and to form appropriate questions to facilitate the discussion is critical. How do you learn how to do this? One essential step is to be familiar with the story or the selection that the students are discussing. Read the text for an overview of its content and organization. To gain insight into the story or passage, note which parts stand out in memory and which are readily lost. Then try to construct a broad outline of its significant content. A second reading of the text may be useful in order to "fill in" the outline, and additional readings may suggest some higher-level interpretive or critical evaluation questions. As we discussed in chapters 8 and 9, some consistent components of stories have been identified (Mandler & Johnson, 1977; Rumelhart, 1975; Stein & Glenn, 1979). Typically, the initial section of a story introduces the main characters and the setting of the story. The story itself is composed of a series of episodes, followed by a final resolution (Rumelhart, 1975).

Learning from Experience

Most teachers know how to read a story and to make a mental outline of the important ideas. Keisha Brown, who teaches a combined first- and second-grade class, was planning to have some of her first graders read the story "Cookies" by Arnold Lobel in order to check their comprehension. As a first step, she carefully read the story to fix in her mind the main information conveyed. In a similar fashion, as you read the story, try to form a mental outline of the important ideas.

Cookies*

Toad baked some cookies.
"These cookies smell very good," said Toad.
He ate one.
"And they taste even better," he said.
Toad ran to Frog's house.
"Frog, Frog," cried Toad, "taste these cookies that I have made."
Frog ate one of the cookies.
"These are the best cookies I have ever eaten!" said Frog.
Frog and Toad ate many cookies, one after another.
"You know, Toad," said Frog, with his mouth full,
"I think we should stop eating. We will soon be sick."
"You are right," said Toad.
"Let us eat one last cookie, and then we will stop."
Frog and Toad ate one last cookie.
There were many cookies left in the bowl.
"Frog," said Toad. "Let us eat one very last cookie, and then we will stop."
Frog and Toad ate one very last cookie.
"We must stop eating!" cried Toad as he ate another.
"Yes," said Frog, reaching for a cookie. "We need will power."
"What is will power?" asked Toad.
"Will power is trying hard not to do something that you really want to do," said Frog.
"You mean like trying not to eat all of these cookies?" asked Toad.
"Right," said Frog.
Frog put the cookies in a box.

---

*Arnold Lobel (1972). "Cookies" in *Frog and Toad Together* (pp. 30–41). New York: HarperCollins. Copyright © 1971, 1972 by Arnold Lobel. Reprinted with permission.

"There," he said. "Now we will not eat any more cookies."
"But we can open the box," said Toad.
"That is true," said Frog.
Frog tied some string around the box.
"There," he said. "Now we will not eat any more cookies."
"But we can cut the string and open the box," said Toad.
"That is true," said Frog.
Frog got a ladder. He put the box up on a high shelf.
"There," said Frog. "Now we will not eat any more cookies."
"But we can climb the ladder and take the box down from the shelf and cut the string and open the box," said Toad.
"That is true," said Frog.
Frog climbed the ladder and took the box down from the shelf.
He cut the string and opened the box.
Frog took the box outside. He shouted in a loud voice.
"HEY BIRDS, HERE ARE COOKIES!" Birds came from everywhere.
They picked up all the cookies in their beaks and flew away.
"Now we have no more cookies to eat," said Toad sadly. "Not even one."
"Yes," said Frog. "But we have lots and lots of will power."
"You may keep it all, Frog," said Toad. "I am going home now to bake a cake."

 Your Turn: Construct a broad outline of the content of this story that is based on your reading. First, identify when and where the story takes place [Setting] and who the main characters are [Character]. Then describe the problem: How did it all begin? What is the predicament of the main character(s) [Problem]? Next, describe the attempts made by the characters to resolve the problem and their reasons for what they did [Attempts and Internal Response]. Finally, describe what happened in the end [Resolution].

After completing your outline of the story, read the story a second time. Then check the outline and fill in additional information. Record your outline in your journal under the heading An Outline of "Cookies."

Our Turn: Keisha Brown read the story with essentially the same purpose in mind. Here is what her outline looks like. See how yours compares with hers.

Setting: Toad's house, Frog's house.

Characters: Frog and Toad.

Problem: Frog and Toad were eating too many of the cookies that Toad had baked.

Attempts and Internal Response: In order to stop eating cookies, Frog said they needed willpower. Frog put the cookies in a box, tied the box, put it up high—but they could still get the cookies. Finally, Frog opened the box and gave the cookies to the birds.

Resolution: When the cookies were gone, Toad concluded that he didn't want willpower and went home to bake a cake.

After summarizing several stories in this way, you will be able to form mental outlines of the stories your students are reading as you read them. This outline can serve as the framework for evaluating children's retelling.

Learning from Experience

Once you have studied a story or selection and have distilled the important ideas from it, you are in a better position to consider the responses of children. In the following Learning from Experience description, Keisha had two of her first graders read "Cookies" and tell her about it. As you read the retellings of the children, consider what they tell you about the comprehension of each of the children. Do they understand the story? Would you want to ask either of them further questions to clarify their understanding?

Lucas's Retelling

Lucas, one of Keisha's first graders retold the story of "Cookies" as follows:

Frog baked some cookies and Frog went over to Toad's house. And Frog tasted some cookies and he thought they were very good. Toad said, "We better stop eating cookies. We might get sick." Toad said, "Let's put it into a box." But Frog said, "I can get it out of the box." Toad said, "Well, let's put a string around it." Then Frog said, "We can cut the string." Then Toad said, "I'll put it up high." Frog said, "We can climb up a ladder." Toad said, "That's true." Toad took the box outside and gave the cookies to the birds. Frog said. "I'm going home to make a cake." Frog said he didn't want willpower.

Rachel's Retelling

Keisha asked a second child, Rachel, to read the story and then tell her about what happened. Here is her retelling:

It was about this Frog and Toad. They had cookies and then they baked a cake. That's all.

Your Turn: Reflect for a moment. What is your assessment of Lucas's retelling? On the basis of his retelling, do you conclude that he understood the story? If not, what aspects would you explore further? Record your assessment in your journal under the heading Lucas's Retelling.

What is your assessment of Rachel's retelling? On the basis of her retelling, do you conclude that she understood the story? If not, what aspects would you explore further? Record your assessment in your journal under the heading Rachel's Retelling.

Our Turn: With regard to Lucas's retelling, most of the information contained in the outline of the story is included in his retelling, even though the two characters are reversed. You can conclude that Lucas's comprehension and his retelling ability are good.

It is less easy to know how well Rachel understood the story. Her reconstruction is extremely brief, although she did remember the character names and that they made cookies. She also reported that they baked a cake, which was mentioned by Toad only as a possible future activity. Because the retelling is so limited, Keisha asked Rachel some questions that would help her to structure the story in order to see if she had understood the story. Here are some of the questions she asked:

1. Who are the main characters and where does the story begin?
2. What is their problem?
3. In order to stop eating cookies, what did Frog say they needed?
4. What did they do to stop eating the cookies? What else?
5. What happened in the end?

Since Rachel was able to give short but relevant answers to these questions, Keisha concluded that she had comprehended the story but had difficulty retelling it. If she had failed to answer the questions, it could mean several different things. It might mean that she really had not understood the story. But it might also mean that, for some reason, she was not able to respond. The reason might have been because she was shy or lacked confidence; it might have meant that she has difficulty organizing her ideas to retell them. Most often, children do respond to some questions with appropriate answers and to others with inaccurate or inappropriate answers. And from such responses, you can begin to see where they are encountering difficulty.

What standards should you use in judging whether a child's comprehension is adequate? If a student remembers all or most of the important information about a passage, you can conclude that his or her comprehension is extremely good, and infer that the student should be able to read this and similar material independently without instructional support. If the student misses 3 or 4 out of every 10 questions, then you would conclude that comprehension is adequate but that the student could profit from instructional support before, during, and following reading. (For specific examples of instructional support, see chapters 4 to 6.) If, however, a student misses half or more of the questions asked, you would conclude that the material is too difficult and that you should find more appropriate selections for the student to read.

This form of retelling is akin to the reflective activity Rosenblatt used with her students in response to Robert Frost's poem (see chapter 1). With mature readers, it is not necessary to assess whether readers have understood the story line; such comprehension is assumed. With children developing skill in literacy, in contrast, it is important to assess whether they follow the story line. As Rosenblatt notes, the assessment of *aesthetic* comprehension should focus on how readers respond *affectively* as well as *cognitively* during the reading event. Thus in assessing the comprehension of children, it is important to ask questions that focus on their affective as well as their cognitive responses. For example, Keisha may have asked children some of the following questions about the story "Cookies" to direct their attention to their feelings: How did you feel as you read about Frog and Toad's trying to stop eating the cookies? How did you feel when Frog gave the cookies to the birds? Why did Toad say, "I am going home now to bake a cake"? Questions such as these will focus children on affective aspects of the aesthetic experiences of reading stories as well as the cognitive aspects.

Informational Comprehension

The procedures you follow in preparing to assess children's comprehension of informational text *(efferent reading)* are similar to those used in assessing the cognitive aspects of narrative comprehension. The first step is to read the passage and to consider the structural characteristics of text and how the information is organized. Sometimes informational articles follow a pattern. The information may be organized according to a time sequence, a set of steps or enumerations, problem and solutions, cause and effect, comparison and contrast, or main assertion and supporting facts and examples. When reading nonfiction selections, you must figure out the organizational pattern that the authors are using to convey the information they believe is important.

 # Learning from Experience

Jason Petersen, a fourth-grade teacher, is helping his students organize a unit on national forests. As part of the science strand, the students will be reading selections on forest fires. Jason is interested in whether any of his students might have difficulty comprehending some of the selections he has available in the class. Consider the following selection on "Forest Fires." Jason reads this selection to assess its structure and the information it contains.

As you read the article, see if you can determine the organizational pattern used by the author. Note the important ideas included in the article and their organization.

Forest Fires*

An important problem for forest rangers is how to protect forests from being ruined by fire. Each year thousands of trees are destroyed by fire. Careless campers do not put their fires completely out. Cigarettes are left to burn on the dry ground. These small fires in dry forests can burn thousands of trees. One solution to the forest fire problem is to man lookout stations and use helicopters to spot fires. Fires that are spotted right away can be put out before they get too big to handle. Then fires will cause less damage to the forest. A second solution to the problem is to have experts and bulldozers ready to move in quickly to fight the fire. Bulldozers can throw huge amounts of dirt on a fire in a short time. The dirt helps put the fire out quickly. A third solution is to build fire lanes in the forests. Fire lanes are long breaks in the forest where there are no trees. These breaks prevent the fire from spreading and getting too large.

 Your Turn: Reread the article through carefully to determine the organizational pattern used by the author. Then write an outline in your journal that includes important ideas and their organization. After completing your outline, read the selection a second time to check the outline and fill in additional information. What specific

---

*McGee, L. M. (1982). The influence of metacognitive knowledge of expository text structure on discourse recall. In J. A. Niles & L. A. Harris (Eds.), *New inquiries in reading research and instruction* (p. 6). Rochester, NY: National Reading Conference. Reprinted with the permission of the National Reading Conference and L. M. McGee.

questions might you ask to assess comprehension? Record your outline in your journal under the heading Outline of Forest Fires.

 Our Turn: Compare your outline with the one that Jason developed.

Main Topic: How Forest Rangers Protect Forests from Fire Damage

> *Causes of Fire*
> > Campfires
> > Cigarettes
>
> *Solutions to Problem*
> > Early detection: Lookout stations
> > > Helicopters
> >
> > Quick extinction: Bulldozers—throw dirt on fire
> > Prevention: Building fire lanes

With this outline in mind, you would be ready to ask students to tell what they learned from the selection. If students neglected important information during the discussion, you might ask one or more of the following questions based directly on the outline:

1. How do many forest fires get started?
2. How are bulldozers used in fighting fires?
3. How do fire lanes prevent fire damage to forests?

You also might want to pose the following higher-level discussion questions:

1. The passage mentioned that "experts" are needed in fighting fires. What sort of things might experts know that would be helpful in fighting fires?
2. What might be done to prevent fires from getting started in the first place?

Assessing comprehension is easier when you work one-on-one with a child, but most of us support student reading in groups. Even in a group setting, you have the opportunity to ask individuals questions and to hear comments from individual students. Particularly in a group, it helps to have an outline in mind to see if students have understood the important ideas in a selection. After group instruction, you need to ask yourself what you know about the comprehension of each student. You may realize that you know very little about some group members and need to be more attentive to them.

Written responses to comprehension tests and other writing assignments based on selections that students have read can also provide information for assessing comprehension. Written responses can be organized in one of two ways. You may ask students to record in their journals their ideas and feelings as they read. These entries will let you know what the student saw as being interesting, puzzling, satisfying, and the like. Alternatively, you can pose a more structured writing task either by asking students to retell what a story or selection was about or by posing questions about characters or themes based on your reading of the selection.

In the following paragraph, a middle-school teacher comments on comprehension assessment in a group setting:

Well, first of all, I evaluate them in terms of just listening to their discussion. . . . Believe it or not, most of the kids do discuss. I do have some verbal kids and I have to kind of stifle them sometimes. Also it's important to look at their journals and their reactions to what they have read. Sometimes I have them write short essays about story characters and themes. I find their written work reveals a lot about their thinking and their reading and writing.

For both written responses and questioning, you must have a clear understanding of what constitutes good comprehension, based on your mental outline of the story or selection. If you believe that a student is having comprehension difficulties, you need to determine why. You need to decide the areas of reading strengths and difficulties and whether the materials being read are at an appropriate level of difficulty.

These assessment procedures, particularly those involving written response, must be used cautiously with special populations because the written responses may underestimate what children actually know. Written responses are especially difficult for students with learning disabilities; they are often more able to respond orally to questions than in writing. Similarly, children who are learning English as a second language may have difficulty expressing what they know in English either orally or in writing. Thus conclusions drawn about the comprehension of special populations should be extremely tentative. Although more difficult to prepare, assessments involving the selection and arrangement of pictures that convey the actions and information in selections may provide a more valid measure of comprehension for such special populations.

Assessing Children's Interests

Some children find reading and writing inherently engaging; others choose other activities. A variety of factors, including past literacy experiences, natural talent, or models at home, may contribute to this predisposition. But beyond these individual inclinations, teachers can create environments that encourage literate activity. Ruddell (1995), for example, describes some of the shared beliefs and motivational strategies of influential teachers. Teachers demonstrate energy, commitment, flexibility, warmth, and caring about individual students. They are sensitive to the needs of individuals and understand where students are developmentally in their literacy learning. Equally important, during instruction they demonstrate enthusiasm, intellectual excitement, and the ability to consider alternative views of text. They make the material personally relevant, stress basic communication, and engage students in intellectual discovery.

Similarly, Oldfather (1993) describes the power of a classroom culture in which respect is shown for students' opinions and students are encouraged to express themselves. Teachers with this attitude create a classroom environment that builds motivation through their intimate knowledge of individual student needs and preferences and encourages it through the development of a supportive and rewarding social system.

What are the ways in which you can learn about your students' interests and preferences? Perhaps most important is to create an environment in which children feel free to speak their minds and show respect for the work and ideas of other students. In such a classroom, by simply listening to what children say you can learn a great deal about their preferences and ways of viewing themselves and others.

You can also learn about their interests by observing the activities in which they choose to participate. Do they ever choose to go to the writing center or select a book from the class library? Are they attentive when you read aloud to the class?

Perhaps the best way to learn about your students' interests and perceptions is through the reading and writing conferences you have with them. During these conversations, students share the goals they have set for themselves and their evaluation of how well they are achieving them. For example, Hansen (1992) reports the comments that first graders made to Chris, their teacher, about writing and reading:

- "I've learned to make spaces."
- "I can write words and pictures that go together."
- "I want to know more sounds."
- "I can read *Mr. Fox!*"

Comments such as these are useful in mapping the progress of children.

More formal procedures also exist for gathering information about students' interests and perceptions. Henk and Melnick (1995) describe the Reader Self-Perception Scale (RSPS) in which students are asked to agree or disagree with such statements as "I think I am a good reader," "My classmates think that I read pretty well," and "I understand what I read better than I could before" (pp. 478–479).

Saccardi (1993–1994) describes a "ballot" in which students evaluate the books they read, rating the book from 1 (Did not like it at all) to 4 (Thought it was great!) and writing reactions they wish to share. When these are gathered for individual children over time, they provide an inventory of the type of book they like.

Several times a year, you may have children examine and evaluate the work they have collected in their portfolios (Paulson, Paulson, & Meyer, 1991). By encouraging students to reflect on their work, you allow them to take charge of their own learning and to set goals for their learning. Students can reflect on the books they have read to identify the ones they found most interesting. This information provides the most direct evidence concerning the sorts of books they are interested in reading.

To keep track of this rich set of descriptive evidence, you will want to develop a file or a notebook with a pocket page for each of your students. As you jot down on a card or sticker what you have learned about the interests and perceptions of students, these notes should go into the file or notebook pocket. You may find that some children have numerous entries and others very few; you will then know the children you need to get to know better.

Assessing Children's Skill with Print

The instructional strategies described in this book are designed to be responsive to the needs of individual children or groups of children with similar needs. In order to use these strategies, you need to learn about the knowledge that children have about print. There are two main windows into their knowledge. The first of these is through *writing:* having children write and determining what it implies about their understanding of print. The second way is through *reading:* having children read aloud to you and noting the strategies they use. By studying the ways in which their oral readings depart from text, we can also learn about their sight word development and their knowledge of letter-sound patterns. We explore these ways of knowing more fully in the remainder of this section of the chapter.

Analysis of Children's Writing

To help you develop skill in analyzing children's writing, we describe a framework to guide your thinking about writing development. Then we discuss procedures for gathering and analyzing writing samples. We include a case study in which Keisha Brown, a first-grade teacher, analyzed the writing of one of her students. We then describe a more formal procedure for assessing children's knowledge of spelling through word writing.

As we discussed in chapter 3, when children read and write, their knowledge of English spelling (orthography) increases. They gradually develop greater understanding of the elements of words, and they do so in a fairly predictable manner. Longitudinal studies of children show how the early spellings of children change over time. These observed changes have been classified by Henderson according to developmental stages (Henderson, 1985/1990). As shown in Figure 10.2, in the first stage of writing (Preliterate), children use letters, numbers, and other marks to represent words; however, the spellings bear no resemblance to correct spellings. Such responses show that children understand that words are composed of a series of letters, but they have not yet solved the problem of the more precise matches that hold between the phonemes and letters of words.

In the second stage, alphabetic writing occurs when children represent some sounds of words in a systematic way, particularly those at the beginnings of words (see Figure 10.2). First, they tend to represent only initial consonants (Initial Consonant); then both initial and final consonants are represented (Consonant Frame).

Correct	Preliterate	Initial Consonant	Consonant Frame	Phonetic	Transitional
BACK	RE	BET	BC	BAK	*
SINK	E	C	SE	SEK	SINCK
MAIL	A	MM	MOL	MAL	MAEL
DRESS	S	DN	JS	GAS	DRES
LAKE	AH	L	LAE	LAK	LACE
PEEKED	TTT	PF	PT	PECT	PEKED
LIGHT	IEIX	LSIE	LAT	LIT	LIET
DRAGON	ATJA	JK	GAN	DAGN	DRAGIN
STICK	F	S	STC	SEK	STIK
SIDE	TC	ST	CI	SID	CIDE
FEET	V	F	FT	FET	*
TEST	ABT	TS	TST	TAST	TEEST

Figure 10.2 *Developmental Spelling Test* Items and Illustrative Spelling at Each Stage. *Source:* L. Ferroli & T. Shanahan (1987). Kindergarten spelling: Explaining Its Relation to First-grade Reading. In J. E. Readence & R. S. Baldwin (Eds.). *Research in literacy: Merging Perspectives.* Thirty-Sixth Yearbook of the National Reading Conference. Rochester, NY: National Reading Conference. Based on D. Morris & J. Perney (1984) developmental spelling as a predictor of first-grade reading achievement. *Elementary School Journal. 84.* Copyright © 1984 by the University of Chicago Press. *No transitional spellings were produced by the subjects for these words.

In the Phonetic stage, children represent within-word patterns more completely, in particular, letters representing vowels and those that mark the pronunciation of vowels (e.g., final *e* pattern) are included. Nevertheless, as shown for the Transitional stage in Figure 10.2, spelling still departs in systematic ways from standard spelling for some words. In the final stage (Correct), children learn to spell words in standard form.

What this development in spelling reflects is growth in the underlying knowledge that children have about words and the letter-sound patterns that compose them. To think of this development in terms described by Ehri (1980), the images of words that children store in memory become more complete. Her research shows that children spell words not simply on the basis of letter-sound knowledge but also on the basis of their stored images of words, because silent as well as voiced letters are represented in their spellings.

Writing samples may be gathered in two main ways. You may wish to examine samples of the writing that children produce daily in your classroom. You may also wish to have children write a set of words. The advantage of the more natural writing sample is that it shows how children select and spell words to represent the meanings they wish to communicate. The advantage of the spelling task is that you have the opportunity to observe how children write a set of words that includes a representative set of consonants, consonant blends, short vowels, and long vowels.

We gain insight into children's knowledge by analyzing the ways in which their writing departs from standard English (Read, 1971). It is not always easy to read children's early writing and to know what words are being represented. Teachers develop skill in reading "invented" spellings over time through the accumulation of experience in having children read what they have written aloud.

Learning from Experience

In order to learn more about how to interpret writing samples to learn about children's knowledge of print, we consider an example from Keisha Brown's combined first- and second-grade class. Keisha is curious about what Jennifer is learning about writing as a form of communication and what knowledge she is developing about letter-sound associations and spelling. To gain insight into this, she looks through the writing samples in Jennifer's portfolio and decides to spend time analyzing the sample shown in Figure 10.3. As you read the sample of Jennifer's writing, consider how well she conveys the message she wishes to communicate. Consider her spelling in terms of the developmental framework previously discussed (see Figure 10.2).

Your Turn: Study Jennifer's writing. In general, is she able to convey the message she wishes to communicate? Now look carefully at her spelling. Which word examples are particularly revealing? Study these examples; what does your analysis lead you to conclude about her knowledge of word elements? In terms of the developmental framework described in Figure 10.2, how do you assess her developing knowledge of English spelling? Given your tentative conclusions, what instructional support might you want to provide? Record your thoughts about this in your journal under the heading Jennifer's Writing and then compare your analysis with that of Keisha.

JeNNiFeR

THiR was a bird Namd Toyiss. He livd IN tHe bqc YIRD of a Hiws. a 7 YeR owld GiRl livd IN tHe Hiws and sHe loved Toyiss.

Figure 10.3 A Sample of Jennifer's Writing. *Source:* Printed with permission from Jesse Blachowicz. We thank her for this contribution.

Our Turn: On the basis of her analysis, Keisha concluded that Jennifer shows many signs of spelling strength. She seems to be at the point where she might profit from encouragement to notice the standard spellings of words. Since there are several other children in her class with similar writing, she will place these children into a study group to focus on words from their writing that are close approximations of standard spelling. She will help the children to become aware of how words are spelled in standard English. This careful scrutiny of words is usually sufficient to encourage them to move from the transitional stage to that of standard spelling.

Keisha used a simple analysis sheet to guide and record her observations (see Figure 10.4). On this sheet, she summarized what she learned. She placed the assessment in the file she had developed for Jennifer.

A second way to assess writing involves a spelling task in which children write a series of words. By studying the relation between the letters written and those expected, you can draw some tentative conclusions about what children understand about letter-sound associations. You can also infer the developmental stage they have achieved in understanding English spelling (Henderson, 1985/1990). Although this procedure may be used systematically at the beginning of a school year, you can also

---

Developmental Spelling Analysis Sheet

Student *Jennifer*   Date *10/15*

Sample: *From writing time following the reading of stories on pets.*

Relevant examples: *thir yird hiws yer bac*
namd livd (note also: loved)

Analysis: *Represents most sounds appropriately, but not all*
in standard form — Is in the transitional stage.

Comments/instruction: *A nice beginning to her story. Has learned*
a lot about spelling words. Needs to learn standard
spellings.

Figure 10.4 Keisha's Notes on Jennifer's Writing

use it more informally during the school year to study the development of your students' knowledge of English spelling.

Although many different lists of one-syllable sight words are available, the Developmental Spelling Test that we describe here (Ferroli & Shanahan, 1987; Morris & Perney, 1984) is particularly useful because it includes words that differ in complexity and is sensitive to changes that occur in the beginning stages of spelling. The spelling task has been used with kindergartners (Ferroli & Shanahan, 1987) and first graders (Morris & Perney, 1984) and found to be a good predictor of later first-grade reading achievement.

The list is composed of 12 words (see Table 10.2 for the list of words). Before administering it, prepare children through a demonstration of spelling. First ask them to listen for the letter names they hear in a few sample words not found on the list, such as *mat* and *dip;* then write these letters on the chalkboard, supplying unknown letters if the children offer only a partial spelling. For example, if the children hear only the *m* and *t* in *mat,* you might say, "Good," write *m—t* on the board, and say, "and there's an *a* in the middle."

Following this modeling, children should be encouraged to spell the list of words "as best they can" by writing the letter names they hear. It is important to praise them for whatever spellings they produce. Each word from the list should be pronounced clearly several times and used in a sentence. You should allow children sufficient time to write what they hear.

On the basis of children's responses to the spelling task, you can determine whether the majority of each child's responses are preliterate, initial consonant, consonant frame, phonetic, transitional, or standard. Instruction in letter-sound associations should be geared to the child's stage of development. For example, for children in the preliterate stage, you should check their knowledge of letter names to determine which, if any, need to be taught; similarly, for children in the initial consonant stage, you should explore their knowledge of consonants and consonant blends to determine what in the area of word elements needs to be taught.

Learning from Experience

In order to show how the spelling patterns of individual children can be interpreted, we describe the case of Antonio, a bilingual child. Because of his good command of English, he was assigned to Keisha Brown's combined first- and second-grade class to receive reading instruction in English.

To understand his knowledge of print, Keisha administered the Developmental Spelling Test. She began the test by demonstrating how to spell two basal words: *mat* and *dip.* She first had him listen to *mat* to see what sounds he could hear. He heard the sound corresponding to *m* at the beginning and that for *t* at the end. His teacher encouraged him to write the letters associated with these sounds. Then she had him say *dip* slowly to himself. He wrote all three of the letters. Next she presented the test words, encouraging him "to write them as best he could." The results are shown in Figure 10.5. As you examine the words Antonio wrote, consider what knowledge he has developed about letter-sound associations and spelling patterns.

Your Turn: Study the words Antonio wrote. Does he seem to have learned consonant letter-sound associations? How good is his command of vowels? Is there a consistent pattern? At what stage is he in terms of developing knowledge about English spelling? Complete your analysis and write your conclusions in your journal under the heading Antonio's Spelling before reading further.

bak
sik
ML
Grs
Lak
peet
Lit
Grn
s
sid
fee
t

Figure 10.5 Antonio's Spelling

Our Turn: An analysis of the results shows that Antonio has good command of consonants in the beginnings and endings of words, and that he is beginning to represent some vowel sounds and some consonant blends. Writing the *dr* in dress and dragon as *gr* is a common substitution for young children. Say the words to yourself and you will see how similar the two are in articulatory position. In terms of his underlying knowledge about words, he is entering the phonetic stage of spelling.

The administration of this task helped Keisha to confirm her impressions about his knowledge of print. His strength in word identification and his underlying knowledge of word elements confirmed that he should be able to participate in many of the activities currently being undertaken by her second-grade students.

Analyses of writing and spelling samples are useful tools for teachers to assess what their students understand about reading and writing. They provide the basis for making decisions about instruction and pinpoint what further assessment is needed. For example, if a child can already write the spelling words in a conventional way, little further assessment is needed in that area of phonics. But if a child correctly represents only some beginning consonants, an inventory of consonant letter-sound associations would specify those which remained to be learned.

Oral Reading Analysis

One of the easiest ways for you to check the skill that your students have with print is to listen to them read aloud. Viewing the reading holistically, you can learn about their reading strategies and fluency. Careful listening reveals their knowledge of sight words and skill in identifying unknown words. These observations collectively provide a basis for you to judge whether the selection is at the right level of difficulty or poses too many problems.

Teachers who have developed their listening strategies gain a lot of information about their students' reading by simply listening. But it is a complex process. For those of you who are learning how to listen to children read aloud, it is helpful to make a tape recording or to make notes about their oral reading. The nature of their corrections and repetitions shows whether they view reading as a meaning-making process.

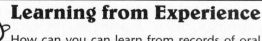 **Learning from Experience**

How can you can learn from records of oral reading? One way is to consider the notes (transcript) that Alice Walker, a first-grade teacher, made of Peter's oral reading (see Figure 10.6). When he read aloud to her, Alice felt that the sample was a valid one. That is, he seemed to "be having a good day" and his reading was typical of his daily reading. His reading lacked fluency, mainly because of the problems he encountered with unknown words. These observations made by Alice add to the knowledge that she has about his reading.

There are two different ways in which you can make records of a child's oral reading.

Text and Alice's notes	Peter's oral reading
ⓟ	
A little boy planted a carrot seed.	A little boy . . . . planted a carrot seed.
The ⓒ *did*	
His mother said, "I'm afraid it won't come up."	The mother did . . . said, "I'm afraid it won't
	come up."
The	
His father said, "I'm afraid it won't come up."	The father said, "I'm afraid it won't come up."
ⓒ *Said* ⓒ ~~brother~~	
And his big bother said, "It won't come up."	. . . . Said . . . And his brother big bother said, '
	won't come up."
Each	
Every day the little boy pulled up the weeds around	Each day the little boy pulled up the weeds . . .
	Each day the little boy pulled up the weeds aro
	ⓟ
the seed and sprinkled the ground with water.	the seed the seed and . . . sprinkled the ground
	with water.
But nothing came up	But nothing came up
And nothing came up.	And nothing came up. And nothing came up.
ⓟ *said* *won't*	
Everyone ⓚⓔⓟⓣ saying it wouldn't come up.	Everyone . . . . . . said it won't come up.
But he ⓢⓣⓘⓛⓛ pulled up the weeds around it every day	But he pulled up the weeds around it every day
and sprinkled the ground with water.	and sprinkled the ground with water.
And then one day,	And then one day,
a carrot came up.	a carrot came up.
knew	
ⓙⓤⓢⓣ ⓐⓢ the little boy ⓗⓐⓓ known it would.	the little boy knew it would.

Figure 10.6 Alice's Record of Peter's Oral Reading. *Source:* Text only from *The Carrot Seed* by Ruth Krauss, illustrated by Crockett Johnson. Text copyright © 1945 by Ruth Krauss, Illustrations © 1945 by Crockett Johnson. Reprinted by permission of Harper & Row Publishers, Inc.

The first method, which involves a photocopy of the story, is particularly useful to record the reading of children reading longer and more difficult selections. This record is shown on the left side of Figure 10.6. As you can see, you record errors by writing a phonetic transcription of the child's miscue over the word. Omitted words are circled, and pauses are indicated by "P" and repetitions by drawing a line with an arrow over the repeated portion.

The second method, shown in Figure 10.7, involves a "Running Record" (Clay, 1993a). In this approach, you use a blank sheet of paper to make the record. You make a check mark for each word correctly read. When an error is made, write the printed word, draw a line over it, and on top of it, write a phonetic transcription of the child's miscue. When a word is omitted, write the printed word, draw a line over it, and on top of it place a dot. Pauses are indicated by "P" and repetitions by drawing a line with an arrow over the repeated portion. Study the oral reading shown in Figure 10.5 and the Running Record of it in Figure 10.7. What impressions do you gain about Peter's oral reading skill?

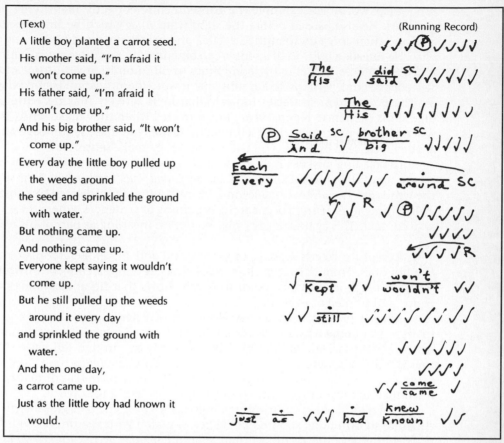

Figure 10.7 Running Record of Ken's oral reading of *The Carrot Seed*. *Source:* Text only from *The Carrot Seed* by Ruth Krauss, illustrated by Crockett Johnson. Text copyright © 1945 by Ruth Krauss, Illustrations © 1945 by Crockett Johnson. Reprinted by permission of Harper & Row Publishers, Inc.

Your Turn: Reread the oral reading shown in Figure 10.6 and the Running Record in Figure 10.7. Think about Peter's oral reading. One useful way to gain insight into his reading is for you to read aloud the story in the way he read it. That is, reconstruct his reading from the typescript shown on the right side of Figure 10.6. Note how Alice recorded the ways in which Peter's reading departed from the text (see Figures 10.6 and 10.7). After your study, write your responses to the following questions in your journal under the heading Peter's Oral Reading.

What reading strategies has Peter developed?

How well developed is his sight vocabulary?

How well developed is his knowledge of word elements?

Is the story too easy, too difficult, or just about right?

Our Turn: In considering Peter's reading strategies, Alice finds it particularly useful to examine pauses and repetitions. Peter seems to pause while he is thinking about unfamiliar words. For example, he paused before correctly identifying *planted* and *sprinkled*. He also paused before the sight word *And*, which he first misidentified as *Said* and then correctly identified as *And*, and before the word *kept*.

He rereads a portion of a sentence, sometimes to reinforce the meaning of a sentence (sentences 1, 7, and 10), sometimes to fill in omitted words (*up* and *around* of sentence 5), and, perhaps, to aid subsequent word identification (*sprinkled* in sentence 5). These repetition strategies indicate that he is actively making sense of text. His omissions (sentences 8 and 10) are not corrected when they make sense, but they are when they do not make sense (sentence 5). If you read these sentences 8 and 10 aloud as they were read by Peter, you will see that they make sense.

His reading miscues indicate several areas of strength. First, he was able to correct three of the nine substitutions *(did/said; said/And; brother/big)*. This suggests that the words are known by him. Second, his difficulties (as indicated by substitutions as well as omissions) tend to occur at the beginning of sentences, where there is less available context. This again suggests his reliance on meaning as part of his reading strategy.

Except for Peter's reading of sentences 8 and 11, spoken words correspond to printed ones. From this, it is clear that he has developed concept of word. In addition, his tendency to voice-point to words shows that he understands how spoken words and printed ones relate.

Alice is pleased with the development of Peter's sight vocabulary. He knows many words immediately, words that were not cued by her introduction of the story. At the same time, she is interested in the words he omitted (all basic sight words), that she thought were in his sight vocabulary. Thus she plans to explore whether he actually knows these words in isolated form. He may have had difficulty with them in context because of the other problems he was trying to solve.

The nature of his substitutions suggests his awareness of graphic cues. Seven of the nine substitutions show some degree of match with the printed words, either at the beginning of the word in initial letter *(big/brother;every/each;known/knew)*, at the end *(said/did;And/Said)*, or both at beginning and end *(wouldn't/won't;came/come)*. Only the repeated substitution of *The* for *His* shows little correspondence in terms of print, but the miscue does make sense in terms of sentence context. Thus we see that Peter is aware of letter cues and makes use of this knowledge. Most of his miscues not only match the print in some way but also make sense in context.

It is more difficult to assess phonemic awareness from oral reading than from writing. There were no cues such as his saying initial sounds that would indicate the development of phonemic awareness. Moreover there was no evidence of any decoding strategies. The words he substituted for others that tended to match in the beginning and/or final consonants could have been made on the basis of visual cues rather than letter-sound cues. Alice wants to know more about Peter's knowledge of letter-sound patterns.

Alice explored his knowledge of letter-sound patterns further by assisting him in the identification of several sight words he seemed not to know. She did this by first showing him the initial consonant (or consonant blend) and then the word ending. For example, she had him look at *his* and asked him if he knew it. He didn't. She then covered all but the initial consonant *(h)*. He was able to give the sound corresponding to *h*. She then covered the initial consonant and asked him to pronounce the word ending *(is)*. He did so successfully. She asked him if he knew the word. He said he couldn't get it. She then supported his blending of the consonant sound into the word ending. On another word *(still)*, he identified *s* and *t* but had difficulty blending the consonants; he did not know the word ending. From this she knew that he is developing knowledge of the sounds that letters represent, but that he has difficulty blending sounds with each other and with word endings.

Finally, Alice considered whether the story was too difficult for Peter. Her judgment was that it was quite challenging for him. Yet he was able to read many of the words in the story correctly (90 of 101 words for 90 percent accuracy). Is this story too hard for him? An accuracy level between 90 to 94 percent is usually considered to be in the borderline range for young children (see Table 10.1). Generally, she was pleased by his sense-making strategies and his growing knowledge of sight words and word elements. From this perspective, Alice considered this story to be appropriate for Peter, particularly with instructional support and rereading.

The nature of Peter's corrections and repetitions shows that he views reading as a meaning-making process. The analyses also reveal that Peter is developing a sight vocabulary. He has fairly good knowledge of initial and final consonants, but is not yet able to undertake more systematic forms of decoding.

Alice believes that he would benefit from rereading familiar stories to consolidate his sight vocabulary. She also believes he would profit from instruction that focuses on the representation of consonant blends in his writing and on blending word parts. In general, she believes that his classroom program is appropriate. Yet she will provide the more specialized support in writing and blending word elements, either individually or as part of instruction.

Working with first graders and other children in the beginning stages of reading demands expertise both in structuring the oral reading task for them and in analyzing the results. Repeated practice is essential. The Running Record procedure Alice used with Peter is particularly valuable for children during their first year of reading (see Figure 10.7). Thereafter, we prefer to make a record of the oral reading on a duplicate copy of the text (see Figure 10.6). Older readers typically read longer segments, and it is easier to compare their responses with the text when the record is marked directly on the text.

Assessing Vocabulary and Prior Knowledge

The method we encourage you to use to identify central vocabulary is similar to that which we recommended earlier in forming an outline of a story or article. You must read the selection yourself and then ask what important information is conveyed and what specific terms are important to understanding that information. Different teachers will come up with somewhat different outlines and somewhat different lists of vocabulary items this way, but more systematic procedures that teachers can easily use simply do not exist. One way to become good at making these decisions is to work with other teachers at your grade level and compare the terms they think are important with those that you select.

Pause and Reflect

Recall how Jason Petersen examined the article "Forest Fires" in preparation for his class to read it. In the same way, you can determine vocabulary that may be new and unfamiliar to your class by rereading the selection. Turn back to page 364 and reread the selection. Are there any important vocabulary words that, if unknown, would make it difficult for students to comprehend the passage? Make a list of these words and write them in your journal under the heading Forest Fire Vocabulary.

You may have listed such terms as *protect, forest rangers, lookout stations, experts, fire lanes,* and *prevent.* These are all important words; students with only a vague sense of what these mean might have difficulty comprehending the selection. When they read the selection, it is as if they are saying "blank" when they come across these words: They must infer on the basis of the remainder of the passage what the author is trying to communicate.

Once the vocabulary items are selected, how can you assess the prior knowledge of your students? You might list these words on the chalkboard and then ask students to share what they already know about each of them. Observe which students rarely contribute, even when called upon, which ones understand most terms, and which ones have only a vague understanding of key concepts. After individual words have been discussed, ask students to speculate about the focus of the reading selection. The purpose of the prereading discussion should be to sharpen the understanding of all class members.

Learning from Experience

The following is an excerpt from a lesson in a fifth-grade class in which Harriet Jones assessed her students' prior knowledge about two words that were important for understanding the selection they were about to read: *diadem* and *nostalgia.* She began by saying that one of the words would be pretty easy for the students because they knew a synonym; the other might be more difficult. Read the transcript of the lesson in order to learn how Harriet assesses her students' knowledge of vocabulary and their abilities to use strategies for understanding vocabulary.

Assesses
vocabulary
knowledge

Assesses
use of
context

Ms. Jones: Let's start with this one. [She points to *diadem,* marks off the syllables, and places vowel markings and accent.] Let's pronounce it. [Students and teacher pronounce the word together.] Does anyone know what it means? [The students have never heard of it.] Okay, here's a sentence: "The queen wore a jeweled diadem." Any ideas about its meaning?

Jennifer: Robe?

Ann: It could be a crown. Shoes or something. No, it couldn't be. It's an a-one thing.

Ms. Jones: Any other ideas?

Peter: Well, it's something she wore.

Checks use of
dictionary

Ms. Jones: Okay, let's look it up and see if any of our suggestions matches a definition.

Rachel: [reads] "A crown or cloth headband, worn as a sign of royalty." Yup, it's a crown.

Assesses use
of word in
context

Ms. Jones: Can somebody give me an original sentence with the word?

Randy: Miss America gets a diadem when she gets crowned.

Ms. Jones: Does anybody disagree? [No disagreement.] Okay. Do you think that was the easy one or the hard one? Right—the easy one. Now let's try this one. [Points to *nostalgia* and marks off the syllables. The students pronounce it, with some difficulty on the *gia*.] Does anyone know what nostalgia means? [The students say they've heard of it, but don't know what it means.] Okay, let's start with a sentence. "Watching her son march into school, she felt nostalgia for her own school days." Any ideas?

Assesses
vocabulary
knowledge
Assesses
ability to use
context

Ann: Sadness?

John: Remembering?

Jennifer: Wanting to be there?

Checks use of
dictionary

Ms. Jones: [Harriet places suggestions in spokes around the word on the chalkboard. See Figure 10.8.] Okay, so you all think it's some kind of feeling. Let's look at the definition.

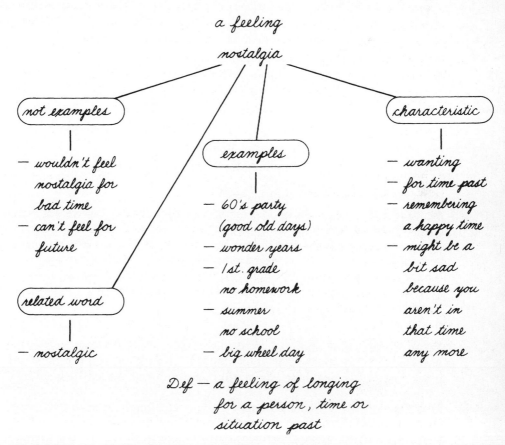

Figure 10.8 Prereading Instruction to Assess and Develop Vocabulary

Checks vocabulary knowledge

Assesses use of word in context

Randy: [reads] "A longing for things, persons, or situations that are not present."

Ms. Jones: Do you know what longing means?

Ann: Wanting?

Ms. Jones: Okay. So what could that sentence mean?

Jennifer: When she saw her son go to school, she wanted to be back when she was in school.

Ms. Jones: [to Ann] Do you want to keep sadness as part of this?

Ann: No. It's got to be a wanting for a happy time.

Randy: But I think sad could be part of it because she's not a kid anymore. It's like remembering a time when you were happy. It makes you happy because you were happy but you're a little sad because it's not then anymore.

Assesses ability to generate examples

Ms. Jones: Can you think of any examples of nostalgia in your own life or in the lives of those around you?

John: My mom and dad went to a sixties party. They dressed up real weird and showed us dances. They said those were the good old days.

Peter: There's a TV show, *The Wonder Years,* which is all about a kid remembering; actually it's a grown-up remembering the fun of being a kid. That would be feeling nostalgia.

Ms. Jones: Would you feel nostalgia for a terrible time in your life?

Jennifer: No, it's got to be happy remembering.

Ms. Jones: Would you feel nostalgia for the future?

Assesses ability to specify definition

Rachel: No, it's got to be in the past so you can long for it.

Ms. Jones: Can you each use nostalgia in a sentence that gives a personal example?

Rachel: I feel nostalgia for summer when we didn't have any school.

Ms. Jones: How about examples not about school!

Randy: I know, I know. Every Saturday when I am lying in bed and I hear my little brother run his big wheels up and down the sidewalk, feel nostalgia for when I was three. I really loved my big wheels. [Everyone laughs.]

Assesses use of word in context

Ms. Jones: These are really good examples. Let's look at what we've got. A new term, it's a feeling, it relates to longing for the past, and here are some examples and some things that are nonexamples. [Harriet reviews the chart on the board.] Why not go home tonight and ask your folks about some examples of nostalgia from their lives and we'll talk about it tomorrow? Now, from just these two words, diadem and nostalgia, do you have any ideas about the story we're going to read today? [The students go on to make predictions about the story.]

 Your Turn: Think about some of the ways in which Harriet assesses her students' knowledge of vocabulary and their ability to use strategies for understanding vocabulary. List as many of these as you can in your journal under the heading Vocabulary Assessment.

Our Turn: She assessed vocabulary knowledge directly by asking whether any of her students knew the meanings of the words. She explored whether students were able to use sentence context to derive the word meaning. She checked their ability to use the dictionary as a source of vocabulary definitions. She then assessed their ability to use each new word in sentence context. In the case of *nostalgia,* she explored whether students were able to specify the word definition. From each question she asked and each request she made, she assessed whether students were able to use new procedures to learn word meanings. All of these procedures are excellent ways to assess your students' knowledge of vocabulary and their strategies for learning the meanings of new words.

At the beginning of this prereading lesson, Harriet simply asked her students to tell what they knew about the two terms. As an alternative, she could have asked her students to write what they believed the words meant and to share their understanding with other class members. Then concepts that were still unclear could have been discussed and clarified as in the foregoing lesson.

Asking students to rate their knowledge of terms in written form works particularly well with older readers who have had writing experience. To do this, students can be asked to place a "++" by words they know well, a "+" by words they know somewhat, a "?" by words they are unsure of, and a "–" by words they are certain they don't know. Alternatively, students can be given a list of words and asked to write a short definition of them. With written ratings and definitions of this sort, however, you should be aware that short responses may indicate that a student has difficulty with writing rather than with vocabulary and other aspects of prior knowledge.

Often it becomes clear during the discussion of a story or article that certain words are unknown. When this is the case, it is appropriate to include some of these difficult concepts in the discussion that follows a selection. For example, for the story "Cookies," it might become clear that children do not understand the concept *will power.* The discussion that follows not only provides the opportunity to assess what students know about the concept *will power* but also to assess children's strategies for learning new word meanings such as the use of context, information shared by other students, and the dictionary. These examples show ways in which prior knowledge and vocabulary assessment can become an integral part of discussion prior to reading a selection or after reading it.

Assessing Comprehension Strategies

In the first part of this section, we discussed the assessment of comprehension—that is, response of students to text. In this section, we consider how you can learn more about the strategies students use for comprehension. A student may have no difficulty with print and be familiar with the meanings of the words and concepts that are central to understanding a passage but still fail to comprehend. Generally, this type of failure stems from difficulty with the integration of information across a text. Readers reconstruct the message of the author by processing words, phrases, and sentences and organizing the meaning from these units into one or several arguments or descriptions.

Some readers experience difficulty unique to this integration process. For example, when readers encounter pronouns, nouns, or phrases that refer back to a previously identified person or topic, they must realize that a new topic is not being introduced but rather that more information is being provided about the same topic or person. Then they must understand what to look for and how to reread and connect the information they missed on first reading.

Other readers encounter difficulty with text structure. They have not yet learned to look for common organizational patterns that authors use to convey information. Because children read so many stories, they are familiar with narrative structure. They know the sort of information that is usually presented at the beginning of the story (characters, setting, problem); and they know that several episodes will follow that typically lead to a resolution. The structures of informational text are less familiar. Often children are not familiar with the key words that signal time sequence (first, then, finally), contrast and comparison, cause and effect, problem and solutions, or a main assertion and supporting facts and examples. To assess whether students are familiar with these organizational structures, when students read text involving common organizational patterns, ask them to describe the structures.

Other readers encounter difficulty because they read in a passive fashion: They have not learned to actively construct expectations about what an author may say and then check their expectations against the information they derive from reading a passage. The instructional strategies described in chapters 4 to 6 represent useful ways to help students become more active readers. During group instruction, you can assess the extent to which students apply these strategies when reading independently through a discussion of the self-monitoring they do.

What can this teacher learn about children's reading abilities during small-group instruction?

Pause and Reflect

Read a selection that is somewhat difficult for you. Assess the reading strategies that you use. Do you read with a purpose? If so, how did you establish that purpose? What do you do when you are reading along and what you are reading fails to make sense? When you finish reading, what do you do to make sure that you remember the important information in the selection? If you have answers to these questions, then you have developed a set of strategies to help you comprehend and remember text. If your answers to most of these questions were "no" or "nothing," then you can conclude from your assessment that you read in a fairly passive fashion. Write a brief paragraph describing this assessment of your strategies in your journal under the heading My Reading Strategies.

Informal questioning during instruction can be used with groups of students or individuals in order to assess how well they are using strategies that have recently been introduced to them. For example, after introducing the K-W-L Plus strategy (Ogle, 1986), look at what children report they have learned, the ways they have organized this information in a web, and their written summary. What does this work show about students' comprehension of text? Such assessment will enable you to make decisions about the follow-up instruction that is needed.

Similarly, with other strategies, examine student responses in order to assess whether they understand the strategy. With respect to the Herringbone strategy, for example, can students find information from text to complete the bones? Can they organize information from the bones to write a summary of text? By assessing their responses at each point in the strategy, you will discover aspects of the strategy that need to be retaught.

Students who have tried to use comprehension strategies during their independent reading should be encouraged to comment on the problems they encountered and whether they believe the approach worked for them. More discussion on the integration of assessment and strategy instruction is included in chapters 13 to 16.

Assessing what students do as they read silently is more of a challenge. Do students establish a purpose for reading? What do they do when something does not make sense? Do they attempt to recall and organize what they have just read? When certain reading strategies are introduced during instruction and students understand what is meant by them, getting answers to questions about the comprehension strategies they use is easier. Often students' journal responses provide the most useful window into their strategy use. Do they reflect the use of reading strategies? Do readers evaluate character motives and actions? Or do students limit their responses to summarizing text? Reflecting on the written responses of students will help you to assess their comprehension and the strategies they are using independently as they read.

The information that you gather through discussion with students and through consideration of their written work represents a main source of information that you will use to guide your instruction. A different window into the learning of students is provided by the samples of work that students collect in their portfolios. In the next section, we consider the development of student and class portfolios.

HOW CAN YOU AND YOUR STUDENTS DEVELOP PORTFOLIOS?

Portfolios are being used for assessment purposes in many K–12 classrooms (Valencia, 1990) and special-education classrooms (Bartoli & Botel, 1989). Different types can be developed depending on the purpose of the portfolio—for example, to provide information on writing products, processes, or even on programs. Simmons (1992) has researched the use of portfolios and suggests different types and levels of information to represent writing development, including process, product, and programs. He compared the perceptions teachers formed about students based on standardized test results versus portfolio samples and found that they gain more detailed information from the portfolios. This type of research, and increasing interest by teachers in classroom assessment, has encouraged many teachers, schools, and districts to investigate the use of portfolios.

Student portfolios usually contain process data that show how a student's performance has developed, as well as reading and writing products, including drafts and final products, questions and personal responses following the reading of a story, and ideas for future reading and writing. Student portfolios can also include self-evaluation information such as students' reflections on their writing products, books they have read, and their personal development.

Teachers can develop their own *class portfolios*. These portfolios organize information teachers have collected on the performances of individual students. In addition to teachers' notes and assessments, summaries of interviews with students about their reading and writing may be included (Hansen, 1992). We describe both student and class portfolios in the following sections.

Building Student Portfolios

What are student portfolios? Student portfolios are like the portfolios of artists; they contain a representative sample of artists' work, which reveals the essence of who they are and what they are trying to accomplish. A similar collection of work can be developed by students in your class. The process of building a portfolio is important for two reasons. It becomes a window into students' thinking, by revealing their aspirations, interests, and goals. It is a powerful educational tool that can encourage students to assume control of their own learning.

Paulson et al. (1991) developed the following definition: "A portfolio is a purposeful collection of student work that exhibits the student's efforts, progress, and achievement in one or more areas. The collection must include student participation in selecting content, the criteria for selection, the criteria for judging merit, and evidence of student self-reflection" (p.60). Although portfolios can be defined in other ways, we have selected this definition because it captures what we believe are several important aspects of portfolios.

Selecting Portfolio Information

First, the collection of student work must be purposeful; it must relate to the goals that you and the student have established in the area of literacy. Do not focus on too many areas in which work is to be collected. For example, it may be sufficient to collect work in three areas: writing samples, a list of books read with brief paragraphs summarizing students' reactions, and writing that relates to other reading activities. More activities related to the development of print may be included for younger children (spelling samples, words known, challenge words, and the like).

Second, the work collected must show the "efforts, progress, and achievements" of the child. The samples must be judiciously selected to show work reflecting effort (e.g., multiple drafts of the same paper) and must be collected over time to show progress. Not all work of the child should be included or the task of examining the work will become overwhelming. The work selected should be included with a purpose in mind. More samples will be collected at the beginning of the year to represent the year's starting point; some of these may be eliminated as the year progresses. The portfolio is organic in nature and profits from being pruned periodically.

Evaluating Portfolio Samples

The student will be involved not only in selecting work samples, but also in establishing the criteria for judging merit. Part of the value of student portfolios lies in students assuming responsibility for their own reading and writing development. This can only occur if the student's goals and values influence what is kept in the portfolio and influence the criteria by which merit is judged. For many teachers, the interactive process of considering work, discussing its strengths and weaknesses, and judging its merits is a new one. Those who have been doing it for some time have learned to become very good listeners when they interact with their students. Teachers who wish their students to keep portfolios must set aside time for individual conferences every week or two for younger students and for conferences at least every three weeks for older ones. Conferences should be more frequent at the beginning of the year than later. Usually the focus of the conferences is on the new work the students have placed in their portfolios. On the basis of the conference, some of this work will be kept in the portfolio and other work will be sent home, displayed, shared, or discarded.

Evidence of student self-reflection will be included in the portfolio. By encouraging self-reflection on work, the portfolio collection becomes an occasion for students to take charge of their own learning. Prior to selected conferences with their teachers (for example, at midyear and a time or two thereafter), students can be encouraged to study the work they have recently collected, compare it with previous work, and draw conclusions about their progress. Paulson et al. (1991) provide some useful illustrations of student reflection. These are shown in Figure 10.9. Writing about what they have learned becomes an important part of the process and becomes an important part of the record.

More formal rubrics for evaluating the samples gathered for student portfolios are usually not necessary. That is, the process is a more individualized one in which

5-11-90

At the beginning of the year.
I havit been yoosng periods
and I am now!.
At the beginning of the year,
I havit been yoosng sentence
and I am now.
At the beginning of the year.
I havit been yoosng elaboration
and I 'am now the End

Today I looked at all my
stories in my writing folder
I read some of my writing since
September. I noticed that I've
impaved some stuff. Now I edit my
stores, and revise, Now I use periods,
quotation mark. Sometimes my stories
are longer I usd to mis:rspell my
words and now I look in a
dictionary or ask a friend and now
I write exciting and scary stories
and now I have very good endings
Now I use capitals I usd to leave out
words and wrote short simple stories.

Figure 10.9 Samples of Students' Reflections on the Writing Samples They Include in their Port-folios. *Source:* Paulson, F. L., Paulson, P. R., & Meyer, C. A. (1991). What makes a portfolio a port-folio? *Educational Leadership, 48*(5), 62–63. Reprinted with permission of the Association for Su-pervision and Curriculum Development. Copyright © 1991 by ASCD. All rights reserved.

each of your students sets goals, develops criteria for judging growth, and then examines samples of work to see whether the changes observed indicate development.

Learning from Experience

The following describes the process followed by Arthur and his third-grade teacher in setting goals for his work in reading and writing. As you read the description, think about whether the goals are good ones. How did Arthur's goals influence the work samples he collected for his portfolio and his assessment of his progress?

Arthur, in consultation with his teacher, set three goals for himself in the fall of the year: to read a book each week, to write longer stories, and to improve spelling. These goals indicate the sort of evidence that Arthur needed to collect in his portfolio. To assess the amount he read, he decided to keep a record of the books he read and when he read them. To assess his writing and spelling, he decided to collect writing samples every month or two.

To assess progress in the spring of the year, Arthur counted the number of books read each month and found that he fell short of his goal during the fall months, exceeded it during the winter, but fell short in the spring (after baseball season began). He also noted that the books that he was reading at the end of the year were longer and harder. Although he had not reached his goal, he believed that he was reading a lot.

He selected first draft and final draft samples of his writing from October, January, March, and May. He found that by spring he was writing three-page stories in comparison with a half-page story in October. Thus he accomplished his goal of writing more. He also thought that his stories were better organized by the spring of the year—the characters and settings were described more vividly, the problem was clear, and how the characters solved the problem was also clearer.

It was difficult for Arthur to assess his spelling development by looking at his writing. Because he was writing much more, he made more spelling errors in the spring than in the fall. He listed the words he misspelled in October and compared them with those from May. The words from May seemed to be longer and more complex. He also noted that he no longer had difficulty writing some words in May that he had had difficulty with in the fall. So he concluded that he had made progress in spelling.

Your Turn: After reading the description of Arthur's goals and self-assessment, what are your reflections on whether the goals were good ones? How did his goals influence the work he collected in his portfolio? How successful do you think he was in assessing his progress? Write your responses in your journal under the heading Arthur's Portfolio Assessment.

Our Turn: Although Arthur's three goals were established in collaboration with his teacher, they focused more on quantitative than qualitative changes. Yet it is important that the student be in control of the goal-setting process, even though the resulting statement of goals is not as sophisticated as it might be. The three goals represented areas in which Arthur believed he wanted to improve.

The work to be collected in the portfolio followed directly from the goals. With respect to the first two, few alternatives to the list of books read and the collection of writing samples would be appropriate. The assessment of spelling is more difficult. What Arthur wanted to improve was the spelling of words in his writing samples; thus a more formal measure of spelling might be inappropriate. Thus the use of the writing samples to judge spelling improvement also seemed appropriate.

Finally, Arthur nicely assessed his attainment of the goals he set. He came to realize that the number of books read was an insufficient gauge of his reading—that he needed to consider book length and difficulty as well. In addition to commenting on increases in the amount he wrote, he also saw changes in the complexity of his writing—in the areas of description and organization. Finally, his assessment of spelling was quite useful; he came to see that the length and complexity of words had a bearing on his spelling and that he was able to spell longer, more complex words.

Building a Class Portfolio

The informal assessments that we have described in this book must be recorded and organized in some way. The procedures that we have just described for student portfolios represent one solution to the problem of organization. Student portfolios are useful educational tools for assessing student learning and progress. They display to parents the work that their children have accomplished. Portions of student portfolios, such as writing samples, lists of books read, and student reflections on their progress, complement the records you will keep on each student. In addition to student portfolios, you will need to build a class portfolio that organizes the information and insights you develop over the course of the year. This information, in conjunction with that from student portfolios, will help you make informed instructional decisions.

This section on building a class portfolio may be among the most important in the book, for if you do not find a way to record and organize the information you have, it will be of limited use to you. How should you go about developing a system to organize the knowledge you are developing about your students? There are many different systems and we shall describe some. The system you develop may turn out to be a unique hybrid.

There are several thinking steps you should undertake in developing a portfolio. These include specifying your goals in the areas of reading and writing, thinking about the activities in your class that may yield valuable information, selecting the types of information that you want to include in the class portfolio, determining the physical form of the portfolio, and, finally, making sense of your portfolio records.

Specifying Your Goals

Your goals in the areas of reading and writing will directly reflect the prior learning of your students. If you are teaching first grade, your goals will differ somewhat from those of a sixth-grade teacher. Furthermore, the children in your class will differ from each other and your goals must reflect these developmental differences. The goals that Alice Walker, for example, has for Peter will differ somewhat from those she has for other students in her class.

Yet there are general learnings in the area of literacy that will apply to all children. These include such areas as knowledge of print, reading fluency, vocabulary development, comprehension strategies, love of reading, reading and writing interests, knowledge of types of writing (narrative and information books), writing fluency, and ability to organize ideas. The Upper Arlington City Schools include among their assessment guidelines for teachers (shown in Figure 10.10) four main categories that capture many of these areas.

From the large set of possible goals, you must select the subset (from 4 to 10) that you will evaluate during the year. Some teachers prefer to define a more limited number of general goals; others identify a larger number of more specific goals. But whatever the number, they will be the areas in which you gather information in an ongoing fashion.

Thinking about Class Activities

Another way to define your set of assessment activities is to think about the activities that your children are undertaking each day or week and identify those that may lend themselves to evaluation. Jason Petersen's class includes large- and small-group reading instruction, Reading Workshop, independent reading and writing time, and book club activities. Each of these activities offers Jason different opportunities to increase his understanding of his students' reading and writing. During the independent reading and writing time, he meets individually with students to discuss their recent work. During the individual conference, he explores his students' understanding of and reflection on books they have recently read, he studies samples of their writing, and he asks questions and listens carefully in order to assess their feelings and reflections about their literacy activities. On an ongoing basis, he reads their journal entries. During Reading Workshop, he notes whether students work individually or with a partner, whether they are deeply or superficially engaged, and what reading activities students choose to undertake. Work samples from some of these activities (for example, student writing and journal entries pertaining to their reading) will be kept in student portfolios. Jason will keep his notes from conferences pertaining to the quality of writing, reading interpretation, and student interests and attitudes in his class portfolio.

Selecting Portfolio Information

The information gathered in a class portfolio should represent areas of literacy that coincide with instructional goals (i.e., that are important aspects of literacy) and that permit assessment of learning over time. Linda Pils, a teacher in a first-grade whole-language classroom (Pils, 1991), for example, gathers the following:

- Writing samples (considered for their content, number of known words, sentence structure, and punctuation)
- Number of words read aloud in 1 minute (assessed in September, January, and May)

UPPER ARLINGTON CITY SCHOOLS
Holistic Reading Assessment
Observation Form

Date _____   Holistic Reading Score _____

Student's Name _____   Grade ____

Teacher _____   Observer _____

BOOK SELECTION FOR HOLISTIC READING ASSESSMENT

Book Title

Child selected __ Teacher selected __

WIDE READING

- *May I see your book list?* (comment on books read)

Book List: Limited __ Adequate __ Extensive __

Comments:

- *How do you choose a book to read?*
- *What is one of your favorite books? Why?*
- *What are you reading now?*
- *What do you think you will choose to read next? Why?*

CONSTRUCTING MEANING/RESPONSE

- *Tell me about the book you have selected for this conference.*

Student discusses story idea __ major events __ characters __

story ending __

(Prompting may be used to elicit additional information; i.e., tell me more about the story idea.)

Prompted with additional questions __ No additional prompting necessary __

- *Why do you think the author wrote this book?*
- *Would you recommend this book? Why or why not?*

SILENT/ORAL READING/USE OF STRATEGIES

- *Find a passage in your book to read aloud. You can read it to yourself first if you like.*

Estimated Accuracy: 95–100% __ 90–95% __ Less than 90% __

Do miscues interfere with meaning? yes __ no __

Rate: slow __ adequate __

Fluency: (Intonation, phrasing, repetitions) fluent __ some fluency __

      nonfluent __

Observation of student strategies: (self-correction, prediction, use of cues) Comments:

- *Tell me in your own words about what you've just read?* (comment on reading and retelling).

ATTITUDE/SELF-ASSESSMENT

- *Do you like to read? Why or why not?*
- *What are your strengths as a reader? (What do you do well as a reader?)*
- *What would you like to improve about your reading?*

PLANNED INTERVENTIONS

Figure 10.10 A Holistic Reading Assessment Observation Form

- 10-minute writing sample (at 3-month intervals throughout the year)
- Lists of books read and to be read (kept during buddy reading time)
- Challenge cards (lists of unknown words and their sources)
- Conference records (students' interests in reading, how themes of books are alike and different, what they are currently writing about)

These samples are either easily obtained (number of words read aloud in 1 minute and 10-minute writing sample) or can be gathered during the course of instruction. All are in keeping with her literacy goals for her first graders.

Some samples that are gathered may be kept best in student portfolios (discussed in the preceding section) and some in a class portfolio. For example, from the samples listed above, the writing samples, the list of books read and to be read, and the challenge cards should be kept by students in their portfolios. The other information (1-minute word reading sample, 10-minute writing sample, and conference records) may be kept best by the teacher in the class portfolio.

Recording Observations

How can a teacher record the ongoing observations made during instruction? Two systems that have been developed by teachers may work for you. One described by Rhodes and Nathenson-Mejia (1992) involve anecdotal records. They offer three guidelines: "Describe a specific event or product. Report rather than evaluate or interpret. Relate the material to other facts that are known about the child" (p. 503, adapted from Thorndike & Hagen, 1977). A sample shown in Figure 10.11 illustrates the nature of anecdotal records.

A somewhat different system is described by Pils (1991). Her portfolio materials include strips of blank mailing labels attached to a clipboard. Each morning she dates several of these and then as she walks around the room, records her observa-

---

Eleanor

STRDAIPADENBSNO

(Yesterday I played in the snow.)

STRDA = yesterday
I = I
PAD = played
EN = in
B = the (said "du" and thought she was writing "D")
SNO = snow

Showed her how to stretch her words out like a rubberband—doing it almost on own by SNO. E does have a fairly good grasp of sound/letter relationships. However, has a hard time isolating words and tracking words in sentences in her mind. That may hold up progress for a while. Asked her—at end—what she did in writing today that she hadn't done in previous writing. She said, "I listened to sounds." Told her to do it in her writing again tomorrow.

Figure 10.11 An Anecdotal Record of Eleanor's Reading. *Source:* Rhodes, L. K., & Nathenson-Mejia, S. (1992). Anecdotal records: A powerful tool for ongoing literacy assessment. *The Reading Teacher, 45,* 503. Reprinted with permission of L. K. Rhodes and the International Reading Association. All rights reserved.

tions of children's works. For example, her records on Stacy might include the following:

> 9/24 Stacy: "I can read Hop on Pop all by myself."

> 10/5 Stacy: Stacy and Alan very good buddies, Stacy helps Alan with words.
> She read all of helper chart when she selected her job. (p. 48)

Linda has a three-ring binder with a section for each child. At the end of the day, she places the labels on the sheets of the children for which the observations were recorded.

Although it is important to use some more formal observational procedures such as the Upper Arlington City Schools Holistic Reading Assessment form or an assessment of spelling, it is also important to assure that your daily observations become represented in your class portfolio.

Determining the Physical Form of the Portfolio

The portfolio may take several different forms. It may consist of a set of manila folders (one for each child) in your file drawer. It may be a loose-leaf notebook with a page or section for each child. It may be an accordion file with a section for each of your children. The form should be one that you believe will be easy to use. You should have the physical form of the portfolio established before the beginning of the school year.

Making Sense of Your Portfolio Records

The final step is the most important. The best-kept records in the world will do you little good if you fail to reflect on what you have observed over time and make sense of the patterns you see. Your records should be descriptive rather than interpretive. At least once a month, for each child in your class, read over your portfolio entries and ask yourself what they tell you about the child's literacy development. You will begin to see recurring patterns in some areas and marked departures in others. When you do this sort of reflection, record your thoughts and ideas in writing as you read the record. It is possible to identify patterns and inconsistencies in your insights and emerging understandings.

On the basis of the patterns you see and the changes that have occurred, identify the current reading and writing strengths and weaknesses of the child. These tentative conclusions will form the basis for setting new short-term goals. During your next conference with the child, you will be able to discuss and confirm the patterns you believe you see and use these as the basis for discussing goals for reading and writing. The insights and new understandings you derive from your study of the portfolio entries should be recorded in brief form in the class portfolio. This assessment will better prepare you for your next observations of the child's reading and writing.

What is the teacher doing to assess her student's portfolio work?

Pause and Reflect

Select a grade level that you either currently teach or would like to teach in the future. Describe your goals in the areas of reading and writing in your journal. What are the activities you will undertake to help your students achieve these goals? What type of information will you want to include in your class portfolio? Describe the procedures you will follow and the physical form of your portfolio record-keeping approach. Record your ideas in your journal under the heading Class Portfolio.

HOW CAN YOU USE KNOWLEDGE FROM ASSESSMENT TO DEVELOP APPROPRIATE INSTRUCTION?

You have now learned something about how to observe the comprehension level and strategies of your students, their print skill, and their prior knowledge and vocabulary. But gathering this information is of little value if you don't know how to make sense of it. What you learn can be extremely useful in answering two questions: In what major areas is the student experiencing success and difficulty? Is the material appropriate in difficulty?

In the prior portions of this chapter, we focused attention on assessment in various areas of reading and writing in which students develop strength or may experience difficulty. We have spent less time on whether the materials are of appropriate difficulty. In other words, is there a match between the difficulty of the material and the skill of the reader? Earlier in chapter 3, we discussed how the books for beginning readers could be arranged in terms of difficulty. Indeed, the Appendix contains a list of books ordered according to difficulty. The judgment of the difficulty of these books was made by experienced teachers who used the books with children learning to read. More challenging materials are often rated by publishers on the basis of the characteristics of text—whether the text contains long words and sentences. There is, however, disagreement on whether more advanced materials beyond the more simple levels can be reliably classified in terms of difficulty.

Ultimately, teachers in classrooms are faced with helping their students read materials that are challenging. That is, for children to learn from text the material must not be too easy for them (Carver & Leibert, 1995). But it is also important that the materials not be so difficult that students become frustrated and overwhelmed. To help teachers make this decision, standards have been developed for assessing when text is too difficult in terms of the demands of print and/or comprehension. Table 10.1 shows the criteria often used to judge whether a certain level of material is too difficult for a student. The table includes criteria only for comprehension and oral reading, but standards similar to those for comprehension can be used to judge prior knowledge and vocabulary. The table shows that if children comprehend less than half the information in a selection, it is too difficult for them. If they recognize fewer than 90 percent of words in the passage, it is too difficult for them. In such cases, you should either try out an easier level of material or offer extensive instructional support so that students are well prepared for reading the more difficult selections.

Learning from Experience

To help you learn how to integrate the information gained through instructional observation, we have developed four case studies in order to demonstrate how assessment information from teacher observation, informal tasks, and portfolio samples can lead to use-

Table 10.1 Criteria for Determining Reading Levels

	Passage Reading	
Level	Oral Reading Accuracy (%)	Comprehension Accuracy (%)
Independent	98–100	90–100
Instructional	95–97	75–89
Borderline	90–94	50–74
Frustration	Below 90	Below 50

ful implications for instructional planning. We present only brief evidence to help you achieve a general overview of how these students' teachers make decisions. As you read the cases, consider the evidence and determine each student's relative strength in comprehension, print skill, prior knowledge and vocabulary, and comprehension strategies.

Case study: Beth

Beth is 7 years old and in the second grade. She is currently in the middle reading group, which uses second-grade-level materials. When she reads aloud during reading instruction, she does so fluently, making almost no errors. However, many of her answers to postreading questions show that she has not understood major events within the story. She typically misses about half the questions she is asked. Questions about important terms within the story reveal that she has a good command of English and is more knowledgeable than other students in the group.

Her writing samples typically focus on familiar events, often about her dog Gracie. Nevertheless, her writing is flawless in spelling and mechanics.

 Your Turn: Consider the following questions. Is Beth's comprehension adequate? How well developed is her print skill? Her vocabulary knowledge? Does she have any problems in reading and writing? If so, in what area or areas? What evidence supports these conclusions? What additional information would you like to have? Write your answers to these questions in your journal under the heading Beth.

 Our Turn: Beth's reading difficulty is not associated with inadequately developed print skill or vocabulary knowledge. Thus Beth should be able to handle second-grade-level reading materials and writing tasks. Her inability to comprehend what she reads may stem from her inability to connect the information of one sentence with that from other sentences. Accordingly, if you were her teacher, you might want to focus on developing Beth's knowledge of comprehension strategies so that she has a better idea of what she should be focusing on as she reads. You might also want to encourage her to read some of the more imaginative tales written by some of her peers in the class to broaden her vision of thematic possibilities in writing.

Case study: John

John is 10 years old and in fourth grade. His teacher immediately noted his difficulty in reading aloud, even when he read from materials that were somewhat easier than those read by most of his classmates. Although John has developed familiarity with some common words, he misreads many one-syllable words and waits for his teacher to assist him on many other words, particularly those of more than one syllable. He avoids writing whenever possible. Consequently, there are few writing samples in his portfolio.

His comprehension of stories read silently is extremely low; however, he comprehends well when others in his group read aloud. He also demonstrates good understanding of key words in the reading selections; indeed, he is one of the most knowledgeable class members when it comes to science activities and social studies discussions.

Your Turn: Consider the nature of John's reading and writing. How good is his comprehension? Is his print skill well developed? How adequate is his vocabulary knowledge? Record your tentative conclusions about the nature of his literacy strengths and difficulties in your journal. What evidence supports your conclusions? What level materials should he be reading? What additional information would you like to have? Write your answers in your journal under the heading John.

Our Turn: John's main difficulty seems to be in the area of print skill. He also has difficulty comprehending selections that he reads, even though his prior knowledge and vocabulary are strong. Therefore we conclude that his comprehension difficulty may reflect his poorly developed print skill. There is evidence to support this conclusion—his good comprehension when he listens to others read. Once he acquires skill with print, he should become a much better reader, given his well-developed prior knowledge. His teacher needs to obtain additional information on his word identification skills to better prepare him for reading selections. It may also be necessary to have him read less demanding materials. Writing may become an important avenue for developing his knowledge of print.

Case study: Rick

Rick is nearly 8 years old and in the third grade. His answers to comprehension questions indicate excellent understanding of what he reads, whether silently or aloud. Furthermore, informal questioning about key vocabulary words indicates a breadth of knowledge and fluency of expression. However, his oral reading is characterized by frequent substitutions of words. He seems to have developed an extremely careless reading style. He loves to write and often develops clever science fiction stories. Nevertheless, he has difficulty with spelling and often omits words when writing.

Your Turn: Consider Rick's reading strengths and difficulties. Does he have a reading problem, and, if so, what is its nature? Be ready to provide evidence to support your conclusions. Are the materials he is reading at the appropriate level of difficulty? What additional information would you like to have? Write your answers to these questions in your journal under the heading Rick.

Our Turn: Rick's strengths are his good prior knowledge and comprehension and his creative writing. Nevertheless, his oral reading and spelling difficulties suggest that his print skills are inadequately developed and should be explored further. Generally, adequately developed print skill is a prerequisite for adequate comprehension. Exceptions occur, however, among students with extremely well developed vocabulary knowledge. Such students, on the basis of their good knowledge with minimal information from print, can make sense of a story or passage. Although we may conclude that Rick has no reading problem at the present time, his print skill may become inadequate to the demands of reading as the materials become more technical and precise in their informational content. Therefore it is appropriate to explore Rick's skill with print and his writing further. He may profit from special instruction in the area of spelling. In order to develop reading fluency, he may need to read materials that pose few problems for him.

Case study: Dan

Dan is 11 years old and in the sixth grade. His teacher has found that he has considerable difficulty understanding not only his social studies and science textbooks but also the stories in fifth-grade-level books. His oral reading, however, is flawless, and he even read the social studies and science passages with considerable fluency. His teacher first noticed that he has extremely vague concepts pertaining to biological terms and then pursued his understanding of more common terms. She found that he knew only superficially, or not at all, words from his reading book such as *revenge, comrade, foundation,* and *craftsmen.*

 Your Turn: Pause for a moment to consider Dan's reading. In terms of the prior discussion, what are his areas of strength and difficulty? Is the level of material he is reading appropriate? What additional information would you like to have? Write your answers to these questions in your journal under the heading Dan.

 Our Turn: The oral reading evidence indicates strength in print skill. Dan's inability to answer the questions posed by his teacher is likely attributable to inadequate prior knowledge and/or poor comprehension strategies. The possibility that vocabulary knowledge is an area of difficulty is suggested by his lack of knowledge about terms known by his classmates. Thus we tentatively conclude that prior knowledge is Dan's major problem area. It is possible that comprehension-strategy difficulties also exist, but this remains to be determined by having him read a passage for which his vocabulary knowledge is sufficiently well developed. We conclude from this assessment that Dan could benefit from more prereading activities to develop his vocabulary knowledge prior to reading selections. He may also need to read easier materials.

SUMMARY

In designing instruction, you need to be able to answer two questions: First, what are the major areas of student strength and difficulty in reading and writing? Second, is the material being read appropriate in difficulty? We described a model that focuses on the relationship between assigned materials and student ability to comprehend them. If problems exist in comprehension, then you need to explore other aspects of reading—reading interests, skill with print, prior knowledge and vocabulary, and comprehension strategies—to determine strengths and weaknesses. We suggested a variety of activities to help you become proficient in assessing students' performances in each of these areas. The assessment skills you develop will enable you to observe student performance on the instructional activities that are ongoing in your classroom.

The observations and more formal assessments you make will provide useful information for your class portfolio.

We recommend that you encourage your students to develop portfolios of their work, so that their progress can be noted over time. This, in conjunction with your class portfolio, will provide a sound basis for assessing the literacy development of your students and for providing appropriate instruction.

In the Field

1. Select a story or an article. Read it and develop an outline based on your first reading. Then reread it and refine your outline. Now have a child of an appropriate age read the selection and tell you about it. Note the points on your outline that are mentioned by the child. What more specific questions, if any, should you ask? Finally, on the basis of the child's retelling and the answers to your questions, determine whether you think the child's comprehension is acceptable. Was the selection easy for the child to comprehend, somewhat difficult, or too difficult? Summarize what you learned in a report or in your journal under the heading Comprehension Assessment.

2. Ask a few 5- or 6-year-old children if they are willing to write some words for you. Take your time as you demonstrate the pronunciation and writing of the first two words *(mat* and *dip)*. Then ask the children to write more words "as best as they can." Watch and listen to them as they say the words and write them. If they have difficulty, discontinue the task. Reflect on your experience. What aspects went well? What problems arose? Study the words the children wrote. Did they seem to have learned consonant letter-sound associations? How good is their command of vowels? Is there a consistent pattern? At what stage are the children in terms of developing knowledge about English spelling? What did you learn from participating in the activity? Summarize what you learned in a report or in your journal under the heading Spelling Assessment.

3. Find a child who is in the beginning stages of learning to read. Select a storybook with predictable text. Introduce the story and tape-record the child's reading. Later, listen to the oral reading. Practice making a record of how the child's reading departs from the text. Examine the record to see what it reveals about the child's reading strategies and knowledge of print. Summarize what you learned in a report or in your journal under the heading Oral Reading Assessment.

Portfolio Suggestion

Select from your journal two examples of your responses to Pause and Reflect or Learning from Experience: Your Turn and include these in your portfolio. If you completed an In the Field activity, include your report from it in your portfolio as well. Write a brief evaluation of your work, commenting on what it shows about your learning.

For Further Reading

Clay, M. M. (1993). *An observation survey of early literacy achievement.* Portsmouth, NH: Heinemann.

Green, F. (1986) Listening to children read: The empathetic process. *The Reading Teacher, 39,* 536–543.

Pils, L. J. (1993). "I love you, Miss Piss." *The Reading Teacher, 46,* 648–653.

Valencia, S. (1990) A portfolio approach to classroom reading assessment: The whys, whats, and hows. *The Reading Teacher, 43,* 338–340.

Organizing Students for Literacy Instruction

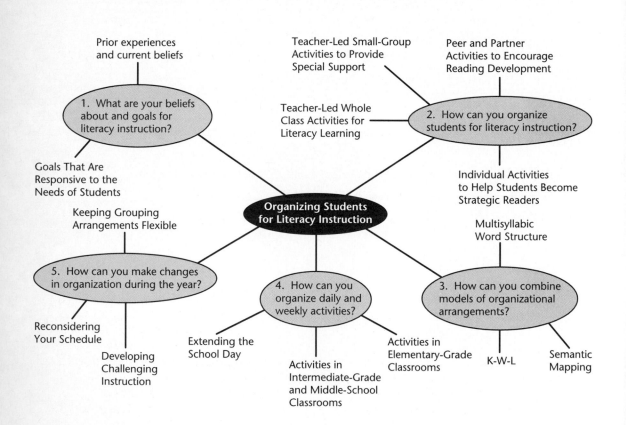

Prior experiences
and current beliefs

Teacher-Led Small-Group
Activities to Provide
Special Support

Peer and Partner
Activities to Encourage
Reading Development

**1. What are your beliefs
about and goals for
literacy instruction?**

Teacher-Led Whole
Class Activities for
Literacy Learning

**2. How can you organize
students for literacy instruction?**

Goals That Are
Responsive to the
Needs of Students

Individual Activities
to Help Students Become
Strategic Readers

Keeping Grouping
Arrangements Flexible

**Organizing Students
for Literacy Instruction**

Multisyllabic
Word Structure

**5. How can you make changes
in organization during the year?**

**4. How can you
organize daily and
weekly activities?**

**3. How can you combine
models of organizational
arrangements?**

Reconsidering
Your Schedule

Extending the
School Day

Activities in
Elementary-Grade
Classrooms

K-W-L

Semantic
Mapping

Developing
Challenging
Instruction

Activities in
Intermediate-Grade
and Middle-School
Classrooms

CHAPTER GOALS FOR THE READER

To consider your beliefs about and goals for literacy instruction

To understand how to organize students for literacy instruction

    To learn about teacher-led total-class activities

    To learn about teacher-led small-group activities

    To learn about partner and peer activities

    To learn about individual activities

To understand models that combine organizational arrangements

To understand how to organize daily and weekly activities

To consider changes in organizational structures during the year

CHAPTER OVERVIEW

How *do* teachers begin reading and writing instruction? Should you instruct your class as a whole or should students be divided into small groups? What other arrangements might you consider? In this chapter, we consider some principles you may follow in organizing your class for instruction. The chapter is divided into five parts. In the first, we describe how your beliefs, prior experiences, and goals, and the needs of your students may influence the instructional arrangements you decided to organize. In the second, we discuss some common forms of organization and how they may help you achieve your instructional goals. In the third section, we recommend that you use a combination of instructional arrangements and describe ways in which you might do so. The fourth section considers how the daily and weekly activities in your class might look, and the final section describes the changes you will need to make in your classroom organization as the year progresses.

 TAPPING PRIOR KNOWLEDGE TO SET A PURPOSE

Think back through your experiences in schools. How were the classes you remember taught? Can you remember how your first- or second-grade teacher organized your instructional activities? How does this compare to your more recent experiences in schools? Were most lessons presented in a total-class format? Was this also true for reading and writing? Now think about your experiences in fifth and sixth grades and your recent experiences in these grades. How were lessons organized? Have changes occurred? After reading the chapter overview and reflecting about your experiences, identify what it is that you most want to learn from reading this chapter. List these in your journal under the heading Chapter 11: Setting a Purpose.

WHAT ARE YOUR BELIEFS ABOUT AND GOALS FOR LITERACY INSTRUCTION?

Prior Experiences and Current Beliefs

Your own past experiences in classrooms may be one of the main influences on how you will organize classroom instruction (Lortie, 1975). These past experiences are the images that we carry with us that shape the visions that we have for classroom instruction. Most of us learned in fairly traditional classrooms where teachers did most of the talking, selected the reading materials, and established the learning assignments.

Recent research suggests that children learn more when they have the opportunity to express their ideas, select some of the materials they read, and influence the tasks they undertake (Paris et al., 1991). Yet teacher-led instruction may not encourage these forms of independence on the part of students. Thus in the past several years, teachers have been experimenting with new ways of organizing instruction so that students may have a greater role in planning, reading, and writing.

Underlying the decisions you make about classroom organization are a set of beliefs about student learning, autonomy, and social responsibility. If you believe that students learn what they are told or assigned to do, if you believe that you are the best person in the classroom to establish learning goals, and if you believe that students have little to gain from working together, then the instructional arrangements that would be most compatible with your values would be teacher-led total-class and small-group instruction. If, on the other hand, you believe that students learn only what they determine they want to learn, that they are the best persons to establish their own learning goals, and that the most important learning occurs through working with peers, then the instructional arrangements that would be most appropriate to your values would be various forms of peer group and individual work. Most teachers fall somewhere between these extremes. Where you place yourself will have implications for how you organize students for instruction. We suggest that you should be aware of your beliefs while, at the same time, trying to adapt and apply what theory and research suggest.

Pause and Reflect

In your journal, reflect on your beliefs concerning how involved students should be in the following: (1) establishing goals for learning, (2) expressing their views openly and freely, (3) selecting the materials they read, (4) determining the assignments they will complete, and (5) determining whether they will work alone or with others. How would you characterize yourself on the continuum between traditional and student-centered instruction? Record your ideas in your journal under the heading Beliefs about Instructional Organization.

The experiences that you have had as a teacher will also influence how you organize your students. When you have had relatively little experience in the classroom, it is appropriate to begin the school year by developing the forms of grouping typically used in your new school. One reason for this is that colleagues who organize their classes in a similar manner will be more able to offer help as problems arise. Another is that students will be familiar with the grouping patterns and how they are expected to behave during literacy instruction.

Although teacher-led patterns may be easier for a beginning teacher to learn than more individual or peer-directed forms, we recommend that beginning teachers begin the year with forms of instruction that entail combined forms of teacher-led and pupil-centered arrangements, such as working with partners, with peers, or individually. (These are described later in the chapter.)

Goals That Are Responsive to the Needs of Students

Instructional Goals

Although some goals are determined in response to the needs of students, some derive from the more general expectation of the school as to what students of a particular grade level should know and be able to do. In chapter 1, we discussed some of the goals that elementary-grade schoolteachers typically have for their literacy program. We believe that teachers at every level should aspire to develop students' love for literacy and the habit of independent reading and writing. Beyond this, teachers must help students to become proficient readers and writers.

Becoming proficient readers means being able to construct meaning from text and critically evaluate authors' ideas. Becoming proficient writers means being able to represent one's own ideas in written form. How teachers promote reading comprehension and writing differs from level to level. For example, in preschools and kindergarten, teachers promote reading comprehension and writing through the development of print awareness and comprehension of stories they read aloud to students. In the primary grades, teachers help students to develop reading comprehension and writing through opportunities to read and to talk about what they've read and through writing and sharing their writing, as well as through instruction in comprehension strategies. In the intermediate- and middle-school grades, when reading and writing in the content areas becomes more important, students need to develop their vocabulary and background knowledge, become familiar with the ways in which text is organized, and develop additional strategies for comprehending. Furthermore, as students engage in more independent projects, they must develop strategies for inquiry and independent study.

The organizational patterns described in the following sections differ in the extent to which they support the achievement of certain goals. Teacher-led total-class and small-group activities are particularly useful for introducing new concepts and modeling new reading and writing strategies. In particular, teacher-led groups are useful for introducing concept of word, sight words, phonics concepts, use of context, vocabulary and prior knowledge, and comprehension and study strategies.

Peer-group structures reinforce and support learning rather than teach an unfamiliar concept; they encourage students to assume responsibility for more independent use of reading strategies. Peer groups are useful for prereading activities, reading support, discussion of selections, and writing support. At all grade levels, they permit students to be responsible for asking and pursuing their own questions. Particularly for those students in intermediate and upper elementary grades, they provide support for more independent projects.

Individual forms of reading and writing are most useful for promoting independence and developing a love for and appreciation of reading and writing. When these individual forms are well supported, they provide the freedom for students to pursue their interests and explore alternative forms of expression.

Often you will use more than one organizational format to achieve an instructional goal. For example, if your goal were to teach students the strategy of K-W-L (see p. 420), you would begin with teacher-led total-class instruction combined with individual reading. But then to encourage more independent use once the approach had been mastered in the total-class setting, you might have peer groups use the strategy when reading a new informational selection. Finally, you might have students use the strategy individually. That is, the organizational context may change as you wish students to assume more responsibility through independent use.

Student Needs

Whether a total-class approach, teacher-led small groups, peer groups, or individual activities should be used also depends on the needs of students. Not only do fifth and sixth graders differ greatly from first and second graders in their instructional needs for reading and writing development, but students also differ greatly within any grade level. Most literacy educators agree that the beginning stages of literacy differ in certain fundamental ways from subsequent stages. Beginning readers and writers must learn about the nature of print and how print relates to their spoken language. Chall (1983b) describes the initial stages of reading as learning to decode and then learning to read fluently.

Typically, this focus on print occurs in the first two or three grades of elementary school. The developmental nature of literacy learning becomes obvious in several ways. Children who are able to read beginning first-grade materials have extreme difficulty reading materials typically read by second or third graders because they have not yet acquired the needed sight vocabulary nor the skill to identify unknown words. Furthermore, studies of reading development show that the learning of first graders is closely tied to instructional content, the printed words, and phonics concepts in the materials they read, and this knowledge accurately predicts their ability to read graded passages and to perform well on standardized reading tests (Barr & Dreeben, 1983). These research findings provide the rationale for the practice of instructing children who are similar in literacy knowledge in flexible groups in the first and second grades.

Once children have learned to identify printed letters and words, they consolidate this learning to become fluent readers. For most children, this integration occurs sometime during the second or third grade. Learning about print is no longer a major emphasis of instruction; instead, reading instruction focuses more intensively on the strategies that children must acquire in order to comprehend effectively and critically. What children need to learn to become effective readers is no longer developmentally organized. Whereas skill with print relates directly to the level of the material that children will be able to read in the early stages, in later stages interest in and prior knowledge about the topic are very determinant (Anderson & Davison 1989). Accordingly, in the intermediate grades and above, predicting whether or not a child can comprehend a particular story or article becomes more difficult. At this stage much instruction in strategies will be designed for the class as a whole, with reinforcement supplied in small flexible groups for students who need more support learning the strategy. Moreover, more of the instruction will occur in the context of reading and writing workshops, book clubs, and the like.

In sum, grouping children in the primary grades so as to achieve a closer match between their skill in dealing with print and the demands of printed material appears to be desirable. In contrast, ability-grouping in the intermediate grades, once fluency has been achieved, seems less appropriate because accurately predicting what will be easy or difficult for students to comprehend is more difficult. Moreover, children frequently watch television programs and movies—the same programs and movies watched by adults. They are exposed to the same ideas, vocabulary, and sentence structure as the adult viewers. That they are attentive and can comprehend the stories suggests that these stories are broadly accessible. We believe that the same is true in the reading of stories. Although the medium of print may pose a barrier in the beginning stages of literacy, once print is mastered, printed stories become what we call "broad-gauged tasks." They can be enjoyed and comprehended by students with a broad range of background experiences.

At the same time, it is important to remember that the individual needs of students in classes must be accommodated. For example, primary classes may include some extremely proficient readers. Although these children might profit from participation in discussion with other students, their continued reading growth may depend on more challenging reading monitored through an individualized reading program. Some intermediate and upper elementary school classes include low-achieving students who experience difficulties with print skills and fluency; special instructional provisions will need to be made to accommodate their knowledge in these areas. They may need to be instructed in a small group with appropriate materials, or to receive special support before or following total-class instruction with the same materials or those that pose fewer problems. As you reflect on the characteristics of each of your students, you must consider two related questions: (1) Given the needs of my students, how will I organize my class for various instructional activities? and (2) Given the organizational structures I have decided to use, what kind of support should I provide each of my students?

Learning from Experience

Tina Moore, a teacher of a split kindergarten–first-grade class, describes how she uses the first month of school to work informally with her students. As you read this interview, note how she uses the information she obtains to organize her kindergarten and her first-grade students for instruction.

Tina: My main goal is to have kids do as much reading as possible and to have them become powerful readers. I try to group them in units that will get them the most time for reading. For example, this year I have four reading groups, three for the first graders. My reason for putting the first graders in particular reading groups is their knowledge of print—how well they read and comprehend stories and how well they spell words. Our main goal in first grade is having everyone learn how to read.

I tell the kids, "The best thing about reading is telling your friends about it." So we do have some activities in which members of groups cross over to tell their friends about what they are reading. But for daily reading, I pretty much stick to ability groups that are— I hate to say—low, medium, high. For the kids that are already reading well, we're really sailing. For those who have already formed concept of word and are just starting to develop a sight vocabulary, they're the ones that I start with books, in the published literacy series. The ones who have not yet formed concept of word are the ones whose primary instruction is their own dictation—language experience stories. I put them on a schedule where they write a story, they work with it the next day, they write another story, they work with it the next day, and then the fifth day I type those stories and I work with them individually.

I am lucky this year that I have a class that's very willing and loves to draw. They're very artistic. So, you see the LEAs [Language Experience Activities] across the board? [Tina pointed to stories posted on the chalkboard.] I put them into Big Books, which I then use with the kindergartners, so it's been a great process for everyone. The LEAs this year have been a real equalizer. When kids write a story, they'll go out and contract some other kids as illustrators for them. So it really ties the class together.

This year I am lucky to have a parent several days a week to help with the average group, which is the group I worry about because they can be neglected. The high-group members are kind of self-propelled, and the ones that don't read, you worry so much about that you always give them lots of time. But the middle group, they're always the ones that in January my stomach hurts and I think, "You know, I don't know if I spent enough time with them."

I work with the kindergarten children as a total group and then individually on language experience stories, Big Books, and the like—lots of reading to them, sometimes finger-point reading to help them to begin to see the connection between what I'm saying and the words I'm looking at.

Your Turn: From reading the interview, how would you say Tina organizes her kindergarten students for instruction? How does she organize her first graders? Why do you think she chose the organizational arrangements she did for the kindergartners? . . . for the first graders? Write your response in your journal under the heading Tina's Instructional Arrangements and then read our response.

Our Turn: As you probably noted, Tina groups her first graders differently from the way she groups her kindergartners. She has divided the first graders into three groups, based on their print awareness and their knowledge about reading. She uses a less formal system for her kindergartners, offering total class reading and writing activities, as well as working with children individually.

We believe that she groups her first graders in the way she does to provide a good match between what they know about print and the demands of the stories. The activities she uses with her kindergartners—language experience stories and Big Books—are broad-gauged activities that can be engaged in by a class of children at various stages of emergent literacy. This is one way to group; other teachers may use ability grouping along with some whole and individualized patterns. A split-grade class is particularly challenging. A different way to form flexible groups would be to do so across grade levels; in this form of grouping, both kindergartners and first graders who are similar in their literacy knowledge would be grouped together for aspects of the literacy program.

HOW CAN YOU ORGANIZE STUDENTS FOR LITERACY INSTRUCTION?

Organizing students for literacy activities is like weaving a tapestry. To develop the patterns that will unfold in your class, you need to consider your goals—the strategies you want your students to develop and the literacy experiences you would like them to have. Some of your goals may suggest individually based reading and writing, while others may imply partner or peer group work. When students are first introduced to new strategies, you may wish to do so using a teacher-led total-class format. Similarly, when you become aware of a general need of the class, you may develop a minilesson for the total class or a small group. In this section, we will consider the major forms of grouping options that you have available to you. In previous chapters, you were introduced to a variety of teaching strategies. We will consider how various forms of instructional organization may be used for their development. In the end, your goal should be to fashion a tapestry that includes a variety of grouping formats. In the final sections of the chapter, we discuss how these may be woven into the school day and how the patterns may change during the school year.

Controversial Issue

Ability Grouping

Ability grouping for reading instruction has been pervasive in American schools (Goodlad, 1984). Ability groups within classes are common at all levels, particularly the primary grades; in addition, cross-class grouping arrangements (tracking) frequently occur in the intermediate grades and high schools. Reviewers of the historical research literature on grouping criticize the adequacy of the studies that have been undertaken and emphasize the equivocal and inconsistent results from study to study (for recent reviews, see Barr, 1995; Barr & Dreeben, 1991; Slavin, 1987). Ability grouping was not found to be clearly advantageous. More important, why we should have expected other than inconsistent results is interesting. A social arrangement, whether it is ability grouping or any other form of grouping, does not lead in any direct fashion to learning. Rather, it is the activities in which children participate, the materials they read and write, and the teaching support they experience that shape what they learn and their feelings about it.

More recent studies have examined grouping from a somewhat different perspective, asking about the quality of the instruction that students received in ability groups. Reviewers such as Allington (1983b), Barr (1992, 1995), Hiebert (1983), and Pikulski (1991) summarize the results from this research as follows: The instruction of children in low-achieving groups tends to include a greater number of intrusions and less time-on-task than in higher achieving groups. Low-achieving group members tend to read less material, work on less complex assignments, and receive instruction that emphasizes smaller units of print and decoding rather than constructing meaning. They experience more drill and skill work, read aloud more often, and tend to be asked questions requiring recall rather than reasoning. They are provided with different prompts from teachers and with more structured activities with advanced organizers than are students in higher achieving groups. Although some instructional researchers also claim that low-achieving group members receive less instructional time, others have not found differential time allocations.

We are currently evaluating our instructional grouping practices. Several factors seem to have precipitated this reexamination. Our increased understanding of the constructive nature of reading and the mutually supportive relation of reading and writing has led us to experiment with alternative forms of literacy instruction. Not only are we finding that we need longer blocks of time to combine reading and writing instruction, but also that our interactive teaching strategies encourage and enable us to change the way we organize students for reading instruction. Students who would have had extreme difficulty understanding a selection can with appropriate prereading instruction now read with comprehension.

At the same time, a variety of cultural forces are at work. The past decade has been characterized by particularly high rates of immigration; this has led to increased cultural and linguistic diversity among students. We are concerned about the de facto segregation that often results from ability grouping. Given these societal pressures, as well as our current ways of thinking about literacy instruction, it is not surprising that we are reconsidering the ways we group students for instruction and searching for new alternatives.

Given the equivocal nature of the research evidence, we recommend against the use of a rigid ability-grouping scheme, because it may lead to lower achievement and negative attitudes among lower achieving children. Instead, we encourage you to develop a repertoire of flexible grouping strategies to meet the individual needs of your students in reading and writing. This does not preclude you from providing supportive instruction for a group of your less able readers. What it means is that all children should have a variety of reading peers to support and encourage their progress (Radencich et al., 1995).

When you are thinking about how to organize your students for different aspects of instruction, consider your goals, the characteristics of your students, and the instructional support that they require to be active participants. If you choose to form groups that are diverse in reading ability, you will need to provide special support for those children who are developing their reading strategies more slowly than others in your class. When you choose to form groups that are homogeneous in reading ability, be certain that lower-achieving readers also have the opportunity to work with more proficient readers at other times.

Teacher-Led Whole-Class Activities for Literacy Learning

Whole-class instruction is special, since with its use, all members of your classroom community share in the enjoyment of literature and writing. This is your opportunity to model the strategies you use and to share your values and ideas; it is the time when students in the class can share their reactions to what they have read and their writings. Through these shared experiences, students come to see the value of reading and writing and the satisfactions inherent in them. This is the time to build a culture in which class members learn to respect the contributions of others, support the development of others in the class, and share in the pleasures afforded by literacy.

Whole-class instruction is useful in achieving a variety of goals. It can be the arena in which literature and the writings of children are shared—the time to focus on the beauty of the language, to share an exciting or moving event, and to explore the power of words to express ideas. Teacher-led whole-class instruction is a useful forum in which to describe and model new strategies to facilitate print skill development, vocabulary growth, and comprehension. It is also a useful format for reviewing previously developed ideas and strategies in order to explore how different students have found them useful.

Before a selection is read, teacher-led discussions can encourage students to establish goals for reading, consider new vocabulary, and speculate concerning the purpose of an author. While a selection is being read, either silently or aloud, students can be encouraged to share their ideas on what is happening and what they believe may occur next. After students have completed reading a selection, teacher-led discussions are useful for sharing the various interpretations of class members and searching back in the text to find the evidence on which conclusions were based.

The whole-class format is an inclusive one in which all students are members of the class literacy community. This inclusiveness is of particular value for the self-esteem of all students, but particularly for the lower performing ones. Students experience the satisfactions of being part of the class group and learn to appreciate the many and various ways that other class members "make meaning."

Although whole-class instruction has many advantages, there are also limitations. Because of interacting with so many different students during the instructional

Why do teachers read aloud to adolescents?

period, you may not develop as clear an understanding of the strengths and problems of each student in the class. That is, it is extremely difficult for you to assess and remember the responses of each class member when you are also overseeing the class discussion. Consequently, it is hard to gain specific information on students' learning and interests that can be used in instructional planning. Moreover, the reading selection or task may be so easy for some students that they are not challenged, and so difficult for others that they may be overwhelmed.

These disadvantages become serious only when whole-class instruction is the only grouping format that you use. For most teachers, whole-class instruction is a point of departure, a unified experience on which other forms of activity can build. In the following sections, we consider other arrangements that serve to complement whole-class instruction.

Teacher-Led Small-Group Activities to Provide Special Support

There are also times when it is important for you to interact with a group of children that is smaller than the whole class. When might you wish to do this? Small groups can be useful as an extension of whole-class instruction. As noted in the preceding section, whole-class instruction usually involves the use of reading selections that may be insufficiently challenging for some students in your class and overwhelming for others. Small groups can be used to address both of these situations.

Small-group instruction may be used to supplement the instruction of those who are insufficiently challenged by what the whole class reads. That is, the small group may be used to suggest other readings and projects that elaborate concepts of the text.

From these small-group discussions, students may define additional work that they are interested in undertaking individually or with a friend.

For children who find the selection read by the whole class to be extremely difficult, small-group instruction can help make the selection more accessible. Experts in reading instruction have for a long time believed that there needed to be a close match between the demands of a selection and the reading proficiency of a child. In recent years, we have come to realize that there are two ways in which we can support reading development. One is the age-old method of finding a more appropriate reading selection. The other is to make a selection more accessible through instructional support (Paratore, 1995). In other words, the manner in which you scaffold a selection can make it easier for your students to comprehend. This approach is based in the notions of Vygotsky (1978) that children can be helped to accomplish tasks that are beyond their ability to accomplish independently when they are given appropriate support and guidance. Thus when selections are first introduced, it may be useful for you to form a group of children who need extra support in order to comprehend a selection. Such support may take the form of introducing and discussing new vocabulary, anticipating word-identification problems, and supporting the application of comprehension strategies.

Small groups can provide the opportunity for you to become more aware of children's literacy strengths and weaknesses. Because there are fewer children in the group, you have the opportunity to reflect on children's comments and to learn about the evidence they use to support their interpretations. When you ask them to read aloud the portion of the text on which they based their response, you can achieve some understanding of their skill with print. You can assess their knowledge of word meanings.

Small-group support can be provided during the various phases when a selection is being read. Through small-group instruction *prior* to reading a selection, you will have the opportunity to build and assess prior knowledge and to understand how students set purposes for reading. You may wish to include those who you know could profit from such discussions and those about whose reading strengths and weaknesses you need to learn more. Through small-group instruction *during* text reading, you may observe students who have difficulty attending while they read and who can profit from discussion at strategic points during the selection. It may also be useful to follow up whole-class discussion of a text with a small group composed of those children who seemed to need greater support with comprehension or with extending their reactions through writing or drama.

There is a danger that the same set of children may always be the participants of the small group. That is, the group may tend to become rigid in membership. Although this may be appropriate in the beginning stages of reading, it should be avoided later. One way to do this is to provide alternatives to the small-group session in the form of peer support and to let children select the group in which they would like to participate. During reading, for example, peer groups and partner reading may be established to provide support, and students may be encouraged to select one of these alternatives instead of participating in the teacher-led small group. It is easy to believe that the only way children will progress is through the direct instruction that you provide; yet some children thrive when working with a supportive friend.

Another solution may be to invite visitors into the small group so that membership beyond the core group changes on a daily basis. Cunningham and Allington

(1994) describe such a plan—Their "lunch bunch" meets after lunch for about 15 minutes to read easy selections. Membership changes on a daily basis, with lower-performing students being frequent members and other students occasional attenders. The main point is that small-group membership should typically not be fixed. Moreover, teacher-led small groups should be only one of a variety of organizational structures in which a child participates.

Peer and Partner Activities to Encourage Reading Development

In the past few years, the use of peer work groups has become more common in elementary schools. Instead of working under the direct supervision of teachers or individually, students work with other students without the immediate presence of teachers. They control their own discussions rather than respond to teacher questions and requests (Barr, 1989).

Peer Group Variations

A variety of procedural formats has been developed to structure the work of peer groups (see, for example, Johnson & Johnson, 1975; Slavin, 1983). We will describe three variations that are particularly useful for reading instruction. In the first two, students work together to complete a teacher-assigned task, while in the third, students may work on assigned tasks or they may define their own task or project.

Partner Reading Having two children work together on assignments promotes dialogue as children complete tasks. When they encounter difficulty with the work, they can usually solve the problem together. This arrangement lends itself to a variety of reading tasks. It complements a traditional reading program by changing the assignments that are normally accomplished by students working alone during independent work into collaborative work. If the assignment is to read a story, children can either read it together softly or take turns reading pages. Paired oral reading is especially beneficial for less able students and second-language learners. Children may also jointly complete questions based on the selection. Similarly, older students may work on assigned reading tasks together even though they read selections silently. Partner reading allows students to help each other and to learn more by explaining their answers to their partners.

Peer Discussion Peer discussion is typically used as an extension of total-class or small-group instruction. Once you have modeled a reading strategy, it is appropriate to see if students can use it without your supervision. For example, over a three-week period a primary-grade teacher modeled the reading strategy of predicting what a selection would be about prior to reading it. Then, prior to reading a new story, she divided the class into groups of three and told each group to examine the beginning portion of the selection and to make predictions as they had learned to do. Following this discussion, the groups shared with the total class what they had predicted and the evidence on which they based their predictions.

Similarly, a middle-grade teacher used peer discussion after the class had read a story. After all students in the class had finished reading it, he showed them how to obtain a more precise picture of a character by gathering evidence in a systematic manner. He asked students to recall descriptive phrases and events from the story that were used by the author to describe the character. As he listed these on the chalkboard, he asked the class to draw conclusions about the character.

As a second phase of the lesson, he then divided the class into heterogeneous groups and had them repeat the process for a second character in the story. Students then reported their conclusions and the evidence on which they were based to the class as a whole. Peer discussion represents an intermediate step between teacher modeling and independent use of a strategy.

Cooperative Teams Although cooperative teams will vary in the extent to which they define their own agenda and the manner in which they report what they have learned, they are typically responsible for determining how they will work on tasks or projects. Usually, the cooperative teams are formed to work together for a period of several weeks. They may be composed of four or five students who are seated as teams during the period of time they work together; desks can be grouped in clusters for this, so that students, as they work cooperatively, do not need to leave their seats. Tasks may integrate such subject areas as social studies, science, math, and art. The group may, for example, select a book for everyone to read and discuss. Alternatively, the work may consist of pursuing a topic related to the Civil War. Typically, the length of time that students have to work before a report is due is established by the teacher, but this too can be negotiated.

One particularly effective pattern for cooperative teamwork in the upper elementary grades and beyond is called Jigsaw (Slavin, 1983). Each group is assigned the same topic, such as understanding the life of whales or the politics of Russia. Each topic is divided into a number of subtopics, with each group member becoming a specialist on a subtopic. Specialists from different groups who are researching the same subtopic will collaborate during the research period of their work and then report back to their respective groups concerning what they have learned. Each group then considers the reports of their specialists; the pieces of the jigsaw puzzle come together. The group then compiles a report covering each of these areas as well as their interconnections.

Management of Peer Groups

Management of peer groups is more complicated than other forms of organization because you are not present as part of the group. You can, however, influence how well groups work together by monitoring groups as they work and by helping students learn to work more effectively together in groups. Generally, when students have not worked in peer groups before, you should start with small groups of students who you know are compatible and assign familiar tasks. Of the three previously described forms of peer groups, it is best to begin either with partner work or with peer discussion. Students may be assigned to groups randomly or on the basis of interest or achievement, but membership should change fairly frequently so that all children in a class have the opportunity to work with each other during the course of the school year. For certain tasks, it is useful to assign roles to children (e. g., scribe, clarifier, reader, "go4").

While students work in groups, you need to be present and circulate near the groups. Your presence helps keep students on task. At the same time, you must be careful not to become involved in group discussions unless problems arise, because this defeats one purpose of the peer-group arrangement. Students should be encouraged to solve any problems that arise as best they can on their own and solicit your help only when these attempts fail.

Perhaps most important, the total-class discussion following group work should include not only reports of what students learned but also a discussion of how well the group worked together. During this discussion, ask students to describe student activity that helped their group work well together (e.g., clarifying comments or questions, summarizing prior discussion, bringing reticent students into the discussion) and list these actions on the chalkboard. You might also have groups describe any problems that arose and how they solved them. When students are learning how to work effectively in groups, this form of "debriefing" helps to focus students on how to be supportive group members.

Strengths and Limitations

Peer-group work gives students greater opportunity to raise questions and to structure their reading comprehension and writing. Students are usually more actively involved during peer-group work than during other forms of instruction. It also lets students learn from each other as they work together. Finally, students can apply strategies they have learned through teacher modeling in a supportive situation.

The main limitations of peer-group work arise from the failure of students to work well together. Sometimes ineffective work results when a group is too large, when students with past histories of incompatibility compose the group, or when students have not been taught how to work effectively through debriefing discussions following group work. Sometimes groups do not work well together when the task is inappropriate. The task may not be sufficiently well defined, or more preparation through teacher-led discussion and direct instruction may be needed. In general, some of these limitations are minimized when peer groups are used in combination with other organizational structures such as total-class instruction. For example, when you are teaching students to use the Herringbone strategy, you will want to introduce and model the approach with the class as a whole. After the strategy has been used with several stories with your support, you may divide the class into heterogeneous groups to use the strategy with a new story. As children face problems in how to apply the strategy, they learn from each other. Following such group work, it is usually useful to meet as a whole class to discuss how effectively they used the strategy.

Individual Activities to Help Students Become Strategic Readers

Individualized reading involves as many different tasks as there are children in a class. Typically, teachers monitor this work through individual conferences. Although teachers rarely have a completely individualized reading program, it is important to understand how this pattern works because of its unique advantages. An individualized reading program demands considerable knowledge on the part of teachers.

Learning from Experience

Rosemary Lane's third-grade students are, for the most part, fluent readers. She assesses their reading by having them answer questions about selections they have read silently. If they have difficulty, she has them read a portion of the passage aloud to her. She uses this information in organizing her students for reading instruction. As you read the interview, think about how she organizes her students in comparison with the previously described way Tina arranges her first graders.

Interviewer: How do you organize your reading program?

Rosemary: Every day we have silent reading for 45 minutes. There was a time when I read silently myself during this time, but every child who's had me knows I read, so I don't have to prove that anymore. Now I use the time for oral reporting, very quietly at my desk. I have a file box with each child's name on it. In the beginning I will put down on a file card (which they don't see) little remarks about their reading. And then I keep an ongoing record of the books they read. Every 10 books they read they get a certificate of achievement. It goes home in their folder on Friday. We also have a bookworm that grows across and around the ceiling. When children finish reading books, they write the title, the author, "why I like the book," and their name on a circle that becomes part of the bookworm. Already this year, the bookworm is about 30 yards long—about 200 books.

Interviewer: Would this individualized instructional approach be appropriate for even younger children or those who don't read as well?

Rosemary: One year I had a child who was in the very beginning stages of reading. When he came in the room and looked around at all the books, he said, "I can't do this; you have only chapter books." So when I left school that night, I went to the school library and the local library; the next morning I brought in 50 picture books. And when he came in the next morning I had the picture books strewn right across this board. And I said, "You can pick any of those you like." Well, his reading started to pick up so fast. I would announce, "Peter has read so many books this week: This is what's on his card." All of the children need this kind of positive reinforcement. Any book a child mentions an interest in, if I don't have it, I make an effort to get it for him or her. I can take out 50 books a month from the local library—I'm sure that other teachers can make arrangements to do that too. And then I'll bring them in. It's amazing to me that I've never had very many fines. We keep these books separate from the room collection. The kids have books at their desks all the time.

To make an independent reading program like this work, I also need the cooperation of the parents. During open house, the second week of school, I tell the parents how very important the reading process is to me and how all my life I have loved books. As a child, I never liked reading in round-robin reading groups. I wanted to read books. And so that's what I provide here: an atmosphere so they can read books.

I also require half an hour every night at home. I tell the parents that their children will have a reading folder. At the back is a simple form that I have shown the children how to fill out with the date and the book they are reading. There's also a small space for parents' initials and comments. I say to the parents, "I don't care if you read to them, with them, if they read to you, if they read to their baby brother; I don't care how it's done, but it must be done every night." That is what you call homework in the classroom. It must be done. I take the folders in every Friday, check them off, and keep the record in their file.

As part of the program, I believe that it is important for children to discuss books with each other. In order to do this, I regularly form reading groups to select and read a book together. Based on my initial assessment of their reading, I make notes on my cards. Because I have used basal series often enough, I will usually record the approximate grade level at which a child reads. And then I will, somewhat arbitrarily, form small groups, sometimes varied in reading ability and sometimes homogeneous. I have to play with the composition because if you get too much diversity either in reading level or interest within a group, they get very frustrated. They can't pick a book. So homogeneous grouping seems to work better in the beginning, but I'm always changing these groups. One of my top groups is composed of boys; they traipse down to the library, they fight, but they come back with multiple copies of a book of their choice. Even though I have a lot of books in the room, I want them to learn to use the library, to be free to choose without my being down there with them all the time.

Interviewer: How can a beginning teacher become familiar with literature?

Rosemary: I'd go to the best children's library and I'd hang out with the librarian awhile. There's no substitute for reading and reading and reading. And I'd look, for instance, at the pamphlet they put out—you know, the "Best Read-Aloud Books." I'd go to the shelves that had Jim Trelease's *The New Read-Aloud Handbook,* or Bayhill, or Sutherland's magnificent book on children's literature. I would spend considerable amounts of time in the library—reading the books and asking questions about them. I don't know a children's librarian who would not be helpful. Another way is to begin with a course in children's literature.

 Your Turn: Once you have read the interview, describe how Rosemary organizes her students for literacy instruction. In order to have an effective individualized program, what are some of the things you would consider? How does Rosemary's individualized program compare with the way Tina grouped her first graders? Write your response in your journal under the heading Rosemary's Individualized Program and then read our response.

 Our Turn: As you read the interview, you probably noticed that Rosemary organized an individualized reading program in which students, for the most part, selected their own reading materials and then conferred with Rosemary after they had read them. Rosemary also uses peer group reading as part of her program. Here, too, groups of children decide what they wish to read. This contrasts with Tina's first graders, in the beginning stages of learning to read, who are grouped on the basis of their print awareness and knowledge about reading.

Being thoroughly familiar with children's literature permits you to suggest books that will match the interests of children. Once they become excited about one book, they are usually able to find other similar books with your help. In addition, you need to know how to select material that is at the appropriate level of difficulty for individual children—at their comfort level. In order to do this, you need to know how to listen to what they say about books they have read, to ask appropriate questions, and to interpret their oral reading.

The structure of an individualized program is not as obvious as that for small-group or total-class instruction. Conferences between teacher and individual students are at the heart of the program: The child describes the book she has just finished, the teacher may ask some questions, and perhaps the child will read aloud. Then if the child needs assistance, the teacher will help select a new book. The teacher sets aside a period each day for reading. For example, Rosemary sets aside a 45-minute period during which some children report to her, and she also requires a half hour of reading every night at home.

The system supporting the approach includes careful record keeping on your part to make certain that children are reading, that they are progressing, and that they solve any problems that they have with reading. As Rosemary suggests, it is important to keep a record of the books that a child reads and to note any problems that are encountered. A literature-based individualized program assumes that reading skill develops from actually reading interesting stories. The young boy who entered Rosemary's class as a nonreader progressed from reading and rereading picture books to gradually reading and rereading easy books with limited amounts of print, some of which had been read to him in the class. Instruction is mainly a one-to-one arrangement in response to problems observed. Rosemary, for example, will help children develop initial decoding skill, when problems arise, through direct instruction and writing activities (see chapters 12 and 13).

An individualized reading program is effective to the extent that you motivate students to read. This is accomplished in a variety of ways. First, you must read books or parts of books to students to give them an idea of what is available and encourage children to report to others when they come across a great book. Second, a wide selection of books must be available to students. You should stock the class library with interesting books, be willing to bring additional books in as children show interest in certain topics or authors, and encourage children to become comfortable users of the school and local libraries. Third, tangible incentives should be provided. In Rosemary's room, for example, the bookworm was displayed for all to see the books the children had read. Parents were also asked to enforce the half-hour reading homework and to initial the reading sheet when books were completed. Moreover, completion of every 10 books was recognized with a certificate. Finally, the reading of self-selected books provides the most direct form of incentive; children like to read when they can choose stories that they find interesting.

This way of organizing reading instruction has some distinct advantages. First, since children read books that they are interested in, they typically find reading a satisfying activity. Through their elementary school program, they become familiar with the best in children's literature. Second, because the time periods set aside for reading are usually about an hour or a little less, children usually do more actual reading than they do when instructed in small groups or as a total class. Third, the need for workbooks and other seat-work activities is typically minimized; instead children read books.

At the same time, managing an effective individualized program is extremely demanding. Unless you are knowledgeable about children's literature and the stages that children progress through as they learn to read, this approach can be ineffective—particularly for those children who experience difficulty learning to read. Furthermore, it makes extensive demands on the teacher, who must secure a wealth of appropriate books and do considerable amounts of record keeping.

Because of these demands, this approach should probably not be used as the main portion of the reading program by a beginning teacher. And yet, as we discuss in chapter 16, we believe that teachers will move in this direction as they mature professionally. More important, we believe that all teachers should have as part of their literacy program a portion that is individualized. To the extent that teachers treat this component systematically through a stimulating class library, motivation to read, and a good record system, this program will contribute to the growth that students make in reading and writing.

HOW CAN YOU COMBINE MODELS OF ORGANIZATIONAL ARRANGEMENTS?

In the day-to-day realities of classroom life, several organizational formats are usually used in combination. New concepts and strategies are introduced in settings where you offer direct instruction, guidance, and some support. Gradually, the responsibility for using concepts and strategies is handed over to students. This occurs best when students have control over activities in peer groups or when working independently. As previously described in chapter 5, Pearson and Gallagher (1983) have called this teaching and learning process "The Gradual Release of Responsibility Model of Instruction" (see Figure 5.10 in chapter 5). This model specifies the proportions of responsibility of teachers and students in learning particular concepts and reading strategies.

When introducing a new strategy or concept, you would need to demonstrate how readers use the concept or strategy to understand and learn from text, illustrate how the strategy is to be used, and explain what information should be selected and when an approach can be used most effectively. Questions such as "Why is the concept important?" and "Which goals can best be satisfied by using the strategy?" can be pursued with the class.

Once students have shown that they need little guidance to apply a given concept or strategy, encourage them to use it in a setting in which they have control, either by reading with peers or independently. Through this process, they will learn to adapt it to their individual needs. Even at this point, most students can still benefit from occasional review and prompting.

In order to illustrate how various organizational forms are used in combination to achieve instructional goals, we have identified several strategies and concepts introduced in the preceding chapters. We will show how the organizational structures shift over time as the concept or strategy becomes more familiar. The concepts and strategies that we have selected for this purpose are multisyllabic word strategies, Semantic Mapping, and K-W-L. We have selected these to show how you may use a variety of organizational formats in developing these strategies, but you will use this approach to develop other concepts and strategies as well. The Gradual Release of Responsibility Model of Instruction applies to each of your instructional goals.

Multisyllabic Word Strategies

In chapter 3, you were introduced to teaching procedures to help students deal with multisyllabic words. If you follow the set of procedures described, you will introduce the procedures to a group of students who are overwhelmed when they encounter longer words (this may be the whole class). During several minilessons spread over a period of two or three weeks, you and the students will focus on longer words from the selections they are going to read and discuss how they may be divided into syllabic chunks and pronounced.

Concurrently, you should encourage students to try the strategy when they are reading independently. In the group setting, discuss with students what they do when they read independently and ask whether any of them have been using the strategy. Inquire about how well it worked for them. By doing so, you are encouraging students to begin applying the strategy when they read on their own.

After several teacher-led minilessons and when students have gained confidence in their ability to tackle longer words, you may wish to divide the group into smaller groups or partners to work together on dividing words into pronounceable chunks without your direct supervision. Small peer groups provide support and the opportunity to clarify what is still unclear for certain students.

In sum, two organizational arrangements can be used during the first phase of helping students deal with multisyllabic words: teacher-led group (or class) instruction and individual application of the strategy. A third may be used after the strategy has been understood: peer groups or partners working without the direct support of the teacher.

Semantic Mapping

In chapter 4, you were introduced to Semantic Mapping, which is an effective strategy for learning sets of conceptually related words. You may either begin with a set of words that are topically related and ask students to explain how the words are related, or you begin with a topic and ask students to free-associate words related to the key term. Since this strategy may be unfamiliar to most students in the class, you may wish to introduce it to the class as a whole. When you first introduce Semantic Mapping, because the approach may be unfamiliar to the students, you may need to encourage their response. After they have used it with several different topics or texts, they will become more confident in its use.

At this time, you may want to shift organizational structures. Instead of working with the class as a whole, you may wish to divide the class into five or six small groups and have each group work on the same topic, either explaining the relation between a set of words or free-associating words related to a key term. After groups have completed their work, the class should meet as a whole to discuss the insights of each group. Often groups differ in their interpretations, and this provides the opportunity for students to learn to appreciate the plausibility of alternative interpretations.

As a final step, you may want students to work individually in defining the relations that hold among words in a Semantic Map. Then have students work together in pairs to share their explanations. Through this set of steps using different organizational contexts, students learn to assume responsibility for understanding and applying the new concepts and strategies being introduced.

As the year proceeds, you may wish to revisit the strategies you have previously introduced. This can be done either with the whole class or by having students work together in small groups. This form of review will help students consolidate their knowledge and remind them to use the strategies when reading independently.

K-W-L

As you learned in chapter 4, K-W-L is an acronym for "What do I **K**now, What do I **W**ant to Know, and What have I **L**earned" (Ogle, 1986). It is a complex strategy that serves to guide students as they read informational text. Students establish what they know and what they want to know before they read. After reading, they consider what they have learned. This strategy should be introduced in whole-class format and used several times a week over several weeks.

Once students understand the approach, it should be used with small groups. The class can be divided into four or five heterogeneous groups to discuss what they know about a topic that relates to a text they will read. They should consider what they would like to know. One student in the group can record both the information they already know and what they would like to find out. After students read the text independently, they should reconvene in the small group to discuss and record what they have learned. Once groups have completed their work, it is important for the class to meet as a whole to focus on some aspect of the group work. You may, for example, ask them to share their ideas about what they learned. You should write their comments on the chalkboard. You may even want to organize their new learning topically in the form of a Semantic Map.

As a final step, it is important to encourage students to use this strategy when they read independently. You can do this by asking students how many of them used the K-W-L strategy when they read an informational selection. One or two students may wish to report to the class on what they *knew,* what they *wanted* to learn, and what they *learned.*

The important point to remember is to be conscious of the potential of different organizational arrangements. In general, teacher-led formats are most useful for introducing and reviewing new concepts and strategies. Student-controlled formats are best for the purpose of students assuming responsibility for applying and extending this learning.

HOW CAN YOU ORGANIZE DAILY AND WEEKLY ACTIVITIES?

Based on our knowledge of the research literature and the practice of outstanding teachers, we recommend that the following components form your literacy program. You may include other activities as well, but these should serve as the basic core.

LISTENING: Children's literature read aloud by the teacher
READING: Literature-based instruction
  • Reading strategies
  • Personal response

Self-selected Reading

• Reading Workshop

• Silent Sustained Reading

WRITING: Process Writing Approach

• Spelling

More traditional activities such as vocabulary development, handwriting, and grammar instruction should be incorporated in meaningful and functional ways.

As you create your daily and weekly schedules, it is important to provide sufficient time for students to read and write. During the past two decades, there have been many studies of reading programs and their effectiveness. A repeated finding is that the length of time children spend on reading activities strongly predicts their achievement (Rosenshine & Stevens, 1984).

In the following sections are examples of how teachers have structured daily activities. Although a variety of alternatives are possible, these provide an image of how some teachers have organized their programs. Other models will be developed in chapters 12, 13, and 14, when integrated perspectives on classroom instruction will be presented. The purpose of the following examples is to make you aware of the variety of ways in which you may structure daily activities and how this organization changes as children acquire literacy skill and become more independent.

Activities in Elementary-Grade Classrooms

In this section, we consider two alternative flexible grouping arrangements. The first was developed by first-grade teachers from Pinellas County in Florida (Radencich et al., 1995). The second, created and piloted by Wiggins (1994) and various teachers from third-grade classes, presents an alternative approach involving published reading programs.

First-Grade Alternative

The first-grade teachers in Pinellas County in Florida developed a two-day cycle of activities. Figure 11.1 shows the activities recommended on the first day. Time is set aside for self-selected reading and writing, as well as reading guided by the teacher. In addition, because of the specific needs of the students, time is set aside for vocabulary practice, phonics instruction, and the alternating time for handwriting or reading aloud to the class. During the self-selected reading and writing and the reading and rereading (small groups), the teacher can form teacher-directed groups to provide extra help and guided reading. The teachers generally follow the order of activities as listed in Figure 11.1, with various pullout subjects such as art, music, and physical education interspersed.

On the second day, time is scheduled for self-selected reading, writing, partner oral reading, discussion of the selection introduced the previous day, strategy instruction, and written work (see Figure 11.2, p. 423). The day ends with some time on projects or in centers and either handwriting or reading aloud to the class.

Day 1

45 minutes	*Self-Selected Reading and Writing (all students)*
	Teacher-directed group (extra help group; guided reading)—20 minutes
	Reread yesterday's story
	Practice words (segmenting and blending)
	Write a group sentence (guided writing)
	Read a new story
	Teacher-directed group (mixed ability)—20 minutes
	Share reading (as a literature circle with teacher as facilitator)
	Share writing in response to reading
15 minutes	*Preparing to Read (whole class)*
	Background, predicting, read-aloud, and/or vocabulary
15 minutes	*Reading and Rereading (small groups)*
	Teacher-directed group (a needs-alike group; guided reading)
	Independent readers (read and write in response)
	Listening center group (listen and write/draw; may be extra-help group that met earlier
	· in the day)
15 minutes	*Vocabulary Practice (partners and small groups)*
	Teacher-directed group (independent readers and listening center students)
	Share writing and drawing
	Discuss vocabulary
	Partner vocabulary practice (students who were in the needs-alike guided reading group)
15 minutes	*Phonics Instruction (whole class)*
	Pat Cunningham's "Making Words"
30 minutes	*Centers*
30 minutes	*Handwriting/Teacher Read-Aloud*

Figure 11.1 First-day Activities Scheduled in first-grade classes in Pinellas County, Florida *Source:* From Radencich, M. C., McKay, L. J., Paratore, J. R., Plaza, G. L., Lustgarten, K. E., Nelms, P., & Moore, P. T., 1995. "Implementing flexible grouping with a common reading selection." In M. C. Radencich & L. J. McKay (Eds.), *Flexible grouping for literacy in the elementary grades* (pp. 49–50). Boston, MA: Allyn and Bacon. Copyright © 1995 by Allyn and Bacon. Reprinted by permission.

Two such cycles might occur per week (Monday-Tuesday and Wednesday-Thursday). Friday is reserved for such special activities as Reading Workshop, Writing Workshop, and integrated curricular projects.

Third-Grade Alternative

Wiggins and his colleagues (1994) developed an alternative approach for using flexible groups within the reading program. Large-group lessons are followed by two forms of small-group activity: the teacher working with one small reading group and other students working in reading, writing, or math centers, or on some form of independent work. The schedule followed is shown in Figure 11.3 (p. 424).

Day 2

25 minutes	*Self-Selected Reading (all students)*
	Teacher-directed group (extra-help group)—15 minutes
	    Reread yesterday's story
	    Practice words (segmenting and blending)
	    Write a group sentence
	    Read a new story
	
	Book chats (two or three individual student chats) or guided reading needs-alike group

25 minutes	*Writing [whole-class (shared) and individual (guided) conferences]*
15 minutes	*Partner Oral Reading (of yesterday's selection and books of students' choice)*
15 minutes	*Discussion of Yesterday's Selection and/or Student Choices (whole class)*
15 minutes	*Strategy Instruction (whole class)* Meeting unknown words
15 minutes	*Written Work (partners, small groups, and individual)* Teacher-directed group (a needs-alike group) Independent practice Partner practice
25 minutes	*Projects/Centers*
30 minutes	*Handwriting/Teacher Read-Aloud*

Figure 11.2 Second-Day Activities Scheduled in first-grade classes in Pinellas County, Florida (Radencich, M.C., McKay, L.J., Paratore, J.R., Plaza, G.L., Lustgarten, K.E., Nelms, P., & Moore, P.T., 1995, pp. 49–50). *Source:* From Radencich, M. C., McKay, L. J., Paratore, J. R., Plaza, G. L., Lustgarten, K. E., Nelms, P., & Moore, P. T., 1995. "Implementing flexible grouping with a common reading selection." In M. C. Radencich & L. J. McKay (Eds.), *Flexible grouping for literacy in the elementary grades* (pp. 49–50). Boston, MA: Allyn and Bacon. Copyright © 1995 by Allyn and Bacon. Reprinted by permission.

Students are randomly clustered into five groups, and each group attends two centers each day (see Figure 11.4, p. 424). As shown, during the course of a week, they go to the reading center on three days; the writing center, math center, and science center, respectively, on two days; and the social studies center on one day. Students can attend either of their designated centers at any time during their seat work. But no center typically has more than three students working there. Students, assigned as center monitors every two weeks, assume responsibility for the number of peers attending the center.

Activities in Intermediate-Grade and Middle-School Classrooms

As students progress into the intermediate grades and middle school, they still need direct instruction, but since their literacy skills are more developed, they are able to work on tasks for longer periods of time and more independently. They become able to assume responsibility for planning and monitoring their work. In this section, we

9:00–9:20	Students arrive, pledge, attendance, etc. Calendar exercise and/or writing assignment on chalkboard
9:20–10:00	Whole class math lesson
10:00–10:40	Special subject (music, art, or physical education)
10:45–11:15	Whole class reading lesson Seatwork and centers
11:15–11:35	—small group 1 meets with teacher
11:35–11:55	—small group 2 meets with teacher
11:55–12:15	—small group 3 meets with teacher
12:15–12:45	Whole class writing lesson
12:45–1:25	Lunch
1:30–2:10	Science, social studies, or library Seatwork and centers
2:10–2:30	—small group 4 meets with teacher
2:30–2:50	—small group 5 meets with teacher
3:00	Dismissal

Figure 11.3 A Typical Day in Third-Grade Classrooms. *Source:* From Wiggins, Robert A. (1994, March). "Large group lesson/small group follow-up: Flexible grouping in a basal reading program" (p. 457), *The Reading Teacher, 47*(6), 450–460. Reprinted with permission of Robert A. Wiggins and the International Reading Association. All rights reserved.

Group	Monday	Tuesday	Wednesday	Thursday	Friday
A	Reading Math	Reading Science	Writing Math	Reading Social studies	Writing Science
B	Writing Science	Reading Math	Reading Science	Writing Math	Reading Social studies
C	Reading Math	Writing Social studies	Reading Science	Reading Math	Writing Science
D	Writing Math	Reading Social studies	Writing Science	Reading Math	Reading Science
E	Reading Science	Writing Math	Reading Social studies	Writing Science	Reading Math

Figure 11.4 Schedule for Groups to Work in the Learning Centers. *Source:* From Wiggins, Robert A. (1994, March). "Large group lesson/small group follow-up: Flexible grouping in a basal reading program" (p. 457), *The Reading Teacher, 47*(6), 450–460. Reprinted with permission of Robert A. Wiggins and the International Reading Association. All rights reserved.

describe the schedules followed by a fourth-grade teacher and by a group of sixth-grade teachers who collaborated in offering thematic units.

Activities of a Fourth-Grade Teacher

Jane Pearson had been teaching the fourth grade for five years. During this period of time, she had shifted from almost total reliance on the publisher's program used by the district to selected use of the program as an anthology, supplemented by trade books and novels. Her students now spend more time on self-selected reading and writing and thematic units. Figure 11.5 shows how she scheduled daily activities.

Her students begin the day reading and writing what they wish. Whereas she had previously formed groups on the basis of ability, now after she has provided prereading support, students read silently and independently or as partners and then meet in peer groups to apply strategies she has introduced to support their deeper interpretation of stories. In the afternoon, she has another period for literature and writing in which students can elect to work independently or with a partner, to form a book club, or to meet with a teacher-directed small group for extra support. Finally, in the final block of the day, she has developed thematic units that focus mainly on science and social studies, with the possibility of expression through drama, art, music, and writing.

Collaborative Sixth-Grade Activities

The three sixth-grade teachers in Hope Schools have undertaken joint planning over the past seven years. During the past three, they evolved a system of sharing their students for reading and writing activities in the morning and topical units during the afternoon period. Figure 11.6 describes two main blocks of scheduled time: one in the morning for language arts and another in the afternoon for thematic units.

The teachers differed somewhat in how they spent their time each morning, although students participated in Reading Workshop one morning and Writing Work-

Activities in a Fourth-Grade Class

45 minutes	Self-selected reading and writing
15 minutes	Total-class prereading activities and strategy instruction for stories or novels
15 minutes	Independent silent reading; shared reading with partners
15 minutes	Peer discussion of stories and application of strategies
45 minutes	Total-class math lesson; partner problem solving; total-class discussion
30 minutes	Language arts independent projects; book club, teacher-directed small group for special support
75 minutes	Thematic units combining science, social studies, and literature; expression of knowledge through art, music, drama, and writing

Figure 11.5 Schedule of Activities in a Fourth-Grade Class

Daily Schedule

90 minutes   Reading and writing activities: Reading Workshop, Writing Workshop, sixth-grade newspaper, book club, self-selected reading and writing

75 minutes   Thematic units integrating science, social studies, mathematics, literature, art, drama, music.

Figure 11.6 Collaborative Activities in Sixth-Grade Classes

shop on another. The other mornings were spent on self-selected reading and writing, book club (peer group) activities, the sixth-grade newsletter, and teacher-directed small groups for students needing special support.

In order to monitor the progress of students, teachers met with each of their students once a week in order to listen to their accomplishments from the week just finished and to share their plans for the coming week. Using a class portfolio file system, teachers made notes on the conferences and recorded whether students had completed the work proposed and their reactions to it.

For the thematic units in the afternoons, teachers built on their areas of interest in ways that combined science, social studies, literature, mathematics, art, and music. Units typically lasted for three or four weeks. Students were drawn from each of the three classes to participate in the units; when one unit was completed, they would work with a second teacher on the unit that teacher had developed. Typically, teachers developed two or three units a year, and after the first one, students helped in the planning of units.

Extending the School Day

In scheduling time for reading and writing, it is important to realize that not all time must come from within the school day. In one of the interviews at the beginning of this chapter, Rosemary Lane described how she set aside 45 minutes for her students to read; in addition, she required 30 minutes of reading as homework. Her students had the opportunity to read for more than an hour each day. By requiring, monitoring, and rewarding reading at home, she nearly doubled the time her students spent reading each day.

But scheduling time is not enough. You must plan instruction so that most of the scheduled time is used productively for reading. You must manage instruction so that time is not wasted. Students, for example, should not have to wait while you locate the materials they need. Similarly, you should attempt to ensure that they will not be interrupted by intrusions from outside the classroom (e.g., by loudspeaker, visitors, deliveries). When you work with only part of a class, appropriate activities must be arranged with the remaining students so that their time is spent productively and so that they are not constantly interrupting the group instruction.

Furthermore, you must make sure that independent or partner work is at an appropriate level of difficulty, that children have other means for getting help, and that they have other work alternatives once they finish their reading or writing tasks. The preventive measures that teachers provide to ensure that reading time will not be interrupted communicates to students the importance of the work.

HOW CAN YOU MAKE CHANGES IN ORGANIZATION DURING THE YEAR?

We have discussed how you can make decisions about grouping students, scheduling time for reading instruction, and selecting appropriate materials. The ways in which you organize students for instruction will influence what they learn and how they feel about themselves. The opportunity they have to read and write makes a difference in how much they learn. Whether the materials are appropriate in their level of difficulty has implications for the reading development of students. Whether students have opportunities to write on self-selected topics and on topics about which they have knowledge and experiences has implications for their writing development. These decisions, made early in the school year, form the structural arrangements for the reading and writing program, and these defining structural characteristics, once established, exert considerable influence on the effectiveness of the literacy program.

Although in most classes the decisions made early on remain unchanged throughout the school year, this should not necessarily be the case. You should evaluate the appropriateness of your grouping, assess the challenge of your instructional program, reconsider your time schedule, and make changes as needed.

Keeping Grouping Arrangements Flexible

This chapter has described various ways in which you can arrange your instructional program. In evaluating your grouping arrangements, you may wish to consider some of the following questions:

1. Do my students have the opportunity to work in student-controlled arrangements as well as in teacher-led formats?
2. Do I use a variety of grouping formats each day?
3. Does the membership of peer groups change on a regular basis?
4. Does the membership of the small groups I lead change on a regular basis?

If your answer is yes to each of these questions, you may feel confident that you are keeping your grouping arrangements flexible. If, however, your response is no, then you may want to make changes in your grouping.

A negative response to the first question would indicate either that students rarely participate in teacher-led discussion or that they rarely experience group work over which they exert control. The solution to either of these imbalances is to consider your goals for student learning and how they may be implemented either through the addition of teacher-led formats or student-controlled peer groups. If, for example, students rarely work in peer groups, you should reread the section on peer-group work and then consider how you can include peer groups as part of your students' daily experience. You may incorporate peer groups as one phase in the teaching of strategies, as was suggested in the previous section on semantic webs and K-W-L. To achieve a balanced learning program, you should strive to provide your students with the experience of learning in both teacher-led and peer-group formats.

A negative response to question 2 suggests that you will have to consider how to achieve a better balance. Students should not experience teacher-led instruction one week and peer group or individual work during successive weeks. Instead, each day should be a tapestry of experiences that includes independent work and peer collaboration as well as teacher-led activities.

A negative response to question 3 indicates a problem that is easy to correct. It may mean that your groups are stable in membership because you have children who are seated together working in peer groups. This arrangement saves time, but it is also one that could easily be changed every several months so that children have the opportunity to learn to work with a variety of class members.

Finally, a negative response to question 4 probably means that you are grouping children together on the basis of performance for teacher-led reading instruction. As described earlier, some teachers find that grouping children in the beginning stages of learning to read on the basis of performance enables them to provide appropriate support with materials that are at the right level of difficulty. We question, however, whether this form of inflexible grouping is necessary beyond the beginning stages of learning to read.

If you have selected this alternative, you must decide if the manner in which you grouped students for instruction is appropriate and determine whether changes should be made in group membership. One frequent change involves moving children from lower performing groups to higher performing ones. Indeed, both Barr and Dreeben (1983) and Rupley, Blair, and Wise (1982) found that their most effective teachers used this mode of grouping adjustment. Moving children from more slowly to more rapidly paced groups seems to enhance motivation, not only of the child in question but also other class members. The result of this grouping strategy is the creation of large rapidly paced groups and smaller more slowly paced ones. Alternatively, moving children from a rapidly paced group to a more slowly paced one seems to be counterproductive. Instead, you should provide additional reinforcement for the child in question through extra afternoon reading sessions.

Moving students from one group to another poses problems for teachers. First, which children can be moved up a group? Those children who learn the concepts presented during instruction more easily than other group members and who read contextual selections confidently, with good comprehension, are good candidates to be moved to a group that is reading more demanding materials. One way to make the change is to have the students be a member of the old group as well as the new group for a transitional period of time. Alternatively, the support of a parent or reading specialist might enable the student shifting from one group to another to read some of the stories that the new group had already read. Changes during the beginning stages of learning to read are more problematic and have to be handled more carefully than changes in later grades.

If you do choose performance-based teacher-led groups as one alternative, it is important that it not be the only small-group activity that children experience. In addition, they should participate with other students in more heterogeneous teacher-led small groups and should have the opportunity to work in peer groups with students who are not in their reading groups.

Developing Challenging Instruction

Reading assignments must be at an appropriate level of difficulty if students are to profit from them (Carver & Liebert, 1995). The instruction should be sufficiently challenging, but not frustrating. If students read only very easy selections, even though they spend much time reading each day, they will not profit as much as when they are assigned reading that challenges them.

What is easy or difficult for students depends to some degree on what they already know. For example, at the kindergarten level, most reading selections will be too difficult for students to read independently. A reading task is made appropriate at this level through teacher support and children's familiarity with the organization and content of the selection. Language experience stories are familiar to the children who participated in their development; at the same time, many children need the support of their teacher to read and reread them.

Many reading selections in the primary grades are not demanding in terms of content; that is, they describe familiar events and things. Words they have not encountered before are difficult for children at this level. Thus, in judging the appropriateness of selections at this level, you need to know whether the words in a story or article will likely pose problems for your students. The criteria described in chapter 10 are useful for determining whether instructional materials are appropriate or too difficult.

After the beginning stages of learning to read, as children become fluent readers, criteria other than reading accuracy become important. Accuracy will continue to be important, however, for those children who have not become fluent with print. From about third grade on, students encounter many selections that are demanding in terms of content, particularly in their social studies and science textbooks, but also in their literature readers and mathematics books. As discussed in chapter 10, you can assess whether selections are of an appropriate level of difficulty for reading instruction through children's retellings and their answers to questions.

Selecting materials that are at an appropriate level is particularly difficult because you need to find a match, not just for a single student but for a group of students who differ in their proficiency with print and in their prior knowledge. Often through supportive prereading activities (see chapter 4) you can provide sufficient support so that students are able to comprehend selections that would be too difficult for them if they read them independently. Thus, in evaluating the appropriateness of reading selections, you need to experiment with alternative forms of prereading support as you assess the appropriateness of selections.

Students need to read selections at their instructional level, but they also should read some selections that are easy for them. For these easier selections, they should experience very few problems with the print (2 or fewer problems for every 100 words read), and they should easily understand most of the ideas conveyed. Such reading is particularly important for children who are consolidating their knowledge of print so as to become fluent readers.

Unfortunately, children who encounter problems with print rarely experience problem-free reading. Typically, every selection they read is demanding for them. For these children, you need to encourage independent reading that is easy and pleasurable. In the beginning stages of reading, reading that is easy is achieved by having students *reread* familiar books, sometimes with a partner, parents, younger siblings, or children in a lower grade. Sometimes, external rewards (for example, charts, book trees or bookworms, or popcorn parties) may be necessary to encourage reading of this sort.

A somewhat different problem occurs for proficient readers. Often these students are not challenged by the instructional program. Particularly when you develop a reading program around a published program, the selections read may represent independent-level reading for these students. They may, therefore, require little in the way of prereading and postreading instruction. These children need to be encouraged to undertake projects with other students or independently that will challenge them conceptually and help them to develop independent-study strategies. You should meet with these students once a week to support and monitor their progress.

In sum, you need to ensure that your students experience reading that is challenging but not overwhelming. The way in which you do this will differ somewhat depending on whether your students are engaged in an individualized literature-based program or whether they read from published programs, and also it will depend on the literacy development of students.

Literature-Based Programs

As described earlier in this chapter, in order to develop instruction that is challenging, you need to be knowledgeable in several areas. Being familiar with children's literature permits you to suggest books that will match the interests of children. Moreover, you need to know how to select materials that are at the appropriate level of difficulty for individual children—at their comfort level. In order to do this, you need to know how to listen to them, ask appropriate questions, and listen to them read aloud. Conferences that you have with individual students are the heart of the program, aided by carefully kept records to ensure that children are reading and making progress.

As Rosemary Lane suggests in the interview quoted earlier, records should be kept of the books that each child reads. It is particularly important to monitor the reading of children who dislike reading or find it difficult. These are frequently the children who fall between the cracks in an individualized reading program. An individualized literature-based program is effective to the extent that you motivate students to read and keep track of their progress. Time for reading, in addition to that available during school, can be expanded through a home reading program. In the end, the reading and writing skill of your students will improve to the extent that they are engaged in reading and writing. Thus changes may need to be made in the support you offer and the time available for reading if children are not doing a sufficient amount of reading and writing.

Published Reading Programs

Although it might seem that all teachers using published programs would offer programs that are similarly challenging, this is not the case. Students may differ markedly in the degree to which their reading programs challenge them. The challenge students experience depends on how teachers pace instruction. By "pace" we mean the amount of reading students engage in each week that determines how fast they proceed through the published program.

Barr and Dreeben (1983) found that the teachers they studied differed greatly in their instructional pace, particularly at the first-grade level. Some groups read nearly three times the amount read by comparable groups taught by other teachers. These differences in instructional pace were directly reflected in reading achievement at the end of the school year.

If you use a published reading program, you must solve two problems that pertain to pace. First, you must establish, through experimentation, how much reading children will do on a daily basis. When children show signs of frustration and confusion about what they have learned, instruction should be paced more slowly, with more opportunity for in-depth discussion and review. By contrast, extremely able students in a class are often not challenged: Stimulating work—often beyond that included in published programs—must be developed with these students.

Second, you must establish appropriate goals for the school year. At the beginning of the school year, you need to determine what students should have accomplished by the winter holiday, by the spring holiday, and by the end of the school year. In order to make such plans, examine a calendar and consider the reading program your school or district has selected and then project the number of stories your students are to read by each of these time periods.

Reconsidering Your Scheduling

The daily or weekly schedule that you established at the beginning of the school year may need to be modified as students gain skill and independence. Typically, periods may be extended as the year progresses. Two questions you may wish to consider are:

1. How has my schedule changed since the beginning of the year?
2. Do students have sufficient time to engage in reading and writing?

With regard to the first question, students at the beginning of the year may have found a 30-minute period for reading or an hour period for writing to be endless. Yet as they develop skill and direction, these time periods may become appropriate or even too short. It is one of your goals that students achieve independence in literacy. As the year progresses, they may profit from longer blocks of time for activities that they plan and for which they are responsible. Your December and spring vacations are useful occasions to consider how the schedule you established earlier needs to be adjusted.

Concerning the second question, during the past two decades many studies of reading programs have found that the length of time children spend on reading activities strongly predicts their reading achievement (Rosenshine & Stevens, 1984). Barr and Dreeben (1983), for example, found that teachers differed greatly in how much time they scheduled for literacy activities and how that time was used. During the

What is this teacher doing to plan for the school year?

course of a school year, these differences mattered a great deal for the learning of students. Hence your schedule should allow for sufficient time for reading and writing activities. Teachers who schedule more daily time, and make certain that scheduled time is well used for reading and writing, allow their students to make good progress.

SUMMARY

Through reading this chapter, you were encouraged to reflect on your beliefs about how children learn and on your goals for literacy instruction. Your beliefs and goals, as well as the needs of your students, serve as the framework for thinking about how you will organize classroom activities. You should have developed a sense of how the four major ways in which you can organize students for reading instruction can be used effectively. The literacy culture you develop should involve a combination of small-group, total-class, individualized, and peer-group instruction. Your schedule should ensure a sufficient amount of time for reading and writing so that children can develop their knowledge of literature and strategies for reading and writing. Your instructional arrangements should evolve during the year to accommodate the increasing proficiency and independence of your students.

In the Field

1. Interview teachers who apply a whole-language philosophy. Ask them about how they organize their days and weeks. Are children involved in peer groups? Are the children in these peer groups of similar literacy development? Ask whether their schedules and activities in the fall of the year differ from those in the spring. Summarize what you learned in a report or in your journal under the heading Whole Language: Teacher Interview.
2. Observe Reading Workshop or Writing Workshop in a primary classroom. Note the different configurations of student groupings that are involved with this activity. Record your observations and your reactions in a report or in your journal under the heading Reading/Writing Workshop.
3. Observe students working together in peer groups. How well do the groups work together? Do they accomplish the work they are undertaking? Interview several students. Do they like working in peer groups? How do they like peer groups in comparison to working independently or teacher-directed work? Summarize what you learned in a report or in your journal under the heading Peer-Group Activities.

Portfolio Suggestion

Select from your journal two examples of your responses to Pause and Reflect or Learning from Experience: Your Turn and include these in your portfolio. If you completed an In the Field activity, include your report from it in your portfolio as well. Write a brief evaluation of your work, commenting on what it shows about your learning.

For Further Reading

Leal, D. L. (1993). The power of literacy peer-group discussions: How children collaboratively negotiate meaning. *The Reading Teacher, 47*, 114–120.

Leland, C., & Fitzpatrick, R. (1993–1994). Cross-age interaction builds enthusiasm for reading and writing. *The Reading Teacher, 47*, 292–301.

Radencich, M. C., & McKay, L. J. (1995). *Flexible groups for literacy in the elementary grades*. Boston: Allyn and Bacon.

Schumm, J. S., Vaughn, S., & Leavell, A. G. (1994). Planning Pyramid: A framework for planning for diverse student needs during content area instruction. *The Reading Teacher, 47*, 608–615.

Wiggins, R. A. (1994). Large group lesson/small group follow-up: Flexible grouping in a basal reading program. *The Reading Teacher, 47*, 450–460.

IV. • • • • • • • •

Classroom Perspectives: The Developmental Nature of the Literacy Program

CHAPTER 12

Supporting Emergent Literacy

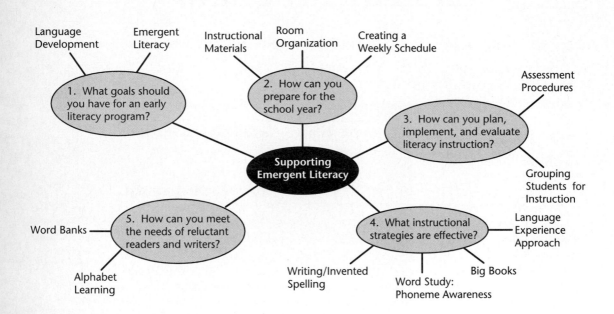

Language Development

Emergent Literacy

Instructional Materials

Room Organization

Creating a Weekly Schedule

Assessment Procedures

1. What goals should you have for an early literacy program?

2. How can you prepare for the school year?

3. How can you plan, implement, and evaluate literacy instruction?

Supporting Emergent Literacy

Grouping Students for Instruction

5. How can you meet the needs of reluctant readers and writers?

4. What instructional strategies are effective?

Language Experience Approach

Word Banks

Writing/Invented Spelling

Word Study: Phoneme Awareness

Big Books

Alphabet Learning

Pam Pifer

▼ CHAPTER GOALS FOR THE READER

To define goals that are appropriate for an early literacy program

To learn how to prepare for the school year

To learn beginning-of-the-year diagnostic and grouping strategies

To become familiar with instructional strategies and materials that are effective with emergent readers and writers

To learn how to meet the needs of reluctant readers and writers

▼ CHAPTER OVERVIEW

In this chapter, we consider the goals for your program and the planning you need to do to prepare for the school year. In particular, we discuss how you can select instructional materials, organize your room, and develop your weekly schedule. Then we examine what you need to do to get started, with an overview of diagnostic procedures and instructional grouping considerations. We include a case study of a kindergarten teacher, Pat Martin, preparing for the school year. We then discuss three instructional strategies that are generally effective with emergent readers and writers: language experience activities, Big Books, and invented spelling. In the final section, we describe two strategies that are useful with reluctant readers and writers who profit from more support: alphabet learning and word banks.

◆ TAPPING PRIOR KNOWLEDGE TO SET A PURPOSE

Have you recently interacted with very young children? What were they interested in doing? What are some of the differences you observed between children before they go to school and children in kindergarten? How do they talk about their experiences? After reading the chapter overview and reflecting on your experiences with young children, identify what it is that you most want to learn from reading this chapter. List this in your journal under the heading Chapter 12: Setting a Purpose.

WHAT GOALS SHOULD YOU HAVE FOR AN EARLY LITERACY PROGRAM?

Language Development

Holistic teaching is child-centered. Effective instruction builds on the prior knowledge of students, is adjusted for their present level of competency, and complements their interests. An important factor for teachers of young children to consider is the language development of their students. Teachers create the contexts in which children practice being effective communicators as well as efficient processors of both written and oral language. Contexts for sharing experiences, ideas, and opinions as well as for asking questions provide the teacher with opportunities to assess and encourage the oral language development of students. Students need to be able to express their thoughts and feelings clearly in complete sentences. Teachers can learn a lot about their students by being good listeners (Heath, 1983).

Emily Cotter, a Montessori preschool teacher in an urban school, likes to join her students for lunch and listen in on their informal conversations. She listens for their ability to make themselves understood and to handle frustrations and anger in reasonable and effective ways. Emily has set her room up in centers so that small groups of children can work together on activities which may inspire verbal narratives as well as negotiation and compromise. There are centers in which the children may play dress-up (clothes and hats are provided), build with blocks and Legos, and create puppet shows (puppets and a staging area are provided). The fantasy play and accompanying conversation are wonderful opportunities for students to fine-tune their verbal abilities. When conflicts arise, Emily steps in and helps her students negotiate reasonable compromises.

On a table near the center of Emily's room is a small bell. When one of her students finishes a "challenging work," the student rings the bell and all the children stop what they are doing while the proud student announces the completion of the project and issues an invitation for the others to come over and take a look. When a small group is assembled, the bell ringer presents the finished project and answers questions.

Emily also has a "line time" when she presents finger plays, songs, poems and limericks to her students. This is also the time when the "calendar work" is done (date, weather, and a record of something interesting that happened that day). Emily may also use this time to present science or social studies content. Students may "share" at this time as well. They often bring in vacation souvenirs or other treasures they want

How can storytelling improve children's reading?

to show the other students. The listeners are expected to be good listeners and are encouraged to ask questions.

As her students mature, Emily encourages them to write about the things they talk about. She will transcribe their ideas if they are hesitant about writing themselves, but she eases them into invented spelling as soon as possible. Language Experience Stories are a wonderful strategy for introducing students to their thoughts in print. Understanding the connection between their own ideas and the text that represents them is critical if literacy skills are going to develop.

Providing opportunities for students to develop their abilities to listen and express themselves is important at this level. They are not only learning necessary communication skills, but are developing confidence and self-esteem as well.

Emergent Literacy

What can a preschool or kindergarten teacher expect from young children in terms of literacy development? Some children will enter school reading! They may have taught themselves, learned from siblings, or learned through the diligent efforts of an enthusiastic parent. Others may enter with an awareness of print functions and conventions, recognition of the alphabet, a vague notion of the relationship between sounds and symbols, and an eagerness to read. Still others may have had very little exposure to print, no knowledge of letter-sound relationships, no knowledge of the alphabet, and no interest in reading and writing.

Many children who are familiar with *Sesame Street* come to school with some knowledge of the alphabet, letter names, letter sounds, and some sight words. The extent to which children absorb what *Sesame Street* has to offer varies from child to child. In addition, *Sesame Street* has been criticized for not demonstrating the usefulness of literacy activities as well as for deemphasizing the meaning-driven purposes of reading and writing (Mates & Strommen, 1996). So *Sesame Street* viewing may not be a clear indication of a child's sophistication in terms of literacy skill development.

Children coming to kindergarten may have had some experience in a preschool program. The academic content of these programs varies greatly, so preschool attendance is also no guarantee that the child will have had reading and writing experiences. As a prepared preschool or kindergarten teacher, you need to be aware of the vast differences among your students and be willing to accept each child's literacy skills for what they are. It is up to you to create an environment that will nurture the emergence of reading and writing in all your students.

Controversial Issue

You have probably heard the terms "reading readiness" and "emergent literacy" used to describe that period when children are first learning about reading and writing. Do they mean the same thing? If not, how do they differ?

Readiness literally means "preparedness to cope with a learning task" (Harris & Hodges, 1981, p. 263). Reading researchers for many years have used this term to refer to the complex pattern of intellectual, experiential, maturational, and motivational factors that indicate a child's preparation to learn to read. Yet the connotation of this term reflects the skills perspective that has influenced thinking about beginning reading instruction for most of this century. Specific, prerequisite skills were identified and instruction in these skills was provided. Traditionally, these skills included alphabet learning, recognizing the relationship between sounds and letters, auditory discrimination, and visual discrimination. It was assumed that students would master these skills sequentially and when enough skills had been mastered, reading would begin. From this perspective, the reading process is divisible into many separate skills, and aspects of it become the focus of direct instruction, particularly for students with limited literacy experience.

The term "emergent literacy" is of recent derivation. It became widely known with the publication of the book *Emergent Literacy Writing and Reading* by William Teale and Elizabeth Sulzby (1986). From this perspective, reading and writing are viewed as communicative activities (e.g., Cochran-Smith, 1984; Edelsky, Altwerger & Flores, 1991; Holdaway, 1979; Strickland, 1994–1995; Strickland & Morrow, 1989; Teale & Sulzby, 1986, 1989). Children become skilled readers by interacting with printed messages that allow them to respond to cues from varied sources simultaneously (print, their memory for stories, pictures, context). Reading and writing are not distinguished from areas that are the prerequisites to them. Rather literacy is seen as emerging from early experiences of being read to and seeing print function in the environment. Proponents of this position hesitate to fractionate text for direct instruction; they seek more natural alternative experiences with print such as those involved in writing.

In spite of the recent shift toward viewing literacy as a holistic process that grows from natural print experiences in the lives of children, some traditional "readiness" issues remain relevant. Certainly familiarity with the alphabet, letter names, and sound-letter correspondences are integral parts of the reading process that must be mastered. But these understandings do not need to be sequentially presented or mastered in order for readers and writers to emerge. In fact, these skills develop in a rather nonlinear fashion from meaningful interactions with print. Environmental print, favorite stories, and attempts at written communication with family and friends provide the impetus and opportunities for sorting out the multitude of cues that surround children every day. Children's early school experiences should include opportunities for meaningful reading and writing. Being able to distinguish a *b* from a *d* becomes much more important to a child writing a note to Daddy than to a child circling *b*'s and *d*'s on a workbook page.

Early literacy instruction should be designed to help children develop proficiency in the following areas: (1) functions of print, (2) concept of word, (3) phoneme awareness (the ability to hear individual sounds within spoken words), (4) knowledge of alphabet names and sounds the letters represent, (5) interest in reading, and (6) adequate prior knowledge. Basic to literacy development is the understanding that print has meaning and function. Children learn that people make things happen and meet their needs when they participate in reading and writing activities: They are informed by reading newspapers, mail, or instructions; entertained by books, magazines, and personal letters; guided by street and traffic signs.

The graphic symbols fluent readers take for granted are a secret code that the beginning reader has to "break" in order to unlock meaning from the printed page. But the code represents ideas that go beyond oral communication and requires an understanding of the difference between print and speech, particularly in the rhythm and cadence of words and sentences. Eventually, children also need to be exposed to language that is unique to the medium of print—expressions and rhythms that are delightfully peculiar to literature (Henderson, 1981).

Concept of word—the way words are separated by boundaries of space—is an awareness that develops at different rates in children (and may have to be taught explicitly to those who don't just "get it") from wide exposure to print. Some children come to school with a firm awareness of how print "works," how groups of letters represent words and ideas, and how the spaces function to separate those words. This awareness may develop as a result of experiences with print in their environment or from the pleasurable experience of being read to at home. But many children come to preschool and kindergarten with a much less sophisticated approach to print and need experiences through which they can learn about the function of spaces and concept of word. Helping children to understand the relationship between printed and spoken words should be an objective in preschool classes and a primary goal of the kindergarten reading-writing program (Morris, 1986).

The names of the letters of the alphabet and the sounds those letters represent are usually taught at the preschool and kindergarten level. Phonics instruction will be effective if it focuses on words the children have in their speaking vocabularies.

Phoneme awareness—knowledge of the discrete, component sounds within words—usually begins with beginning consonant sounds of words children use regularly. The ability to segment words into their component sounds develops most effectively as children attempt to write. When children are given the opportunity to invent spellings of familiar words, they begin to solidify the relationships between sounds and letters, and they develop a set of rules that guide the spellings they create. Children are first able to hear sounds as separable units at the beginning of words, then at the end of words, and finally in the middle of words. Children work diligently to build the most accurate representation of words they are trying to spell when they write to communicate. The sentences and, ultimately, the stories children write should be made available to be read repeatedly by the author as well as by the other children in the class. Figuring out the words represented by their own invented spellings is excellent practice in developing decoding strategies that will eventually enable them to read unfamiliar text. Critics have suggested that encouraging invented spelling leads to the establishment of poor spelling. Teachers need to recognize the point at which a student's reading has become skilled enough to provide that student with regular exposure to common sight words and spelling patterns. When a student is no longer relying on invented spelling to solidify the connection between sounds and letters, invented spelling needs to be phased out and instruction that encourages conventional spelling must begin.

Is this young child reading?

In addition to nurturing basic print awareness skills, preschool and kindergarten provide an opportunity for cultivating children's interest and enthusiasm for reading and writing. Young children need lots of positive experiences hearing favorite stories, being read favorite books, getting messages from friends, expressing themselves through drawing and writing, and playing with language (Cochran-Smith, 1984). School is a place where children's imaginations should be stimulated and urged to grow. You need to plan a variety of activities that will expose your students to new concepts in meaningful and exciting ways. At the same time, you need to be aware of the prior knowledge each child possesses and if it will be enough to enable that child to understand the new concepts being presented. If you find the children's prior knowledge is lacking, first-hand experiences need to be planned to help the children develop new concepts.

The preschool and kindergarten programs should be rich and *participatory*, thereby maximizing the children's experiences and guiding the connections they make between the new experiences and what they already know. Let's take a detailed look at what you as a preschool or kindergarten teacher need to consider as you plan a literacy program.

HOW SHOULD YOU PREPARE FOR THE SCHOOL YEAR?

Instructional Materials

If you are teaching preschool or kindergarten, you need to create an environment that is filled with opportunities for children to interact *formally* and *informally* with print. Before school begins, make certain that you have many books and magazines in your classroom with which children can interact, and set up a comfortable place for the children to hold, hear, or experience books in some personal way. They will look at the pictures, pick out familiar words, tell themselves familiar stories, find the funny parts, and share them with friends as well as read them.

They need many experiences with good children's literature if they are going to learn to love reading. Frog and Toad books by Arnold Lobel, the Frances books by Lillian Hoban, *Goodnight Moon* and *The Runaway Bunny* by Margaret Wise Brown, *Are You My Mother?* by P. D. Eastman, books by Dr. Seuss such as *The Cat in the Hat, Green Eggs and Ham,* and *One Fish, Two Fish, Red Fish, Blue Fish,* as well as *Bringing the Rain to Kapiti Plain* by Verna Aardema, *Brown Bear, Brown Bear* by Bill Martin, Jr., *The Napping Game* by Don and Audrey Wood and *Chicken Soup with Rice* by Maurice Sendak are examples of literature that children enjoy.

Big Books that can be shared with small groups or the whole class should also be chosen for the classroom (see the section on Big Books later in this chapter). Check publishers' catalogues frequently for the titles that are available as Big Books. In addition, consider making Big Books out of the children's dictated language experience stories. The time and effort it takes are well worth it.

Collections of poems and songs that appeal to children are also a rich source of predictable language. *Ride a Purple Pelican* by Jack Prelutsky, Shel Silverstein's books

(Where the Sidewalk Ends, A Light in the Attic), Jack Prelutsky's holiday collections *(It's Christmas, Thanksgiving, Valentine's Day)*, and his collection of poems, *New Kid on the Block*, are excellent sources of poems children love to hear and repeat.

Preschool and kindergarten classrooms should have an abundant supply of paper. Children enjoy drawing and writing on various sizes, colors, textures, and shapes of paper. It is especially important to provide paper that has space for a picture and lines for accompanying text and a variety of writing implements, so children can experiment with pencils, markers, crayons, colored pencils, and chalks. Pat Martin, a kindergarten teacher whose case study we discuss a little later in the chapter, rotates materials throughout the year, putting several kinds of paper and writing implements out for a while and then replacing them with a new supply when the children seem to be growing complacent with the first batch. The new materials rejuvenate the children's interest in writing whenever the supplies in the writing center change. Index cards on which children can write important words and individual envelopes in which to keep those word banks should also be ready to use. Pictures that can be used to encourage vocabulary development or teach phonics generalizations are also something teachers need to prepare ahead of time.

When considering instructional materials for kindergarten reading instruction, you need to be familiar with the published reading program or programs if any are used in first grade. Most published reading programs begin with an emergent literacy component that is generally considered to be a central part of the kindergarten reading curriculum. The kindergarten materials usually address print awareness skills (including developing left to right orientation), listening skills, awareness of the organization of a story, poetry appreciation, basic sight vocabulary recognition, phoneme awareness, and names and sounds of the letters of the alphabet recognition.

When planning instruction using a published program, focus on the activities that help you achieve your instructional goals. For example, the Scott, Foresman kindergarten book *Here We Are* (1989) contains a familiar fairy tale ("Goldilocks and the Three Bears") and a well-known folktale ("Stone Soup") to be read to the class. Several lessons are planned around the themes these stories provide. Opportunities to retell and to dramatize the stories are also provided in the suggested activities. The Scott, Foresman kindergarten book also includes poems and other nursery rhymes ("Old Mother Hubbard" and "Star Light, Star Bright") for the teacher to read to the children. The Harcourt Brace kindergarten book *All Ears* (1995) is an anthology of literature that includes popular trade books and appealing poetry. After reading Eric Carle's engaging story "Do You Want to Be My Friend" (also available in Big Book format), students are encouraged to brainstorm a "friendship web," detailing things friends like to do together. After reading Ann Shelby's "Potluck," the students are invited to create their own potluck book following the format of her book: ———— brought————to the potluck. (The name of the person and the name of the contribution begin with the same letter).

Some activities included in the teacher's manual are not appropriate for every child. Auditory discrimination activities may not be thorough enough for children who are struggling with phoneme awareness and phonics. In addition, these activities are often too teacher-directed to be really useful in helping children to hear sounds in words. Working on the recognition of the phoneme /p/ and the letter *p* that represents it may be redundant and boring to a child who has mastered consonant letter-sound associations.

In summary, a variety of materials are needed to help children develop skill in reading and writing: good children's books and magazines to which the children have hands-on access and that are good read-aloud choices, Big Books, paper for developing Language Experience Stories, lined paper with space for illustration, and paper and things with which children can draw and write. The early literacy component of a published program may also be used selectively. Read through the teacher's manual critically and assess what meets the instructional goals you have set for your particular group of children.

Learning from Experience

Pat Harvey teaches kindergarten in an inner city school in which some children respond well to instructional support in developing phoneme awareness and knowledge of letter-sound associations. The teachers in several of the first-grade classes to which her students will go next year use the Harcourt Brace reading program selectively. Thus Pat reviews the kindergarten reading program to see if it might be useful in developing phoneme awareness. Several pages from the program are shown in Figure 12.1.

Your Turn: Consider the workbook pages shown in Figure 12.1. What must children be able to do to perform these tasks? What additional related tasks can you think of that would further develop children's awareness of initial sounds and their letter associations? Write your ideas about these pages in your journal under the heading Analysis of Workbook Pages.

Our Turn: The tasks shown in Figure 12.1 might inspire opportunities for the children to create phonics displays of things they have brought from home beginning with the sounds corresponding to *s, m,* and *d.* They might create games based on pictured words cut from magazines, some of which begin with the letters *s, m* and *d.* Or the tasks might be linked to opportunities to spell inventively as the children become more aware of letter-sound associations. Such activities in which children are actively involved in understanding letter-sound associations are useful in helping children build solid phonics concepts. They are important extensions from activity pages in the kindergarten materials that ask them to circle pictures and trace letters.

Room Organization

Children at this age learn by exploring things with their own hands and eyes. Teachers need to bring in things children can hear, feel, smell, and taste as well as see, and provide places for children to display things they've brought in from home. Pat Martin often changes her displays to reflect the season, current interests, social studies and science projects, favorite authors, or the kinds of books in which her children are currently interested. The room should be organized so that children may move about freely and still have places where they can work without interruptions.

We believe that it is important for preschool and kindergarten rooms to have a class library, set up in an area where the children can comfortably look at a book or share it with a friend. Many teachers of young children equip this area with a large rug, some pillows, or even a large overstuffed chair that has been donated to the classroom.

Figure 12.1. Workbook Pages from the Harcourt Brace Reading Program *Source:* Illustrations from *Treasury of Literature,* Writer's Journal, Practice Book, All Ears, Grade K, Level 1, pp. 7 and 13, copyright © 1995 by Harcourt Brace & Company, reproduced by permission of the publisher.

Also important is an area where the children can write (whether they are writing conventionally or not). It should include a variety of paper (some lined, some unlined) cut into a variety of shapes and sizes, different writing/drawing instruments (pencils, markers, pens, and crayons), scissors, tape, stapler, hole punch, glue, and other things with which to construct "books." Children often enjoy sharing their ideas with each other as they draw and write, so the writing area should be a place in the room where conversation won't bother children who need a quiet place to work.

The room should also include areas where children can engage in physical activities such as building with blocks, playing in dress-up clothes, shopping in a grocery store, or working in a restaurant or a kitchen. These activities provide a forum in which language is practiced and enhanced and also provide real opportunities for the children to read and write functionally as they make signs, write shopping lists, menus, and invitations, and use their reading and writing skills to practice daily activities.

A science center where students can make records of weather observations, care for classroom pets, sort and categorize things like rocks, shells, seeds, and buttons, and plant seeds and watch them grow will not only lay the foundation for scientific understandings but will also provide opportunities for oral language development and for authentic literacy activities as students record predictions, observations, procedures and findings in journals.

Betty Roth, a kindergarten teacher in a suburban school, created a Student of the Week center where students brought in things from home to display that helped them to share who they were with their classmates. The student of the week was encouraged to talk and write about the items displayed in the center.

Areas for large- and small-group instruction should be a part of the classroom plan. One area should be large enough for the whole group to sit comfortably without being crowded, and another should allow children to meet in small groups with the teacher with few interruptions to disrupt instruction.

Pause and Reflect

Take a blank piece of paper and plan the room organization for a kindergarten classroom. How would you divide the areas of the room? What materials would you provide in each area? Include your plan and your responses to these questions in your journal under the heading Kindergarten Room Plan.

Creating a Weekly Schedule

In September you will want to plan your weekly schedule so that it includes large blocks of uninterrupted time each day for the children to interact with print and for you to engage them in explicit instructional activities. They should write, hear stories, and participate in some kind of reading activity each day. These activities are crucial to developing positive attitudes about literacy in general and about themselves as potential readers and writers.

Look at the sample schedule shown in Figure 12.2. The teacher, Cynthia Inness, has to plan her instructional time around many other scheduled activities—music, science labs, library, art, gym, and drama. At least two days a week (Thursday and Fri-

Time	Monday	Tuesday	Wednesday	Thursday	Friday
8:30 8:50	AM Routine (Leaders, Helpers, Calendar, Weather chart)				
8:50 10:00	Reading and writing	8:50–9:30 Reading and writing	8:50–10:30 Reading and writing	8:50–10:50 Reading and writing	8:50–10:50 Reading and writing
10:00 10:40	Library	9:30–10:00 Music			
10:40 10:50	Washroom	10:00–10:50 Reading and writing	10:30–10:50 Music		
10:50 11:10	Gym				
11:15	Lunch				
12:30 1:00	Math	12:30–12:50 Story time			
1:00 1:30	Drama	12:50–1:30 Math		12:50–1:45 Math	12:50–1:30 Math
1:30 1:50	Science	1:30–1:50 Quiet time		1:45–2:10 Science lab	1:30–1:50 Quiet time
1:50 2:30	Art	1:50–2:20 Science	1:50–2:20 Social studies	2:10–2:25 Snack	1:50–2:20 Social studies
2:30 2:45	Snack	2:20–2:35 Snack		2:25–2:45 Social studies	2:20–2:35 Snack
2:45 3:00	Story time	2:35–3:00 Story time		2:45–3:00 Story time	2:35–3:00 Story time

Figure 12.2. Weekly Schedule for Cynthia Inness's Kindergarten class

day) she has a two-hour block of time from 8:50 to 10:50 for reading and writing. On the other mornings, she has to do the best she can with one-hour (or shorter) slots that are interrupted by activities that require the children to leave the room. She must schedule time carefully so that the children feel they have adequate time to "write," even if they are at the stages in which they primarily scribble or draw as they tell a story. She also has to plan her instructional time carefully so she can fit all the children in as many times as they need to be seen in the course of a week. Most children will need instructional time on a daily basis. This need can be accommodated only by teaching them in combinations of large and small instructional groups.

Notice that Cynthia plans a story time after lunch and at the end of every day. She reads to the children at least once and often twice a day, because it is crucial that young children hear as much good literature and other examples of quality writing as possible.

Activities during the language arts period will change from day to day. You might want to write a Language Experience Activity (LEA) on the first day, read it to the children several times, and encourage them to read along. On the second day, you might target certain words to be read aloud. Have the children take turns reading, or ask them questions that require the targeted words to be used in response. Use the LEA or another story, and have the children finger-point to targeted words as they read. Read the LEA story again on the third day and give out individual copies for students to illustrate. On the fourth day, you might want to change your focus to a favorite poem, copied on very large chart paper. Have the children read it aloud, and focus on specific words. On the final day, you might ask the children to find words from the LEA story or the poem that begin with certain initial consonants or rhyme with certain words. Don't forget to leave out copies of whatever text you are working on during the remainder of each day, so children can read it again—and don't forget to have children write every day!

When the children have been in school several months, the pace may be picked up. Supporting reading of LEA stories or Big Books won't take as long. The children should exhibit more strategic thinking so that newer, harder material is not such an obstacle. Since you will have been asking them to focus on certain words in their LEA stories and predictable books, an improvement in sight word recognition, decoding, and perhaps in their invented spelling ability should be apparent for some children. In kindergarten, this may be the point at which you put them into small groups and work through more guided activities. Remember to be selective; everyone won't need to work on recognizing upper- and lowercase letters. Everyone won't be ready to play sight-word bingo at the same time. The children will still benefit from (and still enjoy) creating LEA stories and reading Big Books with you.

HOW CAN YOU PLAN, IMPLEMENT, AND EVALUATE LITERACY INSTRUCTION?

During the first weeks of school, you will learn a great deal about your students. In this section, we consider how you assess the needs of your students. We also consider when and how you may wish to group your children for literacy instruction. In the following section, we describe alternative instructional activities and how you use information about your students in planning appropriate instruction for them.

Assessment Procedures

Assessment takes place continually as children engage in reading and writing activities each day (see chapter 10). You need to allow the children to become accustomed to you and to their new environment before attempting any formal assessment of their literacy skills. At the same time, you should look for signs of interest in reading and writing: Do the children listen attentively when stories are read aloud? Do they have favorite books? Do they try to scribble or write notes to other children, to their parents, or to the teacher? Do the children ever pick up books independently and look through them? Do they attempt to read any of the labels you have in the classroom? When you ask the children if they can read, what do they say? Do they write their own names? Do they use upper- and lowercase letters?

Children need to be engaged in meaningful conversation. During this interaction, you need to notice the language development of your students. Do they speak in complete sentences? Is their vocabulary adequate? Do they understand what you are saying to them or asking them? Pat Martin, whose kindergarten class we describe in detail later, says she gets solid diagnostic information just by asking her students if they want to write their names on tape to identify their hall cubbies. If they do not want to write themselves, Pat asks them to spell their names so she can write them. When children cannot do that, she writes their names and asks them to choose their own names from several she has already written. This conversation tells Pat if children recognize, know the letters of, or can spell their own names. It also tells her something about children's willingness to take risks and their comfort with simple reading and writing tasks. If students are asked to sign in on a daily basis, the teacher can monitor the gradual progress they are making in letter formation.

More formal assessment will probably not be needed at the preschool level. But after several weeks at the kindergarten level, you may wish to undertake more formal assessment to determine, for example, whether or not children know the names of the letters of the alphabet, the difference between the upper- and lowercase letters, and the sounds the letters usually represent. An informal assessment using flash cards and pictures is sufficient: Put out five uppercase letters and five matching lowercase letters and ask the child to match them up. Show a picture and ask what letter the child thinks it starts with (see the photograph on p. 451). Let children know if they are right or wrong. If a child is relatively successful, continue through the alphabet. If the child experiences considerable difficulty with either task, do not continue. Assess the child's ability to recognize and produce rhyming words. This can be done as a game: Say two words to the child and arrange a signal that the child can use to show whether or not the words rhyme; or ask the child to give a rhyming word for words you supply.

If the children are relatively competent at these tasks, administering a developmental spelling test will provide a great deal of information about their phoneme awareness, phonics knowledge, and the sophistication of their conventional spelling knowledge. (These procedures were described in detail in chapter 10.)

Keep in mind that you do not want to overwhelm children with assessment situations in the beginning of the year as they attempt to make the adjustment to their

What does this child know about letters?

new classroom, teacher, and peer group. Much information can be obtained from careful observation during the instructional activities planned for the first few weeks of school. When the children dictate a Language Experience Story, who is able to read it back after you write it on chart paper? Who can point to words you ask the class to find? Who memorizes the story easily? Who understands concept of word, pointing at the individual words as they are read, acknowledging the function of the spaces?

If you use Big Books in your classroom, who listens attentively to the story? Who watches the print as you draw your finger across the page under the line you are reading? Who can point to words you ask the students to find? Who figures out new, unfamiliar words in the text? Who reads strategically and what strategies are being used? Are the children using phonics to figure out the "hard words"? Are they relying on their memories of the story to read every word? Do they go back to the beginning of the line or read ahead to figure out the words that have them stuck?

When you ask them to write something, who insists on dictating every word to the teacher? Who scribbles or writes in letter strings? Who spells inventively? Who hears beginning consonants? Final consonants? Medial consonants? Vowels? Is there any evidence of conventional spelling patterns (like a silent final *e*)?

All of this information should help you to plan an instructional program that will meet the needs of the children in your class. For some, you may have to plan many activities that will familiarize them with books and their exciting stories. Some may profit from informal tasks that will help them develop the ability to discriminate beginning sounds. Some may have to work on learning their upper- and lowercase letters. Many will probably need to work on developing concept of word. Still others may be reading already and you will have to plan opportunities for them to read. Children need to be engaged in meaningful literacy activities. They start school with a variety of strengths and weaknesses, and a good program lets each child grow in proficiency from that unique starting point.

Grouping Students for Instruction

Many preschool and kindergarten teachers like to teach the whole group at once (assuming the class size is reasonable), because the children support each other and often act as models as some develop skills more quickly than others. Teaching to the whole group is usually seen as more time-efficient, although instruction is rarely individualized and the chance of missing a child who is having significant difficulties is greater than in a small-group instructional format. (For an overview of grouping, see chapter 11.)

Other teachers divide the children into instructional groups depending on the assessment that has been made during those first few weeks of school. These groups are usually flexible, and children move in and out of them whenever it is necessary for the benefits of instruction to be maximized for each child. Some children need extra time developing certain strategies while others will experience growth spurts and need to be moved ahead more rapidly. Grouping as a result of teacher observation and informal diagnosis usually yields two or three groups.

Some children will have had very little exposure to reading and writing, may not know the alphabet or the sounds of the letters, and have no concept of word. They may have some difficulty expressing themselves in complete sentences, and their vocabularies may seem somewhat underdeveloped. These children will need many opportunities for oral language development. You may wish, for example, to encourage them to share their experiences with you and the other children, to retell stories or books that have been read in class, to participate in activities and writing Language Experience Stories about them, or to play games requiring verbal responses such as 20 Questions and I Spy. A significant part of their instructional program will be devoted to building concepts, expanding their vocabularies, and increasing their prior knowledge by engaging them in many hands-on experiences. These children will enjoy hearing predictable books, stories that rhyme, and books that are playful with language. They will also benefit from rereading their own LEA stories.

Other children may come in with more knowledge about sounds and letters, some sight vocabulary, and some rudimentary knowledge about the relationship between speech and print. Their overall language skills and their prior knowledge may be stronger than those of the previously described group. These children will also benefit from creating and reading Language Experience Stories. The related skill work will be more complicated as they work quickly toward developing the strategies they will need to become fluent readers. Rhyming stories and predictable Big Books are also good to use with this group, since they will "catch on" quickly as you finger-point while reading these materials out loud. In kindergarten, a group such as this may also benefit from working with published reading materials designed for the emergent reader/writer. Be selective about the activities you choose to do with them. Those activities should supplement a whole-language program that encourages children to participate in meaningful, functional literacy activities based on their own interests and their own language.

Yet another group of children, particularly at the kindergarten level, may have very sophisticated skills and may even be reading. You may want to move these children right into word banks (described more completely later in this chapter) or trade books and to focus on developing their independent word attack skills as well as their comprehension abilities. Published materials at the kindergarten level may be too simple for this group, and using them extensively may cause confusion over the nature of reading as well as behavior problems in the children who are bored with work that is not challenging or interesting.

Some teachers prefer to teach children individually. Opportunities that arise in class when children write stories or ask to listen to stories allow you to seize the teachable moment when a child's need to know is strong. Skills and strategies needed to become fluent readers are developed as children realize discrepancies between what they know and can do and what they want to know and do.

Any of these grouping models can be employed in the classroom when they are appropriate. Often a combination approach works best. Whole-group instruction may work best in the beginning of the year when instruction focuses on reading Big Books, creating Language Experience Stories based on whole-class activities, learning, reciting, and trying to read nursery rhymes and encouraging beginning writing skill. After a month or two, when you have had opportunities to assess each child's knowledge of sounds and letters, concept of word, sight vocabulary, attention span, and interests, small-group work may seem more feasible and beneficial. It is always a good idea to keep the schedule flexible enough to allow spontaneous interaction on a regular basis with individual children in your class.

Most teachers move to a more individualized program that is primarily child-centered rather than teacher-directed as the teachers grow in confidence. The teacher who has internalized appropriate expectations for children based on realistic appraisals of their developmental needs and levels notices subtle signs of potential growth and frustration and adjusts the curriculum to meet the needs of individual children.

Learning from Experience

The inner city school in which Pat Martin teaches is characterized by a high degree of teacher autonomy in terms of both curriculum development and student evaluation. It is organized so that there are large blocks of uninterrupted instructional time in every classroom. Pat has a full-time assistant and approximately 25 students each year in her kindergarten class. As you read this case, note in particular how Pat assesses her students' knowledge about reading and how she organizes the class for instruction.

 In September, Pat prepares her room by setting up interest centers in which the children will find many things to touch and explore on their own, with friends and with her help. She might begin the year with a collection of leaves on display for the children to touch, smell, draw, put in order, or categorize by shape or color. She has several kinds of paper and a variety of drawing and writing implements in this area; it also contains several books about leaves, trees, and plants for the children to look at and try to read. Pat believes her children's natural curiosity and personal experiences with leaves will inspire conversation that will help her assess and encourage language development.

One September, Pat created an interest center that consisted of postcards and some souvenirs that she had collected from her own vacation and those of friends and relatives. Again, she had different kinds of paper and writing implements, travel brochures and books about new places, and some teacher-created materials designed to introduce some basic sight vocabulary and travel concepts. She listened to the conversation between children and she engaged the children in meaningful conversation about traveling and about vacations in order to assess their language development and background knowledge about this subject.

In addition to interest centers, Pat labels things in the room so the children will begin to recognize words they use every day, and she displays the alphabet up on the wall as well. Pat sets up a reading area with a variety of books and magazines for the children to read. She has collected good books to read to her children: books whose stories she likes and knows children enjoy, books with rhyming words or patterned language, books she buys and books she makes. She also has several Big Books that she uses with the whole group. Pat reads to the children every day. When she reads aloud, she often stops and asks the children to respond in a personal way to the text. "What do you thing will happen next?" or "Is that what you would have done?" or "Have you ever seen anything like this?" By monitoring their responses, Pat finds out who can follow the narrative, who has adequate background knowledge, who sustains interest in the text, and who has knowledge of any specialized vocabulary.

Pat encourages the children to draw pictures, and she offers to write sentences they dictate to her about their drawings across the bottom. She begins to give them subtle suggestions about writing notes to her or writing stories. Many children don't wait for her to suggest it. They see the paper and writing tools and immediately begin to use them. Some need more coaxing, and there are a few who may be quite intimidated by the task of writing and need more time to warm up to it. As the year progresses, she gently nudges children who may be reluctant writers by saying something like, "I haven't heard one of your good stories in a long time!" Sometimes just changing the shape of the paper that's available for them to use is impetus enough for a flurry of writing activity. All the children who write are given the opportunity to share their stories with the rest of the class. The latter are expected to listen attentively and respond by saying what they liked about the story that has been read and by asking questions. Pat puts the children's stories into a class book that they like to hear over and over again.

Writing is an important activity in Pat's room, because, in the process of spelling inventively, the children are solidifying phonic concepts that they will need when they begin to read. Pat is able to ascertain alphabet knowledge (familiarity with upper- and lowercase forms of the letters), phoneme awareness, and knowledge of sound-symbol relationships when she watches the children write. She looks for solid beginning-sound knowledge and the ability to follow a story when it is read to the child as indications of readiness for reading instruction. Besides assessing skill development, by paying attention to their writing topics, Pat gets an idea of what is going on with them socially and emotionally. She finds out what is important to her children.

Pat does not place the children into instructional groups. She prefers to deal with them on a one-to-one basis, encouraging them as they write and helping them to grow in acquiring the skills they need. As their skills and confidence grow, the children often pick up the books Pat has read to them or new books they are interested in and ask Pat to listen to them read. She can often nudge children in that direction if she senses they are ready for that step by having them join a small group that is listening to or reading a story. Through Language Experience Stories, the stories they write themselves, and word bank activities, the children begin to develop a healthy sight vocabulary and some strategies for figuring out words they don't know.

Pat's assessment centers on the children's enthusiasm for reading and writing activities, their ability to listen actively when she reads aloud, and evidence of phoneme awareness, phonics knowledge, and concept of word when they read Language Experience Stories to her, follow along in a Big Book, or read one of their own invented-spelling stories to her. Pat is not likely to push a child who is too reluctant to venture into literacy activities, but she does make sure there are many opportunities for children to model reading and writing for each other and that there are authentic opportunities for the children to engage in functional, even necessary, literacy activities.

 Your Turn: From this brief description of Pat's class, what did you learn about how she assesses the knowledge her students have about literacy and how she organizes them for instruction? Write your thoughts about this in your journal under the heading Assessing the Knowledge of Kindergartners.

 Our Turn: You may have noticed that Pat uses every literacy activity to assess the knowledge of her students, from reading name cards on the first day of school to later language experience and writing activities. Through her experience working with young children, she has learned what it is she wants to learn about each child and is able to seek this information while working with students.

You may also have noticed that she doesn't group her students for instruction but works with them on an individual basis. At least in part because of her experience, she is able to use this organizational arrangement effectively so that all the children, even her most immature ones, make progress.

WHAT INSTRUCTIONAL STRATEGIES ARE EFFECTIVE?

Young children need to continue their language development; they also need to begin to understand the basic connection between print and speech and, more specifically, between their own ideas and the printed words that represent them. This can be accomplished in many ways, but basically young children need to see their own words in print—over and over again. As you write dictated captions to accompany pictures the children draw, they carefully watch you transcribe each word. This type of activity provides the basis for helping children develop that crucial concept of word and awareness of the phonemic structure of words. The activities described in this section provide opportunities for language development as well as emergent literacy.

Language Experience Activity

Description

To develop an LEA story, have children dictate several sentences about an experience they have shared and carefully write down every word exactly as the children say it. This is important because the children will rely on their memories to "read" the story, and so it must say exactly what they dictate. Through a process of support reading by the teacher that occurs as many times as it's needed and a myriad of word-study and comprehension activities, the children begin to focus on individual words and their component parts as well as on the story content, which is inherently meaningful to them because they wrote it.

LEA stories serve as a gentle way to introduce young children to a beginning understanding of the nature of spoken language in relation to written language. Later in kindergarten, children's dictated sentences can be used for a variety of instructional purposes: to develop concepts about print, word recognition, phoneme awareness, phonic generalizations, and concept of word as described in chapter 3. LEA stories can also be used diagnostically.

Procedure

Stories may be the product of experiences planned just for the purpose of writing and reading stories or they may be the natural result of spontaneous events that occur in the rest of the preschool or primary curriculum (e.g., a trip to the grocery store as a part of a nutrition unit, a math project in which every child is weighed and measured, a children's theater group that performs at your school, their first gym class, or a fire drill).

Write exactly what the children say as they watch you write. Write the story on large paper with large letters that everyone in the group can easily see. Be sure to use upper- and lowercase letters appropriately. As children watch the words and spaces appear, they will begin to solidify their ideas about the functions of print, concept of word, and sound-symbol relationships. Do not let the story get too long. Children need to be able to remember the sentences they have dictated to you, and it will require a significant amount of concentration for them to be able to read them.

When the story is complete, read it deliberately but naturally to the children, pointing at each word as you read to emphasize the connection between the familiar spoken word and its unfamiliar graphic representation. This will also help the children separate the ideas they have spoken into the discrete words that compose them. Read it a second time, encouraging the children to join in if they can read any of the words. Depending on the group's sophistication, some may be able to read their story immediately upon seeing it in print and others may have to hear the story over and over again before they begin to recognize any of the words.

At this point, your use of the story will vary depending on the children and on your specific purpose. If it is just a record of an interesting event, you might display it for the children to read when they are interested. If your group's print awareness skills are undeveloped, you might have them take turns finger-pointing at the words as they read the sentences with you. If your group has solid print-awareness skills, you might want to work on word recognition activities. For example, you might ask, "Can you find the word that rhymes with bake?" or "Can you find the word that is something to eat?" You might make word cards of the significant vocabulary in this story and work on helping the children memorize these words. They can practice their words with a friend, draw pictures to go with the words, match the words on the cards with the words in the story, or fill in a cloze version of the LEA story in which the significant vocabulary has been deleted.

The children should have access to their stories for as long as they're interested in rereading them. You might hang the stories on the walls of your classroom; it might, however, get a bit crowded! You could make a Big Book of their illustrated LEA stories. Individual copies of the stories can be made so that each child has a personal copy to read and take home.

One of the benefits of using the LEA stories is the children's familiarity with the vocabulary, sentence structure, and subject matter of this reading material. They are able to use a variety of strategies as they contemplate the text because they can rely on their prior knowledge of the subject to help them use context and phonic skills to read their stories.

Learning from Experience

The following instructional excerpt represents a conversation between Mary Johnson and a small group of preschool children as she helps them write a story about a field trip to the local park. As you read the lesson transcript, note the way in which she structures the initial portion of the story and then leads the children through the main events in which they participated.

Focuses on topic for story

Teacher: I thought we would write a story today about going to the park to collect insects. Remember the other day when we did that? How are we going to start the story?

James: We went to the park to get bugs.

Helps student elaborate on idea

Teacher [writing]: "We went to the park to get bugs." Why?

James: 'Cause the teacher said.

Teacher: Why did the teacher say?

James: So we could write about them.

Teacher: Okay. Let's write that: "[writing] So we could write about them."

James: Somebody broke the glass.

Jacob: Yeah, Catherine broke the glass. Write: "Catherine broke the glass when we was going to the park."

Helps students add details

Teacher [writing]: "Catherine broke the glass—" Can I say "the glass jar"?

James: The glass jar!

Jacob: Glass—glass jar is harder.

Helps students develop a sense of audience

Teacher: Glass jar is harder but they might not know what glass you're talking about.

James: Glass jar!

Jacob: Okay. Glass jar.

Teacher [pointing while reading]: "Catherine broke the glass [now writing] jar—"

James: With the . . .

Jacob: While . . .

Teacher: While what?

Jacob: When we was going to the field.

Teacher [writing]: "when we was going to the field." Okay. Did we get bugs?

Clifford: Yeah.

James: Grasshoppers.

Jacob: Centipedes. [James had asked a man playing tennis at the park if he could have one of his tennis balls, but the teacher said he couldn't take it when she realized what was going on because he wasn't supposed to talk to strangers. James wanted to include this incident in the story. At first the teacher said no, because it didn't happen to all the children in the group. But James seemed insistent, so she offered to put it in at the end after more sentences about the group's experiences.]

Brings students back to the topic

Teacher: Let's talk about collecting bugs. What did we get?

Ann: Centipedes, beetles, a tree-hopper bug.

Teacher [writing]: "We got centipedes, beetles, a tree-hopper bug, . . ." Anything else?

James: No.

Teacher: How about a bee?

Jacob: Okay.

Teacher [writing]: "a bee."

Jacob: The bee died.

Helps student clarify his thinking

Teacher: Do you want to say, "The bee died"?

Jacob: Yeah.

Teacher [writing]: "The bee died." Okay. James, do you want to say our sentence now about the man with the tennis balls?

James: I got a tennis ball.

Teacher: We can't really say "I," since this is all of our story. We need to say, "James got a tennis ball."

Jacob: I got lots of tennis balls.

Teacher: Let James finish. "[writing] James got a tennis ball . . ."

James: . . . at the park.

Teacher [writing]: "at the park." Then what happened?

James: But Ms. Johnson told him throw it back over the fence.

Teacher: Why?

James: Because not to talk to strangers.

Teacher [writing]: Ms. Johnson told him throw it back over the fence because not to talk to strangers. Okay. This is a long story! Let's read it. [Ms. Johnson reads the whole story while pointing to the words. Figure 12.3 shows the story they wrote.]

Teacher: You're going to read this with me this time. I'll go slow and you read as I point to the words. [The children try to read along, chiming in on most words.]

Brings
closure to
the story

:

Uses
support
reading to
engage
students

← **Your Turn:** In what different ways did Mary structure and support the retelling of this Language Experience Story? Record your answer in your journal under the heading Retelling an LEA Story.

→ **Our Turn:** As you probably noted, Mary structured the initial portion of the story by describing the shared activity (going to the park to collect insects) in a sentence and asking the children to remember it. She recorded the students' offerings, although occasionally she posed a question to lead the children to specify their thinking ("Why did the teacher say?") and their description ("Can I say 'the glass jar'?"). At one point, she also chose to get the children back on topic ("Let's talk about collecting bugs. What did we get?").

Big Books

Description

Big Books are oversize books with large print that can be read to a group of children who can follow the text as you read aloud and point to the text. The Shared Book Ex-

We went to the park to get bugs
so we could write about them.
Catherine broke the glass jar
when we was going to the field.
We got centipedes, beetles, a
tree-hopper bug. The bee died.
James got a tennis ball at the
park. Ms. Johnson told him throw
it back over the fence because
not to talk to strangers

Figure 12.3. Language Experience Story: "Going to the Park"

perience (Holdaway, 1979) using Big Books works very well with familiar stories and stories with predictable and/or repetitive language. Children love to read along as they get to know the story by heart. Some teachers make Big Books out of the children's own work by recopying their LEA stories on large chart paper and allowing the children to illustrate them.

Big Books can be used to introduce children to books they can read and to vocabulary that will interest them. Used effectively, they can help children develop knowledge about reading and books in general: front to back, top to bottom, and left to right orientation; knowledge that most of the information is carried in the print, not the pictures; and knowledge that the words printed in the book will always say the same thing.

As you read Big Books to the class, children begin to notice discrete, high-interest words and the spaces that surround them, as well as sound-symbol relationships in the words they learn to recognize. They may even begin to identify conventional spelling patterns. Most important, this may be their first exposure to the rhythm and cadence of written language, which is very different from the rhythm and cadence of speech.

Big Book experiences can also be used diagnostically, to identify children who don't sustain interest in narrative or remember the story or significant vocabulary—abilities that are crucial for the development of reading skill. Using Big Books can help you identify children who have a developed concept of word if they are given the opportunity to follow the text and point at targeted words or read the text aloud independently. Through teacher-directed word study, you can determine whether or not children recognize isolated words and identify beginning sounds and/or letters. Finally, by giving children an opportunity to read Big Books with you, you can begin to identify the strategies they try to use when they approach an unfamiliar word. Do they rely on their memories of the familiar story? Do they use the context of the surrounding words? Do they attempt to "sound it out"?

Procedure

Big Books can be commercially produced or created for the class or by the class. Commercially produced Big Books are usually oversized versions of books the children enjoy in a more conventional size, such as *Brown Bear, Brown Bear* by Bill Martin and *Chicken Soup with Rice* by Maurice Sendak. Most published reading programs now have Big Book components for their beginning reading levels, and publishers of whole-language materials such as Rigby and the Wright Group are also a source of Big Books.

Big Books can be read to the whole class or to small groups, as long as everyone who should be listening can follow the text visually as it is being read. Read the text at a natural, even pace, pointing to the words as you read them (or drawing your hand under the line of text you are reading). Pause during the reading of the story to ask the same kinds of engaging questions and encourage the same kinds of personal response that you would ask and encourage when you read any story to your class, but when you are actually reading the text aloud, the children should be focused on the words you are reading. After you've read the story several times over several sessions, ask the children to read it with you. You may have to slow the pace a little as the chil-

What do children learn from finger-point reading?

dren try to read the words on the page as you point to them. If there are any children who think they can read the story alone, let them try, helping them when they get stuck.

As the children gain proficiency with their Big Books, you can do a number of activities with them. Have them draw their favorite parts and dictate sentences for you to write about their pictures. Ask the children to identify certain words, or to find words that begin with the same sound or letter as a sample word you will give. Ask them to find rhyming words. Make Big Books available for the children to use at other times of the day as well; the more familiar they are with the story and the text, the more beneficial your work with the Big Books will be.

Word Study: Phoneme Awareness

As we discussed in chapter 3, phoneme awareness is the conscious awareness of sounds within words. Learning to hear sounds within words enables children to relate sounds to letters, which in turn leads to improved reading (Ball & Blachman, 1991; Bradley & Bryant, 1983; Clarke, 1989; Lundberg et al., 1988). Emergent readers may need support as they begin to develop an awareness of sounds within words. One natural approach is to encourage children to compare and contrast words as they say them. Another way is to invent spellings during writing. When instruction is offered in the context of meaningful literacy activities, students are likely to develop real skills and understandings that will enable them to use phonics as an effective word attack strategy. Opportunities to analyze familiar words (names of children in the class, classroom labels, words in personal word banks, lists generated by the students or by the teacher) will provide students with needed practice using genuinely interesting materials. As the teacher, you can decide when to allow open-ended scrutiny and analysis and when to direct the students' attention to word beginnings, medial vowels, spelling patterns, and the like. That decision will be determined by your instructional goals as well as by the competency of the particular group of students with whom you are working.

In this section, we describe a *Word Study* activity that can be used to develop phoneme awareness. It is an activity that can be embedded into classroom sequences, including those having to do with housekeeping. As part of the activity, children compare a set of words and search for those with similar elements. The search may be open ended or it may be focused by asking children, for example, to find words that begin or end the same. The purpose of the activity is to encourage children to become aware of the sounds in words and their spelling.

Procedure

Some children profit from having their attention directed to parts of words in order to note similarities; they also benefit from having the correspondence between printed and spoken forms made explicit. The following steps can be followed in preparing and directing this activity.

1. To begin with, you need to identify a set of words for children to study that contain within them a number of similarities that you want them to notice.
2. You may ask children to pull a set of word cards from their word banks or you may write the words in list form on the chalkboard. The set of words should have some elements in common that you wish children to discover.
3. Begin simply by asking children what they notice about these words. Alternatively, you may structure the task by asking them to focus on word beginnings, middles, or endings.
4. Each child's discovery should be noted, by pointing to the similar elements and emphasizing the relation between print and pronunciation.
5. Continue the activity by asking children if they notice anything else. Discontinue when no new discoveries are made.

Word study can also be developed as a minilesson whenever the opportunity appears. The following example shows how a kindergarten teacher, Leslie Shaver, used the word study activity as helpers were selected to perform classroom tasks.

Learning from Experience

Leslie Shaver and her kindergarten students had just arrived in the morning, and they were gathering in the activity area to discuss who would be helpers for the week. During this minilesson, Leslie encourages the students to look carefully at words and to make comparisons. As you read the lesson transcript, notice the ways in which Leslie directs their attention to studying the names included in the list of helpers written on the chalkboard along with each student's job for the week.

Calendar	Paula
Weather	Jason
Girls' Line	Shana
Boys' Line	Peter
Pet Feeder	Jennifer

The students read the list aloud in unison and then reviewed what was involved in doing each of these activities (it was early in October). Then Leslie asked the children to look carefully at the list of five names and to share what they noticed. They had the following conversation:

Encourages open-ended analysis

Jennifer: My name is the longest.

Emphasizes the syllabic nature of name

Mrs. Shaver: Yes, let's say it together: "Jen ni fer." It looks long and it sounds long. Is there anything else you notice?

Peter: Jason and Jennifer look the same [Peter points to "Jason" and "Jennifer"].

Mrs. Shaver: Interesting. How do they look the same?

Reinforces the phoneme /j/

Peter: At the beginning. They both start with "J" [Peter points to "J"].

Mrs. Shaver: Let's say them: "Jason, Jennifer." Can you hear that? They both sound the same at the beginning. Does anyone else have a name that begins with "J"?

John: Mine does.

Encourages generalization to other names

Mrs. Shaver: [Mrs. Shaver writes "John" on the chalkboard.] Let's say them: "John, Jennifer." Can you hear the sound that goes with the "J"? Does anyone notice anything else about these names?

Reinforces awareness of phoneme /p/

Kevin: "Paula" and "Peter" begin the same.

Mrs. Shaver: Let's say them: "Paula" and "Peter." Can you hear the sound that goes with the letter "P"? Does anyone notice anything else?

Angela: "Paula" and Shana" end the same—just like "Angela"

Mrs. Shaver: That's right. Lets say them "Paula, Shana, Angela." Can you hear the sound that goes with the letter "a"? Anything else? [Pause, no response.] Okay. Great job. You're really starting to notice a lot of things about names.

Your Turn: Think about this minilesson. What concepts about print were developed? Before you read our response, write your response in your journal under the heading Concepts about Print.

Our Turn: Some children in the group were still learning the alphabet, so the activity served to make them more aware of letters in words. Others were ready to profit from the part of the activity that reinforced phoneme awareness, and still others were beginning to learn letter-sound associations. The word study activity, repeated over time, provides the basis for developing phoneme awareness and learning letter-sound associations.

Writing/Invented Spelling

Children at this stage need ample opportunities and lots of encouragement to write. For very young children, you will encourage their exploration of writing and their interest in it. For children with a more developed understanding of print, writing helps them solidify their knowledge of letter-sound relationships that is so crucial to the development of fluent reading. As their phonic skill develops, children will try to spell the words as they think they hear them. This is a crucial stage in which the relationship between sounds and symbols is literally invented by each child in much the same way each child invents spoken language while learning to communicate with others (Read, 1971).

Research shows that children are hypothesis testers: They construct the syntactical and phonological rules that enable them to communicate with other human beings (Bruner, 1983). Learning to process written language should be allowed to develop in the same way. Successive approximations that come closer and closer to conventional representations are applauded as the children sort out for themselves "what works." Phonic generalizations that are invented by the child and refined through constant exposure to words in print become internalized and are available when the child needs to apply them during the act of reading.

Many activities will reinforce these generalizations once they are discovered. Some examples include: finding all the words in an LEA story that begin with a certain letter; playing I Spy, a game in which the children are asked to select an object from a group of objects on the basis of a phonetic component (beginning sound or vowel sound, for example); asking the children to bring something from home that begins with a certain letter; having a vowel search in the classroom; sorting pictures or objects according to a phonic rule (beginning sounds, vowels, etc.); word-family work (word recognition exercises that focus on groups of rhyming words and their graphic relationship: e.g., pan, tan, fan, fat, hat, cat, etc.); sorting words in their word banks.

Purpose

Invented spelling and other forms of writing help the children solidify their understanding of the functions of print, the consistency of print (written words have single, consistent oral counterparts), concept of word (words are discrete units separated by boundaries of space), and letter-sound relationships (phoneme awareness and phonic generalizations). The more children write, the more comfortable they feel with print and the ideas embedded in it. Figuring out how to write a word so that they or others may read it requires intense phonemic analysis and also a fairly thorough knowledge of the names and sounds represented by the letters of the alphabet.

Children's writing can also be used diagnostically to ascertain whether or not children understand the consistency of print principle, concept of word, and letter-sound relationships; and when children are writing extended text, it provides an opportunity to assess their ability to express thoughts completely, sequence ideas, and describe something adequately.

Procedure

Give children many opportunities to write. They often begin "writing" by scribbling; encourage exploration of this form of expression by asking them to read to you what they've written. As their awareness of print and knowledge of the alphabet grow, scribbling is often replaced by strings of letters. Sometimes these strings are a random assortment, and sometimes they represent at least some of the sounds in the words the children are trying to write. Again, give children opportunities to read their writing to you in whatever form it appears. Children can write notes to you, to their parents, and to each other. They can write stories to be read to their classmates. They can label their own things as well as things in the classroom. Remind them in these beginning stages that it is important for them to read their writing just after they have written it. If they need to have someone else read their writing, you can always help them to use the letters that will make another person understand the message.

Invented spelling is the first stage in the development of conventional writing skills. Children initially become aware of the beginning sounds of words and attempt to use their knowledge of the names of the letters of the alphabet to write those sounds. Often a word will be represented by just one letter—its beginning sound. You can encourage children to write letters before scribbles or letter strings when you think they can identify the beginning sound. As the children become more aware of the phonemes within words, each word will be represented by more letters. Usually words are represented by first and last sounds, and then medial consonant sounds are added, with vowels being the last sounds to appear.

You also need to encourage spontaneous writing in kindergarten. As the children's writing skills develop, you may consider adding to the daily schedule a short writing period when everyone writes and, if time permits, shares what has been written with the whole group or with a friend.

HOW CAN YOU MEET THE NEEDS OF RELUCTANT READERS AND WRITERS?

Alphabet Learning

Purpose

Often when you talk about reading and writing in the classroom you refer to letters by name; thus it is important for children to have learned the names of letters of the alphabet in order to understand and be part of the discussion. Beyond this, as described in chapter 3, many of the letter names contain the sound related to the letter. As Charles Read (1971) described the process, children make use of this knowledge in their invented spelling. In this way, knowledge of letter names provides one basis for spelling and learning letter-sound associations. The purpose of the following activities is to help children learn letter names informally in preschool classes and through more direct instruction in kindergarten.

Procedure

Activities that focus on letters and their names should be part of all preschool curricula. A variety of wonderful materials exist that focus children's attention on letters, their form, and their names. Discussions focused on letters also develop children's oral language abilities. Although alphabet books can be used as valuable resources much beyond preschools and kindergartens (Chaney, 1993), they are an exceptionally useful way to engage children in "learning their letters." Such books as *A. My Name Is Alice* by J. Bayer (1984) and *Alphabet Puzzle* by J. Downie (1988) contain word games that encourage prediction and language use. Similarly, books such as *A, B, See!* by T. Hoban (1982) and *From Letter to Letter* by T. Sloat (1989) include a variety of pictures relating to letters that promote vocabulary learning, in addition to letter names. These books are particularly useful with children who speak a language other than English.

A second natural way to help children learn the names of the letters of the alphabet is through poems and rhymes. Anthologies such as *Poems in Your Pocket, Three Bags Full,* and *A Pocket Full of Licorice,* collected by Debbie Powell and Andrea Butler and published in Big Book form, represent a useful focus for instructional activities. They allow children to see a poem in print as they hear it read aloud.

 ## Learning from Experience

Markesha Smith teaches a preschool class of four- and five-year-olds. Every day on three or four occasions she reads aloud to her children. One poem she reads aloud is "One Potato."

One Potato*

One potato, two potato,
Three potato, four;
Five potato, six potato,
Seven potato, MORE.

Traditional

 Your Turn: Consider the poem "One Potato." If you were Markesha Smith, what questions might you ask to encourage students' language development and to sensi-

---

*"One Potato," from *Poems in Your Pocket,* selected by Debbie Powell and Andrea Butler, p. 21, 1989, Crystal Lake, IL: Rigby. Reprinted with permission.

tize them to letter names? Write your ideas in your journal under the heading En-couraging Language Development.

Our Turn: Markesha's main purpose in reading poems is to have children enjoy them and gain a sense of the rhythm. To do this, she has children clap as they repeat the poem together. In this case, she then had children hold up the number of fingers corresponding to the number of potatoes in the poem. She asked how many had ever seen a potato. She then showed them a large potato she had brought to class and cut it into bits so that they could taste it. After they reread the poem again, she asked [pointing to the "P"], "Does anyone know what letter this is?" Pat immediately raised her hand and said "P." Markesha then asked Pat to take a picture of a potato and paste it in the class alphabet book under "P."

Markesha embedded this brief focus on the letter "P" and its name in an instructional sequence focused on enjoying a poem. Some children already had learned letter names; some were attentive and seemed to be learning letter names; others were not yet interested.

For kindergarten children who have not yet learned letter names, more direct instruction is appropriate. A small group should be formed of children who have not yet learned letter names as well as some children who are interested in participating although they already know letter names. Some of the latter may be children who have learned English as a second language who could profit from the language and vocabulary development aspects of alphabet learning.

The small group will develop an Alphabet Big Book. One way to begin is with the first letters in the names of children in the group. For example, the letter "D" may be selected first because of David, who is one of the group members. Each page in the alphabet book will contain names and other words that are important to children in the group, but mainly pictures that children have collected from magazines in the room and from home. A week can be devoted to each letter, with a brief instructional session each day in which pictures children have brought from home are discussed and pasted in on the "D" page and poems featuring the letter "D" are read (for example, "Diddle, Diddle, Dumpling"). Children can be helped to print the letter "D" and any words they know beginning with "d." Phonemic awareness should be developed as words beginning with the letter "d" are pronounced slowly. A week on a letter is a sufficiently slow pace so that most children who have not yet learned letter names will do so. Some will begin to learn letter sounds through these activities.

Word Banks

Purpose

A "sight word" is "a word that is immediately recognized as a whole and does not require word analysis for identification" (Harris & Hodges, 1981, p. 295). As children engage in reading, words become familiar as units. Most children, through reading and rereading books, build a sight vocabulary; that is, they are able to recognize a set of words immediately without analysis.

Some children, however, do not develop a sight vocabulary readily through repeated reading. How can you support the reading of such children? Helping children develop individual word banks significantly increases their sight vocabularies. These children should each build unique collections of words that are important to them (Ashton-Warner, 1963). High-frequency and function words may also be included in word banks if the children are ready for them. Writing and pronouncing the words in their collections strengthens the children's phoneme awareness and develops their abilities to segment familiar words into their phonemic components. Arranging their own words into phrases and sentences also helps them develop concept of word. The extent to which you will use word banks depends on the language development and sophistication of the children in your class.

Word banks can be used to help children learn vocabulary and develop print awareness skills, concept of word, and phonic generalizations based on familiar vocabulary. They can also be used for diagnostic purposes to determine (1) the level of the child's language development (vocabulary, sentence structure), (2) the child's concept of word, (3) the child's memory for sight vocabulary, and (4) the child's knowledge of phonics generalizations.

Procedure

Have children maintain personal banks containing the words they want to know how to read and the basic sight vocabulary that will help them create coherent sentences using those high-interest words. Word banks are useful with individuals or in a small-group format. This is not, however, an activity that can be done with a large group or an entire class.

When you begin word banks with your children, write a simple sentence like "I play with my _____" on a board or large piece of newsprint easily seen by everyone in the group. "I like to eat _____" or, simply, "I eat _____" is also a good sentence with which to start this activity. Ask the children to tell you what they play with, and as each child mentions a favorite toy, write it on an index card that will be kept in a small box or envelope for the child. Repeat the word as you hand it to the child who asked for it and ask the child to "read" it to you. Then have the child hold the word up to the end of the incomplete sentence and read the sentence with the new word in it. For example, if the word is "bike," you will write "bike" on the card and the child will hold it up to the end of the sentence and read, "I play with my bike."

Give each child the opportunity to read a new word in the unfinished sentence. Invite the other children in the group to read their friend's sentence too, or give them a second word on that first day that is also something they play with and let them draw pictures of the two words they have requested. If your group of children is very sophisticated, you might also use the "I like to eat" sentence and give them a food word to use in it. Give them ample opportunities to use their words in these two simple sentences. It's fun to let them make silly sentences like "I play with my pizza" or "I like to eat Legos." They quickly learn words as they entertain their friends and themselves.

The next time you meet, write the sentence beginnings you used on the board (or paper) again and let the children hold their words up and read the sentences they can make. If they know their own words (and they usually do), you can write all the words in the sentence on index cards and give them to the children. It is a good idea to color-code the words according to their part of speech: for example, all the nouns in blue, verbs in green, adjectives in red, and so forth. Don't tell children the names of the parts of speech at this early stage, but color coding helps them begin to develop an intuitive sense of the function each word fulfills in a sentence and allows you to refer to the words by categories (the naming words, the describing words, etc.). Ask them to construct the sentence they see on the board with their own words at the end. When they've put all the cards in order, let them take turns reading their sentences out loud. If their attention span holds out, you can give them the additional words they would need to construct and read the second sentence. (It is a good idea to have the children initial the backs of all their cards as they get them because the cards can easily get mixed up.)

Each time you meet with the group, review the words they have accumulated and ask them to make sentences. Eventually you will add other words they want to know how to read and words you would like them to be able to read. You might add color words or concentrate on basic sight vocabulary ("and," "have," "see," etc.). Give the children many opportunities to read aloud the sentences they make and their friends' sentences as well, perhaps by rotating around the table at which they are working.

Remember that this activity works because the children feel a great degree of success reading the sentences they are creating. To keep this activity successful, don't introduce too many new words at one session. The burden on the students' memories can easily become overwhelming. Each child's memory capacity is different, however, so there is no magic number of new words that can be introduced at one time. Be sensitive to the ease or difficulty each child is having reading the words and making sentences. It's okay to have days when no new words are introduced and you just have fun making sentences with the old words.

All kinds of worthwhile seat work can be generated using word banks. The children can, for example:

- Copy a sentence or two and make an illustration.
- Write a sentence for a friend to illustrate.
- Make lists of all the "green" words that have a certain vowel sound or begin with a certain consonant sound
- Work with a friend to find all the cards they have that are the same, and read to each other the cards that are different.
- Construct the longest sentence possible with their words.

You can:

- Write sentences using their words for them to illustrate.
- Tell them to draw pictures representing words you choose.

These activities represent some of the alternative ways in which you can extend the learning of children using word banks.

Learning from Experience

To illustrate the use of word banks, we present a lesson in Mary Johnson's kindergarten classroom. All of her children have their own word banks. The reading group with whom Mary is working is composed of boys. The group has participated in several word bank activities previously. During this lesson, Mary introduced the word *they* to add to their banks. As you read the lesson transcript, note the ways in which Mary supports the children in learning the word *they*.

Introduces new word	**Teacher:** This is the word *they*. [She shows a card with *they* printed on it.] Say it: "*they.*"
	Children: They.
	Teacher: What does it begin with?
	Children: th
	Teacher: And that stands for what sound?
	Children: [Most produce the *th* sound accurately, but there is some confusion over the *th* sound for the Spanish-speaking boy in the group.]
Clarifies and models target sound	**Teacher:** Fernando, put your tongue between your teeth. [She demonstrates this procedure.] *They* . . . There's a *they* for you and a *they* for you . . . [She hands each child a card with *they* printed on it.] Make a sentence with *they: They* went . . . *They* have . . . *They* play . . . You make a sentence with *they*.
	Jacob: They swim?
Encourages elaboration	**Teacher:** Sure! Where would *they* swim?
	James: At the Y.
	Jacob: At the pool.
	Teacher: At the Y, at the pool, at the lake . . .
	Jacob: At the swimming pool.
Focuses attention on category of words	**Teacher:** Everyone's going to need a green word after *they* because those are your action words. *They* . . . do something. So find an action word. Jacob found *swim* and Fernando used *play*. You [to Clifford] need to find an action word that you can use with *they*.
	Fernando: [looking at his stacks of words]: Where's *my*?
	Teacher: It's a red word. *My* starts with an /m-m-m/.
	James: Where's *with*?
	Clifford: Can I have *here*?
	Teacher: I don't want to give you any other new words because I really want you to learn the new word *they*.
Sets limits on lesson to ensure focus on target word	**Clifford:** I want to make "Here *they* are."
	Teacher: Try to make a sentence that has five words in it. That's the rule. [This is a guideline the teacher had established earlier in the year to encourage sentences with more content words that could be illustrated and remembered.]
	Clifford [to himself]: They go to . . . [to Ms. Johnson] Ms. Johnson, I need *school*.
Reinforces routine	**Teacher:** Let's see if there's another place they can go in here. [The teacher goes through his stack of nouns.] They can't go to He-Man, can they? They can't go to pizza, duck, football . . . [She comes to zoo.] How about zoo? They could go to the zoo! You would have to use your card too. [The teacher lets Clifford think about this possible sentence.]
	Teacher [to James]: Okay. Read your sentence.
	James: There are . . .
	Teacher: They are . . .

James: They are Ghostbusters having pizza.

Demon-strates inflectional endings

Teacher: James's sentence actually said, "They are Ghostbusters have pizza." [He had for-gotten to add a card with an *ing* on it to the root word *have.*] Having? Then you need to put *ing* on there [pointing at the word *have*]. [James adds *ing* to *have*.] They are Ghost-busters having pizza.

James: Mmm-mm yes.

Clarifies difference between "they" and "there"

Teacher [pointing at *they* and *are*]: It's not "there," you know. It's not "There are Ghost-busters having pizza." It's "They are . . . [The teacher waits for James to understand the difference between "They are" and "There are."] Why don't you make: "They are having pizza with Ghostbusters"?

Clifford [meanwhile]: I don't have the word *the.*

Encourages peer support

Teacher: You should look again. [Clifford has, indeed, misplaced his *the* card because all of the children had at least one.] Does anyone else have an extra *the*? [Some of the chil-dren have multiple copies of certain high-frequency words.]

James: I have two *the*'s.

Teacher: Why don't you let Clifford use one of your *the*'s and I'll make him one later. Let's read our sentences. Fernando, you read yours.

Fernando: [Fernando gets stuck when he attempts to read the new word *they*]

Teacher: That's your new word. What's your new word? Everyone, what's our new word?

Everyone: They.

Reinforces the natural language of the student

Fernando: They playing with my cars. [Fernando is a Spanish-speaking boy who is just learning how to speak English. This sentence represents the syntactical level at which he speaks. He would not use the word *are* before *playing* when he speaks, and the teacher doesn't expect him to use it in this activity with his word bank.]

Teacher: Very good! [Repeats his sentence.] "They playing with my cars." James, read your sentence.

Immediate feedback to misreading "there" for "they"

James: There . . .

Teacher: No.

James: They are having pizza with Ghostbusters.

Teacher: [Repeats James's sentence.] "They are having pizza with Ghostbusters." Clifford, read your sentence.

Clifford: They go to the zoo.

Teacher: Good. [Repeats Clifford's sentence.] "They go to the zoo." Jacob, read your sen-tence.

Jacob: They swim with Frankenstein.

Teacher: Good. [Repeats Jacob's sentence.] They swim with Frankenstein. Now everybody get up and change places.

Provides opportunity for students to generalize knowledge

Clifford: Change places?

Teacher: That's right! And read the sentence that's in front of you now. Jacob, read the first one. [The children take turns reading each other's sentences, reinforcing their knowl-edge of basic sight vocabulary, particularly the new word *they,* and being exposed to some high-interest vocabulary as well. At the end of the session, the children return to their own sentence, copy it, and draw a picture to illustrate it as independent seat work.]

Your Turn: Think about this lesson. What were the variety of ways in which Mary introduced the word *they?* Write your response in your journal under the heading Using Word Banks and then read our response.

Our Turn: Mary used a variety of ways to help her students learn the word *they*. She had them look at it printed on a card and note the sound that goes with the initial letters (th). She encouraged them to build sentences including the word *they,* had each child read the sentence he developed, and then had the group take turns reading each other's sentences. This activity shows how children can practice reading words already in their word banks as they become familiar with a new word. The lesson also models a productive group activity.

SUMMARY

In this chapter, we discussed the goals that you as a preschool or kindergarten teacher would likely have for your students. These will focus on the language development of children and their emergent literacy. In the area of literacy, you will help children to develop: (1) interest in reading and writing, (2) language facility and adequate prior knowledge, (3) an understanding of functions of print, (4) concept of word, (5) phoneme awareness, and (6) knowledge of alphabet names and the sounds the letters represent.

We discussed how you can prepare for the school year. Three areas received special focus: becoming familiar with instructional material (published programs as well as children's literature and other material), organizing the classroom, and creating an effective weekly schedule. We then described important activities that you will undertake during the beginning months of kindergarten. We focused on assessment procedures through which you can learn more about the knowledge of your students and ways to organize your students for instruction.

In the final sections of the chapter we introduced three generally useful instructional strategies and revisited three that are especially useful with reluctant readers. Kindergartners need to understand the basic connection between print and speech and, more specifically, between their own ideas and the printed words that represent them. This can be accomplished in many ways, but basically the young child needs to see his or her own words in print over and over again. One instructional procedure, LEA, allows children to see the relation between stories they tell and their written representation. Similarly, instruction involving Big Books also permits children to map the relation between speech and print while at the same time enjoying and responding to well-formed children's literature. Word study and invented spelling allow children to become aware of the phonemic composition of words in a natural fashion. Each of these activities is a useful means for you to achieve your objectives for the literacy learning and development of your preschool and kindergarten students.

At the kindergarten level, you may wish to provide more structured support for the learning of reluctant readers and writers. Activities that promote concept of word can be the path through which some children begin to make sense of the relations between spoken and written language. The word bank is a specific instructional strategy that encourages children to focus on words to form meaningful sentences and to study their letter-sound composition. Finally, some kindergartners need encouragement and specific instruction to help them master the letters of the alphabet and their associated sounds. As a teacher of young children, you use these activities and the stimulating print-rich classroom environment you have created to help children gain confidence as they learn to read and write.

In the Field

1. Visit a kindergarten classroom where children are encouraged to write. Get the teacher's permission to engage a few children quietly in discussions of their writing. Ask them to "read" what they have written. If they say they cannot read, ask them to "pretend read" it. Make notes on a separate paper about what they read and then compare it with what they wrote. How well formed were the stories and to what extent did the "reading" reflect oral versus written language patterns? If the writing contains some letters, to what extent do the letters correspond to the sounds of the words read? What does this evidence indicate about the reading development of the particular child? Summarize what you learned in a report or in your journal under the heading Kindergarten Writing and Reading.

2. Interview some preschool or kindergarten teachers concerning the decisions they make at the beginning of the school year: How do they determine the books they will read to their students and the materials they will have them read? The time schedule they will follow? The organization of their rooms? Once school begins, what do they do with children on the first day? On the second day? On the third day? How do they assess the knowledge that their students have about reading and writing? How do they organize (group) their students for instruction? Summarize what you learned in a report or in your journal under the heading Interview with Preschool (Kindergarten) Teachers.

3. Select one of the instructional strategies described in this chapter. Plan how you might use it with a small group of preschool or kindergarten children. Ask a teacher if you can try out the strategy. Reflect on your experience. Did the activity proceed as expected? What things went as anticipated? What were aspects that were puzzling or unexpected? Summarize what you learned in a report or in your journal under the heading Using an Instructional Strategy with Preschool (Kindergarten) Children.

Portfolio Suggestion

Select from your journal two examples of your responses to Pause and Reflect or Learning from Experience: Your Turn and include these in your portfolio. If you completed an In the Field activity, include your report from it in your portfolio as well. Write a brief evaluation of your work, commenting on what it shows about your learning.

For Further Reading

Coate, S., & Castle, M. (1989). Integrating LEA and invented spelling in kindergarten. *The Reading Teacher, 42,* 516–519.

Kupinsky, B. Z. (1983). Bilingual reading instruction in kindergarten. *The Reading Teacher, 37,* 132–137.

Martinez, M. (1993). Motivating dramatic story reenactments. *The Reading Teacher, 46,* 682–688.

Strickland, D. S., & Morrow, L. M. (1989a). An emergent literacy perspective. *The Reading Teacher, 42,* 722–723.

Strickland, D. S., & Morrow, L. M. (1989b). Young children's early reading and writing development. *The Reading Teacher, 42,* 426–427.

Teale, W. H. (1982). Toward a theory of how children learn to read and write naturally. *Language Arts, 59,* 555–570.

Developing Literacy in the Primary Grades

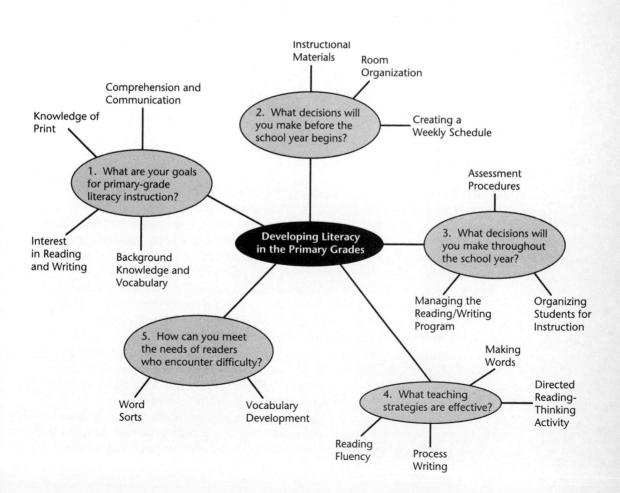

Instructional
Materials

Room
Organization

Comprehension and
Communication

Knowledge of
Print

2. What decisions will
you make before the
school year begins?

Creating a
Weekly Schedule

1. What are your goals
for primary-grade
literacy instruction?

Assessment
Procedures

Interest
in Reading
and Writing

Developing Literacy
in the Primary Grades

3. What decisions will
you make throughout
the school year?

Background
Knowledge and
Vocabulary

Managing the
Reading/Writing
Program

Organizing
Students for
Instruction

Making
Words

5. How can you meet
the needs of readers
who encounter difficulty?

Directed
Reading-
Thinking
Activity

Word
Sorts

Vocabulary
Development

4. What teaching
strategies are effective?

Reading
Fluency

Process
Writing

▼ CHAPTER GOALS FOR THE READER

To define goals that are appropriate for a primary-grade literacy program

To understand the decisions you will make before the school year begins

To understand the decisions you will make as the school year begins

To learn about instructional strategies appropriate for primary-grade students

To learn how to meet the needs of readers who encounter difficulty

▼ CHAPTER OVERVIEW

In this chapter we consider the decisions that primary-grade teachers make in developing effective reading programs. We begin the chapter by discussing important goals for literacy instruction in primary grades. We believe that goals are the cornerstone of a quality program. A balanced set of goals provides the framework within which you assess the knowledge of your students, evaluate instructional materials, organize students for instruction, and plan instructional activities.

In the second section, we consider decisions you will make before the school year begins: selecting appropriate materials, forming a workable schedule, and organizing your room. In the third section, we describe useful assessment procedures and how you may use information from assessment in organizing children for instruction and managing it. We follow these sections with the case study of a first-grade teacher, Marcy Lee, and the decisions she made. The fourth section on teaching strategies considers (1) Making Words, a word study approach, (2) DR-TA (Directed Reading-Thinking Activity), a strategy to develop comprehension and prior knowledge, (3) process writing, and (4) ways to develop reading fluency. Some children in your class may encounter particular difficulty with print. Thus, in the final section, we describe teaching approaches for vocabulary development and word sorts to guide their learning.

TAPPING PRIOR KNOWLEDGE TO SET A PURPOSE

Have you recently interacted with primary-grade children? What were they interested in doing? What are some of the differences you observed between children in the first and third grades? Did they talk about their experiences in school? Drawing on the chapter overview and your reflections about your experiences with young children, identify what it is that you most want to learn from reading this chapter. List these in your journal under the heading Chapter 13: Setting a Purpose.

WHAT ARE YOUR GOALS FOR PRIMARY-GRADE LITERACY INSTRUCTION?

As we discussed in chapters 1 and 2, learning to read is a complex process that occurs over several years. The essence of reading involves interacting with print to construct meaning. Yet the emphasis of reading instruction changes as children progress through the grades. When children first come to school, a major goal is to have them develop awareness of the nature and functions of printed messages. Some ways in which you can help children to achieve this goal were discussed in the prior chapter. The primary grades are a time when children need to develop a "sense of story" and become proficient with print through reading and writing. Typically, children who enter first grade differ in their knowledge about reading. Most are in the beginning stages of learning about print, but there will be some who are already fluent readers. During the primary grades, instruction should be designed to help you achieve four major goals: (1) develop children's knowledge of print, (2) promote comprehension and communication, (3) enhance the development of prior knowledge, and (4) develop interest in reading.

Knowledge of Print

Children in the primary grades make major changes in reading and writing. Many entering first grade are struggling to understand the nature of print and how it functions. With experience, they begin to see that print relates to speech and meaning in complex ways. Once they determine the match between printed and spoken words (concept of word), they are ready to develop more systematic knowledge about the nature of words and letters through their reading and writing experiences and through more formal instruction. A rich literacy environment in which children read and write and are given the instructional support they need leads to spectacular growth in literacy.

By second grade, some children have already become fluent readers and writers; others are on the brink of consolidating the knowledge and strategies they have learned for dealing with print. Children are comfortable reading longer and reading less predictable selections, and they are beginning to be comfortable reading selections silently. Some children in the class have become prolific readers; others are more hesitant, preferring alternative leisure activities. They are writing longer stories and messages that are better structured. Their spelling for the most part reflects traditional spelling patterns. It is as if many are now beginning to internalize their knowledge about English spelling.

Exceptions to this trend are children who experience special difficulties with print and those who do not speak English as a first language. Both of these groups require special support in second grade. Children who experience difficulty learning about the nature of print often need additional instructional support to help them to learn about the patterns of English. This can be done through such activities as shared writing, spelling, and the Benchmark Word Identification Program (see chapter 3). Those who are learning English as a second language will profit from activities to develop their English vocabulary (see chapter 4) and their general language facility (see chapter 12).

Third graders are in a transitional phase. Compared to first graders, they are extremely competent and independent in their reading and writing. But compared to fourth graders, they are still in the process of learning self-monitoring strategies that will let them function well independently. They are learning to work well with peer groups with relatively little teacher supervision. They want their writing to please an audience, and they are responsive to editorial guidance. A system of peer editors that requires much teacher support at second grade, will work with less supervision at third grade. Children, through their wide reading, will for the most part have become fluent readers.

This brief discussion shows that although you may have a general goal of helping children to improve their reading and writing, the focus of this goal changes during the primary grades. During first grade, considerable attention is directed toward helping children understand the nature of print. After basic understandings are established, reading and writing for a variety of purposes serves to consolidate and extend this skill into fluent performance.

Controversial Issue

Beginning reading instruction periodically becomes the focus of intense controversy. The old debate between meaning versus code methods of teaching reading (Chall, 1967/1983a) has become recast in more sophisticated terms through the development of theoretical perspectives and supporting evidence.

On the one hand, increased understanding of reading as a communicative language act provides the theoretical rationale for integrating reading, writing, and other language arts and for viewing the emergence of literacy in developmental terms. Holdaway (1979), Strickland and Morrow (1989), Teale and Sulzby (1986), and Sulzby and Teale (1991), among others, believe that children become skilled readers by interacting with printed messages that allow them to respond to cues from varied sources simultaneously (print, their memory for stories, pictures, context). They view literacy as emerging from the early experiences of being read to and seeing print function in the environment; they do not believe that prerequisite skills should be taught. Instead, all children, particularly those with limited literacy experience, should begin reading and writing in ways that are personal and generally meaningful to them (Goodman, 1986; Wells, 1985).

On the other hand, sustained research by cognitive psychologists reveals the importance of phoneme awareness as children learn to read. Adams (1990), in her book *Beginning to Read,* provides evidence showing that what we think we do as skillful readers is not necessarily what we do. We do not sample textual evidence in a manner informed by our expectations, nor do we see words as wholes, but rather we perceive individual letters in the form of spelling patterns.

This evidence and the model of skilled reading it supports sharply conflict with models that propose selective sampling of print by good readers. A major rationale of some "meaning-based" approaches to reading has been that children *do not need* to read words accurately as long as they obtain the author's meaning, because that is how proficient adults read. Teachers consequently believe that it is not necessary to help children develop knowledge of spelling-sound patterns and that it is not useful to encourage accurate reading of print. The evidence summarized by Adams on skilled reading disputes this rationale for not teaching children about spelling-sound relations.

Based on the research evidence, we believe that children must learn to link spelling patterns with the sounds and meanings of words as they learn to read. We are not convinced, however, that these understandings need to be induced *early* through direct instruction (e.g., Bradley & Bryant, 1983; Lundberg et al., 1988; Tunmer, Herriman, & Nesdale, 1988). Instead, we believe the appropriate time to focus on phoneme awareness is when children are learning to write, usually in kindergarten, but certainly in first grade. Through such activities as shared writing, word sorts, Making Words, and invented spelling, children learn to listen for the sounds of words in natural ways (e.g., Clay, 1975; Morris, 1988). In other words, we argue that reading and writing alone may not be sufficient for some children to become familiar with the spelling patterns of English. Instead, they need to be engaged in supervised tasks in which they learn through focused instruction to hear the sounds in words and to think about the sounds that go with letters.

Comprehension and Communication

When children are in the beginning stages of learning to read, they are often most comfortable reading aloud (Goodman, 1976). It is as if hearing as well as seeing the messages reinforces their comprehension. You may also find that their reading aloud provides a window into how well they are able to cope with the print, and this enables you to determine when they need support. Yet you must also have as one of your goals the development of silent reading comprehension. This can be encouraged in first grade by having your students reread stories silently that they have previously read aloud or have heard you read aloud many times.

By second grade, most children have acquired a sight vocabulary, have developed print-identification strategies, and are becoming fluent readers. At this point, you should encourage and provide support for them to read sections of a selection silently. Moreover, they should be able to read some stories silently without your instructional support. As children achieve fluency, they are able to direct their undivided attention to comprehension of the meaning conveyed in selections. Activities such as Reading Workshop that became common in the second part of first grade should become a mainstay in second and third grade. Moreover, children in these grades, particularly third grade, become sufficiently independent to function well in Book Clubs (Raphael & McMahon, 1994). Reading informational text becomes more common at this level; thus discussion will focus more on conceptual development and interpretation.

In all primary grades, when children read, they should be given opportunities to discuss sections of stories or articles that they found to be particularly interesting or challenging. They should compare with others what they believe to be the themes of stories. Such discussions should occur when you are reading books aloud to the class as well as when students read themselves.

Parallel developments occur in writing. In first grade, children are preoccupied with getting the words down. As they become comfortable writing, they become more able to focus on the message and its structure. By third grade, children desire to see their writing communicate what they intend it to and to be in good form. Because of this, third grade is a good time to focus on the editorial process and to establish a peer-review support system.

Although your general goal for comprehension and communication will stay the same from grade to grade, its implementation will take different forms depending on what students are able to do in reading and writing. Yet, at the same time, and particularly with your students who have special needs, it is important to make sure that *all* your students participate in dialogue that is rich in substance. This can occur through the discussions that accompany selections that you read aloud to your class and through literacy groups that are heterogeneous in composition.

Background Knowledge and Vocabulary

In all primary grades, you need to ask yourself if the literary diet that you prepare for your students will expand their background (or prior) knowledge. Will they encounter new concepts that will enrich their thinking? As we learned in chapter 4, the development of background knowledge is closely related to the development of reading comprehension. As children acquire knowledge about people, concepts, and situations, they increase their power to understand events described in stories and information books. Indeed, once children have developed fluency with print, prior knowledge is a main predictor of their reading comprehension. And yet, because of the low conceptual complexity of many primary-grade reading materials and the frequent neglect of instruction in social studies and science, the vocabulary and prior knowledge of children are often not developed during this period of schooling. Accordingly, children who come to school with extensive prior knowledge do well in intermediate-grade comprehension while those entering school with limited experiences do less well.

Because of the importance of background knowledge, you must take an active role in developing prior knowledge during the primary years, so that your students with more limited background knowledge will not show declining comprehension during the intermediate grades (Blachowicz & Fisher, 1996). One way to enrich the background knowledge of your students is through "directed listening-thinking activities," in which children make predictions and reason and become deeply engaged with characters and story themes that are written at levels often too complex for these young children to read independently. These listening-thinking activities lay the basis for interpretive reading comprehension strategies that are characteristic of mature readers.

Interest in Reading and Writing

Children come to school curious about a variety of things and with many emerging interests. What our goal should be is to build on these areas of interest. Reading and writing activities provide opportunities for children to pursue their questions, develop their knowledge, and expand their interests. The *content* of reading and writing can intrigue and capture the interests of children. Particularly in the primary grades, it is important that the pleasures to be gained through reading and writing are not sacrificed through preoccupation with print. A primary teacher who emphasizes decoding and, in the process, destroys children's intrigue with the stories has failed. Children become good readers by reading. Those who read extensively expand their prior knowledge, form flexible reading strategies, and develop new interests.

How can you provide for students who are interested in reading? We suggest three main ways. First, develop a class library that contains trade books of various genres, magazines, and the writings of children in the class. Research suggests that young children may be more interested in reading information books than narratives (Pappas, 1993). Children should be able to select materials for reading at home and at school, and time should be provided in school for such reading. Second, read aloud to children every day and discuss the selections, not only to increase their pleasure but also to enhance their knowledge and interpretive strategies. Carefully select books to be read aloud, both for their substantive interest and their literary value. Finally, encourage children to read books at home. Help them find books they enjoy, either in the class or the school library, and acknowledge their home reading in some way.

In sum, your goals will include developing knowledge of print, comprehension and writing strategies, background knowledge and vocabulary, and interest in reading and writing. Although these goals are appropriate for most children entering the primary grades, some who begin first grade with less well developed literacy skills may need to receive a somewhat different type of instruction. Often, they cannot recognize letters of the alphabet, have little sense of how stories are organized, and/or have not developed a concept of printed words. Since they have had so little experience with print, it is particularly important that their literacy program include Language Experience Stories, being read to, and exploratory writing. The literacy program you develop for them will look very much like the programs described in chapter 12 for preschool and kindergarten children.

WHAT DECISIONS WILL YOU MAKE BEFORE THE SCHOOL YEAR BEGINS?

Instructional Materials

You need to create an environment that invites children to read and write, one in which they can't resist being drawn into looking at books and writing. Before school begins, look over the books that you have in your classroom library. You will want to include some books that children learned to love in preceding grades and some favorite old folktales such as *The Gingerbread Boy, The Tale of Peter Rabbit, Jack and the Beanstalk, Cinderella,* and *Rumpelstiltskin.*

What other books might you select for your class library? If they are going to learn to love reading, students need a variety of opportunities to become engaged with good children's literature. Some of the books suggested in chapter 12 for kindergarten are appropriate. Children love to read and to hear read the Frog and Toad books by Arnold Lobel, books by Don Freeman such as *Corduroy* and *A Pocket for Corduroy,* books by Ezra Jack Keats such as *Peter's Chair* and *Whistle for Willie,* books by Judith Viorst such as *Alexander and the Terrible, Horrible, No Good, Very Bad Day,* and those by Bernard Waber such as *Ira Sleeps Over.*

A variety of literature from such publishers as Rigby and the Wright Group should be secured and placed into open boxes on the basis of level. (See the appendix for a list of books for beginning readers.) Books such as *Brown Bear, Brown Bear, What Do You See?* by Bill Martin are classified as predictable pattern books. These books are easy for children to read because they use familiar vocabulary, common language patterns, repetitions of those patterns, and illustrations that closely portray the meaning and language of the story (Levels 1–4).

Books such as *Where's Spot?* by Eric Hill (Level 8), the *Very Busy Spider* by Eric Carle (Level 14), and *Frog and Toad Are Friends* by Arnold Lobel (Level 19) include more complex concepts and vocabulary and provide less support in the form of repeating sentences and picture cues. The most advanced levels feature sequences of episodes that extend over several pages and the language is literary in style. You will want to select from a variety of levels that match the reading proficiency of your students.

Select a variety of Big Books that can be shared with groups of students or with the whole class. There are two reasons for selecting Big Books. The easier-to-read ones are for the children to read. The more difficult ones are for enjoyment and listening comprehension. Some of these such as *Brown Bear, Brown Bear, What Do You See?* by Bill Martin and *Chicken Soup with Rice* by Maurice Sendak also have regular-size counterparts. Both the Big Books and their smaller counterparts are often included in commercial literacy programs. After children have participated in reading the Big Books, they can then reread the same stories to encourage independent reading. Other Big Books from such publishers as Rigby (for example, Gail Jorgensen's *Guess Who's Coming for Dinner* and *On a Dark and Scary Night*) and from The Wright Group (for example, Mary Rees's *Ten in a Bed* and Joy Cowley's *If You Meet a Dragon* and *Hairy Bear*) and *Polar Bear, Polar Bear, What Do You Hear?* by Bill Martin are wonderful for enjoyment and developing listening comprehension. If the little books corresponding to the Big Books are not available, children also love reading the Big Books, either by placing them on the floor or on a stand.

Don't forget to include collections of poems that appeal to children, such as those by Shel Silverstein, John Ciardi, Harry Behn, and Jack Prelutsky. These are excellent sources of poems children love to hear, repeat, and begin to read. Also, favorite poems can be put on charts, illustrated by the children, and added to the class library.

Some books included in your library should anticipate thematic units you plan to develop during the school year. Units that draw on understandings from science, social studies, and literature can revolve around such themes as work, neighbors, and growing. Alternatively, you may build an integrated unit around a book that you enjoy reading with your children. Whatever thematic units you have selected to pursue,

Why is it important to have a wealth of children's literature in your classroom?

begin thinking about what children's books may be relevant. In the second and third grades, you will build your collections partly in response to the interests of your students. Librarians and reading specialists can be a wonderful resource in identifying appropriate titles.

Primary-grade classrooms should have an abundant supply of paper. As in kindergarten classes, children enjoy drawing and writing on various sizes, colors, textures, and shapes of paper. At this level, they enjoy writing their own books and having them illustrated. In chapter 11, Tina Moore described how her kindergarten and first-grade students, once they had written a story, would contract with another student to have it illustrated. Children's writing—Language Experience Stories and Big Books—provides another source of books for your library. The authors and other children particularly enjoy reading these books.

Finally, the set of materials you have for your children to read may be enhanced by a published literature-based program. The extent to which this program is the mainstay of the reading program or simply a source of additional stories (an anthology) will depend on your beliefs and experiences, school and district policies, as well as the needs of your students. The process of establishing and maintaining your own literacy program is complex. Read again the comments made by Rosemary Lane in chapter 11 concerning her individual literature-based program. For Rosemary, the published program became another source of stories for children to read. The sequences of activities within her program emerged from her interaction with specific children and groups of children.

If you are a relatively new teacher, you may wish to develop a program that relies closely on the published program selected by your district. The stories in the program are sequenced in terms of complexity, although the initial stories may be less supportive for beginning readers than the literature described earlier. You may also want to use the published reading program as a source of ideas for teaching word identification and comprehension. Again, both the stories and suggested activities should be used selectively, depending on the needs and level of your students.

Later in this chapter, you will read the case of Marcy Lee, who is entering her second year of teaching first grade. Although she follows the sequence of stories in the published program, she has modified the beginning part of the program to focus exclusively on language experience activities and reading from Big Books and little books. She uses the teaching strategies from the published literacy program selectively and has incorporated many additional activities. For example, she developed several thematic units involving the reading of trade books. Writing is also an integral part of her program. Although she uses the published program, she is well on her way to developing her own literacy program.

In summary, a variety of materials can be used to create an environment in which children love to read and write: children's literature, Big Books, predictable books, paper for publishing students' writing, and published literacy programs. The materials and activities in published programs should be used selectively. It is important for you to read through the teacher's manual critically to determine what meets the instructional goals you have for your children.

Room Organization

Students in the primary grades learn by being able to explore things, particularly in the areas of science and mathematics. They also learn through reading and writing and by listening and talking about their ideas. Your room should be organized so that the children can meet and discuss ideas with their peers; yet they also need to be able to move about freely and to have places to work without interruption. You are creating an environment where children can discover new ideas and pursue them to learn more about themselves and their world. The walls of your classroom represent an opportunity. You will want to change your displays frequently to reflect the season, current interests, thematic units in social studies and science, and favorite authors. At the first- and perhaps second-grade level, you will also want to have some bulletin boards that aid students' writing, through such displays as *Word Walls,* where words selected by you or students are displayed alphabetically. Words, about five per week, may be chosen because they are sight words, patterned words, words frequently misspelled, and the like. These words can then become part of word study activities (Cunningham & Allington, 1994).

The organization of your room in first grade will support the emerging knowledge of children about books. In order to provide appropriate support for children's developing knowledge of print, you may need to set aside an area of your room for small-group work. While you are working with some children, others may be undertaking activities in activity areas that focus on math concepts and thematic units. You will need to have space for children to work as partners as they pursue reading and writing activities.

As children progress into second and third grade, they become much more independent in their work. Not only will they spend more time reading and writing independently, but they also will form peer groups to read and discuss selections. Often desks are clustered to form peer working groups. These groups may form Book Clubs, or they may work on thematic research projects.

Particularly at the third-grade level, children will show increased interest in editing their writing and in receiving peer support for the editorial process. Having a computer in the classroom is essential so that children can write and then easily edit their writing. Having a class library continues to be important, although students will increasingly rely on the school library and resource centers. Students need quiet areas in which they can read, perhaps in a loft or an alcove.

Pause and Reflect

Take a blank piece of paper and plan the room organization for a third-grade classroom. Assume that there are 20 students in this third-grade class and that all are reading fluently and interested in writing. How will you organize the desks of these students? What special areas might you wish to have in the room? Assume that you have space for either three activity areas or for two areas and a larger space for all students to sit on the floor. What would you choose to use these areas for? What materials will you provide in each area? Include your third-grade plan and your responses to these questions in your journal under the heading Third-Grade Room Plan. Please comment on how your plan for a third-grade room differs from the plan you made for a kindergarten classroom in chapter 12.

This is a difficult task unless you know the size of the classroom and its layout. Yet what it encourages you to do is to think about the aspects of third-grade work to which you might give priority. Composing five clusters of four desks might be a useful arrangement for independent work (Reading Workshop and Writing Workshop) as well as the peer-group work of Book Clubs and thematic unit work groups.

What were some special areas that you represented in your drawing? Did you include a class library where the children can comfortably look at a book or share it with a friend? You may wish to equip this area with a rug and some pillows, or a table with chairs. In some classrooms, teachers have had a loft built. The library is kept in the space under the loft, and children who wish some privacy climb up to the carpeted loft to read.

Did you include an area where your children can share their writing and edit it? You might have included a computer and printer so that children can more easily edit and publish what they write. Having an area in which students can work independently on their various writing projects, including those for science, social studies, and integrated units, is extremely important.

Creating a Weekly Schedule

You will want to plan your weekly schedule so that it includes large blocks of uninterrupted time each day for reading and writing activities. The schedule may also establish a form of flexible grouping that combines large-group lessons with small-group follow-up similar to the system developed by Wiggins (1994) and his colleagues in third-grade classrooms (see chapter 11, page 422). Your schedule will also need to consider periods for such activities as library work and physical education, when your students will be out of the classroom.

The weekly schedule should be considered in relation to the goals you have for your students. They should hear stories, write, and participate in several kinds of reading activities each day. Most children who are puzzling over the way speech is represented by print need periods of sufficient duration and frequency to develop into proficient and enthusiastic readers and writers.

Pause and Reflect

Look at the sample schedules shown in chapter 11 (Figure 11.4 and Figure 11.5). Which to you seems most appropriate for first graders? Which for third graders? Consider these schedules in terms of how much time children will have for reading and writing. Are the blocks of time for reading and language arts sufficient? Is there enough time for writing? When would you have time to meet individually and in small groups with children who need more support? Many children, particularly those at the first-grade level, will need instructional time on a daily basis. This may be accommodated only by teaching them in small instructional groups. Is there time for reading a story aloud to children at least once and sometimes twice a day? Write your responses to these questions in your journal under the heading Evaluation of Schedules.

Activities during the language arts period may change from day to day. You may schedule Reading or Writing Workshop one or several times a week; you may have a sequence of activities that focuses on a story being read over the course of a week. Many activities will be undertaken as a group or by children working individually or with one or several other children. In the first grade, however, you will probably reserve some time each day to work with small groups on reading and spelling. This may also be true for selected groups of children in second grade. Generally, children will grow familiar with the pattern of activities that you have selected to follow during your language arts periods each week.

A major difference exists between the beginning of first grade and the other primary grades. Considerably more time must be spent on establishing classroom routines for accomplishing work and for transitions at the beginning of first grade, since children are not yet familiar with many of them. Older children are familiar with work routines and are used to working independently. The major similarity is that all children need to read and write every day in order to become confident students.

WHAT DECISIONS WILL YOU MAKE THROUGHOUT THE SCHOOL YEAR?

You will learn a great deal about your students during the first weeks of school. In this section, we think more deeply about how you can assess the needs of your students. We also consider ways in which you can organize your students for literacy instruction.

Assessment Procedures

Assessment takes place during the school year on an ongoing basis. Through both formal and informal activities, you will become familiar with how well your students are reading and writing and whether they are enjoying it (see chapter 10 for a more detailed discussion of assessment). Through informal observation you will note signs of student interest in reading and writing. You will ask some of the following questions: Do your students choose to write and what do they write? Do they listen attentively as you read stories aloud to the class? Do they ever pick up a book on their own and look through it? Do they have favorite types of books? If you are able to answer most of these questions for most of your students, you have already achieved considerable understanding of their reading and writing.

How can you assess the vocabulary and background knowledge of your students? During individual conferences and informal conversations, note their language development. Are they able to express themselves clearly? Do they understand what you are saying to them or asking them? How complex are the words and sentences that they use to express their ideas? What kinds of questions do they ask? Are they able to make inferences and develop logical conclusions?

When you ask students to write something, which students write with ease? Which cannot yet form letters? Which students are very dependent on you for support during their writing? Which are able to spell using invented spellings? Are their spellings logical and easy to discern?

More formal assessment can provide more systematic evidence. You may wish to administer a spelling task, such as that developed by Morris and Perney (1984), to see how children write words that are not familiar in printed form (see chapter 10). This will provide a great deal of information about the phoneme awareness, phonics knowledge, and conventional spelling knowledge of your students. You may use the results from this test in forming word study groups composed of children who are similar in their knowledge of print.

You may also ask children to read a section of a story aloud in order to assess the quality of their reading strategies and their sight vocabulary, and to further assess their knowledge of print. Methods for recording oral reading were described in detail in chapter 10.

Keep in mind that you do not want to overwhelm children with assessment situations in the beginning days of school, since they are adjusting to a new class and teacher. Much information can be obtained from careful observation during the instructional activities planned for the first few weeks of school. When you and your first-grade class, for example, develop a Language Experience Story, who can point to words you ask them to find? Who indicates the development of concept of word by being able to point to individual words as they are read? You may wish to develop a chart with names of students down the side and concepts about print across the top to be able to check off what each child knows and to remember who knows what.

The information you gain from informal and formal assessment should help you plan instruction that is responsive to the needs of the children. For some children in the beginning stages of reading, you will have to plan many activities that will familiarize them with books and help them develop the ability to discriminate beginning sounds. Others may be reading already and you will give them a variety of opportunities to read and write. Children begin each school year with a variety of strengths and weaknesses. Your goal as their teacher is to develop instruction that lets each child grow in confidence and proficiency.

Organizing Students for Instruction

Many preschool and kindergarten teachers like to teach the whole group at once (assuming the class size is around 25), because the children support each other and often act as models for each other as some develop skills more quickly than others. Teaching to the whole group is usually seen as more time-efficient, although instruction is rarely individualized and the chance of missing a child who is having significant difficulties is greater than in a small-group instructional format.

First-grade teachers often divide their students into instructional groups depending on their assessments during the first few weeks of school. These groups should be flexible; children should move in and out of them on a regular basis. The goal is to maximize the instructional benefits for each child. Some children need extra time developing certain strategies while others experiencing growth spurts will no longer need to come to a special teacher-led support group.

In second and third grades, most reading and writing activities may occur for the class as a whole, within peer groups, or with children working individually or with partners. In addition, using the information from their observations, teachers may form an instructional group that is flexible in membership for children encountering reading difficulties. This group may need to meet on a regular basis. Other instructional groups will be formed as children display special needs. For example, a group may be formed for children who are interested in editing and publishing their stories. One may be created for children who encounter difficulty reading multisyllabic words. Another may be organized for children interested in reading science fiction or for those who are reading far above the level of their classroom peers

Managing the Reading/Writing Program

Children in the primary grades, can be clustered together according to their needs. Some children in kindergarten and first grade, for example, may have had very little exposure to oral communication. They may have some difficulty expressing themselves in complete sentences, and their vocabularies may seem somewhat underdeveloped. These children need many opportunities for oral language development. You may wish to develop small-group activities to encourage them to share their experiences, retell stories that have been read in class, write Language Experience Stories about them, and play games requiring verbal responses such as 20 Questions and I Spy. Show and Tell is a useful activity if you model and set expectations for student contributions. For example, to foster descriptions, you may guide a child to "tell about what you have and where you got it," or to encourage sequencing, ask the student to "tell how it works." A significant part of the instructional program will be devoted to building the concepts of children, expanding their vocabularies, and increasing their prior knowledge by engaging them in many hands-on experiences. These children will enjoy hearing predictable books, stories that rhyme, and books that are playful with language. They will also benefit from rereading their own Language Experience Activity (LEA) stories.

Some children with good language facility may not know the alphabet or the sounds of the letters; they may have no concept of word. Other children will come to your class with more knowledge about sounds and letters, some sight vocabulary, and some rudimentary knowledge about the relationship between speech and print. Both of these groups of children, as in the case of those with more limited language development, will benefit from creating and reading Language Experience Stories. Rhyming stories and predictable Big Books are also good to use with this group, since they will "catch on" quickly as you finger-point while reading these materials out loud.

Yet another group of children may be independent readers and writers. They already know what they like to read and will read whenever given the opportunity.

The challenge for you is to organize a set of reading and writing activities for this diverse collection of children. As discussed in chapter 11, the traditional instructional solution has been to form three groups and to plan activities for each. As we learned from the interview with Tina Moore in chapter 11, she prefers to use this form of grouping for her first graders.

Other first-grade teachers and many teachers of second and third graders prefer a more flexible arrangement in which all members of a class participate in the same activities: shared writing, Writing Workshop, and Reading Workshop. This permits children with more limited experience in reading and writing to work and interact with those with more experience. If you follow this way of organizing your class, you will also need to have conferences with children on a weekly basis to learn about their discoveries and to monitor their progress. You will also need to plan teacher-led small-group instruction for a cross section of children, including those needing special instruction for language development. Particularly for first graders but also for second and third graders who encounter difficulty with print, you will develop special word study, spelling, reading, and writing activities to further their understanding of the nature of print. You may gather a small group to focus on learning new vocabulary—those who need support in this area as well as enthusiastic learners. Minilessons growing out of total-class activities can focus on an area of special need or interest, such as thinking about the characteristics of a particular literary genre or learning about the editing process.

Some teachers prefer to teach children individually. Problems that arise in class when the children read and write their own stories allow you to seize the teachable moment when a child's need to know is strong. Skills and strategies needed to become fluent readers are developed as children realize a discrepancy between what they know and can do and what they want to know and do. Yet the reality of being 1 teacher with 20 to 30 children means that there will be limited time for this form of one-to-one instruction.

Most teachers develop a combination of organizational formats. For example, in first grade, whole-group instruction may work best in the beginning of the year when instruction focuses on reading Big Books, creating Language Experience Stories based on whole-class activities, learning, reciting, and trying to read nursery rhymes and encouraging beginning writing skill. After a month or two, when you have had opportunities to assess each child's knowledge of sounds and letters, concept of word, sight vocabulary, attention span, and interests, small-group work along with total-class activities may seem feasible and beneficial. In second and third grade, more of your activities such as Book Clubs, Reading Workshop, and Writing Workshop may involve students working with peers or independently. It is always a good idea to keep the schedule flexible enough to allow spontaneous interaction on a regular basis with individual children in your class.

Many teachers move to a more individualized program that is primarily child-centered from one that is mainly teacher-directed as they gain teaching experience. Once you have internalized expectations for students based on realistic appraisals of their developmental needs and levels, you will notice subtle signs of potential growth and frustration and adjust the curriculum to the needs of individual children.

In the following section, we describe the case of Marcy Lee, who is in her second year of teaching a first-grade class in a town near a large city. In addition to speaking English, two children in her class speak Spanish as a first language, and one speaks Vietnamese. Many of her students are enthusiastic readers and writers. Some, however, seem to need more systematic instructional support to develop knowledge about print. Marcy is required to use the reading program selected by her district.

Learning from Experience

As you read this case study, notice the major decisions that Marcy makes as she forms the reading and writing instruction for her students. Are there any areas in which you agree or disagree with her decision making? How might you have done it differently and why?

As you read, identify what you believe were three particularly significant decisions. Write your responses in your journal.

 THE DECISIONS MARCY MADE BEFORE THE SCHOOL YEAR BEGAN

During August, Marcy reexamined her copy of the reading and language arts curriculum and the first-grade literature-based program she had used the previous year. She had already gathered a set of books for her class library. Her principal had told her when out-of-class activities would be scheduled each week. Using this information, she began planning how she would organize instructional activities each day. She spent a lot of time in her room, determining how she would cluster the desks, where her own desk would be, what board displays were needed, and where she would meet with small groups of children for reading and writing instruction. Although she made other decisions as well, we will focus here on those she made about reading materials, time scheduling, and room organization.

Reading Materials. As a result of her use of the literacy program the previous year, Marcy had become aware that she needed to expand her classroom library. She spent several days in June and July visiting a children's library in a university near her home. Each day she read and filled note cards on the books she read. After reading many sources, she made a list of books to order for her class library. The principal had given her a budget for this purpose.

She was particularly interested in obtaining predictable books that she could organize into levels according to difficulty. The year before she had discovered that sets of Big Books and accompanying little books were available in the school library to be checked out on a weekly basis. She wanted to purchase some of these books to have available for rereading in her class. From her previous year's experience, she knew that she particularly needed books that ranged in difficulty from Level 1 to Level 8 (see the appendix).

In developing the list of books for the class library, Marcy discussed her choices with the school librarian and with the other first-grade teacher. She found that some of the books on her list could be borrowed from the school library for a month at a time; in addition, she found that the nearby public library was willing to loan books to teachers. In the end, she decided to purchase some books that duplicated those in the school and public library because she believed they were books that the children would like to read and reread. She purchased others that were not available in the school library and decided to subscribe to two magazines.

The previous year Marcy had been overwhelmed when she first looked over the published program because there were so many parts to it. This year these parts were familiar, and she began to reconsider the teacher's guide and the pupil's reading books and practice materials. Last year none of her students had completed the reading program. She looked over the materials to see how she could have most children complete the program during the school year. Marcy knew that some students who were already in the beginning stages of reading and writing would not need the units for emergent readers that were included; moreover, she anticipated that they would sail through the beginning stories.

For other children last year, these emergent literacy activities had been insufficient. Marcy decided to develop her own program for all children and others in her class based on LEAs, predictable books, and Big Books during the first months of school. She also planned to have them, along with other class members, participate in shared writing and word study activities. On the first day of the week, for example, she might develop a shared writing experience to read with students. On the second day, she might have children work with partners to finger-point-read the story the class had written. On the third day, children might shift to a new set of literacy activities such as listening to her read a Big Book aloud; Marcy might then work with small groups as they reread the story. On the fourth day, the class might focus on word study, taking words from the shared writing story and the Big Book, along with previously learned words. Word building and word sort activities may be used to focus on initial consonants or endings. On the final day of the week, she might plan to have her children participate in Reading Workshop and Writing Workshop.

After this initial set of activities, Marcy planned to incorporate stories from her reading program into her ongoing set of reading and writing activities. She planned to use activities from the program that were suitable to reinforce phoneme awareness, the learning of letter-sound activities, and vocabulary development. In addition, last year she had found that children enjoyed some of the activities presented under the headings of Whole Language Activities, Extending Thinking Skills, and Enriching Understanding in the published program; she decided to use some of them.

Time Schedule. The daily schedule was fairly straightforward: Children entered the building at 8:30, left for lunch at 11:30, returned from lunch at 12:30, and were dismissed at 3:00. Marcy learned from the principal that her pupils were scheduled for library on Wednesday from 1:45 to 2:30 and for physical education on Friday during the same time period. She was delighted that she would have the "prime time" each morning to work with her students on reading and writing.

Pause and Reflect

Imagine that you are Marcy Lee. Get a blank piece of paper and fill in the days of the week and the hours available to Marcy for instruction. How would you schedule activities during each day? After you complete your schedule, compare it with the one developed by Marcy. Include the schedule and your comments in your journal under the heading Schedule for Marcy Lee's Class.

Marcy decided to begin each day with 15 minutes devoted to talking about the day, selecting children for jobs, and writing a story about past or anticipated events. She scheduled reading and language arts for the mornings. Language arts would begin with total-class writing instruction. During the first months of school, she would then have all children participate in shared writing, reading predictable books, and reading Big Books and accompanying little books. Later on, they would also read stories and other selections from the literature-based program, in addition to those from the class library. Because of extreme differences among the children in knowledge of print, she organized flexible groups in which she introduced children to predictable books and focused on word study and spelling.

Marcy decided to follow a weekly sequence for reading and writing activities related to stories from the reading program:

Monday: Reading aloud, vocabulary, word study and writing activities related to a story from the program, and spelling activities related to children's developmental level in spelling.

Tuesday: Reading and discussing a story from the program or the class library; assigning activities for study of spelling words.

Wednesday: Rereading of the Tuesday selection or other stories independently or with a partner; focus on word study and spelling activities.

Thursday: Discussion of the selection and writing or dramatizing activities based on the story; writing spelling words.

Friday: Independent reading and writing through Reading Workshop and Writing Workshop.

Marcy planned to begin the afternoon with a half hour of math, followed by a half hour of work time in which students could do math problems, independent reading, or other self-selected activities while she worked again with students who were experiencing reading and writing difficulties and/or who needed support for their oral language development. For the next hour on Mondays, Tuesdays, and Thursdays, she planned to focus on science, social studies, art, music, and health as integrated units, with as much reading and writing as possible. The final half hour of the day would be used for reading poetry and short stories aloud. Figure 13.1 (p. 494) shows Marcy's tentative schedule.

Room Organization. Twenty-six children were assigned to Marcy's class. She wished she had more space for activity centers, but the classroom was large enough only for a library/listening center in one corner and a small-group instructional area in another. She bought a rug and some pillows for the quiet library area. The room already had two bookshelves and a small table she would use there as well. She placed her computer and printer on a nearby desk. She had a loft built so that children who wanted a quiet place to read could escape.

She had few chairs in addition to those used at children's desks. Since she didn't want children to have to bring their own chairs to reading group, she requested and received a half dozen more chairs for the small-group instructional area. Blackboards were already in place, and she requested an easel for Language Experience Stories. She arranged the children's desks in clusters and decided that, at least at first, she would let children select their own seats. Later, she would rearrange them.

The classroom had three large bulletin boards. Marcy decided to use the one near the library corner for children's writing and a Word Wall and one for science and social studies displays. She decided to let the children help her decide how to use the third. She created labels for many of the objects and areas in the room—doors, windows, library, reading circle, and so on.

Marcy thought about traffic patterns and walked through the room to make sure no passageways were too tight. She put her own desk near the door and the cloakroom storage area, since she rarely used it during class time. See Figure 13.2 (p. 495) for a diagram of Marcy's room.

Time	Monday	Tuesday	Wednesday	Thursday	Friday
8:30–8:45			Sharing time—Preparation for day		
8:45–9:30			Language arts and reading		
9:30–10:30			Language arts and reading		
10:30–11:30			Language arts and reading		
12:30–1:00			Mathematics lesson		
1:00–1:30			Independent work: Math—Reading—Writing Reading for Group 3 ———		
1:30–2:30	Science/Social Studies (Art, Music, Health)		Library	Science/ Social Studies (Art, Music)	P.E.
2:30–3:00			Teacher reading aloud		

Figure 13.1 Weekly Schedule for Marcy Lee's First-Grade Class

THE DECISIONS MARCY MADE DURING THE SCHOOL YEAR

Managing Reading/Writing Activities. There were many things Marcy hoped to accomplish during the first weeks of schools. One was to convey to her students a sense of what they would be doing and the rules and routines she wanted them to follow. Here are some of the activities she planned for the first week.

Day 1. • The first day was a Tuesday. Marcy decided to plunge right in and follow the schedule she had planned for the week, devoting the morning to reading and language arts activities. She began by asking the children to talk about their summers. Then she introduced them to the various parts of the room, including the library, where she explained how to check out books and rules for using the quiet loft area. She read a book from the classroom library aloud and asked students to speculate about what might happen in the story, first on the basis of title and pictures, and then again after hearing the first section of the story. She made a mental note

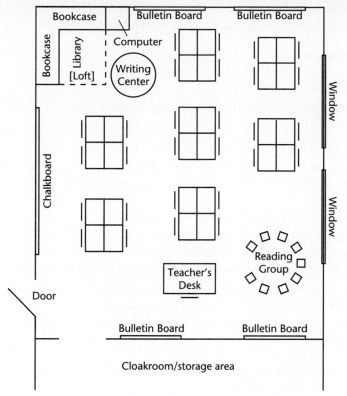

Figure 13.2 The Floor Plan of Marcy Lee's First-Grade Class

of which students appeared interested in the story, which ones participated in the discussion, and which ones made logical predictions.

After a recess and bathroom break, Marcy asked the children to draw a picture of something they liked from the story or from their summer vacation. She circulated around the room as the children drew, admiring the drawings and asking the children who had completed theirs to write something on the picture. She noted which children were confident writers, which ones responded when she encouraged them, and which ones wanted her to spell the words for them or write what they had said.

After lunch, Marcy introduced the math book and the first lesson in it, and then she discussed activities that might be undertaken independently. During the next hour, she began a science unit on plants, and the day ended with something especially fun: Marcy read aloud a book about popcorn, and then the whole class made—and ate—popcorn. At 2:50, it was time to clean up and line up to go home.

Day 2. • On the next day, Marcy began the language arts period by leading a discussion of the popcorn-making experience the previous day. Children dictated sentences about the experience, which Marcy wrote on a large sheet of chart paper. She followed a shared writing approach in which she encouraged children to help her spell the initial sounds of words. She noted which children already seemed to be comfortable with the writing process. Here is the story they wrote:

Making Popcorn

We made popcorn yesterday.
We put salt on the popcorn.
We ate the popcorn.

Marcy read this Language Experience Story aloud, pointing to each word, and then had the children join her several times in choral reading, again as she pointed to each word (Morris, 1986). She also asked some informal questions:

Who can point to where we start reading?

Where do we go when we finish the first line?

Where does the story end?

Who would like to finger-point-read the first sentence? (Marcy marked the first sentence with her hands.) Someone else? The second sentence? (She continued until all students who wanted to read had had a turn.)

Who knows this word? (Marcy pointed to *popcorn*.) Can someone else find it in a different place?

She made mental notes about the children who volunteered to read and the ones who were able to identify words.

Upon returning to the classroom after recess and a bathroom break, they all read the popcorn story several times in unison again as Marcy modeled finger-point reading. She then asked children if they could think of any words that began in the same way as "popcorn." Marcy recorded the word provided by a child. She asked the class if they knew what letter the word started with and then wrote the letter and the remainder of the word on the chalkboard. The class read the list of words (popcorn, puppy, pumpkin, party) in unison, emphasizing the initial sound.

After lunch and math class, Marcy accompanied her class on their first visit to the school library. She helped children find appropriate books; this gave her more information on their likes and dislikes.

Day 3. • Marcy transferred the popcorn story to the bottom of an 8 1/2 × 11 sheet of paper and made copies for the whole class. They reread the story in unison from the chart one more time as Marcy pointed, and then she distributed the copies. As they read the story again, Marcy asked the children to follow along on their copies, pointing to the words themselves. Then she asked children sitting next to each other to read the story as partners, pointing to the words as they read. After they had read the story together several times, she suggested that they could write something more or illustrate the story. As they wrote or drew, she moved from child to child, asking each one to finger-point-read the story. She asked those who were successful to iden-tify individual words that she pointed to in the text. When they had difficulty, Marcy read the first line while pointing to the words and then asked the children to do the same. If the children were successful, they continued through the second and third lines; if not, they read the story together. She also noted which children were writing and which ones chose to draw.

Day 4. • On Friday, Marcy announced that Friday mornings were special times in which the children could plan their own reading and writing work. They could read their library books or books from the classroom library; they could write a story or make a sign. Those who had difficulty getting started could begin by drawing a picture or a cartoon. Marcy went from child to child, discussing their plans and presenting alternatives.

Marcy established a number of routines during the first few weeks of school. The most complicated of these involved transitions from one place to another: lining up for recess, lunch, and dismissal; waiting for turns to use the bathroom; lining up for fire drill. She gradually introduced other routines—handing out papers and books and collecting them—during the first weeks. For spelling, she demonstrated how children should write their names on their papers and write numbers down the left side. She noted which children were able to follow directions and which ones had difficulty writing their names or numbers.

Regarding language arts, Marcy made clear her expectations as to how students should complete work at their desks and participate in class discussions. She talked about how to get help from classmates, how to get supplies, when to sharpen pencils, and what to do when they had finished their work. She outlined rules during the first week for listening carefully when others were speaking in class discussions and raising hands when they wished to speak. She also talked about working as partners and how important it was for them to help each other.

Assessment Procedures. A second important thing Marcy hoped to achieve was to get to know about the interests and understanding of her students. She quickly identified the children who could follow directions during lining-up routines, total-class instruction, and independent work. Many children had difficulty with instructions the first few days but were working well on assigned tasks by the end of the second week. Marcy spent considerable time the first few weeks walking around the classroom and explaining procedures to children who needed more support.

Marcy used many opportunities in the first few weeks to learn about her pupils' interests. From their descriptions of their summers, she identified the sports fans, the animal lovers, and so on. In helping her students select books, she discovered that some didn't want to read and some knew exactly what kind of books would please them. Marcy also spent time during the Friday morning period talking with students about their interests and how those interests could be developed into reading and writing activities; some children who were reticent during language arts came alive during science and social studies.

She was particularly interested in learning more about how proficient in English her three bilingual children were. Both children who spoke Spanish as their first language had lived in the United States for three years. They responded quickly and accurately to Marcy's questions in English; Juan was outgoing and seemed comfortable conversing with classmates in English. It was more difficult to assess the extent of Maria's knowledge of English because she was shy. For the time being, no special instruction seemed to be indicated. The third child, Ling Chi, had only recently come to the United States. Although she was extremely quiet and seemed able to speak little English, Marcy noted how attentive she was when other children spoke. She seemed to particularly enjoy the Big Book activities where English language was objectified in print and pictures. Marcy had already conferred with several specialists in the school to learn what special support might be available to support her English language development. She decided to seat her next to one of the more mature girls in the class who had taken an interest in being her interpreter.

Marcy also had many opportunities in the first weeks to assess her students' reading and writing. Nine children were already reading. Seven others could not finger-point as they read; they had not yet established concept of word. All but three could easily write their names and numbers. From writing and spelling tasks, she learned that seven children knew all or most of the letter-sound associations, and nine knew some. Ten children, including Maria and Ling Chi, lacked this knowledge; all were attentive during shared writing experiences. Marcy made notes about all the children on her file cards—their reading of the Language Experience Story, their consonant knowledge, and their writing ability.

Organizing Students for Instruction. Marcy used her observational evidence to begin thinking about her students—who might require special support and who to keep her eye on. After several weeks, she decided to seat children who were already reading next to those who needed support; she hoped that they might work well together during partner reading. She knew that she would have to spend more time discussing how partners should work well together, taking turns and providing support.

During the afternoon work period, she collected together the children who knew no consonant letter-sound associations. She focused on word learning through the use of word banks. She used such activities as shared writing and picture sorts to develop phoneme awareness. She taught letter-sound associations by using word study activities and word sorts. She followed the sequence in which letter-sounds were developed in the published program and used practice activities from the program when they were appropriate.

Marcy found during the course of the year that some children learned more quickly than others. She accommodated individual differences by providing small-group instruction for children who needed more direct instructional support, and she encouraged those who were not challenged by the literacy program selections to form Book Clubs and partnerships to read self-selected books and to develop projects.

During the last two weeks of May, Marcy had the class read a trade book. She prepared children by reading aloud short stories containing similar new concepts to build their background knowledge. Once children began reading the book, she provided special support for less proficient readers during the afternoon work period. She formed peer groups of three students to develop a play based on the story, and she was delighted to see that some of her students who struggled with reading and writing were leaders in translating actions from the book into dramatic form.

 Your Turn: Marcy was involved in making decisions on many levels. Identify what you believe were three particularly significant decisions. Briefly describe these in your journal under the heading Three Important Decisions Made by Marcy Lee. Would you have made the decisions that Marcy did? Why or why not? Include your responses in your journal.

Our Turn: We believe that it is useful to think about decisions in terms of those made prior to the school year (about reading materials, time schedule, and room organization), and those made during the first weeks of school (managing the reading/writing program, assessment, and organizing students for instruction). All these decisions are important in establishing an enticing literacy environment.

Marcy's reading and writing program changed from a fairly traditional one that closely adhered to a published reading program during her first year of teaching. During her second year, she developed a program that incorporated a greater variety of reading materials and more flexible forms of grouping. We believe that Marcy's decisions will show even further change as she gains more experience assessing the needs of students, greater familiarity with children's literature, and more confidence in her teaching.

WHAT TEACHING STRATEGIES ARE EFFECTIVE?

Making Words

Making Words is an activity to foster children's awareness of phonemes, letter-sound associations, and spelling patterns (Cunningham & Cunningham, 1992). It does so by actively engaging children in the construction of words. From this activity, they can also see that changing just one letter results in a quite different word. Drawing children's attention to the features of words in this way is particularly useful for first- and second-grade children and those from higher grades who encounter difficulty in spelling and word identification.

Each child in a group is given the same set of letters to use to make words. During a period that lasts 15 minutes, 12 to 15 words are made, beginning with two-letter words and progressing to words that are three, four, five, and even more letters in length. The final word includes all the letters the children were given. For example, children may be given the letters *i, c, k, r, s, t.* The words that could be made, beginning with two letter words, would include *is, it, kit, sit, sir, stir, sick, Rick, tick, skit, skirt, stick, trick,* and the long word *tricks.*

To prepare a lesson for Making Words, the Cunninghams (1992) recommend that the following steps be followed:

1. Select a final word for the lesson. In the preceding example, this word was *tricks.* When you choose this word, consider the number of vowels (more vowels permit words of greater complexity), child interest, relation to the curriculum, and the letter-sound patterns to which you would like to draw children's attention.

2. Make a list of the words that can be made using the letters of the final word.

3. From the set of possible words you have listed, select 12 to 15 by using some of the following considerations: They are (a) words that most children will be familiar with in their listening vocabularies, (b) words composed of familiar

spelling patterns, (c) words representing a change in letter sequence (bran, barn) to highlight the difference a letter sequence makes in word pronunciation, and (d) a proper name or two (Rick) to remind children about using capital letters.

4. Write all words on index cards; arrange them in order from shortest to longest. Study these words to identify letter patterns you wish to identify, letter sequences that change word pronunciation, and letter substitutions and additions that lead to different words. These differences will become the focus of your instructional activities.

5. Store the cards in an envelope, showing on the envelope the words (in order) and the patterns that can be emphasized. A Word Sort (see page 509) can be used as a culminating activity.

The materials that you will need for this activity include (a) letter holders for individual students (cardboard holders with a tray that holds about 10 letters; by folding the holder in half, it can be made to stand upright in front of each child); (b) multiple copies of letter cards, with the uppercase letters on one side and the lowercase ones on the other, and consonant letters in black and vowels in red (the multiple copies of each letter can be kept in a reclosable bags); (c) a pocket chart for children to use to build words at the board, and (d) large-size letters corresponding to those of the children.

To begin the Making Words lesson, you will place the large letters you have selected for the lesson in the pocket chart on the front board. Assign children (corresponding to the number of letters in the lesson) to pass out letters to each of the children. For example, if the lesson includes a *d,* one child would take the *d* bag and pass out one *d* to each child; a second child would distribute a different letter, and so on. Each passer can keep the reclosable bag to collect that letter at the end of the lesson. Activities during the lesson consist of the following:

1. To begin the lesson, hold up and name the large letters and have children hold up matching small letters. Then write the number "2" on the board, name the first word, use it in a sentence, and ask children to take two letters to make the word.

2. Have a child who has made the word correctly use the large letter cards to make the same word. Have children who did not make the word correctly look at the model and fix their word.

3. Continue with the remaining words, writing the number of letters on the board as that number changes, saying the word, and using it in a simple sentence to make sure that the meaning is understood. Cue children if only one letter changes, if the sequence changes, if the total set changes, and if a proper name is being made.

4. For each word made, have a child who made the correct word reproduce it with the large letters.

5. For the last word, ask if anyone has figured out what word can be made with all the letters and have them make it with the large letters. If no one knows, say, "I love it when I can stump you. Use all your letters and make ———" (Cunningham & Cunningham, 1992, p. 108).

In addition to their use in the Making Words phase of the lesson, the index cards can be used for a Word Sort activity. (This is described further on page 509.) Following up on the patterns introduced, you can reinforce the learning and its transfer to other words by having children use the patterns to spell a few new words.

Learning from Experience

The following transcript demonstrates a Making Words lesson that Marcy Lee did with a group from her class in December of first grade. This is one of the easier lessons, since it involves only a single vowel (Cunningham & Cunningham, 1992, pp. 110–111). As you read the following description, think about the teaching strategies that Marcy uses to focus children's attention on spelling patterns and letter-sound associations. At the end of the case, we will ask you to write your response in your journal.

Five consonant letters *(g, n, p, r, s)* and one vowel *(i)* are distributed to the children. At the front of the room, Marcy places six large cards with the same letters on them in the pocket chart.

Reviews role of vowels

Ms. Lee: What vowel will we use to make words today? [The children hold up their red *i* card.]

Ms. Lee: Why are vowels important?

Children: Because every word has to have at least one.

Ms. Lee: [She writes the number "2" on the board.] The two-letter word I want you to make today is *in.* Put the stamps *in* a box. [She watches as most children complete the word accurately.] Patty, please go to the board to make *in* with the big letters.

[Patty makes the word.]

Enables children to see what happens to pronunciation with addition of letter

Ms. Lee: That's exactly right. [She places the index card with *in* on it on the chalk ledge.]

Ms. Lee: [She erases the "2" and writes "3" on the board] Add just one letter to *in* to make the three-letter word *pin.* [She notices that most children make the word correctly.] Juan, please make the word with big letters.

[Juan makes the word.]

Ms. Lee: Now change just one letter to make *pig.*

[The children do this and one reproduces the word in large letters.]

Focuses on change in letter and change in pronunciation

Ms. Lee: Now make another three-letter word, *rig.* Sometimes a big truck is called a *rig.* [Children then make the word *rig,* and one child makes it with big letters.] Now make another three-letter word, *rip.* I have a rip in my pants. [Children quickly take the *g* away and replace it with *p* in their holders.] Great, you are really good word builders.

Add just one letter to *rip* to make *rips.* [The children do this and one reproduces the word in large letters.] Now change just one letter to make *nips.* [The children do this, and one reproduces the word in large letters.]

Focuses on letter reordering and change in pronunciation

Ms. Lee: Now, this is really tricky! Don't take any letters away and don't add any, but just change your letters around and like magic you can change your *nips* into *spin.* [The children do this; one child reproduces the word *spin* in large letters.]

Ms. Lee: Believe it or not, there is another word we can make with this same four letters. Move your letters around to change *spin* to *snip.* The barber began to *snip* my hair. [Marcy then has them make the words *pins, sing,* and *ring.*]

Focuses on shift in pronunciation with addition of letter

Encourages word sort on the basis of initial consonant and word ending

Ms. Lee: [She then erases the "4" and writes "5" on the board.] Add a letter to *ring* to make *rings*. [The children do this; one child reproduces the word *rings* in large letters.]

Ms. Lee: Now the tough one. What word can we make with all six letters?

[The children look puzzled and try various combinations without coming up with a word.]

Jason: I've got it! The word is *spring!*

Ms. Lee: Great, Jason. All right, can you make the word *spring* using all of your letters? *Spring* is coming soon. Jason, make it with the big letters.

Ms. Lee: Now let's see what patterns we can find. [She puts the following words in the pocket chart: *in, pin, pig, rig, rips, nips, spin, snip, sing, ring.*] Okay. Which words can you find that begin the same? [Children pronounce the words and listen to the letters. They identify three sets of words that begin with *p, r,* and *s.*] Now which words end the same? [Children identify the words *in, pin,* and *spin, pig* and *rig, rip* and *snip, rips* and *nips, sing* and *ring.* As children identify the words, she clusters them together on the pocket chart.]

Your Turn: What teaching strategies does Marcy use to focus children's attention on word patterns and letter-sound associations? Write your response in your journal under the heading Making Words.

Our Turn: You may have noticed that Marcy has children construct words that retain the same ending pattern but that change in only the beginning letter. For example, she had children change the word *in* to *pin, pig* to *rig, rips* to *nips,* and *sing* to *ring.* She developed children's knowledge of letter-sound associations by having them notice what happened to the pronunciation of words when one letter was changed, as for the initial consonants in the words of similar pattern. She also gave them the opportunity to become aware of how word pronunciation changes as the order of letters is altered, by having them listen to words composed of the same letters that shift in pronunciation: for example, *nips, spin, snip,* and *pins.*

Directed Reading—Thinking Activity

Children make sense of what they are reading by actively drawing on what they already know; and this combination of prior knowledge applied to new situations yields new knowledge. But this learning might not occur if the prior knowledge of readers were not considered. Analyses of classroom instruction (Beck, McKeown, McCaslin, & Burkes, 1979; Durkin, 1978–1979) suggest that too little time before reading is devoted to developing and activating the prior knowledge necessary for effective comprehension. In this section, we revisit a strategy, the Directed Reading-Thinking Activity (DR-TA, Stauffer, 1969), that is effective in activating prior knowledge and helping students to actively monitor their own reading.

The DR-TA approach models the comprehension process by having participants walk through a selection bit by bit rather than locating all discussion after reading. In this way you help students experience the thinking process that expert readers use in comprehending a text (Davidson & Wilkerson, 1988; Stauffer, 1969). The steps to be followed include:

1. Before reading a section of text, use clues to make predictions about what the author will say.

2. Stop at a preselected point to refine or reformulate predictions.
3. Repeat steps 1 and 2 throughout the selection.

To plan a DR-TA, you need to select an appropriate reading selection, one at an appropriate instructional level that lends itself to making predictions. After analyzing the selection, choose several points when your students might be stopped and ask for a prediction about what will happen next in the selection. The title, picture, caption, first paragraph, or some combination of these often serves as the basis for the first prediction.

After each chunk is read, you and your students will discuss their predictions in light of the clues the author has given them. You may ask such questions as:

What makes you think so?

What did the author say that supports (or refutes) that?

What will ——— do about ——?

Why do you think the author said that?

Students will go back to the selection to find more information, clarify a point, and resolve conflicts. Oral reading is used to substantiate opinions. It may also, particularly in first grade, yield diagnostic information about a child's reading development.

By progressing through the text in this manner, the students come to a full construction of the message so that the final discussion can focus on evaluating the author's message and craft. For second and third graders, writing also fits naturally into the DR-TA: students can write predictions and evidence at various points, and they may want to rewrite sections of narratives that they find unsatisfactory. (For a more detailed description, see chapter 5.)

Process Writing

Process writing is an instructional methodology that reflects the stages through which successful writers produce pieces that communicate clearly and effectively (see chapter 7). As described earlier, the stages in this process are (1) developing a topic, (2) creating a draft (writing), (3) conferencing, (4) revising, (5) editing, and (6) publishing. In the following paragraphs, we review these steps of the process.

Developing a Topic

Children need to select and develop their own topics. Creating interesting, readable writing depends on the child's interest in the chosen topic, the child's level of expertise, and the child's voice coming through the information being presented. Guide the children's choices by listening to each child's interests and concerns, making suggestions based on that information when the child seems stuck for a topic, and developing broad guidelines within which children can explore specific topics of personal interest.

Creating a Draft

Encourage children to write down all of their thoughts on the subject they've chosen without immediate regard to spelling and organization. Children need to write freely and need to know the importance of creating content from which to work when they write; they need uninterrupted writing time that, when provided regularly, will be expected and respected by the children.

Conferencing

When a child finishes the first draft of a piece, provide feedback to the student author through a conference. An effective conference can help the author identify what is memorable and what holes exist in the piece. This conference can take any number of forms:

Teacher–student: You can provide one-on-one attention to the student author by listening to the ideas being expressed as well as by noting any problems with organization that can be dealt with later in the process.

Student–student: Students listen to each others' stories and give feedback about what works and ask questions about anything that is either ambiguous or provocative.

Student–group of students: Conferences can take place between an author and a small group of students who give feedback to each other after each piece is read aloud to the group.

A successful conference format is based on three questions:

What did you hear the writer say in the piece?

What did you like best about the piece? (With this information, the writer knows what was communicated well, what was memorable, and what caught the reader's or listener's attention.)

What questions do you have about the piece? (This identifies the holes in the piece or areas of special interest to the audience that bear expansion.)

The tone of the conference needs to be positive; writers should see conference partners as allies who want to help make the piece the best it can be. You need to set the tone of conferencing in the classroom by modeling effective interactions. Guided discussions about the success of conferences help students identify constructive ways of interacting.

Revising

After a conference, the author goes back to the piece and adds to it or changes it according to the feedback given during the conference. The choice of what to change and what to leave the same is always the author's ultimate responsibility, but you as a primary-grade teacher will help the writer to see how the piece can be improved by taking into account the thoughts of friendly listeners. Eventually, as the concept of audience becomes internalized, the questions asked by listeners become self-imposed. But this self-monitoring develops gradually, and audience reaction continues to be an important part of the process throughout the elementary grades. Most first and second graders do not make many revisions. It is not until third grade that revision is really understood and developed.

Editing

At this stage, the children stop focusing on content and examine the grammar, spelling, and format of their pieces. Effective editing techniques, however, become established through your modeling. Conventions of punctuation, spelling, and grammar need to be followed to make the writing accessible. Minilessons on an individual, small-group, or large-group basis are appropriate when children realize there are mechanical errors to be fixed. The children work on editing independently, with a partner, or in a small group. You will usually have a final editing conference with the child once all that can be done without your intervention has been accomplished.

Publishing

The final stage when the piece is made ready for everyone to read can be done by simply rewriting and displaying it. More elaborate preparations can include typing the text and stapling it into a hardcover book. By offering a variety of formats, you give students the opportunity to decide how they want their writing to be published.

Reading Fluency

Reading Practice

Contextual reading practice is the most effective means for developing fluency. Many less able readers fail to achieve fluency because they are continually asked to read materials that are too difficult. They have little opportunity to experience the pleasure of problem-free reading and to develop reading fluency. Thus, for practice to improve fluency, the material read must be easy for the reader. It should pose almost no word identification problems and no comprehension problems.

Having students reread selections can eliminate many problems posed by a selection. After a first reading, students are familiar with the content of the selection and can recognize most difficult words. Thus they are more able to focus directly on

What are the benefits of Sustained Silent Reading?

meaning and to read at a faster rate. The method of repeated readings can be used in a more formal way (Chomsky, 1976; Lopardo & Sadow, 1982; Nelson & Morris, 1988). (This approach is described in detail in chapter 14.)

Modeling Fluent Reading

It is sometimes useful for you or an older student who is a proficient reader to read to a student in order to demonstrate the nature of fluent reading. One method effective for readers lacking fluency is to model phrase reading (Walker, 1988). First, you tape the student reading a short selection that is of appropriate difficulty for the student. Then read a sentence, with brief pauses between phrases of the sentence, and have the student read the same sentence with similar phrasing. Once adequate phrasing has been demonstrated, read more than one sentence and have the student follow. Finally, have the student read the remainder of the selection independently or along with you. You may wish to tape the reading of individual students to compare their phrasing and general fluency on the final reading with their phrasing and fluency on the first reading.

An alternative method is to have a student read with or slightly after a proficient reader. The model reads slightly ahead and somewhat louder than the student, finger-pointing to the line of print as it is read. Once the student reads fluently, you or the student model can relinquish control to the student by reading more softly and somewhat behind the student. In general, the purpose of providing a model of fluent reading is to show clearly the nature of fluent reading and to get the student to compare nonfluent reading with that which is fluent.

HOW CAN YOU MEET THE NEEDS OF READERS WHO ENCOUNTER DIFFICULTY?

Increasingly, attention has focused on interventions in the early phases of school that will get children off to a good start in reading and writing. Prompted by programs such as Reading Recovery (Clay, 1993b; Lyons, Pinnell, & DeFord, 1993), educators have developed a variety of other early intervention programs (Hiebert & Taylor, 1994). The instructional strategies involved offer guidance for the classroom teacher about ways to support the early literacy development of students. In this section, we describe two approaches that can be used to support the learning of primary-grade students. These, along with other teaching strategies, can help you develop a program that gets all your students off to a good start.

Vocabulary Development

Many students easily expand their sight vocabulary and their meaning vocabulary through contextual reading alone. These children do not require the intensive instruction described in this section. Other children profit from seeing and studying words in a focused manner. The strategy we describe here can be used effectively with beginning readers as well as those beyond the initial stages of reading.

In thinking about how to help students learn new words, we need to distinguish between words whose meanings are unfamiliar and words whose meanings are known. For unfamiliar content words, a systematic instructional approach involving three steps can be used: (1) seeing, (2) discussing and defining, and (3) using and writing (see Johnson & Pearson, 1984, for a similar approach). Words that are familiar in meaning (basic sight words) require only the first and last of these steps. Although teachers are often advised to introduce new words before children encounter them in stories, we have found that the approach discussed here may be used after reading, to reinforce word learning, as well as before.

Seeing

In the first step, select several words that are key in comprehending the story but that may not be familiar to most children. Write one of these on the chalkboard and pronounce it. Use each word in a sentence so that its meaning can be easily derived from context. The word in the example sentence should be used in the same manner as the word is used in the text.

Draw attention to features of the words (initial letters, word endings). Once children have developed strategies for scanning new words, they will need less help from you in focusing on the features of the word. Nevertheless, when students encounter new multisyllabic words, it is often useful for them to focus on them syllable by syllable.

Discussing and Defining

When the meaning of the new word is unfamiliar to the students, it is important to discuss the word. Some children in the group may have some understanding about what the word means, and you should elicit these hunches. You may wish to develop several sentences that include the word to enable your students to venture some guesses about its meaning. They should form a definition of the word. If they are unsure or if competing hypotheses exist, check the meaning in the dictionary. If the word is totally unfamiliar, you can help the group by identifying synonyms and antonyms, if such exist.

Using and Writing

Following the discussion, encourage children to use the new word in their speaking and writing. For example, ask children individually or in groups to suggest several sentences that include the word and write each of these sentences on the chalkboard, overhead projector, or chart paper. The meaningful sentences that children develop should be included in their personally developed dictionaries. Children at the beginning stages of learning to read may wish to include the new words in their word banks.

Newly learned vocabulary becomes mastered in two main ways. The first is through repeated exposure to the words when they recur in the stories and articles children read. Beck and McKeown (1983) suggest that from 13 to 20 exposures are needed before a word is learned. The second way is when they are used frequently in the children's writing. Thus it is useful to encourage children to use newly learned words in their writing.

Learning from Experience

The following brief excerpt from a first-grade lesson shows how Ms. Lee helps her students focus on the features of new words. She is introducing a group of her students who have difficulty reading to a set of words that they will encounter in the story they are about to read, *The Great Big Enormous Turnip* by Alexei Tolstoy. She has selected two words as being of central importance to the study: *turnip* and *enormous*. As you read the transcript, try to identify the cues she focuses on to help her students to learn the word *turnip*. Write your responses in your journal.

Uses word in sentence

Ms. Lee: Here is a new word that will be in your story today. [She writes the word *turnip*.] The word is *turnip*. The *turnip* grows in the garden. Does everyone know what a *turnip* is?

Sam: I'm not exactly sure, but it's like a carrot, but it's white. Sometimes we have turnips for dinner.

Focuses on word meaning

Ms. Lee: Yes, that's exactly right. Let's look at the picture in the book so that we can see what a turnip looks like. [She has her students look at the picture.]

Ms. Lee: Let's look at the word. What other words do you already know that begin the same as *turnip*?

Focuses on initial letter

Pedro: It starts the same as *top*. Oh, it starts the same as *take*.

Focuses on letter-sound association

Ms. Lee: [She writes *top* and *take* on the chalkboard.] What sound goes with *t*?

Group: /t.t.t/

Ms. Lee: Can you think of any other words that begin the same as *turnip*?

Latisha: *Turn!* Turn begins exactly the same.

Focuses on word ending

Ms. Lee: Good. Very good! [She writes *turn* on the chalkboard and then points to the *turn* in *turnip*, tracing the letters.] Okay, now I have a tough one! Who can think of a word that ends the same as *turnip*?

Simon: *Nip nip. Sip. Dip. Lip. Tip. Nip.*

Ms. Lee: That's right, all of them: *Sip. Dip. Lip. Tip* ends the same as *nip*. [She writes *nip* and *sip* above the *nip* in *turnip*.] They both end with the sound of *ip*. They rhyme. Okay, now, I want you to look again very carefully at the word *turnip*. See if you can close your eyes and remember what *turnip* looks like. Can you? Okay.

Visualizing word

Your Turn: What strategies did Marcy Lee use to help her first graders learn the word *turnip*? Write your response in your journal under the heading Vocabulary Development.

Our Turn: You may have noted that she first used the word in a sentence and checked to see that all children knew the meaning. As they listened to the initial sound, she had her students recall other words that begin with the same sound. She then wrote the word, noting the initial letter corresponding to the initial sound. Finally, she drew their attention to the ending of the word and other words that sound the same. She focused on the features of the word (beginning syllable and word ending) so that students might remember it.

Word Sorts

Word Sorts are activities in which children examine a set of words and group them according to shared features, such as the same initial consonant or word ending (Gillet & Kita, 1979). Marcy used the word sort as a culminating activity when she involved her students in Making Words. At the end, she selected a subset of the words and had students sort them first on the basis of initial consonant and then on the basis of word ending.

Word sorts are useful activities to use with small groups of children who are learning about spelling patterns and letter-sound associations. By sorting on the basis of initial consonant, children become aware that words that begin with the same initial letter also have the same initial phoneme, and they learn the initial consonant letter-sound associations. In a similar way, they can focus on final consonants, initial consonant blends, and vowel patterns.

In addition to focusing children's attention on print, the word sort can also be used to direct their attention to word meaning. For example, children can sort words on the basis of similar meaning or base words. They can sort words on the basis of their prefixes or suffixes. Word sorts can be used to help children become sensitive to parts of speech. For example, children can sort words that name things from those that describe an action.

In order to prepare children for a word sort, they must have a set of words to sort. For a group lesson that will be making use of a pocket chart, these words should be printed on large cards. This form of the activity is particularly useful when you are introducing children to what sorting words entails or when you are wanting to reinforce the prior learning of a lesson, as was the case for the Making Words lesson. Most often, you will have children do their own word sorts. In chapter 12, you read about helping children build word banks. Words from the word bank can serve as the basis for a word sort. Begin by providing two or three examples of the pattern for which they are to search. For example, you may ask them to find words from their bank that end the same as *bat* and *dot*. Children can then refer to these examples as they search through the words in their word banks, identify those fitting the pattern, and place the cards in a pile. To begin with, children may sort on the basis of a single letter or pattern. Soon, however, they are able to sort words on the basis of two or three letters or patterns.

Learning from Experience

As you read the following description of Marcy Lee's class doing a word sort, think about the teaching strategies that she uses to focus children's attention on the sound corresponding to the letter *p.* Write your response in your journal.

Ms. Lee: Let's read these words. [They read each word slowly, with the teacher emphasizing the initial sound.].

popcorn
puppy
Peter
Patty

Focuses on word features	**What do you notice about these words?**
	Sam: They all have two of the same letter.
	Ms. Lee: That's right. Anything else you notice?
	Peter: They all begin with the same letter.
	Ms. Lee: That's right. Anything else you notice?
	Yit Tseng They sound the same at the beginning.
Focuses on initial sound	**Ms. Lee:** That's great. They begin with the same letter and they sound the same. Can you hear the beginning sound? What sound do you hear?
	Group: /p/ /p!/
	Ms. Lee: Let's read the words again.
	Group: popcorn, puppy, Peter, Patty
Requests words beginning with initial sound	**Ms. Lee:** Now, I want you to take the words out of your word banks. As you read through them softly, see if you can find any words that begin like popcorn and puppy.
	Sarah: I found *pie.*
	Tim: I got *pitcher.*
Encourages word sort on the basis of the initial consonant *p*	**Ms. Lee:** Great. Now sort through the rest of your words. When you sort through all of them, then we'll compare the words you found. [The children in the class are hard at work looking through their word bank cards.] Okay Peter, what words did you find?
	Peter: I found *pumpkin, party,* and *park.*
Encourages word study	**Ms. Lee:** Good! [She writes the words on the board.] Let's say these together slowly. [The children and Marcy read the words in unison.] Do you hear the beginning sound? [Children respond with the phoneme.] Now if we were going to write a word that begins with that sound, what letter would we write first?
	Children: p.
	Ms. Lee: Okay. Sarah, what words did you find?
Focuses on letter sound	**SARAH:** I found *pretty, pink, pussy,* and *pie.*
	Ms. Lee: Good! [She writes the words on the board.] Let's say these together slowly. [She and the children read the words in unison.] Do you hear the beginning sound? [Children respond with the phoneme.] Now if we were going to write a word that begins with that sound, what letter would we write first?
Encourages word study	
	Children: p.
Focuses on letter sound	**Ms. Lee:** Very good work. Tim, what words did you find?
	TIM: Well, I got *pitcher, pick,* and *percentage.*
Encourages word study	**Ms. Lee:** [She writes the words on the board.] Let's say these together slowly. [She and the children read the words in unison.] Do you hear the beginning sound? [Children respond with the phoneme.] Now if we were going to write the word *percentage,* what letter would we write first?
Focuses on letter sound	
	Children: p.

Ms. Lee: Okay, the next time you meet a word such as *party, pat,* and *pig,* what will be the first letter that you will write?

Applies to writing

Group: p.

Ms. Lee: Good. And what will you know when you see a word with the letter *p* at the beginning?

Reviews letter-sound association

Sarah: That it begins the same as *party* and *pig.*

Your Turn: What teaching strategies does Marcy Lee use to focus children's attention on the sound corresponding to the letter *p?* Write your response in your journal under the heading Word Sorts.

Our Turn: You may have noticed that Marcy begins by listing words that are familiar to the children on the chalkboard. She then has them listen to the words and their initial sound. Then she has them sort through the words in their word banks to find other words that begin with the letter *p.* Finally, she focuses their attention on the letter and emphasizes the sound with which it corresponds. She applies the new knowledge by having the children think about how they would write words. This example also shows how the relationship between reading and spelling can be developed.

SUMMARY

In the first part of this chapter, four main goals were discussed. A literacy program is balanced if it promotes the development of knowledge of print, comprehension and communication, background knowledge and vocabulary, and interest in reading and writing. If you are using a published literacy program and the activities provided do not enable you to achieve all of your goals, then you need to evaluate the program to determine what should be omitted so that more appropriate activities can be incorporated.

A variety of decisions shape the development of a balanced literacy program: appropriate materials must be secured and activities for their use developed, and the classroom must be organized in a way conducive to reading and writing activities. The schedule must allow for extended periods of reading and writing.

To develop your classroom literacy program, you must learn a great deal about what your students already know about reading and writing and about what interests them. Given a group of children that vary greatly in their proficiency and interests, you must then determine how they can be grouped flexibly so that you can offer them the guidance and support they need.

The case study included in the chapter exemplifies the complex thinking that must go into preparing for the school year, getting started during the first weeks of school, and managing the reading program throughout the year. In this book, one of our goals is to help those of you who are beginning teachers to establish a sound literacy program; at the same time, it is our goal to encourage you, once you have acquired experience, to develop your own literacy program.

To develop an effective reading program, you also need to develop a repertoire of teaching strategies. In this chapter, we discussed instructional strategies for Making Words, revisited the DR-TA and process writing, and discussed strategies for developing reading fluency. Some children, those who encounter difficulty learning print, may profit from additional instructional support, including vocabulary development and word sorts.

In the Field

1. Select a word from a children's LEA story or a book that children are reading; introduce it to them as a sight word. First, plan how you will complete the "seeing" portion of the lesson. Second, do you think that the children are familiar with the meaning of the word? If not, consider how you will help them to become familiar with the meaning of the word? Finally, what writing or oral language activities will be appropriate to reinforce the learning? After developing your plans, work with the children to help them learn the word. Reflect on the instruction you provided: Did the children learn and remember the word? What parts of the instruction went particularly smoothly? What parts would you change? Summarize what you learned in a report or in your journal under the heading Vocabulary Development.

2. Select a group of second or third graders and an appropriate story or article that lends itself to making predictions. Analyze the selection and choose several points where you might stop the reading of the group to encourage predictions and confirm prior predictions. During the confirmation process, ask probing questions. During the final discussion, have students evaluate the author's message and craft. Reflect on the DR-TA instruction you provided. What parts of the instruction went particularly smoothly? What parts would you change? Summarize what you learned in a report or in your journal under the heading DR-TA.

3. Interview some primary-grade teachers concerning the decisions they make at the beginning of the school year: How do they determine the books they will read to their students and the materials they will have them read? The time schedule they will follow? The organization of their room? Once school begins, what do they do with children on the first day? On the second day? On the third day? How do they assess the knowledge that their students have about reading and writing? How do they organize (group) their students for instruction? What reading and writing strategies do they plan to teach their students? Summarize what you learned in a report or in your journal under the heading Interview with a Primary-Grade Teacher.

Portfolio Suggestion

Select from your journal two examples of your responses to Pause and Reflect or Learning from Experience: Your Turn and include these in your portfolio. If you completed an In the Field activity, include your report from it in your portfolio as well. Write a brief evaluation of your work, commenting on what it shows about your learning.

For Further Reading

Ernst, G., & Richard, K. J. (1995). Reading and writing pathways to conversation in the ESL classroom. *The Reading Teacher, 48,* 320–326.

Goldenberg, C. (1993). Instructional conversations: Promoting comprehension through discussion. *The Reading Teacher, 46,* 316–326.

Raphael, R. E., & McMahon, S. I. (1994). Book Club: An alternative framework for reading instruction. *The Reading Teacher, 48,* 102–116.

Swift, K. (1993). Try Reading Workshop in your classroom. *The Reading Teacher, 46,* 366–371.

Tancock, S. M. (1994). A literacy lesson framework for children with reading problems. *The Reading Teacher, 48,* 130–140.

Trachtenburg, P., & Ferruggia, A. (1989). Big Books from little voices: Reaching high risk beginning readers. *The Reading Teacher, 42,* 284–289.

Young, R. A., & Vardell, S. (1993). Weaving Readers Theatre and nonfiction into the curriculum. *The Reading Teacher, 46,* 396–406.

Developing Literacy in the Intermediate Grades

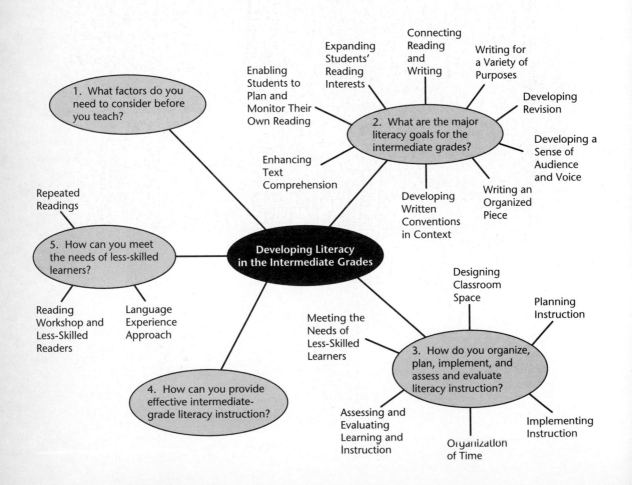

1. What factors do you need to consider before you teach?

Enabling Students to Plan and Monitor Their Own Reading

Expanding Students' Reading Interests

Connecting Reading and Writing

Writing for a Variety of Purposes

Developing Revision

2. What are the major literacy goals for the intermediate grades?

Enhancing Text Comprehension

Developing Written Conventions in Context

Developing a Sense of Audience and Voice

Writing an Organized Piece

Repeated Readings

5. How can you meet the needs of less-skilled learners?

Developing Literacy in the Intermediate Grades

Reading Workshop and Less-Skilled Readers

Language Experience Approach

Meeting the Needs of Less-Skilled Learners

Designing Classroom Space

Planning Instruction

3. How do you organize, plan, implement, and assess and evaluate literacy instruction?

4. How can you provide effective intermediate-grade literacy instruction?

Assessing and Evaluating Learning and Instruction

Organization of Time

Implementing Instruction

CHAPTER GOALS FOR THE READER

To recognize factors affecting literacy learning during the intermediate grades

To identify instructional goals for literacy during the intermediate grades

To be able to organize, plan, implement, and assess literacy instruction for intermediate-grade students

To link goals with appropriate instruction and assessment

To meet the needs of all learners

CHAPTER OVERVIEW

What factors affecting literacy learning during the intermediate grades do you need to consider before you teach? What are your instructional goals for literacy development? How do you design your classroom for literacy instruction? How do you plan, organize, and implement literacy instruction? How do you assess and evaluate students' literacy development? How can you meet the needs of diverse learners? These are typical questions beginning teachers as well as experienced teachers who are developing or changing their instructional philosophy and practices ask. These are the questions we address.

In this chapter, we identify the factors that impinge on your planning, organization, implementation, and assessment of literacy instruction. To learn about intermediate-grade literacy instruction, we interviewed Sharon Gleason, a fifth-grade teacher, to share her ideas and insights. We chose Sharon because she presents an integration of philosophical perspectives—that is, combines a holistic-collaborative approach and a direct instruction approach to teaching and learning.

We begin this interview by initially discussing Sharon's literacy goals for her fifth graders and compare them to those we consider important for all intermediate-grade students. Later in the chapter, we resume our discussion with Sharon to learn how she designs the physical space in her classroom for literacy instruction; how she plans, organizes, and implements instruction and assessment; and how she addresses the needs of less skilled readers. In the remainder of the chapter, we provide additional instructional activities to address the needs of less skilled readers.

 TAPPING PRIOR KNOWLEDGE TO SET A PURPOSE

Reflect on your own schooling experiences as an intermediate-grade student and also consider classroom observations and your own teaching experiences. Describe these experiences in your journal. Before reading this chapter, use these experiences to help formulate purpose-setting questions. Write your questions in your journal. Respond to these questions as you read or after you have read the chapter.

WHAT FACTORS DO YOU NEED TO CONSIDER BEFORE YOU TEACH?

One of the most difficult tasks facing you is presenting a coherent and cohesive picture of instruction and learning to students. Interfacing goals, instruction, grouping, and assessment and evaluation to meet individual student needs require thinking, reflection, and decision making. Many factors impinge on how you organize and implement literacy instruction in your classroom. These include curricular and administrative demands of school and district, diversity of learning needs, parent and community expectations, classroom size and interpersonal dynamics, and instructional resources. Therefore no one correct plan or prepackaged program can exist; rather, you need to consider and accommodate these factors.

Organizing and designing classroom literacy instruction present a set of complex problems that change from school to school. Each classroom is different in composition and dynamics and requires ongoing observation and experimentation to create an effective environment for learning. Hence it is your thinking about learning and instruction and the ways in which you as an artist shape the classroom into a beautiful work of art that make a difference in students' literacy development.

WHAT ARE THE MAJOR LITERACY GOALS FOR THE INTERMEDIATE GRADES?

Intermediate-grade students who are reading at or above grade level are fluent oral readers who are able to apply phonic principles, use context, and have a sight vocabulary commensurate with their grade level. As a teacher of these students, you should focus on nine major goals: (1) enhancing text comprehension; (2) enabling students to plan and monitor their own reading; (3) increasing students' reading interests; (4) connecting the reading and writing processes; (5) writing for a variety of purposes; (6) developing revision; (7) developing a sense of audience and voice; (8) writing an organized piece; and (9) developing written conventions in context. These general goals are important, but you must also go beyond these goals to consider the individual students' needs and to collaboratively establish goals with your students. These more finely tuned individual goals address specific individual needs and encourage students to have a vested interest in achieving their literacy goals.

Enhancing Text Comprehension

Comprehension is the most important goal in reading; it is the heart and soul of reading. Developing comprehension is a constructive process that includes understanding vocabulary, developing personal responses, understanding and applying text-based ideas, and critically evaluating these ideas. As intermediate-grade materials become increasingly complex—with longer sentences, dependent clauses, and embedded phrases—comprehension also becomes more difficult. Stories include more events and problems. Characters are developed in greater detail; they have motives and desires that go beyond actions to resolve problems. Reading vocabulary is not always a familiar part of students' listening or speaking vocabulary, especially in nonfiction where technical words appear. During the intermediate grades, students are also reading more expository materials and need to become familiar with different expository text structures to facilitate their text comprehension. Thus text factors place a greater demand on comprehension.

Besides their need to cope with greater text complexity, students should broaden both their experiences and prior knowledge, since they are reading a wider variety of materials and becoming acquainted with a plethora of topics. Instead of *activating* prior knowledge, you may need to *develop* students' knowledge and experiences so the students can better construct meaning from text.

Enhancing text comprehension is best accomplished by reading and discussing good literature. Providing students with opportunities to choose their own literature can increase students' motivation and desire to understand and learn. Both are essential instructional ingredients that can help students increase their comprehension of text.

Enabling Students to Plan and Monitor Their Own Reading

Intermediate-grade students need to hone their strategic reading skills. They must learn how to plan for different kinds of reading and to self-monitor their understanding and learning of text. Reading for pleasure and reading to learn are two quite different things. Quick, rapid reading may characterize recreational reading whereas verbal rehearsals and rereading of important parts tend to characterize textbook reading. Self-monitoring reading comprehension before an exam is quite different from enjoying recreational reading. In reading for pleasure, readers are more likely to tolerate ambiguity and to ignore vague or confusing text information. Strategic readers plan for these differences and make adjustments according to their purposes or goals.

For students to become strategic readers, they need to read a variety of texts and discuss the strategies they used to comprehend text. Allowing students to choose their own topics, develop their own purposes, and share their reading strategies with peers promotes strategic reading.

Expanding Students' Reading Interests

It is during the intermediate-grade years that students' commitment to reading as a leisure time activity and a tool for lifelong learning should deepen. Students who read widely understand the world, its problems, and its challenges better than those who do not. Wide reading stimulates thinking, enables students to better interpret ideas and events, and creates new interests. Erikson (1983) refers to this developmental period as the Stage of Industry, in which students seek to learn and to become proficient at adult activities. Wide reading that includes nonfiction can help satisfy the developmental needs of students in this age group.

The strategies and materials you choose as teachers have a great effect on encouraging or discouraging recreational reading. The teacher who reads aloud to students and allocates time for independent reading, or who shares informational books and magazines about daily events, does much to stimulate the love of reading as well as curiosity about and interest in our world. Teachers who encourage and provide time for personal inquiry do much to help students achieve this goal.

Connecting Reading and Writing

Intermediate-grade students need to recognize and use the relationships between the reading and writing processes to increase literacy development. Writing provides opportunities to reconstruct meaning of text. Students become acutely aware of what they know, believe, and value by making a written response to a text; they internalize the meaning of that text. Writing encourages reflection so that students become involved with the writer's ideas.

The principles of process writing instruction need to be incorporated as you connect reading and writing. For example, brainstorming and discussion should precede the act of drafting. Students should be given ample opportunities to revise, with attention to a sense of audience and voice. Analyzing literature from the writer's perspective and understanding the author's craft do much to enhance students' writing as well as facilitate text comprehension.

Writing for a Variety of Purposes

Intermediate-grade students should be able to use writing to accomplish different tasks. Writing stories and poems is creative and entertaining, but students need to be competent in other forms of writing such as exposition. Are students able to persuade and present a good argument with supportive evidence? Can students explain directions for completing a project or provide directions for getting to the library? Can they write friendly letters and business letters, thank you notes, and other forms of correspondence? Can they conduct personal research and write reports? Do they recognize

How might this cooperative project involve reading and writing?

and use functional forms of writing such as making a shopping list, writing directions to their home? Do they use the writing of diaries or journals to enhance personal understanding and for enjoyment? It is important that intermediate-grade students recognize these different forms of writing and be able to practice them. By using these different forms of writing in authentic and meaningful contexts, students will achieve this goal.

Developing Revision

Revision is central to good writing. The notion that writing is a recursive process needs to be firmly developed during the intermediate grades. Students need to write many pieces and make critical choices about which ones they will revise. The power of revision comes with students' sharing and receiving of peer and adult responses to their written pieces. The reason for revision becomes apparent during sharing: writers elicit giggles, excitement, and maybe tears from their audience as they read particular parts of their writing. A confused expression or a question may cause writers to recognize that they need to rethink and possibly revise.

Developing a Sense of Audience and Voice

Developing voice is also an important goal, since it provides a natural, authentic, and continuous flow to writing. Written pieces that exhibit a voice are enjoyable to read. The writing seems real, and the language is not stilted.

For a writer's piece to have a sense of audience and voice, it needs to be more than a listing of events, actions, facts, and details. Good authors understand their audience and are able to choose appropriate words and phrases and a suitable writing style to communicate their ideas in an enjoyable and convincing manner. Intermediate-grade students need to consider such questions as: Who will be reading this piece? Would the story be more convincing and enjoyable if it were told from the first-person point of view rather than from another point of view? Would the use of metaphors and similes make an expository piece more understandable? Does the dialogue illustrate the personality of the character? Is enough information included for readers who know nothing about the hobby being described? These questions can be easily used during instruction when students are engaged in writing for a variety of purposes and audiences. But the writing must accomplish a "real" purpose and not be a contrived assignment; otherwise audience and voice seem less important to students.

Writing an Organized Piece

Intermediate-grade students need to strengthen their skills in organizing their writing. Organization refers to logical development of a written piece. In a story, there is the logical sequence of beginning, middle, and end. In expository pieces, students are engaged in writing topic sentences and providing supporting details. During the intermediate grades, students learn to develop a coherent piece by writing cohesive paragraphs and using transitions between paragraphs. Given numerous opportunities to write, share their writing, and discuss and analyze other authors' writing, intermediate-grade students can demonstrate organized writing.

Developing Written Conventions in Context

Intermediate-grade students need to increase their abilities to use appropriate grammar, punctuation, spelling, and usage in their writing. These developing writers learn that readers are more able to understand and respond to text that contains few or no errors. Readers can focus on content and not be distracted by a misspelled word, sentence fragment, or other failures to eliminate inappropriate written conventions.

Publishing and writing for real audiences cause students to be concerned about following written conventions. Publication develops ownership and pride, since there is a real purpose for writing that directly affects the use of appropriate written conventions. Thus, correct spelling, grammar, and usage are best understood and developed during editing. At this time, students are more likely to edit, since their writing is intended for public use. Using a grammar and punctuation checklist during editing can provide guidance and improve students' editing.

Learning from Experience

We interviewed Sharon Gleason, a fifth-grade teacher, and invited her to share her goals for literacy instruction. We were interested in learning about Sharon's thinking and decision making in establishing goals for her fifth graders. As you read, consider the process she employed to establish goals by answering this question. How did Sharon formulate these goals? And, lastly, identify her goals.

Sharon Gleason has a master's degree in reading and has been teaching for over 15 years. Sharon has a heterogeneous classroom of approximately 23 students that includes a less skilled reader and a learning-disabled student. Her school district is not unlike other schools in the Chicago suburban area in which the teachers are developing an integrated curriculum where reading and writing processes are connected and developed in all subject areas. Before her district educational board members became committed to an integrated, interdisciplinary approach, Sharon personally worked on an integrated approach for several years by drawing upon her daily classroom experiences, her graduate work in reading, membership in a local reading council, and her principal's support. These professional experiences affected Sharon's philosophy of teaching and learning. As a consequence, her instruction changed and gradually evolved until it is now an integrated curriculum that is literature-based and concerned with developing instructional strategies and students' understanding of the reading and writing processes.

Sharon bases her instruction partially on goal settings that are collaboratively developed by teacher and student. In September, each of her students reads aloud an excerpt from children's literature, typically of interest to intermediate-grade students. Sharon and the student listen to the taped oral reading, discuss their observations, and establish individual goals.

Sharon also identifies a general set of goals based on her teaching experiences, district goals, and her training as a reading specialist. Sharon shares these goals with us.

My overall goal was that I wanted them to have an enthusiasm for reading and knowing what good literature was. When those students walked out of there and said, "I am a reader!" I mean, those words were just music to my ears. It was just so exciting to see them so involved and immersed in literature and enjoying it and wanting to do it. There were a lot of pluses that stemmed off. Then I saw the improvement in the writing, they go like hand in hand, and was seeing the similes, the metaphors, the imaging, the descriptions, the feelings and understanding the characters and the conflicts. All of these things that they had been reading about I saw being transferred over to the writing. The transfer occurred through direct teaching. I really feel very strongly that you have to model what you expect these kids to learn. We went through *Tuck Everlasting* and *Bridge to Terabithia*. We scrutinized, and we read those pages, and we drew pictures of what the words were saying to us. We spent a lot of time visualizing what was read and looking at the details and looking at the vocabulary of good literature.

Sharon's statement not only identifies her goals but also illustrates her belief that reading and writing must be connected. Sharon uses reading as a springboard into the writing process. Sharon also points out that the teaching of instructional strategies and skills are important goals to accomplish. Throughout the interview, Sharon talked about teaching different instructional strategies such as think-aloud predictions, and questioning to develop both aesthetic and efferent stances of reading, and subsequently using these strategies to inform their own writing.

Sharon also wants her fifth graders to read a variety of genres and to posses knowledge of literary elements such as characterizations, plot structure, conflict, and foreshadowing. She notes that understanding these elements leads to appreciation and then improved writing. But again, she expresses the need for teacher guidance to help students understand how literary elements can facilitate comprehension and enjoyment of text.

I feel strongly that you still have to instruct. There needs to be modeling. I don't think that you can just say—you have a choice of books and just read. I think the appreciation comes from seeing these things that the kids never noticed before, but at the same time I think it's so important for them to get the things that they wonder about, because they can see it in so many different ways. I also made a chart where I make sure that they read every type of genre. I didn't want them just to have the choice— "Gee, I love mysteries so I'm going to read mysteries all year." That was not an option. They had to read, sometime, every single solitary type of genre.

Sharon explains that instruction has to be balanced. Students can benefit from direct instruction of strategies, but, at the same time, they need opportunities to develop their personal responses to text. Students need choice; yet they need to be familiar with all genres in order to make informed choices and have a "balanced diet." Hence her fifth graders can choose specific titles to read but are expected to read all different types of genres.

Sharon also includes specific skills as goals. Critical reading, vocabulary, and study skills are emphasized. She talks about the need for reflection, relating personally to text, and using prior knowledge as well as questioning everything that is read. Thinking while reading is essential. Since Sharon teaches reading and writing across the curriculum, she uses the social studies textbook as a vehicle to teach study skills. She elaborates:

That's when I taught Reciprocal Teaching. I used it to teach how to take a test and how to detect distractors. I used it to teach outlining—organization and mapping out ideas, to teach the boldfaced headings.

Your Turn: How does Sharon formulate her goals, and what are her specific goals? Write your responses in your journal before reading our response.

Our Turn: Sharon's goals are partially influenced by her philosophy, classroom teaching experience, graduate education, involvement in professional organizations, and administrative support. Over the years, she has been able to use these different sources to formulate a philosophy and thereby create goals. Sharon's statement shows the interconnectedness among goal setting, beliefs, instruction, and observation; these form a loop of information that influences teacher decision making.

Sharon uses informal assessment to help her and her students establish goals in a collaborative manner. She also refers to the local district goals to ensure that she addresses the goals all fifth graders are expected to accomplish.

Many of Sharon's goals are similar to the ones we discussed as being necessary for all intermediate-grade students to develop. Sharon's number 1 goal is to create enthusiastic and voracious readers—students who view themselves as readers. Sharon also places great emphasis on students reading a variety of genres so that they are not limited to a particular type of book, such as mysteries. She stresses the need for students to have a "balanced diet" and know what good literature includes. They need familiarity with a variety of genres, so they can make informed choices about reading for pleasure and learning.

Sharon also identifies strategic reading as important. She talks about the need to model different instructional strategies such as think-alouds, prediction, and visualization, as well as skills such as critical reading and vocabulary, so that students can comprehend and learn information from a textbook or find pleasure and beauty in reading.

Although Sharon does not elaborate on specific writing goals beyond writing's direct link to reading literature, she does talk about connecting writing and reading to other content areas and about using a process-writing approach. In Sharon's classroom, students read and analyze different genres and use them as models for their own writing, in which they also incorporate revision, editing, sharing, and publishing. Sharon feels that her fifth graders are being mentored by experts when they analyze the author's work and try to write in the particular genre of the author. More specific goals could be developed to increase her fifth graders' writing.

Sharon requires her students to read a variety of reading materials and to use different forms of writing. She stresses that her students learn different literary elements and genre characteristics so that they can communicate effectively.

Reading and writing goals must be directly linked to instruction and assessment if we are concerned about students' growth and learning. In the next section on organizing, implementing, and assessing literacy instruction, you learn how Sharon used her goals to provide guidance for instructional planning.

HOW DO YOU ORGANIZE, PLAN, IMPLEMENT, AND ASSESS AND EVALUATE LITERACY INSTRUCTION?

As Sharon suggested, instruction begins with goal setting—establishing a course or plan with logical outcomes of learning and enjoyment. The importance of goal setting is also supported by the research, which indicates that if teachers have formulated and clearly communicated goals to their students, learning is enhanced (Anderson, Evertson, & Brophy, 1979; Emmer, Evertson, & Anderson, 1980).

Sharon established three major goals: (1) creating enthusiastic and voracious readers, (2) developing strategic readers and developing critical thinking and vocabulary, and (3) connecting reading and writing to develop literacy. She used these goals to think about creating an effective classroom environment and talked to us about the following areas of literacy instruction: (a) designing the physical space in her classroom, (b) planning instruction to address goals, (c) implementing instruction, (d) establishing a schedule for instruction, (e) assessing and evaluating literacy instruction and learning, and (f) meeting the needs of less skilled readers. In the following Learning from Experience, Sharon shared information about these areas of literacy instruction.

Learning from Experience

Read and examine Sharon's thinking about teaching and learning. There will be six sections: (a) designing the physical space in her classroom, (b) planning instruction to address goals, (c) implementing instruction, (e) establishing a schedule for instruction, assessing and evaluating literacy instruction and learning, and (f) meeting the needs of less skilled readers. For each subsection, we ask you to focus on a particular question as you read about and reflect on Sharon's thinking and decision making. Write the question in your journal.

Designing Classroom Space

How would you design your classroom? In your journal, jot down your design. Compare your design to Sharon's design in Figure 14.1. What does Sharon's design of her classroom communicate about her instruction? Write your responses in your journal.

Sharon organizes her students' desks into groups of four. Two desks face the other two, so small-group discussions can occur during language arts, social studies, science, and mathematics. She has a reading area, where bookshelves with all different types of books, a large-area rug, and beanbag chairs make for an inviting space for reading. Three tables are placed around the perimeter of the room to further en-

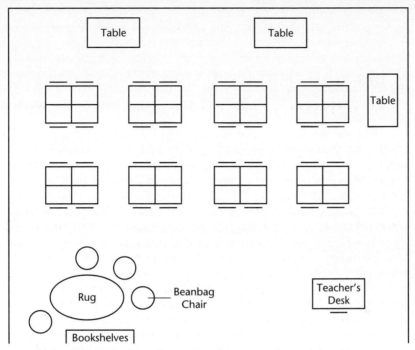

Figure 14.1 The Floor Plan of Sharon's Fifth-Grade Classroom

courage discussions, small-group work, and conferencing. Students can choose to sit at tables or desks—whatever seems to be the most suitable for the individuals and the tasks they are doing. The fifth graders' projects are displayed to indicate that the classroom is a shared community of learners.

 Your Turn: How does the layout of your classroom compare to Sharon's? What does Sharon's design of her classroom communicate about her instruction? Consider this idea before you read our response.

 Our Turn: Using tables and placing desks together so that students are facing each other demonstrates Sharon's beliefs about the importance of conversation about books and the importance of learning from peers. She shows children that learning is developed in a social context. Including books, rug, and beanbag chairs in the environment demonstrates the importance Sharon places on students' reading for enjoyment. Sharon shows that all types of reading are important and valued by including a variety of genres in her classroom library.

Planning Instruction

In this subsection, we talk about Sharon's instructional planning. As you read, think about this question: What did you learn about instructional planning? Write your responses in your journal.

As Sharon plans for instruction, she considers her beliefs and goals about developing lifelong readers. She knows that becoming a better reader requires students to read daily and select their own titles. They need to have opportunities to share with their peers so they will have a myriad of recommended titles and be able to continue the reading adventure. To accomplish this task, Sharon incorporates a form of Reading Workshop (Atwell, 1987). The fifth graders select their own books, read, and share them with their peers.

Sharon also believes that strategy and skill instruction are important and organizes her instruction into units based on a particular theme or genre. She develops her own units and includes themes identified by her school's faculty. These themes then determine the selection of appropriate trade books made by Sharon or her students.

Frequently, Sharon uses Samara and Curry's (1990) unit framework to design differentiated activities, based on Bloom's Taxonomy (1956), that include simple to more complex levels of thinking. In Figure 14.2 (pp. 528–529), Sharon outlines activities for each category of thinking as it relates to her unit goals. In this science fiction unit, Sharon chooses Madeleine L'Engle's *A Wrinkle in Time* as her core literature book. Sharon wants students to identify and discuss the characteristics inherent in science fiction and the themes and character development in *A Wrinkle in Time,* and to relate science fiction concepts to social studies and science. For each goal, Sharon identifies and develops activities that help students think at a variety of levels about different ideas in *A Wrinkle in Time.* Sharon also considers her students' diversity in learning styles, and she designs different activities that emphasize visual, auditory, and kinesthetic learning modes. She wants the fifth graders to choose their own projects to stimulate interest and encourage ownership.

One lesson about character development in *A Wrinkle in Time* is highlighted in Figure 14.3 (p. 530), illustrating Sharon's instruction plan. This lesson is a detailed lesson plan of square 13 from Figure 14.2 denoting the third goal: character development in which the student demonstrates knowledge of character. Sharon uses large-group instruction to brainstorm ideas about the topic, hypnosis. She then provides additional texts to increase the students' understanding of this concept. Using this information on hypnosis, Sharon has the students reread sections of *A Wrinkle in Time* and think about the effects of the hypnosis on the character's behavior. The fifth graders are then divided into dyads to dramatize the story events. She concludes the lesson with sharing and discussing the students' dramatizations.

For this unit, the fifth graders also discuss the book in small groups and participate in whole- and small-group instruction that is similar to the lesson outlined in Figure 14.3. Sharon maintains that the Curry and Samara unit model provides a structure. It allows for differentiated instruction, with the result that everyone is challenged; for self-selection of activities and literature so that students develop ownership; and for stimulating activities that require students to think about what they are reading.

For the science fiction unit using L'Engle's *Wrinkle in Time,* students read the same book, but in most units Sharon gives her students a choice of titles. Discussion groups are formed according to book selection, with no more than four groups being formed. Sharon's discussion-group concept gradually evolved into literature circles (Short & Klassen, 1993). In literature circles, Sharon and her students select and read literature and then engage in book conversations, with all discussants being equal participants. Students are expected to share insights and to respond to their peers' questions, and also to provide needed instruction. Sharon believes that this shared participatory framework in discussion groups empowers students to value their own thinking and insights and thus encourages them to develop responsibility for their own learning. She describes the effects of these discussion groups on developing responsible learners and strengthening peer instruction.

I find that it's been so common for them, if you've really got a question, you can always ask somebody from the class. I find that helps so much when I'm working with others, if they have a question about something, I would say 90 percent of the time they're going to go ask a classmate. And that's Okay. It's serious. They're working on it, and they wonder about it. I guess it's again developing that responsible child. The world doesn't revolve around me. They have to make their own decisions. We talk about—what do I do if I'm conferencing with someone and you don't understand a vocabulary word? What could you do? And we'll sit there and brainstorm. What are the options that you have? And I think this has to be made clear that there are other options and it's not just the teacher.

At these book conversations, Sharon observes her students and listens to their ideas. As a consequence, she plans what Atwell (1987) has labeled minilessons—a short period to share, analyze, and appreciate literature. Sharon plans a 10- to 20-minute minilesson focused on literary elements common to the books being discussed in literature circles as well as reading and writing skills and strategies addressing students' demonstrated needs. Occasionally, Sharon forms additional small groups based on specific needs. These groups are flexible in membership and are disbanded when students' needs have been met.

Sharon believes that vocabulary is an integral part of comprehension and identifies words she thinks will cause her fifth graders difficulty in understanding the fiction or nonfiction text being read. But instead of planning specific vocabulary activities to develop word knowledge, she gives this responsibility to her students. They self-assess their knowledge of her targeted words and also select unknown or interesting words to teach their peers. The students are then given opportunities throughout the unit to teach vocabulary they have selected.

To develop writing, Sharon plans for her students to engage in daily free writing in order to connect reading with writing and to increase writing development. For daily free writing, Sharon uses journaling to provide opportunities for prewriting activities such as brainstorming, experimenting with writing a particular piece, and receiving teacher response. The free writing focuses on the genre the fifth graders are reading in a particular unit. For example, if the fifth graders are reading mysteries, they write a mystery. Reading and analyzing mysteries, for example, serves as a model for increasing writing development. After they have engaged in free writing, Sharon guides her fifth graders through the process-writing approach that includes drafting, revising, editing, sharing, and publishing.

Key Products:
- Auditory
- Visual
- Kinesthetic

Interdisciplinary Relationship:
Social Studies
Science
Math
Language Arts

A Wrinkle in Time by Madeline L'Engle	Knowledge	Comprehension	Application	Analysis	Creative thinking/ Synthesis	Creative thinking/ Evaluation
1. Concepts of space a. Time b. Location of planets c. Travel d. Tesseract	1. Draw a picture of our solar system and Milky Way. Place Camazotz on the picture. • Banner	2. List 12 vocabulary words from the novel that describe something in space. • Card game	3. Construct a travel brochure for Camazotz or Uriel using concepts of space. • Travel brochure	4. Collect information on how stars disappear. Differentiate between the story Mrs. Whatsit tells the children and the info. gathered. • Oral report	5. Create a new form of space travel. • Model/diagram	6.
2. Themes a. Love conquers all b. Goodwill overcomes evil c. Individualism self-worth making choices growing up	7. Find examples of individualism. • List	8.	9.	10. Combine Meg's and It's views of It controlling Charles Wallace. List the pros and cons of each. • Chart	11. Predict what would happen if the "dark thing" enveloped the earth. • Panel discussion	12. Justify/ criticize emotions (Meg) vs. intelligence (It) in ruling. • Speech
3. Characters a. Character of each b. Strengths and weaknesses c. Educational influences d. Changes e. Motivation f. Influences on one another	13. Recognize the scenes that demonstrate mind control. • Dramatization	14. Summarize the main events in the novel that revolve around Meg. • Swatch watch	15. Relate a character in the story to yourself, considering the differences in motivation, strengths, weaknesses, etc. • Letter	16.	17.	18. Justify/ criticize the right of Mrs. Whatsit to steal Mr. Buncombe's sheets because she "needed them." • Debate

A Wrinkle in Time by Madeline L'Engle	Knowledge	Comprehension	Application	Analysis	Creative thinking/ Synthesis	Creative thinking/ Evaluation
4. Contemporary issues related to A Wrinkle in Time a. Pollution b. Space "junk" c. Space travel d. Mind control e. Coups f. Peer pressure	19. List the sequence of events that occur after the landing on Camazotz. Include the synchronization scene. • Flow chart on block picture story	20. Summarize the research Mr. Murry was working on for the CIA that caused his imprisonment. • Essay	21.	22. Compare/contrast the "black thing" with today's problem of pollution or space "junk." • Venn diagram	23. Speculate what the "black thing" is. Design a symbol for it and formulate possible solutions to conquering it. • Display	24.
5. Independent study options a. Dimensions b. Space Travel c. How stars die d. Different types of governments e. Decision making f. Read A Swiftly Tilting Planet or A Wind in the Door (sequels)	25. Collect information on different forms of government. • Oral presentation	26. List resources that describe different dimensions or how stars die. • Computer printout	27. Discuss and apply decision-making skills to Meg's decision to go back and get Charles Wallace or another problem she had. • Mock interview	28. Develop a profile of the "perfect" planet in the universe. • Advertisement on videotape	29. Develop a profile of a "stereotypical" Charles Wallace using information from at least one sequel of Wrinkle in Time. • Diagram	30. Determine the best place to go in the universe if given the opportunity to "tesser." Justify. • Poem in greeting card
Independent study	I. Select a Topic.	II. State a Challenge.	III. Design a Plan.	IV. Gather information.	V. Organize information.	VI. Present the Findings.

Figure 14.2 Instructional Unit on the Book *A Wrinkle in Time*, Based on Curry and Samara's Framework

Content: Mind control in *A Wrinkle in Time*
Product: Dramatization
Process: Knowledge
Research: Gather information on mind control/hypnosis; record information
Learning Objective: In their study of a *A Wrinkle in Time,* students will use what they have learned to demonstrate mind control used in the novel, and they will share their results through a dramatization.

Description of Activity: The teacher will:

1. Ask students what they think they know about mind control or hypnosis. Write on chart paper (with outline of brain on it) under column What I Think I Know.
2. Distribute handouts with more information on mind control. Give students time to read and then discuss new information that could be added to the chart. Place information under column in brain outline that says What I Know.
3. Reinforce mind control by having the class read some lines that demonstrate mind control (see chapters 6,7,8).
4. Review the knowledge level or thinking by reminding students that the dramatization will focus only on recognizing and speaking the lines that demonstrate mind control.
5. Discuss the guidelines for the dramatization.
6. Assist dyads in preparing the dramatizations.
7. Allow students to add more on the mind control chart under the column What I Learned during the planning or after the dramatization.

Evaluation: Discussion of chart—emphasis is on students noting how much they learned from the beginning to end of activity.

Figure 14.3 Lesson on Character Development Based on Curry and Samara's Framework

Sharon points out that writing is not limited to this single classroom period. Writing is incorporated into everything the fifth graders do all day such as social studies and other content areas. For example, Sharon talks about the social studies simulation of discovering the new world, and part of this simulation requires the students to keep a daily log of their journey. They need to include daily events and records of their food supply, the weather, and other information.

Your Turn: What did you learn about instructional planning? Write your response before reading the next paragraph.

Our Turn: Sharon clearly uses goal setting to plan instruction. Her beliefs about teaching and learning guide instructional planning. She understands and uses theories about teaching and learning to plan instruction and is able to explain, modify, and present rationales for specific educational practices. Sharon's planning shows that she is a decision maker. She does not rely on a literature-based program; rather, she develops her own themes and units and selects children's literature, develops instructional activities, and identifies strategies and skills based on goal setting and students' needs. Sharon recognizes that reading and writing are learned in the context of natural and meaningful activities. Fifth graders are reading and responding to good literature and using this literature as a model for writing a particular genre. She uses a unit approach to provide in-depth thinking about, for instance, a particular genre, topic, and theme. As a consequence, students receive many opportunities to develop and apply learning. Sharon also embeds minilessons to address instructional goals and students' needs.

The portrait of Sharon as decision maker is not complete unless we consider the role of student collaboration and empowerment in the instructional process. A large part of Sharon's instruction invites students to self-select literature and instructional activities and to provide their own personal responses in literature circles as a means to guide discussion. Students have choices. They select their own titles during Reading Workshop and usually have some choices during the literature units.

Sharon has a vision of literacy instruction and provides direction for the types of reading and writing experiences she believes fifth graders need. She tries to achieve a balance between teacher and student choice so that students will receive the benefits of her knowledge of reading and writing processes and yet have opportunities to develop ownership and responsibility. Sharon refers to this kind of instruction as "guided choice," which she believes provides a balance between teacher- and student-centered instruction.

Implementing Instruction

As you read this section, consider the following question: What did you notice about Sharon's implementation of instruction?

 Sharon points out that a single type of grouping does not address the diversity of students' needs. She uses whole- and small-group instruction and also meets with individual students to address instructional goals and individual needs. Cooperative groups are sometimes formed to discuss literature and complete a particular project. Small-group book discussions, in which students freely exchange ideas, questions, and curiosities, are regularly employed. All members are responsible for participating, and the teacher becomes a group participant. Sharon rotates from group to group to participate and learn about all the students. Partner reading is also used. Flexible groups are formed to help students who are experiencing difficulties with particular literacy skills or strategies. These groups are disbanded as students learn the particular skill or strategy. Large-group instruction incorporating minilessons on reading and writing strategies and skills related to literature is a routine part of instruction. Time for independent individual reading and writing is also a part of daily instruction. Hence grouping remains flexible because of the use of different units, student choice, coverage of varied goals, and the change in observed needs.

Literature circles are a regular part of Sharon's instruction, since they provide students with opportunities to explore their own ideas and discuss their personal responses to literature. About eight students meet to lead their own discussions by sharing their ideas about a particular book they have selected. Discussions are usually divided by chapters, with each group making their own decisions about the amount to be read. Students are asked to bring questions they are wondering about to discuss with the group. The students' natural curiosity and their reflections usually promote good discussions.

In the past, Sharon specifically taught students different types of questions: explicit types in which the answer was found in the text, the inferential or implicit types in which students had to put text-based ideas together with their own knowledge to answer the question, and evaluative types in which readers had to use their own knowledge to respond. But Sharon noted that teaching students different types of questions wasn't always necessary. Instead of providing direct instruction for different question types, for example, her instruction evolved into observing students' needs before she planned to teach a specific skill such as questioning. Sharon had her fifth graders take notes on things they wondered about and write questions. A page number needed to be included so that students could refer to the author's ideas during discussions. Using Post-its in their books for note taking proved to be a helpful technique. By participating in the discussion groups, Sharon observed, modeled, and provided feedback on questioning as needed. She contextualized questioning as she participated and did think-alouds.

These small-group discussions also focus on applying specific literacy strategies and skills Sharon teaches during minilessons. For example, Sharon wants her students to understand a particular character and uses mapping as a reading strategy to enhance character development. Sharon explains mapping in greater detail:

They share their maps, and we develop a group character map. Everybody adds in and we look and see what we've got and then we've got a whole picture of everybody's thoughts of this particular character. We leave that up for a couple of days because there might be something more throughout the whole book. We're constantly adding to it. Maybe in a week or two we'll say, 'Let's look back at our map that we made, and is there something else we want to add on to it?'

Journaling is a regular routine. The free-writing journal occurs daily and focuses on developing the writing process. The students' writing does not necessarily relate to a particular book; they are encouraged to write their own pieces. Other journals

How does this teacher organize intermediate-grade literacy instruction?

are also used but are not a part of every unit. With some units, Sharon pairs students to write and share their personal responses and questions about characters, events, and other things that occur in the book they are reading. Sharon implements this peer-response journal with books that tend to be more difficult for students to comprehend.

Sharon responds to each student's journal writing, but to read and respond to 23 journals is time-consuming and requires an efficient management system. Instead of responding to all journals in one day, Sharon staggers the days student journals are due. Each day of the week a different group of five students submit their journals for her feedback.

Your Turn: What did you notice about Sharon's implementation of instruction? Write your journal response before reading ours.

Our Turn: Sharon uses a variety of groups to accomplish different purposes. No one grouping scheme meets all goals or needs. Students are not labeled as skilled or less skilled readers and writers who remain in fixed groups. In this way, students' motivation and learning are not hindered. Heterogeneous grouping provides models for learning. The class learns that all students have strengths to share and that everyone also has weaknesses. Strengths and weaknesses change according to topic, interest, prior knowledge, and experiences.

Although Sharon believes in the collaborative nature of instruction, she recognizes the importance of both implicit and explicit models of instruction. Creating a community of learners in which she participates rather than leading literature discussions demonstrates Sharon's beliefs in an implicit model of creating a literacy environment and allowing learning to emerge. However, direct instruction is another side of instruction Sharon believes in and practices. In her minilessons, she models and uses think-alouds to teach literacy strategies and skills that can improve students' comprehension and learning. It is this balance of both types of instruction that characterizes Sharon as teacher and decision maker. Achieving a balance of teacher- and child-centered instruction is difficult, but it addresses a variety of students' learning needs so that more students both enjoy and increase their learning.

Sharon's instruction evolved from teaching specific skills to observing students' needs and providing a general strategy, such as note taking with Post-its to assess if instruction was needed. Sharon reflected critically on her teaching to learn about students' needs and hence was able to use instructional time more effectively.

Organization of Time

Organizing instruction is often a perplexing task for preservice teachers. Typical questions include: How often do you read aloud to your students? How long is a minilesson? How do you ensure that students receive enough reading, writing, speaking, and listening instruction? If you are working with one small group, what are the rest of your students doing? As you read, consider the following question: How does Sharon organize different activities into a language arts period?

Sharon integrates the teaching of reading, writing, speaking, and listening into a daily block of instruction that occurs between 9:30 and 11:45 (see Figure 14.4) Language arts begins with 30 minutes of journaling in which different types of writing occurs. The form of writing is often based on the instructional unit being studied. From 10:00 to 10:40 students are involved in Reading Workshop in which all students are silently reading books of their own choice while Sharon meets individually with students for book conferences. In the next five minutes, students share their reading with two or three people. For the last hour, the fifth graders are immersed in different types of literature activities such as discussion groups, minilessons, and unit projects. While students work on unit projects, Sharon meets with small groups to address specific instructional needs.

 Your Turn: How does Sharon organize the literacy activities into a language arts period? Write your ideas in your journal before reading our response.

Time	Monday	Tuesday	Wednesday	Thursday	Friday
9:30–10:00			Journaling		
10:00–10:40			Reading Workshop and conferencing		
10:40–10:45			Book sharing		
10:45–11:45			Literature unit		

Monday	Tuesday	Wednesday	Thursday	Friday
Minilesson whole group 10:45–11:05 Literature circles 11:05–11:45 •read •discuss	Self-selected unit projects or Flexible groups 10:45–11:45	Minilesson whole group 10:45–11:05 Literature circles 11:05–11:45 •read •discuss	Self-selected unit projects or Flexible groups 10:45–11:45 •read •discuss	Self-selected projects 10:45–11:05 Literature circles 11:05–11:45

Figure 14.4 Sharon Gleason's Language Arts Schedule

Our Turn: Sharon does not separate the teaching of reading and writing during the language arts block. There is a natural flow from writing to reading. Students' interests and instructional needs are considered by incorporating self-selection of books and projects, by meeting with large and small groups, and by having individual conferences. Both guided instruction and peer discussions are included to provide a balanced perspective on teaching and learning. This schedule allows students to be involved in a variety of activities to address all students' needs.

Assessing and Evaluating Learning and Instruction

In this subsection, we explore literacy assessment and evaluation by sharing Sharon's assessment practices in her fifth-grade classroom. As you read, think about the following question: How does Sharon assess and evaluate students' learning and instruction? Jot down some responses in your journal.

Sharon begins the school year by listening to her students read aloud a grade-level passage so she can learn about their strengths and weaknesses and instructional needs. She uses this reading to establish initial goals that she and the student agree upon during an individual conference.

In Sharon's classroom, the fifth graders keep literacy folders or portfolios that include what they know about reading and writing and what they accomplish. The students select their own work for the portfolio. Some work shows areas that need improvement while other samples illustrate the students' best work and demonstrate their achievement. The students are expected to establish their own goals, self-assess their literacy development in writing, and discuss their strengths and difficulties during quarterly conferences with Sharon.

Reading logs are another document the fifth graders and Sharon use to note changes in students' reading development. Students keep a record of the books read during Reading Workshop and note whether the books were easy or difficult and whether they completed the book.

During quarterly conferences, Sharon again listens to each student read aloud, and they discuss individual strengths and weaknesses. Sharon finds that fifth graders can talk about themselves as readers and are able to collaboratively set goals and activities to meet a particular goal. Sharon provides instructional guidance by designating activities to meet that goal. For example, for a student who needs assistance with reading fluently, Sharon would demonstrate and provide time to use the Repeated Reading strategy (Samuels, 1979). (A description of this strategy appears later in this chapter.)

The quarterly reading conference and portfolio also help Sharon to determine if her students are accomplishing her fifth-grade literacy goals and those established collaboratively. For example, by reviewing the reading log, she recognizes if they are experiencing a variety of genres. If the student's reading is narrowly focused, then Sharon identifies wider reading as an additional goal, and together they decide which genres to include and discuss books to be read.

To conduct these quarterly conferences, Sharon has parent volunteers come in to help the other students as she meets individually with students. Each conference takes approximately 10 minutes, and she spends about 1 hour a day over a 3-day period in conference with each student.

Besides teacher- and self-evaluation, peer evaluation is an important part of assessment. For example, students design games about the literature they are reading, play the game with their classmates, and receive feedback about many different aspects of the game, such as providing a complete set of directions, identifying the goal or object of the game, recognizing the relationship between the game and the literature, and developing an interesting and enjoyable game. Other examples of peer evaluation take place in the author's corner where students share their stories or meet in groups and do peer editing.

Because Sharon's school assigns letter grades to students' language arts efforts, Sharon develops a point system. She associates points with each unit project, with the simpler projects receiving fewer points and the more complex ones receiving more points. Students gather points over the duration of the unit and receive a letter grade based on this total. In choosing activities, students know the point value of each activity and add these points together to receive a specific letter grade. By choosing simple activities, students achieve a lower grade than they would achieve if they chose more complex activities.

Before students are assessed, Sharon provides models of the assignment, specific criteria in which students are evaluated, and the total points for the assignment. Sharon recognizes the importance of providing a completed model, but she also recognizes the need for analyzing and discussing her thinking process so that students can achieve success in completing the project as well as learn about a particular concept. For example, Sharon wants the fifth graders to understand the different types of maps, such as political, relief, climate, or other type of map. To demonstrate their knowledge, students use their special interests as vehicles for applying their understanding about a particular map. Since Sharon's interest is jogging, she develops a relief map of the fictitious country of Jogland and explains how she decided on the shape of the country configured as a gym shoe. Sharon talks about how she associates different running terms with physical features of the land such as "Nike" Mountains linking Nike's high sales volume to the massive heights of a mountain. Modeling both process and product is important, since both are evaluated.

Your Turn: How does Sharon assess students' literacy development? Write your response before reading the next paragraph.

Our Turn: Sharon focused on developing individual growth and achieving specific goals by assessing students' reading at the beginning of the year, establishing goals, checking progress quarterly, and developing new goals. These are important points to assess.

Sharon uses portfolios to demonstrate growth in reading and writing, but also to examine students' thinking about reading and writing. Students are able to take ownership in their learning by selecting particular projects, self-selecting pieces for their portfolio, discussing their progress in quarterly conferences, and establishing goals collaboratively. They have criteria to help them in their self-assessment, and this again illustrates Sharon's strong beliefs about providing students with models and direction for learning.

Meeting the Needs of Less Skilled Learners

All classrooms have students who are challenged by learning. Some have been labeled learning-disabled. Others have limited English proficiency while others are just not reading and writing as well as their grade-level peers. You have the responsibility to meet these children's needs and help them improve their literacy development. Sharon's classroom includes students who experience difficulties with literacy, and she shares ways to address these children's needs. As you read, note in your journal how Sharon addresses the needs of less skilled learners in her classroom.

Sharon has two students who experienced difficulties with learning. One receives services from a learning disabilities teacher while the other is a less skilled reader. At the beginning of the year, the LD student's mother spoke to Sharon about her son's inability to read aloud and his dislike of reading. Reading programs, in the earlier grades, did not use literature. He was placed in a low reading group, and he lacked self-esteem. Through reading, writing, and discussing literature in natural, functional, and meaningful ways, this LD student became a voracious reader. Through direct instruction and discussion, he learned that reading every word correctly was not important. He learned how to develop an awareness of content words that carried the message. By the end of the year, he was even volunteering to read aloud.

Thomas, the less skilled reader, also had poor self-esteem and told Sharon he couldn't read. By the end of the year, this fifth grader had joined the literacy club and he was a reader. Sharon recounted one of her fifth graders' reactions to Thomas's success: "Thomas says he's a reader now. And he just needed to realize the joys of literature." At the beginning of the year, Sharon noted that Thomas was a very choppy reader; he stumbled over words. What he needed was much practice with reading good literature! In her program, Sharon provided ample opportunities to read and discuss books. Through Reading Workshop, reading books for discussion groups, and specifically planned activities to address his reading needs such as Repeated Readings, Thomas was able to consolidate his print skill knowledge and develop fluency. Literature and self-selection opened the doors to success and enjoyment.

Your Turn: How did Sharon meet the needs of these two less skilled learners? Write your response before you continue to read.

Our Turn: Sharon provided time for reading literature to develop her students' reading abilities. She allowed them to self-select much of their reading. Sharon also individualized instruction to address these students' specific needs. These students were also reading literature rather than rewritten text or other contrived materials designed to teach particular skills. Reading literature helped them to realize the value in becoming a good reader and also to develop an interest in reading. They became involved and committed to reading. Frequently, intermediate-grade students who are experiencing difficulties with reading need many opportunities to practice. They need to read good literature that captures their interest and doesn't overwhelm them. They

cluded on a daily basis during Reading Workshop. The students were able to read books that met their needs. They had the opportunity to practice reading strategies with material at an easier, independent level. Students were writing daily and using writing to facilitate discussion, and this permitted less skilled readers time to prepare and reflect on a topic before discussion. This writing was not evaluated—another factor that allowed students to reflect, organize, and take the risks that are requisite for learning. Literature circles were incorporated that included student-centered questions instead of the more traditional teacher-centered questions and interpretations. The peer-group discussions encouraged students to ask questions about confusing and vague ideas in reading and writing literature. Students were not expected to have all the answers. They were not being tested by teachers and rewarded for correct answers—a practice that has for so long dominated reading instruction. Sharon emphasized the teaching of reading and writing strategies that, according to theoretical research, are especially necessary for less able learners (Paris, Lipson, & Wixson, 1984). They also learned strategies to handle reading and writing through direct instruction, which included modeling and feedback.

Sharon recognized that less skilled readers needed practice, often in the form of Repeated Readings (an approach that is supported by Chomsky, 1976, and Samuels, 1979). But employing the Repeated Reading strategy may not be the sole answer. Sharon used Repeated Readings within the context of collaborative goal setting. During individual conferences, she and the student jointly assessed and evaluated reading progress and then together established goals. Sharon then suggested a plan to address these goals so that the student knew why particular strategies and activities were being assigned. In this setting, we can see the roles of purpose, function, and ownership in engendering commitment and facilitating learning. It is less skilled readers who need to be convinced that a particular plan of action will be successful because earlier plans have failed them. In the remainder of this section, we provide greater detail about meeting the needs of students who experience difficulties with literacy.

Repeated Readings

Repeated Readings develop print skill and fluency. Poetry presents great opportunities for enjoying reading and for the experience of wanting to reread the same poet. The rhyme and cadence that are characteristic of poetry enables students to identify words automatically, and thus enhance fluency. Poetry may be the key to understanding the phonological qualities of our language, qualities that may have been inaccessible through phonics or writing that employs invented spelling.

Most poetry tends to address all grade levels, so students are not insulted by factors associated with story, such as age of character, problems, and situations of particular age groups. Contemporary poets such as Silverstein, Moss, Prelutsky, and Ciardi have done much to create a renewed interest in poetry. Their poetry, and poetry in general, begs to be read aloud and to be read in choral fashion. Thus it's a perfect fit for Repeated Readings.

Tape recordings are often used in Repeated Readings to give students an expert model to emulate. They listen to the tape and follow along with the text, read simultaneously with the tape, and then read the text independently. Commercial tapes are available and may be motivating because many are read by the author. The only problem with some of these tapes is that the reading pace is often too fast. Teacher and parent volunteers can easily make tapes. If they do, they should adopt a smooth but not too rapid pace and use a bell or other indicator to note pagination and pauses between pages.

Students need instruction as to how to employ these tapes. Letting students choose their own reading material for taped readings enhances interest and commitment. Encouraging students to graph their progress in using taped readings can also increase commitment and highlight progress. For example, students can note their time for independent reading of the selection. From their first to their last reading, they should realize a decrease in time. Students can tape their first reading and some of their subsequent readings to note changes in fluency. The tape can also help them examine factors inhibiting fluency.

Besides taped readings, interactive computer programs can increase fluency. Computer discs (CDs) are used in conjunction with personal computers to allow students to see and hear books being read. With the use of a mouse, for example, students can repeat and highlight words, phrases, and sentences. Students can also play with the illustrations to stimulate interest and enhance comprehension. In most programs, students can listen to the entire story, read along with the CD, and stop at any point to repeat and highlight words.

Language Experience Activity (LEA)

Language Experience Activity has been described as an approach for teaching beginning readers (see chapter 3). This instructional system is best used with second-language learners who are not fluent speakers of English and are reading below grade level. Dictation can help second-language learners read text that is based on their present language development. It also allows them to work with materials that interest them. Reading their own dictated materials exposes them to longer and more complex text than the typical text written for beginning or less skilled readers. Consider Mei, an 11-year-old Vietnamese girl who spoke and read very little English. She had completed less than a year of schooling in the United States, where she received her first exposure to the English language. Her dictation is a retelling of the wordless picture book *Pancakes for Breakfast* by Tomie dePaola.

Mei's Dictation about Pancakes

It is early. And her sleep on the bed. Her wash her face. She put on apron. She get a book out. And she read it. And she get out the bowl. And she fill the flour in the sifter. And she fill the flour in the bowl. And she looked for the egg. And she go in the barn and get some egg from the barn. She look for the milk but don't have anymore. And she go out the door get some milk from the cow. Then she got the milk and go home back. And she fill the milk in the pitcher. And she make the butter and she got the butter. And she look for syrup. She·buy the syrup. She break egg put in the bowl. She mix stuff. Then she fill the pancake. She pop it up and coming back. And she happy. And she surprised. She smells the pancake. And she ran out door and she go another door. And then she knock the door. She come right in and eat the pancake. She feel happy.

Mei's dictation provides a sense of story. There is a clear beginning, a middle, and a definite ending. As Mei uses her dictation for reading instruction, she is continually exposed to basic story structure. Moreover, Mei's dictation is based on a folktale that appeals to a wide variety of ages, and it is innately interesting to Mei herself, since she has created it.

The language patterns in Mei's dictation mirror her own second-language learner patterns, so she is able to read the text with great fluency; research suggests that children's comprehension is enhanced when materials are written with frequent rather than infrequent oral language patterns (Ruddell, 1965; Tatham, 1969–1970) and that children have difficulty comprehending print that contains unfamiliar syntactic structure (Christie, 1980). Typically, commercial materials contain syntactic patterns unfamiliar to second-language learners, and, consequently, they may not facilitate reading.

The sentences and vocabulary in Mei's dictation look more complex than the typical text written for beginning or less skilled readers, and yet, since Mei dictated the text herself, we can feel confident that she understands what it means and is familiar with both vocabulary and concepts.

You may understandably be concerned about Mei continually reading her own dictation, which does not conform to acceptable written language patterns. As Mei becomes more conversant in spoken English and receives continual instruction in oral language, her language patterns will change. Consequently, her dictations will also change; her language patterns will become more and more like those of a native speaker. If the teacher changes the language patterns of her dictation to conform to the rules of written English, however, two things are likely to occur. First, the second-language learner will be less capable of reading the dictation, thus diminishing the positive effects of the LEA. And second, the second-language learner's self-esteem may be negatively affected. Language is so closely tied to how people view themselves that we cannot recommend changing a student's dictation. Reading professionals such as Russell Stauffer (1970) have documented second-language learners' progress through dictations; reading and language patterns have improved through the use of LEA in which language patterns were not changed.

Less skilled readers who are reading three or more years below grade level will also benefit from LEA. Typically, the less skilled readers' language development is advanced far beyond the books they would be reading (such as the I Can Read series). Their interests also differ substantially from those of children of this age level. Hence the early reading books do not sufficiently address the reading needs of the very poor reader, whereas the LEA focuses on a student's interests so as to stimulate and encourage that student to discuss the selection, dictate a version of it, and learn to read the dictation. Reading materials created by students and based on their own interests are a true incentive for those who have frequently failed at reading.

Less skilled readers experience the same problems that second-language learners do in other subject areas—inability to maintain grade-level achievement. Textbook reading becomes more common as students progress through the elementary grades, and since these students are reading far below grade level, textbooks are often frustrating and even incomprehensible to them. These students can benefit from connecting LEA to social studies and science topics within the school curriculum—from discussing, dictating, and reading about the content area concepts and vocabulary. This additional instruction can substantially improve their achievements in other subjects and thereby encourage them to read.

Learning from Experience

As you read about Mr. Ryan's use of LEA with special learners, explain how he used it with less skilled learners.

Mr. Ryan's fifth-grade class includes four less skilled readers and two students who are learning to speak and read English as a second language. Mr. Ryan knows all these students like baseball, so he decides to use this as a topic for dictation. Before dictation, Mr. Ryan asks the students to identify their favorite baseball players and to discuss the great plays each of these players had made in different games. After about 10 minutes, Mr. Ryan asks each student to dictate about one great play made by his favorite player. Mr. Ryan writes down the students' names and exact words.

Kevin: I like when a guy hits it to the outfield and then the outfielder throws it to the catcher and the catcher throws it to third and gets him out.

Jose: I like Mark Grace, a first baseman. He is an announcer in the winter. He plays for the Cubs, and he can catch wild throws.

Rick: A batter hit ball to second base and there is a man on third. The second baseman throw it to catcher and get him out.

Santo: I like Mitch Williams, and he is a relief pitcher. He throws lots of wild pitch and then he throw them clear across plate.

After the dictation, Mr. Ryan asks the students to listen as he reads it aloud and to point out words and sentences that they want changed in their own selections; finally he has them read the dictation chorally.

In the second session, Mr. Ryan wants to work on fluency and quick identification of high-frequency words. To develop fluency, he has the students read the dictation chorally, and each student then reads his own section. Mr. Ryan listens carefully to each reading. Finally Mr. Ryan uses a window card—a card with a rectangular hole cut in it—to isolate high-frequency words. When the students cannot identify a word isolated in the window, he lifts the card and has them reread the sentence. The students are fairly successful with word identification and are also able to read their own sections fluently.

In the third session, Mr. Ryan discusses the reason for developing fluency in reading and models it for the group. The students read the dictation in unison. Then Mr. Ryan divides the group into dyads and has one student read while the other serves as listener. After five minutes, they switch roles. Mr. Ryan visits each dyad to check for fluent reading.

The fourth session includes more fluency practice in dyads as well as development of the students' abilities to formulate questions. After 10 minutes of fluency practice, Mr. Ryan brings the group back together. These students rarely ask questions and have difficulty formulating questions when they do not understand the text. Mr. Ryan wants them to realize the value of asking questions, and he begins instruction by explaining how questioning could help them be better readers. He provides several examples of various kinds of questions. Then he asks the students to reread the dictation and develop questions of their own; each student asks his question of another student, who attempts to answer it. All the students are able to form questions, but every question requires factual recall. Mr. Ryan concludes his instruction by giving examples of questions that require the responder to interpret the text, rather than simply remember it. He will focus on this again in subsequent instruction.

Your Turn: How did Mr. Ryan use LEA with these special learners? Write your response in your journal before comparing it to ours.

Our Turn: Mr. Ryan motivated his students by using an interesting topic—baseball—for the dictation. He used instructional time efficiently by asking each child to report on only one favorite baseball play; this way the students could become familiar with the dictation without being overwhelmed by learning all the reported plays. Those who advanced quickly were encouraged to read other students' favorite plays. Over several days of instruction, students were given repeated opportunities to read the dictation; repetition and modeling increased their fluency and word identification.

This is only one example of several sessions incorporating LEA. Other reading skills and strategies can be taught with the dictation. Observing students during literacy instruction and using the school's reading curriculum or reviewing the scope and sequence chart from the literature-based program, you can decide which strategies the students are ready to learn and if the strategies identified are necessary to becoming skillful readers. This type of decision making can be difficult for beginning teachers. Through experience, you will learn to identify the appropriate strategies students need; it's an evolving process that you will continue to develop as a professional.

Reading Workshop and Less Skilled Readers

Reading Workshop addresses the needs of all readers, including those of the less skilled. In this framework, students can read and respond to books whose level of complexity is commensurate with their ability. They can read books that interest them. Unlike many programs for the less-skilled, Reading Workshop emphasizes reading and responding to text. Students are receiving the much needed practice they need to increase their expertise. The workshop provides a great opportunity for these students to become members of the "literacy club"; for many of these students, membership to this club has been denied. By reading self-selected literature on a daily basis, students are likely to find an author or genre that stimulates and entices them to choose reading for recreation and relaxation. Minilessons include the teaching of instructional strategies so that students can apply them to their own personal reading. In Reading Workshop, teachers respond to individual students' journals and address the needs of the individuals. Students work within their "zone of proximal development," an area that Vygotsky (1978) identifies as being beneficial to increasing student learning. But along with Reading Workshop, these students may need to learn specific strategies that are developed during minilessons. Some individual or small-group time should be allotted for this extended development of reading strategies.

SUMMARY

There are many factors to consider when organizing and planning instruction. Interfacing goals, instructional strategies, flexible grouping patterns, and assessment and evaluation are the main factors teachers need to consider in relation to the students' needs and school and community expectations. It is a highly complex process that requires reflection and teacher decision making. The teacher is the artist who selects the right medium, colors, and perspective to create a masterpiece. It is the teacher's thinking about learning and instruction that is important, and the way in which the teacher as artist formulates the classroom into a beautiful work of art. As each teacher's masterpiece differs from another's, so is each classroom different. Its unique composition and dynamics require ongoing observation, experimentation, and design of instruction to create an effective environment for learning.

The case study of one fifth-grade teacher's design in thinking and planning literacy instruction stimulates insights into the complex process of developing an effective literacy program for the intermediate grades. Sharon Gleason provided us a lens for investigating her thinking and reflection about instruction and learning. She illustrated the skillful orchestration that is necessary for effective instruction. We learned how she interpreted research and theory and linked them to practice. Sharon illustrated how individual teachers rethink and reformulate instructional practices in response to their own beliefs about teaching and learning and their students' needs. She amalgamated instructional ideas to exemplify best practices. Sharon also showed that teachers continually develop and improve their professional skills. Teaching reading and writing is a process that never ceases to develop, so that it will always be a challenge to provide effective instruction.

In the Field

1. If you have access to an interactive computer and software, try out interactive animated stories for children. One good example is Living Books published by Broderbund, a series that includes Marc Brown's *Arthur's Teacher Trouble*. This book can be enjoyed by intermediate-grade readers, since animation is included and the print size is not large. An additional benefit of this book is that the text can be read in English, Japanese, and Spanish. For example, Spanish-speaking students who can read their native language can use Spanish to build a bridge to the English reading. In your journal, write your reactions to the program.

2. Interview a few intermediate-grade teachers and find out their goals for literacy instruction. Write their goals in your journal. Use a Venn diagram to compare these teachers' goals with the target goals discussed in the previous section and those of Sharon Gleason, a fifth-grade teacher. Respond to the similarities and differences in these teachers' goals.

Portfolio Suggestion

Select from your journal two examples of your responses to Learning from Experience or In the Field activities. Write a brief evaluation of your work. Explain what you learned and how it will affect your planning and implementing instruction.

For Further Reading

Atwell, N. (1987) *In the middle: Writing, reading, and learning with adolescents.* Portsmouth, NH: Heinemann.

Block, C. C. (1993). Strategy instruction in a literature-based reading program. *Elementary School Journal, 94,* 139–152.

Klassen, C. (1993). Literature circles: Hearing children's voices. In B. E. Cullinan (Ed.), *Children's voices: Talk in the classroom* (pp. 66–86). Newark, NJ: International Reading Association.

Peterson, R., & Eeds, M. (1990). *Grand conversations: Literature groups in action.* New York: Scholastic.

CHAPTER 15

Developing Literacy across the Curriculum in Middle and Junior High Schools

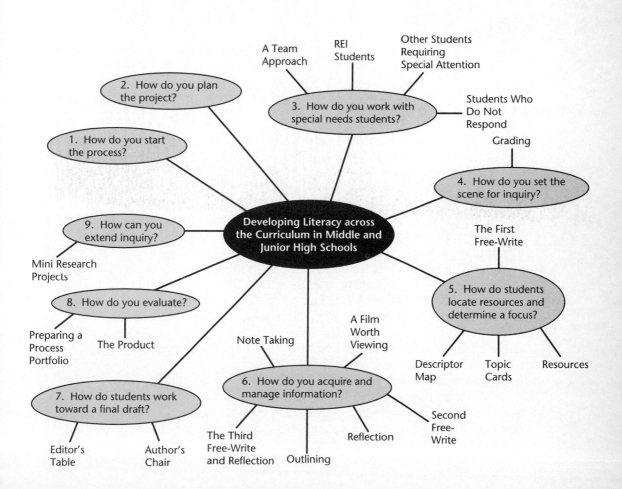

Developing Literacy across the Curriculum in Middle and Junior High Schools

2. How do you plan the project?

1. How do you start the process?

3. How do you work with special needs students?
- A Team Approach
- REI Students
- Other Students Requiring Special Attention
- Students Who Do Not Respond

4. How do you set the scene for inquiry?
- Grading
- The First Free-Write

9. How can you extend inquiry?
- Mini Research Projects

8. How do you evaluate?
- Preparing a Process Portfolio
- The Product

5. How do students locate resources and determine a focus?
- Descriptor Map
- Topic Cards
- Resources

7. How do students work toward a final draft?
- Editor's Table
- Author's Chair

6. How do you acquire and manage information?
- Note Taking
- A Film Worth Viewing
- The Third Free-Write and Reflection
- Outlining
- Reflection
- Second Free-Write

Claudia Katz and Sue Ann Johnson Kuby

▼ CHAPTER GOALS FOR THE READER

To explain the research process and put it in small, manageable steps
To help the teacher make the research process successful for every student
To show how the research process forms a firm foundation for Writing Workshop as well as for literature extensions

▼ CHAPTER OVERVIEW

In this chapter, we describe the entire process we use when our students are doing research. We set the stage by having them consider many topics before choosing one. Enthusiasm for the self-selected topic helps maintain the student's energy level throughout the process.

Once topics are selected, students are taught the individual skills that contribute to being able to complete a research project successfully. They learn to formulate a topic question and create a map with descriptors, both of which help the student maintain a focus. We invite the support personnel in our school to be involved. The learning center director becomes involved at the early stage of topic selection and continues guiding the students as they search for materials. The learning disabilities teacher lends support to all students. We teach the students how to gather information in an organized way, to record it efficiently, and to put it in a logical order. The rough draft is examined through both author's chair and editor's table before the student writes a final draft. We explain the methods we use to ensure student success. We relate this project to Writing Workshop as well as to further applications for research.

Although this chapter is focused on middle and junior high school students doing research, younger elementary-grade students can and should engage in research. Intermediate-grade teachers can use the same procedures described in this chapter to help their students conduct research, but teachers of younger primary-grade students can use a modified version wherein children use drawings, pictures, and captions to share information about a particular research question. The complexities of using multiple resources and note cards that are typically associated with research are eliminated for primary-grade students.

TAPPING PRIOR KNOWLEDGE TO SET A PURPOSE

When you were in junior high school, how did your teacher approach doing research? In what class did you learn the research process, and in what class or classes did you put it to use? How was topic selection handled? Were you allowed to choose any topic, choose one topic from a list prepared by the teacher, or did the teacher assign a specific topic? What were your feelings about doing research then? How did you use the research process later in your education? How did the way you learned to do research affect you? In your journal, record what you remember about learning to do research and your feelings or frustrations concerning it.

HOW DO YOU START THE PROCESS?

Ours is a middle-class community in which most parents are supportive of the schools and want their children to have a strong educational experience. We have some minorities in our population—Latino, Asian, African-American, east Indian—with a few who enter our classes with limited English proficiency. We have an English as a Second Language (ESL) teacher who works with those students both in the classroom and in a pull-out situation. Our ESL and learning-disabled (LD) students are integrated into the regular classrooms. The LD teachers offer support by being in the classroom to hear instruction and give added help to anyone struggling. They offer a limited pull-out situation for catch-up time for further explanation. Any Regular Education Initiative (REI) students are provided with aides who accompany them all day and help them with organization, timeliness, and note taking. The REI aide adapts the material to fit the needs of the individual.

Our school day is divided into nine periods, six for academics, two for physical education and the arts, and one for lunch/recess. We are fortunate that students are scheduled for two periods with the reading/writing teacher, and those two periods are back to back in eighth grade. The periods are 39 minutes long, with a 4-minute passing time provided. With the exception of the gifted students who are put into one section, the student population is heterogeneous in each class grouping. Our class size is 24 to 27 students per class, and we each see three groups of students in a school day.

Our classrooms are next to each other. In one room (Sue Ann's), desks are arranged in an arena setting, with the desks in a U-shaped arrangement so that everyone can see everyone else as well as the screen and chalkboard. In the other room (Claudia's), desks are in straight rows, with everyone facing the front of the room (see

Figure 15.1). The desks are all movable and we frequently move them into pairs of desks or triads, depending on the activity we are doing. When we want all of the students in the same room, we add chairs to the arrangement to provide seating for the "guests." We usually assemble both groups in Sue Ann's or the arena room, where the arrangement lends itself to adding stacking chairs in front of the existing rows and along the walls. After moving from room to room a few times, the students handle it quietly and efficiently.

Pause and Reflect!

What factors need to be taken into consideration before a research project can begin? What do you think could contribute to the success of this project? List your ideas in your journal.

HOW DO YOU PLAN THE PROJECT?

Planning a research or inquiry project carefully is important. We have found doing inquiry during the first quarter of the year is of optimum benefit to our students. It serves as a wonderful foundation for future mini-inquiry projects and for Writing Workshop. For us, this process and the product determine the grade for writing for the first quarter, so it is essential that we be finished in nine weeks. We begin planning by looking at the district calendar and finding the date for the end of the quarter. A big calendar is drawn on unlined paper, two weeks to a sheet. First we write in all the school days and then mark the days that school will not be in session, any days the students will not be in attendance, any shortened or half days, and any days on which an assembly has been scheduled. Now we have the skeleton calendar into which the flesh of the process can be added.

Our learning center (LC) operates on a fixed schedule. All reading/writing teachers have an assigned day for taking their classes to the LC to check out books and use the other materials provided there. Teachers of content-area subjects may also schedule time for their classes in the LC for the entire school year or for a shorter time during which they wish to do a specific project. In addition to our scheduled time, we add extra periods in the LC when the use by other teachers and students is lowest. Our students have access to all of the materials and the space is less crowded then. The librarians are also more available to assist our students with helpful suggestions and resources.

Now we know how many days we have available and when the LC is open to us. We then fill in the steps of the process on the calendar and adjust the amount of class time we can provide. Sometimes the students will have to work on this project at home, so the LC will check out materials overnight or we will photocopy them.

The next step in planning is to coordinate the tasks in the process with the dates available on the calendar. We call this document the track—the students, parents, and teachers all follow the timetable to stay "on track" (see Figure 15.2). We list the tasks

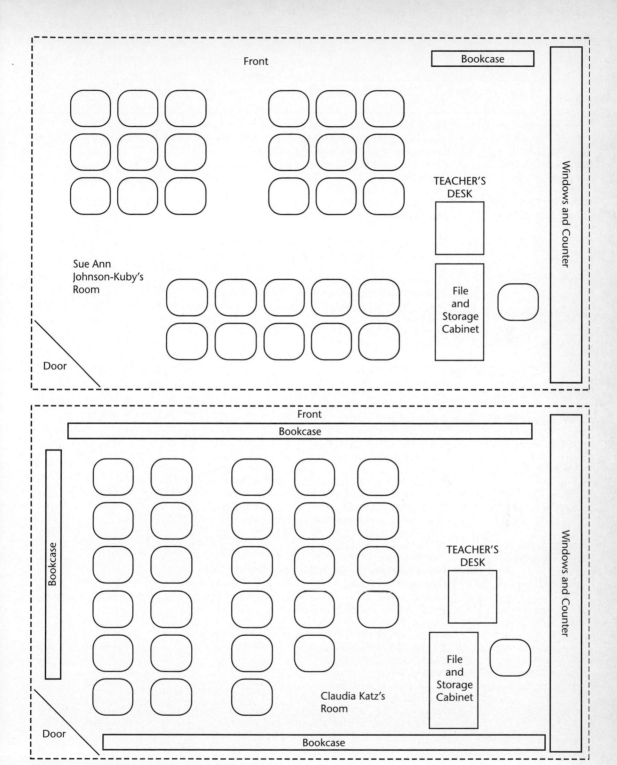

Figure 15.1 Eighth-Grade Classroom Floor Plans

Topic_____ Name_____

Date	Assignment	Check-off
Monday, August 29	Research Paper letter goes home	
Tuesday, August 30	All classes to the learning center	
	Homework: Read *Write in Style,* pp. 7–12	_____
Wednesday, August 31	Complete and turn in Frame Strategy Sheet	
	Teach Works-Cited Card	
	Make a Works-Cited Card	_____
Thursday, September 1	All classes to learning center to discuss topic selection	
Friday, September 2	Topic selection due	_____
	Free-Write due	_____
	Library: Locate an article on topic, read it,	
	create and check in one *perfect* Works-Cited Card.	
	Begin viewing film *The Mind's Treasure Chest*	
Tuesday, September 6	Continue viewing film *The Mind's Treasure Chest*	_____
	All classes to the learning center to create a topic	
	map using article found on Friday	
	Topic map due	_____
	Homework: *Write in Style,* pp. 5–6, pp. 13–18	
Wednesday, September 7	Complete Cloze Strategy Sheet	
	Teach Topic Card	
	Topic Card is due	_____
	Teach Note Cards	
Thursday, September 8	Work on Note Cards in the library	
	Continue viewing *The Mind's Treasure Chest*	
Friday, September 9	Catch-up day	
	Three perfect Works-Cited Cards due	
Monday, September 12	One perfect Note Card due	_____
	Continue to work on the Note Cards in the library	
Wednesday, September 14	Johnson to learning center to work on Note Cards	
	Katz to learning center to work on Note Cards	
Thursday, September 15	Continue to work in the learning center	
Friday, September 16	20–25 Note Cards due	_____
	Continue to work in the learning center	
	Homework: *Write in Style,* pp. 17–18	
Monday, September 19	40–50 Note Cards due	_____
Tuesday, September 20	Catch-up day	
	Last opportunity to work in the library	
Thursday, September 22	Second Free-Write due	_____
	Reflection due	
	Teach Outline and prepare Outline	
Friday, September 23	Outline due	_____
	Rough Draft of Introduction taught	
Monday, September 26	Rough Draft of Introduction due	_____
	Teach Rough Draft of Body	
Tuesday, September 27	Work on Rough Draft of Body	
Wednesday, September 28	Rough Draft of Body due	_____
	Teach Rough Draft of Conclusion	
Thursday, September 29	Rough Draft of Conclusion due	_____
	Fictional Free-Write and Reflection due	_____

Figure 15.2 Inquiry Project Track

Friday, September 30	Catch-up day
Monday, October 3	Self-Corrected Rough Draft due with two signatures of adult readers. Begin Author's Circle. (One day past Author's Circle appearance, Rough Draft due for photocopying for Editor's Table, with *black ink, lines numbered, pages numbered*)
Tuesday, October 4	Continue Author's Circle
Wednesday, October 5	Last day for Author's Circle Check in Author's Circle appearance
Thursday, October 6	Begin Editor's Table
Friday, October 7	Editor's Table
Tuesday, October 11	Editor's Table
Wednesday, October 12	Editor's Table—final chance to pass Editor's Table and check in Check in after passing Editor's Table
Thursday, October 13	Teach smoothing Rough Draft
Friday, October 14	Check in Smooth Rough Draft with page numbers in place. Teach Works Cited and Appendix. Lottery for due dates.
Monday October 17	Works-Cited page due. Title Page taught.
Tuesday, October 18	Final Papers due
Wednesday, October 19	Final Papers due
Thursday, October 20	Final Papers due

Figure 15.2 Inquiry Project Track *(continued)*

down the left-hand side of the paper, including all the pieces that need to be accomplished in a day, and make sure they are in the correct order. In front of each task is the date it is to be taught or checked in. To the right of each task is a box for a check and a line for the teacher's initials. These are filled in when the task is done correctly. This document is a great help to the students because they can easily see what they have accomplished. It serves the teachers because we can assess at a glance if anyone is falling behind and can then supply help. It also allows parents to be informed about the progress of their child.

Students need specific materials to participate in the process. We ask each student to buy a copy of *Write in Style* (available through Perfection Form). Students also need 3 × 5 white, lined note cards; two black ballpoint pens; wide-lined notebook paper; and a folder for housing these materials. We charge a fee that covers the cost of all of these materials and then do the purchasing for the students. This system eliminates the problem of students who expect others to supply them with note cards or who use the lack of materials as an excuse to avoid starting. For this quarter, the folder is the "textbook" for writing class. Items such as editor's marks will be added. These will serve as a foundation for Writing Workshop, so everyone is expected to save everything for use later in the year.

Pause and Reflect!

What special-needs students might you expect to encounter in your classes? How would you adjust the requirements of this project to help these students succeed? Write your ideas in your journal.

HOW DO YOU WORK WITH SPECIAL-NEEDS STUDENTS?

A Team Approach

Our school employs teams of teachers and specialists who routinely follow a child through the grades, ensuring that core and remedial programs are cumulative and that current approaches build on what has taken place before. In the fall, the teaching team meets with the assistant principal, who is in charge of student discipline, the social worker, the learning disabilities teacher, and the guidance counselor to discuss the history of any child assigned to the team who has had difficulties in the past. Often parents and community workers are invited to attend these meetings. This communication lends support by giving teachers an insight into strategies that have worked in the past to ensure the student's success. The special service personnel meet weekly to update the team with information and to offer suggestions. Often these specialists will work with the child and the teacher in the classroom setting.

REI Students

At our school, the LD teachers like to come into the classroom and assist students who require special help. They will also help all the students, even ones who are not identified in the LD program. We provide them with copies of all the materials we give to students. We also inform them as soon as possible if any student is falling behind or having difficulty getting the idea of what is required.

We will often modify requirements to reflect the REI student's ability. For example, we might require only one bibliographic citation. We might reduce the number of note cards and the paper length. We will still expect that the student complete most of the steps in the process and that the final product be in good form. The LD teachers and the REI aide will support us. Even an REI student should be able to feel pride in completing the process.

Other Students Requiring Special Attention

Even with this support, there may be some students who will require special attention from the teacher. There are always a few students who will not or cannot work independently. Even after a parent is informed, these students lag behind the others or just stop doing the work on the project. By eighth grade, most students with identifiable special needs have been diagnosed. Frequently there is no reason for these students to fail to accomplish the task at hand. In this situation, we find that placing the student near us as we check in work keeps the student on task. In the library, we invite the student to sit at our table. This usually takes the student away from the distractions other students produce and keeps the student focused. We check on progress, we cajole and encourage, and as the work is completed, we cheer the student on. In the classroom we follow the same pattern. We seat the student near us. We set small goals for the students, such as "Finish this paragraph," "Complete three cards," and the like. We check on the work frequently to make sure the student is proceeding correctly. As a task is completed, we ask the student to reflect on the way it feels to have the step completed. We ask the student to concentrate on that feeling. It is that good feeling of accomplishment that will help the student complete all the steps required for this project.

Learning from Experience

As you read, think about the following question: What do LD teachers do to help their students? Write these points in your journal.

Sharon Aspinall has earned a Bachelor of Arts degree in education with a major in special education and a master's degree in administration. She has taught Educable Mentally Handicapped (EMH) and physically handicapped children for nine years and learning-disabled children for six years.

Q: What help would you give a teacher when the school year begins, and what information would you like a teacher to give you?

A: I want to sit down with the teacher and let her know some of my needs and the children's needs so that we can work collaboratively to get through the projects and activities she assigns. I need to set up lines of communication, and I need to know about the paperwork that goes with the assignments. I would like a syllabus or schedule—whatever the teacher is giving to the students. I would also like a copy of any texts that would be used now or in the future so I can prepare myself. It is important to meet with the teacher to determine her teaching style and see what her needs might be. That way I can support her because I know what she is going to do. When the student comes to me, I know what the student is supposed to be doing. I am not teaching the course; I am supporting the course.

Q: What procedure should a teacher follow in working with LD students within a class?

A: If students are in class, they could be able to handle the day-to-day work with support. They should be able to attempt an assignment and begin to do some work. It would be my responsibility to let the teacher know what the needs of the child are. If the child is an auditory learner or if the child is a visual learner, the teacher can work with the child in the appropriate manner after we have discussed it.

Q: Give us an example of a student who really needs teacher adjustments.

A: Tom is a child who is lost when given only verbal instructions. He wouldn't be focusing on the assignment. He would need someone to say directly to him, "Tom, this is the assignment." It would be helpful to have the assignment in writing on his desk so he could keep referring to it. If he hears more than two or three instructions, he is lost after the second one. He needs the assignment broken down.

Q: What adjustments should be made to accommodate an LD student?

A: Sometimes length should be adjusted because the processing of some students is so slow that asking them to do 25 note cards could be the same as asking another student to do 50. If our objective is to get them to learn the process, to have good content in the paper, and to have a finished product, sometimes we need to cut down the amount required. This is the only adjustment I would see for them.

Q: How would you want teachers to handle grades for LD students?

A: I think you must look at all the kids individually, decide what you expect from each one, and if what you got is what you expected, then I think an A is warranted. For instance, Becky came in with major writing difficulties in usage. She couldn't even finish a project. She put in every bit of effort that was needed. She spent a lot of time on it and I didn't see much goofing off. Her content was good for her. She wrote so much better than she had the previous semester. I would look at her and say she wrote an A paper. If she had received a C, I think it would have knocked her down so much in self-esteem that she would have said, "Gosh, I worked so hard, I did so much and I only got a C on this paper."

I look at a kid like Barry, who probably didn't put in the amount of work that he should have. He goofed off and I had to pull him out of class and back him up. He didn't put in all the effort he should have. He didn't deserve an A because he probably wasted time. He did not give it his all.

Your Turn: In your journal write your response to the question What does the LD teacher do to help her students? and then compare your response to ours.

Our Turn: Sharon meets with each classroom teacher who has REI students and establishes rapport, so she can learn about the teacher's assignments, materials, and expectations in regard to the students. She informs the teacher of the students' specific needs and collaborates with the classroom teacher to develop ways the students can successfully complete the project. Sharon knows and understands the students' assignments so she can aid her REI students.

Students Who Do Not Respond

Almost every teacher has had a student who will not respond to any type of support, even when a great deal of support is given. If it appears that you have encountered such a student, you should begin to keep anecdotal records of the student's behavior. Record every time a parental call is made and make a note of the subject of the call. Inform the administrator in charge of discipline that you are concerned about the student and that you are keeping records of your attempts to bring the student on board. If your school has an after-school tutoring program or detention program, consider recommending the student for it. If your school has a process for retention, now, early in the school year, is the time to proceed with it. Ask other teachers how they have dealt with the student's avoidance of work. Do not abandon the entire project because a few students do not respond. These students will always exist. They should not influence the educational process.

Learning from Experience

Cynthia Locke is a guidance counselor in the Libertyville School District. As you read the interview with Cindy, think about this question: How does Cindy support her students? Write your response in your journal.

Q: How do you see your work in relation to how you work with teachers?

A: A big part of counseling needs to be consultations with staff. My role is to serve as a consultant and a collaborator with teachers to assist them in being able to work with the students. To be an effective middle school guidance counselor, you have to have people who buy into the middle school philosophy and are willing to behave as a team.

Q: What information can teachers give you that can help your work?

A: I still have a hard time asking teachers to keep anecdotal records. I have difficulty sometimes saying, "You need to write that down." But in case work, documentation is needed. Whether we're trying to identify a problem or investigate it, all the pieces of a case need to be pulled together if we are going to act on it, whether that be to initiate some kind of treatment or move into the realm of special education. The only way you can take action is through the actual solid recording of data. The only way that you can really adequately communicate that to a family is through the data collection.

Q: How about a phone call home and documentation right away?

A: The teacher's willingness to initiate communication with the home is the most powerful tool that can be used to demonstrate to a kid, "Hey, you're accountable and I'm going to be working with your parents. It's not going to be you playing all the manipulative games that kids learn how to play."

Teachers should act on a situation when it happens. You need to stop at the moment that you're seeing the behavior and try to address it. I know it sounds easy when I say that, but it's certainly more effective than coming back later and realizing that you have a kid out of control. It would be helpful if teachers could deal with students more immediately. Because we know that you don't teach a lesson later. You teach it when the opportunity arises.

A phone call home can do so much in terms of relationships between the teacher, the parents, and the kid. If the teacher gets to the parent first, the teacher can say, "Help me understand your child. You know her better than I do. You know her better than anyone. Tell me what works at home. This is what I think is going on with her." The teacher enlists the parents and begins to collaborate with them. A phone call can save a teacher so much trouble in the long run.

Q: That behavior, right in the beginning of the school year, has an enormous effect on whether students are going to be successful. Every time I've done it, kids perceive it as, "You care about me."

A: But if the teacher waits and doesn't initiate that . . .

Q: The kid goes home and tells a whole different story.

A: And then you're back tracking and you're trying to intervene in a situation where the system's already developed. You're trying to act on it, and it's so much harder. If people only knew that it would be easier for them in the long run to just call when something happens. That's something really important for a new teacher to develop. Once you become adept at it, it's just another skill in your bag of tricks.

Q: What can teachers do when they've exhausted all their solutions? When there are no solutions left? The teachers have done everything. They've had the parents in. They've scheduled a meeting and the parents didn't show up. They've called home. They've documented the classroom behavior. They've enlisted you. They've had the LD evaluation. The administration, as well as it can, supports them.

A: That's when you stop and you reflect back on everything that you've done. What that enables you to do is to lay it all out logically and look at the reality. The reality is you have behaved professionally. You have used all your resources and you have exhausted them. You have done a fine, professional job and you stop and pat yourself on the back. Then you realize—and this is really important to your survival in working with middle school kids—the limits and the boundaries of what you can accomplish with this particular child as a teacher. You realize that you should self-evaluate yourself, not according to how this kid is doing, not according to whether the kid turns in homework, or whether the kid's grade is good. You self-evaluate according to all the things you just did. You say, "That was what I needed to do. I've done my job as well as I possibly can. I need to emotionally distance myself from this situation over which I have no control. If I continue to throw energy and effort at it, it will be a case of diminishing returns. I will become increasingly frustrated and angry because I cannot change what is here. I've done my best and now I need to emotionally distance, so that I can continue and I can use my energy on the kids who perhaps will benefit from it." When you emotionally distance, you have put it in a place in your head that will not allow you to be angry at the child. The child is going to continue to function poorly and the kindest thing you can do is just treat the child with the same respect that you would any other human being, with compassion. That's one of the teacher's greatest tools, compassion.

Q: I focus on a kid like Sid. We did all those things for him and it made a difference. Sid's behavior changed and he became a happier kid. A kid who smiled more often, had more friends, got his work in, felt some satisfaction about doing his job, celebrated graduating as he should have. That was where my attention was.

A: You adjusted your lens. Celebrating is a really good verb that needs to be applied more, and used more, in schools. I think we think of it as a luxury, so we tend not to want to do it because it doesn't seem to fit in with our notion of work. It's such a key component of climate. For a school to be an effective community, there has to be some spirit and some celebration. That's what you do. You change your focal point. When you've done everything you can do with a kid and you can't do anything else, then you shift and you look for where you can do the good.

Sometimes people ask me, "How come you do what you do? You only work with problems." As a counselor you have to be able to let go. If I judged my effectiveness on how well my kids were doing, I'd be crying. They're not all doing so well.

Q: Even when you're really successful with most kids, and you handle the reluctant learners in the best way possible, there are still some people who come at you, unexpectedly and often with no rational motivation. Sometimes there is just nothing you can do to stop that.

A: What helps me with that is a phrase that I've repeated often in school context: "You can't deal rationally with irrational people, so you just have to identify them as irrational and then distance." That's what you have going in that kind of situation. Who knows what the issue is? It isn't rational. So there isn't a heck of a lot you can do. Even if you went back and said, "Well, how could I have handled this differently?" Some people are irrational. Therefore for me to waste my time trying to reconstruct their personalities is silly.

Your Turn: How does Cindy support teachers and students? Answer this question in your journal before reading our response.

Our Turn: Cindy acts as a consultant and as a collaborator. She recognizes the difficulty in keeping anecdotal records, but this data gathering is necessary if teachers and students are to receive the needed assistance. Teachers need to respond immediately to their students' needs if the students are going to learn from the problem. Communication with the home is paramount to show accountability and to facilitate student success.

HOW DO YOU SET THE SCENE FOR INQUIRY?

Students should report on topics that interest them. We seek ways to invite students to initiate topics they might not think of easily on their own but that reflect their real interests.

We composed a survey, but before distributing it, we pose the question, "What issues are of concern to young people today?" Students suggest some ideas such as death, disease, family values, and violence. These ideas are written on the chalkboard. Later, they become our topics for categorization. We collect a set of recent issues of news magazines and invite students, divided into groups of three, to browse through these magazines to locate articles that deal with issues that reflect their concerns. We also include some science magazines and about a week's worth of local newspapers. We want this exploration to have a *now* feeling. We distribute Post-its and invite students to mark the stories that they find interesting. Later, these stories become resources for some of the inquiry projects. Each group is encouraged to find at least three articles. After about 30 minutes of exploration, we bring the students together and they begin sharing what they have discovered. We list these ideas on the board and begin to classify them under the topics the students had previously generated.

Now we distribute the survey (see Figure 15.3). It consists of three questions: *What personal decisions do you make every day? What are the most important issues faced by young people today? And what are your biggest concerns for young people today?* We ask students to question four people: an adult relative or parent, an adult neighbor, another student, and themselves. We define as adult anyone of driving age. We ask the

YOUR _____

NAME _____

GENDER (male) (female)

YOUR AGE _____

1. What personal decisions do you make every day?

_____

_____

2. What are the most important issues faced by young people today?

_____

_____

3. What are your biggest concerns for yourself today?

_____

_____

GENDER (male) (female)

AGE (16–20) (21–30) (31–40) (41+)

1. What personal decisions do you make every day?

_____

_____

2. What are the most important issues faced by young people today?

_____

_____

3. What are your biggest concerns for young people today?

_____

_____

****

GENDER (male) (female)

AGE (16–20) (21–30) (31–40) (41+)

1. What personal decisions do you make every day?

_____

_____

2. What are the most important issues faced by young people today?

_____

_____

3. What are your biggest concerns for young people today?

_____

****

GENDER (male) (female)

AGE (16–20) (21–30) (31–40) (41+)

1. What personal decisions do you make every day?

_____

_____

2. What are the most important issues faced by young people today?

_____

_____

3. What are your biggest concerns for young people today?

_____

Figure 15.3 Inquiry Survey

students to return with the survey results as well as a brief list of possible issues (3) for their inquiry project.

The next day we examine the survey results and tabulate them, comparing the five issues that most concern adults with those that most concern young people. We invite students to briefly reflect in their journals on the results and compare the similarities and differences of the responses. We also invite students to collect five or six words that keep popping up in relation to their topics. These words are also listed in the journals we ask students to keep during this unit.

Topics in hand, students meet in the LC where the librarian confirms whether materials are available. Students suggest topics. They are told whether material for the topic is available in the LC. When material on a topic such as heavy metal music is not readily available, the student is encouraged to choose a different focus. In this case, a student insisted on this unusual topic. He was required to locate three texts that could be kept at school for at least six weeks, so the research process could proceed smoothly.

At this point, a letter is sent home to the parents informing them of their child's choice of topic and asking them to express any concerns (see Figure 15.4, p. 562).Popular topics such as witchcraft or drugs have been a concern to parents, and we are reluctant to have students begin work only to have their parents voice concerns later and cause the project to be interrupted.

Grading

In our grade books, we write all of the steps on the track across the bottom of the page. The students' names are down the left side of the books, and we add the date each item is due on the top of the page. Now we are ready to check in student work and keep records of it. Students can bring their completed work to either of us and have the initials written on the blank on the inquiry project track form (Figure 15.2).

We both keep a binder that contains detention slips, demerit slips, and midterm notices. Plain paper is inserted so conversations with parents can be recorded. If a student is a consistent problem, an entire page can be devoted to that student. It is efficient to keep a list of parental phone numbers at home and at work right in the binder too. When problems need to be handled through a conference with parents, we have an ongoing record of contacts made and subjects covered that is organized and easy to maintain.

Daily assignments are handled differently by each of us. We both believe that teachers should keep close track of daily assignments. This is especially important at the start of the school year when teachers are establishing themselves as educational components in a student's life. If assignments are checked frequently, teachers can quickly tell which students might be falling behind in their work. The teacher can speak personally to a student. If a gentle reminder fails, it is time to inform the student's parents that assignments are missing. Parents like to know early that their child is missing assignments. A few assignments can be easily made up; numerous assignments are a different matter. Faced with more than three missing assignments, a parent sees the task of getting the assignment done as daunting. Catching missing assignments early can really put parents on the teacher's side.

Monday, August 26, 1996

Dear Parents,

Today Mrs. Johnson and Mrs. Katz will begin teaching the term paper. This year, students are to select a topic about which they would like to know more. The final paper is short—2 to 3 pages—so the topic should be limited in scope. We would like you to discuss the topic proposed by your child or other topics he or she may have in mind. When you have agreed with your child on one that suits you both, please write it on the form provided and send this letter, signed, with your child on Tuesday, August 30. We will review the topics during the first week of the project.

We are providing learning center time for research, but your child must expect to work on this project at home as well. It will fill all of first quarter, so it is a major influence on the first quarter grade in language. Please ask to see your child's track sheet to monitor the progress the student is making. As steps are completed, the teachers will initial the track sheet. (This sheet will be distributed to students later this week.) Today we are sending home a PLANNING CALENDAR for the first three weeks. We hope you will get a sense of how the project will flow.

We will be using the text *Write in Style.* Over the years we have found this text to be useful for learning term-paper style as well as process. At the end of the project, students usually want to keep this useful resource. Thus, we are asking you to purchase a copy for your child. The cost is $6.00. Please make a check payable to Mrs. Katz. (The books have been ordered on her credit card.)

If you have any questions, please call either of us (Mrs. Katz or Mrs. Johnson) at Highland 708/362-9020. Thank you for your cooperation in signing this and having your child return it with the check for $6.00 promptly.

Sincerely,

Mrs. Katz and Mrs. Johnson

✄ ....

My child _____, would like to do research on _____ .

_____I am enclosing the check made payable to Mrs. Katz for $6.00.

_____
Parent signature

Figure 15.4 Sample Letter to Parents

How I Handle Grades: Claudia

I want students to take a risk and turn work in. To prime the pump, I give only two grades, A or O. A student turning in a daily assignment, or completing a step on the inquiry project track, gets an A in my grade book. If an assignment is late, the A drops to a B and so on until the grade becomes a U if it is more than five days late. A series of grades other than A can indicate that a student is developing a pattern of turning in work late, and parents should be informed. I make my grade book available to students. They can check on their grades at any time.

How I Handle Grades: Sue Ann

I record a check when items are completed correctly on time. When something is not in, I check with the student (maybe Claudia had seen it and initialed the track), and if I find it is not done, I put a zero in the box. Once the step is done, I enter a check in my grade book, but I also have a record that says the work was late. If a student has two or three zeros in a row, it is time to call home and let the parents know the student is falling behind and needs to be working at home and/or making better use of the time provided in class. In my class, the quarter grade is determined by the grades earned on the product only. However, the student who "stays on track" and is doing quality work (the only kind that earns a signature on the track) is probably going to have a quality product as well. Because there are so many built-in checkpoints, most students do very well on this project.

HOW DO STUDENTS LOCATE RESOURCES AND DETERMINE A FOCUS?

The First Free-Write

When students have determined a general topic, they are invited to do a free-write. To complete a free-write, students write fast for 5 or 10 minutes without worrying about grammar, punctuation, or spelling, and they concentrate on what they know about their topic (Macrorie, 1988). They are asked to fill a page with information. At this point in the project, most students find it difficult to fill a page and often must settle for part of a page. These attempts are checked off on the inquiry project track, recorded in the teacher's grade book, and stored by the student in the writing folder.

Resources

After students have selected their topic, they are ready to search for resources. Before the search begins, the chapter on resources in *Write in Style* is assigned and the form of a citation is taught. Students copy an example and create another example as part of their notes for the project. These samples are placed in their writing folders.

Students proceed to the LC, where they are invited to find three resources. We would like them to find one book, one magazine, and one encyclopedia entry. If it is apparent that three *different* kinds of resources are not available, teachers may adapt this requirement. If three resources are not available, students are encouraged to alter their topic so that they can locate three resources. Students record their resources on 3 × 5 note cards. Each resource card is checked at this point to make sure it follows the proper form. Cards that are incorrectly constructed are "slashed" with a red marker and students are sent off without additional instruction to locate their error. A student might do a single card over and over until it is correctly completed. Students collaborate with others, comparing cards and searching for errors until they determine

Student's Name_____ Date _Sept. 6, 1996_

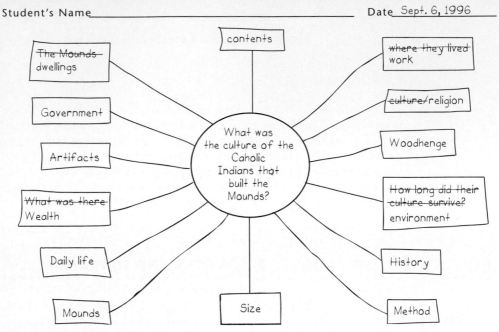

Figure 15.5 A Student's Descriptor Map

their own mistakes. A demand for perfection at this point pays off later when students are constructing their final draft and their bibliography. The final construction of the paper becomes easier because in the opening steps a high standard is set. Later, students might find additional resources and add cards.

Topic Card

Defining and selecting a specific topic can be the most important single act in the construction of an inquiry paper. Our students are invited to focus on their topic and state it in the form of a thesis question. For example Matt's topic, UFOs, becomes, "What are some sightings of UFOs and Extraterrestrials?" and it is improved to read, "What happened in Rosewell, New Mexico?" Transforming a topic to a specific question can be difficult. Topic questions should be as specific as possible.

We approach this activity together. After modeling the construction of a few questions, we invite students to try their hand at writing a specific question for themselves. In a whole-class setting, students share the questions they produce. The class evaluates, edits, and adjusts each question until everyone is satisfied that the question can be answered.

The Descriptor Map

A descriptor map breaks the topic down into subheading categories. These categories (descriptors) become the labels on the top of the note cards and, later, the organizing categories for the body of the paper. The student places the topic question in the center of the map. Initially, the teacher models the creation of a map in the form of a minilesson. With the help of a partner, the student brainstorms the subcategories of the topic and adds them to the arms of the map. It should be understood that these descriptors might change. Students can cross out useless descriptors and add additional descriptors. After it is checked in, the map need not be rewritten. We have found that eight categories are usually sufficient. A completed map is shown in Figure 15.5.

HOW DO YOU ACQUIRE AND MANAGE INFORMATION?

We want the students to have enough time to complete the necessary explorations in the LC, but not so much time they feel they are being provided with a social hour. We also want them to be well prepared so their efforts are directed and efficient. One valuable resource in the LC is the director who loves seeing students doing research and ferreting out great resources and information. The director helps the students by reviewing the use of the *Reader's Guide to Periodic Literature,* since many students choose contemporary topics and need very current information. The director also does a quick review of the kinds of resources our LC has available, where they are located, and the kinds of information found in them. The LC subscribes to a limited number of magazines and keeps back issues on file so the students can fill out a request slip for issues they think will have applicable information. If they find others listed in the *Reader's Guide to Periodic Literature,* they are encouraged to write those down and ask for them at the public library. We encourage the students to make good use of their time in the LC; for the most part, they are able to complete their note cards without any of their materials being photocopied for note taking at home.

Learning from Experience

We talked to the school and public librarians to learn about their roles in helping students with their inquiry projects. Karen Mueller has been a school librarian for 20 years, working in both elementary and middle schools. Eileen Tanguay has been a volunteer and paid library aide in a variety of schools. Eileen Sullivan has been the children's services librarian at Cook Memorial Library in Libertyville, Illinois, for 15 years, and Eileen Kloberdanz has worked at Cook Library for 20 years, 8 of them as coordinator of adult services. As you read the following interview, think about this question: How do school and public libraries provide research assistance? Write your response in your journal.

Q: What is your role in topic selection with the students?
Karen: Sometimes we are presented with the topics we will be working with, but it works better when we can be involved with the students as they select their topics. They may choose a topic that might need to be narrowed or broadened. It's better for them to ex-

How does newspaper reading enhance reading and writing development?

plore and bounce that off of us right away rather than being two weeks into the topic and discovering the topic is too narrow or too broad. They may intend to do a report on World War II, but that is a bit much. Sometimes if they want to do something very specific, that can be a problem as well.

Q: Give an example of a perfect situation.

Karen: The teachers come in and we talk about the project ahead of time. They say, "This is what we are thinking. Would it work?" They work with me and let me work with the students on selection of topics. They set up a schedule ahead of time for bringing students in. That is when it really works.

Q: What advantages do you see as a result of our preparing students by teaching them the research process?

Eileen S.: I think students learn as the year progresses to work more independently. I think they ask us fewer basic questions. They may ask us to help them find something specific, but they will go right to the encyclopedia or the *Reader's Guide* and they will look for information and then they will come to us. They are less intimidated by the whole process as the year goes on.

Q: Are there rules that teachers make that drive you nuts?

Eileen S.: Yes! Some teachers say that the students can't use certain books because they are too simple or too short. It drives me crazy. Personally, if I want to learn a craft, I make a beeline for the children's books because these books are going to put it in the simplest terms. I'm going to be able to understand it, and I can always go on to a more sophisticated level at another time. If the book is short or it is simple, maybe that's what the student needs.

Karen: A limitation on page length on any kind of book is definitely a problem. Biography is a good example. Teachers have students read a biography. They require that the book be over 110 pages and it can't have a lot of pictures in it. If I want to tell you about my family, I'm going to pull out my photo album and then tell you about my family via my photo album. There are many books purchased and not used as well as they should be because they are "too small and have too many pictures."

Q: How would you like teachers to involve you in the process when they ask their students to do research?

Eileen S.: I think it would be really helpful if, before the teachers made the assignments, they would call the library and give us a background in what they are assigning and what their expectations are and let us investigate what we have that the students would be able to use. If they would like to come in in person, it's really helpful. We can have a better questioning process. We can show the teachers the types of materials that we have, and I think I would like to ascertain from them what they truly expect the kids to produce—to be able to find. Many times for the assignments they give, there just isn't lots and lots of information available either at the proper reading level or even in existence within the library. Lots of things need to be interlibrary-loaned, and sometimes those research skills are well beyond your average middle school student.

Eileen K.: Often we will see an assignment that is written out on a sheet of paper and the student doesn't understand it, the parent doesn't understand it, and we certainly don't understand it. And lots of times I think we all make it more difficult than the teacher ever expected it to be. I think if the teacher would communicate with us exactly what is expected on this assignment, none of us would be quite as stressed out over it.

Eileen S.: I think lots of times the kids either think they've got it so they ask no questions, or they don't want to appear before their peers to be either asking to make everyone do more work or showing the fact that they don't understand. They come here and say they have to do a report on, say, the Civil War. That's impossible! It probably never was the initial assignment, but if we know what the assignment really is, that is helpful.

Eileen K.: And sometimes the parents come along to work with the student. If we could say to them, "We have spoken to the teacher and this is what the expectations are. You don't need to do research beyond a certain level."

Eileen S.: The other thing we need to mention is to let us know the assignment is being made. We need to know of it before the first kid comes in and takes everything out.

Eileen K.: That's a real problem. It takes us at least two students to realize that this is a class assignment and not an individual research project. And if we know it is a class assignment, we will pull all of the books and put them on reference, so there is something available for everyone who comes in. But if nobody notifies us, the first one or two students literally clean us out and we have nothing that we can give other students. We have to just scrounge to find bits and pieces in reference books because our major sources have gone out.

Eileen S.: "You can't use an encyclopedia" drives me through the ceiling.

Eileen K.: That's a big issue.

Eileen S.: Any book with the word "encyclopedia" on the cover the kids won't look at. I presume the teachers mean *World Book* and that type of thing.

Eileen K.: We buy some very expensive encyclopedias that are highly specialized, and the kids won't touch them because they have the word "encyclopedia" on the cover. That's a big problem.

Eileen S.: That's an interpretation problem. I say, "The teacher means you can't copy from the *World Book,*" but they take the instructions very literally.

Eileen K.: "But the teacher said"! And here sits *The Encyclopedia of Scientific Biography,* which is the only place with the answer and the student won't use it.

Eileen S.: There are some wonderful new endangered-species books, but they are in an encyclopedia. They are the only way to find some information.

Your Turn: How did the librarians provide research assistance? Write your response in your journal before reading our response.

Our Turn: All the librarians suggest that classroom teachers meet with them to help plan a research project. This communication can save much work and frustration by students, librarians, parents, and classroom teacher. Helping students narrow or broaden a topic is important, since the school library may have insufficient items or too many that will overwhelm the students. By allowing the librarians to suggest a narrower or wider topic focus, librarians can again save the teacher time and frustration. Putting page limits on books and other general and arbitrary requirements can be problematic. As a result, important materials can be overlooked because they don't meet the criteria. Thus these librarians would welcome fewer restrictions and greater focus on locating meaningful information that would help the students answer their questions. Communication and flexibility are key factors in enabling students to succeed in locating and using resources.

Note Taking

Once students have located at least three sources of information in the LC and have written the bibliographic information, they are ready to start taking notes. In the mini-lesson where we teach the making of the cards, we emphasize reading a sentence, a group of sentences, or an entire paragraph before taking a note. The student must put only one idea on a note card, and it must be in the student's own words. Also, each card must have a descriptor in the top left-hand corner that has been taken from the map the student has prepared. The information written on the card needs to be related to that subtopic. In the bottom right-hand corner, the student writes the citation (first word on the works-cited card and the page number of this information).

It is very important to have each student check in the first note card for accuracy, because, by carefully checking the first one, we can help the student avoid repeating an error that might have been made. One common error is using the general topic for the descriptor on the card. We ask the students to bring their maps to us whenever they check in note cards. We ask, "Where is this word on your map?" At the beginning of the note-taking process, students are puzzled by that question. As the purpose of putting descriptors on the cards is explained again, understanding registers on the students' faces and they grab their materials and return to their tables to reconstruct the note cards. One perfect note card must be completed, checked off in the teacher's grade book, and recorded on the tracking sheet before the student goes on to write any more cards. The next check-in is at five cards. For all students, the question is asked again, "Where is this word on your map?" At this point, most students can readily point to the map and indicate the descriptor. Some are still baffled, and the explanation is given again. This is the time to clear up any mysteries about descriptors, citations, and note taking. We don't want a student to end up with 20 or more note cards that are done incorrectly. It is discouraging to the student to have to start over, but it does happen if students fail to check in the note cards at the prescribed times.

The note card check-in process is repeated after 20 cards and after 30 or more cards. When the student feels that enough cards have been made to cover the topic, it is time to sort the cards by descriptors. If there are six or seven cards with strong information for a descriptor, there is probably enough information for writing two or three paragraphs on that subtopic. But if there are fewer than six cards, the student may need to return to the searching process and find a new resource, so more information can be added. Naturally, any new resources must have works-cited cards made for them. At this point, students may discover that they have no cards or just one or two cards for a subtopic. They have two options—to look for more information or to eliminate the subtopic from the map. Usually, by now, the student who has been making a good effort at reading will make the best decision.

A Film Worth Viewing

As we are exploring topic selection, topic limiting, and note taking, we like to show the film *The Mind's Treasure Chest* (the Follett Software Company, 809 North Front Street, McHenry, IL 60050-5589, 1/800-323-3397). In it, Jack, a high schooler with political ambitions but no research skills, is running for class president. In his American history class, he is challenged by his teacher to present the lesson the next day. He needs to look well informed in order to win the election, but he knows nothing about John F. Kennedy and the Cuban Missile Crisis. It occurs to him that he must research the topic, but he doesn't even know where the library in his school is located! He has lots to accomplish in 24 hours. Jack, with the help of a fellow student and a sympathetic librarian, explores most of the research facilities in the school and in public libraries. The story is funny and far-fetched, so eighth graders love it, and, in spite of themselves, they learn about the library and how to use it. It is with great delight that they realize that our LC has a vertical file, although not nearly as tall as the one Jack encounters! We show the film over a number of days and the library discoveries that Jack makes correspond very closely with the discoveries our students are making.

Second Free-Write

When students have completed their note cards, they are invited to compose another free-write. Once again students focus on their topic and write what they know about it without being concerned about spelling, grammar, or punctuation. Second free-writes are limited to the front of *one* piece of notebook paper. This limitation is significant.

Students become aware that they have acquired a large amount of information. Keeping their writing under one page is difficult. The second free-write becomes a kind of first rough draft. Students see that they can write about their topic without copying information directly from a book. This goes a long way toward eliminating plagiarism.

Reflection

Metacognition, observing one's own learning, is an important task for middle school students. Reflection is a meaningful activity to promote metacognition. After the second free-write is completed, students are invited to prepare a reflection sheet comparing their first free-write with their second one. Students complete these sentences.

I chose this topic because

When I started, I knew

The steps I followed to find my information were

What I learned after my research is

My second free-write is different from my first because

What I learned from doing the free-writes is

Outlining

Once the students have assembled enough note cards so they feel their topic is evenly covered, it is time to create an outline. For this minilesson, we write a sample outline on the overhead projector. Students may copy ours or create their own as we work. Usually we ask for a student who would like to volunteer note cards for the sample.

The first item on this outline is the question from the topic card. As the students have been exploring and gathering information, they have always had the option of rewording the question. As they research, they become more informed on the topic and discover a related subtopic that is fascinating to them, realize their question is too broad, or realize their question is too narrow. Here is another spot at which some students reevaluate the question they have posed and wish to rewrite it.

The second item is the title the student would like to give the paper. This requires some brainstorming and sharing. Basically, what the students are doing is using major words from the question to form a title. Students look at the sample and generate a title together. Then students look at their own questions and work on formulating titles. We listen to the questions of the students struggling for ideas and make some suggestions. At this point we review the capitalization rules for titles, and the titles are written on the outlines.

The students look at their maps and decide the order in which the information is going to be presented. They might wish to write numbers on the legs of the map as they consider how to make this paper logical and understandable.

We follow the procedure for developing an outline that is presented in *Write in Style*. This outline is important. We believe this is where the paper is actually written.

Once the outlines are done and checked in, it is time to begin the actual writing of the paper—usually the easiest part of the process. The students must have their note cards in front of them, and if they haven't already done so, they must sort them by descriptors and pick out the ones they feel will work in the introduction. They also need wide-lined paper and a black pen to begin. The introduction needs to include one or two paragraphs of general background information and, in a paragraph by itself, the question the body of the paper will answer. We model this with a student's note cards. It is usually hard for eighth graders to understand what an overview is, so we try to model that a number of times. Students need to skip lines, leave margins, and write on only one side of the paper. All of this contributes to ease of editing later in the process.

When the introduction is finished, we are ready to begin writing the body. The student needs to find the note cards for the first descriptor. The student reads them and puts them in a logical order. Meanwhile, we are doing the same thing as the overhead projector. We read a volunteer's cards aloud to the class to see if the ideas sound logical as arranged. We decide how to group them to form paragraphs and how to formulate the information back into sentences. We write the text we have generated together on the overhead projector, demonstrating how to put in the citations. At this time we explain what plagiarizing is, why it is bad, and how to avoid it. Once the students see how to organize the cards, break the information into paragraphs, and write proper citations, they need to complete the body of the paper.

The introduction and body must be completed before we write the conclusion. The simplest way to make sure that all the points of the paper are covered in the conclusion is to write a one-sentence summary of each paragraph of the body. Each sentence must be to the point and devoid of detail. Students tend to want to say *everything* again! The final paragraph is a one-sentence answer to the question asked in the introduction. This calls for a bare-bones attitude, and it usually shows if the student understands the "big picture" drawn by his research. The first draft of the paper is written, but there is much yet to learn.

Controversial Issue

Plagiarism

Teachers often express dismay when faced with teaching research. They point out that students are likely to copy most of their work directly from a single text or multiple texts. Encyclopedias seem to be the most used source, and for this reason, in an attempt to stem plagiarism, teachers often forbid students the use of encyclopedias. Teachers also attempt to devise alternative projects or abandon the study of library research and the resulting formal research paper altogether.

In an article in the *Middle School Journal* in January 1994, Susan Davis suggests a number of techniques that go a long way toward eliminating plagiarism:

1. Teachers should attempt to "develop topics for research reports that would lend themselves to the creation of original work" (p. 57). She suggests that students research an area that is of personal interest to them. If a specific curricular area is to be covered, the teacher should find some way of connecting the students' personal interest to the curricular area. For example, during an investigation of Russian life and culture, a student interested in ballet could study Russian ballet dancers.

2. "When assigning research reports, teachers should assume that their student knows nothing about the topic" (p. 57). Teachers can build background information by using picture books and then encourage students to discuss what they have learned

either in topic-centered groups or with a peer partner. We ask our students to free-write at various places in the research project. Davis states (and we agree) that "students who free write about their topic in a journal, can begin to understand what they have learned already" (p. 57).

3. Students should be allowed to revise their topic as their research progresses. "Topic selection is a compromise between the writer's own ideas and preferences, the course material available, and the time allowed for searching" (Kuhlthau, 1984). We try to delay a final commitment to a topic until the outline for the first rough draft has been written.

4. Students should use source material that is easy to understand. If a teacher observes a student struggling with a text, unable to take any notes, or lifting information, Davis (1994) suggests "having students read the text and explain the 'gist' of the passage" (p. 57).

5. Teachers should emphasize the organization of data. Davis (1994) suggests the use of graphic organizers. "Students should brainstorm main ideas and examples from their reading and write them on the charts" (p. 58). We find the construction of an outline is a valuable tool and makes writing the final paper easy. As Joe said, "Once I organized my note cards and wrote my outline, the paper wrote itself."

6. Try not to set a predetermined length. Some students will find that their topics are so specific, their paper can be very short. Other students find that a wealth of information appears and they are unable to adequately address even a pared-down topic in a short format. Davis (1994) suggests assigning a range of paragraphs rather than a specific number of pages. She suggests "students think of three subheadings for their topic and write from two to four paragraphs for each section" (p. 58). We find that the cutting process we used when students take the Author's Chair is an excellent method to address papers with information that is not directly related to the topic.

7. Invite students to think of some method of presenting their findings. "Asking students to develop their own methods of presenting findings helps keep the idea of an audience forefront in their minds" (Davis, 1994, p. 58).

Third Free-Write and Reflection

After the students complete a rough draft, they are invited to complete a fictional free-write. We hope students see that their own research can inform fiction. In a miniles-son format, we brainstorm with students, listing different fictional formats. The research might result in a story or an alphabet book. Polly, a student researching dolphins, created a story with dolphins as the main characters. The adventure of the dolphins was based on the research Polly had done. Tom, a special-needs student, was able to get started when we suggested he create an alphabet book of soccer terms. In Writing Workshop, this free-write becomes the first writing project and often results in the creation of a charming picture book. When students complete their third free-write, they are invited to complete another reflection. This reflection asks the following questions:

How is my third free-write different from my first and second?
What did I learn?
How have I changed it to make it different?

Pause and Reflect!

How do the free-writes and the reflections inform the learning process for the students? Reflect on a response and write it in your journal.

HOW DO STUDENTS WORK TOWARD A FINAL DRAFT?

Students come to class proudly clutching a sheaf of papers. It is now time to examine what has been written and work on getting it into the correct format. Eighth graders often lapse into using first- and second-person pronouns, even in a formal piece of writing. Once they understand that this is inappropriate, they can usually find the words, but they don't know how to change the wording. This is a time to demonstrate one or two transformations. Brainstorming for each other not only helps for this project, but it also allows students to see how writers help each other work through problems in the text. The student should read the body of the text several times and correct the problems in the draft. The skipping of lines that we require leaves room for eliminating and rewriting.

No new information may be introduced in the conclusion, so there should be no citations. The student should have one or two paragraphs of summary sentences followed by a separate paragraph where the question is answered in one sentence.

Sometimes students have photographs or charts or other artifacts they wish to put in the paper. At this point, we briefly explain how to add any appendices, how to label them, and how to write the citation. This part of the paper counts for extra credit and is not required, so we touch on it briefly and give help to individuals who wish to add an appendix to their papers.

Our goal is to have each student produce a three- to five-page paper; often their papers are much longer at this point. It is very painful for the students, but usually they must eliminate some of what they have written. Our instruction is to cut anything that does not directly answer the question asked. The student needs to reduce the length of the paper before it is brought to Author's Chair.

Author's Chair

Author's Chair is the first public sharing of the paper. We follow this procedure. The student writes the question the paper is to answer on the blackboard. The reader sits on a chair at the front of the room next to the teacher. The paper is read to the class. As soon as someone hears information that does not directly answer the question, a hand goes up and the problem is discussed. The student reading aloud also hears repetitions of words and sentence patterns as well as illogical statements and incomplete thoughts. These can be marked for later revision. Sometimes when we are done listening to the paper, the conclusion we draw is that the information is adequate but that it does not answer the question asked. We offer the writer some alternatives for a new question. This is a time-consuming process, but later readers learn from the first few papers and become very serious about making cuts before reading their papers to

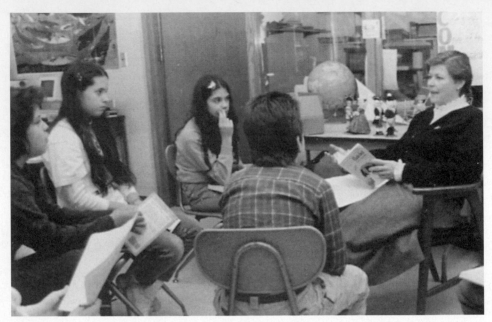

How can discussion promote literacy development?

the class. Soon we speed along. As painful as this procedure might be, it is a very important step in the process.

Editor's Table

As students finish making the cuts, they write a fresh copy to send to Editor's Table (Harste, Short, & Burke, 1988); the form used is illustrated in Figure 15.6. In this step, students work in groups of three, each person having a specific responsibility in the editing process. The teacher provides everyone with a list of standard proofreader's marks and demonstrates how to use them in a minilesson. In advance of the groups meeting, we have made two photocopies of each paper, and two of the editors may write on these copies. The editor reading the paper aloud should use the original copy. One of the editors is the spell checker, who is equipped with a dictionary and a highlighter marker. If anyone in the group questions the spelling of a word in the paper, the spell checker looks it up in the dictionary. If it is correct, the group moves on; if it is incorrect, it is highlighted for the writer to fix. The grammar checker is equipped with a red pen and uses it to add editor's marks. When the group has read and discussed the entire paper, they collaborate on filling out the cover sheet so the owner of the paper can make improvements.

Although Editor's Table provides an authentic audience for their work, students cannot expect perfection from eighth-grade editors. The students need to carefully examine their papers once they have been returned from the editors. Sometimes the editors make mistakes and overlook errors. The students are told they are responsible for the further editing of their papers and for making good use of what the editors did

EDITOR'S TABLE

Name of author _____

Date submitted _____

Author's check:

Are the lines and pages numbered?

Have you stapled the copies?

Is the clip on the original?

Editors' names _____

_____

_____

Date of actual editing _____

Editors please note:

Do not write on the original.

Use highlighter to mark spelling errors.

Use red pen to mark grammar, punctuation, capitalization, and usage errors.

Indicate line and page number where the error occurs.

COMMENTS: All comments should be either factual (e.g., "There are seven spelling errors") or positive.

CONTENT (Amount and quality of information)

_____

_____

ORGANIZATION

_____

_____

PARAGRAPHING

_____

_____

SENTENCE STRUCTURE

_____

_____

SPELLING

_____

_____

PUNCTUATION AND CAPITALIZATION

_____

_____

GENERAL COMMENTS:

CIRCLE ONE: PASSED   FAILED

REASON: (You must give three factual reasons for failing a paper.)

Date returned: _____

Figure 15.6 Form Used for Editor's Table

mark. If a spelling error was marked by the editors and not corrected by the author, that is a major error when we grade the final product. At this point, the papers are ready for an adult edit done by someone at home—parent, older sibling, neighbor, or any adult except a teacher at school. This draft needs to be signed by the adult editor.

The papers need to be put into final form with a final minilesson in which the teacher explains the form and spacing of the title page, the numbering of the pages, the margins, and the works-cited page. (At this point students always ask if they should leave out the citations in the final paper; of course, we say they must be included and reemphasize their importance.) The *Write in Style* book explains each step and provides handwritten and typed examples of every page so the students have an excellent way to check their form. The works-cited page is put together quite easily if the student did the works-cited cards correctly, because they are arranged alphabetically by first word on the card. Even the works-cited page is double spaced for easy reading.

HOW DO YOU EVALUATE?

The Product

The students are given the grading sheet (see Figure 15.7) a few days before the papers are due so they can ask questions about anything they don't understand. The form shows in what ways we are going to be evaluating the work, so the students have every opportunity to write a paper that conforms to the expectations. We find it is best to stagger the due dates of the papers. To accomplish this, we hold a lottery for the three or four due dates. Thus only seven or eight papers are due in each of the three classes each day. We choose a movie that relates to our next focus in literature and have the students watch it while we are busily grading papers. Because of the layers of conferencing and editing, the quality is usually high and the papers are enjoyable to read. Most of the papers can be returned the day they are handed in. Students love the immediate feedback to their work of nine weeks. We love the paper-free weekends that this system produces. We are never seen taking home baskets of ungraded papers.

 ## Pause and Reflect!

What is a portfolio? How can a portfolio be used as a strategy to focus on the inquiry process? Write your response in your journal.

Preparing a Process Portfolio

A portfolio is a collection of student-selected artifacts that represent growth over a period of time. It should be open and wide ranging in its inclusions in order to capture a profile of the whole learner. "Portfolios are an integral part of an extended learning process and are themselves a learning strategy" (Crafton, 1991, p. 174). In our classes,

EVALUATION SHEET FOR INQUIRY RESEARCH PAPER
NAME OF STUDENT _____ DATE DUE _____
TITLE OF PAPER _____ DATE IN _____

FORMAT: Title page correct
Pages double spaced, one side, black ink
Page format correct—margins, numbering _____
Works-cited page correct _____

INTRODUCTION: Has label
 Has at least two paragraphs
 First paragraph provides overview or background or history
 Last paragraph states question _____

BODY: Begins with title
 Is divided into paragraphs
 Paragraphing is logical
 Resources are cited correctly _____

CONCLUSION: Has label
 First paragraph summarizes
 Last paragraph answers question _____

MECHANICS: Spelling is correct _____
 Commas are used correctly _____
 Capital letters are used correctly _____
 End punctuation is used correctly _____
 Other mechanics and usage problems are avoided _____

TIME LINE: Deadlines were consistently met _____

CONTENT OF PAPER: Answers the question asked _____
 Presents information logically and understandably _____
 Presents complete information _____
 Uses a variety of sources _____
 Maintains the interest of reader _____

REFLECTIONS:

EXTRA CREDIT: APPENDIX

        EXTRA SOURCES

Figure 15.7 Inquiry Research Paper Evaluation Form

we use portfolios as a place for students to gather their best work, reflect on their accomplishments, and celebrate their growth.

As the students are involved in building their inquiry paper, they are making a series of decisions and acting on a number of problem-solving procedures. When they complete the project, we ask our students to retrace their steps and reflect on their learning. Students are asked to keep all the artifacts associated with the creation of the paper. Even cards that are wrong are saved.

When we are ready to prepare the process portfolio, we invite students to bring all their artifacts and materials to class. Students spend a few minutes browsing through these items. Selecting a student who has a complete collection of materials, we revisit the process by selecting an artifact from each step of the process as an example of that step. At the same time, a student is writing the list of process steps at the chalkboard. Students are asked to answer the following three questions, supply an artifact, and write a complete response to each question.

Which part of the process was most helpful for doing the research? Why?

Which part of the process would you eliminate? Why?

At what place in the process did you realize you were learning? Explain.

The artifacts are mounted on 18″ × 12″ construction paper that has been folded in half. Usually three sheets are sufficient for a portfolio. Students are encouraged to create a neat cover for the portfolio and to place pages in the back for responses from an adult, at least three students, and one teacher. Students share their portfolios with the class. If time permits, the portfolios are passed around and students are allowed to respond to each other's work.

Pause and Reflect!

Brainstorm ways students might use the information gained through research for other projects. List the projects in your journal and then compare them with the extensions listed here.

HOW CAN YOU EXTEND INQUIRY?

Although learning the process of inquiry is a fine goal, we see this nine-week investment as a foundation for Writing Workshop. The opportunity to write is enhanced when it is coupled with instruction. Writing Workshop is modeled after the process many published authors use. They do research to make the subject, time, place, and events authentic. We want our students to realize that a strong base of knowledge informed by research is a useful tool for a fiction writer. We expect that the first piece of writing students will do in workshop is a fictional story based on the information learned while researching. It is often hard for the students to make the transition from a formal paper filled with facts and statistics to a story with a beginning, middle, end, characters, and a setting. Again, a minilesson is used as the vehicle to inform students of what is expected and as a springboard for discussion. The class suggests ways of incorporating each topic into a fictional format. Some students decide to use their fictional free-write as the basis of this piece, although it usually needs expanding and refining. Others wish to take a whole new approach. Either choice is fine with us.

Many students research endangered animals, so the suggestion is often made to have the sea turtle, for example, be a character and place the animal in a situation that represents danger to its survival. A story grows quite naturally from this setting and gives the student the opportunity to incorporate authentic details as the story develops. As students listen to the suggestions being made for everyone in class, they begin to see more and more possibilities for their own story development. Anyone who studied a disease can create a character who has the disease, or who is the parent of someone with the disease, or who is the doctor who treats the disease. What seems impossible at the start becomes exciting, and students can hardly wait to begin.

Developing this piece takes several weeks of workshop time. We present many minilessons. The students learn to use a story sketch (outlining the plot) that commits them to a story line with an ending. They generate an extensive list of writing formats that they might use in future pieces, such as a story, picture book, diary, or journal. They fill the blackboard with words that can be used as substitutes for "said" in dialogue. These lists are placed in their writing folders and used as references for the rest of the year.

Mini-Research Projects

We return to the LC for mini-research projects throughout the year. We start with a focus on historical fiction. Each group of three students chooses a novel. The group decides on a research topic, based on some aspect of the book.

The LC director suggests new sources for information. Each student in the group needs a separate source on the topic selected, so the group is searching for three good sources. They need to be sure they are recording different information on their note cards and therefore should compare these often. When they are ready to share what they have discovered with the class, they will have at least nine interesting facts. We spend two or three class periods gathering information and one more period in the classrooms in which we allow the students to decide how they are going to share the information with us. The reporting can be very simple or made more complex with the addition of a visual aid. This project helps students realize that authors use research to add authenticity to their books.

We repeat this type of research project many times during the year. For example, during the mystery unit, the students research the life of the author of the book they are reading. They make connections between the author's life and details of the book. Our LC has a number of books with biographical sketches of authors of books for adolescents. Students are given some time to prepare a presentation, and we all discover what they learned.

SUMMARY
....

Careful planning is the key to success. When we know how many days the learning center is open to us, we fill in the steps of the process on our calendar and adjust the amount of class time we can provide according to what is available on our schedule. We construct an inquiry research paper track containing dates and places, breaking the investigation process down to small incremental steps. When students have a general topic, they do the first of three free-writes. They attempt to fill a page with information about their topic. Students use a descriptor map to break their topic down into subheading categories that become the labels on the tops of note cards and later the categories for the body of the paper. Our students are invited to transform a topic into a specific question. The group begins working with print resources in the learning center, and when learning center research is completed, the students are invited to compose a second free-write that is focused on their topic and limited to the front of *one* piece of notebook paper. Students become aware that they can write about their topic without copying information directly from a book. After the second free-write is completed, students are invited to prepare a reflection sheet comparing their first with their second free-write.

An outline is created and students decide the order in which the information is going to be presented. They complete the first draft and a final fictional free-write. In Writing Workshop, this free-write becomes a writing project. Author's Chair teaches students to cut information that does not directly answer the question. At the Editors' Table, the editing group reads and discusses the entire paper, noting corrections in grammar, punctuation, and spelling. The students are given a grading sheet that demonstrates the way the work will be evaluated by the teacher. Teachers only collect seven or eight papers due each day. Most of the papers can be returned the same day. Finally, students construct process portfolios to examine and reflect on the process strategies.

In the Field

1. Choose a topic that would be appropriate for a middle school student to research. Go to a school or public library and locate materials on that topic. In your journal, write observations about the process.

2. Make a list in your journal. What directions would you give students before they visit a library? What instruction would you provide on a specific resource? What materials would you advise students to take to the library?

3. Interview a teacher who does a research project with the students. How is the project presented to the students? What instruction is given on the research process? What methods are used to evaluate the research project? Take notes in your journal.

4. Review our conversations with support personnel. What details stood out in the responses? How would you alter your teaching approach to incorporate their insights and suggestions?

5. Review your journal entries. Which reflections do you feel will be of value to you later on? Which reflections are less useful? What surprised you when you reread your entries? What did you learn about yourself when you reread your entries?

Portfolio Suggestion

Select from your journal two examples of your responses to Learning from Experience or In the Field activities. Write a brief evaluation. Explain what you learned and how it will affect your planning and implementing inquiry research.

For Further Reading

Beane, J. A., & Lipka, R. P. (1987). *When kids come first: Enhancing self-esteem.* Columbus, OH: National Middle School Association.

Burns, J. H. (1992). *They can but they don't: Helping students overcome work inhibition.* New York: Viking.

Calkins, L. M. (1986). *The art of teaching writing.* Portsmouth, NH: Heinemann.

Crafton, L. M. (1991). *Whole language: Getting started . . . moving forward.* Kahtonah: Richard C. Owen Publishing, Inc.

Davis, S. J., & Hunter, J. (1990). Historical novels: A context for gifted student research. *Journal of Reading 5,* 602–606.

Davis, S. J. (1994). Teaching practices that encourage or eliminate student plagiarism. *Middle School Journal, 1,* 55–58.

Davis-Lenski, S. J. (1994). The research process of middle school students. *Reading Improvement, 31*(4), 224–242.

Forte, I., & Schurr, S. (1993). *The definitive middle school guide.* Nashville: Incentive Publications.

Freeman, E. B. (1991). Informational books: Models for student report writing. *Language Arts, 68*(10), 470–473.

Graves, D. H. (1989). *Investigative nonfiction.* Portsmouth, NH: Heinemann.

Harste, J., Short, K., & Burke, C. (1988). *Creating a classroom for authors.* Portsmouth, NH: Heinemann.

Hill, B. C. (1995). *Practical aspects of authentic assessment: Putting the pieces together.* Norwood, MA: Christopher-Gordon Publishers, Inc.

Johnson, D. W., Johnson, R. T., & Holubec, E. J. (1994). *The new circles of learning: Cooperation in the classroom and school.* Alexandria, VA: Association for Supervision and Curriculum Development.

Joyce, M. Z. (1995). The I-search paper: A vehicle for teaching the research process. *School Library Media Activities Monthly, 11*(6), 31–37.

Macrorie, K. (1988). *The I-Search paper.* Portsmouth, NH: Boynton-Cook.

Routman, R. (1991). *Invitations: Changing as teachers and learners K–12.* Portsmouth, NH: Heinemann.

Von der Porten, E. P. (1988). *Write in style: A guide to the short term paper.* Logan, Iowa: The Perfection Form Company.

V

Communication
and Professional Growth

Communication with Others and Professional Development

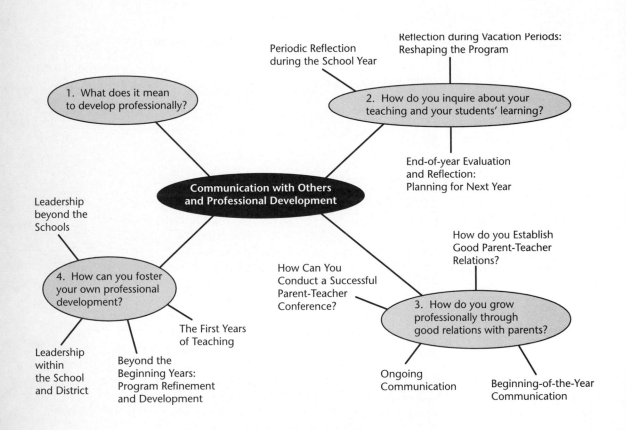

Reflection during Vacation Periods:
Reshaping the Program

Periodic Reflection
during the School Year

1. What does it mean
to develop professionally?

2. How do you inquire about your
teaching and your students' learning?

End-of-year Evaluation
and Reflection:
Planning for Next Year

**Communication with Others
and Professional Development**

Leadership
beyond the
Schools

4. How can you foster
your own professional
development?

How do you Establish
Good Parent-Teacher
Relations?

How Can You
Conduct a Successful
Parent-Teacher
Conference?

3. How do you grow
professionally through
good relations with parents?

The First Years
of Teaching

Leadership
within
the School
and District

Beyond the
Beginning Years:
Program Refinement
and Development

Ongoing
Communication

Beginning-of-the-Year
Communication

CHAPTER GOALS FOR THE READER

To reflect on what it means to develop professionally

To understand how to inquire about your teaching and your students' learning

To learn how to develop good relations with parents

To learn how to foster your own professional development

CHAPTER OVERVIEW

In the past 15 chapters, we have described the thinking and decision making that you as teachers engage in. The nature of that thinking and decision making changes as you learn more about students and how they learn and about your own strengths and weaknesses. It is our purpose in this chapter to deal directly with these themes. The chapter is divided into four parts. In the first, we provide a model of professional development generated by researchers in the field. In the second, we discuss the importance of regular reflection on and evaluation of your instructional progress, and how such assessment can enhance your instruction and better enable your students to achieve the goals you set for them. In the third, we consider how you can grow professionally through good relations with the parents of your students. Although reflection on your instructional program and your relationship with parents promotes professional development, you also need to go beyond the classroom for new ideas and experiences. In the final part of this chapter, we focus on professional development beyond the classroom. We also present two interviews, one with a beginning teacher and one with a more experienced teacher, in which we ask them to reflect on their professional growth.

TAPPING PRIOR KNOWLEDGE TO SET A PURPOSE

It is now time for you to reflect on your own professional goals. What are your goals for your professional life a year from now? What do you hope to be doing? What are your goals for your professional life five years from now? What do you hope to be doing at that time? After reading the chapter overview and reflecting on your goals, identify what it is that you most want to learn from reading this chapter. List these goals in your journal under the heading Chapter 16: Setting a Purpose.

WHAT DOES IT MEAN TO DEVELOP PROFESSIONALLY?

In the past decade, professionals have focused on the ways teachers change as they gain experience. A particularly important development has been that teachers have become important contributors to writing on practice (see, for example, Atwell, 1987; Branscombe, Goswami, & Schwartz, 1992; Cochran-Smith & Lytle, 1993; Gallas, 1994; Wells, 1994). Through study of their practice, teachers provide rich descriptions and "insider" perspectives on life in their classrooms.

In addition, recent studies are exploring the knowledge of teachers as they learn to teach. Some studies trace the thinking and insights of teachers from the time they are in training through their first years of teaching (Grossman, 1990); others explore the knowledge of more experienced teachers (Connelly & Clandinin, 1988; Elbaz, 1991). Through this literature, we are beginning to gain an understanding of the ways in which teachers conceptualize and think about their teaching.

From case studies about individual teachers, we can derive a sense of how careers evolve. One attempt to systematize this literature was undertaken by Burke, Christensen, and Fessler (1984). We present the stages they identify in Figure 16.1.

When you examine these stages, remember that they should not be seen as a linear progression. Instead, teachers tend to move in and out of stages in response to various events and influences in their lives, both personal and professional. Teachers may pass through some but not necessarily all of these stages at some point in their careers. Ideally, of course, you will remain at the "enthusiastic and growing" stage throughout most of your teaching years. One purpose of this chapter is to describe ways in which you can enhance your own professional development, with the goal of remaining enthusiastic and growing as long as you remain a teacher. To that end, we discuss ways in which you can build your competency as a teacher through reflection on your instructional practice, by enhancing your communication with parents, and through a variety of other professional development activities.

Preservice. The period of preparation for a specific professional role. Typically, preservice is the initial preparation in college or university, although it might also include retraining for a new assignment through either university attendance or staff development within the work setting.

Induction. The first few years of employment. The teacher is typically socialized into the system, strives for acceptance by students, peers, and supervisors, and attempts to achieve a level of comfort and security in dealing with everyday issues. Teachers may also experience induction when moving to a new grade level, building, or school district.

Competency building. The teacher strives to improve teaching skills and abilities, and seeks out new materials, methods, and strategies. Teachers at this stage are receptive to new ideas, attend workshops and conferences willingly, and enroll in graduate programs on their own initiative. They see teaching as challenging and are eager to hone their repertoire of skills.

Enthusiastic and growing. The teacher has reached a high level of competence but continues to progress as a professional. Teachers in this stage love their jobs, look forward to going to school and to interaction with their students, and constantly seek new ways to enrich their teaching. These teachers are often helpful in identifying appropriate inservice education activities for their schools.

Career frustration. Job satisfaction is waning, and teachers begin to question why they are doing this work. This stage reflects much of what is described as "teacher burnout." Although this tends to occur most often at the career midpoint, increasing evidence suggests that it is happening more often in the early years, particularly for those teachers facing the continual threat of "last hired/first fired" policies.

Stable but stagnant. The teacher is resigned to putting in a day's work for a day's pay. Teachers at this stage do what is expected but little more; their work is acceptable, but they are not committed to excellence or professional growth. These teachers tend to be the most difficult to deal with in terms of development: they are at best passive consumers of inservice efforts.

Career wind-down. The teacher at this stage is preparing to leave the profession. For some, this is a pleasant period in which to reflect on positive past experiences; for others, it may reflect bitterness at a forced job termination or the end of an unrewarding career.

Career exit. The period after a teacher leaves the job, although not necessarily retirement. It may be an involuntary period of unemployment or a temporary career exit for child rearing or health reasons. It may also be a time of alternative career exploration or moving to a nonteaching position within education.

Figure 16.1. Representation of Teaching Career Stages *Source:* Adapted from "Teacher Career Stages: Implications for Staff Development," by Peter J. Burke, Judith C. Christensen, and Ralph Fessler, 1984, *Phi Delta Kappan* pp. 14–16. Copyright © 1984 by Phi Delta Kappa Educational Foundation. Adapted with permission.

HOW DO YOU INQUIRE ABOUT YOUR TEACHING AND YOUR STUDENTS' LEARNING?

Teaching is an extremely complex act—so complex that many consider it an art. By this, they mean that no simple prescriptions or formulas invariably result in effective teaching. We agree that teaching is an art; the complex acts of teaching are given life by the visions of teachers. Teaching that involves simply following a set of established routines has lost its "soul," its ability to engage others in a living enterprise. We believe also that it is virtually impossible to "teach" this artistic aspect of teaching. For some, the artistic elements of teaching may be developed by modeling master teachers. But for us all, the artistry comes primarily from our personalities and our beliefs and commitments as teachers. As we gain experience and reflect on that experience, we become more able to develop the visions that moved us to become teachers in the first place. Each of us forms a classroom learning community in a slightly different way, and this artistic event reflects our talents and beliefs about teaching.

Although we would argue that teaching is an art, we also accept that teaching includes some elements of craft (Lortie, 1975). That is, ways of proceeding can be and have been identified that enable the artistic core of teaching to become manifest. Consider for a moment the making of pottery. A potter must have not only visions of graceful pots but also a set of procedures for preparing the clay, centering it on the wheel, and forming the end product. A novice potter, like a novice teacher, does not yet have the knowledge to assess progress and adapt strategies in response to what is observed as the pot is being made. As potters become expert, decision making becomes so internalized that the artists are often unaware of the observations they make and the actions they undertake in response to what they observe.

Expert teachers, like expert potters, are constantly observing and making adjustments as they go along. The ability to respond quickly to emerging events seems related to experience, and to the degree to which teachers can free themselves from preestablished plans. Research shows that teachers differ in the extent to which they adhere to a plan, even when things are going badly (Zahorik, 1970). Some teachers continue a lesson that is failing simply to cover material; others continue because they have not developed suitable alternatives. In reading instruction, some teachers adhere closely to commercial programs, while others show considerably more willingness to deviate from suggested scripts (Barr & Sadow, 1989).

The craft that underlies teaching artistry can be improved through reflection on

How is this teacher refining her craft?

practice. Through reflection and evaluation, you can identify areas of strength and weakness, build on your strengths, and work to correct your weaknesses. Refinement of the craft of teaching should occur during the first years of teaching, but once you develop the habits of reflection and evaluation, you will continue these activities throughout your professional career. The nature of the problems that preoccupy you will change over time, however. As a beginning teacher, you will no doubt focus primarily on class management procedures and effective instructional programs. Once these basic patterns have been internalized, you may focus more on refinement of strategies, integration of curriculum, and enhancement of instructional skills. At the same time, you may develop professionally in other ways—by becoming more active on school and district committees, for instance, or by writing about your instructional activities or taking further course work.

In the remainder of this section, we identify ways in which you can begin the process of reflection by examining the nature of your reading program. One of our goals is to help beginning teachers establish a sound reading and writing program; we also hope to encourage experienced teachers to refine, or even develop their own, literacy programs. The questions we pose in the following section should be equally useful for beginning teachers considering their first reading programs and experienced teachers contemplating the programs they have refined or developed. In both cases, further growth results from teachers reflecting on their instructional programs and evaluating their effectiveness in achieving their goals.

We believe strongly that the process of reflection and evaluation should be ongoing and that it should intensify periodically throughout the year. We urge you to use vacation times—in particular December and mid-spring—and the end of the year for intensive reflection and evaluation.

Periodic Reflection during the School Year

Ongoing reflection should center on three main areas: the involvement and success of your students; the effectiveness of your management, teaching strategies, and scheduling; and the appropriateness of your instructional materials.

Are Your Students Involved and Successful with Their Work?

Discovering whether or not students are involved with their work is one of your easiest tasks. Simply look at students during discussion and circulate around the room during independent work to gauge their involvement and assess the accuracy of their work. Check with students informally about the work they do outside class on the topics you present. Little or no involvement is often associated with lack of success, although success or lack of it depends on many other factors as well. When many students do not understand a concept, you will want to revisit it with the whole class; otherwise, individual children or small groups may need to reread or rethink an issue. In addition, your assessment of your students' involvement and success in learning should suggest to you paths for your own development and growth.

Are You Managing Your Time Effectively?

This question is more complicated than it appears. First, you need to ask whether the schedule you planned represents a workable sequence of activities, and whether your students have learned this sequence. Do they make transitions quickly and do they know what to do next when activities change? Do they understand the options available when they finish their work? Do they know how to get help when they encounter a problem, particularly when you are otherwise engaged? Second, you need to ask whether time is well used within lessons. Is time wasted during lessons because of poor planning or intrusions? How much of each 30-minute segment do children actually spend on reading and writing activities? Most important, are your students engaging in activities that will help them achieve the goals you have set? Students need to sense that the classroom is a place for important work—that the time you spend together is a valuable experience.

Are Your Instructional Materials Appropriate?

We have emphasized throughout this book the need to select materials at the appropriate level of difficulty. It is equally important that the materials be interesting. Do the selections permit students to become involved in compelling experiences, to identify with characters facing problems significant for them? And finally, the materials need to be appropriate to your goals. If a main goal is to develop independent readers, are you using strategies and materials that encourage independence rather than concentrating on defined tasks that limit student choice? You must always keep your goals in sight and ask continually whether the materials you use and the tasks you select will let your students grow in the areas that you value.

Reflection during Vacation Periods: Reshaping the Program

The questions in the preceding section should be the focus of ongoing reflection throughout the school year, but we believe that intense reflection at major junctures in the school year will allow you to reshape your instructional program as you go. Such reflection should focus on the following questions.

Are Your Lessons Appropriate to Achieve Your Goals for Student Learning?

Think about the lessons you typically develop for your students. What activities do students engage in *prior to* reading? Are they learning strategies that will make them independent readers? What activities do they engage in *during* reading? Are they learning strategies that will help them identify and solve problems as they read? What activities do students engage in *after* reading? Are they learning strategies that will help them organize and evaluate what they have learned through reading? Do you encourage them to write, to listen, to speak? To be sensitive to style and organization?

Have you incorporated instructional support and modeling into your lessons, particularly when students are first learning new strategies? Do you discuss why and when to use strategies? Do you provide sufficient practice, with appropriate peer support, and do you encourage independent use of strategies through discussion? Do you talk about your own reading and writing and the strategies you use?

Is Your Literacy Program Properly Balanced?

Step back from particular lessons to focus on the total program. Consider the nature of the activities you provide in relation to the goals you have for reading instruction. In chapter 1, we discussed five main goals for literacy instruction. A balanced program promotes the development of comprehension and communication, pleasure from reading, knowledge of print, prior knowledge and vocabulary, and strategies for reading comprehension and writing.

Pause and Reflect

Turn back to chapter 13 and read about the instructional program developed by Marcy Lee. What are Marcy's instructional goals? Make notes about how she went beyond the basal reading program in order to create a balanced literacy program. If you were the teacher, would you want to modify the program even further? What would you include or eliminate? Write your response in your journal under the heading A Balanced Literacy Program.

Marcy's program relies to a great extent on what the published reading program authors define as useful activities. In particular, she found that print knowledge and comprehension strategies were well developed. She supplements the Level I program with Language Experience Stories and Big Books to provide a more natural and accessible introduction to literacy. To support fluency, she encourages rereading and independent reading, and she focuses on development of prior knowledge through content area instruction. She increases interest by reading aloud, encourages use of class and school libraries, and has children talk about books they like.

Marcy has also integrated writing activities into her program through Writing Workshop and time for self-selected writing. She also provides instruction involving shared writing and spelling.

Finally, an effective literacy program results from the right balance between the introduction of new concepts and the practice of previously learned ones. Children learn huge amounts of information about print in the primary grades; they need to reread and read independently to consolidate this knowledge. Particularly in second and third grades, children should read material that is easy for them in order to consolidate skills and achieve fluency. Instruction should always build on what children have recently learned.

As you review the reading and writing activities in your instructional program, consider the relative emphasis you give them. How much time should children spend on word study and phonics versus contextual reading? How much on developing background knowledge versus discussing the story itself? Do your students spend enough time actually reading and writing? Winter and spring breaks offer you the opportunity to refine your literacy program by eliminating activities that are not productive and adding others that may better achieve your goals.

Given the Progress of Individual Students, Is Your Grouping Appropriate?

If you group students on the basis of their reading and writing development, winter and spring breaks offer a good time to consider whether the group memberships need to be modified, and whether the pattern of groups is effective. In chapter 11, we discussed grouping and regrouping students during the year and the ways in which you can prepare students for group changes. You may want to reconsider the overall structure you are using as well. Do your students have opportunities to receive instruction in heterogeneous as well as homogeneous ability groups? Do they have time to work cooperatively in peer groups? If students spend most of their time grouped by ability, you will want to plan alternative group experiences for them.

End-of-Year Evaluation and Reflection: Planning for Next Year

Reflection at the end of the school year is particularly important, because it guides your reflective activity during the summer and may help you select summer activities that enhance your professional development. Focus on these questions at the end of the year:

What Does the Evidence You Have about Your Students' Progress Mean?

During the school year, you will have gathered a variety of evidence of what your students have learned. Compare a writing sample made by each student at the beginning of the year with ones made at the end. Similarly, compare taped samples of oral reading. What changes do you see? How would you characterize student progress? To what extent is growth of comprehension reflected in what your students write or in their discussions with their peers? How many books did each of your students read during the year? Are you providing sufficient support for children who experience difficulty with reading and writing?

What Should Your Goals Be for Next Year and How Will You Achieve Them?

Your response to this may simply be: "The same as last year and in the same way." If you are like most teachers, however, you will identify one or more areas in which you would like to introduce some alternative activities. Targeting these areas is a major step forward in improving your literacy program.

What Do You Want to Learn during the Summer to Enhance your Teaching?

By responding to this question, you can set an interesting agenda for yourself and, because you continue to learn, increase your own excitement about your work. You may also develop bonds with other teachers who are pursuing similar agendas. An almost endless variety of programs is available to you for professional growth and enhancement of your skills.

HOW DO YOU GROW PROFESSIONALLY THROUGH GOOD RELATIONS WITH PARENTS?

In recent years, the importance of involvement by parents in their children's schooling has been recognized. Parents are their children's first teachers and have much to contribute to their continuing education. Yet, establishing good working relations with parents can be time-consuming and produce unexpected results, particularly for beginning teachers. In the Controversial Issues section that follows, we consider a study by Wildman, Niles, Magliaro, and McLaughlin (1989) that describes the experiences of three beginning teachers in Virginia as they form relations with their students' parents.

Controversial Issue

Parental Involvement

The controversial issue arises from the recent strong support for greater involvement by parents in their children's schooling and the real ambivalence of many teachers who encourage such involvement. The dilemmas may be amplified in the case of beginning teachers.

All three teachers studied—Margaret, Janet, and Karen—were confident, enthusiastic, energetic first-year teachers with specific ideas about how children learn but with open minds to new educational ideas as well. Margaret's kindergartners were from upper middle-class backgrounds; their parents were well educated and kept tabs on their children's schooling. Margaret was able to develop a positive relationship with them through back-to-school night and parent-teacher conferences, until, at the end of the year, she recommended retaining one kindergartner. The child's parents were outspoken, questioned Margaret's lack of experience and professional abilities, and eventually called for her dismissal. Margaret had expected parents to be supportive and to trust her professional judgment; this incident changed her mind. The following year she developed a careful plan for communicating with parents through home visits and conferences, but she weighed everything she said to make sure that unpleasant reactions would not ensue. Her ability to communicate openly with parents was inhibited.

Janet's students were from a blue-collar, low-income background, and Janet limited her interaction with parents during the early part of the year, in the belief that they would not be of much assistance. A few parent-teacher conferences brought good results, so that Janet decided to ask parents to assist in her fourth-grade classroom. She quickly discarded the plan, however, when parents whose ill-behaved children Janet disciplined began to accuse her of racial prejudice. Such conflicts caused Janet considerable frustration and eventually resulted in her decision to leave teaching.

Karen, also a beginning teacher, was assigned to average and low-average ninth graders. Karen was in her mid-thirties, the mother of two, and a longtime volunteer in both private and public schools. In her first year, Karen called all parents early in the year to report on their children's achievements and progress. She made notes on her calls and filed this information in her class portfolio. These early phone contacts accomplished two goals: Karen learned more about each adolescent so she could better meet individual needs, and she began building a positive relationship with parents. Parents appreciated her phone calls and noted that previous teacher contacts had been about student problems rather than accomplishments. Karen was quite satisfied with her relationship with parents during her first two years of teaching. During her third year, she was given all low-ability English classes, and for a variety of reasons, failed to make these initial contacts. She later found that calling parents about problems was difficult and not satisfying, since she had not previously established rapport.

Parents play a major role in beginning teachers' professional development (Wildman et al., 1989). Some beginning teachers find that parents are supportive. Others find that parents cause them to become uncomfortable and challenge their abilities. In any case, one of the most demanding tasks teachers face is establishing an effective relationship with parents. Developing effective parent-teacher relationships takes careful thinking and planning.

How Do You Establish Good Parent-Teacher Relations?

How can you develop good relations with the parents of your students? Two key areas for developing effective parent-teacher relationships include your attitude toward parents and the plan for communication that you develop. We present different ways you can make initial contacts with parents to begin building positive and trusting relationships and then to explore how you can continue an ongoing dialogue with parents.

Attitude

To develop effective relationships, you must have a positive attitude toward parents in general. You must believe that parents want the best for their children and can have positive effects on their children's learning. Respect for parents entails listening to their questions, concerns, and criticisms without interruptions and distractions. It requires a sincere interest in learning about children from parents' perspectives and maintaining objectivity, even when you may have encountered somewhat different experiences with their children. Parents may not always be friendly and congenial, as you have learned in the previous examples, but an effective working relationship rests on a positive attitude toward and respect for parents.

Communication

Communication between parent and teacher needs to be honest, open, and frequent so misunderstandings do not develop. It is important to work toward developing a bond of trust, so parents believe you have their child's interest in mind when you make decisions. As you communicate with parents, create a nonthreatening and nonjudgmental atmosphere; using technical teacher jargon such as "metacognition" can be threatening and annoying, and sounding like "the authority" on learning and children can stifle communication. Both parties need to feel they have valuable information to share and are working together for the betterment of the child. Parents have much information that teachers need in developing an effective reading program.

Why is it important to have parents involved in their children's literacy development?

By listening and asking questions, you can better understand how parents interact and teach their children, what kind of learning environment the parents provide, and what parents value and believe about reading, writing, school, and learning. Your sensitivity to and awareness of these factors can do much to facilitate children's learning. There are many ways to establish open lines of communication. Communication should begin at the start of school, continue throughout the school year, and include gathering information, reporting on students' progress, and informing parents about the school reading program. It should also show parents how they can provide support and assistance. Not all parent-teacher contact can or should include all these considerations; however, during the course of a school year, all these topics should be covered.

Beginning-of-the-Year Communication

The best time to initiate communication is at the beginning of the school year, before any problems have arisen. Making contact when feelings are neutral or positive avoids putting the parent on the defensive and allows for more open communication. Moreover, communication with parents at the opening of the school year can provide you with valuable information to improve children's learning. Research has indicated that establishing a parent-teacher relationship prior to the school year improves children's attendance and grades (Duncan & Fitzgerald, 1969). There are various ways to establish parent-teacher communication at the beginning of the school year.

Writing to Parents

At the beginning of the school year, send a letter to each student's parents in which you introduce yourself and briefly tell them about your educational background and experience with children. This information conveys both your openness and your professionalism. Use the letter to present one area that you will emphasize during the first marking period. For instance, if you have planned a reading unit on biographies in October, tell parents about some of your reading goals for this unit. Suggest one or two simple ideas for parent involvement, such as helping their children select some interesting biographies at the library that they can read and share together, or identify specific museums that families can visit to learn about famous people in history. Conclude your letter by encouraging parents to contact you if they have questions, concerns, or criticisms. Include specific times when they can talk to you and information on how they can make an appointment. Making yourself available to parents indicates openness, professionalism, sincerity, and self-confidence, all of which indicates that you will do the best you can to meet their children's needs.

Before sending your letter to parents, have your principal read it to make sure it conforms with school policy. See Figure 16.2 for a sample letter that a fifth-grade teacher sent to her students' parents.

Calling Parents

Too often, teachers call parents only when something is wrong, and the parent is put on the defensive. A telephone call during the first few days of school avoids the hazards of having to make an initial contact with parents when their child has a problem.

In your phone call, introduce yourself and encourage parents to call if they have questions, concerns, or criticisms. Include a positive comment about their child's first week (e.g., "he is eager to learn" or "she is cooperating beautifully") and gather some information by asking about their child's interests. Inquire about their perceptions of their child's strengths and weaknesses and how you can best help their child learn and enjoy school. Conclude by telling them you are looking forward to getting to

Dear Mr. and Mrs. Jones:

My name is Ms. Harris and I will be your son's fifth-grade teacher. I am looking forward to having Matthew in my classroom and having an opportunity to meet with you in the near future. This is my third year teaching at Washington School. Before teaching at Washington, I attended National-Louis University and graduated with a degree in elementary education.

During this coming year, the fifth graders will be involved in reading and enjoying many different types of books. I have chosen some interesting science fiction, nonfiction, poetry, historical fiction, and mysteries to share with the children. Some books I will read aloud. Others will be read for reading instruction, and still others, I hope, will be read for leisure reading at home. If children read about a variety of topics, they increase their vocabulary, knowledge, and comprehension. I've enclosed a bibliography of books Matthew and the other fifth graders may enjoy reading or hearing you read. These books can be found in the school and local public library. I hope we can work together to encourage reading as an enjoyable, satisfying activity.

If you have any questions or comments, please do not hesitate to call from 3:00 to 4:00 on Monday through Friday (295-1000). If this is an inconvenient time, call during school hours and leave a message with the school secretary. I will return your call as soon as possible.

Sincerely,

Figure 16.2 Sample Letter to Parents (Fifth Grade)

Dear Linda:

In this upcoming school year, you will be in my classroom. I am looking forward to meeting you and having some wonderful and enjoyable learning experiences. We will be doing some exciting things such as going on field trips, writing to our favorite children's authors, and writing to pen pals in another state. But these are only a few of the interesting things we will be doing. We will also be involved in many other activities that directly focus on your interests.

To become familiar with your interests, I would like to find out what you have been reading this summer. Choose your favorite book and be prepared to share it with me and your classmates during the first week of school.

I hope that you enjoy the rest of your summer vacation and look forward to hearing about your favorite book and experiences.

Sincerely,

Figure 16.3 Sample Letter to Students (Third Grade)

know and working with their child. This kind of phone call usually prompts parents to take you up on your offer that they call if they have any questions or concerns. This is a great way to start off a new school year.

Writing to Students

Another way to communicate with parents is by writing a letter to each of your students before school begins in the fall. Ask children to share the letter with their parents, which in an indirect manner can establish positive relations with your students' parents. They recognize that you have taken personal time to write to their child in a gesture of welcome to your classroom. Figure 16.3 is an example of a letter sent each year by a third-grade teacher to all her incoming students.

Compare the type of information parents would learn from a parent–teacher conference with what they would learn at an open house.

Open House

In most schools, an open house or parent-teacher meeting is planned at the beginning of the school year so teachers can meet parents and introduce the school curriculum. This is a good opportunity to tell parents about one or two goals that you hope their children will accomplish during the school year. You might also suggest one or two ways in which parents can generally support their children's learning and even present a brief simulation of a reading or writing strategy you use routinely so parents can develop an understanding of the reading approaches their children are using. If parents want to ask questions about their children's progress, suggest they set up a separate appointment so that individual situations can be kept private and confidential. Have your calendar available so you can set up appointments. Parents are likely to appreciate your efficiency and promptness in meeting their requests.

Ongoing Communication

The focus of ongoing communication should be reporting students' progress and informing parents about the classroom literacy program. Most teachers necessarily inform parents of children's progress during parent-teacher conferences and with report cards, but parents want and appreciate a running report of their children's learning before the quarterly report card period. If their children are not making progress, parents should have this information before a quarter of the school year is completed. One good way to establish ongoing communication is to send students' daily work home on a weekly basis. Attach a short note pointing out strengths and weaknesses; parents are then alerted to their children's progress throughout the year.

Learning from Experience

Mrs. Lewis, a junior high school language arts teacher, uses summary writing to inform her students' parents about their children's reading progress. Her seventh graders routinely write and revise summaries of articles they read, and at the end of each month, Mrs. Lewis has them choose one final summary and its drafts for their parents to review. Choosing their own summary not only gives her students a sense of participating in their own review process but also provides an opportunity for them to develop skill in evaluating and critiquing their own work—an unplanned outcome of this project.

Along with the drafts and the final summary, Mrs. Lewis includes a brief statement explaining the purpose of summary writing and the natural process of revision. She asks parents to indicate that they have seen the material by signing the summary and encourages them to include comments and questions.

Your Turn: Write your ideas on why summary writing may be an effective communication strategy in your journal under the heading Mrs. Lewis's Communication with Parents.

Our Turn: The strategy may be effective because students select what their parents will receive, parents have the opportunity to examine their children's actual writing as it is being revised over time, and the parents' comments as well as their signatures are requested by Ms. Lewis.

This kind of reporting procedure can help you develop an effective parent-teacher relationship. Teachers who keep parents informed about their children's progress on a regular basis are better able to establish positive relations with parents; parents are aware that the teacher is competent and knowledgeable about their children's abilities, and that she encourages as well as respects parental feedback.

Goal-Setting Meetings

Goal-setting conferences at the beginning of the year provide an opportunity for parent-teacher dialogue before a quarter to a half of the school year is completed. Parents can be invited to give their comments and ideas regarding your initial assessment and goal setting. This is also a good opportunity to elicit parental support and to initiate learning partnerships. In the Park City School District, for example, teachers assess students during the first month of school and schedule a parent-teacher conference to identify initial strengths and weaknesses and to discuss instructional goals derived from their assessment. Figure 16.4 shows the instructional goals for one student, Julianne, that the teachers shared with Julianne's parents.

Teacher's Letters

Short letters sent on a regular basis help parents develop an understanding of the reading and writing program and how their child is or is not achieving increased proficiency in reading and writing before they receive report cards. Ms. Garcia, a first-grade teacher, periodically writes letters to the parents of her students about their children's literacy program and often makes reasonable requests for their assistance (see Figure 16.5).

McPolin Elementary School
2270 Kearns Blvd.
Park City, UT 84068
(801) 645-5630
Linda Singer, Principal

Student Education Plan

STUDENT: *Edward Johnson*

TEACHER: Jeanette Raymer

GOALS:

Writing: *Ed* will show growth in writing skills and fluency as documented by writing samples from writing portfolio.

Reading: *Ed* will develop behaviors of an independent reader, able to self select and discuss a variety of literature at an appropriate instructional level, as evidenced through greater periods of sustained reading, formal written responses and increased participation in class literature discussions.

Math: *Ed* will demonstrate an understanding of multiplication and division by solving written equations as documented by quizzes and post-tests from Scott-Foresman Mathematics. *Ed* will use a variety of mathematical problem solving strategies and be able to apply them to real world situations.

Date: October 18, 1995

Parent: *Barbara Johnson* Teacher *J. Raymer* Student: _____

Evaluation of Goals: June 12, 1996
        Math:
        Reading:
        Writing:

Figure 16.4. A Statement of a Student's Instructional Goals to Be Shared with Parents

600

Dear Parents,

We are working hard at developing sight vocabularies through echo reading and language experience stories. Each time the class writes a story your children receive their own copies which are read individually with them. They then point to words that they recognize. The following day, your child is shown these words one more time to see if he or she still recognizes them in isolation. The words then become part of his or her sight vocabulary or "word bank."

All the children will be keeping their own "word bank" in reading. Each time your child recognizes a word in isolation for two consecutive days, he or she will be able to place it in the bank. "Word bank" words will then be used for drills, assignments, and writing activities.

Would you mind sending a small recipe holder (index card size) box to school for this purpose? Osco has them in metal or plastic. Your child will also benefit from a set of 26 file dividers labeled A through Z. These look like this:

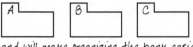

and will make organizing the bank easier.

Thank you very much in advance.

Figure 16.5. A Teacher's Letter to Promote Ongoing Communication with Parents (First Grade)

This type of letter can do much to build a positive parent-teacher relationship. The parents feel informed and knowledgeable. They understand what is being done to help their children become good readers, and such knowledge develops trust and instills confidence in their children's teacher.

Children's Letters

Some teachers also use children's correspondence to keep parents informed about the literacy program. For example, once a month, Mr. Stuart's fifth graders devote part of their Friday writing workshop to telling parents what they are learning in reading class. Before writing, they share what they have learned during the past week. Mr. Stuart records the gist of their points and guides the discussion through questioning. Then the children write and share their letters with peers, and Mr. Stuart provides suggestions for revision. The revised letters are not flawless; they reflect each child's present capabilities, so there are mistakes in spelling and sentence structure. For parents to understand and accept less than perfect letters, however, you must be careful to explain not only the purpose of this activity (to let parents see firsthand their children's strengths and weaknesses) but also that through continued practice and instruction their errors will become less frequent.

Parents' Visits

A very traditional way of keeping parents informed is to invite them to visit your classroom during literacy instruction. Identify several days when parents can visit, choosing days that are representative of typical reading and writing instructional activities. Suggest that they observe and then ask questions during a designated time when you are not teaching. Be sure to discuss your plans for parent visitation with your principal before issuing invitations; most principals will welcome this idea and appreciate your willingness to communicate with parents.

How Can You Conduct a Successful Parent-Teacher Conference?

Parent-teacher conferences typically create some discomfort and uneasiness, but there are two ways to overcome these feelings. First, if you have established a good relationship with your students' parents from the beginning of the school year, conferences will hold no threat. In all likelihood, however, you will not be able to establish a parent-teacher partnership with every parent every year. With those parents you have not yet met, we recommend you consider the seven elements we discuss in the following sections.

Friendly Atmosphere

Your first objective should be to establish a nonthreatening atmosphere in which parent and teacher communicate openly and objectively. Parents should feel that you and they are on the same team, working to improve their children's reading and writing ability. How do you create such an atmosphere? We provide a few simple suggestions:

- Provide chairs outside the classroom for parents who arrive early. If possible, set out some coffee or juice.
- Provide full-sized chairs for parents inside the classroom. Sitting in primary-school-size chairs can make parents feel patronized.
- Sit next to rather than across from parents, so parents feel like team members rather than passive receivers of information from the authority.
- Welcome parents as they arrive and thank them for coming.
- Begin by providing a quick overview of what the meeting will cover, so parents feel comfortable with the agenda, rather than plunging right into evaluations.
- Make clear how much you value parental input and listen when parents talk.

Objective Comments

Frame your statements in objective terms, beginning with a positive statement that notes the child's strengths, continuing with a review of weaknesses, and ending with a statement about the child's progress.

 ## Learning from Experience

Consider how a second-grade teacher presents Susan's reading behaviors in objective terms to her mother. What are some of the important points the teacher made to convey the nature of Susan's reading? Write your response in your journal.

Describes strengths, then weaknesses

Teacher: Susan is doing very well with phonics. She's able to apply phonics as she reads a story, and that's great. My main concern is that she may rely too heavily on phonics and disregard meaning as she sounds out words in a story. I'd like you to listen to part of a tape in which Susan is reading a story for the first time.

Illustrates
weakness

Mother: Yes, I've noticed Susan does sound out words well. I thought that was good, and I've encouraged her to do it. Am I doing something wrong?

Teacher: No, absolutely not. We want children to sound out words—it's a good tool for solving the pronunciation of unknown words. What I'm encouraging Susan to do is check if it makes sense in the sentence. If her first attempt doesn't make sense, then she needs to try again before she continues to read on. Let's listen to Susan's tape. [Tape is played, and both listen.]

Listens and
responds
to mother's
concern

Mother: I see what you mean. She just keeps reading even though the word doesn't make a bit of sense in the story. What can I do?

Teacher: It sounds as if Susan reads to you. Does she?

Mother: Yes, she loves to read aloud.

Offers
specific
guidelines
for ways in
which
mother
can help

Teacher: As she reads and comes to an unknown word, encourage her to read to the end of the sentence. Tell her to go back to the unknown word and sound it out. After she identifies a word, ask Susan to reread the sentence and check if it makes sense. If it doesn't, encourage her to try again. As she reads to the end of the sentence, Susan should be able to focus on sentence meaning and then combine it with her excellent phonic abilities. After she gets used to this strategy, she should notice a positive change in her reading.

Your Turn: What were some of the important things the teacher said and did to convey the nature of Susan's reading? Write your ideas in your journal under the heading Conference with Susan's Mother before comparing them to our ideas.

Our Turn: During this segment of the parent-teacher conference, the teacher began with Susan's strength—phonics—and then identified a weakness that was inhibiting Susan's progress in reading. A tape was played to illustrate the nature of Susan's over-reliance on phonics. All teacher statements focused on objective, observable reading behaviors. The teacher offered specific guidelines for ways in which the mother could help Susan.

Good Listening

It is essential that you listen to parents' comments during a conference. This is difficult; you have to be alert and able to develop appropriate comments and suggestions on the spot. Let's look again at the conference about Susan. Did you notice Susan's mother's comment after she heard that Susan was relying too heavily on phonics? She seemed to blame herself for Susan's bad habit. Instead of continuing with the agenda—playing the tape of Susan's reading—the teacher immediately responded to this sign of uneasiness. The teacher's attention to the mother's comment allowed the conference to run smoothly and to focus on Susan's behaviors as well as ways to improve them.

Children's Work

Showing parents examples of their children's work is a powerful tool. It communicates much better than a letter grade of A, B, C, D, or F, since parents can see for themselves their children's strengths and weaknesses in reading and writing. In Susan's conference, the teacher used a tape recording of Susan's reading to illustrate how she used phonics with little or no attention to context clues. Susan's mother could hear for herself how Susan read and could easily note her daughter's strengths and weaknesses in word identification. The audiotape is a good example of how teachers can use meaningful tools to illustrate children's strengths and weaknesses. Such examples can also illustrate progress, plateaus, and regressions. At a subsequent conference with Susan's mother, for example, this teacher might play an audiotape that illustrates Susan's new attention to context clues.

Many teachers are using portfolios to show children's progress. As discussed in chapter 10, portfolios of children's work demonstrate their learning and growth. Often they are prepared for parent-teacher conferences by the child in collaboration with the teacher, and, with the teacher's support, explained by the child during the conference.

Written summaries of stories children read can be used to illustrate comprehension and summarization abilities, and children's written responses to a story or book can shed some light on their attitude to and enjoyment of reading. Written responses to comprehension questions covering a text selection can indicate children's abilities to comprehend and express themselves in writing. These are only a few ways to show parents their children's reading and writing behaviors. Using children's work communicates and supports your statements about children's literacy abilities and instills parents' confidence in your abilities to teach.

Avoiding Jargon

Jargon and technical vocabulary are often not only meaningless but also offensive to parents, who feel excluded from the process of educating their own children. Look for clear and understandable ways of saying things. Susan's teacher, for example, does not use the term "context clues," but instead points out that Susan needs to check the meaning of sentences to verify her attempts at unknown words.

Parental Involvement

Try to get parents involved in their children's learning. The nature of parental help should reflect the child's needs and the parents' time and abilities. Provide specific suggestions for how parents can support and increase their child's learning, perhaps by designating a given time each night for reading or doing homework. Susan's teacher provided specific suggestions, since Susan's mother was already engaged in oral reading activities with her daughter. The suggestion was quick, easy, but very helpful, and Susan's mother was led to understand how this specific suggestion could contribute to her daughter's reading success. For parents to be able to carry out our suggestions, they need a clear understanding of how to do an activity and of the prospect of progress or success. Write out your suggestions so parents can refer back to them, or allow parents an opportunity to ask questions after you explain an activity. Be careful that the activities you suggest are not too complicated or time-consuming.

Inviting Parental Input

Do not suggest that you know everything about a child: Parents almost always have things to teach you. In order to acquire information from parents, give them ample opportunity to make comments and ask questions. In Susan's conference, the teacher listened to the mother's observations and used them to create more effective learning for Susan at home. Since parents do not always volunteer comments, provide time for questions: If they do not ask questions, you may need to ask your own questions to gather additional information. Although the questions you ask should be shaped by the dynamics of the parent-teacher conference, they may be along the following lines:

- Have you noticed this behavior as your child reads or writes at home?
- Has your child ever experienced this problem before?
- Do you know of anything that could provide me with additional insights?
- What are some of your thoughts about your child's reading and writing?
- Is there additional information I need to know to improve your child's reading and writing?

Before the conference concludes, make sure parents have opportunities to comment on how you might better meet their child's reading needs.

At the conclusion of a conference, parents need to feel they have learned valuable information. They need to understand their children's strengths and weaknesses in reading and writing and recognize how both you and they can contribute to their child's growth in literacy. And, finally, parents must feel that their questions are answered and their comments are heard and respected.

Having good relations with parents will foster the learning of your students. Moreover, as you learn to look carefully at your instructional program and to assess the learning of your students, you form a clearer understanding of the needs of students, which in turn enables you to be clearer in your communication with parents. Learning to communicate with parents is one important aspect of your professional growth. In the following sections, we explore other opportunities.

HOW CAN YOU FOSTER YOUR OWN PROFESSIONAL DEVELOPMENT?

Growth in any area consists of solving new problems and resolving old ones. Because of the inherently complex nature of teaching, not all problems can be solved in a single year; indeed, the best teachers are those who continue to identify and solve problems—or challenges—throughout their careers. They do not allow themselves to be satisfied with existing solutions that are merely workable: They explore new approaches to find the best possible answer. They continue to develop as "enthusiastic and growing" teachers.

The First Years of Teaching

Your first year is typically filled with learning about children, developmental processes in reading and writing and the other content areas, teaching, the school, and the school community. Although most of us never really stop learning in these areas, after the first year the classroom becomes a more predictable and manageable place.

This initial learning occurs best when supported by other teachers working in the same school. Some schools have formal mentoring programs, in which new teachers are assigned to work with more experienced colleagues. Unfortunately, many beginning teachers must identify their own support systems, and sometimes they are hesitant to ask for help. But if you are in this position, keep in mind that teachers who have been on the job for four or five or more years often profit greatly from having to think about what they do, in order to understand the problems confronting a new teacher. Try to develop close working relationships with your colleagues that do not focus simply on problems in the classroom; ask other teachers about the school, the community, the nature of their literacy programs, and so on.

The kind of reflection and evaluation that we recommend in the previous sections of the chapter are particularly important during your first year. In the following Learning from Experience activity, we share the reflections of Nedra Winter, who had just completed one year of teaching third grade and was beginning her second year when we interviewed her.

 # Learning from Experience

As you read this interview, note what Nedra learned about getting along with other teachers in her school and with parents. Consider the reading and writing activities that Nedra uses. How do these compare with those developed by Marcy Lee? Why does Nedra believe that beginning teachers should take risks? Do you agree? Write your responses in your journal.

Interviewer: What are some of the things you feel you learned from your first year of teaching?

Nedra: I came out of school full of theories about individualized learning and making sure that children had options so that they could express themselves, particularly in writing. So I was giving three exercises a day where each paper was different. There was no way you could grade it without reading it. I found myself at the end of the week with just hundreds of papers that I had not read. So a big problem to solve was how to structure the classroom in a way that I could give them immediate individual feedback on their work and yet not make it impossible for me to do it.

Another thing was dealing with parents—recognizing that they all have real specific agendas and trying to identify those agendas before I got sucked into them. Often I found that parent agendas had nothing to do with the academic program, but with the social agenda, for instance, wanting their children interacting with children of friends of theirs. Some parents really did have academic concerns—their kids were not doing well in math or something. But many of these were overachieving parents who had kids who were not overachieving. At first I didn't realize that these kids were getting browbeaten every night with homework assigned by their parents. Heaven forbid I should send more because they already had their parents' homework to do. And when the parents came to talk, they didn't seem so tense at first, but as I learned more about them, I found they were really extremely anxious. I needed to find ways of helping them to be at ease about the academic program.

Another area is dealing with other teachers. You walk into the building, Miss Eager Beaver, you know. You're busy running around putting this up and it's all so exciting and you're so happy to be there. You come early, you greet the children in the morning and try to make a certain kind of atmosphere and you actually go onto the playground or into the lunchroom, you know, where heaven forbid any teacher should ever go unless you're on duty. But anyway, the other teachers are really not all that thrilled about this. I think teachers coming out of training programs now have a whole different approach to discipline and teacher-student interaction than some of the people who have been teaching 20 years. Some are used to establishing discipline in a hierarchical way. You know, I'm the teacher, I'm the authority figure, you're the kid, you have no power, you do what I say and that's that.

So when I came in, the kids responded—a child has never been disrespectful to me, but they're very much my friends in the sense that they come in and tell me about stuff, and they want to be in the room even if they're not in my class. And we get to talking, and some of the older teachers come in, and they aren't so sure—they're not comfortable with that. They really think there should be a separation and teachers should have a distinct role and function outside of the social lives of the students. They act as if you're just trying to make kids like you and not like them. So there's a lot of that.

But it's important to work well with the other staff—learning how to do it and finding out where the bodies are buried, how to become effective in a building. You know, if you come in and side with the principal—"Great idea! Love this idea!"—then you've got 23 other people who let you know, "We never do that. You know, we just don't do that. You just don't show unbridled enthusiasm for the principal's ideas when they are first offered because you just don't." That's part of the unspoken etiquette. So with something that seems like a good idea, you're supposed to hold your reactions in until all have decided it's a good idea.

In addition, getting along involves a lot of little things—learning how to get your materials back; you know, people come in and borrow stuff and never bring it back. Learning how to fit into the life of the building is not easy. One thing I've found is I have to make more phone calls to my colleagues. The more I make a call here and there, the more I call to ask about something outside of the school environment, the more we seem to be comfortable with each other. It seems to establish a network that goes beyond the school building and seems to make it easier to be accepted and to know where people are coming from with their ideas. So often what people say in front of a principal or somebody else on the team is not what they are thinking at all. At first, I was operating on what I heard at meetings. I'd say, "So that's what they want," and I'd go off trying to do that. It'd turn out that it wasn't what anybody wanted and there was no support. So the calls really helped, you know, asking, "What did you think about XYZ?"

Interviewer: Sounds as if you have figured out quite a bit about how your school works. I'm curious, though. How did you solve the problem of giving students feedback on their writing?

Nedra: Well, I'm still working on it. I tried having the reading groups be small editorial boards. They'd bring their writing and we'd sit around and start discussing it. But if we got hung up on one, it would take the whole period. So this year, I'm limiting the kids. They have to choose one piece of writing from a week that they want to develop. We've been doing all kinds of writing—short poems, story ideas, whatever. On Friday they choose one piece that they'd like to develop more. They put it in a file at the back of the room. The editorial board reads everybody's writing and we rotate them every three weeks. We have times when people get to go back there—they can either go back to write more or to edit. The kids who are doing editing check for spelling and they ask, "Does this indicate a clear idea or did I get confused?" The sheet I'm having them do this on has a place for editor's comments and they write their responses. When kids are finished with what they're doing, they go back there and pull out their work and then form their own groups. Usually it's one-on-one. Sometimes there's two editors, one writer. Last Friday there were three writers to one editor because everybody wanted this one kid to read what they had written. My room is great because I've got an isolated area back there. Now I'm crossing my fingers that they don't start playing there, but so far they haven't. They love the idea that we're going to publish the stuff. So they're all hot to get it right.

Interviewer: What advice would you give to new teachers as they begin their careers?

Nedra: For me a really important thing is being willing to take some risks. You come out of school and you think, "I'm not sure how I'm going to do this, but I've got these beliefs, these theories about teaching." You've got to realize that the kids are not going to die while you are finding out what works. And I think we owe it to the kids to do what we learned to do, to figure out how to put those theories we believe in into practice. And we owe it to ourselves. Because otherwise it's like you wanted to be the boss, but you end up being the secretary. You become a slave to the curriculum rather than a creator of learning experiences. You just have to go for it and know that the kids aren't going to be ruined and nobody's going to fire you. They may send a teacher or two in to say, "Let's try doing it this way," but that's not bad.

At first I found myself so focused on me and what I was supposed to be doing that I wasn't listening to the kids. It was just like, "Okay, I'm doing my thing, let's go." But by the end of the year, and I don't know how it happened, things changed. Their moans and groans stopped, and what I was saying and doing made sense to them. They tell you if what you're doing is working. They master stuff. I mean, they demonstrate it. They show you they have the skill.

Interviewer: Learning to teach really is a complicated task. Is it worth it?

Nedra: The first time a child called me "Mama," it floored me. I didn't realize until that first year in the classroom that teachers serve that kind of intensely important function in a child's life. I just didn't. You know, you intellectualize about it. Teachers are very important, education is very important, and so on. However, you are Mama, you are Dad—they call me Daddy. Whoever is important in their lives. There are points where that's what they call me. You know, they want something and they call you that. That really brought home to me my responsibility to take risks—to do the work—to always be ready for them. Because they give—they truly are giving us themselves. They really are. They go along with this stuff. "Do you want me in this room six hours a day? Okay." They give us themselves. And they're going to be the people we help them to be—in whatever way, good or bad. I'd like to feel that I'm helping kids in a way that'll help them be a productive part of the society rather than misfits. Yeah, you are very much identified as an important person in their lives.

Your Turn: In thinking about this interview, did you notice the understandings that Nedra gained about the teachers in her school and the parents of her students? What did she learn about children and teaching that impressed you? Write your thoughts in your journal under the heading Nedra's First Year of Teaching.

Our Turn: This interview reveals the extremely complex set of learnings that a beginning teacher faces. It is most unusual for a teacher who has just completed her first year to demonstrate the insight that Nedra does into how she, with her eagerness and new knowledge, might appear to other teachers in the school. The interview vividly demonstrates the extent to which "risk taking" is essential in becoming an effective teacher. It also provides a clear and compelling answer to the question of whether teaching is "worth it."

The interview also shows how Nedra incorporates the ideas she learned during her preservice course work into her writing program. Nedra followed a process writing program in her class (see chapter 8 for further description of process writing). The interview reveals what she has learned about managing this program. The extent of Nedra's reflection and evaluation is unusual for a first-year teacher.

Beyond the Beginning Years: Program Refinement and Development

Burke and his colleagues (1984) define the stage of competency building as the period when teachers improve their skills by seeking out new methods, materials, and strategies. Teachers are receptive to new ideas, attend conferences and workshops willingly, and often enroll in graduate programs on their own initiative.

End-of-the-year reflection and evaluation are particularly important for teachers who have solved the challenges of their first years. Summer presents an opportune time to refine the reading program for the coming year and to stay current and hone professional skills. Take a reading or writing course; check with other teachers about which colleges or universities offer the most current and informative ones. Experience from the first few years of teaching provides you with a broader perspective from which to view new ideas about literacy development.

Third-grade teacher Nedra Winter is entering into the stage of competency building. We might expect Nedra to expand her knowledge during the next few summers by taking a course or two on reading, by exploring children's literature in local libraries and bookstores and reading a wide selection of recommended titles, and by involving herself in a writing workshop (see, for example, Calkins, 1986; Cochran-Smith, 1984; Temple, Nathan, Burris, & Temple, 1988). She might also want to plan for more parent involvement in her literacy program by talking with teachers who have used parents as volunteers.

Teachers entering the competency-building stage should familiarize themselves, if they haven't already done so, with professional journals and organizations. Survey the journals in your teachers' lounge and at a local college or university, to see which ones most directly address the concerns you are facing in your classroom. At minimum, elementary school teachers should subscribe to a journal such as *Language Arts* and *The Reading Teacher,* and upper elementary and middle-grade teachers should subscribe to a journal such as *The Journal of Adolescent and Adult Literacy.*

You will probably learn about the committee structures of your school and district, how members are selected, and when major curricular decisions are made. As you begin to build your own knowledge in various areas, you may wish to serve on a committee that considers issues of interest to you: a reading committee charged with reviewing published literacy programs, the school library committee, or a committee formed to develop a writing strand for the curriculum.

We want to add one cautionary note to all this. Your career will be, we hope, a long one; you should not try to accomplish everything in one summer or even one year. During each year, set for yourself a single focus to guide your learning and reflection—one year to expand your knowledge about reading instruction; the next to explore children's literature; a third on writing, and so on. Staff development in your district may be organized around a continuing agenda that includes some of these topics, and you may want to coordinate your personal learning with this adenda. Try to find other teachers—some at the same stage of development but also others searching for renewal—with whom you can share your learning.

Leadership within the School and District

Once you have developed competency in the ways described above, you may want to seek further growth by assuming leadership in your school or district. We end this chapter by exploring some of the paths available to you at this level.

Program Development

It is not unusual for teachers at this stage of development to design their own literacy programs, in order to expose students to a wider range of trade books, to integrate writing into the program, and to free themselves from dependence on workbook activities for seat work. Not all districts provide teachers with opportunities to move away from published programs to develop their own plans of instruction, but we believe this will happen more often in years to come.

One reason that many districts require close adherence to published programs is that the content and organization of the programs reflect a considerable body of knowledge about how children learn to read. If such programs are given up, we run the risk of abandoning much that is useful. The reading series, for example, include stories that increase systematically and gradually in level of difficulty through carefully controlled vocabulary and language patterns, so that stories are accessible to beginning readers and provide a balance among different kinds of literacy activities. These strengths can also be weaknesses, since controlled vocabulary and word patterns sometimes result in unnatural and difficult language, and the balance of activities sometimes ignores the need for emphasis in certain areas.

In designing your own literacy program, you need to develop methods to incorporate the strengths of published programs while avoiding their weaknesses. You will need to select materials carefully and sometimes modify them to ensure that you are providing students with selections at the appropriate reading levels. To make stories accessible, you will need to employ instructional strategies like those discussed in chapter 3, in which children read and reread stories several times before they engage in independent reading.

One of the most extensive efforts to order stories in terms of difficulty has been undertaken by the Reading Recovery staff (see appendix B). Part of the effectiveness of Reading Recovery methods lies in the fact that children are challenged by stories of increasing complexity once they demonstrate fluency with stories at an easier level (Lyons et al., 1993). When you develop your own program, you need to be aware of the extent to which children are challenged by the selections you include. For the beginning stages of reading, the lists developed by Reading Recovery are extremely helpful; beyond this level, you need to evaluate the difficulty of your selections by assessing oral reading and comprehension as outlined in chapter 10.

How can journals help teachers grow professionally?

Further Learning

After a few years of taking courses of immediate interest to you, you may shift your focus to a degree program, perhaps to completing your master's in a field of specialization such as reading, writing, literature, or mathematics. Programs are being developed for experienced teachers that differ in important respects from more traditional, course-by-course master's programs and offer new ways of thinking about instructional practice.

Leadership

After some years of experience, one of the most satisfying activities you may want to undertake is mentoring a teacher just starting out. Mentoring can occur through formally structured programs in which master teachers are selected to support beginning teachers, or on an informal basis when experienced teachers simply make themselves available to novices to answer questions and provide support. An extremely helpful service for the beginning teacher, mentoring yields equal benefits for the mentor, who is forced to consider teaching from new perspectives. You can also demonstrate leadership on school and district committees; once a member, you will find many opportunities for extending your leadership, both formal and informal, within and beyond the committee. Being active in the school and district allows you to influence the conditions of your own workplace. The following interview with Barbara Rogers, an experienced teacher, demonstrates how teachers can provide innovative leadership through committee work and program development. It also shows that no career is an entirely smooth progression from one step to the next. Most important, it reveals the attitudes and ways of thinking that characterize a teacher who continues to grow throughout her career.

 ## Learning from Experience

As you read the transcript of this interview, note the things that Barbara was concerned about early in her career and those that preoccupy her now. What are the things in which she has had a continuing interest? Write your responses in your journal.

Interviewer: Take us back to the early days of your teaching and talk a little about how your career has developed.

Barbara: I graduated in 1975, and in order for an inexperienced teacher to get a job at that time, it was necessary to move. So I found a job in Appalachia in the Blue Ridge mountains where they badly needed teachers. I taught second graders in a remote corner of Virginia. It was probably a pretty good place to start because I wasn't in a spotlight. They were very happy to have me there, and I could close my door and make my mistakes and sort of teach myself as I went along. I think probably the hardest things for a first-year teacher are classroom discipline and getting things flowing smoothly, and it's very hard to know how to pace yourself, what things to give a lot of attention to, what things to skip. I really didn't feel that I had a strong background in what specifically a second grader should know, and what I should focus on.

They had just started a new reading program in my school district. They were very proud of it, but there was so much of it that you could spend weeks on lesson number 1. I had reading groups, but it was hard to organize and to keep the groups who were not working with me productively on task. I began to cut back on reading groups and tried to find things that the whole group could do. I probably read to them about an hour a day. The librarian in town had a wonderful children's library that nobody seemed to use, so I brought back armloads of books and surrounded my students with literature and read to them. And I ordered some really good books for kids just beginning to read.

I found when I got down there that Virginia certification requirements were different from those for Illinois, so I needed something like 14 more courses. That summer I took a course in reading. The course was taught by a very traditional, experienced classroom teacher. I learned "everything there was to know" from her about primary-level teaching— from language experience and phonics on up. I acquired a wonderful repertoire of teaching activities. When I went back the second year I felt powerful, like I knew what I was doing and I had some options. I had a better idea of how to sort out what kids already knew, so I probably had them more correctly placed.

Still, after two years, now looking back, I knew nothing. I mean, I had very limited ideas about what could or should be done. When I came back to Illinois to teach in the city system, I felt very good and powerful after those two years in Virginia. I thought I had a lot to offer inner-city students and hoped I could translate my success in teaching rural disadvantaged students, but it didn't work. I still have no idea about what you do in that situation. When they had a strike and a big juncture in the school year, and I got "bumped" from my assigned classroom, I quit. I didn't feel any support. Everybody was out at 2:45 and tried to forget about teaching and school as fast as possible. I'm overgeneralizing, but teachers were required to leave right after school. You couldn't get to know the kids or the staff more informally, and there was absolutely no sense of faculty development.

I've learned that professional growth is not a solitary thing. It's like forming a community within a community. There are certain teachers who sort of gravitate together who are very serious about what they are doing. For instance, when I changed to the school where I'm still teaching, I ran into Linda [the reading teacher in Chapter 1]. Very quickly, we began sharing ideas. I had so many questions based on course work that I had done, and Linda and a few other classroom teachers were eager to discuss them. I'd go to Learning Institute sessions and come back to school full of more questions. I heard about Learning Institute through *Learning Magazine,* which I always subscribe to. They had some excellent speakers, like Dorsey Hammond and Bill Halloran. Schools are always getting solicitations to attend conferences and workshops. I think as you go along you become more savvy about which ones to pay attention to. If you've had a couple of good experiences with Learning Institute, you look at those flyers. If you've had a few bad experiences with another organization, you're going to ignore those. Also, I think by reading you begin to hear who are some of the well-known people who share some of your beliefs and interests.

When I first started out I just subscribed to the very teacherly magazines. You know, *Learning Magazine, Instructor,* and there used to be a magazine called *Teacher.* I really looked forward to receiving them every month—especially down in Virginia, where I was more isolated. You'd get all sorts of ideas. They were specific and classroom-oriented. You'd get some good thinkers in the field, too. Herb Kohl used to write in *Teacher* most months. I still continue to subscribe to them, but I find myself not reading them cover to cover anymore. I'm more interested now in sort of midlevel, professional journals—*Language Arts, Reading Teacher, Arithmetic Teacher,* and the like.

Interviewer: When you reflect on your teaching at the end of the year, what are the questions you ask yourself? How do you know you've done a good job and how do you identify those areas you would like to do better in?

Barbara: I think you're modifying all year long, trying things and seeing how they work. I generally have a pretty positive outlook, so I look back and see what things I thought were outstanding about that year that I really liked or that I tried that I hadn't done before. This past year I changed to a different grade level, which was really energizing. It was something that I asked the principal to do. I felt like I'd done a good job in fourth grade. But it gave me a chance to sort of rethink what I'd been doing when I made the change. For instance, in reading class I'd always been one of the lesser users of the published reading program. The program is our curriculum, and teachers have to give the unit tests, but I've found that nobody's looking over your shoulder to see if you've done every workbook page or that it is the main thing you've used. Each year I've included more literature and fewer reading subskills. I work on the reading committee, and one of the outcomes of our reading committee was to build a huge trade-book library, a multiple copy library with a dozen copies of at least 20 titles per reading level. So it's a nice resource. Once the school bought that, you certainly have permission to make good use of it. So I try to use it as much as possible and still go through most of the reading program stories. When I decided to go to third grade, my goal was to see how far I could push that—how much I could do based on really good literature. Now I use the reading program much less, and not too much of the skills. I just cross out the ones that are a total waste of time for kids. So this grade-level change challenged me to go even further in developing my own literacy program, and it gave me the chance to look more critically at what I was doing.

Interviewer: You said that you try new things usually every year. Can you give us an example of something you've tried recently that you learned from?

Barbara: This year, for the first time, I tried something called Lit Logs—reader response journals. It's a dialogue journal about the things that students are reading. The year before I had asked permission to go to one of the regional conferences of IRA [International Reading Association], where I heard someone talking about them.

This year I decided to try them as a new way to get the kids to make better use of their independent reading time. I wanted them to know that independent reading was part of a program that counted rather than just filler time. So they would have the opportunity to write their thoughts about whatever they were reading, and I would model how you think about things you read by writing back to them, asking questions and saying what I thought about the books when I read them. And we wrote back and forth about some of the books we were reading together as a group, too. I would send them back to their seats and say, "Okay, write in your Lit Logs now." We'd write back and forth, probably at least once or twice a week.

It was something I had never tried before, and it was so exciting to me. Besides deepening students' response to literature, I really felt that it made a major impact on my relations with the students. The logs helped to form a bond among my students, most of whom were from other homeroom classes. The logs helped me to get to know them all and to get them to want to behave and be interested in reading, because they took themselves seriously and were committed. We were all kind of working with a common purpose, and we were all readers and discussers. All the students had all sorts of interesting thoughts on what they were doing. It's very exciting!

I had an opportunity to share what I was learning about the logs. Fairly early on in the year, the principal asked me to share my ideas with another teacher. I was excited about this and talked with her at one of our staff meetings. She asked me to share some of the logs and tell the other teachers about it. I'd say that by the end of the year there were probably at least 10 or 12 teachers who were trying it on a regular basis. And one of my personal goals for the year was to explore Lit Logs further. When I took a reading research course this spring, that was the topic that I investigated, and I'm still involved in writing a paper about it. Maybe I'll be able to share my experience in using response journals with other people in a magazine or something.

Interviewer: Is there anything else that you want to add about the next steps in your professional development?

Barbara: The more you feel you know about something, the more you want to share it. And you begin to look for outlets, like volunteering to give an inservice in your school or accepting an invitation to talk about something you're doing in different schools. I was involved in an inservice project last spring. From it, I learned to see things in a somewhat different way. When I assisted in teaching a practicum course at the master's level in reading this summer, I found that some of the student tutors I worked with were particularly interested in the work I'd done with Lit Logs, and they incorporated this procedure into their tutoring. So I continue to learn by sharing what I've learned.

Your Turn: What were some of the things that concerned Barbara earlier in her career? What preoccupies her now? What are the concerns that have characterized her career at every stage? Write your responses in your journal under the heading Barbara's Professional Development.

 Our Turn: As you probably noticed, Barbara's commitment to learning more about teaching and her interest in children's literature characterize every phase of her career. She sought new ideas from colleagues and from professional magazines, and learned from her experience. Although she was concerned early on about discipline and how to establish a reading program, these concerns quickly gave way to pursuing more effective ways to engage children in authentic literacy experiences. Recently, she has assumed leadership roles within her school and district. There is no sharp line delineating leadership within schools from that beyond schools. Indeed, as can be seen from Barbara's interview, as she began to assume active leadership within her school, broader leadership opportunities also developed.

Leadership beyond the Schools

Leadership opportunities within schools lead directly to similar opportunities beyond the schools. For example, as you begin developing workshop presentations for colleagues in your school, teachers in other schools may request similar presentations. This may also lead you toward a central role in shaping the staff development activities for your district. The knowledge that you develop during a competency-building phase provides the basis for program development in your school and district. Thus a natural extension from one's own exploration is the sharing of successful practice with other teachers. Enthusiastic and growing teachers may build a relationship with faculty at local colleges or universities. What begins with workshop participation and occasional course work may lead to completing a degree program or assisting in teaching courses as a guest speaker. This, in turn, often leads to enrollment in advanced programs and the opportunity to teach college-level courses. A deeper level of understanding develops as you learn to communicate your knowledge about teaching with others who are facing problems you encountered earlier. Collaborative teaching activities with other teachers or university faculty may also develop into collaborative inquiry projects. You may in this way become involved in the generation of knowledge that shapes our thinking about practice in the field of literacy.

Finally, the communicative skill that you develop through teaching and other leadership activities leads directly to opportunities to write about your practice for other teachers. Just as Barbara Rogers was encouraged to write about her Lit Log project for other teachers, you may feel compelled to share your knowledge with a broader range of teachers. Teaching is truly an exciting field in which to be involved.

SUMMARY
••

In this final chapter of a very demanding book, we have developed some of our ideas about reflection and professional growth. We hope that you will refer to this chapter frequently as you begin the process of reflecting on your own teaching. The questions we have suggested can serve as a beginning framework from which you can consider the effectiveness of your program. One area of particular challenge is in developing positive and productive relations with the parents of your students. We offered specific suggestions for how you may accomplish this. We have, also in this chapter, tried to challenge you to continue to grow. Identify where you are now in this odyssey of professional development and set your sights for further growth.

In the Field

1. Interview some elementary school teachers from the grade level you would like to teach. Ask them whether and how they reflect on their instructional program. Is the process ongoing or does it occur at specific times? How do they know if activities are effective in terms of student learning? What leads them to change their instructional program or to try new things? What did you learn from the interview that will be useful in your own teaching? Summarize what you learned in a report or in your journal under the heading Teacher's Reflection on Teaching.

2. Role-play with another person a parent-teacher conference in which you want to inform parents that their child is experiencing difficulties with comprehension. The child is able to read text fluently but is unable to retell what has happened in the story. Remember the seven points you have just learned about conferences. Summarize what you learned in a report or in your journal under the heading Parent-Teacher Conference.

3. Interview experienced elementary school teachers about their professional development. What were their first years like? How have they sustained and expanded their expertise? Have they mentored teachers during their training? How did they find this experience? What aspects of the interview did you find to be particularly valuable and why? Summarize what you learned in a report or in your journal under the heading Teacher's Reflection on Professional Development.

Portfolio Suggestion

Select from your journal two examples of your responses to Pause and Reflect or Learning from Experience: Your Turn and include these in your portfolio. If you completed an In the Field activity, include your report from it in your portfolio as well. Write a brief evaluation of your work, commenting on what it shows about your learning.

For Further Reading

Cairney, T. H., & Munsie, L. (1995). Parent participation in literacy learning. *The Reading Teacher, 48,* 392–403.

Cochran-Smith, M., & Lytle, S. (1993). *Inside/outside: Teacher research and knowledge.* New York: Teachers College Press.

Edwards, P. A. (1995). Empowering low-income mothers and fathers to share books with young children. *The Reading Teacher, 48,* 558–564.

France, M. G., & Hager, J. M. (1993). Recruit, respect, respond: A model for working with low-income families and their preschoolers. *The Reading Teacher, 46,* 568–572.

Stieglitz, A. L., & Oehlkers, W. J. (1989). Improving teacher discourse in a reading lesson. *The Reading Teacher, 42,* 374–379.

Wildman, T. N., Niles, J. A., Magliaro, S. G., & McLaughlin, R. A. (1989). Teaching and learning to teach: The two roles of beginning teachers. *Elementary School Journal, 89,* 471–493.

Appendix

Children's Literature for Young Readers

This bibliography includes just a sampling of the many hundreds of wonderfully exciting books for beginning readers that can be found in public and school library collections.* Level designations are only approximations, since text difficulty can most effectively be evaluated with real readers in the context of authentic classroom and teaching situations. Books at higher levels can be introduced early in the school year for shared reading or as read-alouds.

Savor the language, explore the illustrations, and return again and again to favorite stories. Link books with similar themes, such as *Rosie's Walk* (Pat Hutchins), *Across the Stream* (Mirra Ginsburg), and *Hattie and the Fox* (Mem Fox), in which the hungry fox just can't seem to catch the tasty hen. Read aloud books too difficult for independent reading, such as Patricia McKissack's *Flossie and the Fox* (illustrated by Rachel Isadora, Dial Books, 1986), the story of a young girl who outwits a wily fox. Browse through library and bookstore collections to make other discoveries!

LEVELS 1 TO 4

Books in Levels 1 to 4 provide strong links to situations experienced by young children who are learning to read through the use of familiar concepts and vocabulary, commonly used oral language patterns, repetition of those patterns, and illustrations that closely portray the meaning and language of the story.

Level 1

Hoban, Tana. *Count and See*. Macmillan, 1972.

Jonas, Ann. *Now We Can Go*. Greenwillow, 1986.

Maris, Ron. *My Book*. Viking Penguin, 1983.

McMillan, Bruce. *Growing Colors*. Lothrop, Lee & Shepard, 1988.

Tafuri, Nancy. *Have You Seen My Duckling?* Greenwillow, 1984.

Wildsmith, Brian. *Cat on the Mat*. Oxford, 1982.

Level 2

Carle, Eric. *Have You Seen My Cat?* Picture Book Studio, 1987.

Gomi, Taro. *Where's the Fish?* Morrow, 1977.

Ziefert, Harriet, and Simms Taback. *Where Is My Dinner?* Grosset & Dunlap, 1984.

Level 3

Hutchins, Pat. *One Hunter*. Greenwillow, 1982.

Minarik, Else Holmelund. *It's Spring!* Illustrated by Margaret Bloy Graham. Greenwillow, 1989.

Sawicki, Norma Jean. *The Little Red House*. Illustrated by Toni Goffe. Lothrop, Lee & Shepard, 1989.

Tafuri, Nancy. *Who's Counting?* Greenwillow, 1986.

Wildsmith, Brian. *All Fall Down*. Oxford, 1983.

Wildsmith, Brian. *Toot, Toot*. Oxford, 1984.

---

*From "Selected Books for Beginning Readers," by Barbara L. Peterson, in *Bridges to Literacy*, ed. by D. DeFord, G. S. Pinnell, and C. Lyons, 1997, Portsmouth, NH: Heinemann. Adapted with permission.

Level 4

Kalan, Robert. *Rain*. Illustrated by Donald Crews. Greenwillow, 1978.

Martin, Bill. *Brown Bear, Brown Bear, What Do You See?* Illustrated by Eric Carle. Holt, 1984.

Peek, Merle. *Roll Over*. Clarion, 1981.

Tafuri, Nancy. *Spots, Feathers, and Curly Tails*. Greenwillow, 1988.

LEVELS 5 TO 8

Books in Levels 5 to 8, like those in the first four levels, provide support for young children's experiences by using familiar vocabulary and language patterns. Gradually, however, language patterns become less repetitive, and some literary language is introduced. Illustrations provide strong support for the meaning of stories through Levels 6 and 7. Around Level 8, as sentences become longer and less descriptive of concrete objects and actions, illustrations provide moderate support. Picture-book versions of familiar songs often fit within this group of levels.

Level 5

Parkinson, Kathy. *The Farmer in the Dell*. Whitman, 1988.

Raffi. *Five Little Ducks*. Illustrated by José Aruego and Ariane Dewey. Crown, 1989.

Stobbs, William. *One, Two, Buckle My Shoe*. Bodley Head, 1984.

Tafuri, Nancy. *The Ball Bounced*. Greenwillow, 1989.

Level 6

Browne, Anthony. *I Like Books*. Knopf, 1988.

Browne, Anthony. *Things I Like*. Knopf, 1989.

Burningham, John. *The School*. Crowell, 1974.

Ginsburg, Mirra. *The Chick and the Duckling*. Illustrated by José Aruego. Macmillan, 1972.

Hellard, Susan. *This Little Piggy*. Putnam, 1989.

Jones, Carol. *Old MacDonald Had a Farm*. Houghton Mifflin, 1989.

Lindgren, Barbro. *Sam's Ball*. Illustrated by Eva Eriksson. Morrow, 1983.

Lindgren, Barbro. *Sam's Cookie*. Illustrated by Eva Eriksson. Morrow, 1982.

Lindgren, Barbro. *Sam's Lamp*. Illustrated by Eva Eriksson. Morrow, 1983.

Lindgren, Barbro. *Sam's Teddy Bear*. Illustrated by Eva Eriksson. Morrow, 1982.

Lindgren, Barbro. *Sam's Wagon*. Illustrated by Eva Eriksson. Morrow, 1986.

Peek, Merle. *Mary Wore Her Red Dress*. Clarion, 1985.

Rounds, Glen. *Old MacDonald Had a Farm*. Holiday House, 1989.

Level 7

Crews, Donald. *Flying*. Greenwillow, 1986.

Shaw, Charles. *It Looked Like Spilt Milk*. Harper & Row, 1947, 1988.

Level 8

Burningham, John. *The Blanket*. Crowell, 1975.

Campbell, Rod. *Henry's Busy Day*. Viking, 1984.

Christelow, Eileen. *Five Little Monkeys Jumping on the Bed*. Clarion, 1989.

Hill, Eric. *Where's Spot?* Putnam, 1980.

Jonas, Ann. *Where Can It Be?* Greenwillow, 1986.

Kraus, Robert. *Herman the Helper*. Illustrated by José Aruego and Ariane Dewey. Windmill, 1974.

Langstaff, John. *Oh, A-Hunting We Will Go*. Illustrated by Nancy Winslow Parker. Atheneum, 1974.

Roffey, Maureen. *Home Sweet Home*. The Bodley Head, 1982.

LEVELS 9 TO 12

Many books in Levels 9 to 12 have a more fully expanded story shape with sequences of episodes in which each new event is a result of the previous action. Repetition often occurs in the form of refrains, and illustrations provide moderate support for the meaning of the written text.

Level 9

Asch, Frank. *Just Like Daddy*. Prentice-Hall, 1981.

Campbell, Rod. *Dear Zoo*. Four Winds, 1982.

Galdone, Paul. *Cat Goes Fiddle-i-fee*. Clarion, 1988.

Henkes, Kevin. *SHHHH*. Greenwillow, 1989.

Hutchins, Pat. *Rosie's Walk*. Macmillan, 1968.

Lloyd, David. *Grandma and the Pirate*. Illustrated by Gill Tomblin. Crown, 1985.

Maris, Ron. *Are You There Bear?* Greenwillow, 1985.

Maris, Ron. *Is Anyone Home?* Greenwillow, 1984.

Stobbs, William. *Gregory's Garden*. Oxford, 1987.

West, Colin. *Have You Seen the Crocodile?* Harper & Row, 1986.

West, Colin. *"Pardon?" Said the Giraffe*. Harper & Row, 1986.

Level 10

Bang, Molly. *Ten, Nine, Eight*. Greenwillow, 1983.

Brown, Ruth. *A Dark Dark Tale*. Dial, 1981.

De Regniers, Beatrice Schenk. *Going for a Walk*. Harper & Row, 1961.

Gerstein, Mordicai. *Roll Over!* Crown, 1984.

Gerstein, Mordicai. *William, Where Are You?* Crown, 1985.

Ginsburg, Mirra. *Across the Stream.* Illustrated by Nancy Tafuri. Greenwillow, 1982.

Goor, Ron, and Nancy Goor. *Signs.* Crowell, 1983.

Rockwell, Anne. *Cars.* Dutton, 1984.

Rockwell, Harlow. *My Kitchen.* Greenwillow, 1980.

Stadler, John. *Hooray for Snail!* Harper & Row, 1984.

Ward, Cindy. *Cookie's Week.* Illustrated by Tomie de Paola. Putnam, 1988.

Watanabe, Shigeo. *I'm King of the Castle!* Illustrated by Yasuo Ohtomo. Philomel, 1982.

Wheeler, Cindy. *Marmalade's Nap.* Knopf, 1982.

Wheeler, Cindy. *Marmalade's Snowy Day.* Knopf, 1983.

Wheeler, Cindy. *Rose.* Knopf, 1985.

Ziefert, Harriet. *Thank You, Nicky!* Illustrated by Richard Brown. Viking Penguin, 1988.

Level 11

Ahlberg, Janet, and Allan Ahlberg. *Each Peach Pear Plum.* Viking, 1978.

Barton, Byron. *Dinosaurs, Dinosaurs.* Crowell, 1989.

Gelman, Rita. *More Spaghetti, I Say!* Illustrated by Jack Kent. Scholastic, 1977.

Hellen, Nancy. *The Bus Stop.* Orchard Books, 1988.

Hennessy, B. G. *The Missing Tarts.* Illustrated by Tracey Campbell Pearson. Viking Kestrel, 1989.

Kraus, Robert. *Whose Mouse Are You?* Illustrated by José Aruego. Macmillan, 1970.

Mack, Stan. *10 Bears in My Bed.* Pantheon, 1974.

Rockwell, Anne. *Boats.* Dutton, 1982.

Stadler, John. *Snail Saves the Day.* Harper & Row, 1985.

Testa, Fulvio. *If You Take a Paintbrush.* Dial, 1982.

Level 12

Barton, Byron. *Buzz Buzz Buzz.* Macmillan, 1973.

Bonsall, Crosby. *The Day I Had to Play with My Sister.* Harper & Row, 1972.

Burningham, John. *The Baby.* Crowell, 1975.

Burningham, John. *The Cupboard.* Crowell, 1975.

Burningham, John. *The Dog.* Crowell, 1975.

Burningham, John. *Friend.* Crowell, 1975.

Burningham, John. *The Snow.* Crowell, 1974.

Crews, Donald. *Ten Black Dots.* Greenwillow, 1986.

Ginsburg, Mirra. *Three Kittens.* Illustrated by Giulio Maestro. Crown, 1973.

Hutchins, Pat. *Titch.* Macmillan, 1971.

Keller, Holly. *Ten Sleepy Sheep.* Greenwillow, 1983.

Kline, Suzy. *Shhhh!* Illustrated by Dora Leder. Whitman, 1984.

Krauss, Ruth. *The Carrot Seed.* Illustrated by Crockett Johnson. Harper & Row, 1945.

Long, Earlene. *Gone Fishing.* Illustrated by Richard Brown. Houghton Mifflin, 1984.

Shulevitz, Uri. *One Monday Morning.* Scribner, 1967.

Stadler, John. *Three Cheers for Hippo.* Crowell, 1987.

Taylor, Judy. *My Dog.* Macmillan, 1987.

Van Laan, Nancy. *The Big Fat Worm.* Illustrated by Marisabina Russo. Knopf, 1987.

Watson, Wendy. *Lollipop.* Crowell, 1976.

Wescott, Nadine Bernard. *Peanut Butter and Jelly.* Dutton, 1987.

West, Colin. *"Not Me," Said the Monkey.* Harper & Row, 1987.

LEVELS 13 TO 15

The language in books from Levels 13 to 15 becomes more descriptive through the use of less familiar and more varied vocabulary, and events are more fully elaborated in longer, more complex sentences.

Level 13

Alexander, Martha. *Blackboard Bear.* Dial, 1969.

Campbell, Rod. *Misty's Mischief.* Viking, 1985.

Goenell, Heidi. *If I Were a Penguin.* Little, Brown, 1989.

Jonas, Ann. *Two Bear Cubs.* Greenwillow, 1982.

Jonas, Ann. *When You Were a Baby.* Greenwillow, 1982.

Kovalski, Maryann. *The Wheels on the Bus.* Little, Brown, 1987.

Rockwell, Anne. *The Awful Mess.* Four Winds, 1973.

Rockwell, Anne, and Harlow Rockwell. *The Tool Box.* Macmillan, 1971.

Stinson, Kathy. *Red Is Best.* Illustrated by Robin Baird Lewis. Annick Press (Toronto). 1982.

Tolstoy, Alexei. *The Great Big Enormous Turnip.* Watts, 1968.

Level 14

Barton, Byron. *Building a House.* Greenwillow. 1981.

Brown, Margaret Wise. *Goodnight Moon.* Harper & Row, 1947.

Butler, Dorothy. *My Brown Bear Barney.* Illustrated by Elizabeth Fuller. Greenwillow, 1989.

Carle, Eric. *The Very Busy Spider.* Philomel, 1984.

Hutchins, Pat. *You'll Soon Grow into Them, Titch.* Greenwillow, 1983.

Kalan, Robert. *Jump, Frog, Jump!* Illustrated by Byron Barton. Greenwillow, 1981.

Kraus, Robert. *Come Out and Play, Little Mouse.* Illustrated by José Aruego and Ariane Dewey. Greenwillow, 1987.

Kraus, Robert. *Where Are You Going, Little Mouse?* Illustrated by José Areugo and Ariane Dewcy. Greenwillow, 1986.

Robart, Rose. *The Cake That Mack Ate.* Illustrated by Maryann Kovalski. Little, Brown, 1986.

Spier, Peter. *Bored—Nothing to Do!* Doubleday, 1978.

Taylor, Judy. *My Cat.* Macmillan, 1987.

Level 15

Ehlert, Lois. *Planting a Rainbow.* Harcourt Brace Jovanovich, 1988.

Fox, Mem. *Hattie and the Fox.* Illustrated by Patricia Mullins. Bradbury, 1987.

Guilfoile, Elizabeth. *Nobody Listens to Andrew.* Illustrated by Mary Stevens. Modern Curriculum Press, 1957.

Hayes, Sarah, and Helen Craig. *This Is the Bear.* Harper & Row, 1986.

Kline, Suzy. *Don't Touch!* Illustrated by Dora Leder. Whitman, 1985.

McPhail, David. *Fix It.* Dutton, 1984.

Nodset, Joan. *Who Took the Farmer's Hat?* Illustrated by Fritz Siebel. Harper & Row, 1963.

Rosen, Michael. *We're Going on a Bear Hunt.* Illustrated by Helen Oxenbury. Macmillan, 1989.

Setrfozo, Mary. *Who Wants One?* Illustrated by Keiko Narahashi. Macmillan, 1989.

Seuss, Dr. *Green Eggs and Ham.* Random House, 1960.

Seuss, Dr. *Hop on Pop.* Random House, 1963.

Wood, Audrey. *The Napping House.* Illustrated by Don Wood. Harcourt Brace Jovanovich, 1984.

LEVELS 16 TO 20

Many books in Levels 16 to 20 feature a sequence of episodes that extend over several pages or are organized into paragraphs. The language is literary in style, and illustrations enhance the story but seldom provide clues to specific words in the text. Although themes may be closely related to personal experiences, the characters are fictional personalities, and episodes develop around fanciful, imaginative events. Falling into this range of levels are many poetry collections, picture-book versions of familiar folktales such as "The Three Little Pigs," and publishers' special series designed for young readers such as And I Can Read Book (Harper & Row) or Ready-to-Read (Macmillan).

Level 16

Alexander, Martha. *We're in Big Trouble, Blackboard Bear.* Dial, 1980.

Barton, Byron. *Hester.* Greenwillow, 1975.

Bennett, Jill. *Teeny Tiny.* Illustrated by Tomie de Paola. Putnam, 1986.

Bonsall, Crosby. *And I Mean It, Stanley.* Harper & Row, 1974.

Charlip, Remy. *Fortunately.* Macmillan, 1964.

Hutchins, Pat. *Goodnight Owl.* Viking Penguin, 1973.

Hutchins, Pat. *Happy Birthday Sam.* Viking Penguin, 1978.

Jonas, Ann. *The Quilt.* Greenwillow, 1984.

Kent, Jack. *The Fat Cat.* Scholastic, 1971.

Kraus, Robert. *Leo the Late Bloomer.* Illustrated by José Aruego. Windmill, 1971.

Kuskin, Karla. *Just Like Everyone Else.* Harper & Row, 1959.

McLeod, Emilie. *The Bear's Bicycle.* Illustrated by David McPhail. Little, Brown, 1975.

Mayer, Mercer. *There's a Nightmare in My Closet.* Dial, 1968.

Minarik, Else Holmelund. *A Kiss for Little Bear.* Illustrated by Maurice Sendak. Harper & Row, 1968.

Ormerod, Jan. *The Story of Chicken Licken.* Lothrop, Lee & Shepard, 1985.

Rice, Eve. *Benny Bakes a Cake.* Greenwillow, 1981.

Riddell, Chris. *Ben and the Bear.* Harper & Row, 1986.

Seuiling, Barbara. *The Teeny Tiny Woman.* Viking, 1976.

Testa, Fulvio. *If You Take a Pencil.* Dial, 1982.

Level 17

Adoff, Arnold. *Greens.* Illustrated by Betsy Lewin. Lothrop, Lee & Shepard, 1988. (Poems)

Bridwell, Norman. *Clifford the Big Red Dog.* Scholastic, 1985.

Clifton, Lucille. *Some of the Days of Everett Anderson.* Illustrated by Evaline Ness. Holt, 1970. (Poems)

Flack, Marjorie. *Ask Mr. Bear.* Macmillan, 1932, 1960.

Galdone, Paul. *Henny Penny.* Clarion, 1968.

Galdone, Paul. *The Little Red Hen.* Clarion, 1973.

Galdone, Paul. *The Three Bears.* Clarion, 1972.

Hurd, Edith Thacher. *Johnny Lion's Book.* Illustrated by Clement Hurd. Harper & Row, 1965.

Hutchins, Pat. *The Doorbell Rang.* Greenwillow, 1986.

Isadora, Rachel. *Max.* Macmillan, 1976.

Johnson, Crockett. *Harold and the Purple Crayon.* Harper & Row, 1955.

Lobel, Arnold. *Mouse Soup.* Harper & Row, 1972.

Mayer, Mercer. *There's an Alligator under My Bed.* Dial, 1987.

Mayer, Mercer. *There's Something in My Attic.* Dial, 1988.

Nicoll, Helen. *Meg and Mog.* Illustrated by Jan Pienkowski. Viking Penguin, 1976. (There are several books about Meg and Mog.)

Peppe, Rodney. *The House That Jack Built.* Delacorte, 1970.

Roy, Ron. *Three Ducks Went Walking.* Illustrated by Paul Galdone. Scholastic, 1979.

Shulevitz, Uri. *Rain Rain Rivers.* Farrar, Straus & Giroux, 1969.

Udry, Janice May. *Let's Be Enemies.* Illustrated by Maurice Sendak. Harper & Row, 1970.

Vipont, Elfrida. *The Elephant and the Bad Baby.* Illustrated by Raymond Briggs. Coward, 1969.

Level 18

Asch, Frank. *The Last Puppy.* Prentice-Hall, 1980.

Carle, Eric. *The Very Hungry Caterpillar.* Philomel, 1970.

Cummings, Pat. *Jimmy Lee Did It.* Lothrop, 1985.

Dabcovich, Lydia. *Mrs. Huggins and Her Hen Hannah.* Dutton, 1985.

DePaola, Tomie. *Charlie Needs a Cloak.* Prentice-Hall, 1973.

Emberley, Barbara. *Drummer Hoff.* Illustrated by Ed Emberley. Prentice-Hall, 1967.

Jonas, Ann. *The Trek.* Greenwillow, 1985.

Joyce, William. *George Shrinks.* Harper & Row, 1985.

Keats, Ezra Jack. *The Snowy Day.* Viking, 1962.

Knight, Joan. *Tickle-Toe Rhymes.* Illustrated by John Wallner. Orchard Books/Watts, 1989.

Krasilovsky, Phyllis. *The Man Who Didn't Do His Dishes.* Illustrated by Barbara Cooney. Doubleday, 1950.

Lionni, Leo. *Little Blue and Little Yellow.* Astor Honor, 1959.

Marshall, Edward. *Three by the Sea.* Illustrated by James Marshall, Dial, 1981.

Martin, Bill, and John Archambault. *Chicka Chicka Boom Boom.* Illustrated by Lois Ehlert. Simon & Schuster, 1989.

Sendak, Maurice. *Where the Wild Things Are.* Harper & Row, 1963.

Seuss, Dr. *The Cat in the Hat.* Random House, 1967.

Shulevitz, Uri. *Dawn.* Farrar, Straus & Giroux, 1974.

Level 19

Brown, Ruth. *The Big Sneeze.* Lothrop, Lee & Shepard, 1985.

Browne, Anthony. *Bear Goes to Town.* Doubleday, 1989.

Burningham, John. *Mr Gumpy's Motorcar.* Crowell, 1976.

Burningham, John. *Mr Gumpy's Outing.* Holt, Rinehart & Winston, 1970.

Carle, Eric. *The Grouchy Ladybug.* Crowell, 1977.

Galdone, Paul. *The Gingerbread Boy.* Clarion, 1975.

Hennessy, B. G. *Jake Baked the Cake.* Illustrated by Mary Morgan. Viking, 1990.

Hutchins, Pat. *The Surprise Party.* Macmillan, 1969.

Lobel, Arnold. *Frog and Toad Are Friends.* Harper & Row, 1970.

Lobel, Arnold. *Frog and Toad Together.* Harper & Row, 1971.

McGovern, Ann. *Stone Soup.* Illustrated by Nola Langer. Scholastic, 1968.

Murphy, Jill. *What Next Baby Bear?* Dial, 1984.

Oppenheim, Joanne. *You Can't Catch Me.* Illustrated by Andrew Shachat. Houghton Mifflin, 1986.

Rice, Eve. *Sam Who Never Forgets.* Greenwillow, 1977.

Rylant, Cynthia. *Henry and Mudge and the Forever Sea.* Illustrated by Sucie Stevenson. Bradbury Press, 1989. (There are seven other books about Henry and Mudge.)

Stevens, Janet. *The Three Billy Goats Gruff.* Harcourt Brace Jovanovich, 1987.

Level 20

Allen, Pam. *Who Sank the Boat?* Coward-McCann, 1982.

Bang, Molly Garrett. *Wiley and the Hairy Man.* Macmillan, 1976.

Bennett, Jill, collector. *Noisy Poems.* Illustrated by Nick Sharratt. Oxford, 1987.

Carle, Eric. *Eric Carle's ANIMALS ANIMALS.* Philomel, 1989. (Poems)

Cauley, Lorinida Bryan. *The Story of the Three Little Pigs.* Putnam, 1980.

Crowe, Robert L. *Tyler Toad and Thunder.* Illustrated by Kay Chorao. Dutton, 1980.

DePaola, Tomie. *The Art Lesson.* Putnam, 1989.

DePaola, Tomie. *Tomie dePaola's Mother Goose.* Putnam, 1985.

Fisher, Aileen. *The House of a Mouse.* Illustrated by Joan Sandin. Harper & Row, 1988. (Poems)

Fisher, Aileen. *When It Comes to Bugs.* Illustrated by Chris & Bruce Degen. Harper & Row, 1986. (Poems)

Galdone, Paul. *The Magic Porridge Pot.* Clarion, 1976.

Heine, Helme. *The Most Wonderful Egg in the World.* Atheneum, 1983.

Hoberman, Mary Ann. *A House Is a House for Me.* Viking, 1978.

Hoberman, Mary Ann. *Yellow Butter Purple Jelly Red Jam Black Bread.* Illustrated by Chaya Burstein. Viking, 1981. (Poems)

Hogrogian, Nonny. *One Fine Day.* Macmillan, 1971.

Hopkins, Lee Bennett, selector. *Surprises.* Illustrated by Megan Lloyd. Harper & Row, 1984. (Poems)

Hutchins, Pat. *The Very Worst Monster*. Greenwillow, 1985.

Hutchins, Pat. *Where's the Baby?* Greenwillow, 1988.

Hutchins, Pat. *The Wind Blew*. Viking, 1974.

Jonas, Ann. *Round Trip*. Greenwillow, 1983.

Kasza, Keiko. *The Wolf's Chicken Stew*. Putnam, 1987.

Kennedy, X. J. *Ghastilies, Goops & Pincushions*. Illustrated by Ron Barrett. McElderry/Macmillan, 1989. (Poems)

Kuskin, Karla. *Dogs and Dragons, Trees and Dreams*. Harper & Row, 1980. (Poems)

Livingston, Myra Cohn. *A Song I Sang to You*. Illustrated by Margot Tomes. Harcourt Brace Jovanovich, 1984. (Poems)

Merriam, Eve. *Blackberry Ink*. Illustrated by Hans Wilhelm. Morrow, 1985. (Poems)

Merriam, Eve. *A Poem for a Pickle—Funnybone Verses*. Illustrated by Sheila Hamanaka. Morrow, 1989.

Orbach, Ruth. *Apple Pigs*. Philomel, 1981.

Preston, Edna Mitchell. *Squawk to the Moon, Little Goose*. Illustrated by Barbara Cooney. Viking, 1974.

Reinl, Edda. *The Three Little Pigs*. Picture Book Studio, 1983.

Rice, Eve. *Peter's Pockets*. Illustrated by Nancy Winslow Parker. Greenwillow, 1989.

Rylant, Cynthia. *When I Was Young in the Mountains*. Illustrated by Diane Goode. Dutton, 1982.

Sendak, Maurice. *Chicken Soup with Rice*. Harper & Row, 1962. (Poems)

Slobodkina, Esphyr. *Caps for Sale*. Harper & Row, 1940, 1968.

Stevenson, James. *"Could Be Worse!"* Greenwillow, 1977.

Tresselt, Alvin. *The Mitten*. Illustrated by Yaroslava. Lothrop, Lee & Shepard, 1964.

Zemach, Margot. *The Little Red Hen*. Farrar, Straus & Giroux, 1987.

Zolotow, Charlotte. *I Know a Lady*. Illustrated by James Stevenson. Greenwillow, 1984.

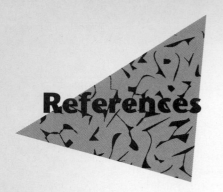

References

Adams, M. J. (1990). *Beginning to read: Thinking and learning about print.* Cambridge, MA: MIT Press.

Allen, V. G. (1991). Teaching bilingual and ESL children. In J. Flood, J. M. Jensen, D. Lapp, & J. Squire (Eds.), *Handbook of research on teaching the language arts* (pp. 356–364). New York: Macmillan.

Allington, R. (1983a). Fluency: The neglected reading goal. *The Reading Teacher, 36,* 556–561.

Allington, R. (1983b). The reading instruction provided readers of differing reading ability. *Elementary School Journal, 83,* 548–559.

Alvermann, D. E., Smith, L. C., & Readence, J. E. (1985). Prior knowledge activation and the comprehension of compatible and incompatible text. *Reading Research Quarterly, 20,* 420–436.

Anders, P. L., Bos, C., & Filip, D. (1984). The effect of semantic features analysis on the reading comprehension of learning-disabled students. In J. A. Niles & L. A. Harris (Eds.), *Changing perspectives on research in reading/language processing and instruction.* Rochester, NY: National Reading Conference.

Anderson, L. M., Evertson, C. M., & Brophy, J. E. (1979). An experimental study of effective teaching in first-grade reading groups. *Elementary School Journal, 79,* 193–223.

Anderson, R. C. (1984). Role of the reader's schema in comprehension, learning, and memory. In R. C. Anderson, J. Osborn, & R. J. Tierney (Eds.), *Learning to read in American schools* (pp. 243–258). Hillsdale, NJ: Lawrence Erlbaum.

Anderson, R. C., & Davison, A. (1989). Conceptual and empirical bases of readability formulas. In G. Green & A. Davison (Eds.), *Linguistic complexity and text comprehension* (pp. 23–53). Hillsdale, NJ: Lawrence Erlbaum.

Anderson, R. C., & Freebody, P. (1981). Vocabulary knowledge. In J. T. Guthrie (Ed.), *Comprehension and teaching: Research reviews* (pp. 77–117). Newark, DE: International Reading Association.

Anderson, R. C., Hiebert, E. H., Scott, J. A., & Wilkinson, I. A. (1985). *Becoming a nation of readers.* Washington DC: National Institute of Education.

Aoki, E. (1992). Turning the page: Asian Pacific American children's literature. In V. J. Harris (Ed.), *Teaching multicultural literature in grades K–8.* (pp. 109–136). Norwood, MA: Christopher Gordon.

Applebee, A., Langer, J. N., & Mullis, A. (1988). *Report of the national assessment of educational progress.* Washington, DC: U.S. Department of Education.

Ashton-Warner, S. (1963). *Teacher.* New York: Simon & Schuster.

Atwell, N. (1987). *In the middle: Writing, reading, and learning with adolescents.* Portsmouth, NH: Heinemann.

Ball, E. W., & Blachman, B. A. (1991). Does phoneme segmentation training in kindergarten make a difference in early word recognition and developmental spelling? *Reading Research Quarterly, 26,* 49–66.

Banks, J. A. (1989). Integrating the curriculum with ethnic content: Approaches and guidelines. In J. A. Banks & C. A. McGee Banks (Eds.), *Multicultural education: Issues and perspectives* (pp. 189–207). Boston: Allyn & Bacon.

Barr, R. (1989). Social organization of reading instruction. In C. Emilhovich (Ed.), *Locating learning across the curriculum: Ethnographic perspectives on classroom research* (pp. 57–86). Norwood, NJ: Ablex, 1989.

Barr, R. (1992). Teachers, materials and group composition in literacy instruction. In M. J. Dreher & W. H. Slater, *Elementary school literacy: Critical issues* (pp. 27–50). Norwood, MA: Christopher Gordon.

Barr, R. (1995). What research says about grouping in the past and present and what it suggests about the future. In M. C. Radencich & L. J. McKay (Eds.), *Flexible grouping for literacy in the elementary grades* (pp. 1–24). Boston: Allyn & Bacon.

Barr, R., Blachowicz, C. L. Z., & Sadow, M. W. (1995). *Reading diagnosis for teachers. An instructional approach* (3rd ed.). White Plains, NY: Longman.

Barr, R., & Dreeben, R. (1983). *How schools work.* Chicago: University of Chicago Press.

Barr, R., & Dreeben, R. (1991). Grouping students for reading instruction. In R. Barr, M. Kamil, P. Mosenthal, & P. D. Pearson (Eds.), *Handbook of reading research* (Vol. 2, pp. 885–910). White Plains, NY: Longman.

Barr, R., & Sadow, M. (1989). Influence of basal programs on fourth grade reading instruction. *Reading Research Quarterly, 21,* 44–71.

Bartlett, J. E. (1984). *Top-level structure as an organizational strategy for recall of classroom text.* Unpublished doctoral dissertation, Arizona State University, Tempe.

Bartoli, J., & Botel, M. (1989). Reading/learning disability: An ecological systems view. *Reading Instruction Journal, 32*(3), 13–19.

Bauman, J. F., Jones, L. A., & Seifert-Kessell, N. (1993). Using think alouds to enhance children's comprehension monitoring abilities. *The Reading Teacher, 47,* 184–93.

Beck, I. L., & McKeown, M. G. (1983). Learning words well: A program to enhance vocabulary and comprehension. *The Reading Teacher, 36,* 622–625.

Beck, I. L., McKeown, M. G., McCaslin, E. S., & Burkes, A. M. (1979). *Instructional dimensions that may affect reading comprehension: Examples from two commercial reading programs* (LRDC Publication 1979/20). Pittsburgh: University of Pittsburgh, Learning Research and Development Center.

Beck, I. L., Perfetti, C. A., & McKeown, M. G. (1982). Effects of long-term vocabulary instruction on lexical access and reading comprehension. *Journal of Educational Psychology, 74,* 506–521.

Bieger, E. F. (1995–1996). Promoting multicultural education through a literature-based approach. *The Reading Teacher, 49,* 308–311.

Bishop, R. S. (1992). Multicultural literature for children: Making informed choices. In V. J. Harris (Ed.), *Teaching multicultural literature in grades K–8* (pp. 37–54). Norwood, MA: Christopher-Gordon.

Bissex, G. L. (1980). *Gnys at wrk: A child learns to write and read.* Cambridge: Harvard University Press.

Blachowicz, C. L. Z. (1985). Vocabulary development and reading: From research to instruction. *The Reading Teacher, 38,* 876–881.

Blachowicz, C. L. Z. (1986). Making connections: Alternatives to the vocabulary notebook. *Journal of Reading, 29,* 643–649.

Blachowicz, C., & Fisher, P. (1996). *Teaching vocabulary in all classrooms.* Englewood Cliffs, NJ: Prentice-Hall.

Blachowicz, C. L. Z., & Johnson, B. E. (1994). Semantic mapping. In A. Purves (Ed.), *Encyclopedia of English studies language arts.* New York: Scholastic.

Block, C. C. (1993). Strategy instruction in a literature-based reading program. *Elementary School Journal, 94,* 139–152.

Bloom, B. (1956). *Taxonomy of educational objectives, Handbook I: Cognitive domain.* New York: David McKay.

Blos, J. W. (1993). Perspective on historical fiction. In M. O. Tunnell & R. Ammon (Eds.), *The story of ourselves: Teaching history through children's literature* (pp. 11–17). Portsmouth, NH: Heinemann.

Bos, C., & Anders, P. L. (1990). The effects of interactive vocabulary instruction on the vocabulary learning and reading comprehension of junior-high learning disabled students. *Learning Disability Quarterly, 13,* 31–42.

Bos, C., & Vaughn, S. (1994). *Strategies for teaching children with learning and behavioral disabilities.* Needham Heights, MA: Allyn & Bacon.

Bowman, B. T. (1989). Educating language-minority children: Challenges and opportunities. *Phi Delta Kappan, 71,* 118–120.

Braddock, R., Lloyd-Jones, R., & Schoer, L. (1963). *Research in written composition.* Urbana, IL: National Council of Teachers of English.

Bradley, L., & Bryant, P. E. (1983). Categorizing sounds and learning to read: A causal connection. *Nature, 301,* 419–421.

Branscombe, A., Goswami, D., & Schwartz, J. (Eds.). (1992). *Students teaching, teachers learning.* Portsmouth, NH: Boynton/Cook, Heinemann.

Brown, R. (1973). *A first language.* Cambridge: Harvard University Press.

Bruner, J. (1983). *Child's talk: Learning to use language.* New York: W. W. Norton.

Burke, P. J., Christensen, J. C., & Fessler, R. (1984). *Teacher career stages: Implications for staff development* (Fastback 214). Bloomington, IN: Phi Delta Kappa Educational Foundation.

Bussis, A. M., Chittenden, E. A., Amarel, M., & Klausner, E. (1985). *Inquiry into meaning: An investigation of learning to read.* Hillsdale, NJ: Lawrence Erlbaum.

Calfee, R., & Hiebert, E. (1991). Classroom assessment of reading. In R. Barr, M. Kamil, P. Mosenthal, & P. D. Pearson (Eds.), *Handbook of reading research* (Vol. 2, pp. 281–309). White Plains, NY: Longman.

Calkins, L. M. (1980). When children want to punctuate: Basic skills belong in context. *Language Arts, 57,* 567–573.

Calkins, L. M. (1983). *Lessons from a child.* Portsmouth, NH: Heinemann.

Calkins, L. M. (1986). *The art of teaching writing.* Portsmouth, NH: Heinemann.

Calkins, L. M. (1991). *Living between the lines.* Portsmouth, NH: Heinemann.

Calkins, L. M. (1994). *The art of teaching writing.* Portsmouth, NH: Heinemann.

Carr, E., & Ogle, D. M. (1987). A strategy for comprehension and summarization. *Journal of Reading, 30,* 626–631.

Carson, J. E. (1990). Reading-writing connections: Toward a description for second language learners. In B. Kroll (Ed.), *Second language writing: Research insights for the classroom* (pp. 88–101). New York: Cambridge University Press.

Carver, R. P., & Leibert, R. E. (1995). The effect of reading library books at different levels of difficulty upon gain in reading ability. *Reading Research Quarterly, 30,* 26–48.

Chall, J. S. (1967/1983a). *Learning to read: The great debate.* New York: McGraw-Hill.

Chall, J. S. (1983b). *Stages of reading development.* New York: McGraw-Hill.

Chall, J. S., & Stahl, S. A. (1985). Reading comprehension research in the past decade: Implications for educational publishing. *Book Research Quarterly, 1,* 95–102.

Chamot, A. U., & O'Malley, J. M. (1994). Instructional approaches and teaching procedures. In K. Spangenberg-Urbschat & R. Pritchard (Eds.), *Kids come in all languages: Reading instruction for ESL students* (pp. 82–107). Newark, DE: International Reading Association.

Chaney, J. H. (1993). Alphabet books: Resources for learning. *The Reading Teacher, 47,* 90–104.

Chiesi, H. L., Spilich, G. J., & Voss, J. F. (1979). Acquisition of domain-related information in relation to high and low domain knowledge. *Journal of Verbal Learning and Verbal Behavior, 18,* 257–273.

Chomsky, C. (1976). When you still can't read in third grade: After decoding, what? In S. J. Samuels (Ed.), *What research has to say about reading instruction* (pp. 13–30). Newark, DE: International Reading Association.

Christie, J. F. (1980). Syntax: A key to reading comprehension. *Reading Improvement, 17,* 311–317.

Church, S. M. (1994). Is whole language really warm and fuzzy? *The Reading Teacher, 47,* 362–371.

Clarke, L. K. (1989). Encouraging invented spelling in first graders' writing: Effects on learning to spell and read. *Research in the Teaching of English, 22,* 281–309.

Clay, M. M. (1967). The reading behaviour of five year old children: A research report. *New Zealand Journal of Educational Studies, 2,* 11–31.

Clay, M. M. (1975). *What did I write? Beginning writing behaviour.* Portsmouth, NH: Heinemann.

Clay, M. M. (1979). *Reading: The patterning of complex behavior.* Auckland, New Zealand: Heinemann.

Clay, M. M. (1993a). *An observation survey of early literacy achievement.* Portsmouth, NH: Heinemann.

Clay, M. M. (1993b). *Reading recovery: A guidebook for teachers in training.* Portsmouth, NH: Heinemann.

Cochran-Smith, M. (1984). *The making of a reader.* Norwood, NJ: Ablex.

Cochran-Smith, M., & Lytle, S. L. (1993). *Inside/outside: Teacher research and knowledge.* New York: Teachers College Press.

Connelly, F. M., & Clandinin, D. J. (1988). *Teachers as curriculum planners.* New York: Teachers College Press.

Crafton, L. M. (1991). *Whole language: Getting started . . . . moving forward.* Katonah, NY: Richard C. Owen Publishing, Inc.

Craik, F., & Lockhart, R. (1972). Levels of processing: A framework for memory research. *Journal of Verbal Learning and Verbal Behavior, 11,* 671–684.

Cunningham, P. M. (1979). A compare/contrast theory of mediated word identification. *Reading Teacher, 32,* 774–778.

Cunningham, P. M., & Allington, R. L. (1994). *Classrooms that work. They can all read and write.* New York: HarperCollins.

Cunningham, P. M., & Cunningham, J. W. (1992). Making words: Enhancing the invented spelling-decoding connection. *The Reading Teacher, 46,* 106–115.

Dahl, K. L., & Freppon, P. A. (1995). A comparison of inner-city children's interpretations of reading and writing instruction in the early grades in skills-based and whole language classrooms. *Reading Research Quarterly, 30,* 50–74.

Daniels, H., & Zemelman, S. (1985). *A writing project.* Portsmouth, NH: Heinemann.

Davis, F. B. (1968). Research in comprehension in reading. *Reading Research Quarterly, 3,* 499–545.

Davis, S. J. (1994). Teaching practices that encourage or eliminate student plagiarism. *Middle School Journal, 1,* 55–58.

Dinan, L. L. (1977). By the time I'm ten, I'll probably be famous! *Language Arts, 54,* 742–749.

Doctorow, M., Wittrock, M. C., & Marks, C. (1978). Generative processes in reading comprehension. *Journal of Educational Psychology, 70,* 109–118.

Dole, J. A., & Osborn, J. (1989). Evaluation, selection, and use of reading materials. In S. B. Wepner, J. T. Feeley, & D. Strickland (Eds.), *Administration and supervision of reading programs* (pp. 109–130). New York: Teachers College Press.

Dowst, K. (1983). Cognition and composition. *Freshman English News, 11,* 1–14.

Duffy, G. G. (1993). Rethinking strategy instruction: Four teachers' development and their low achievers' understandings. *Elementary School Journal, 93,* 231–248.

Duffy, G. G., & Roehler, L. R. (1987). Teaching reading skills as strategies. *The Reading Teacher, 40,* 414–418.

Duffy, G. G., Roehler, L., & Herrmann, B. A. (1988). Modelling mental processes helps poor readers become strategic readers. *The Reading Teacher, 41,* 762–767.

Dulay, H., & Burt, M. (1974). New perspective on the creative construction process in child second language acquisition. *Language Learning, 24,* 253–278.

Duncan, L. W., & Fitzgerald, P. W. (1969). Increasing the parent child communication through counselor-parent conferences. *Personnel and Guidance Journal, 47,* 514–517.

Durkin, D. (1978–1979). What classroom observations reveal about reading comprehension instruction. *Reading Research Quarterly, 14,* 481–533.

Durkin, D. (1981). Reading comprehension in five basal reader series. *Reading Research Quarterly, 16,* 515–543.

Dyson, A. H. (1989). *Multiple worlds of child writers: Friends learning to write.* New York: Teachers College Press.

Dyson, A. H., & Freedman, S. W. (1991). Writing. In J. Flood, J. M. Jensen, D. Lapp, & J. Squire (Eds.), *Handbook of research on teaching the language arts* (pp. 754–774). New York: Macmillan.

Edelsky, C. (1982). Writing in a bilingual program: The relation of L1 and L2 tests. *TESOL Quarterly, 16,* 211–228.

Edelsky, C. (1986). Writing in a bilingual program. *Habia una vez.* Norwood, NJ: Ablex.

Edelsky, C., Altwerger, B., & Flores, B. (1991). *Whole language: What's the difference?* Portsmouth, NH: Heinemann.

Ehri, L. C. (1980). The development of orthographic images. In U. Frith (Ed.), *Cognitive processes in spelling* (pp. 312–338). London: Academic Press.

Ehri, L. C. (1984). How orthography alters spoken language competencies in children learning to read and spell. In J. Downing & R. Valtin (Eds.), *Language awareness and learning to read* (pp. 119–147). New York: Springer-Verlag.

Ehri, L. C. (1991). Development of the ability to read words. In R. Barr, M. Kamil, P. Mosenthal, & P. D. Pearson (Eds.), *Handbook of reading research* (Vol. 2, pp. 383–417). White Plains, NY: Longman.

Ehri, L., & Robbins, C. (1992). Beginning readers need some decoding skill to read words by analogy. *Reading Research Quarterly, 27,* 12–27.

Elbaz, F. (1991). Research on teacher's knowledge: The evolution of a discourse. *Journal of Curriculum Studies, 23,* 1–19.

Elbow, P. (1981). *Writing with power.* New York: Oxford University Press.

Elkonin, D. B. (1963). The psychology of mastering elements of reading. In B. Simon (Ed.), *Educational psychology in the U.S.S.R.* (pp. 165–179). London: Routledge & Kegan Paul.

Emig, J. (1971). *The composing processes of twelfth graders* (Research Report No. 13). Urbana, IL: National Council of Teachers of English.

Emig, J. (1983). *The web of meaning.* Upper Montclair, NJ: Boynton/Cook.

Emmer, E. T., Evertson, C. M., & Anderson, L. M. (1980). Effective management at the beginning of the school year. *Elementary School Journal, 80,* 219–231.

Englert, C. S., & Hiebert, E. H. (1984). Children's developing awareness of text structures in expository materials. *Journal of Educational Psychology, 76,* 65–74.

Englert, (1992). Writing instruction from a sociocultural perspective: The holistic, dialogic, and social enterprises of writing. *Journal of Learning Disabilities, 25,* 153–172.

Erikson, E. H. (1983). *Identity, youth, and crisis.* New York: W. W. Norton.

Farr, R., & Tone, B. (1994). *Portfolio and performance assessment.* Orlando, FL: Harcourt Brace.

Ferreiro, E. (1984). The underlying logic of literacy development. In H. Goelman, A. Oberg, & F. Smith (Eds.), *Awakening to literacy* (pp. 154–173). Portsmouth, NH: Heinemann.

Ferreiro, E., & Teberosky, A. (1982). *Literacy before schooling* (K. Goodman Castro, Trans.). Exeter, NH: Heinemann. (Original work published 1979)

Ferroli, L., & Shanahan, T. (1987). Kindergarten spelling: Explaining its relation to first-grade reading. In J. E. Readence & R. S. Baldwin (Eds.), *Research in literacy: Merging perspectives* (pp. 93–99). Thirty-sixth Yearbook of the National Reading Conference. Rochester, NY: National Reading Conference.

Fisher, C. W., & Hiebert, E. H. (1990). Characteristics of tasks in two approaches to literacy instruction. *Elementary School Journal, 91,* 3–18.

Flexner, S. B. (Ed.). (1993). *Random house unabridged dictionary.* New York: Random House.

Foorman, B. R. (1991). How letter-sound instruction mediates progress in first-grade reading and spelling. *Journal of Educational Psychology, 83,* 456–469.

Forrest, D. L., & Waller, T. G. (1980). *What do children know about their reading and study skills?* Paper presented at the annual meeting of the American Educational Research Association, Boston, MA.

Frost, R. (1949). *The poetry of Robert Frost.* (C. E. Lathem, Ed.) New York: Henry Holt.

Gallas, K. (1994). *The languages of learning: How children talk, write, dance, draw, and sing their understanding of the world.* New York: Teachers College Press.

Gambrell, L. B., & Bales, R. J. (1986). Mental imagery and the comprehension-monitoring performance of fourth- and fifth-grade poor readers. *Reading Research Quarterly, 21,* 454–464.

Garner, R., Hare, V. C., Alexander, P., Haynes, J., & Winograd, P. N. (1984). Inducing use of a text lookback strategy among unsuccessful readers. *American Educational Research Journal, 21,* 789–798.

Garner, R., & Kraus, C. (1982). Monitoring of understanding among seventh graders: An investigation of good comprehender differences in knowing and regulating reading behaviors. *Educational Research Quarterly, 6,* 5–12.

Garner, R., & Taylor, N. (1982). Monitoring of understanding: An investigation of attentional assistance needs at different grade and reading proficiency levels. *Reading Psychology, 3,* 1–6.

Gaskins, I. W., Anderson, R. C., Pressley, M., Cunicelli, E. A., & Satlow, E. (1993). Six teachers' dialogue during cognitive process instruction. *Elementary School Journal, 93,* 277–304.

Gaskins, R. W., Gaskins, J. C., & Gaskins, I. W. (1991). A decoding program for poor readers—and the rest of the class, too! *Language Arts, 68,* 213–225.

Gentry, J. R. (1981). Learning to spell developmentally. *The Reading Teacher, 34,* 378–381.

Gentry, J. R., & Gillet, J. W. (1993). *Teaching kids to spell.* Portsmouth, NH: Heinemann.

Gersten, R., & Carnine, D. (1986). Direct instruction in reading comprehension. *Educational Leadership, 43,* 70–78.

Gersten, R., & Jimenez, R. T. (1994). A delicate balance: Enhancing literature instruction for students of English as a second language. *The Reading Teacher, 47,* 438–449.

Gersten, R., & Woodward, J. (1992). The quest to translate research into classroom practice: Strategies for assisting classroom teachers' work with "at risk" students and students with disabilities. In D. Carnine & E. Kammeenui (Eds.), *Higher cognitive functioning for all students* (pp. 201–218). Austin, TX: Pro-Ed.

Gillet, J. W., & Kita, M. J. (1979). Words, kids and categories. *The Reading Teacher, 32,* 538–542.

Gilligan, C. (1982). *In a different voice.* Cambridge: Harvard University Press.

Gipe, J. P. (1980). Use of relevant context helps kids learn new word meanings. *The Reading Teacher, 33,* 398–402.

Gipe, J. P. (1981). *Investigation of techniques for teaching new words.* Paper presented at the meeting of the American Educational Research Association, Los Angeles, CA.

Golinkoff, R. A. (1976). A comparison of reading comprehension processes in good and poor comprehenders. *Reading Research Quarterly, 11,* 623–659.

Goodlad, J. I. (1984). *A place called school: Prospects for the future.* New York: McGraw-Hill.

Goodman, K. S. (1976). Reading: A psycholinguistic guessing game. In H. Singer & R. Ruddell (Eds.), *Theoretical models and processes of reading* (pp. 497–508). Newark, DE: International Reading Association.

Goodman, Y. M. (1978). Kid watching: An alternative to testing. *National Elementary School Principal, 57,* 41–45.

Goodman, Y. M. (1986). Children coming to know literacy. In W. H. Teale & E. Sulzby (Eds.), *Emergent literacy: Writing and reading* (pp. 1–14). Norwood, NJ: Ablex.

Goswami, U., & Bryant, P. E. (1990). *Phonological skills and learning to read.* Hillsdale, NJ: Lawrence Erlbaum.

Goswami, U., & Mead, F. (1992). Onset and rime awareness and analogies in reading. *Reading Research Quarterly, 237,* 152–162.

Gough, P. B. (1972). One second of reading. In J. F. Kavanaugh & J. G. Mattingly (Eds.), *Language by ear and by eye: The relationship between speech and reading* (pp. 331–358). Cambridge: MIT Press.

Grabe W. (1991). Current developments in second language reading. *TESOL Quarterly, 25,* 375–406.

Graves D. H. (1976). *Balance the basics: Let them write.* New York: Ford Foundation.

Graves, D. H. (1983). *Writing: Teachers and children at work.* Portsmouth, NH: Heinemann.

Graves, D. H. (1994). *A fresh look at writing.* Portsmouth, NH: Heinemann.

Gregg, N. (1983). A comparison of the written language mechanical error patterns of college learning disabled, normal and basic writers. (ERIC Document Reproduction Service No. ED 241 948)

Grossman, P. L. (1990). *The making of a teacher: Teacher knowledge and teacher education.* New York: Teachers College Press.

Haggard, M. R. (1982). The vocabulary self-selection strategy: An active approach to word learning. *Journal of Reading, 26,* 203–207.

Haggard, M. R. (1985). An interactive strategies approach to content reading. *Journal of Reading, 29,* 204–210.

Halliday, M. A. K. (1973). *Explorations in the functions of language.* London: Edward Arnold.

Halliday, M. A. K. (1975). *Learning how to mean: Explorations in the development of language.* London: Edward Arnold.

Hansen, J. (1992) Students' evaluations bring reading and writing together. *The Reading Teacher, 46,* 100–105.

Harris, T. L., & Hodges, R. E. (1981). *A dictionary of reading and related terms.* Newark, DE: International Reading Association.

Harris, V. J. (1992). *Teaching multicultural literature in grades k–8.* Norwood, MA: Christopher Gordon.

Harste, J., Short, K., & Burke, C. (1988). *Creating a classroom for authors.* Portsmouth, NH: Heinemann.

Hartman, D. K. (1992). Eight readers reading: The intertextual links of proficient readers reading multiple passages. *Reading Research Quarterly, 30,* 520–561.

Hartman, D. K., & Hartman, J. A. (1993). Reading across texts: Expanding the role of the reader. *The Reading Teacher, 47,* 202–211.

Heath, S. B. (1983). *Way with words: Language, life, and work in communities and classroom.* Norwood, NJ: Ablex.

Heimlich, J. E., & Pittelman, S. D. (1986). *Semantic mapping: Classroom applications.* Newark, DE: International Reading Association.

Heller, M. F. (1995). *Reading-writing connections: From theory to practice.* White Plains, NY: Longman.

Henderson, E. H. (1981). *Learning to read and spell.* DeKalb: Northern Illinois University Press.

Henderson, E. H. (1985/1990). *Teaching spelling.* Boston: Houghton Mifflin.

Henk, W. A., & Melnick, S. A. (1995). The Reader Self-Perception Scale (RSPS): A new tool for measuring how children feel about themselves as readers. *The Reading Teacher, 48,* 470–482.

Herber, H. L. (1970). Teaching reading in content areas. Englewood Cliffs, NJ: Prentice-Hall.

Herman, P. A., Anderson, R. C., Pearson, P. D., & Nagy, W. E. (1987). Incidental acquisition of word meaning from expositions with varied text features. *Reading Research Quarterly, 22,* 263–284.

Hiebert, E. H. (1981). Developmental patterns and interrelationships of preschool children's print awareness. *Reading Research Quarterly, 16,* 236–260.

Hiebert, E. H. (1983). An examination of ability grouping for reading instruction. *Reading Research Quarterly, 18,* 231–255.

Hiebert, E. H., & Taylor, B. M. (1994). *Getting reading right from the start: Effective early literacy interventions.* Needham Heights, MA: Allyn & Bacon.

Hillocks, G. (1984). What works in teaching composition: A meta-analysis of experimental treatment studies. *American Journal of Education, 93,* 133–170.

Holdaway, D. (1979). *The foundations of literacy.* Sydney, Australia: Aston Scholastic, Houghton Mifflin.

Hollingsworth, P. M., & Reutzel, D. R. (1988). Whole language with LD children. *Academic Therapy, 23,* 477–488.

Hornberger, N. H. (1992). Biliteracy contexts, continua, and contrasts: Policy and curriculum for Cambodian and Puerto Rican students in Philadelphia. *Education and Urban Society, 24,* 196–211.

Horowitz, R. (1985a). Text patterns: Part I. *Journal of Reading, 28,* 448–455.

Horowitz, R. (1985b). Text patterns: Part II. *Journal of Reading, 28,* 534–541.

Houghton Mifflin Reading Series. (1981). Boston: Houghton Mifflin.

Hudelson, S. (1984). Kan yu ret an rayt en Ingles: Children become literate in English as a second language. *TESOL Quarterly, 18,* 221–238.

Invernizzi, M., Abouzeid, M., & Gill, J. T. (1994). Using students' invented spelling as a guide for spelling instruction that emphasizes word study. *Elementary School Journal, 95,* 155–168.

Jenkins, J. R., Pany, D., & Schreck, J. (1978). *Vocabulary and reading comprehension: Instructional effects* (Technical Report No. 100). Urbana: University of Illinois. Center for the Study of Reading. (ERIC Document Reproduction Service No. ED 160 999)

Johnson, D. D., & Pearson, P. D. (1984). *Teaching reading vocabulary.* New York: Holt, Rinehart, & Winston.

Johnson, D. D., Toms-Bronowski, S., & Pittelman, S. D. (1982). *An investigation of the effectiveness of semantic mapping and semantic feature analysis with intermediate grade level students* (Program Report No. 83-3). Madison: Wisconsin Center for Education Research, University of Wisconsin.

Johnson, D. W., & Johnson, R. T. (1975). *The use of cooperative, competitive, and individualistic goal structures within the classroom.* Englewood Cliffs, NJ: Prentice-Hall.

Juel, C. (1991). Beginning reading. In R. Barr, M. Kamil, P. Mosenthal, & P. D. Pearson (Eds.), *Handbook of reading research* (Vol. 2, pp. 759–788). White Plains, NY: Longman.

Kameenui, E. J., Carnine, D. W., & Freschi, R. (1982). Effects of text construction and instructional procedures for teaching word meanings on comprehension and recall. *Reading Research Quarterly, 17,* 367–388.

Katz, C. A. (1995). Trekking with an accidental traveler. *Illinois Reading Council Journal, 23,* 51–58.

Kirst, M. W. (1991). Interview on assessment issues with James Popham. *Educational Researcher, 20,* 24–27.

Kohlberg, L. (1981). *Essays on moral development: The philosophy of moral development.* New York: Harper & Row.

Kuhlthau, C. C. (1984). Library research process: Case studies and interventions with high school seniors in advanced placement English classes using Kelly's theory of constructs (Doctoral dissertation, Rutgers University, 1983). *Dissertation Abstracts International, 44,* 1961.

Ladson-Billings, G. (1994). *The dream keepers: Successful teachers of African-American children.* San Francisco: Jossey-Bass.

Langer, J. A. (1986). *Children, reading, and writing: Structures and strategies.* Norwood, NJ: Ablex.

Lapp, D., Flood, J. & Farnan, N. (1993). Supporting and encouraging diversity: Literacy learning for all. In J. Tinajero & A. Ada (Eds.), *The power of two languages* (pp. 294–303). New York: Macmillan.

Lesser, M., & Blachowicz, C. L. Z. (1995). Using technology for literacy learning in one primary ESL classroom. *Illinois Reading Council Journal, 23,* 35–41.

Liberman, I., Shankweiler, D., Fischer, F., & Carter, B.

(1974). Explicit syllable and phoneme segmentation in the young child. *Journal of Experimental Child Psychology, 18,* 201–212.

Linn, R. L., Baker, E. L., & Dunbar, S. B. (1991). Complex, performance-based assessment: Expectations and validation criteria. *Educational Researcher, 20,* 15–21.

Lipson, M. Y. (1984). Some unexpected issues in prior knowledge and comprehension. *The Reading Teacher, 37,* 760–765.

Lipson, M. Y., & Lang, L. B. (1991). Not as easy as it seems: Some unresolved questions about fluency. *Theory into Practice, 30,* 218–227.

Lopardo, D., & Sadow, M. W. (1982). Criteria and procedures for the method of repeated readings. *Journal of Reading, 26,* 156–160.

Lortie, D. C. (1975). *Schoolteacher.* Chicago: University of Chicago Press.

Lukens, R. J. (1976). *A critical handbook of children's literature.* Glenview, IL: Scott, Foresman.

Lundberg, I., Frost, J., & Petersen. O. (1988). Effects of an extensive program for stimulating phonological awareness in preschool children. *Reading Research Quarterly, 23,* 263–284.

Lyons, C. A. (1990). Reading Recovery: An effective early intervention program that can prevent mislabeling children as learning disabled. In *Early reading difficulties: Their misclassification and treatment as learning disabilities* (ERS Digest, pp. 17–23). Arlington, VA: Educational Research Service.

Lyons, C. A., Pinnell, G. S., & DeFord, D. E. (1993). *Partners in learning: Teachers and children in Reading Recovery.* New York: Teachers College Press.

Macrorie, K. (1988). *The I-Search paper.* Portsmouth, NH: Boynton/Cook, Heinemann.

Mandler, J. M., & Johnson, N. S. (1977). Remembrance of things parsed: Story structure and recall. *Cognitive Psychology, 9,* 111–151.

Margosein, C. M., Pascarella, E. T., & Pflaum, S. W. (1982). *The effects of instruction using semantic mapping on vocabulary and comprehension.* Paper presented at the meeting of the American Educational Research Association, New York, NY.

Markman, E. M. (1977). Realizing that you don't understand: A preliminary investigation. *Child Development, 43,* 986–992.

Mason, J. (1980). When do children begin to read: An exploration of four-year-old children's letter and word reading competencies. *Reading Research Quarterly, 15,* 203–227.

Masonheimer, P. E., Drum, P. A., & Ehri, L. C. (1984). Does environmental print identification lead children into word reading? *Journal of Reading Behavior, 16,* 257–271.

Mates, B. F., & Strommen, L. (1996). Why Ernie can't read: Sesame Street and literacy. *The Reading Teacher, 49,* 300–306.

McGee, L. M. (1982). The influence of metacognitive knowledge of expository text structure on discourse recall. In J. A. Niles & L. A. Harris (Eds.), *New inquiries in reading research and instruction.* Rochester, NY: National Reading Conference.

McGee, L. M. (1992). Exploring the literature-based reading revolution (Focus on Research). *Language Arts, 69,* 529–537.

McGee, L. M., & Richgels, D. J. (1985). Teaching expository text structure to elementary students. *The Reading Teacher, 38,* 739–748.

McGinley, W. J., & Denner, P. R. (1987). Story impressions: A prereading/writing activity. *Journal of Reading, 30,* 248–253.

McGinley, W., & Tierney, R. J. (1989). Traversing the topical landscape: Reading and writing as ways of knowing. *Written Communication, 6,* 243–269.

McMahon, S. I., & Raphael, T. E. (1990). Creating an environment to encourage classroom discourse about text: A preliminary investigation. Paper presented at the National Reading Conference, Miami, FL.

Meyer, B. J. F. (1977). The structure of prose: Effects on learning and memory and implications for educational practice. In R. C. Anderson, R. J. Spiro, & W. F. Montague (Eds.), *Schooling and the acquisition of knowledge* (pp. 179–200). Hillsdale, NJ: Lawrence Erlbaum.

Meyer, B. J. F., Brandt, D. M., & Bluth, G. J. (1980). Use of top-level structure in text: Key for reading comprehension of ninth-grade students. *Reading Research Quarterly, 16,* 72–103.

Mezynski, K. (1983). Issues concerning the acquisition of knowledge: Effects of vocabulary training on reading comprehension. *Review of Educational Research, 53,* 253–279.

Miller, G. E., Giovenco, A., & Rentiers K. A. (1987) Fostering comprehension monitoring in below average readers through self-instruction training. *Journal of Reading Behavior, 14,* 379–393.

Moll, L. C. (1988). Some key issues in teaching Latino students. *Language Arts, 65,* 465–472.

Monson, R. J., & Monson, M. P. (1994). Literacy as inquiry: An interview with Jerome C. Harste. *The Reading Teacher, 47,* 518–521.

Morris, D. (1986). *Teaching reading in kindergarten: A language-experience approach* (Occasional Paper No. 13). Evanston, IL: The Reading Center, National College of Education.

Morris, D. (1992). Concept of word: A pivotal understanding in the learning to read process. In S. Templeton & D. Bear (Eds.), *Development of orthographic knowledge and the foundations of literacy:*

A memorial festschrift for Edmund Henderson. Hillsdale, NJ: Lawrence Erlbaum.

Morris, D. (1993). The relationship between children's concept of word in text and phoneme awareness in learning to read: A longitudinal study. *Research in the Teaching of English, 27*(2), 133–151.

Morris, D., Blanton, L., Blanton, W. E., Nowacek, J., & Perney, J. (1995). Teaching low-achieving spellers at their "instructional level." *Elementary School Journal, 96,* 163–177.

Morris, D., Blanton, L., Blanton, W. E., & Perney, J. (1995). Spelling instruction and achievement in six classrooms. *Elementary School Journal, 96,* 145–162.

Morris, D., & Perney, J. (1984). Developmental spelling as a predictor of first-grade reading achievement. *Elementary School Journal, 84,* 441–457.

Murray, D. (1982). Teaching the other self: The writer's first reader. In *Learning by teaching: Selected articles on writing and teaching*. Portsmouth, NH: Boynton/Cook.

Myers, M., & Paris, S. G. (1978). Children's metacognitive knowledge about reading. *Journal of Educational Psychology, 70,* 680–690.

Nagy, W. E., & Anderson, R. C. (1984). How many words are there in printed school English? *Reading Research Quarterly, 19,* 303–330.

Nagy, W. E., Herman, P. A., & Anderson, R. C. (1985). Learning words from context. *Reading Research Quarterly, 20,* 233–253.

Nelson, L. J., & Morris, D. (1988). Echo reading with taped books. *Illinois Reading Council Journal, 16,* 39–42.

Ogle, D. M. (1986). K-W-L: A teaching model that develops active reading of expository text. *The Reading Teacher, 40,* 564–570.

Oldfather, P. (1993). What students say about motivating experiences in a whole language classroom. *The Reading Teacher, 46,* 672–681.

Olson, D. R. (1994). *The world on paper*. New York: Cambridge University Press.

O'Malley, J. M., Chamot, A. U., & Walker, C. (1987). Some implications of cognitive theory for second language acquisition. *Studies in Second Language Acquisition, 9,* 287–306.

Osborn, J. (1984). *Evaluating workbooks*. Urbana, University of Illinois, Center for the Study of Reading. (Eric Document Reproduction Service No. ED247 543)

O'Sullivan, J. T., & Pressley, M. (1984). Completeness of instruction and strategy transfer. *Journal of Experimental Child Psychology, 38,* 275–288.

Palincsar, A. S., & Brown, A. L. (1984). Reciprocal teaching of comprehension-fostering and comprehension-monitoring activities. *Cognition and Instruction, 1,* 117–175.

Pappas, C. (1993). Is narrative "primary"? Some insights from kindergartners' pretend readings of stories and information books. *Journal of Reading Behavior, 25,* 97–129.

Paratore, J. R. (1995). Connecting assessment and instruction in the flexibly-grouped classroom. In M. C. Radencich & L. J. McKay (Eds.), *Flexible grouping for literacy in the elementary grades* (pp. 113–133). Boston: Allyn & Bacon.

Paris, S. G., Calfee, R. C., Filby, N., Hiebert, E. H., Pearson, P. D., Valencia, S. W., & Wolf, K. P. (1992). A framework for authentic literacy assessment. *The Reading Teacher, 46,* 88–98.

Paris, S. G., Lipson, M. Y., & Wixson, K. K. (1984). Becoming a strategic reader. *Contemporary Educational Psychology, 8,* 293–316.

Paris, S. G., & Myers, M. (1981). Comprehension monitoring, memory, and study strategies of good and poor readers. *Journal of Reading Behavior, 13,* 5–22.

Paris, S. G., Wasik, B. A., & Turner, J. C. (1991). The development of strategic readers. In R. Barr, M. Kamil, P. Mosenthal, & P. D. Pearson (Eds.), *Handbook of reading research* (Vol. 2, pp. 609–640). White Plains, NY: Longman.

Paulson, F. L., Paulson, P. R., & Meyer, C. A. (1991). What makes a portfolio a portfolio? *Educational Leadership, 48,* 60–63.

Pearson, P. D. (1976). The effects of grammatical complexity on children's comprehension recall, and conception of certain semantic relations. In H. Singer & R. B. Ruddell (Eds.), *Theoretical models and processes of reading* (pp. 67–102). Newark, DE: International Reading Association.

Pearson, P. D., & Fielding, L. (1991). Comprehension instruction. In R. Barr, M. L. Kamil, P. Mosenthal, & P. D. Pearson (Eds.), *Handbook of reading research* (Vol. 2, pp. 815–860). White Plains, NY: Longman.

Pearson, P. D., & Gallagher, M. C. (1983). The instruction of reading comprehension. *Contemporary Education Psychology, 8,* 317–344.

Pearson, P. D., Hansen, J., & Gordon, C. (1979). The effect of background knowledge on young children's comprehension of explicit and implicit information. *Journal of Reading Behavior, 11,* 201–209.

Peregoy, S. F., & Boyle, O. F. (1993). *Reading, writing, and learning in ESL*. White Plains, NY: Longman.

Peterson, R., & Eeds, M. (1990). *Grand conversations: Literature groups in action*. New York: Scholastic.

Piccolo, J. (1987). Expository text structure: Teaching and learning strategies. *The Reading Teacher, 40,* 838–847.

Pikulski, J. J. (1991). Grouping for literacy instruction: A need for thoughtful reconsideration. *Florida Reading Quarterly*, June, 7–12.

Pils, L. J. (1991). Soon anofe you tout me: Evaluation in a first-grade whole language classroom. *Reading Teacher, 45,* 46–50.

Pinnell, G. S., & McCarrier, A. (1994). Interactive writing: A transition tool for assisting children in learning to read and write. In E. H. Hiebert & B. M. Taylor (Eds.), *Getting reading right from the start: Effective early literacy interventions* (pp. 149–170). Needham Heights, MA: Allyn & Bacon.

Pressley, M., El-Dinary, P., Brown, R., Schuder, T. L., Pioli, M., Green, K., & Gaskins, I. (1994). *Transactional instruction of reading comprehension strategies* (University of Georgia and Maryland Perspectives in Reading Research, No. 5). National Reading Research Center.

Pressley, M., Johnson, C., Symons, S., McGoldrick, J., & Kurita, J. (1989). Strategies that improve children's memory and comprehension of text. *Elementary School Journal, 90,* 3–32.

Pressley, M., Levin, J. R., & Delaney, H. D. (1983). The mnemonic keyword method. *Review of Educational Research, 52,* 6–91.

Radencich, M. C., McKay, L. J., Paratore, J. R., Plaza, G. L., Lustgarten, K. E., Nelms, P., & Moore, P. T. (1995). Implementing flexible grouping with a common reading selection. In M. C. Radencich & L. J. McKay (Eds.), *Flexible grouping for literacy in the elementary grades* (pp. 42–65). Boston: Allyn & Bacon.

Raphael, T. E. (1984). Teaching learners about sources of information for answering questions. *Journal of Reading, 28,* 303–311.

Raphael, T. E. (1986). Teaching question-answer relationships, revisited. *The Reading Teacher, 39,* 516–523.

Raphael, T. E., & McMahon, S. I. (1994). Book Club: An alternative framework for reading instruction. *The Reading Teacher, 48,* 102–116.

Raphael, T. E., Myers, A. C., Tirre, W. C., Fritz, M., & Freebody, P. (1981). The effects of some known sources of reading difficulty on metacomprehension and comprehension. *Journal of Reading Behavior, 13,* 324–334.

Raphael, T. E., & Pearson, P. D. (1982). *The effect of metacognitive awareness training on children's question answering behavior* (Technical Report No. 238). Urbana: University of Illinois. Center for the Study of Reading.

Read, C. (1971). Preschool children's knowledge of English phonology. *Harvard Educational Review, 41,* 1–34.

Rhodes, L. K., & Nathenson-Mejia, S. (1992). Anecdotal records: A powerful tool for ongoing literacy assessment. *The Reading Teacher, 45,* 502–509.

Richek, M. A., List, L. K., & Lerner, J. W. (1983). *Reading problems: Diagnosis and remediation.* Englewood Cliffs, NJ: Prentice-Hall.

Roehler, L. R., & Duffy, G. G. (1984). Direct explanation of comprehension processes. In G. G. Duffy, L. R. Roehler, & J. Mason (Eds.), *Comprehension instruction: Perspectives and suggestions* (pp. 222–280). White Plains, NY: Longman.

Rogoff, B. (1990). *Apprenticeship in thinking.* New York: Oxford University Press.

Rosenblatt, L. M. (1978). *The reader, the text, the poem.* Carbondale: Southern Illinois University Press.

Rosenblatt, L. M. (1985). Viewpoints: Transaction versus interaction: A terminological rescue operation. *Research in the Teaching of English, 19,* 96–107.

Rosenblatt, L. M. (1989). Writing and reading: The transactional theory. In J. M. Mason (Ed.), *Reading and writing connections* (pp. 153–176). Boston: Allyn & Bacon.

Rosenshine, B., & Stevens, R. 1984. Classroom instruction in reading. In P. D. Pearson, R. Barr, M. Kamil, and P. Mosenthal (Eds.), *Handbook of reading research* (Vol. 1, pp. 745–798). White Plains, NY: Longman.

Ruddell, R. (1965). The effect of the similarity of oral and written patterns of language structure on reading comprehension. *Elementary English, 42,* 403–410.

Ruddell, R. B. (1995). Those influential literacy teachers: Meaning negotiators and motivation builders. *The Reading Teacher, 48,* 454–463.

Rumelhart, D. E. (1975). Notes on a schema for stories. In D. O. Bobrow & A. Collins (Eds.), *Representation and understanding: Studies in cognitive science* (pp. 211–236). New York: Academic Press.

Rumelhart, D. E. (1977). Toward an interactive model of reading. In S. Dornic (Ed.), *Attention and performance VI* (pp. 573–603). London: Academic Press.

Rupley, W., Blair, T., & Wise, B. (1982). Specification of promising teacher effectiveness variables for reading instruction. In J. Niles & L. Harris (Eds.), *New inquiries in reading research and instruction* (pp. 232–236). Thirty-first Yearbook of the National Reading Conference. Rochester, NY: National Reading Conference.

Saccardi, M. (1993–1994). Children speak: Our students' reactions to books can tell us what to teach. *The Reading Teacher, 47,* 318–324.

Samara, J., & Curry, J. (Eds.). (1990). *Writing units that challenge: A guidebook for and by educators.* Portland, ME: MEGAT.

Samuels, S. J. (1979). The method of repeated readings. *The Reading Teacher, 32,* 403–408.

Santa, C. (1993). *Teacher's implementation guide from Pegasus*. Dubuque, IA: Kendall/Hunt.

Saville-Troike, M. (1984). What really matters in second language learning for academic achievement. *TESOL Quarterly, 18,* 199–220.

Schwartz, R. M., & Nicholas, S. (1982). *The effect on vocabulary acquisition of instruction in the concept of definition*. Paper presented at the American Educational Research Association meeting, New York.

Schwartz, R. M., & Raphael, T. E. (1985). Concept of definition: A key to improving students' vocabulary. *The Reading Teacher, 39,* 198–205.

Seto, T. (1995). Multiculturalism is not Halloween. *The Horn Book, 71,* 169–174.

Short, K., & Klassen, C. (1993). Literature circles: Hearing children's voices. In B. Cullinan (Ed.), *Children's voices: Talk in the classroom* (pp. 66–85). Newark, DE: International Reading Association.

Short, K. G., & Pierce, K. M. (1990). *Talking about books*. Portsmouth, NH: Heinemann.

Shunk, D. H., & Rice, J. H. (1987). Enhancing comprehension skill and self-efficacy with strategy value information. *Journal of Reading Behavior, 3,* 285–302.

Simmons, J. (1992). Portfolios for large scale assessment. In D. Graces & B. Sunstein (Eds.), *Portfolio portrait*. Portsmouth, NH: Heinemann.

Slavin, R. E. (1983). *Cooperative learning*. White Plains, NY: Longman.

Slavin, R. E. (1987). Ability grouping: A best-evidence synthesis. *Review of Educational Research, 57,* 293–336.

Sloan, G. D. (1991). *The child as critic: Teaching literature in elementary and middle schools*. New York: Teachers College Press.

Slobin, D. (1966). English abstract of Soviet studies of child language. In F. Smith & G. Miller (Eds.), *The genesis of language*. Cambridge: MIT Press.

Smith, F. (1988a). *Joining the literacy club*. Portsmouth, NH: Heinemann.

Smith, F. (1988b). Understanding reading (4th ed.). Hillsdale, NJ: Lawrence Erlbaum.

Smith, J. L., & Johnson, H. (1994). Models for implementing literature in content studies. *The Reading Teacher, 48,* 198–209.

Smith, M. L. (1991). Put to the test: The effects of external testing on teachers. *Educational Researcher, 20,* 8–11.

Stahl, S. A., & Fairbanks, M. M. (1986). The effects of vocabulary instruction: A model-based meta-analysis. *Review of Educational Research, 56,* 72–110.

Stahl, S. A., McKenna, M. C., & Pagnucco, J. R. (1994). The effects of whole-language instruction: An update and a reappraisal. *Educational Psychologist, 29,* 175–185.

Stahl, S. A., & Miller, P. D. (1989). Whole language and language experience approaches for beginning reading: A quantitative research synthesis. *Review of Educational Research, 59,* 87–116.

Stanovich, K. E. (1980). Toward an interactive-compensatory model of individual differences in the development of reading fluency. *Reading Research Quarterly, 16,* 32–71.

Stanovich, K. E. (1991). Word recognition: Changing perspectives. In R. Barr, M. Kamil, P. Mosenthal, & P. D. Pearson (Eds.), *Handbook of reading research* (Vol. 2, pp. 418–452). White Plains, NY: Longman.

Stauffer, R. G. (1969). *Directing reading maturity as a cognitive process*. New York: Harper & Row.

Stauffer, R. G. (1970). *The language-experience approach to the teaching of reading*. New York: Harper & Row.

Stein, N. L., & Glenn, C. G. (1979). An analysis of story comprehension in elementary school children. In R. O. Freedle (Ed.), *Advances in discourse processes: Vol. 2. New directions in discourse processing* (pp. 53–120). Norwood, NJ: Ablex.

Stotsky, S. (1983). Research on reading/writing relationships: A synthesis and suggested directions. *Language Arts, 60,* 627–642.

Strickland, D. S. (1994–95). Reinventing our literacy programs: Books, basics, balance. *The Reading Teacher, 48,* 294–302.

Strickland, D. S., & Morrow, L. M. (Eds.). (1989). *Emerging literacy: Young children learn to read and write*. Newark, DE: International Reading Association.

Strom, I. M. (1960). Research in grammar and usage and its implications for teaching writing. *Bulletin of the School of Education. Indiana University, 36,* 1–21.

Sulzby, E. (1985). Kindergartners as writers and readers. In M. Farr (Ed.), *Advances in writing research: Vol. 1. Children's early writing development* (pp. 127–200). Norwood, NJ: Ablex.

Sulzby, E., & Teale, W. (1991). Emergent literacy. In R. Barr, M. Kamil, P. Mosenthal, & P. D. Pearson (Eds.), *Handbook of reading research* (Vol. 2, pp. 727–757). White Plains, NY: Longman.

Swaby, B. (1977). *The effects of advanced organizers and vocabulary introduction on the reading comprehension of sixth grade students*. Unpublished doctoral dissertation, University of Minnesota, MN.

Tatham, S. M. (1969–1970). Reading comprehension of materials written with select oral language patterns: A study of grades two and four. *Reading Research Quarterly, 5,* 402–426.

Taylor, B. M., & Berkowitz, S. (1980). Facilitating children's comprehension of content material. In M. Kamil & A. Moe (Eds.), *Perspective on reading re-*

search and instruction (pp. 64–68). Twenty-ninth Yearbook of the National Reading Conference. Washington, DC: National Reading Conference.

Taylor, B. M., & Samuels, S. J. (1983). Children's use of text structure in the recall of expository material. *American Educational Research Association Journal, 20,* 517–528.

Taylor, D. (1983). *Family literacy: The social context of learning to read and write.* Portsmouth, NH: Heinemann.

Teale, W. H., & Sulzby, E. (Eds.). (1986). *Emergent literacy: Writing and reading.* Norwood, NJ: Ablex.

Teale, W. H., & Sulzby, E. (1989). Emerging literacy: New perspectives. In D. Strickland & L. Morrow (Eds.), *Emerging literacy: Young children learn to read and write* (pp. 1–15). Newark, DE: International Reading Association.

Temple, C., & Gillet, J. W. (1984). *Language arts: Learning processes and teaching practices.* Boston: Little, Brown.

Temple, C., Nathan, R., Burris, H., & Temple, F. (1988). The beginnings of writing (2nd ed.). Newton, MA: Allyn & Bacon.

Templeton, S. (1991). Teaching and learning the English spelling system: Reconceptualizing method and purpose. *Elementary School Journal, 93,* 249–275.

Thorndike, R. L. (1973–1974). Reading as reasoning. *Reading Research Quarterly, 9,* 135–147.

Thorndike, R. L., & Hagen, E. P. (1977). *Measurement and evaluation in psychology and education* (4th ed.). New York: John Wiley.

Tiballi, B., & Drake, L. (1993). Literature groups: A model of the transactional process. *Childhood Education, 69,* 221–224.

Tierney, R. J., Leys, M., & Rogers, T. (1986). Comprehension, composition, and collaboration. In T. Raphael (Ed.), *The contexts of school literacy.* New York: Random House.

Tierney, R. J., & Pearson, P. D. (1983). Toward a composing model of reading. *Language Arts, 60,* 68–80.

Tikunoff, W. J. (1988). Mediation of instruction to obtain equality of effectiveness. In S. Fradd & W. J. Tikunoff (Eds.), *Bilingual education and special education: A guide of instruction* (pp. 99–132). Boston: Little, Brown.

Tolstoy, A. (1971). *The great big enormous turnip.* Glenview, IL: Scott, Foresman.

Tompkins, G. E. (1994). *Teaching writing.* New York: Merrill.

Topping, K. J. (1995). Cued spelling: A powerful technique for parent and peer tutoring. *The Reading Teacher, 48,* 374–383.

Treiman, R. (1985). Onsets and rimes as units of spoken syllables: Evidence from children. *Journal of Experimental Child Psychology, 39,* 161–181.

Tuinman, J. J., & Brady, M. E. (1974). How does vocabulary account for variance on reading comprehension tests? A preliminary instructional analysis. In P. L. Nacke (Ed.), *Interaction: Research and practice in college-adult reading.* Twenty-third Yearbook of the National Reading Conference. Clemson, SC: National Reading Conference.

Tunmer, W. E., Herriman, M. L., & Nesdale, A. R. (1988). Metalinguistic abilities and beginning reading. *Reading Research Quarterly, 23,* 134–158.

Vacca, J. L., Vacca, R. T., & Gove, M. K. (1991). *Reading and learning to read* (2nd ed.). New York: HarperCollins.

Valencia, S. W. (1990). A portfolio approach to classroom assessment: The why, whats, and how. *The Reading Teacher, 43,* 338–340.

Valencia, S. W., & Pearson, P. D. (1986). Reading assessment: Time for a change. *The Reading Teacher, 40,* 726–732.

Vygotsky, L. S. (1978). *Mind and society.* Cambridge: Harvard University Press.

Walker, B. J. (1988). *Diagnostic teaching of reading: Techniques for instruction and assessment.* Columbus, OH: Merrill.

Watson, D. J. (1990). Show me: Whole language evaluation of literature groups. In K. G. Short & K. M. Pierce (Eds.), *Talking about books* (pp. 157–176). Portsmouth, NH: Heinemann.

Weaver, C. (1990). *Understanding whole language.* Portsmouth, NH: Heinemann.

Wells, G. (1985). Preschool literacy-related activities and success in school. In D. Olson, N. Torrance, & A. Hildyard (Eds.), *Literacy, language, and learning: The nature and consequences of literacy* (229–255). New York: Cambridge University Press.

Wells, G. (Ed.). (1994). *Changing schools from within: Creating communities of inquiry.* Portsmouth NH: Heinemann.

Wiederholt, S. L., & Hammill, D. D. (1971). Use of the Frostig-Home visual perception program in the urban school. *Psychology in the Schools, 8,* 268–274.

Wiggins, R. A. (1994). Large group lesson/small group follow-up: Flexible grouping in a basal reading program. *The Reading Teacher, 47,* 450–460.

Wilde, S. (1990) A proposal for a new spelling curriculum. *Elementary School Journal, 90,* 275–289.

Wildman, T. M., Niles, J. A., Magliaro, S. G., and McLaughlin, R. A. (1989). Teaching and learning to teach: The two roles of beginning teachers. *Elementary School Journal, 89,* 471–493.

Wittrock, M. C. (1984). Writing and the teaching of reading. In J. M. Jensen (Ed.), *Composing and com-*

prehending (pp. 77–83). Urbana, IL: National Council of Teachers of English.

Wixson, K. K. (1979). Miscue analysis: A critical review. *Journal of Reading Behavior, 11,* 163–175.

Wixson, K. K., Peters, C. W., Weber, E. M., & Roeber, E. D. (1987). New directions in statewide reading assessment. *The Reading Teacher, 40,* 749–754.

Yolen, J. (1994). An empress of thieves. *The Horn Book, 79,* 702–705.

Zahorik, J. A. (1970). The effects of planning on teaching. *Elementary School Journal, 71,* 143–151.

Zutell, J., & Allen, V. (1988). The English spelling strategies of Spanish-speaking bilingual children. *TESOL Quarterly, 22,* 333–339.

Index